A HISTORY OF RUSSIA

A

HISTORY OF RUSSIA

BERNARD PARES

*Formerly Professor of Russian History,
Language, and Literature, University of Liverpool, 1908–18;
University of London, 1919–36*

DEFINITIVE EDITION

WITH A NEW INTRODUCTION BY

RICHARD PARES

A Caravelle Edition

VINTAGE BOOKS

A DIVISION OF RANDOM HOUSE

New York

VINTAGE EDITION, 1965

VINTAGE BOOKS

are published by ALFRED A. KNOPF, INC.

and RANDOM HOUSE, INC.

Reprinted by arrangement with Alfred A. Knopf, Inc.

MANUFACTURED IN THE UNITED STATES OF AMERICA

FIRST PUBLISHED 1926
SECOND EDITION REVISED 1928
THIRD EDITION REVISED 1937
FOURTH EDITION REVISED 1944
FIFTH EDITION REVISED 1947

*Definitive Edition, reset and printed from new plates,
with a new introduction and bibliography and new maps, 1953*

T O

The Honourable Charles R. Crane

UNFAILING FRIEND OF RUSSIA

INTRODUCTION

My father, who wrote this book, was quite unlike any other academic person I ever knew. Gifted as he was, it was not scholarship, nor insight, nor even style that distinguished him from other historians, but his unusually dynamic will. He gave the impression, not merely of a man of action strayed into academic life—there are many of them, they sit on committees and, if they are wise, become principals of universities— but of something more: a man with a mission. This mission was to interpret Russia to the English-speaking world, and even to bring the two worlds into political partnership with each other.

He was born, at Albury in the county of Surrey, 1 March 1867, into the midst of a happy, religious, and somewhat Philistine family of five brothers and five sisters. My grandfather came of a midland family of country bankers; he had an unearned income, and no occupations but such as he chose for himself. He was a high church Anglican, in politics a Liberal—a combination by no means uncommon, best exemplified in Gladstone, whom he admired with a devotion which must have been slightly absurd. My father reacted against this Liberalism, but only on the surface. As a pert little boy, he used to make disrespectful verses about Gladstone and, upon remonstrance, only turned them into Latin, in which form they were still more disrespectful. As a man, he prided himself on belonging to no party. But fundamentally all his ideas and sympathies were Liberal, and he seems to have allied himself somewhat more definitely with Liberal parties in Russian politics than in British, though many of his best friends, such as Guchkov and Homyakov, were moderate Octobrists.

The chief preoccupations of the five brothers and five sisters, besides churchmanship, appear to have been practical jokes, light verse, cricket, and football. Of the practical jokes, the less said the better; they do not stand the test of time. The light verse was not all very subtle, but my father developed an astonishing verbal dexterity: when he had nothing better to do, he amused himself by composing rhymes upon the names of the railway stations on his journeys, and I have always thought that a man who could find a plausible rhyme to "Worplesdon" could have rhymed anything. This gift served him particularly well in translation.

He rendered German student songs into very singable English verse (many of them were published in the *Liverpool Students' Song-Book*). His masterpiece was the translation of Krylov's fables, in which he contrived to reproduce exactly the complicated metrical structure of the original, without undue contortion or loss of idiom—it was, perhaps, a somewhat wry idiom, but an idiom nevertheless. Nor was this dexterity confined to verse. When I was a boy, I used to spend hours playing with him what was called the "Sir George Back game": I was to make any remark I liked, and he was to introduce, with some appearance of relevance, the name of his great-uncle Sir George Back, an Arctic explorer, into the first or at least the second sentence of his reply. He always won.

The cricket and football were a more serious matter. Three of my uncles were rather distinguished players at a time when amateur and professional sport were less sharply separated than they are today; and my father, who was far the most talented member of the family in other respects, was long content, even proud, to be known as its fourth-best footballer. He kept up an interest in these games to the end of his days, and continued, in his seventies, to visit his old school, largely for the purpose of inspecting its performance at cricket. There was a reason for all this. In that age and class, the manly character was thought to be formed, tested, and exhibited in outdoor games. My father held this belief; and I think he may have been partly right, for, certainly, by his account of it, he had often discerned nobility, resourcefulness, or egoism in an innings at cricket or a run up the football field. For those who have the patience to watch character unfolding at the leisurely pace of a three-volume novel, a cricket match is still a good school of life. For my father, character was everything, intellect of no more than secondary importance. I do not think I ever heard him express admiration for cleverness unaccompanied by moral excellence—awe, yes, but never admiration. It was perhaps for this reason that he had a penchant for over-rating the intellect of men of character. His favourite term of praise was "simple"; but he liked to think that in the simple there was more than met the eye. Thus he admired most of all men like Sir Edward Grey and Sir George Buchanan, who were really, I suspect, more commonplace than he believed. Perhaps, at the bottom of his heart, he liked them because they reminded him of my grandfather, who was stable, generous, and moderately wise, but obviously not at all clever.

He was a promising boy, and his career started well. He was a scholar at Harrow, then at its greatest, the nurse of great politicians and great teachers. He shared a room with a future Prime Minister, Stanley Baldwin, but found difficulty in remembering anything about his character forty years later. He went on to Cambridge with a scholarship at Trinity College. There he came to grief. Probably he had had too much of the classics; he would have liked to specialize in history, but there was no escape from the classics in those days. He made matters worse by confusing himself in an attempt upon ancient philosophy; his cast of mind was essentially historical, undistinguished in abstract thought. Yet he seems to have worked out for himself, from the study of Plato, some elementary principles which made part of his religion ever afterwards; and this is more than many people retain who get much higher marks for ancient philosophy than he did. At the time, however, the result was disaster: he did badly in his degree examinations, and an academic career seemed to be out of the question. He was destined to spend his next few years teaching at a second-rate school. I think he felt this very much: when I won a College Fellowship, his pleasure seemed to be much heightened by the feeling that he would have liked to hold one himself.

It is important to remember that he was, at this stage of his career, a failure: if he had succeeded more easily at the first, he would probably have been a less remarkable man later, for his strength of will and sense of mission were nourished in the bitterness of frustration and in the determination to make his mark on the world in spite of all disadvantages. Also, perhaps, the paltriness of the daily task left his mind more open to new impressions than the preoccupations of a successful professional career would have done.

It is not easy to say when he discovered his passion for Russia. In his *Memoirs* he suggests that Russia had drawn him unconsciously, like a magnet, from the first. But I think his memory may have deceived him. He may, indeed, have felt keenly the impression of the great war scare of 1877–8, when every English schoolboy of ten was either a "Russian" or a "Turk," and he, as the son of a Gladstonian Liberal, must undoubtedly have been a "Russian." Perhaps it was at this early age that he formed the opinion (which he still expressed in the last year of his life) that the British had no right to keep the Russians out of Constantinople. But there is not much other sign of an early interest in Russia. After he left Cambridge he visited, as a student or as a sightseer, almost every European country before Russia; and he learnt French, German, and Italian thoroughly before he knew a word of Russian. At one time he was particularly interested in Italy—not only in Dante, Ariosto, and Tasso but also in the *Risorgimento*—and it was he who first interested his friend G. M. Trevelyan in *Garibaldi* by giving him a copy of the *Autobiography* as wedding-present: surely one of the most momentous wedding-presents in literary history. Russia came last in time. I may mis-remember, but I certainly got the impression that he first went there in order to visit the Napoleonic battlefields. He had a passion for battle-fields, especially those of Napoleon, and would speak of them in the same tones in which other connoisseurs might have spoken of a vintage claret. He had seen all the others, and none now remained to visit but the Russian.

Whatever the reason for his going, his first two visits to Russia changed the whole course of his life. The charm of the Russian peas-antry captivated him. Those who have experienced this charm at first hand are better able than I am to explain why this son of an English *rentier*, whose experience of peasantry had been confined to the de-pressed yokels of Surrey and Cambridgeshire, should have been so com-pletely overpowered by it as to make Russia his second homeland, one might almost say his first. His emotions seem to have been comparable to those of the *Narodniki*, who felt that they had not begun to live until they had got into immediate and unsophisticated contact with the peo-ple. It was much easier, at that time, for an Englishman of the middle class to indulge these feelings in Russia than in England, where rustic society was especially vitiated by snobbery and subservience. Add to this, that Russian politics had reached a stage peculiarly interesting to an English Liberal, when it seemed likely that all the institutions and ideas which were taken for granted as the foundations of English politi-cal development would be domiciled and established in Russia under the observer's eyes. Here was history, which my father had always wanted to study and, what was better, history in the making.

These are the best reasons I can give for the new orientation of my father's life, which came to appear to him so natural and necessary that he hardly ever explained it; and if he did try, it is likely that the expla-nations were quite trifling in comparison with the thoughts and feelings which moved him.

The mission which he now took up brought him, in time, a position almost unique in British life. There were other passionate experts, who interpreted to the British public the feelings and the needs of Yugoslavs, Arabs, Albanians, Persians; but none of them, except Colonel T. E. Lawrence, made such an impression as my father. This was chiefly be-cause none of them specialized in a country half so important as Russia. By luck or by skill, he had backed the best horse in the stable. But he had to pay for his eminence. The mission almost became an obsession. It ate up nearly all his other interests. Some of his friends thought him a club bore, because he would talk about nothing else. He could read about nothing else: the former student of Michelet and Ariosto could hardly be tempted to open a book even about cricket, and, when he was not reading, writing, or talking about Russia he would spend hours playing patience with *élan*, puffing furiously at a rather dirty pipe and, no doubt, thinking about Russia. Also, he planned his journeys to Russia without much consideration for his family, who were often left for long periods, sometimes in difficult circumstances.

This concentration of his interests did not come about all at once. In the meantime his knowledge of Russia had led him back to academic life. He had already made half the journey from schoolmastering when he became a lecturer under the Cambridge University Extension Scheme. (It is difficult now to realize the importance of the University Extension Schemes, both as education and entertainment, before the days of cinema and radio; the Workers' Educational Association did not exist, and even some of the newer universities themselves were only half-fledged.) Probably it was in the service of this movement that he perfected his skill as a lecturer, equally effective with the deadly serious miners of County Durham or the genteelly curious middle classes of the Home Counties. He was by far the best lecturer I ever heard: he had a peculiar gift for characterization and for dramatic narrative, but everything he said was exciting, for his mind was full of it. He used a few scribbled notes, but they can hardly have been necessary to the performance, for he could not always have found them in the appalling chaos which he stuffed into his pockets, nor can they have been easy to decipher when found. He could never see why certain elderly ladies used to come, year after year, to the course of public lectures which he gave in the University of London; but I have no doubt that they went as one goes a second or third time to an exceedingly well performed play. It was as good as a play even to listen through the door. If he had gone into politics or had taken Holy Orders (which he once thought of doing), he might have had an electrifying effect in the pulpit or on the platform.

His first real university post was at Liverpool. That was the heroic age of the English provincial universities: they had only just been founded, and were pervaded by a mood of generous enterprise and unbounded optimism; for the limits to the potential number and quality of the students, which have since become apparent, could not then be perceived. Not only the early professors, but the city fathers too had the *goût de la fondation.* My father's Chair was itself an example of this civic and mercantile enterprise; for there was then no other Professor of Russian in the country. Even the academic controversies were heroic: there were two factions, known as the "Old Testament" and the "New Testament," and their campaigns in the Senate, as recounted by my father, sounded to my youthful ears like the War of Troy. My father belonged to the New, so I have never discovered what the Old stood for; by his account, they were a set of mere *routiniers* without an idea in their heads—I have sometimes wondered if they were as bad as that. The New Testament won, but itself dissolved, soon after, in intricate personal feuds; and the great days were over before the War of 1914.

My father described his war experiences so fully (in a book published at the time, *Day by Day with the Russian Army*, and later in his *Russian Memoirs*) that I need not describe them again. He spent nearly the whole of the first three years in Russia. His status was undefined, and changed from time to time; but that made no difference, for he never cared about his status any more than he cared about his appearance. His mission was really personal, and it seems to have been on his own initiative that he did the most important things, as when he brought home the list of the shortages in munitions and other supplies to the British government. Most of the time he was at the front or near it (he was nearly fifty, but very tough and quite indifferent to hardship). Finally, when society and the army began to dissolve behind the lines, he ceased to have any British status at all, and virtually became a Russian: as such he found himself joined with four Mensheviks—two civilians, an army lieutenant, and a sailor—in a curious body called "The League of Personal Example," which toured the country making speeches in order to revive morale and keep Russia in the war. Luckily for him, he was in England when the October Revolution came, and was stopped in Stockholm on his way back to Russia. Then followed the queerest journey of all—the British government sent him out to Siberia, with a roving commission to keep up the spirits of the farmers behind Kolchak's lines and give them the (largely illusory) impression that Great Britain meant to see the intervention through. From this nightmare he was lucky to escape in a fur-trading vessel down thousands of miles of Siberian river and through the Arctic Circle.

Thus he had been repelled from the front door of Russia and from the back door. It was sixteen years before he saw the country again. They were very unhappy years for him. At first he believed, like many other people, that the working-class unrest of 1919–21 might lead to some kind of revolution in Great Britain itself; he therefore engaged in a tournament of public debates, up and down the country, with British Communists and sympathizers with the Soviet government. These debates, conducted with "sportsmanlike" fairness on both sides, first made him a public figure in his own country. Even after the danger of a British revolution had obviously receded, he was not happy. He was, in a certain sense, an exile; cut off from the country whose current history was his chief interest and his business, and necessarily influenced by other exiles who (as always) underrated the stability and overrated the difficulties of the regime they hated, he found it difficult to maintain in London an advanced post of observation from which developments in Russia could be reported or judged with scholarly detachment. He tried to condemn the Soviet authorities out of their own mouths, using only facts and figures provided by their own newspapers. But even thus he was misled, for he continued to believe, down to the advent of Hitler, that the end or at least the total transformation of the Soviet regime was just round the corner. His only opportunity for constructive work was the establishment of the School of Slavonic Studies in the University of London. Here his astuteness and determination in committee work and his standing with the general public enabled him to free the school from influences that might have cramped it and to obtain for it an independent status and an international reputation. He enjoyed this work: it had not quite the same excitement as the wars of the Old and New Testaments, but he met foemen worthy of his steel.

The rise of Hitler, which caused the Soviet government to reorient its foreign policy, also made a great change in my father's life. He revised his attitude to the Soviet government, and it revised its attitude to him. He had, for many years, been a Russian Liberal rather than a British Liberal, and perhaps a Russian patriot rather than a British patriot. For Russian Liberalism, in the narrower sense, there was no more hope: my father's friends had had their hour in 1917, and lost it. Even so, he could take comfort in the apparent liberalization of Russian institutions and in the triumph of Stalin's common sense over doctrinaire Marxism in certain fields of art, literature, and education. Moreover, when Russia was once more in danger, his feeling of Russian patriotism returned in full force. Already he had welcomed the victory of Stalin, the Russian national leader, over Trotsky, the international revolutionary. Now he was well on the way to becoming once more the partisan of an Anglo-Russian alliance. The Soviet government, on its side, had a use for such partisans, in the days of national and international "Popular Fronts."

The *rapprochement* took some time to bring about: there were even more than the usual delays about visas and so forth. At last, towards the end of 1935, my father set foot in Russia once more, and any remaining doubts vanished at once. He had not left the Moscow railway station before his mind was flooded with the realization that the Bolsheviks were, after all, Russians. The second conversion was even more instantaneous than the first.

He was an old man, but the best part of his life was still to come: he had his best books to write, and he was, for the first time, the oracle of a cause in which nearly everybody wanted to believe. For a few months in 1939–40 the Russo-German pact and the Finnish War put him out of his stride: he was hardly popular with the general public, and still less so with the Foreign Office, which was understandably irritated by his pursuing a private foreign policy of his own in interviews with the Russian Ambassador, although he was in its employment. But Hitler's invasion of Russia proved him right, in his own mind and in that of the public. He now became more active, and had more influence, than ever before. He lectured up and down the country, regardless of blackout and even air raids. He wrote a little book in paper covers—perhaps the best of all his books—which sold more than half a million copies. Finally, at the age of nearly seventy-six, he crossed the winter seas infested by submarines to start the same career on an even larger scale in America.

He ought to have died about that time, at his finest hour. It is a pity that he lived to undergo a second disillusionment and some confusion of mind. He stayed on in America after the war, and found useful work to do in advising American universities on the creation of schools of Slavonic studies such as that which he had built up in London. But the breakup of the wartime alliance which he had preached made him very unhappy. He did not pretend that the faults were on one side, but the faults he minded most were on the British and American side. I think he would have accepted almost any extension of Russian power, if only the Soviet government had not shown that it meant to return to rigid Communism at home. Thus, suspected of un-American activities on the one hand and scurrilously abused by Communists on the other, he hardly knew what to think or what to hope. He died in New York, 17 April 1949.

He was not one of the great scholars, in the sense in which the word is commonly used; but he was a creator, which is, perhaps, something more, even in academic life; a great orator, a vivid and magnetic personality, and a man of indomitable will.

RICHARD PARES

Preface

In attempting a history of the Russian people it seemed best to start from the data of prehistoric times, in order to catch such a glimpse as they give us of the characteristics of the Slavs and in particular of the Russians before they received a state organization. Later, I have tried throughout, so far as the compass of the book allowed, to direct especial attention to the living conditions of the people and especially of the vast majority of it, the peasantry; but I think it would be misleading to consider the term people as limited to any particular class. The tendency of the present time to concentrate on economic conditions in history is nowhere better justified or more necessary than in the case of a history of Russia. Here the main outlines of geography and the movements of peoples have a specially dominant bearing on everything else.

Constitutional history in the more narrow Western sense hardly existed at all in Russia; and the history of the institutions, though it is very important and claims more thorough study than it has received, is yet there more than elsewhere associated with rulers and administrators who were even formally by class distinctions separated from the mass of the people which they administered.

I cannot follow my teacher and master Professor V. O. Klyuchevsky in the comparatively secondary importance which, in the plan of his incomparable course on Russian history, he assigns to the influence of individual characters and of individual thought, as it is expressed in literature; and I find that Klyuchevsky has himself given the student more brilliant and informing suggestions in this field, too, than any other Russian historian with whose works I am acquainted. With the help of the admirable Russian Chronicles, so wonderful in their simplicity, directness, and clearness of vision, and of other later authorities, I have tried where possible to enable the more interesting of the characters to speak for themselves in their own words; and I have also endeavoured to voice in the same way, sometimes from written records and sometimes in the last period from my own personal experience, the running chorus, so intelligent and so suggestive, of the best wisdom of the Russian peasantry; in these respects I took as a model Professor York Powell's short textbook of English history up to the Tudors.

Though church history is a special study, no story of Russia can be complete without taking account of it. Indeed it is at times difficult to distinguish the religious from the national; and though the Church never did its duty in education or in provision for the public welfare, and though too often the best of the work of religion was left to the lower ranks of the clergy whether monastic or parochial, Orthodoxy was itself the major part of Russian civilization, and has perhaps done more than anything else to shape the distinctive Russian consciousness.

Military history cannot be isolated in a separate compartment from general history, of which it is an essential and illuminating part; its scope is much wider and it reaches much further back than is sometimes thought; in a broad sense it covers a large part of earlier Russian history; the career of Suvorov has been emphasized because he is the best manifestation of the Russian people in arms. On the other hand, diplomatic history is much more a special province and, particularly in Russia, has had much less to do with the common life of the people; it is here treated in detail only where great issues or remarkable personalities are involved. Annexations are in the main simply recorded—except where they lead to a struggle between nationalities or have a great economic importance—but in view of the long-drawn conflict of centuries between Russia and Poland, it has seemed necessary to give a parallel summary of Polish history by the side of the Russian.

Russia, segregated early from Europe of which she had at first formed a part, developed a pride of her own without any evident justification except for the vague feeling of the capacities that were in her people; and this developed her distinctiveness and made a creed of it. This peculiarity has reflected itself in the course which the study of Russia has followed in Western Europe. It was right, at the outset, that emphasis should be laid on the necessity of beginning this study from the inside and not from the outside; otherwise the study could not be intelligent. But now the time has come, as in the history of Russia herself, for the portcullis to be removed altogether and for every aspect of Russian life to be connected with all that is akin to it elsewhere. Consequently, this book attempts throughout to link up Russia with her neighbours and to find what is her part in the common history of Europe and the world. This is necessary in the first and last periods, both of which are European; but it is none the less necessary in the period of segregation, when assuredly the flow of influence and also, for a time, of power, was from outside onto Russia.

Two interests, in the later period closely interwoven, exact both

study and sympathy, not only for their cardinal importance but because
they are distinctive of Russia and are more or less foreign to the experience of other countries. If the story of the people as a whole is the subject of study, it is almost throughout—I would not apply this so much to
the glowing life of the Kiev period—the history of an underworld. Government and people are here more separate, even more foreign to each
other, than elsewhere; in the main, it is the doings of the government
that are chronicled, not the life of the people, so that of the latter we get
ordinarily only glimpses. If these glimpses showed nothing more than a
subject world of servants, we might not look further; but it is just in this
underworld that we find those suggestions of shrewd wisdom, patient
toil, a morale of suffering and endurance, and a broad humanity which
have always encouraged even the most matter-of-fact of foreign observers
to see in the Russian people the potentiality of a great future. This sense
of potentiality was never entirely absent with their administrators, generals, or teachers; as for the educated class, from the first stages of its
formation the instinct which gave shape to its thoughts and ideals was
the powerful sense of solidarity which it felt for the peasant world below
it and its sense of shame in presence of the standing contrast between
the actual and the possible conditions of peasant life. This second peculiarity produced even more distinctive results. It was as if, among educated Russians, there were a kind of suppuration of the conscience; and
it is only by taking account of this that we can get an understanding of
the engaging but baffling mentality of the Russian intelligentsia.

Members of this educated class might and, in more cases than elsewhere, did serve in the system of administration, but as such they were
the servants of a quite different mental attitude. Thus, the intelligentsia, as such, was ordinarily deprived of the opportunity of directly applying its ideas, which therefore remained for the most part in the domain
of the abstract and theoretical: a contrast between thought and action
which only heightened the strained consciousness of which I have spoken. Add to this that the Russian consciousness, so distinctive and independent, had always the sense of its disadvantage as compared with the
more civilized West of Europe. The phases of thought and action produced on the groundwork of these conditions, and in particular the last
and most confusing period from 1858 to 1917, have causes which lie far
back in Russian history and must be studied from its beginning; and
they demand of the student not only often a very wrestle of thought but
also a very special gift of sympathy. This is one of the chief of those
factors which attract just the best minds to the study of Russia; and they

find invariably that it helps to broaden all their conceptions even in the study of other countries. From this point of view, it is essentially the moral factors that count for most in the story of the Russian people; taking the word in its broadest sense, the problem throughout is a problem of education, and in all Russian history there is nothing that has ever counted so much as character.

On the other hand, the separation of government and people has given free scope in the latter to an instinctive anarchy, which has sometimes, as in the most recent period, broken out into sheer savagery. One cannot possibly, therefore, refuse all sympathy to the efforts made by the government, for instance in the reigns of Peter I and Catherine II, to achieve the triumph of order over chaos. It is still the continuation of that struggle, of Apollo and Minerva on the one side against the Titans on the other, which inspired the gospel of the Rome of Horace; yet, the epic of Peter and Catherine—far more with the second than with the first—is not a classic, only a pseudo-classic, because it is not, as with Republican Rome, based on the production of individual character, so that after all the chief thing which it explains to us is the inevitableness of the Russian Revolution.

A bibliographical note deals with the main materials of Russian history and with some of those special studies and books relating to particular periods which the writer has found to be of most value. Other lists of authorities are also given, in some cases with short comments. Of the ten maps some deal with the movements of peoples. For the use of students, the book contains a full index of names and subjects, in which the Russian names are accentuated to assist pronunciation, and also some tables which may be of service.

To several of my colleagues I am indebted for much help in different aspects of the subject, though any mistakes which remain must be credited to me and not to them: to Prince D. Svyatopolk Mirsky, who has a rare knowledge of the detail of various periods in Russian history and literature and has made several valuable suggestions and corrections; to Baron A. F. Meyendorff, who has helped me to shape some of the passages relating to Russian law; to Dr. Harold Williams, who kindly read through all the manuscript and, with Sir E. Denison Ross (Director of the London School of Oriental Studies), verified several of the Tartar names; to Mr. N. B. Jopson, who helped me in revising the passages relating to philology, and to Professor W. T. Gordon, who did the same for those that concern geology; and to Professor R. W. Seton-Watson, whom I consulted on certain points relating to Balkan history. I am indebted to the *Anthology of Russian Literature* compiled by Professor Leo Wiener of Harvard University for some parts of the translations contained in it, and to Professor Robert J. Kerner of the University of Missouri for his kindness in allowing me to make free use of his valuable work, *Slavic Europe: a Bibliography*.

Preface to the Fourth Edition

In this revision I have given a more consequent account of the Soviet period of Russian history up to the date of writing. The chapters mark themselves off as the story develops, and all serious students in Russia or outside are agreed on the main demarcations. The story of the Provisional Government of 1917 is really an appendix to that of the Monarchy. "His Majesty's Opposition," as Milyukov once called it in a speech in London, disappears soon after "His Majesty." Communist rule, beginning with the Communist Revolution of November 1917, really ends in the spring of 1921; and after it comes the rule of Communists without the practice of Communism, except for the weak socialized industry in an agricultural country. But the socialist principle, namely the national ownership of the means of production, though undergoing many modifications in practice with strong encouragement of the profit motive, was later immensely strengthened under Stalin by the enormous development of the national industries and by the collectivization of agriculture. Stalin's Russia has a story of its own, so far unfinished. The "Second Fatherland War," as it is now officially called in Russia, is a new chapter; but it is clearly also the consummation and, in a sense, the vindication of Stalin's Russia.

We are terribly short of full materials for the whole Soviet period. The Russian materials are very seriously prejudiced by the requirements of propaganda. Professor Michael Pokrovsky, the Communist historian, whose own work is permeated by this defect, freed himself of it most honourably in the historical accuracy with which he supervised the publication of the inestimable private material on preceding history which the Revolution placed in his hands; but the Party's monopoly of publication made impossible a fully informed record of the contemporary course of events. The serious specialist publications were noticeably more free of this taint. Under the Soviets, Russian laws were really enforced, and the successive legislation was the best index of changing policies; but much could also be gained from an honest chronicle of events based on a thorough analysis of the current Soviet press.

With the very fewest exceptions, it was no way possible for a Mackenzie Wallace or a Harold Williams to live and study for years in Russia. This is the first thing needed if the Soviet government wishes us to know and love the people of Russia—the two go together almost automatically for an Anglo-Saxon. A few, a very few of our students have contrived to manage this of themselves. Young American and British technicians rendered a real service by entering, while they were able to do so, into the full working life of the country. The "carpetbagging" escorted visitor was no substitute, so that there was a lamentable falling off in our contacts, very easily explained by the circumstances of the time. Most of the earlier "carpetbaggers" were attracted much less by Russia than by what they believed to be a confirmation of their own particular theories.

Some really valuable work was done by journalists, generally American, especially by W. H. Chamberlin; but they worked under the most disheartening difficulties. This is all the more important because peculiarly in Russia, where, as Kipling has put it, every word in the jungle means something different from what it says, understanding is more important than simple knowledge; and it is only the observer on the spot who can get it. Samuel N. Harper, of the University of Chicago, eminently had this understanding; and his work, from the time of his return, was invaluable. We also owe very much to the wonderfully vivid and convincing pictures of contemporary Russian scenes given us by Maurice Hindus. Some Russian emigrants have done honourable work; but, intelligibly enough, they have in general been hopelessly cut off, and they have never been able to witness the extraordinary and rapid changes in Russia during the Soviet period.

Of books in English on this period, conspicuously the best are the contributions of Sir John Maynard, *Russia in Flux* and *The Russian Peasant and Other Studies.* Each is a *tour de force*, for he never had all the contact that he needed; but his study of the first materials, both before and after the Revolution, is as comprehensive as that of any Russian, and his grasp generally much firmer—although he is not easy to read. His work towers over that of Sidney and Beatrice Webb. It is not possible to transfer ready-made a deservedly great reputation acquired in one subject to the study of another quite different. There is much of detail to be learned from the Webbs' work; but if they had known Russian and lived even for a short time among Russians in Russia, they would have been saved some fundamental misapprehensions. The Bibliography (page 583) contains, along with a few brief notes, a list of some books in which I find that understanding goes with knowledge.

I am greatly indebted for valuable help to my American colleagues and in particular to the American Russian Institute.

April 3, 1944

Note on Old and New Style

After September 1752, when the New Style was adopted in Great Britain, the dates are given in that style. This is noted in the text. The New Style is in advance of the Old (which was retained in Russia till 1918) by eleven days in the eighteenth century, by twelve days in the nineteenth, and by thirteen days in the twentieth.

Spelling

Usage has made a completely consistent spelling of names impossible. Accepted Western spellings are in general retained. H initial is used in place of Kh initial for Russian names, but not for others. In Polish names the diacritics are omitted. The names of Byzantine Emperors are given in the Latinized form. The name "Ivan," in the case of Moscow sovereigns, is in Russian textbooks written "Ioann," and is given here as "John," on the analogy of "Peter" (for "Petr"), "Alexander" (for "Alexandr"), and others; in the case of John IV, "Dread" represents "Grozny" better than "Terrible"; "Ivan" is retained in the other cases.

Transliteration

а — a	ж — zh	м — m	у — u	ъ — omit
б — b	з — z	н — n	ф — f	ь — omit
в — v	и ⎫	о — o	х — kh	ы — y
г — g(h)	i ⎬ — i	п — p	ц — ts	ѣ — e
д — d	й — y	р — r	ч — ch	э — e
е — e	к — k	с — s	ш — sh	ю — yu
ё — e	л — l	т — t	щ — shch	я — ya
				ѳ — f
				ѵ — i

This system follows in the main the principles adopted in the so-called Liverpool scheme, in that adopted by the British Academy, and in that accepted by the British Conference of University Teachers of Russian and Slavonic Languages; there are some slight differences between these three schemes. Keeping to the same general lines I have allowed myself a few departures of detail as follows: A medial y is inserted in names such as Dostoyevsky. In names such as Belyaev and Chernyaev I have transferred the position of the ʏ, with a view to simplicity and to preserve a similarity to the Russian pronunciation. x, in Russian words, is written ʜ, when initial. Φ and θ are written ᴘʜ and ᴛʜ in words derived directly from the Greek.

Contents

Beginnings (*to 1533*)

John III: the foundations of his "greatness"—he subdues Novgo-rod, 1465–88—the significance of the struggle—other acquisitions—the fall of Constantinople, 1453; John marries Sophia Paleologa, 1472—end of the Tartar yoke, 1480—increased ceremony and claims of Moscow; "the Third Rome"—position of the boyars: order of precedence—John and Lithuania; Crimea and Kazan—Basil III—church controversy—the first critics.

Moscow (1533–1682)

of God"—rivalries of boyars; Boris Godunov prevails—a Russian Patriarchate established, 1589—death of Prince Dmitry, 1591—Boris Tsar,
1598—his wise rule—ambiguous character of Boris—he crushes the
Romanovs—famine and robbers—the first Pretender—he invades from
Poland, 1604—changing fortunes; Boris dies, 1605—the Pretender on
the throne: his ability and daring—Basil Shuisky overthrows him, 1606
—Shuisky's turbulent reign—more Pretenders; Bolotnikov's slave war—
the Brigand of Tushino—Tushino and Moscow; siege of the Trinity
Monastery—the "flitters"—successes of Skopin Shuisky—King Sigismund of Poland besieges Smolensk—Tushino treats with Sigismund;
constitutional guarantees, Feb. 1610—Skopin's triumph and end—Moscow surrounded by enemies—Basil Shuisky deposed—the Poles admitted
to Moscow—patriotism of the Patriarch Hermogen—the Moscow envoys at Smolensk—Prince Wladyslaw invited—the Brigand of Tushino
dies—Lyapunov and the first national host—fall of Smolensk—the first
host fails—letters of Hermogen and Dionysius—Minin raises Nizhny
Novgorod, Oct. 1611—the second national host—the Kremlin recovered
—Michael Romanov elected Tsar, Feb. 21, 1613—Poland's lost chance.

A critical period—recent Tsars and the Zemsky Sobor—the first
Romanovs and the Sobor—disorders and unrest: the restoration of authority—the claims of Russia's weakened position in Europe—financial
needs of the State.

The peasants under the recent Tsars—the gentry demand the return of fugitive peasants—time limit for recovery abolished, 1646—the
peasants registered—serfdom confirmed by the Statute of Alexis (*Ulozhenie*), 1649—reticences and reservations of the State—but practice
turns the peasants into chattels, and legislation follows practice—flights
—robber bands—the Cossacks—peasant risings—state man hunts and
penalties—risings of 1648—the rising of Stephen Razin, 1667–71.

Centralization; the local elective institutions wither away—defects
of the Zemsky Sobor: no fixed constitution, competence, or procedure
—gradually it ceases to be summoned.

Orthodoxy on its defence in Lithuania—correction of the Russian
church books—Patriarch Nikon—his power—strength of the opposition
—unwisdom of Nikon; Avvakum—Nikon falls, but the schism remains
—the rising of Solovetsk Monastery—the significance of the schism.

Corruption of the officialdom—the *Ulozhenie* rivets the system of
class compartments—military and fiscal burdens; more monopolies—
the coinage debased.

The causes of the burdens—the advance through Siberia—three
barriers in the West: Sweden, Poland, and Turkey—three conflicts not
to be avoided—wars of liberation against Sweden and Poland—treaties
for breathing space: Stolbovo (with Sweden), 1617; Deulino (with Poland), 1619—failure of resumed challenge to Poland, 1632—the Cossacks capture Azov, 1637—Michael returns it to Turkey, 1642.

Tsar Alexis, 1645: crisis of the Ukrainian question—the Uniat compromise in Lithuania, 1596—counter-educational work of the brotherhoods and of Mogila—the Dnieper Cossacks and Poland—Bogdan

The Nineteenth Century (1796–1881)

Contemporary Russia (1881–1947)

XXIII. THE LIBERATION MOVEMENT (1904–12)   447

XXIV. WAR AND REVOLUTION (1905–17)   467

"friendly neighbors"—Germany again the decisive factor—knowledge vitally important: the obstacles.

Maps

Beginnings

(TO 1533)

NOTE

FOR AN EXPLANATION of the Old and New
Style dates, the system of Western spelling,
and the method of transliteration see preceding pages xxiii-xxiv.

CHAPTER I

Country and Peoples

[*To 882*]

Russia is halfway between Europe and Asia. This position has of itself led to infinite searchings of heart on the part of Russians. There is of course a single Eurasian Continent. Europe is a conventional term. At one time it could only be applied to the Greek world in which the term was first used; later it was the Roman Empire; now, in all but its unmeaning geographical sense, it includes America and Australia. Europe, then, is a civilization, a set of ideas and habits; and Asia differs from Europe in having either no such settled morale, or others which are different. Asia, on the other hand, which includes the centre of the whole continent, has from time to time poured down warlike tribes onto Europe. It was through Russia that many of these invaders had to pass; and Russia has been a battleground between Europe and Asia.

This was so in nature before it was so in history. Before the battles of peoples there was a battle of contrary winds. By the northwest of Russia the sea winds of Europe make a faint entry; the Baltic is but a brackish sea; it is only the almost uninhabited north of the Arctic coast that is just touched by the Gulf Stream. But these European winds, weak as they may be, are counted among the beneficent factors in the climate of Russia. On the opposite side, by the southeast, enter the arid and devastating winds of the deserts of central Asia. They tear up the soil or bury the surface with ruinous sandstorms, which fill up lakes and ponds, block rivers, wreck harvests, and ruin estates.

The winds sweep easily over Russia. The mountain ranges are all, or nearly all, on the circumference and outside the original Russia, which grew outwards towards them. Finland is rocky though not high. In Livonia there is a considerable district picturesque enough to be sometimes called the Livonian Switzerland. Russian population even now ends southwestwards at the Carpathians, which are outside political Russia. In the south of Crimea there is a mountain range which hedges off from the north the Russian Riviera, a district in which grows the flora of southern Europe. There are mountains yet higher on another frontier, in the Caucasus. The Ural range, running from north to south, is not very high, and the districts on both sides of it are quite alike in character; one does, however, come to an altogether new country at the Altay Mountains, rather more than halfway through Siberia; but beyond that there are only Russian colonies, not any actual Russia. Within all the other mountains which I have named lies the vast plain of European Russia, the battleground between Europe and Asia of which I have spoken. It is really a low plateau, or to be more accurate, a series of low plateaux, nowhere rising over 1500 feet and usually very much lower. The watersheds not being high, it is very easy to pass from the headwaters of one river to those of another. As there is nowhere, west of the Urals, a main range from north to south, there is nothing to bring down a large rainfall from the winds which come from the ocean. As there is no such range from east to west there is nothing to break the advance of the Arctic climate, which reaches as far as Crimea with only gradual variations. As one penetrates eastward into the block of the Eurasian Continent, the extremes of heat and cold become greater; the isotherms, or lines of equal temperature, deflect further and further southward, so that St. Petersburg, in the latitude of the Shetlands, has the same yearly temperature as Orenburg, in the latitude of Ipswich; but at Orenburg, though much hotter in the summer, it is much colder in the winter. The cold in Siberia is proverbial, but it is less realized that the summers are very hot.

The rocks of Finland are among the most ancient in Europe, and Russia, with the exception of the mountains at its circumference, appears to have been less disturbed by geologic convulsions than other parts. Geologists consider that the Caspian Sea formerly extended northward over a very much wider area. During the glacial epoch a vast sheet of ice, probably of considerable thickness, covered central and southern Russia. The erosion of the rocks by this ice-sheet produced clayey material which, being redistributed by the wind and thereby mixed with decaying vegetation, formed the "black soil" (*chernozem*), which is as rich as any in Europe. In the north, it is only a thin upper layer, but it becomes deeper as it extends southward. Trees will not easily grow on it unless they can make their way through to the clay subsoil beneath. But it produces grasses of every kind, which grow high enough to give cover to a horse and wither yearly in autumn. This black soil begins on a broad base (north to south) in the neighbourhood of the Altay Mountains. It narrows as it goes westward and enters Russia like a wedge, which runs into a point in Galicia. To the south of it, near the Caspian Sea, lies a barren area; here the surface of the soil is often worn away and there are a great number of salt lakes; this part of the plain, which amounts to about one tenth of European Russia, is almost entirely useless for cultivation.

Both these great areas, the black soil and the salt plains, are almost entirely treeless and are known as steppes. The area to the north of them has a poor clay soil (which the Russians call grey), giving little reward to agriculture and covered, especially in central Russia, with thick forests. In the neighborhood of Moscow and southward there are deciduous trees—oaks, elms, beeches, and so on. But not far to the north of Moscow begins the zone in which one finds practically nothing except the trees of Scandinavia, pine, fir, larch, silver birch. The Grand Army of Napoleon marched to Moscow mostly among trees of this kind. The forest zone at the beginning of Russian history seems to have reached further to the south than now.

To the north of this forest zone the trees sink in size until in the Arctic regions one has nothing but crawling scrub, and ultimately little but marshes frozen through most of the year. The population in these northern parts is very scanty and mostly savage. Here, too, then, there is a vast area which is useless to cultivation and civilization.

We have thus two important zones in European Russia: the forest zone of the north and centre, and the black-soil zone of the centre and south. The north has a superfluity of timber, but produces grain only with difficulty; the south as soon as it could be cultivated became the richest of granaries, but has practically no timber. These two Russias were supplementary and necessary to each other, and it was not for nothing that the political centre of the State should for so many centuries have been fixed at Moscow, near to the point where the two zones join.

The watersheds of Russia are in no cases high. The principal watershed is the Valday Hills in the province of Novgorod. From this low range flow some of the greatest and most majestic rivers in Europe: the Western Dvina and the Volkhov to the Baltic, the Dnieper to the Black Sea, and the Volga to the Caspian. The headwaters of the chief Russian rivers are so near to each other that it was easy to establish portages between them, nor were there any great heights to traverse. Thus Russia is before all things a country of waterways, which are among the finest in the world. Not descending from great heights, these rivers wind

MAJOR GEOGRAPHICAL ZONES OF RUSSIA

onward slowly and sinuously, watering vast basins, seldom disturbed by rapids (although there are such both on the Dvina and the Dnieper), passing through a crumbling soil which makes little resistance and fills itself to the full with their moisture. The innumerable marshes of northern and central Russia serve these great rivers as reservoirs. No country in Europe has so large a proportion of marsh. Here in the north, the springs are close to the surface, and they feed and control the rivers which, as has been remarked, have more regular habits than any of the other inhabitants of Russia. Often by a certain tilt of the earth the western bank of a Russian river dominates the eastern, presenting thereby a line of natural fortresses to any enemy coming from Asia. The best and the driest land is often to be found close to this high western bank of the river. The hinterland between the rivers is frequently covered with marsh as well as with forest. We may therefore in earlier Russian history—and as far as Siberia is concerned, even now—dismiss from our minds almost all that is not river or road. The huge hinterlands of marsh and thicket were practically closed. The rivers, so to speak, draw lines of light through this vast wilderness. It was mainly along them that human colonization could travel forward, and the whole history of Russia from the beginning till now is a history of colonization. Meanwhile there is between them plenty of waste space to be filled up when necessary in the halts of advance, or in the times of retreat to serve as natural lines of least resistance into the nowhere. Thus it is that in the great disturbances to which invasions from the East subjected the inhabitants of this plain, they almost seemed to play with this vast area, moving from one point to another of it, giving a history by turns to this or that region in the course of their desultory wanderings.

One may with advantage follow the example of Klyuchevsky in his *Course of Russian History* in comparing the influence on the Russian character exercised by the three chief features of the country. The steppe, which in the stable seasons of the year is all an open road, is the land of vast horizons, distant dreams, active life, and constant danger. It has created in Russian history first the type of the old *bogatyr* or frontier peasant knight of Christendom holding the gates of Europe against the heathen nomads, and later that of the roaming Cossack, also a frontier fighter, ready to sell his labour or turn his sword wherever it would bring him most profit, full of resource, ready horseman, scout, soldier, trader, or thief. The forest, which for the greater part of Russian history was the home of much more than half of the population, teaches different instincts. Working with his axe in this wilderness, the peasant must with infinite slow labour conquer a living from an ungracious soil, clearing arable patches by firing trees and moving on to the same task elsewhere after some seven years, when the land refuses to give more to the primitive implements which he commands. The forest teaches caution; every tree may hide a danger. But the lesson of the rivers is before all things that of sociability and of brotherhood. Every Russian has the instinct of what he vaguely calls socialism, because most Russians were ordinarily condemned to conditions of savage individualism. In their long story of colonization the Russians were always travellers, with little to leave behind them and with ready resource to make some primitive kind of a settlement in a new district. The road of this colonization was the river, and one could not easily depart from it to the right or to the left, except to settle on some tributary stream. Along this great main road met what there was of population, and it met in an environment of solitude, so that every meeting was a spur to comradeship. These lordly water roads could not be of much use to anyone while they remained only scenes of warfare. Thus the river taught peace, and the river taught trade.

Above all, in this vast plain with no natural boundaries where rovers were often meeting, there was the foundation for a great language, a great race, and a great empire. The Russian has a historical feeling for Christendom. But he has also a world-sense, living in his earliest songs, not to be flaunted, very deep-rooted but all the more real for that, which is the heritage only of an imperial race of travellers.

Talking in terms of civilization, Russia is at the back end, the least European part of Europe. Elsewhere peoples have grown up amid the ruins of an earlier culture—which of itself is an education. In Russia there was very little of this. On the other hand, Russian history is in a wide sense more military than that of other countries. With few natural barriers, the great hosts from the East moved wholesale, bag and baggage, men, women, and children, horses and cattle, and even habitations. Every such invading people was a vast army, torn from its bearings, holding land by no title but war, and bound to fight to a finish. These marches drew broad lines through the military map, which otherwise was almost a wilderness and without a history.

Archæological finds reveal the existence of palæolithic man only in southern Russia on the line of Kiev, Poltava, and Ekaterinoslav. Of neolithic man the most numerous traces are in the south, but there are such traces in the neighbourhood of Moscow. It is probable that the Indo-European family to which the Slavs belong was in Europe before the transition to the metal age. The theory that it came from Asia is now generally abandoned; philologists affirm that the most ancient and unchanged of still-spoken Indo-European languages is that of Lithuania; this might imply that it was from the centre of Europe itself that the distribution of the Indo-European family proceeded. The Lithuanians, when first met with, form geographically a kind of inset among the Slavs, to whom they are more closely akin than to any other branch of the Indo-European family. They lie along the coast of the Baltic between the West Slav Poles and the East Slav Russians. As to the origin of the Slavs, there are not any fixed data till some centuries after the Christian era. But as this people appears from the start as one of cultivators and more or less peaceful, its forefathers probably occupied from the earliest times part of the area in which it appears later, namely the middle country between Lithuania and the Carpathians around the rivers Vistula, Pripet, Dnieper, Dvina, Southern Bug, and Dniester. To the north, the basin of the Niemen is the home of the Lithuanian race. To the east, the earliest known inhabitants of what is now central, eastern, and northern Russia were not of Indo-European stock at all, but Finns. The river names in all this part of Russia are evidently of Finnish origin, with the terminations *va, ga, ma, sha,* predominating. The Finns were scattered through the forests all over this area. Patches, large or small, of this race still remain in Finland, Estonia, the neighbourhood of the upper Volga, and the northeastern provinces. They had no corporate life but waged their struggle with the beasts of the forests as savages little removed from them. Their character was anything but aggressive, and they seem to be indicated in a sentence of Tacitus (*Germania*) describing an eastern people who have solved the problem of human existence by having no requirements at all.

This northern forest zone of Russia, whether Lithuanian, Slav, or Finnish, was still dormant; as far as history was concerned, the world began to the south of it. Here in the steppes of the south, at the time of the first historical references to Russia, those of Herodotus in the fifth century before Christ, Ionian and Dorian Greeks had established themselves along the coastline of the Black Sea from the mouth of the Dniester to the Sea of Azov, in the colonies of Olbia, Chersonese, Panticapæum, Tanais, and Phanagoria; but the hinterland was occupied by other peoples, under the headship first of the Cimmerians and then of the Scythians. Both these dominant tribes were in race akin to the Persians and were therefore members of the Indo-European family. Scythian became a term applied to the whole of this area and to all its peoples, who apparently talked as many as seven different languages. The Scythians themselves, whose principal nucleus was called the Royal Scythians, spoke a language which has been identified by the philologist Šafařik and others with the Iranic or Persian branch of the Indo-European family. The southern inhabitants of this area had close touch with the Greek colonists; some Scythians even went to Greece for study; the finds of Kerch (Panticapæum) and Nikopol show that rich ornaments of Greek manufacture were acquired by Scythians. Greek colonies of this region in turn borrowed from their Iranian neighbours the principle of despotism practised by the Persians. In the fourth century before Christ the predominance passed from the Scythians to a kindred tribe formerly lying to the northeast of them, the Sarmatians. These, at the beginning of the Christian era, dwelt between the Sea of Azov and the Danube. They were more nomadic than their predecessors, like other races which were to follow them in these steppes. They lived in felt huts which they could carry about. They fought in brass helmets with bows and swords, and some of them wore mail. They were fair-haired, and their costume was similar to the Persian. Of this Iranic stock there were various branches, such as the Yazygi, who inhabited from the Danube to the river Tisza, and the Roxolans or White Alans. It is important to realize that all these Iranian races were not mere Asiatic savages, but a section, if a remote and frontier section, of the civilized world of their time, grouped around the Mediterranean.

In the second century after Christ these tribes were disturbed by an invasion from an unexpected side, the north. The earliest of the great river roads of Russia that became full of historical movement was that which ran from the Baltic to the Black Sea. Boats could ascend the Western Dvina in the direction of Smolensk; but more ordinarily they passed up the Neva, through Lake Ladoga up the Volkhov, across Lake Ilmen, up the Lovat, crossed the upper Dvina by means of tributaries and portages and so reached the Dnieper at Smolensk, from which the passage was comparatively easy to the Black Sea. This river road was to be the first Russia, but even as early as the second century the river served as a road of invasion for Goths descending from the Baltic. These Baltic Goths, who belonged to the Teutonic branch of the Indo-European family, conquered those whom they passed on their road, which lay through the Slavs, and ultimately created a conglomerate empire of different races under the rule of King Hermanric.

In the second half of the fourth century came a greater invasion from another side, that of Asia. Mention has been made of the broad wedge of black soil which runs westward into Europe, narrowing as it advances. This was a ready-made road for Asiatic invaders. China attained a measure of organization and political stability long before Europe and the nomad tribes living on the poor soil of Mongolia, finding themselves compelled to move as they increased in numbers, were not able to break through to the Pacific. It was against such attacks that the Great Wall of China was constructed. Compelled to seek another outlet, these tribes found it easy to move westward along the great natural track which supplied them all the way with fodder for their cattle and horses. Such were the Huns; they conquered and absorbed other tribes to which they extended their name. In the second century they were already west of the Caspian Sea. Next they are to be heard of northeast of the Don, and about 370 they crushed the Iranian Alans living between the Don and the Sea of Azov. Joined by the Roxolans they then marched on the Goths, and conquering the Ostrogoths, or East Goths, they compelled them to fight against their kinsmen the Visogoths. Two hundred thousand Visigoths were driven across the Danube into the Byzantine Empire in 376; and both branches of the Goths ultimately passed further to found the new kingdoms of the Visigoths in Spain and of the Ostrogoths in Italy. In the fifth century the empire of the Huns extended to the Danube and the Tisza. Ammian Marcellinus describes the Huns as of hideous physiognomy, huge heads, deep sunken eyes, broad shoulders, bow-legs like sticks. Their habits, too, were to the civilized Romans repulsive and terrifying. They lived, conversed, and even slept on horseback, and never changed their clothes until they dropped off. This is the picture of the real nomad Asia, with which Russia later had to fight hopelessly for so many centuries. It was in modern Hungary that Attila their king received in 448 the embassy from the Byzantine Emperor, Theodosius II, of which its chief, Priscus, has left an account. It appears from river names and other details of this account that there were a large number of Slavs incorporated in the short-lived Hunnish Empire.

The Huns passed westward as far as France, where they were defeated by a mixed army of Romans, Goths, and other Teutonic tribes (451). After the death of Attila in 453 their empire broke up, but they had made an epoch in history by driving the Teutons (including the Goths) into the western Roman Empire, which broke under the strain. The Huns themselves, who are still remembered as the most typical and most terrible of Asiatic invaders, disappeared from history after accomplishing this task. But in this there is nothing so very strange. They were a snowball empire including many Mongolian elements and, as we have seen, Iranians, Goths, and Slavs. Of their actual kinsfolk, many reappear under other names.

Such were the Bolgars, who figure in history from the fifth century. In the sixth, they were divided into two main groups, west and east of the Don. They invaded the Greek Empire in alliance with Slavs and exacted tribute. Such were also the Avars, the Obry of the first Russian Chronicle, a tribe of which traces still remain in western Mongolia. Halfway through the sixth century they are found in the steppes of Russia. A little later they demanded and obtained tribute of Byzantium and were used to combat its other enemies, for instance the Bolgars, Slavs, Franks, and Gepids. On the departure of the Lombards from the plain of the Danube to Italy, the Avars took their place. Allied with the Western Bulgarians they drove out the Eastern, some of whom made their way eastward to the junction of Volga and Kama and there founded a kingdom which appears in the beginning of Russian history. Others of the same race retreated to the Caucasus, where they were later conquered by the Khazars. The Western Bolgars lived for a time in what is now Hungary and occupied the territory between the Danube and the Dnieper. They at first kept peace with Byzantium, but in 670 crossed the Danube and conquered their present home. Here they found as many as seven Slavonic tribes and were soon so thoroughly absorbed by them that their tongue later became the original church language of Slavonic peoples.

The Slavs, like everyone else, were set in motion by the Hun impact; but not being militarily organized they did not, like some other peoples, move wholesale. Already, as opposed to their nomad conquerors, they must have reached a considerable development as a people of cultivators, for the words which are practically common to their very distinctive group of languages—and therefore probably existed before their dispersion—include not only the family names such as father and mother, but the house with its simpler articles of furniture, the farm and its outhouses, the domestic animals, and even the simpler implements of agriculture. In those days of conglomerate empires there was no reason why they should appear at once as a political unit. They were rather materials which entered into different such empires—for instance, in all probability into that of Hermanric on the Dnieper, and later more certainly into the Hun Empire with its centre in the present Hungary. Certainly there were Slavs in present-day Roumania and Bulgaria (the Roumanian language, though derived from the Roman settlers of Trajan, includes numerous Slavonic elements), and also much further to the south of their original home.

It is after the Hun Empire breaks up that we first see the Slavs as a unit. They still hold the basins of Vistula, Pripet, Dnieper, Desna, Bug, and Dniester, but they have spread out in every direction. On the west side vast regions were left empty by the irruption of the Goths and other Teutons into the Roman Empire, and much of this ground was taken up by Slavs. The departure of great German tribes such as the Goths, Burgundians, Vandals,[1] and Lombards enabled the Slavs to settle westward up to and beyond the river Elbe (in Slavonic, *Laba*), and this was their western frontier about the time of Charlemagne. Hamburg was a fortress erected to hold them in check, and the Bodrichi (or Bold Ones) and Lyutichi (or Fierce Ones) resisted the German counter-advance eastward for many generations after the foundation of the Frankish Empire. Behind these were the seacoast people of Pomerania. In modern Germany a number of place names are Slavonic in origin, and these include Dresden and Leipzig. Descendants of these Slavs of the Elbe, still speaking a Slavonic language, survive in the Spreewald near Berlin under the name of Wends, a term applied by early writers to the whole Slavonic race (*Veneti*). East of them were the Poles on the Oder, Warthe, and Vistula. South of the Wends were the Czechs in Bohemia and Moravia. Eastward of the Czechs were the Slovaks in the north-western Carpathians. All these tribes are called West Slavs.

Further to the south the Serbs spread over the area known later as Serbia, Bosnia, Dalmatia, and Montenegro, which are all peopled by a stock speaking a distinctive Slavonic language. The same language is spoken by the Croats, of whom one branch, the White Croats, lingered in Galicia into the beginnings of Russian history. At the head of the Adriatic Sea were the Slovenes, closely akin to the Serbs and Croats. There were little to distinguish the Serbs from the Slavs living in present-day Bulgaria or Roumania; and all are known under the name of South Slavs.

Meanwhile, within the original home of the Slavonic family the West and South Slavs still joined immediately onto the eastern branch of the Slavs, to be known later as the Russians. These also had spread far out, in another direction, into the basin of the Don. This is testified by many of the river names and by references of Arab writers; from this district, for instance, large numbers of Slavs were carried away as prisoners into Asia Minor in the time of the Khazars.

[1] The Vandals appear to have had at least an admixture of Slavonic blood.

The Slavs of the Carpathians made themselves known to the civilized world by innumerable incursions into the still unconquered Greek half of the old Roman Empire, populating large areas and penetrating as far as the Peloponnesus, where traces of their language are still to be found. These Slavs did not invade as an organized state. They were an agricultural people and their wars, which were of a peculiarly planless, inconsequent, and irritating kind, seem to have been mainly conducted by small military groups drawn out of the various tribes and acting in unison for the occasion only. Their earliest social basis was the clan. Their marriages, for instance, were ordinarily made between near kinsfolk, and property was held in common under the headship of the chief of the clan. They would seem to have been approaching some larger measure of unity by a kind of federation of clans when they were overwhelmed by the Avars.

The yoke of the Avars was a peculiarly heavy one: we are told, for instance, that they harnessed women to chariots. They also made the Slavs fight in the front line in their wars against Byzantium. By driving this wedge into the Slavonic world the Avars further helped to send them radiating in all directions, and it was in wars with the Avars that the Czechs under a Frankish chief, Samo, were first able to assert their independence (623). The Avars as a political unit disappeared even more completely than their kinsmen the Huns, so that in the earliest Russian Chronicle they are held up as the very type of a vanished people. But none the less they vitally affected the future of Russia.

Numbers of East Slavs, seeking safety from the Avars, made their way as best they could to the great water road of the Dnieper. On this journey, which took many years, the old clan basis gradually gave way to the new basis of the family, for each small unit was compelled to fend for itself. The earliest historical centre of these new settlers was Kiev, which traces its name from a Slavonic princeling, Kiy. On the steep right bank of the Dnieper are a group of hills which were entrenched and fenced by Kiy and his brothers.

We can now have some kind of a picture of those Slavs who were ancestors of the Russian people. To the south were the Slavs of Kiev and its district on both sides of the Dnieper, who had come eastward from the Carpathians and founded an important city on the south of the water road. These were called the Polyane or people of the plain. They were the most civilized of the Eastern Slavs, for they had had more contact with the civilized Greek Empire. With these we must associate the Severyane, who crossed the Dnieper eastward and founded on its eastern tributaries branch depots of river trade, Chernigov, Pereaslavl, and Lyubech. Also we must here mention the Radimichi and Vyatichi, who came last from the west and passed northeastward up the Desna; the Vyatichi occupied the upper Oka and Don. Further east beyond the Severyane, in the basin of the Don, were those far-eastern Slavs who without any military or political organization had settled eastward after the collapse of the Hunnish Empire or even earlier and now entered into the composition of the Khazar State. Next, let us pass from Kiev northward up the water road. Here in the thickets and marshes west of the Dnieper we find the Drevlyane or forest folk, who led a primitive existence without organization and without towns, and north of them the Dregovichi, another forest folk even more primitive. In these remote districts the old clan basis lingered on much longer. Athwart the middle of the water road were the Krivichi, a savage people who in time formed another trading depot at Smolensk. These three tribes had probably never left the original home of all the Slavs. Still further north, extending from this central home, were the East Slavs of the water-systems of the Western Dvina and the Volkhov; and on the last-named river grew up in a prehistoric mist the notable trading centre of Novgorod (the New Town), probably founded from westward, which was later second in importance only to Kiev. Novgorod, which had a small sister city westward at Pskov, owed its main importance to this road, and in particular to its nearness to Scandinavia.

These East Slavs already possessed their commercial waterways not only past Estonia to the Baltic and southward to the Black Sea, but also eastward by the system of the Volga, where they had a trading depot at Rostov. By this road they obtained access to the kingdom of the Eastern Bulgarians at the confluence of Volga and Kama, and it was probably by this road that their merchants were later able to make their way even as far as Baghdad.

All these tribes belonged to the eastern branch of the Slavs. To the north of these East Slavs were the primitive and savage Lithuanians and the Finns of Estonia, known to the people of Novgorod under the name of Chud or foreigners. Finns extended over the north, centre, and east of present-day Russia to the Urals and beyond.

It will be seen that the East Slavs spread over a complete and linked system of waterways: Dnieper, Desna, Pripet, Dvina, Lovat, and Volkhov, with their two most important towns at the two extremities of this system, Novgorod on the north and Kiev on the south. Here was a unit out of which might be created a state, even a commercial state; and the water road was the first Russia. The chief towns along it grew up not as tribal centres, not as provincial capitals, but as trading depots; and there was active movement and trade to the Black Sea, Constantinople, and Asia Minor.

In the seventh century, at the time when some of these Slavs settled around Kiev, they found on their eastern side a people of Turkish origin, the Khazars (or Khozars), who had already founded a considerable state. The Khazars engaged in wars both with the Persians to the south of them, and later with the Arabs, contesting with them the possession of the Caucasus. This the Arabs secured; but the vast region to the north remained in the hands of the Khazars. They had frequent relations with Constantinople and through them passed the important eastern roads of Byzantine trade. These relations went as far as a marriage with Constantine V, Copronymus (761–75), whose son Leo IV was known as the Khazar. The Khazars offer an interlude between the savage irruptions from Asia which preceded and followed them. Their rule was not heavy and they were less military than commercial. They showed tolerance to all religions, and the form of belief adopted by their Khakan or prince was the Jewish. As has been pointed out, there was already a considerable Slavonic population between the Sea of Azov and the Dnieper, and this was absorbed in the Khazar State. The Khazars demanded and obtained tribute of the new Slav settlers who had come from the Carpathians to the Dnieper. We are told that the tribute sent from Kiev included a two-edged sword and that the Khazar prince, on receiving it, remarked that his own people had only one-edged swords and that the present tributaries would later conquer not only the Khazars but other peoples. Under Khazar rule the trade of the water road developed very greatly. The Khazars, who had their capital Itil at the mouth of the Volga, took only one tenth in toll of the goods which passed through their country, and merchants from Russia were able to make their way as far as Baghdad, where some of them were seen by the Arab writer Hordad Bey in 846. Large numbers of Arab coins passed back to the water road of the Dnieper; most of those which have been found date from the ninth and tenth centuries. We have then already important trading centres growing up along the water road. To this growth contributed another element, which was to be of the first importance in Russian history— the Vikings.

At this time (from 830 onwards), warrior traders of Scandinavia were bursting out in all directions from their sterile country. Even at home in their difficult fjords and estuaries they possessed a great school of navigation; the man who could sail the fjords need not be afraid of the North Sea. We are told that Charlemagne before his death saw their ravaging squadrons off his coast and wept. We know that the Vikings changed the whole history of England and of France. With their small ships propelled either by sail or oars or both, they not only crossed the sea but mounted all the main rivers of western Europe. For instance, there was a Dane Hrörekr (Rurik) possibly even the same as the Russian Rurik, who ascended the Elbe and the Rhine, hired Normans, obtained parts of Friesland as a fief from the Emperor Lothair, betrayed him, and was driven out by the Frisians. Viking enterprise in a more organized form founded realms in Normandy and in Sicily, and later even in the Levant. The Vikings would establish a kind of headquarters at the mouth of a great river or in an estuary, seize towns, demand tribute, hire themselves perhaps to the reigning sovereign and fight for him against other bands of Vikings, and obtain from him territory as permanent fiefs in reward for service. Exploits such as these, possible in the West, were very much easier in eastern Europe. Here there were no organized states to resist, and there was the most magnificent water road then known. The population, such as it was, was mostly gathered along this road, so that the name which the Vikings gave to this early Russia was Gardarik, or the land of homesteads or towns. The towns themselves were ready-made trading depots, the Slavs were commercial and not warlike. The Vikings therefore often passed along this road.[1]

But the main significance of a road is the place which it leads to, and this road led ultimately to the one remaining centre and repository of Roman civilization, Byzantium, the great natural fortress discovered by Constantine, which prolonged the life of the Roman Empire by a thousand years after the fall of Rome. The waterway was called at that time the road from the Varangers (Vikings) to the Greeks. Some of these Vikings passed the whole length of it to Constantinople, where there was a Norman Guard of the Emperor, come by another route, and entered his service. Others by loose temporary arrangements entered the service of the trading towns along the road, or without arrangement established themselves there. Trade and war alternated as chance suggested. The Viking came as a trader but was always pre-

[1] Lomonosov and some writers of the Slavophil school have tried their hardest to prove that the Vikings of Russia were not Scandinavians but Slavs. Against their fanciful suggestions and strained philology one must set the Scandinavian names of the first Varangers, the Scandinavian sagas that record their wanderings, and the Scandinavian foundation of early Russian law.

pared to be a warrior; in Kiev, for instance, as we shall see, the adventurers Askold and Dir (Höskuldr and Dyri), finding many Vikings
there, seized the city. On this route you might at any time meet someone
stronger than yourself; it was a series of reconnaissances, in which one
could not get off the main road. The Vikings went even further afield,
whether alone or associated with Slav merchants; and before Russian
history opens, the Black Sea itself was called by their name, Rus. Before
850 some of them crossed over into Asia Minor and sacked towns there.

Such are the factors which we have before us in the middle of the
ninth century—Slavs, Khazars, and Varangers. Further west a Slav kingdom had grown up in Moravia, which received a guarantee of its independence from King Louis, the German, by treaty in 874. Moravia contributed toward the conversion of the West Slavs to Orthodoxy by
inviting from Byzantium two Greeks of Salonica, St. Cyril and St.
Methodius. These invented a Slavonic alphabet which was later adopted
by several Slavonic peoples. Culturally, at least, it seemed as if the
Moravian kingdom might inaugurate some kind of common history of
the Slavs; but it was just now that another sharp turn in their story took
place. Asia was labouring again, and two new hordes arrived at the back
of the Khazar kingdom—the Ugry or Magyars, who were akin to the
Finns, and the Pechenegs or Patzinaks. The new invaders fought fiercely
with the Khazars and with each other. Already in 839 envoys of Scandinavian race sent from the Khazar Khakan to the Western Emperor,
Louis the Pious, found their way back cut off, and the Khazars appear
to have appealed to Byzantium for the help of military engineers. Their
realm was overrun, and leaving a Khazar kingdom still in existence at
Itil, the invaders passed further westward and disputed with each other
the Lower Dnieper. Byzantium set itself, as usual, to play them off
against each other, and ultimately the Magyars, caught between two
fires, passed the Dnieper not far from Kiev (898), and, crossing the
Carpathians with bag and baggage, established themselves in the fertile
plain of the Middle Danube which is now called Hungary. The Moravian kingdom was already in decline, and the Magyars dealt it the final
blow. Thus they drove a final wedge into the vast area of Slavonic
Europe, which now separated the South Slavs both from the Western
and from the Eastern and has ever since presented an insurmountable
obstacle to any achievement of Slavonic political unity.

The Pechenegs had a more immediate bearing on the very beginnings of Russian history. They were as remarkable among Asiatic invaders for their savagery as the Khazars for their mildness, and oc-

cupying both banks of the Lower Dnieper they blocked the outlet of the northern river trade to the sea and to Byzantium. This compelled all who were interested in the water road to take measures for its defence. Already the Slav towns often employed forces of Vikings. From the romantic story of the Russian Rurik contained in the first Russian Chronicle, which naturally tended to glorify the origins of the princely family, we may infer as follows: A band of Vikings had been employed in this way in the service of the large town of Novgorod. These Vikings returned to Scandinavia, and others who took their places were found unsatisfactory. The people of Novgorod decided therefore to invite back the earlier company, whose head was the Rurik of Russian history (862). He hesitated for a time "because of the savage habits of the people," and when he did come he did not at first settle in the city but only a long way off on Lake Ladoga, thus keeping open his road of retreat. Ultimately he quarrelled with the city, possibly demanding a bigger contribution than it was used to give, and there followed a rising led by one Vadim. Rurik however prevailed, and from this time onward his position in Novgorod was that of Prince. He detached two of his brothers to outlying depots, Izborsk in the neighbourhood of Pskov and Belozersk eastward. He also seems to have put a deputy in Rostov.

On his death in 879, one of his kinsmen, Oleg, ruled instead of Rurik's infant son, Igor. Already two companions of Rurik, Askold and Dir, who have already been mentioned, had passed on to Kiev and seized it. It is possible that they set about reducing to some obedience the more primitive tribe of Drevlyane. Anyhow they at once responded to the claims of the water road by conducting an expedition to Constantinople, where it appears that Viking traders had been killed in a fray. This expedition in 865 is the first announcement of the new Russia to civilized writers, and a record of it has been left by the Patriarch Photius. The Varangers were apparently well enough informed; for they came during the absence of the Emperor Michael III on a campaign against the Saracens, and at a time when favourable winds could take their light flotilla through the Bosphorus. They landed and treated the inhabitants with great savagery, but the Emperor Michael returned and very quickly beat them off, though their wild daring left a great impression. The leaders, who suffered another reverse on the shore of the Black Sea, escaped with only a few ships to Kiev. In 882 Oleg followed them down the water road and, appearing outside Kiev with superior forces, summoned them to his ship and treacherously murdered them— according to the Chronicle representing them as traitors to the infant

Igor. Oleg had as little difficulty in taking possession of Kiev as they had had. This event may be regarded as the first foundation of the Russian Empire.

Relying on a few historical allusions and still more on the data of language, we have attempted to trace the Slavs through these misty beginnings of their story. The account which has been given is at least in consonance with the character of their later history. Those who ask always for clear-cut events, for powerful and organized states, those who are inclined to regard history as a record of kings and wars, will in the case of the Slavs often lose sight of a factor less striking but in the long run far more important—population. Wars and conquests are not the best way of perpetuating a race. Throughout Slavonic and especially Russian history we meet at every turn references to the great numbers of Slavs, sometimes with the suggestion that if they could only organize themselves politically they could conquer the world. The Slavs did something else; they settled and tilled; and that, for a race which has always been peculiarly prolific, was the surest way not to conquer the world but to occupy it. They are pushed about the map not only during the great barbarian invasions, but sometimes also in much later history; their map is empty and gives them room to move. They enter into the composition of other states not bearing their name. To take one recent and very conspicuous instance, how many foreigners realized in 1914 that Austria-Hungary consisted three fifths of Slavs, and that these Slavs were all ready to welcome the Entente Powers as deliverers? Russia itself, as we shall see, has frequently been governed by rulers and administrators of foreign origin. But it is the bottom of Russia, not the top, the infantry of the country, not the cavalry, that has in the long run decided not only the economic but the political life of the State. Any record which does not take account of it must inevitably be inconsequent and unintelligible. It is necessary to seize from the outset this conception so strongly suggested in the beginnings of Slavonic history, that the history of states may be something very different from the history of peoples, and that, however little chronicled, it is, in the long run, the history of peoples that counts.

Let us sum up our conjectures as to the movements of the Slavs to the ninth century, when they already occupied something like their present ethnographical position on the map of Europe. We will regard them as living originally outside any contact with the history of those times on the Middle Dnieper, the Vistula, and the Carpathians. They come into contact with the Iranian Scythians and Sarmatians, who have left certain traces on their language. They naturally pass into the composition of the Gothic (that is, Teutonic) Empire of Hermanric, and later into the Hunnish (that is, Mongolian) Empire of Attila. They are also conspicuous in the wars waged by the Mongolian Avars. During these convulsions, many of them are forcibly moved and many move of themselves. Yet they keep their Slavonic identity and even, as in the cases of the Bulgarians and the Varangers, imprint it on their conquerors.

The Slavs spread out westward and southeastward. Some press forward to the Elbe but ultimately go down under the weight of the organized counter-advance of the Germans, leaving remnants in the Wends. The Czechs and the Poles, after a beginning of evangelism from the Greek Church through Moravia, accept Latin Christianity and become strong states. Both the Bulgarians and Serbs have periods of independence before they are conquered by the Turks. The East Slavs, concentrating along the water road of the Dnieper with its ramifications, are wrought into a State by the Varangers. Thus the Slavs by the tenth century cover the major part of what could then be called Europe, of which Russia guards the frontier from the nomads of Asia. Novgorod, Pskov, and Polotsk in the north, Smolensk and Rostov in the centre, and Kiev, Chernigov, and Pereaslavl in the south are outposts in a chain of communications which enable the imperial Vikings to make by water the circuit of Europe.

CHAPTER II

Kiev and the Water Road

[*882–1132*]

Aɪ along the water road and its connections there were already
Slavonic towns engaged in active trade, serving as depots for their ad-
joining districts. It is notable that hardly any one of these districts coincided with the boundaries of a given tribe. The chief of these towns
were Novgorod in the north, Smolensk in the middle, and Kiev at the
south of the road. But as Constantinople was the principle objective of
this trade there was around Kiev a bunch of other towns, some of them
on the lateral streams to the eastward, and this was the centre of commerce and life. The trade did not only pass along the water road and its
tributaries. Use was certainly already made of the Volga, with its trade
depot at Rostov. The Finnish tribes of this area, Ves, Merya, and
Muroma (around the present Murom), being politically unorganized,
offered no obstruction to transport. The kingdom of the Volga Bolgars,
near the junction of Volga and Kama, was an important depot of this
trade.

The unit of territory with which Oleg (Helgi) had to deal was
therefore an economic one and was closely bound together by means of
transport and by commercial interests. The task of Oleg and his successors was threefold, and his three different duties were closely connected. Firstly, they had to obtain obedience within the limits of their
economic area. This they could easily do along the water road itself, for
there the unity of interest was apparent to all. Thus Oleg in winning
Kiev did not lose Novgorod, and he had no difficulty in conquering
Smolensk. The Slavs of the Ilmen (Novgorod), therefore, who did not
even have a tribal name and included in their area also an alien Finnish
population, with the Krivichi of Smolensk and the Polyane of Kiev,
formed one realm. The Severyane on an eastern tributary close to Kiev
also naturally fell into this orbit. It was the distant tribes in the backwoods who offered a stubborn resistance—the Drevlyane and Dregovichi

in the area of the Pripet, west of the Dnieper, and the Radimichi and Vyatichi along the Desna and the Oka. The Vyatichi remained for a long while an unfriendly people through whom a way could only be made by leaders of peculiar daring.

The task of the early Grand Princes of Kiev has been described in detail in the works of the Byzantine Emperor Constantine Porphyrogenitus, contemporary of Olga, whom he entertained in Constantinople. In November, when the rivers were frozen, the Grand Prince would make his way up to the extremities of his domain and levy tribute, sending deputies where he could not go himself. The tribute consisted principally of furs (which came to be a standard of exchange), wax, honey, and slaves. Slavery was common before the coming of the Vikings. The Varanger princes, who were from the start associated with the more well-to-do Slav merchants, would enslave Slavs or Finns indiscriminately. Tribute had gradually to be defined, and part of it (called *povoz*) was brought in small boats by the inhabitants themselves to Kiev.

Visiting their domains, the Grand Princes had every interest also in administering justice. Their law was Viking law. The Prince after hearing both sides gave judgment according to his lights and to earlier customs. If either side in a civil suit were dissatisfied recourse to arms was allowed, and the winner could then impose his own terms. Penalties for offences were in the form of money fines (*viry*). These were regulated far more with reference to property than to person. For instance, there was a similar penalty for knocking out a tooth, for killing another person's slave, for taking a hound, or for enslaving a free peasant. Particular emphasis was laid on insults, and bodily harm was subject to a lesser penalty. It was clearly a law of the rich and the strong. A bankrupt was sold as a slave, and a thief who could not pay his fine was hanged.

In April, when the rivers opened, both the Prince and many of his subjects would make their way down the Dnieper to Kiev. Those who brought tribute would sell their boats in Kiev for the coming trade expedition to Constantinople, by which the Prince and the merchants would dispose of their wares. Convoys came from the principal towns, which had already a direct order of seniority—Kiev, Chernigov, Pereaslavl (all three at the southern end of the water road), Novgorod, and Smolensk. Distant Polotsk, with insufficient water communication, took little part either in these expeditions or in the public life of the realm. At Vitichev, some way below Kiev, there was a halt to wait for the last convoys and to rig out the expedition for the dangerous journey.

This brings us to the second task of the Grand Princes of Kiev. When

Oleg seized Kiev, the Pechenegs had already passed over the Dnieper westward and thus blocked the direct road to Constantinople. Throughout the whole of the great period of Kiev the sovereigns of this vast empire had the foreigner almost at their gates—one day's journey according to Constantine Porphyrogenitus, and two days' according to the German missionary Bruno. A way had therefore to be broken through by each successive water expedition. The Dnieper south of Kiev bends far to the eastward, and at its furthest eastern point before the new curve that carries it to the coast the river is full of rapids for a distance of some forty miles. At points the stream goes six times as fast. Some of the rapids could be passed by unfreighting the ships, others completely blocked the course of the river, and here the whole force had to disembark. The slaves—the most convenient of merchandise, for they could help to convey themselves to the market—would be marched along the bank in chains under escort, and they would carry not only the other goods but the boats as well. Here the Pechenegs would be sure to be waiting, and a flanking force had to be detached into the hinterland to secure the passage of the expedition. When the battered traders ultimately reached the coast at St. Eleutheria (Berezan), even in heathen times they offered thanks for their passage. The dangers were by no means over here. The flotilla had to keep close to the coast and the Pechenegs molested it in every way possible. It was only after passing the mouth of the Danube that the traders were in comparative security. The princes were now in a position to deal with the third of their tasks, commerce with Constantinople.

Constantinople was now at the height of its power. This wonderfully well chosen fortress, after beating off the waves of invasion that were fatal to the western half of the Roman Empire, was in the act of collapsing before the Arabs, when Leo III the Isaurian (717–41) gave it a new lease of life and so strengthened its administrative, financial, and legal machinery that it ultimately outlived the military power of Rome by a thousand years and preserved its monuments and traditions till there was a new Europe capable of making them a new starting-point of progress. Constantinople was an imperial city with no national basis. Its original Roman aristocracy had died out; in its politics Asiatics predominated over Greeks. The great majority of its European population was Slavonic, and for centuries the Slavs occupied much the greater part of the open country in Greece itself. Slavs were among its most prominent politicians and a Slav, Basil I, the Macedonian (867–86), was the founder of the victorious dynasty that now ruled the Empire.

SETTLEMENTS OF THE EARLY SLAVS

Yet the Slavs of Thrace and Thessaly often troubled it with serious risings and sometimes made common cause with the powerful kingdom of Bulgaria, whose sovereigns Krumn and Simeon were several times at the gates of Constantinople, as were also the Magyars more than once; and Basil II, the contemporary of Rurik's great-grandson Vladimir, had for nearly twenty years to wage with them a struggle of life and death. For all that, the Empire continued to extend eastward at the expense of the Caliphs of Baghdad; sea connections, in spite of the corsairs, were more or less preserved; and at least more of order, security, and civilization was maintained than anywhere in the Western Europe. Constantinople was far the greatest trade centre of Europe and, north of the dominions of the Caliph through the empire of the Khazars with which it had close relations, it traded with India and China, of whose wares and especially of bullion it was the chief purveyor to Europe, so that it was as much interested in the Russian water road as were the Varangers themselves: Greece was the centre of European industry.

The long iconoclast controversy, which was at once a protest of Asiatic thought against superstition and a plea for the supremacy of the imperial authority over the Church, after resulting in the definite triumph of the Emperors, was settled in favour of religious paintings (icons) at the close of the Isaurian dynasty. But the political and ecclesiastical claims of the Popes, which stood in the way of the solution of theological differences, ultimately (in 1053) led to a final rupture between the Churches of the East and the West. At the same time the stiffening of the Eastern Church, the complete triumph of the imperial authority, and the decay of local initiative and even of the governing class led to a fatal formalism beautified by a wonderful culture of architecture, church music, and ceremony, which made St. Sophia and the imperial palace seem to any traveller from the west or north almost like another world.

Constantinople maintained its trade connections north of the Black Sea through the ancient Greek colony of Kherson which still preserved till the ninth century its republican institutions, guaranteed by a charter of Constantine I in return for effective aid against the Goths.

Like Askold and Dir, Oleg, after he had established himself in Kiev, made an early campaign to Constantinople (907). Trade relations had again been disturbed, and the object of his expedition was to restore them. His expedition is not mentioned by the Greek writers, and the Russian account is probably very exaggerated, at least as to the number of boats (2000) which are said to have taken part. Oleg claimed to have brought back tribute from Byzantium. It is, however, certain that the expedition was followed by a trade treaty of the most detailed kind, which was regarded as re-establishing former relations that had existed between the two countries. Oleg's successor Igor made two military expeditions. The first (in 941) caused great alarm in Constantinople. The Russians landed on the coasts of Thrace and Bithynia, which they ravaged cruelly, crucifying, burying alive, and driving nails into the heads of priests. The main fleet of Byzantium was away; but the patrician Theophanes boldly attacked with fifteen ships. The Russians made desperate attempts to board them but were driven off by the famous "Greek fire" with huge losses. Their landing parties were destroyed, and all prisoners were beheaded. Theophanes overtook their flying fleet on its way back, and very few escaped to Russia. In 944, according to the Russian Chronicle, Igor invaded again, in league with the Pechenegs; on receiving the alarming news from Kherson, we are told, the Deputy Emperor Romanus I sent envoys to the mouth of the Danube where Igor, doubting his strength, concluded peace. Igor's expeditions also resulted in a treaty (943). In all there had been so far four expeditions: Askold's in 865, Oleg's in 907, Igor's in 941 and 944; and they were followed by four treaties, two of Oleg, one of Igor, and later one of his son Svyatoslav I, of which only part of the preface has been preserved.

These treaties are of remarkable interest. Merchants were admitted yearly to Constantinople, so we may presume that in the intervening years when there was no warfare the commercial expeditions were proceeding regularly. The Russian Grand Prince was expected to send a list of the members of his *druzhina* or company and of the private traders who were licensed to take part in the expedition. Such lists are on record and the names both of the *druzhina* and of the merchants are in the first list exclusively Scandinavian; in the second list preserved there are a few Slavonic names. The Russians were maintained free of cost by the Emperor and had free use of steam baths. They had to live in the suburb of St. Mamant. They might enter the city only unarmed, only by a certain gate, and never more than fifty at a time. A bailiff of the Emperor attended them and supervised their sales. The Emperor himself had the first right of buying from them. Disputes were tried by a mixed court which had regard to the laws of both nations; the law of Constantinople was of course Roman law, that of the Russians consisted of Scandinavian custom. The traders had to go home before the winter and received free of charge not only food but rigging for their journey. They were bound to succour any shipwrecked Greek crew which they met and to take it to the nearest port. The treaties contained detailed arrangements not only for the return of lost property, but even for extradition of criminals.

Igor (Ingvarr) succeeded Oleg and reigned from 912 to 945. He died in attempting to secure an extravagant tribute from the Drevlyane. He had visited them with his bodyguard and tribute had been given, but he returned with the smaller nucleus of his guard to obtain more, and was ambushed and destroyed. As his son Svyatoslav was a minor, the realm was governed by his widow Olga (Helga), who came of a Scandinavian family established in Pskov. Olga was one of the wisest and most energetic of Russian rulers. She regulated the tribute and travelled round the country establishing depots for its collection, which were called *Pogosty*—the name now sometimes given to a Russian parish, as these were the points where later a church would be built. She took signal vengeance on the Drevlyane. She was also the first of the family of Rurik to accept Christianity. Already, it would appear, there were Christian members of the *druzhina*; some of these took the oath to Igor's Greek treaty in a Church of St. Elias in Kiev. Olga saw the emptiness of the vague heathenism of her people and went to Constantinople, where she was baptized (957). Constantine Porphyrogenitus has left an account of her reception. According to the Russian account, she persuaded him to act as her godfather and afterwards, when he made her a proposal of marriage, adroitly reminded him that by Christian law a man could not marry his god-daughter. Olga's son Svyatoslav was now growing up, but he was unwilling to become a Christian because he thought his *druzhina* would laugh at him.

Svyatoslav I was the first prince to bear a genuinely Slavonic name. Undoubtedly Slav elements now entered freely into the *druzhina* itself. In fact this company or bodyguard, to which alone the name Rus was at first applied, had something even of a cosmopolitan character. Adventurers came to it from any country, Lithuania, Hungary, Poland, or the nomads of the steppe. The name Rus probably comes from the word Rothsmen or seafarers, a corrupted form of which (Ruotsi) was used by the Finns to describe the Varangers who came to Russia. It was used long before the coming of Rurik. It now came to mean the upper class of the Kiev realm, which was a mixture of Scandinavian and Slavonic elements.

Svyatoslav did not limit himself to a campaign against Constantinople. He engaged all his forces in a desperate war southwards and, establishing himself on the Danube in Bulgaria, he even thought of moving his capital thither. The reasons which he gave were purely commercial. There, as he said, he would be able to concentrate silver and horses from Bohemia and Hungary, gold, wines, fruits, and silks from Greece, and from his own Russia honey, furs, wax, and slaves. One can see from this how much of the trading adventurer still remained in the Varanger princes and how little there was of the national sovereign. Nor is this the only time that the ruler of Russia wished to plant his capital outside it.

The occasion was an invitation from the Emperor Nicephorus II to join with him against the Bulgarians, who had demanded a former tribute. Kalokyres of Kherson, the Byzantine envoy, brought with him 1500 pounds of gold. Kalokyres, however, treated for himself and not for his master, and declared himself Emperor. Svyatoslav invaded and thoroughly defeated the Bulgarians in 968, capturing the capital Pereaslavl (Preslava) and conquering the country. Svyatoslav was recalled to drive the Pechenegs from his own capital, and with Byzantine help Bulgaria was reconquered. Svyatoslav, however, having made peace with the Pechenegs and allied himself with the Magyars, returned with an army of 60,000 men. He conquered Bulgaria over again and, entering Thrace by the westward pass through the Balkans, took Philippopolis where he massacred 20,000 of the inhabitants. Demanding tribute, he advanced towards Constantinople, but on the defeat of one of his detachments by Bardas Sclerus he recrossed the Balkans to Bulgaria. Hither, in the spring of 971, he was followed by the Deputy Emperor John Zimisces, perhaps the greatest general of Byzantine history, who also sent 300 ships to cut his communications on the Danube. Passing unopposed through the eastern passes, Zimisces beat the Russians in an obstinate battle in which they lost 8500 men and stormed Pereaslavl, which was stubbornly defended by 7000 Russians and Bulgarians. After celebrating Easter here, Zimisces marched to Dorystolon (Silistria), which Svyatoslav and his men defended with desperate bravery. He was investing the town with trenches when the Russians tried to force their way through in squares, relying on the protection of their long shields. Their equipment however was not a match for his armoured cavalry and archers, and after a whole day's fighting they were driven back. They came out to battle again and again but with no more success; a last and still more determined sally was repulsed, and after two months' siege Svyatoslav, whose army was reduced to 22,000, declared himself ready to make terms. Zimisces, who felt that it would be dangerous to drive his enemy to despair, gave him honourable conditions. Svyatoslav engaged not to invade Kherson or Bulgaria again, and the old commercial treaties were confirmed. He was allowed to retire with all that remained of his force and was even given maintenance for the journey. He suffered further disasters in the Black Sea, and with the relics of his army found the Pechenegs blocking the rapids of the Dnieper. In his attempt to break his way through he was killed, and his skull became a drinking cup for his conqueror (972).

Svyatoslav, who cared so little for Russia, had made a division of his domains before he started on his last enterprises. His eldest son Yaropolk I, a mere boy, was in the hands of his advisors. The powerful Svineld, to gratify a personal grudge, stirred him up to fight his brother Oleg, who was defeated and perished in the retreat. Another son Vladimir thought it wisest to fly to Sweden, but the hearty support which he got from Novgorod brought him to the gates of Kiev; as before and later, the North proved stronger than the South. Yaropolk, whose chief fault seems to have been his mildness, was shamefully betrayed by his counsellor Blud and was murdered. Vladimir established himself in Kiev, reigning as sole ruler after the manner of his predecessors (980). He also conquered another Viking prince, Rogvolod, who ruled in Polotsk.

Vladimir I at his accession was a savage and zealous heathen. He showed great brutality after his triumph at Polotsk. He had a large number of wives. Heathenism in Russia was very vague and lacking in content. There were various beliefs as to what happened after death. Some thought it was the end, others that the dead passed into a new country, so that their tombs were sometimes supplied with articles for the journey; others that the spirit passed to heaven, and these cremated their dead; a Russian expressed surprise to the Arab writer Ibn-Fadlan that "they should put their best and fondest in the earth where there are worms and corruption." There was no caste of priests, no regular public worship. There is some suggestion that Yaropolk was inclined to Christianity, and Vladimir began his reign with an orgy of paganism. He put in front of his palace figures of all the old Slavonic gods: Svarog the father of gods, Dazhd-Bog his son the god of the sun, Veles the patron of cattle, Stribog the wind god and, chief of all, Perun the god of thunder, with a huge silver head and moustaches of gold. Vladimir's favourite boyar Dobrynya set up another idol of Perun in Novgorod. Vladimir celebrated his triumph by sacrificing close on a thousand lives to his gods. One of the victims on whom the lot fell was the son of a boyar who had become Christian. This boyar refused to give up his child. "Yours is not a god," he said, "but a piece of wood." He and his son

were killed by a furious crowd, but this was the last outburst of heathenism; Vladimir himself came to be convinced of the need of choosing a
new faith.

The record in the Russian Chronicle is in the nature of a legend, but
the story is very suggestive. Vladimir was well able to hear the merits of
various religions discussed in Kiev, which was a highway for the travellers of many nations. The Khan of the Khazars had professed the Jewish
faith, and there were many Jews in Kiev, in all probability before the
Varangers. The Polish king Mieszko I had accepted Catholicism in 966.
Also there was contact with Mahometan peoples. Vladimir is reported
to have discussed the question with various strangers. He asks the Jews
the home question of a statesman; why they are scattered over the face
of the earth; and they reply "for their sins," so that Judaism is discarded.
Islam is also rejected because, as Vladimir explains, it is quite impossible
to be happy in Russia without strong drink. Papal Christianity was
hardly likely to appeal to Vladimir; with Rome the spiritual chief is
above all secular rulers. Much stronger and also much nearer was the
attraction of the Orthodox confession. Envoys whom Vladimir sent to
Constantinople returned entranced with the beauty of the Orthodox
services which have ever since made so powerful an appeal to Russian
hearts, and they also pointed to the example of Vladimir's grandmother,
Olga.

Once the form of belief had been chosen, the next thing was to
conquer it and not merely to accept it as a gift. Civilization is usually
offered to the uncivilized at a price, and the price is often independence.
This is the significance of the curious anecdote, already quoted, as to
Olga's baptism. Vladimir marched on the Greek colony at Kherson,
which he conquered after a long siege. To the two Greek Emperors of
the time, Basil II (Bolgaroctonus) and Constantine VIII, he made it
known that he would desist from further attacks if they would send
him their sister in marriage; otherwise "it will be the same with your
town as with Kherson." The terms were complied with, and the Princess
Anne was married to Vladimir in Kherson. Before the wedding Vladimir
became a Christian (989).

The conversion of Russia was the act of the Prince, and it was an act
of statesmanship. The acceptance of Christianity by his subjects was
in the first place an act of obedience. We are told, for instance, that the
people of Kiev accepted baptism wholesale in reply to a direct injunction of the Prince; some fled to the woods rather than do so. In the
more distant towns it was the Prince's deputies who were the champions

of the new religion. Dobrynya imitated his master's conversion, and it was with fire and sword that he forced Christianity on Novgorod. But in general Christianity, along the water road at least, was in the main not received unwillingly. Many conversions were the result of the preaching of Christian bishops and monks. It was in the far corners that heathenism lingered longest: for instance, in Rostov, where both Russian and Finnish inhabitants joined against the Christians and there were several martyrdoms. The first bishops came from Constantinople; but Vladimir took early steps to provide for the training of young men of good family for the priesthood, and it was not long before the highest post, that of Metropolitan, was filled by a Russian, Hilarion. The first Christian priests in Russia did much to adapt themselves to the existing beliefs where possible. Perun the god of thunder becomes Elijah, with his chariot of fire; Veles becomes St. Blaise, and is still the patron of cattle. Far later there remained very strange blends of Christian and heathen ideas.

Vladimir from the start made use of the higher clergy as counsellors. Passing from heathen savagery to Christian weakness, he even expressed himself as reluctant to punish highway robbers with death; and it was the bishops who urged him that he was put in office by God as a menace to evil-doers. On the other hand, it was the bishops who obtained of him that slavery, instead of death, should be the punishment for robbery, arson, and horse stealing. The priests, as the only literate persons, were invaluable for civil purposes: for the keeping of records, which was probably begun in this or the next reign, for embassies, and for other public services.

Vladimir left twelve sons by the most various mothers. At the moment of his death he was preparing to drive his son Yaroslav from Novgorod for refusing tribute. The news of his death was kept secret. The eldest son Svyatopolk I, ambitious and unscrupulous, wanted an undivided inheritance and was afraid that the choice of the bodyguard for Grand Prince would fall on Boris who, like his brother Gleb, appears to have been born of the Byzantine princess Anne. Boris, however, refused to oppose his elder brother, and when the bodyguard had dispersed he was brutally murdered while at his prayers by order of Svyatopolk. Svyatopolk next sent murderers who dispatched Gleb. Yaroslav, getting word of his danger from a sister, made up a bad quarrel which had broken out between his bodyguard and the men of Novgorod and sailed with them for Kiev. Svyatopolk was driven out but returned with powerful help from his father-in-law, Boleslaw the Brave, who was one of the most brilliant kings of Poland. Many of the Polish troops, however, were killed off when quartered out among the population; the Poles withdrew and Svyatopolk was again expelled, once more by the army of Novgorod. Svyatopolk turned to the Pechenegs but was betrayed by them on the very spot where he had had Boris murdered. Boris and Gleb were canonized by the Church as types of the brotherly love which was so sorely needed in the Russia of Kiev; and Svyatopolk comes down to us with the name of "Accursed."

Yaroslav's long reign (1019–54) was comparatively peaceful. His final victory over the Pechenegs was more or less decisive, and we hear no more of them as a menace to Russia. For a prince of his time, he was a notable scholar and provided for the copying and translating of Greek books, of which he made a permanent library in one of the new churches which he built. Yaroslav I so greatly beautified Kiev that it was later described by Adam of Bremen as "the glory of Greece." He had, like the Byzantine Emperors, his Golden Gates and his St. Sophia, which did not, however, follow the model of the original. He had the passage from his palace to the church painted, as in Constantinople, with scenes of hunting, music, dancing, and other amusements. He filled Kiev with churches and founded the monastery of St. George.

Already there existed outside the city the beginnings of the famous Monastery of the Caves, which was the first centre of the Orthodox Church in Russia. This great refuge and sanctuary has all sorts of subterranean passages through the friable stone of the high cliffs overhanging the right bank of the Dnieper; for centuries afterwards one could see the remains of those monks who in final triumph over earthly things had themselves half buried before death, and received food only at increasing intervals till they died. The Monastery of the Caves became the first nursery of the Russian Chronicles, which were systematized at the beginning of the twelfth century and continued in ever widening streams of local narrative. Each individual district developed its own psychology in its chronicles; Kiev, radiant and many-coloured, Novgorod, short and drastic, Suzdal, dry and plain. The task of recording events faithfully was therefore regarded as a holy work, and the chroniclers took great pains to secure accuracy. These annals were a school of history in which man was taught to use the past for guidance in the present and to see always before him the great choice between good and evil. They have exercised a deeply moral influence on all succeeding Russian historians.

It was also the clergy who first brought precise ideas of law into

Russia. The princes still judged by custom in their own courts. Church law, as such, was imported wholesale from Constantinople by the translation of all the chief Byzantine models. This of itself established a new standard, in conflict with the old; the standard of sin as distinct from the standard of crime. The church jurisdiction covered domestic matters —relations between man and wife, desertion, adultery, mixed marriages, women's rights of property, daughters' share in inheritance; in every way the Church heightened the consideration paid to women. But apart from this, the Church had under its civil jurisdiction whole categories of the population; firstly, all the servants of the Church itself from the highest to the lowest; and further, those who were indirectly in its service, for instance the first doctors and nurses; besides these, all those who lived in almshouses, and all the bereaved who were called *izgoi* or "excluded," the term extending to all who had no fixed place in society, for instance bankrupt traders, sons of priests who were too illiterate to enter the priesthood, slaves who had managed to purchase their freedom, and even those princes who, by the early death of their fathers, lost their place of seniority in the reigning family. For those who were under its civil jurisdiction, the Church needed a code of its own, and this is the origin of the first monument of Russian law, *Russkaya Pravda*. It is based on Byzantine secular models, in particular the Ecloga of Leo III, the Isaurian (717–41) and the Procheiron of Basil I, the Macedonian (867–86), but applies them to the customs which the priests found already obtaining in Russia. It is notable that the modifications of the Greek codes made for use in Russia are all in the direction of greater mildness. It is also interesting to find that the code possesses the most minute regulations as to commerce, showing how fully developed the trade of the water road then was. For instance, there are precise distinctions between a friendly loan and one with agreed interest, between short credit and long, between a trader's commission and a shareholder's dividend, between malicious and accidental bankruptcy. In sales of the property of bankrupts by auction, the first claim belonged to the Prince, the next to foreign creditors, and only after that the remainder went to the home creditors.

Yaroslav fought with the Poles and conquered back present-day Galicia. He was the last of the old Russian sovereigns to fight the Greeks, sending his son against them at the head of an expedition because of the murder of a Russian merchant in Constantinople. The long struggle with the Pechenegs he brought to an end in 1036. He was one of the greatest sovereigns in the Europe of his time and formed many foreign connections. He married his sister Mary to King Kazimir I of Poland—whom he helped in his internal wars—his daughter Elizabeth to King Harald Hardrada of Norway, his daughter Anastasia to King Andrew I of Hungary, and his daughter Anne to Henry I of France, by which marriage Yaroslav is one of the ancestors of the reigning family in England. His favourite son Vsevolod he married to a daughter of the Greek Emperor Constantine Monomachus.

These early Russian princes are not national sovereigns but adventurers in a vast foreign land which is comparatively empty. Thanks to the Chronicles, the type stands out clearly enough. With most of them, guile and caution play as large a part as valour. It is not so with Svyatoslav I, but it is for that very reason that his deeds do not belong to Russian history. Rurik feels his way into Novgorod, keeping his line of retreat open. Oleg, who is called the Knowing, pretends to be a merchant on his way to Constantinople when he entices Askold and Dir to their death, and is held up as one who has proved a match for Greek cunning. He wins and holds Kiev because he has prepared not a raid but an expedition. He conquers his hinterland systematically (the Chronicles give one year to each conquest) and he brings all his forces to bear at Constantinople. Igor turns back from his second expedition, and it is irresolution, not daring, that brings him to his death. Olga trusts entirely to her wits. She avenges her husband's death on the Drevlyane by a series of four successful deceits. In the end she gives them peace in return for a tribute of pigeons and sparrows and, fastening torches to each bird, sends them back to burn the town. Vladimir I and Yaroslav I are soon disheartened; they flee when the odds are against them, Vladimir even when there seems no need; but his conversion is the story of a man who knows his mind.

Their task is to "think for the land of Russia"; a good prince takes counsel with his comrades, with whom he shares his great commercial profits, chiefly derived from the sale of his other subjects. Svyatoslav is reproached for leaving Kiev with his aged mother to be besieged by its dangerous neighbours the Pechenegs. But Vladimir, attending to his duties, holds the enemy at bay by a system of frontier military colonies drawn from all parts of his realm and even from Poland. He is also commended for his bountiful feasts, in which he himself thinks of sending some of the good cheer to the sick and infirm. Yaroslav is extolled by the first Russian Metropolitan, Hilarion, as a Solomon following a David. From the time when the clergy become the conscience keepers of the princes, a prince is expected to honour the Church, to be good to the poor, to keep the princely family in harmony and to fight the heathen.

Before Yaroslav died in 1054, he wished to avert such a feud of brothers as had preceded his own accession and that of his father. He foresaw, though vaguely, the difficulties of a joint rule. He therefore made his younger sons promise to accept the eldest, Izyaslav, in the place of father, and Izyaslav was pledged in his turn to protect any of his brothers who was wronged. He also divided his realm between them. Izyaslav was to have both ends of the water road, Kiev and Novgorod. The next son, Svyatoslav, was to have Chernigov and also two distant appendages—Murom and Ryazan on the Middle Volga and the distant Russian colony of Tmutorakan near the Caucasus. The third son, Vsevolod, was to have Pereaslavl close to Kiev, and also the distant province of Suzdal in the neighbourhood of present-day Moscow. The fourth, Vyacheslav, got Smolensk in the middle of the water road. The fifth, Igor, obtained the outlying district of Volhynia; and Rostislav, the child of Yaroslav's own eldest son who had died before his father, was to receive Rostov. The interest of the peculiar division lies in its obvious aim of preserving the unity of the family domain as a whole. It set up a tradition which was later preserved as Yaroslav's command to his descendants to stand together as a united family.

In the first generation this new and difficult order of succession was at least in the main observed. It was no long respite that the vulnerable eastern frontier obtained after Yaroslav had crushed the Pechenegs. Their place was taken by a more powerful Asiatic people, the Polovtsy, or Kipchak Turks, known to the Western world as Cumans, who continued to harry the district of the Lower Dnieper to the end of the period of Kiev's predominance. Once the people of Kiev themselves expelled Izyaslav I because he was not competent to defend them from these new invaders. He was also suspected by his two next brothers of wishing to defraud them of their inheritance, and to refound the undivided monarchy. They therefore expelled him from Kiev again, and Svyatoslav of Chernigov took his place. On Svyatoslav's death Vsevolod succeeded in Kiev. Izyaslav now returned with Polish assistance and Vsevolod, without opposing him, retired to Chernigov. When Izyaslav died, Vsevolod at last became lawful master of Kiev. Yaroslav had said to him that if he ever possessed Kiev without having contravened the family order, he was to be buried beside himself. Svyatoslav II had not observed this rule, and that was one reason why the claims of his descendants were so often subsequently challenged.

If Vsevolod I, Yaroslav's favourite son, who at last reigned in Kiev, had been succeeded from son to son in the direct line, for no fewer than six generations Kiev would have been under the rule of strong, able, and even brilliant princes. Not only in distant Novgorod, where the prince was almost regarded as the nursling of the city, but in central Kiev, the bone of all contentions, the townsmen were beginning to have their say. They had expelled Izyaslav I and had told him with convincing bluntness that if he could not defend them from the increasing incursions of the Polovsty, "they had nothing left but to go off to Greece." They dearly longed to keep Vsevolod's eldest son Vladimir Monomakh as Grand Prince; but the conscience of Yaroslav was still a heritage for his descendants, and Monomakh refused to encroach on the claim of his cousin Svyatopolk, whose father, the futile Izyaslav, had reigned before Vsevolod in Kiev. This chivalry was all the more disastrous, because Monomakh was himself the flower of the Kiev dynasty and Svyatopolk II was weak, false, and cruel. But while patiently waiting his turn, Vladimir Monomakh, in the words of Solovyev, set himself "to fight all the evils in the Kiev system and even make it satisfy the needs of the time."

In a remarkable letter, manly and unselfish, he asked for peace with his cousins of Chernigov, over whom he was already prevailing in war, and secured a congress of princes at Lyubech at which their wrongs were righted, though only by the arrangement that each should rule where his father had ruled, the very principle of which he himself had refused to take advantage. But almost immediately afterwards a crying outrage broke the peace. One of the junior princes, Vasilko, was already renowned for knighthood and chivalry; a rival, Prince David, who was jealous and fearful of Vasilko, enticed him to the house of Svyatopolk; he was seized and bound, carried away in a cart, and blinded after a desperate resistance. Monomakh was no weak man; he declared that David had thrown a sword among the family when all efforts were needed to keep the heathen at bay. A second congress was called at Vitichev (1100), and Svyatopolk was required to deprive David of his domain. Svyatopolk acted halfheartedly; but the blinded Vasilko, with his brother Volodar who made common cause with him throughout, proved too strong for David, who died in disgrace in the north.

When order was restored in the family, Monomakh was able to achieve his long-cherished wish to unite all the princes in a crusade against the heathen. The effects of the union were an object lesson. In two successive expeditions (1101, 1103) the princes carried back the war into the heart of the Polovtsy country, ending with a signal triumph, which drew from Monomakh the words: "This is the day which the Lord hath made; let us rejoice and be glad in it." In 1111 Monomakh prompted a third great crusade, which was everywhere victorious. In 1113 when Svyatopolk died, and Monomakh again thought of standing down in favour of the senior line of Chernigov, the people of Kiev would take no denial, and for twelve happy and victorious years the best of the family was Grand Prince in Kiev.

Vladimir Monomakh is the King Alfred of Russian history. He left a striking "Charge" to his children in which the whole man is apparent. Throughout life he has been in constant travel—he reckons eighty-three "long journeys"—often sleeping in the open. He has made his way through the forests to the distant Oka by the dangerous "straight road" of the Desna. He has been thrown by a bull, butted by a stag, trampled by an elk, bitten by a bear, borne to the ground by a wolf. He tells his sons to pray before sleeping and when alone on a journey, not to let the sun find them in bed, to judge the poor in person, never to kill innocent or guilty, and to shed no blood except in battle. "Children, fear neither battle nor beast. Play the man. Nothing can hurt you unless God wills it. God's care is better than man's."

Vladimir Monomakh ruled in Kiev from 1113 to 1125 and was followed by a son worthy of him, Mstislav I, who, till his death in 1132, firmly maintained the peace and order established by Monomakh and kept the family united against the heathen. He even went so far at to send to imprisonment in Constantinople the Prince of Polotsk, who had refused to join in a common effort against the Polovtsy, and annexed his domain. His death was the real end of the great period of Kiev. Kiev with such a constant succession of rulers could not develop a strong local government. Kiev was a prize clutched at by all. But by the very nature of things, a strong territorial power was developed by the able rulers of the frontier domains, especially in Volhynia by the line of Izyaslav II and in the opposite corner of Russia, the distant northeast of Rostov, Suzdal, Vladimir, and Moscow, where Monomakh's last son Yury and his successors Andrew and Vsevolod III thought first of strengthening their own domains. It was with their strong local forces that these two lines were able to dispute between them the empty sovereignty of Kiev.

On the death of Monomakh's son and successor Mstislav, his next brother Yaropolk, who has gloriously repulsèd an invasion of the Polovtsy singlehanded, succeeded him in Kiev (1132–9). On his death, a Chernigov prince, Vsevolod II, claimed and held the throne on the ground of seniority. This was tolerated, but before his death in 1146 he tried to establish a permanent Chernigov dynasty in Kiev; the city called in Izyaslav II of Volhynia, son of Mstislav I, but this incensed his uncle Yury Long-Arm of Suzdal. In the incessant wars that followed, princes of the Chernigov line were to be found in both the Monomak-hovich camps, and Izyaslav II was supported by the kings of Poland and Hungary, while each side employed "Polovtsy of its own." Izyaslav II put forward another uncle, Vyacheslav, who was senior to Yury, and governed Kiev for some time in his name. But Izyaslav died before Vyacheslav, and Yury was at last able to establish himself permanently in Kiev. When Yury I died (1157), Izyaslav's son Mstislav II of Vol-hynia, who could claim no right of seniority, was invited to rule in Kiev by the citizens. But Yury's son Andrew, when the succession came to him, as we shall see, did not care to take it and put in a deputy.

In the curious gyrations in the succession which followed, we need only note the main features. From the start there were formidable princes excluded from the succession, often eldest sons of eldest sons. Such were the princes of Polotsk, the heirs of Vladimir I's eldest son, whom he separated off from the succession and established on the north-west frontier of his realm. Such also were Vasilko, who was blinded, and his loyal brother Volodar, sons of the eldest son of Yaroslav I; these by the intervention of Monomakh were guaranteed their domains on the southeast frontier in Galicia. Such again were the sons of Monomakh's own eldest son, Mstislav; two of them, Izyaslav II, who was peculiarly able in war and government, and Rostislav, renowned for his piety and fairness, at different times reigned in Kiev by invitation of the citizens; but Izyaslav's domains were in Volhynia, again on the frontier. Izyaslav's eldest son, Mstislav II, also ruled in Kiev by invitation; his descendants were able to annex Galicia on the extinction of its dynasty and thus created a strong frontier province, always disturbed by the selfishness and treachery of its boyars, who did not scruple to call to their aid the neighbouring kings of Poland and Hungary, but maintained in honour and power by two exceptionally able princes of this line, Roman and his son Daniel. Rostislav received Smolensk as his domain; from him sprang two brilliant princes, his son Mstislav the Brave and his grandson Msti-slav the Daring.

But apart from all these *izgoi* or excluded princes, there was the eternal feud between the two lines of Chernigov and of Vladimir Monomakh, sprung respectively from the second and third sons of Yaro-slav I. Kiev would have none of the Chernigov line, as it showed plainly enough when Monomakh for the second time wished to give way to a cousin. But Chernigov never gave up hope, and three of its princes sat on the throne of Kiev. Add to all this that Yaroslav I had intentionally interlaced the domains of his various sons all over Kiev Russia, so that each feud meant civil war all over the country. By this time the supremacy had departed from Kiev, and political importance in Russia was divided between the frontier principalities of Vladimir in the northeast, of Galicia in the southwest, and the merchant city of Novgorod in the north.

The order of seniority, with succeeding generations, became an absurdity. According to the principle of Yaroslav, every death in the family would be succeeded by a movement of princes, each being promoted to a senior district. Two values were set by side: the exact order of seniority in the whole family and the exact order of importance of the various principalities. Of these two values the first became so confused as to be ultimately useless. The princely family grew fast. Early marriages were usual and, with the multiplication of the various branches, it was often impossible to say whether the nephew of one line was not senior to the uncle of another. Close kinsmanship disappeared as a factor; it was impossible to expect unanimity from a generation of second cousins. In practice, at least, the principle was from the first partly modified by not taking account of any beyond the third brother. The fourth brother was very often the coeval of the first. For instance, Yury Long-Arm's fourth brother (he himself was the fifth) writes to him, "I had a beard before you were born." Inevitably also the idea of patrimony began to receive a new interpretation. Originally it had meant the right to the first place in the whole family. Later it came to mean, as at Lyubech, the right to succeed to the territory held by your father. The towns continued to grow and naturally spoke with increasing vigour in these disputes. They were of course entirely opposed to the continual disturbances caused by princely transferences and princely feuds. They preferred the son of the prince who had ruled in their city and was known to them. The princely family came to be a kind of upper stratum of society, movable and detached from the rest of the community, and their general politics brought incessant confusion. Most princes took no account of any rules. One of them, Izyaslav II, boldly declared that "the place should not go to the head but the head should go to the place" and established himself in Galicia by his head, that is, by battle. With the multiplication of princes went a multiplication of *druzhiny*, or fighting companies. Every prince had his *druzhina*, and several of these numbered as many as two thousand men. This, when there came to be nearly a hundred princes, was a simple scourge to the country. The astonishing thing is that such a system could last as long as it did.

For all that, the system was at least a great effort of chivalry, and, as such, it even had practical results which were of great importance to the future of Russia. The princes were at least in principle a band of brothers, and quite late, even among third cousins, there were very striking examples of family loyalty. The princes were all kinsmen; and from this family grew up a corporate sense among the scattered communities. Novgorod, at the far end of the water road, was compelled to follow closely all that happened in Kiev; the new prince in Kiev would be entitled to send his son as deputy to Novgorod. There was sense in this, for the road, if split up into pieces, ceased to be a road. Thus it was always in the hinterlands that the territorial principle gained ground fastest; the road kept together as long as possible—in fact, until it was itself devastated. The fellowship of the family meant the supremacy of Kiev. Kiev was the victim of the system, for it was the object of all intrigues and ambitions; yet Kiev, as the recognized centre of the State, was able to spread a whole civilization over the area of the water road and its side communications. Kiev architecture had owed its origin to Constantinople, but it had its own character with its own distinctive mural decorations, and it became a model as far as the Middle Volga. All roads led to Kiev, or as the Russians said: "To Kiev your tongue will find the way." Greek law, as adapted by the Russian priesthood, spread over all this area and gave new conceptions of right and wrong, which were to bear fruit far into the future.

CHAPTER III

Breakup of Kiev: Migrations: The Tartars

[*1132–1263*]

KIEV did produce a galaxy of princes even after Monomakh: indeed the trouble was that there were too many of them. In the Galician line, we have in direct succession the two able and popular rulers of Kiev, Izyaslav II and Mstislav II; next, Roman of Galicia, who summed up his successful struggles with his boyars in the grim words, "You cannot eat the honey until you have crushed the bees," and lastly, Daniel, described in the Chronicles as "without blemish from head to foot," in the saddle from his childhood, as a boy with his ever faithful brother Vasilko working to restore his questioned right and triumphing by sheer courage, wisdom, and perseverance, leading the advance guard in the chivalrous attack on the Tartars on the river Kalka.

The two Mstislavs of Smolensk, the Brave and the Daring, dash round Kiev Russia as knight-errants, putting their heads into every wasps' nest. Mstislav the Brave, when Andrew of Vladimir sends his peremptory orders to "get out of Kiev," shaves the envoy of his powerful senior, who commands instead of asking after the old manner of "elder brothers," and sends him back with a message of open defiance. When Andrew marches on him with an enormous mixed host, Mstislav holds out against it till it breaks up of itself. Next he appears in Novgorod, where he again defies the princes of Vladimir and fights the battles of the city against its incessant assailants. His son, the Daring, also rules in Novgorod and defies the new centre of power, Vladimir, at one time leading an invading army to its walls. In Galicia he drives out the Poles and sets Daniel on his feet again. It is he who insists on facing the Tartars before they have conquered the Polovtsy, and he is the leader of the attack in the fatal battle on the Kalka. These two are types of the Russian knights of the frontier "swaddled under trumpets, cradled in helmets, fed from the end of a lance." The glorious literary monument of this race of fighters is the *Tale of the Host of Igor*. A prince of Chernigov makes his own bold plunge into the country of the Polovtsy: "he had a strong wish to try the Don." Soon they are swallowed up in the steppe: "O land of Russia, thou art already beyond the hills." Omens all around accompany them to the fatal battlefield, "and there the brave sons of Rus finished their feast." Nature weeps for them: "the grass bends with pity and the tree bows to the earth for grief . . . and the heathen from all sides come victorious into the land of Russia."

Kiev was a great and generous attempt to do the impossible: along a single thin road running almost on the frontier of Europe, with a nascent civilization, a scattered population and a hopeless political organization which had little in it but the fine spirit that prompted it, to keep at bay the unceasing and successive waves of population which were driven by economic necessity out of Asia's storehouse of peoples along that other great road of the black soil that brought them into Europe. It is in the right angle of these two roads, the black-soil and the water road, that lie the meaning and pathos of early Russian history; and they bisect each other at Kiev which was at once the capital and the frontier fortress of Russia. The Pechenegs in ceaseless wars, finishing with the crushing victory of Yaroslav, were indeed worn out and exhausted, and in the end became allies; but their place had been taken almost at once by the Polovtsy, more numerous and better organized, and the whole of the Kiev period was spent in the struggle to keep them at bay. In fact, nothing else but this prime danger to the all-essential water road could have kept the Kiev State together so long. In the annals of Kiev is expressed very much the same despair of Europe and of civilization as is found in Roman records at the time of the irruption of the barbarians into Italy. It seemed as if history and Christendom were themselves going backward, to be drowned in a deluge of extermination and savagery. It is this that is the charm of the history of Kiev—that against such hopeless odds the chivalrous fight was kept up so long. Klyuchevsky has said that a people become a nation by passing through some great common danger, which remains afterwards as a great national memory. Russian patriotism glows in the period of Kiev. We find more of it here than at any later time except at such tense moments as the invasion of Napoleon in 1812.

The Kiev period naturally defined further the distinction between classes. The prince's bodyguard itself splits up into three sections: a group of seniors who form his natural council and are the origin of the later Council of Boyars; the juniors, trained by special tasks, who have their descendants in the attachés and staff officers of a later period, and the house guard itself. There were local forces of townsmen, and the princes also impounded for military service all the better-off of the peasants, who were ranked as *smerdy* and thus attained a higher value in the scale of fines for murder. The population of the towns was increasing, and before the end of this period all inhabitants had the right to be present at the meetings of the town assembly, or *veche*, which later became the governing body of its district. Slaves in this period greatly increased in number, and there developed a class of tenants not far removed from them who received stock to conduct agriculture on behalf of a prince or boyar. Princes and boyars, as they came to be deprived of the wealth derived from commerce and trade dues, devoted themselves more and more to agriculture.

The end of the Kiev period comes of itself through the devastation of the environs of Kiev and of the neighborhood of the water road. It will have been seen that the Kiev system of government was impracticable. It continued so long, partly because the Vikings who came to Russia were and long remained trading and fighting companies, with an interest which all the members shared in common. This common interest was the water road, which retained its value only if it were united. The other principle reason was that Kiev Russia as a whole had one common enemy who helped to keep it together.

The Polovtsy made a raid of some kind into Russian territory every year, killing the cultivators, burning their barns, and taking their wives and children away into captivity. Every now and then there was some more serious invasion or some joint counterattack from the Russians. But the devastation went on, and the principalities on the side rivers to the east of the Dnieper—that is to say, Chernigov, then accounted the second city of Russia, and Pereaslavl, accounted as the third—suffered incessantly from them. "The Polovtsy," we read, "are carrying away our land piecemeal." A prince of Chernigov finds that his inheritance when it comes to him is reduced by half; a prince of Pereaslavl complains that he cannot send any help or tribute to Kiev because there are no people left in his principality "except kennel-keepers and Polovtsy." The Russians entered into frequent relations with these heathens; Monomakh, for instance, concluded with them no less than nineteen treaties, but none of them appear to have been kept. "How many times have you sworn not to make wars?" he says to the captive leader Beldiuz when refusing him mercy. Several princes married daughters of the Khans of the Polovtsy, but these alliances too were of no service to Russia, rather, as will be seen later, the reverse. These endless struggles wore out the fighting strength of the country, not merely the princely families and their bodyguards, but those splendid knights of the frontier, sometimes of the humblest origin, known as *bogatyrs*, who are the forerunners of the Cossack, acting as a kind of peasant chivalry of Christendom. On the road from Kiev eastward in the sixteenth century was found a common tomb of *bogatyrs* fallen in battle. The earlier princes of Kiev—Vladimir I and Yaroslav I—had constructed lines of ramparts with military posts and established military colonies in which they utilized prisoners of war, adventurers from the neighbouring countries and men picked from all parts of their empire, including even the Finnish tribes near Novgorod. Yearly there was fighting on the eastern rivers. More and more the princes complain that the nomads are "taking away from us our roads."

The feuds of the princes themselves were interminable. It was impossible to observe one order of seniority for the whole family. As it became larger and larger and the deaths of its members were therefore more frequent, the changes came to be almost incessant. The tie of a common patrimony, a common claim to Kiev, came to give way to the principle that each prince should rule in the local territory held by his father. The innumerable large bodyguards could no longer be fed by trade as the roads came to be more and more blocked, and they remained large fighting units carrying, it is true, the ideal of a common State, but ruinous to the prosperity of every district by their endless civil wars. When one prince stormed the town of another, he would give it over to pillage and carry off all the inhabitants as slaves. Monomakh himself tells us that he did so in the Russian principality of Minsk. The towns therefore came to interfere more and more in the conduct of affairs. Novgorod, powerful and far from Kiev, usually ruled by junior princes, came to make its own treaties with them and was well able to restrict their rights. In the early days of Kiev one hears often of the national assembly, or *veche*, which was common in so many other Slavonic countries, and now the *veche* comes to be the deciding authority for local affairs. It has no fixed procedure or competence; it is attended in principle by all free men; it is summoned by a town bell and deals impromptu with any question which is raised. In principle its decisions are supposed to be unanimous, and unanimity is secured wherever necessary by force.

As trade was blocked, the supply of money and valuables to Russia came to be very restricted. The bodyguards, who had formerly shared in the profits of their princes, had now to be paid in some other way. Meanwhile, like other articles of earlier export, slaves could no longer be carried out for sale to Constantinople. Slavery had at first been more or less limited to prisoners of war; but as the Kiev period developed, there came to be many occasions of slavery, such, for instance, as marrying with a slave, or wilful bankruptcy, or service without a fixed agreement. The princes were the first to see that the new use to which these slaves could be put was agriculture. It is a striking circumstance that Kiev Russia, so well placed for working the black soil which is now one of the chief granaries in Europe, was originally commercial; agriculture now began to increase at the time when the black soil was about to be lost. Instead of direct payment, princes gave to their bodyguard estates and slaves. Thus were formed very large establishments with thousands of slaves and thousands of cattle and horses. When one prince defeated another, he would seize all his possessions.

Free cultivators found it more and more necessary to seek some kind of protection. Many of them took up work on the estates of the princes or boyars, a word which probably meant at first the landowning members of the *druzhina*. The peasant would be provided with land and with stock. If he went away without repaying what he had received, or even if he tried to escape before the end of his contract, he became legally a slave. Hired workers of this kind were called *Naimity* or *Zakupy*; if they were engaged exclusively in the agriculture and house-service of their employers, they were often called *Roleinye*.

From the middle of the eleventh century, the Kiev area was emptying. This is one of those all-important economic movements which are so seldom chronicled in history, The evidence, however, speaks for itself. It was precisely at Kiev, the goal of all ambitions, and, on the water road, as the centre of all movement, that conditions became intolerable; and as the life was not worth living, the cultivator without ceremony went off by himself elsewhere. This involved a displacement of the Russian population and of all its subsequent history. The undoubted emptying of the Kiev area—both at this and still more at a subsequent time—was certainly in large measure due to sheer destruction of human life. But we see also in the history of the period an evident strengthening of the circumference at the expense of the centre, which would only be in keeping with the previous and subsequent migratory character of the people.

Refugees from the central area around Kiev took different directions of retreat. Of those on the right bank of the Dnieper many naturally returned by the road by which their ancestors had come to Kiev from the Carpathians. It was as if, defeated in their endless struggle with the

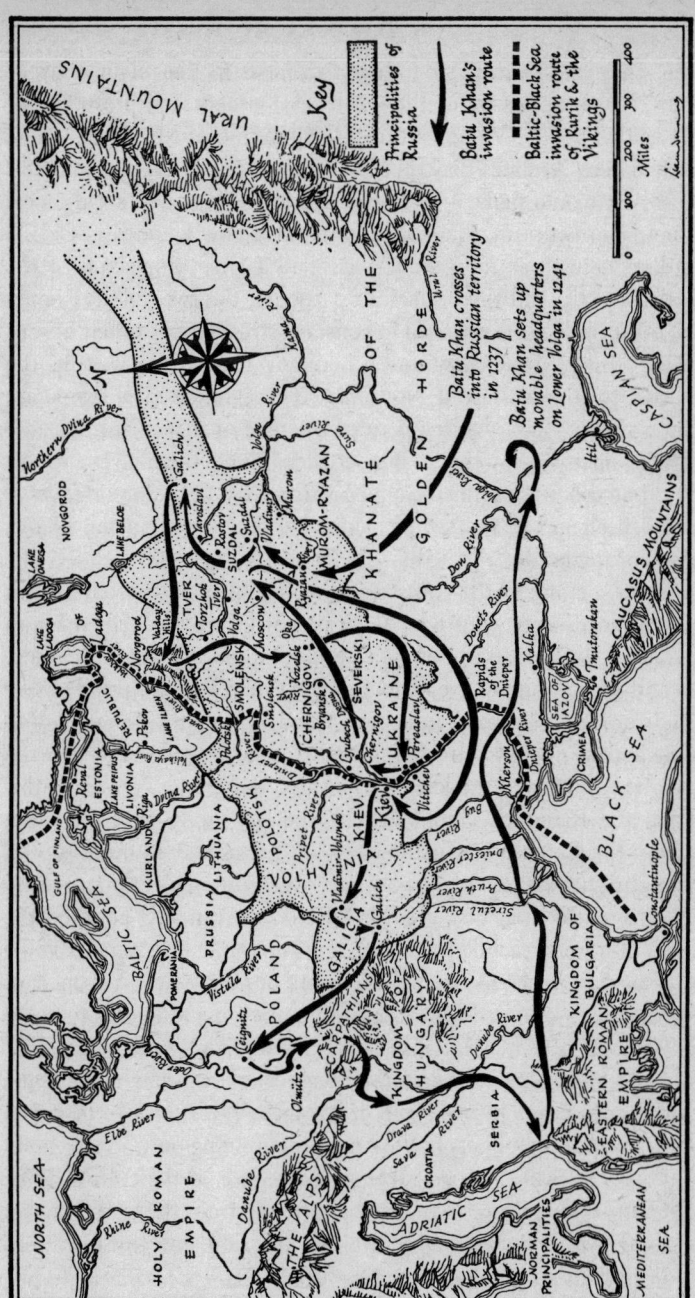

BREAKUP OF KIEV RUSSIA, THIRTEENTH CENTURY

heathen, they had retreated on their natural base, the main body of Europe. This is the reason of the great development and prosperity of Galicia in this period. Vigorous princes of the line of Monomakh were established here. At times they thought of moving to Kiev, but no doubt felt that they would make a great mistake in leaving their strong local base for an empty dream. Many new towns were now founded in Galicia to accommodate these refugees. Galicia had a large proportion of the nobility of Russia; and the princes, in particular the two ablest, Roman and his son Daniel, were engaged in constant struggles with their boyars.

Other refugees from Kiev and Chernigov made their way up the water road to Smolensk and Novgorod. There followed a temporary brilliance of Smolensk, which was ruled by some of the valiant descendants of the line of Monomakh. These often found themselves masters of Kiev, but did not sacrifice Smolensk for Kiev. The importance of Novgorod itself in the succeeding period no doubt owes much to this same line of migration.

However, neither of the two streams of migration which have so far been mentioned—westward to Galicia or northward to Smolensk and Novgorod—was equal in importance to that which remains to be mentioned and was to initiate the history of the Great Russian people. Kiev was itself originally in the forest zone, though later the forest had already, it appears, partly retreated. Almost opposite Kiev falls into the Dnieper its tributary of the left or east bank, the Desna. It was up this river that the Radimichi and Vyatichi, the last group of the Eastern Slavs from the Carpathians, had had to push their way in order to find a home. In the extensive network of river communication of Kiev Russia, this road had at first been little used: the outlying posts on the Middle Volga were reached by passing right up the Dnieper and crossing by very short portages to the upper waters of the Volga. Yet men of valour, such as Vladimir Monomakh, sometimes made their way up or down what was called "the straight road" from Kiev to the Volga, that is the road of the Desna. It passed through dense thickets, such as are indicated for instance in the name of Bryansk (*Debryansk* from *debry*, thicket), infested by robbers but otherwise containing only a very scanty population. This was the road taken now by most of the cultivators of the east bank of the Dnieper and probably many from the west. Russian history has always been a story of river colonization, and this migration was to begin a new period, that of Moscow.

To pass northward into the thickets, even though in a northeasterly direction, was the surest way of avoiding the attacks of the nomads. In the matter of defence, the forest area and the steppe are radically the opposite of each other. The steppe brought the nomads because they lived by cattle and on horseback, and it could supply them with fodder. On the other hand, wholesale marches of peoples of this kind were much less possible in the forest area. The Russian peasant, therefore, by taking this line of least resistance, obtained what he most of all craved—security.

It need not be supposed that such a migration was the sole source of population in this district. The Vyatichi had pushed their way on to the basin of the Oka. In the same direction, when the steppe again became a field of battle, had probably retired many of those East Slavs who had lived on it under the mild rules of the Khazars. Also from the outset of Russian history there had been a line of Slavonic advance down the long west-to-east reach of the Middle Volga. Thus from various sides and for varying reasons this district attracted to itself a considerable population.

In these forests the Russian cultivator came into close contact with the scattered Finnish population. It was entirely unorganized and made no resistance whatever. On the contrary, it yielded to what it regarded as a superior and by no means unfriendly race. The Russian peasant was a man of peace and he did not come to the forest area to start new conflicts, but to avoid them. He would settle along the lines of the rivers, clearing a small patch in the forests by laboriously burning down the trees and digging out the stumps, perhaps in a little colony of three or four houses, keeping close to the river both for fishing and transport. Thus it is in an unpropitious forest area and on the poor clay soil of central and northern Russia that begins the real history of Russian agriculture.

The Russians, in time, came to blend with the Finns. To this connection are generally attributed several physical features which distinguish the Great Russian from all other Slavs: the stocky shoulders, the high cheekbones, the olive complexion, often the dark hair, and, most typical of all, the distinctive and unmistakable Great Russian nose, squat and stretching in flanges on either side. Finnish connections in the same way left their mark on the language; and it is now that the Little Russian and Great Russian manners of speech drift apart. These distinctions need not be dwelt on here; they include the Great Russian hard G as answering to the Little Russian H. Some attribute to the same cause the strong development of the aspects of the verb in Great Russian.

The Finns were heathens with the vaguest beliefs. They worshipped stones, trees, water, and fire. They spoke of gods of their own, but these they regarded as inferior gods, unable to hold their footing in the company of the gods of the Russians. It is typical of earlier relations that when Christianity reached Rostov near the Middle Volga, which was an early Russian outpost in Finnish territory, heathen Finns and Russians alike joined together against it; but there was no settled and regular opposition to Christianity. The boyar Yan on duty for Kiev on the Middle Volga discovered that certain sorcerers were killing men or women on the plea that they were holding up supplies of food, and would produce from their bodies by some trick of conjuring a fish or a piece of meat, or so on. Yan has a talk with these sorcerers and they give him an interesting account of the origin of mankind. Shaytan (our Satan) is trying to mould a man. This, however, he cannot do, and only produces pigs, dogs, or other unsatisfactory results. Ultimately he bribes the flying mouse to watch when Champas, the good god, is bathing, to wrap himself in Champas' towel and thus bring it down to earth. In the towel of Champas Shaytan finds the image of God and from it he succeeds in moulding a human form. However, that is useless to him, for he cannot put any soul in it. At this point Champas comes up and the whole question is settled by compromise. Shaytan may make man, but Champas will give him his soul, and that is why at death the body goes down to the earth to Shaytan and the soul ascends to heaven to Champas. The Finns explained that their gods were black with wings and tails, and did not dare to come out except in the twilight when they watched to see what the Russian gods were doing.[1] There are curious intermixtures of Finnish heathenism and Russian Christendom which have endured to the present day.

The new type of cultivator, the peasant, with difficulty clearing his way through the forest, was to be the founder of a new and great people which was to spread itself over a large part of the earth. The severe climate is against him and for months of the year prevents any useful outdoor work. The Russian peasant therefore works ordinarily in great bursts, and is capable of an extraordinarily prolonged effort. The Russian soldiers of the Great War would go four days without food, though they would say that they could not go for more than four days without sleep. After such privations they would charge the enemy; heavily wounded men who had lain for a day or more between the lines would crawl back, and in a short time their healthy faces would show hardly any trace of what they had gone through. During the short northern

---

[1] Klyuchevsky: Vol. I Lecture 17. I have also made a partial use of the brilliant passage which follows on the mentality of the Russian peasant.

summer, when as far south as Tver hardly a week goes by without a
night's frost, the peasant is afoot with the early dawn and works hard
through all the lengthening summer day. On the other hand, he must
have prolonged intervals, when he sinks into lethargy and musing. But
his thought is full of fancy, and in the long winter evenings he will turn
out the most artistic work in wood or lace or netting. In the forest he
is alone and is forced to be an individualist. Danger may come on him
at any moment, and he is full of a resource which has shown itself in
centuries of scouting in the Russian army. He is cautious and thinks far
more than he says. He does not trust appearances, but is ready to gamble
on the chances that nature gives him. The roads which he makes
through the marshes and forests are full of endless windings, but nothing is gained by leaving them. His loneliness has developed very strongly
in him the longing for the society of his fellow creatures, and this is the
real basis of the loose and dreamy "socialism" which is common practically to all Russians. One of his highest words of praise is the word
"sociable," and he likes to assume this quality in all whom he meets.
He has no greater pleasure than in taking part in some common task
in which his neighbor will find as much profit as himself, and cooperation
is in the very genius of the Russian people. But wariness is prescribed
to him by all the conditions of his life. The constant moving stream of
the energy of the Russian peasantry, which is principally responsible for
the making of the Russian Empire, was always being held up to be
exploited by one dominator or another, and in general, the government
had the class consciousness of an upper stratum lying on the top of the
real people. This, as nothing else could have done, taught the Russian
peasant the art of evasion. He is a man of peace and agriculture, and he
has a genius for following a line of least resistance to escape the insistence of those who would dominate him. He gives you an answer that
will satisfy you, enough for you to go away and leave him in peace. He
is a master at escaping unnoticed from the army or from captivity. He
is talked at by everyone and says the least in reply that he can, pursuing
his own road as far as he is not hindered and usually succeeding in doing
more or less what he intended all along. The constructive work in the
country is much more largely his than might be supposed, and it is done
under this constant weight of domination.   The migration along the
Desna and Oka did not stop there. The peasant has continued to make
his way further, always, if possible, along some water road, reaching in
the end the Pacific Ocean and the west coast of America. The un-
tenanted areas were those where he would be most left in peace and

retain most profit out of his toil. Thus the Great Russian population was, and still largely is, fluid. It presented no basis on which could be founded such a network of feudalism as grew up in Europe. It was only by fixing the peasantry to the soil that there could be based upon it the whole hierarchy of vassaldom under some great lord. At the time of which we speak, there were many princes and it was not difficult to move from one domain to another. The princes, on the other hand, were before all things interested in retaining labour on their domain. There was an endless superfluity of land in Russia but, especially with the primitive implements then employed, land was of infinitely less importance than labour. The prince who could attract labour would be a rich and powerful prince.

Such was Andrew Bogolyubsky, a grandson of Vladimir Monomakh, born in 1111. The line of Monomakh, to the disprofit of the Yorkists of Russian history—the princes of Chernigov—reigned in the three principal groups which resulted from the general migration—in Galicia, in Smolensk and, above all, in Rostov, the birthplace of Andrew. This district, known as Suzdal, had so far been left to minor and junior princes. Being on the extremity, it was now one of the first to drift outside central politics and to find a local basis of territorial sovereignty. Andrew's father, Yury of the Long Arm, youngest son of Vladimir Monomakh, utilizing and increasing the new resources of his district, engaged in constant wars with his eldest nephew Izyaslav II for the throne of Kiev, which after various vicissitudes he held until his death. Andrew, acting as his lieutenant in these wars, showed conspicuous courage and enterprise; at Lutsk it almost seemed as if he thought he could take the fortress by charging it on horseback; but he differed essentially from the other princes in the alertness with which he reaped the full fruits of a victory and turned at once from war to politics. He was disgusted with the princely quarrels. "No one at peace," he said, "and the heathens free to ravish Russia." "Let us make peace," he urges his father. "We have nothing more to do here. Let us go back home while it is warm. There it is quieter." Established as his father's deputy at Vyshgorod, he takes French leave and goes off to Suzdal. When he himself could occupy Kiev he entirely refused to move, putting deputies in his place, and in 1169 his troops stormed the city, showing themselves utterly ruthless to man, woman, and child. It was as if Kiev for him was a foreign town.

He took for his new capital Vladimir on the Volga system: it is not far from present-day Moscow, a town of which the first mention occurs in 1147. Rostov and Suzdal were older towns, with boyars of the Kiev kind and *yecha,* or national assemblies; in Vladimir Andrew was sole master. His *druzhinniki* complained that he did not even share their amusements, and his reign was marked by several plots against him. Both Yury and Andrew founded a whole number of new towns which were evidences of the migration from Kiev. In many cases the old Kiev names were repeated, and the *byliny,* or popular legends, travelled undiluted to this new home, to pass later as far as Archangel and the White Sea. Vladimir was described by its rivals Rostov and Suzdal as a city of "our slaves and masons." Andrew was a great builder. He made his own Golden Gates, his own St. Sophia; at Vladimir are still to be seen some of the most beautiful remains of Russian architecture; when the Italian Fioraventi later came to Moscow to build the Cathedral of the Assumption for John the Great, it was here that he found his model. Andrew was well aware of the credit which a prince could derive from his devotion to the Church. He wished to establish a separate Metropolitan of his own in Vladimir. He stood as the friend of the poor man, the cultivator, against the ravenous class of boyars. Vladimir received settlers not only from all parts of Russia, but from surrounding countries, from the Bolgars on the Volga, from Poland, Hungary, and Germany. Andrew's authority was recognized, if it was also often contested, in Novgorod and in South Russia. It was his dictatorial manner towards his brother princes that aroused all the spirit of Mstislav the Brave.

In 1174 a band of conspirators found Andrew alone and without his sword; he nearly succeeded in beating them off; the would-be murderers went out of the house "trembling all over"; but they heard him groaning from his wounds and came back and dispatched him. His palace and capital were sacked, and there followed a sharp civil war which lasted for two years. It was, however, different in kind from the old princely feuds. Apparently it was a struggle between the brothers of Andrew and their nephews. Really it was a fight to the finish between Vladimir on one side and Rostov and Suzdal on the other. All the odds seemed to be against Vladimir. It was, however, Vladimir that won, and in their celebration of their victory the conquerors described themselves as "poor miserable people who have triumphed over the great of the earth." It is notable that when Vladimir established Andrew's brother Vsevolod in power, it swore allegiance not only to him but to his sons.

Vsevolod III reigned from 1176 to 1212, and had a numerous family, which won him the nickname of Big-Nest. In every way he continued the policy of Andrew, eschewing the showy exploits of the Kiev period and silently accumulating real power based on a territorial sovereignty. Even the princes of Smolensk and Kiev were compelled "to do as he wished." Their vigorous protests and appeals to the old family system have no effect. From elder brother, the prince of Vladimir becomes "father and master." He puts his own son as deputy in the neighbouring principality of Ryazan, which belongs to the rival line of Chernigov. He chooses the princes of the merchant city of Novgorod, and there they punish without trial. The poet of the epic of Igor, appealing in vain to him for help against the Polovtsy, describes him as able "to splash all the Volga with his oars and to drain the Don with his helmets."

Vsevolod before his death replaced his heir Constantine in the succession by a younger son, Yury II. There followed feuds and battles not unlike those of Kiev, in which Mstislav the Daring played an outstanding part. Also, by force of habit, the new grand principality of Vladimir began to divide up, as Kiev itself had done earlier. It was at this time that there fell upon Russia the heaviest of all the invasions that came from the east. At the far end of Asia, in the neighbourhood of Lake Baikal and the Gobi Desert, lived a numerous and fast-multiplying people, the Tartars. Up to about 1202 they were subject to a foreign ruler, Ong Khan, possibly a Chinese governor. They appear to have migrated northward to escape the rigours of his rule and ultimately challenged it under the leadership of Temuchin, who now took the title of Chingiz Khan. Ong Khan was overcome in a great battle; and his conqueror built up a vast empire, and sent out on all sides an avalanche of warriors, aiming at the dominion of the world. The Polovtsy, threatened in their turn, showed signs of confusion in their rear and sent urgent messages to the princes of South Russia, of whom the two most famous, Mstislav the Daring and Daniel of Galicia, were allied to them by marriage. Mstislav, with a soldier's instinct, declared for rescuing the Polovtsy before they were absorbed in the Tartar army. He and six other princes went forth to help the Polovtsy. Two large bands of Tartars faced them on the river Kalka (June 16, 1228). Mstislav crossed the stream but was not properly supported. The Tartars were retreating when the Polovtsy fled in a panic, throwing into disorder the Russian reserves. Some princes defended themselves for three days but were induced to surrender. Nearly all the princes and seventy *bogatyrs* perished. The Tartars constructed a wooden floor on the top of their captives and feasted above them, crushing them to death.

The Tartar menace disappeared into the deserts as quickly as it had come. The bishops more insistently than ever begged the princes to unite for the defence of Russia and of Christendom; but the feuds went on exactly as before: feuds of the Chernigov line against that of Monomakh; internal feuds in the line of Monomakh itself.

Chingiz Khan himself died about 1227, but his son and successor Ögödai granted to a nephew Batu the whole territory from the Urals to the Dnieper; and with an enormous host of 300,000, mostly Turks and Tartars, Batu in 1236 annihilated the kingdom of the Bolgars on the Volga and crossed in the winter of 1237 into Russian territory. This time the Tartars recognized the transfer of power from Kiev to Vladimir by aiming straight at the new centre. The small principality of Ryazan made a plucky resistance. In reply to the usual Tartar summons to surrender a tenth of everything, population and property, the princes replied: "When there is none of us left, then all will be yours." But their army was overwhelmed, their town stormed, and the population put to the sword. The Tartars advanced, enveloping their antagonists from all sides, killing, taking prisoners, laying waste, and burning. They had a kind of crude siege artillery, and no town could stand against them, the more so as their endless numbers enabled them to keep up the attack in relays night and day till the few defenders were overcome by sheer physical exhaustion. Vladimir itself was surrounded; the town was taken, and the cathedral, in which nearly the whole princely family had taken refuge, was burned. The Grand Prince Yury had gone northward to raise a new army. The Tartars followed him, taking all the Volga towns from Yaroslavl to Galich, and on March 10, 1238, they came up with Yury in the marshy country north of the Volga on the river Sit and routed and destroyed him and his forces. They passed on westward towards Novgorod, but with the spring the roads broke up: Novgorod is surrounded with marshes, and seventy miles from the city the Tartars turned away southward. After mastering the especially resolute resistance of the small city of Kozelsk, which put 4000 of them out of action, they came down from the north on to the Polovtsy whom they destroyed or enslaved wholesale, driving the remainder to seek refuge in Galicia, the Balkans, Asia Minor, and even Egypt. In 1238 the Tartars stormed and destroyed what was left of Pereaslavl and Chernigov. In the winter of 1239 they again entered Suzdal Russia and burned some of the remaining towns; everywhere the inhabitants took refuge in the forests. In the winter of 1240 Batu marched on Kiev. The city was deafened with the rattle of wagons, the neighing of horses, and the noise of camels. Battering rams pounded the walls day and night. The inhabitants, who under the boyar Dmitry made a stout defence, built new walls of wood in the centre of the town; but on December 6 these too were stormed and there was the usual wholesale extermination, especially in the crowded churches. Batu passed further westward, treating the capitals of Volhynia and Galicia, Vladimir-Volynsk and Galich, as he had treated Kiev. His main army was accompanied by raiders stretching far on either flank. He crossed the Carpathians and routed the Hungarians on the Sajo (March 1241). He laid Poland waste and defeated a Polish army at Liegnitz in Silesia; but next day the Czechs faced him under their king, Vaclav I. Failing to take Olmütz and repulsed by the Czechs, the Tartars returned to Hungary, whence they tried to enter Austria but were again stopped by King Vaclav and the Duke of Austria. They reached the Adriatic, but Batu returned to eastern Europe where he ruled from a movable headquarters in the neighbourhood of the Lower Volga. Plano Carpini, journeying eastward six years after the sack of Kiev, describes the city as having now only two hundred houses left. Everywhere in the country around he saw skulls and bones. The ruined cities of Russia were full of such remains.

Plano Carpini and Rubruquis, Minorite friars who visited the Tartars after their triumph, were struck with their absolute docility, which was the real basis of their power. They never seemed to quarrel among themselves; but inured by forty years of victorious war, they despised other races and believed they were destined to carry out their master's command to conquer the world. Chingiz Khan had organized them in multiples of ten; and if some of a "ten" were taken prisoners, the rest on their return were put to death. Hand-to-hand fighting they avoided where possible. They would put their subject troops in the centre and keep the flanks for themselves. They liked to envelop an enemy by sheer numbers or to retreat before him, drawing him under a cross fire of their archery. "In this sort of warfare," writes Marco Polo, who later lived in Tartary for seventeen years (1275–92), "the adversary imagines he has gained a victory, when he has in fact lost the battle." They could live for a month, he tells us, on mare's milk, of which they made a kind of porridge; they could stay on horseback for two days on end, and sleep while their horses grazed. Each man took about eighteen horses with him and rode them in turns; if without other food, they would draw blood from their veins. In battle they executed their cavalry manœuvres like one man with extraordinary rapidity. Besieging an important town, they began by building a wooden wall all round it, which blocked all outlet and gave cover to their men. They gave no quarter, quoting a saying of Chingiz Khan that "regret is the fruit of pity." But they showed a remarkable tolerance to all religions and spared their ministers: their Khan even attended indiscriminately Christian, Mahometan, and heathen services; this tolerance disappeared after the Tartars became Mahometans.

There is no better way of estimating the harm which the Tartar invasions did to Russia than to note how from that time forward even Russian historians have difficulty in maintaining their sense of the integrity of the Russian people. Russia was where men spoke Russian, but she had concentrated herself at her extremities, and now the extremities were sundered.

At the northeastern extremity of Russia, Vladimir, after the Tartar invasions Vsevolod's remaining son Yaroslav II, who was much the ablest of the family, set about restoring order and "comforting" the inhabitants, most of whom had fled to the woods in despair on the Tartars' second appearance in force in 1239. He was confirmed as Grand Prince when he answered Batu's summons, but was ordered to visit the court of the Grand Khan himself, where he was poisoned in 1246. His responsibilities passed to his son Alexander who, like his contemporary Daniel of Galicia, was a light to Russia in her darkness. In 1236, just before the Tartar invasion, Alexander, as Prince of Novgorod, had to meet an invasion of the Swedish Jarl Birger whom the Pope had incited to a crusade against the Orthodox. Alexander, marching only with his smaller bodyguard, came up with him on the Neva on July 15 and thoroughly routed him, sinking several of his ships. The people of Novgorod, who quarrelled with all their princes, quarrelled with Alexander; but when the German knights on the Baltic besieged Pskov, seized Novgorod territory, and set up a fort blocking the trade of the city, Alexander was hastily called back. He took the fort (1241) and relieved Pskov (1242); and invading in his turn, he attacked the Germans on the ice of Lake Peipus (April 5, 1242). The "iron wedge" of the knights went through the Russian centre, but by a flank attack Alexander turned their victory into a rout and pursued them five miles over the ice to the shore. In 1245 he drove off the Lithuanian raiders from Torzhok and, pursuing them only with his personal retinue, inflicted two more defeats on them.

In 1242 Alexander Nevsky had to make the visit to Batu. The Tartars thought that no prince was his equal, and he was ultimately appointed by them to the onerous dignity of Grand Prince. In 1247, when the Tartars came to Novgorod for tribute, the city, which had never received them as conquerors, was greatly stirred, and there were riots which endangered the safety of the envoys. It was the Prince who had saved Novgorod from the Swedes, Germans, and Lithuanians who now insisted that the odds were hopeless and that there was no way but submission. In 1263 a number of towns on the Volga refused tribute to the Tartar tax-gatherers and drove them out. A large Tartar army was already on its way when Alexander made his fourth journey to the Tartar headquarters and succeeded in begging his people off. This was the most difficult of his services to Russia, and it was the last. He died on the return journey on November 15, 1263; and his death was announced in the cathedral of Vladimir by the Metropolitan Cyril with the words: "My dear children, know that the sun of Russia has set."

Daniel of Galicia fought the Tartars when and where he could, beginning on the Kalka in 1228. He had only just defeated an invasion of the Chernigov princes, who continued their feuds after the Tartar conquest, when he was summoned to the terrible Batu; and though his manliness won him a respectful reception, he said afterwards with tears and mortification: "Worse than all evils is honour from the Tartars." He attacked a Tartar army but was compelled himself to superintend the dismantling of his own fortresses, though his brother managed to save Chelm from this fate by a stratagem. His work of reparation was crippled by the second Tartar invasion of Galicia. He asked Innocent IV for a crusade and, when hard pressed, even accepted a union of the churches and a kingly crown from the Pope; but the Pope's appeal to Europe and that of the Emperor Frederick II brought no response. Daniel held good in Galicia and continued to build strong places. But cut off from the rest of Russia, he and his successors had to struggle for the existence of their kingdom with the Poles, with the Hungarians, and with his contemporary the wily and able Mindovg, who at this time was building up a strong Lithuanian realm.

We will anticipate, in order to follow further the fortunes of this kingdom of Galicia and Volhynia. Under Daniel and his immediate successors, it more than held its own with Poland and with Lithuania, of which his son Shvarn seems at one time to have been acknowledged as Prince. But with the rise of another notable Lithuanian sovereign, Gedimin, Volhynia itself passed, apparently by marriage, into Lithuanian hands; and in 1321, after a victory over the local princes and a two months' siege, they made themselves masters of Kiev, with an army which already consisted mainly of Russians of the water road whom they had annexed. Galicia later passed by marriage to the Polish Prince Boleslaw of Mazovia and after two campaigns was annexed to Poland by

Kazimir the Great, from which event dates the present Ukrainian question in eastern Galicia. When in 1386 the Polish and Lithuanian crowns were united on the head of the first of the Jagellons, the Russians of the water road also passed, first indirectly and then directly, under Polish rule.

CHAPTER IV

Western Neighbours: Novgorod the Great

THE TARTAR conquest completed the displacement of Russian history begun by the Polovtsy. The new Great Russia of the Middle Volga was crushed almost at its birth. It was not merely that great numbers of Russians were killed and the rest terrified and abased. This new Russia was taken out of the orbit of Europe. A growing culture and civilization was practically extinguished except for one saving force, the national church, which remained one in a Russia hopelessly sundered. With a devastated country and a crushing yearly tribute, there could be little thought for anything beyond the daily bread. Vladimir had so far learned little or nothing from Kiev, and the domains of Vsevolod Big-Nest were parcelled out into smaller and smaller fractions. The way was barred to all high enterprise, and in the subject Russia of the Volga life was sunk in parochial littleness.

But equally great, or even greater, were the indirect consequences of the conquest in western Russia. The very water road itself and the flourishing Russia of Galicia passed under foreign rule. They must not pass out of Russian history; and to preserve the integrity of our story we must now acquaint ourselves more nearly with the western neighbours of Russia.

In the time of Charlemagne, the Western Slavs extended west as far as Hamburg and even Westphalia. Their first attempt at unity was the notable but short-lived kingdom of Moravia in the ninth century, which was finally overthrown by the Magyars. In spite of Cyril and Methodius, the Orthodox Church was not to strike permanent roots here.

A strong principality developed in the ninth century among the Bodrichi, who lived near the mouth of the Elbe and at one time received eastern Holstein as a fief. Charlemagne established Marks, or military colonies, along the Elbe; other such frontier colonies were set up against the Southern Slavs (the Slovenes and Serbs), and it was one of these southern Marks which developed later into the Austrian State. The Bodrichi in the twelfth century, after constant struggles with the Germans, united into a kingdom of the Wends the rest of the Slavs of the Elbe; but in 1126 this kingdom broke up.

Almost as short-lived was the independence of the Sea Slavs (Pomoryane), the modern Pomerania. But they were still vigorous and warlike in the twelfth century, when they were able to make a sturdy resistance to Poland.

More fortunate was the Czech principality which, like the rest of the Slav states, was at first a union of Slav tribes governed by their tribal and family leaders. From 874 began the line of princes of the House of Przemysl, which soon founded a strong monarchy and in 1028 conquered Moravia.

The Poles even more quickly developed a strong central authority, no doubt as a result of their wars against the Germans and Magyars. The first known king of Poland was Mieszko I, who ruled in the middle of the tenth century. His successor Boleslaw I, the Brave (992–1025) subdued Pomerania, took Silesia from the Czechs, won Slovakia in the Carpathians, conquered from the Germans many of the Slavs of the Elbe, and became master even of Bohemia and Moravia. This last conquest he was compelled by the German Emperor, Henry II, to restore. For a time he restored Svyatopolk I in Kiev. Boleslaw was visited by the Emperor Otto III in Gniezno and was there crowned by him and declared to be his friend and ally, a patrician of the Holy Roman Empire. In 1025 he conducted a second coronation of his own.

He was succeeded by a number of princes in the direct line who maintained a strong monarchical authority. Mieszko II lost Slovakia; the Czechs recovered Moravia; the Danes conquered Pomerania; the Germans again made themselves masters of the Elbe; and Yaroslav I of Kiev drove the Poles out of Galicia. After Yaroslav's death, however, Poland intervened for a time with effect in the affairs of Kiev. Boleslaw III recovered Pomerania at the beginning of the twelfth century, and feudal quarrels in Germany and the contests between the Emperors and the Popes tended to strengthen the position of Poland. The Kings developed a court with high officials and a strong military class. This was already a kind of hierarchy with barons and prelates at the top and, below them, a numerous class of gentry, formed of the leaders of various families and of knights. The Polish State rested largely on slave labour.

The country had accepted Latin Christianity in 966. The Bishopric of Posen was founded in 1000; under Boleslaw the Brave the Primate of Poland, the Archbishop of Gniezno, was made independent of external control. A very general rising of the oppressed heathen population was crushed in the middle of the eleventh century and church schools were introduced.

The Polish princes based their authority on the simple conceptions of power and property, and it was not disturbed until 1138, when on the death of Boleslaw III (Wry-Mouth), the kingdom was divided up between his different sons very much after the manner of Yaroslav I of Kiev. In the ninth and tenth centuries the Poles, like the Russians, had derived wealth from the part which they took in eastern trade. Now that the eastern roads were blocked by the Polovtsy, money ceased to come into the country, and the kings had not only to live largely off agriculture themselves but to endow their children and reward their followers by gifts of land. In 1138 Boleslaw III divided up the kingdom between four sons. The division did not even last for their lifetime and it was ultimately the fifth son, Kazimir II the Just (1177), who succeeded to what was left of the authority of Grand Prince, with some central territory in the neighbourhood of Cracow. The appanage system, however, continued, and Poland really ceased to have a national existence, being subdivided into an increasing number of petty principalities.

The Elbe Slavs were finally conquered by Albert the Bear and western Pomerania by Henry the Lion—two notable champions of the German eastward push which was so strong in their time. In 1230, Conrad, prince of Mazovia (in the neighbourhood of Warsaw) called in the Teutonic order of knights to fight against the heathen Prussians. The knights after their victory refused to go, and remained masters of this important outlet of Poland to the Baltic. As already mentioned, in 1241 the Tartars streamed into Poland in two great hosts. There was no common resistance. The Tartars came again in 1259 and 1287; whole villages were swept away, cattle were killed or taken, and the peasants took refuge in the forests.

Even when left to herself, Poland remained under a reign of violence. In this period the barons and clergy ruled unchecked. They chose princes, dictated to the nominal sovereign, and even received foreign envoys. The great court posts became hereditary in their families. Vast lands passed free of all taxes and of lay jurisdiction into the hands of the Church, whose prelates could even hand them on to their children till in 1215 Pope Innocent III insisted on the practice of celibacy. The necessity which drove all the powerful of the land to develop agriculture only strengthened the tight hold which they had on the peasantry, whose condition was, in general, not far removed from slavery to their local owners. Landed property was taken up by barons, gentry or knights, with a military authority over those who were settled on it (*jus militare*).

It was at this time that Polish landowners extensively settled their domains with German colonists. There sprang up a large number of German emigration agents, who brought in masses of settlers and became their local leaders. With the German settlers came German law. Local self-government was secured to the Germans and later was extended to Polish peasants also, which was a great gain for the country as a whole. At this time also another element of population, the Jewish, became very important in Poland, and finance and usury were largely left in its hands. A statute of Henry the Pious of Kalisz, in 1264, left the Jews free to judge their own cases, secured their freedom of faith, their synagogues and their cemeteries, and gave them inviolability of person and of property; it was later extended to the whole kingdom.

In 1295 Poland, thus thrown backward and divided, had fallen under the rule of the Czech king Vaclav II. A Polish prince of Brest, Przemyslaw II, led a national movement against the Czechs and had himself crowned in that year. He was killed a year later, and Vaclav again became King (1300). He strengthened his authority by putting local governors (*starosty*) all over the country, and these officers were continued after him. Vaclav died in 1305, and his son was killed a year later. This gave an opportunity to another Polish prince, Wladyslaw Lokietek (the Dwarf), who invaded his native country from Hungary and was crowned King in Cracow in 1320. Wladyslaw re-established a strong monarchical authority in Poland and took an active part in international politics, allying himself with Hungary and Lithuania against Bohemia, Brandenburg, and the Teutonic Order. After a reign full of wars, he left the throne to his singularly able son Kazimir III the Great (1333–70).

Kazimir did not follow up the chivalrous enterprises of his father. He treated with Bohemia and sacrificed some disputed claims in Silesia and elsewhere, obtaining in return the recognition of his own right to Poland. From the Teutonic Order he got what bargain he could, but had to abandon Pomerania. His position with regard to Bohemia, however, he managed to improve by a subsequent treaty, and the extinction of the line of Daniel enabled him, as already mentioned, to acquire the very valuable province of Galicia and part of Volhynia. Here he founded a special Metropolitan for the Orthodox population, wishing to sever their ties with the rest of Russia, and also introduced Roman Catholic bishops. He found here space enough to grant large domains to the Polish gentry. The lawlessness of his country, which was full of robberies and every kind of violence, he suppressed by the sternest measures, and his *starosty* judged without appeal. By new statutes he consolidated the reign of law (1347); trials were conducted with a regular procedure and with advocates for the defence. He abolished the mischievous principle of corporate family responsibility for crime. Peasants, if wronged by their master, were authorized to leave him; fugitive peasants, if not recovered within a year, were regarded as free; the Jews were restricted in the practice of usury, in which they were refused the assistance of the law courts; the German law courts were centralized, and their principles were applied to the Poles in many parts of the kingdom; the number of colonists from Germany was increased; Cracow was beautified and fortified; military service in return for land was made obligatory on all and not confined to a privileged warrior class. Merchants received definite rights, which included a claim on goods passing on transit through Poland. Good roads were made, and better inns. The church schools spread everywhere. Many Poles went abroad to study or to travel. Cracow University was founded in 1364.

Kazimir died in 1370. He had no children, and long before his death he had arranged that he should be succeeded by King Louis the Great of Hungary, of the House of Anjou. But at this point began the repeated concessions of the monarchy consequent on a number of disputed successions. Louis had to promise to wage the foreign wars of Poland at his own expense, to appoint only Polish officials, and to levy no new taxes. The succession was secured to his sons only. He had, however, no sons, only two daughters, Mary and Hedwig (Jadzwiga); and when he died in 1382 the question of succession came up again. Mary, in spite of the Salic Law which obtained in Hungary, was crowned Queen there. But it was found impossible to retain the union with Poland. After some negotiations the Poles accepted as sovereign her younger sister Jadzwiga. Mary was betrothed to Sigismund, brother of the Emperor Wenzeslas (Vaclav of Bohemia), whom he himself was to succeed in 1411. Poland was disturbed by wars between Sigismund and a Polish suitor for the hand of Jadzwiga, Ziemowit, during which both adversaries lost adherents in the country. Jadzwiga was in love with a friend of her childhood, Wilhelm of Austria; he came to Cracow and was secretly married to her in the Franciscan Monastery. But the barons and prelates who governed the country entirely refused to recognize him as her husband and drove him away. Their intention was to accept the offer of Yagailo (Jagellon), Grand Prince of Lithuania, who was prepared to embrace Latin Christianity, not only for himself, but for his subjects (of whom the majority were Orthodox Russian), if he were accepted as husband of Jadzwiga and King of Poland. Jadzwiga, on whom the match was pressed as a sacrifice to her religion, reluctantly consented and the marriage took place in 1386. Thus Poland and Lithuania became united under one ruler, an event of supreme importance to the future of Russian history and in particular to the Russians of the water road.

From Poland we must turn to the southeastern shore of the Baltic. We must first fix our eyes on the territory to the south of the Gulf of Finland around Reval, known as Estonia. The Estonians, like the Finns, are not of Indo-European stock. Many of them entered the orbit of Novgorod, a city which rested rather on a commercial than on a racial basis. Estonia was conquered by the Danes in the reign of Canute the Great of Denmark (1014–36). From the other side, Yaroslav of Kiev (1019–54) founded here the town of Dorpat, which was then called Yuriev after his baptismal name. Early princes of Smolensk and Polotsk made other conquests for Russia.

The Estonians adjoined on the southwest a race of Indo-European origin, known generally as Lithuanians, and nearer akin to the Slavs than to the other branches of this stock, who are believed to have been the first inhabitants of the district in which they still live. This race extends from near Dorpat westward beyond Königsberg, and nearly as far as Danzig. It was an inhospitable land with little natural wealth, and history did not assail it until well on in the twelfth century. Its people were heathen and lived on a tribal basis scattered about their gloomy forests, heaths, and marshes. The principal groups were as follows: furthest eastward and next to the Estonians were the Letts, centering now round Riga; westward along the coast were the Semigalls; and still further westward in the land which still bears their name, were the original Prussians, who were of the same stock. In the hinterland to the south behind these tribes, lived two kindred peoples, the Zhmud near Kovno and the Lithuanians proper, whose chief settlement was Vilna.

Towards the end of the twelfth century this seaboard was visited by German traders. The monk Meinhard, sent by the Archbishop of

Bremen, converted many of the Letts and became their first bishop. The second bishop was killed in battle in 1198 and the Letts again became heathen. Hereupon Pope Innocent III preached a crusade against them, and the third bishop entered the Dvina with a fleet of war. In 1198, at the mouth of this fine river, was founded the German city of Riga. A year later descended on this coast an Order of crusading knights enrolled under the old statute of the Knights Templar, and known as the Knights of the Sword, most of whom came from western Germany. In 1206 the Letts tried hard to capture Riga but were defeated. Their country was gradually but systematically conquered. The German knights built castles everywhere, and the people were reduced to the condition of serfs. A strong merchant class gathered in Riga and the city became one of the prominent members of the Hanseatic League.

In 1230, as already mentioned, another order of knights, the Teutonic Order, was established further westward along the same coast. Called in by Conrad of Mazovia to conquer the Prussians, it conquered them and almost destroyed them, taking from them not only their country but later their name. The kings of Poland proved unable to dislodge them. This was the occasion of the long wars between the Order and Wladislaw Lokietek. In 1257 at the command of Gregory IX, the two crusading Orders for a time united under a common Grand Master.

These two Orders have a great importance in history, altogether disproportionate to their numbers. In character they were both alike; in each case they were a foreign band of warriors imposing themselves as the ruling class upon two populations entirely alien to them—the Letto-Lithuanians and the Estonians. Here prevailed for centuries that mischievous structure of society in which class coincides with race. Both Estonians and Letts were crushed beneath the ruling caste. The Knights of the Sword were to supply in the future the Baltic barons of Russia. The Teutonic Order was to prove the germ out of which grew modern Prussia. Prussian militarism itself grew up on this soil.

The Letts were conquered, the Prussians almost destroyed, but the Lithuanians proper in their backwoods were still independent. They had long plagued their neighbours with savage raids but remained disunited under various chiefs. The danger that threatened them brought them political union. A crafty and savage chief, Mindovg, persuaded his rivals to march on Smolensk and, while they were on campaign, he made himself master of the country. Daniel of Galicia invaded it, and Tevtivil, one of Mindovg's rivals, sought help of the German knights, and was baptized in Riga. But Mindovg too was christened, in Grodno (1252), and the Pope sent a bishop to crown him. Mindovg's conversion was only a move in the game. He wished to take away any pretext for the "crusaders'" attacks on his people; he continued to make sacrifices to his heathen gods. His son Voishelk, who is described as feeling unhappy when he did not kill three or four persons a day, took Christianity more seriously; he suddenly became a monk and wished to go to an Orthodox monastery on Mount Athos; the heathen Lithuanians, surrounded by Christians, might have turned either to the Eastern Church or to the Western. In 1262, Tevtivil made himself Prince of the Russian city of Polotsk on the Dvina. Mindovg now ceded territory to the German knights and even bequeathed Lithuania to the Order, but he continued to raid them and, winning a crushing victory on the Durba, he offered up his prisoners in burnt sacrifice to his old gods. He brought about a rising of the Prussians and publicly threw off his Christianity. On the death of his wife he possessed himself of the wife of another chief, Dovmont. With the help of the chief of the Zhmud, Dovmont killed him and fled to Pskov where he was baptized and became Prince, serving the city loyally till his death.

Voishelk now threw his monkhood to the winds, killed off his enemies and with the help of Shvarn of Galicia, who was married to his sister, made himself Prince of Lithuania. It was at this point that it seemed possible that Lithuania would come under the headship of Russian and Orthodox Galicia. The Yatvagi did indeed become tributary to Vasilko, the brother of Daniel. A time of confusion followed, and we have little light on the next strong ruler Gedimin (1315–39), who, by one account, was a groom, killed his master and established a dynasty. He could not drive the German knights from their firm foothold on the coast and liberate his oppressed kinsmen in Prussia, Kurland, and Livonia; but following a line of less resistance in the opposite direction, southward, he did make himself master of the Russians of the water road. He finally conquered White Russia with the towns of Pinsk, Brest, and Polotsk. About 1320 he took Vladimir-Volynsk and in 1321, or later, he captured Kiev.[1] His rule was more easily accepted because he did not disturb local arrangements, left the Russian princes in their domains, and only put in his deputies and garrisons. The new Lithuania, which was of vast extent, was not a national kingdom but an empire.

[1] Some put this event considerably later; in general the history of Gedimin is very obscure.

Russian became the official language of the State. Religion was not persecuted; Orthodox churches sprang up at Vilna and Novogrodek.

Gedimin was buried after the heathen fashion and was succeeded by his son Olgerd (1339–77), the ablest of the dynasty and a master builder of empire. We read that he spoke several tongues, did not care for amusements, worked day and night at the government of his country, was temperate and eschewed alcohol, and showed great political wisdom. He is said to have conquered far more towns with his head than by his army. Throughout he was helped by his brother the valiant Keistut, who always made common cause with him; to him he largely owed his throne. Another brother, Evnuty, whom the two expelled from Vilna, took refuge with Simeon the Proud of Moscow and joined the Orthodox Church; he was the first but by no means the last of Lithuanian princes to take service with Moscow, and later we shall see discontented Muscovite princes and boyars taking service in Lithuania.

Olgerd broadened out his dominions eastward at the expense of Russia. He won Vitebsk on the Dvina, Mogilev on the Dnieper, Bryansk on the Desna, Kamenets in Podolia, and even the coast of the Black Sea, from the Dnieper to the Dniester. One of his sons, Andrew, was at times Prince of the Russian city of Pskov; another, Lugveny or Simeon, governed a province of the republic of Novgorod. Olgerd, whose mother was possibly Russian, married thrice, and two of his wives were Russian, the last being Juliana, a princess of Tver. This connection brought him thrice almost to the walls of Moscow in the wars between Moscow and Tver; but Olgerd always showed extreme caution, and usually the enemies, after facing each other for days, made a truce. Generals in this empty part of Europe have often been chary of their reserves; but Olgerd, with the loose hold that he had over his Russian domains, had even greater reasons for avoiding a sharp decision. He preferred to stir up the Tartar Khan against Moscow, but the brother whom he sent for this purpose was handed over by the Khan to Simeon the Proud, and had to be ransomed back. At times Olgerd in the same way challenged Novgorod, but here too he took no decisive action. He was always busy with the German knights. In 1336 his fortress of Pune made a stubborn defence against them, the garrison killing themselves when the fortress was stormed; in 1341 he went to the help of Pskov when it was besieged by the Germans, but refused to remain there as Prince; in 1360 he was badly defeated by the knights; Keistut was taken prisoner, but twice made a daring escape; in 1362 the Germans took Kovno, but Olgerd relieved the town and in 1370 invaded Prussia. He defeated the Tartars and cleared them out of Podolia: in 1368 he routed them on the Lower Dnieper and seized and sacked the old Greek colony of Kherson. He was a Christian and died a monk.

Everything pointed towards closer relations between Lithuania and Moscow and the entry of Lithuania as a whole into the Eastern Church, but history decided otherwise. On Olgerd's death his son Yagailo (1377–1434) plotted to destroy Keistut; when faced by superior forces in the field he proposed a negotiation, during which he seized Keistut and had him killed. In 1386 Yagailo, as we have seen, accepted the Latin form of Christianity in return for the crown of Poland. Now, under Polish pressure, the heathen Lithuanians were baptized off in batches into the Latin confession. The priest, to save time, sprinkled water over a whole company at once, giving it the name of Peter or John or any other.

The two countries were not actually amalgamated, and Keistut's son Vitovt, who was full of spirit and ability, led a determined opposition, at one time besieging Vilna, with the result that from 1392 Yagailo was glad to leave him as Grand Prince of Lithuania under his own suzerainty. Vitovt by treachery made himself master of Smolensk, and married his daughter to the Grand Prince Basil I of Moscow. He led against the Tartars an enormous crusade, heading a host of Lithuanians, Poles, Russians, Mongols, and knights of the Orders, but he was overthrown by the Tartar general Edigei on the river Vorskla (1399). Though he lost here two thirds of his army, in 1410 he led an almost equally large force against the knights of the Teutonic Order, consisting of Poles, Lithuanians, Czechs, Moravians, and Silesians, with Magyars and a big contingent of Tartars. The Teutonic Order was completely crushed in the battle of Tannenberg, and from this blow it never really recovered. Vitovt set up a separate Metropolitan for his Orthodox subjects, Gregory Tsamblak (1429); and at a meeting with the Emperor Sigismund he obtained the promise of a kingly crown. The crown and sceptre though duly sent never reached him, for the Poles refused to recognize Vitovt's independence and intercepted them. He was already eighty years old and died at the moment of his disappointment in 1430.

Yagailo, who ruled Poland under the name of Wladyslaw V, had no children by Jadzwiga; and his sons by another wife had but a poor claim to the Polish crown. They were, however, accepted there: first Wladyslaw VI, who was often absent from the kingdom and was defeated and killed by the Turks at the battle of Varna in 1444, and then Kazimir IV, who was less willing than his predecessors to accept the constant diminutions of the royal prerogatives. Kazimir relied on the gentry for support against the barons and prelates, and the representation of the gentry class came to be put on a much more regular foundation. After his death, however (1492), the gentry themselves took the place of the prelates and barons in constant struggles with the throne and limitations of its rights. Poland became an aristocratic republic in which all was sacrificed to the interests of the gentry, and the peasant was completely enslaved.

Lithuania meanwhile was at times detached, at times re-attached to Poland. Vitovt, we shall remember, had made a strong bid for independence. On his death such a movement was headed by a brother of Yagailo, Svidrigailo, whose authority was only acknowledged in the eastern parts of Lithuania. Kazimir IV was at first Grand Prince of Lithuania, while his brother Wladyslaw VI reigned in Poland. On Wladyslaw's death he reunited the two countries; but after him one of his sons, Jan Albrecht, reigned in Poland and another, Alexander, in Lithuania. Alexander succeeded later to the crown of Poland. His brother Sigismund I succeeded him in both countries, as did later Sigismund's son, Sigismund II Augustus. Sigismund II was the last of the Jagellon dynasty. Poles and Lithuanians had long been wrangling, especially over the provinces of Volhynia and Podolia, which the Poles wished to transfer from Lithuania to Poland. Now, however, with the extinction of the dynasty impending, an agreement was reached; and in 1569, by the Union of Lublin, in the interests chiefly of the Polish gentry, the two countries were consolidated into one kingdom—with an elective king to be chosen in common, a single general assembly and coinage, and freedom for all the gentry to settle or hold office in either province. Thus the gentry of Lithuania gradually became Polonized.

The union of Poland and Lithuania was a menace to the rest of Russia. The moment when the western Russians first passed under the rule of Polish kings was the beginning of a standing quarrel, certain to lead to ceaseless wars and to cause endless sacrifices both to Poles and to Russians.

A great Russian city remained through all this period comparatively independent and indeed established an empire which in extent was far larger than any of the states mentioned so far.

At the top of the water road, an intact survival of the Kiev empire, stood the primeval Russian city of Novgorod, on both sides of the river Volkhov. On the western bank stood the market of Yaroslav. This was the more aristocratic side of the city; the eastern, where was the cathedral of St. Sophia, was the more democratic. The city as a whole was divided into five wards which seem to have been at first independent communities. The name of Novgorod the Great given to the whole was an analogy with the grand principalities of other parts of Russia; only here it was the city that was great and not the prince. The wards, or, as they were called, ends, had each its own separate organization with its own assembly, local council, and officials. The ends were divided into hundreds and the hundreds into streets, and throughout the system ran the same principles of local self-government and administration. The city territory extended on all sides, but was much more limited towards the western. Of the original territory of the city each of the five wards or ends possessed its part, roughly radiating outwards from itself (under Moscow rule these districts were called fifths). Beyond that was the far vaster territory acquired later on the eastern side, which was incapable of such a division. These areas were styled Lands or *Volosti* (domains). They extended down the northern Dvina to the White Sea, along the Volga and Kama to the Urals, and even to the far northeast corner of Europe, the straits separating Nova Zemlya from the mainland. The greater part of this territory was practically uninhabited except for alien tribes, Finnish or others. But it owned no other rule than that of Novgorod, and this sovereignty was very jealously guarded by the city.

Quite early Novgorod obtained the means of defining its own privileges. There was an active city life here before the Vikings came, already based on commerce; and there were not only rich city merchants but city troops and officials. During the Kiev period Novgorod was often left to itself. To preserve the unity of the water road, the Grand Princes of Kiev preferred to send as their deputies not their brothers but their eldest sons. Up to the reign of Yaroslav I, Novgorod paid tribute direct to Kiev. But as Yaroslav had refused the Novgorod tribute to his own father, Vladimir, and himself owed the Kiev throne entirely to the support of Novgorod, he could not himself exact tribute, and this is one of the landmarks in the liberties of the city (1019).

Later, when the order of seniority came into operation, the independence of Novgorod greatly increased. As time went on the changes at Kiev came to be more frequent, and it was impossible for Novgorod to follow suit with constant changes of deputy princes. Quite early the men of Novgorod protested that the princes whom "they had fed up for themselves" should remain with them. Soon they were able to choose between different candidates, and each choice gave an opportunity for defining the privileges of the city. Circumstances were especially favourable to the liberties of Novgorod when Kiev had lost all hold and was itself disputed between the two lines of Chernigov and Monomakh, while bold spirits such as Mstislav the Brave and Mstislav the Daring questioned the new authority of Andrew and Vsevolod III of Vladimir. Andrew twice sent large armies of his discontented vassals against Novgorod, and one even tried to storm the city; but each time he was routed by much smaller forces, and his soldiers were sold for almost nothing in the Novgorod markets; he seemed more likely to be successful with the population of the Novgorod hinterland, who were exploited for the city trade.

Vsevolod III engaged in a long struggle with the city, already instructive as showing its strength and its weakness. On the one hand, the marshes more than once turned back an invading force, as in 1237 they turned back the Tartars themselves. On the other hand, a prince who could control the food supplies of the Middle Volga had no need to capture Novgorod; he could always starve it out. The farthest he had to advance was to Torzhok; then sooner or later he would receive a proposal of peace and if the terms did not satisfy him, he would hold the envoys and await a second more amenable batch. As early as Vsevolod III these tactics were followed; and his son Yaroslav II (later Grand Prince after the Tartar invasion), when expelled from Novgorod, sat down in Torzhok, intercepted the supplies, and awaited results. We read in consequence of terrible famines, when the dead were too many to bury or for the dogs to eat, people living on birch bark; and we can understand how Mstislav the Daring, who flew in his muddleheaded way to the rescue of Novgorod, declared that: "Torzhok shall not be Novgorod and Novgorod shall not be Torzhok"; though he had evidently no means of settling the question. Even when he later made his celebrated invasion of the Middle Volga during the feuds of Vsevolod's sons, he secured nothing more than an apparent success: and the invaded pithily taunted him and the men of Novgorod that they were like a fish who has struggled too far onto the land.

Yet it was from Vsevolod III that Novgorod received the widest definition of its liberties. Thanking off the city forces after a successful joint campaign in the south, in the words of the Novgorod Chronicle, "he gave them all their will and the decrees of their former princes, all that the men of Novgorod had wished for," and he said to them: "Who of you is good, him love: but punish the bad." This was taken to cover the rights of judgment and of electing their own officials, both of which had long been in practice (1209). Under an earlier date, 1196, we read "and all the princes set Novgorod at liberty: whence it pleased them, thence they might take to them a Prince." In 1218 Novgorod refuses to give up its mayor Tverdislav, because the Prince has not brought any definite charge against him. In 1315 the city makes another such refusal, but gives in under pressure. In 1340 it protests to Simeon the Proud of Moscow: "Thou hast not yet taken thy seat among us [i. e., enthroned himself]; yet thy boyars are already doing violence." In 1380 Dmitry of the Don "gives all the old rights and the old charters." His son Basil I makes "the old terms" with Novgorod in 1390; but three years later he quarrels over a matter of church jurisdiction and apparently gets his way. These assertions of liberty are interspersed with very different incidents, where Novgorod yields at discretion. It was generally a question as to how much food there was in the city.

The Archbishop of Novgorod, who was originally sent from Kiev, was later chosen by the city itself, two names being placed on the altar of St. Sophia where a child or a blind man or cripple decided the election by the name which he chose. The archbishops, who only went to Kiev and later to Moscow to be consecrated, came to have a strong local authority. The city also chose its *posadnik* (deputy or mayor), as it was impossible to depend on the choice of absent and changing princes. It also chose the second official of the city, the *tysyatsky*, or thousandth man, who led the troops and was responsible for the police.

The successive treaties with different princes defined their position very closely. The Prince was as necessary to Novgorod as he was to other cities at the outset of Russian history, to watch over its defence. While there was a military ruling class in Russia, it was necessary to seek the city general from among it. The Prince, however, had to live outside the city in the fortress (*gorodishche*); in judgment of all important matters he had to sit together with the elected *posadnik*. Preliminary investigations were divided between the two, but the decision was given in common. The Prince's revenues were also clearly defined. Certain villages were set apart for him, and he was not allowed to acquire any other landed property. Any trading of his own he had to conduct through the merchants of the city. He was not allowed to hunt further than thirty miles from it. Some areas his officials were never allowed to penetrate, others only at certain times. Princes chosen from the outside, for instance from Suzdal, were not to rule the land of Novgorod from their own capitals.

The authority of the city or, as it was called, the Word of Lord Novgorod the Great, was concentrated in the city assembly or *Veche*.

The Veche had in theory unlimited power; any question could be raised and dealt with. The Prince was free to raise questions, but was not able to decide them. The Veche was summoned by the ringing of the town bell and was held in one of the market places of the city, generally in that of Yaroslav. Any free citizen could attend. There was no regular procedure, nor were there any regular times of meeting. It met when summoned, and in principle it could be summoned by anyone.

This, of course, was not a working system, nor was it ever actually in operation. There came to be formed a special "council of masters" (*Sovet gospod*) with a permanent office and archives, which prepared all proposals for the Veche. This council numbered not less than fifty persons; it included those *posadniks* who had passed the chair; to it also belonged the archbishop and members of the ruling families. In the same way were created various institutions of justice. The prince and the *posadnik* judged important matters in common after due preliminary investigation; but there was also the archbishop's court; and the control of trading suits was left to the richer merchants themselves, incorporated in the guild of St. John. The collection of tribute was a peculiar concern of the city administration.

Local government authorities existed in the older territory of the city. Elders were locally elected, but the *posadniks* or governors were sent down from Novgorod. The further areas were traversed by armed expeditions which took little or no account of the inhabitants except for the purpose of taxation, in other words for the collection of merchandise. There were therefore constant complaints from these parts. Novgorod was peculiarly tender and suspicious as to the Zavolochie or territory running along the Northern Dvina. As early as Andrew of Vladimir, the inhabitants joined Suzdal against Novgorod (1169), and under Basil I of Moscow they definitely tried to throw off the city rule, and were made to pay a fine of two thousand roubles and three thousand horses. The town of Rzhev on the Upper Volga also showed signs of independence, and the neighbouring merchant city of Pskov conducted a long struggle which ultimately achieved this result. The larger cities of the realm were called *prigoroda* (dependent towns) and were expected to receive their administration direct from Novgorod. Pskov, however, secured an independent prince in Dovmont of Lithuania, who was left in undisturbed possession by Novgorod. From 1322 Pskov chose her own prince independently, and from a rather earlier date she had her own *posadnik* who governed in company with a *posadnik* sent from

Novgorod. In 1347, by the treaty of Bolotovo, Novgorod acknowledged the full independence of Pskov, which was later, by another analogy with the princely family, styled "younger brother" of the main city.

Novgorod was certainly not a democracy in practice. There was a complete hierarchy of classes. At the top were the boyars, or men of great possessions; these, though they did not themselves trade, financed the commerce of the town out of their capital by loans to the merchants, who were therefore quite dependent on them. It was practically from this class alone that the highest officials were chosen. There were two main parties—the richer against the poorer; but the leaders of the poorer were by party tradition members of the richest class. After them came the well-to-do (*zhityi*), a kind of gentry who like the boyars possessed country estates but often engaged in trade; these usually acted with the boyars and only in cases of extreme discontent against them. Next came the *zemtsy* or country folk, really inhabitants of the city possessing small estates outside it; after them the merchants; then, inside the city, the artisan and workman class, who were also free to attend the V*eche*; and, in the country, the *smerdy*, or independent peasants; next the *polovniki*, who as elsewhere in Russia cultivated on the principle of a division of the crop with the landowner, receiving one quarter or one half of it; and at the bottom of the social scale, as elsewhere, a great number of slaves.

Novgorod could not grow enough corn to feed her large city population. In some years the whole crop was nipped by frosts. Trade was therefore the nerve of her existence. First the city took an active part in the trade of the water road, and eastern coins and ornaments have been found on Lake Ilmen. When the water road was cut off, Novgorod became an intermediary no longer between north and south but between east and west: that is, between the new mercantile Europe and the city's own enormous resources on the Northern Dvina and the Urals. Scandinavian traders came from Wisby in Gothland, where later Novgorod had a church of her own; and the "Varangers" had their warehouse in Novgorod. This last was later absorbed in the German commercial settlement, and Novgorod became a very important member of the Hansa —the member which possessed far the largest hinterland. On the other hand, if Novgorod itself was a city of middlemen, the Hansa were middlemen among middlemen, and Novgorod had to struggle hard to keep her commercial independence. No Russian was allowed to join the German company, or to enter its warehouse: retail sale was forbidden.

Meanwhile throughout her whole story Novgorod was engaged in frontier warfare against the Estonians, the Lithuanians, and the German knights; and defeat by the last-named enemy brought with it a blockage or domination of her trade.

Earlier Novgorod politics consisted in organized opposition to the princes for the extension of the liberties of the city. Later the choice of the Prince was still one of the most vital questions, for the choice usually implied a desire to open trade routes on the side on which his domains lay. This, in the end, came to a question between Moscow and Lithuania; and before the union of Lithuania with Poland, when she almost seemed likely to create a Greater Russia, there seemed not so much harm in the casual practice of taking a Lithuanian prince into the junior service of Novgorod while receiving the Prince of the city from Vladimir or Moscow. But here too the marriage of Yagailo and Jadzwiga in 1386 marks a new epoch.

Much of the politics however was increasingly concerned with social questions; there were also sharp conflicts between the great families which monopolized the power. By no means infrequently a *Veche* would break up in confusion. It was the Slavonic principle—which lay later at the bottom of the *liberum veto* of the Polish gentry, and is also to be found in the procedure of a Russian village commune—that decisions should be unanimous, and unanimity had often to be secured by force. The bridge over the Volkhov, near which had once stood the heathen image of Perun, was frequently the scene of these conflicts, and legends said that when Perun was hurled into the river he threw back a sword to the men of Novgorod as an omen of these battles on the bridge. In a city of so small a compass and with so large a population, the riots assumed the bitterest character, often ending in murders, looting, and burning. The Archbishop had sometimes to come on to the bridge with sacred banners and emblems, to put a stop to these battles.

Pskov, governed on the same democratic principles as Novgorod, realized them much better in practice. It did not have such sharp contrasts of wealth and poverty. Its *Pravda* or code of justice was very humane. Pskov was so long the frontier town of Russia and was kept so busy holding superior forces at bay, that the citizens took their liberty in the main as a very serious responsibility.

Sometimes with, sometimes without the Word (or permission) of Novgorod, young adventurers made up companies of a piratical kind to explore and exploit the hinterland. At one period, soon after the Tartar conquest, these rovers were more troublesome to the Middle Volga than the Tartars themselves. It was an early expedition of this kind that led to the foundation of Vyatka, near the Urals, where the houses still retain the features of Novgorod architecture. Vyatka became a semi-independent republic.

CHAPTER V

Rise of Moscow

[*1263–1533*]

As we have seen, the Tartar invasion was a wholesale calamity, destroying possibilities of development in Galicia, isolating Novgorod from the rest of the water road, leading indirectly to the subjugation of much of the water road itself to Lithuania and, through Lithuania, to Poland. The new Russia of the backwoods of the Middle Volga and Oka was thus politically cut off from Europe. Not far off, on its eastern side, were the frontiers of Tartar occupation, and it was itself squeezed dry by the exactions of their tax-gatherers and reduced to a sheer struggle for existence. This destroyed all common political interest. This newly settled area split into a number of principalities, which constant subdivision made smaller and smaller, till many of them were little more than private estates. Here civilization had been completely thrown back, learning was almost lost, art in decline; and it is from this state of subjection, demoralization, and individual egotism that we must trace the beginnings of the power of Moscow.

First mentioned in 1147, when Yury Long-Arm met a guest here and entertained him to a "mighty feast," this town was surrounded with wooden walls in 1156. At first it was only an appanage of younger sons. Of these, Michael Khorobrit, younger brother of Alexander Nevsky, made himself conspicuous by ousting an inoffensive uncle (Svyatoslav) from the office of Grand Prince of Vladimir. The permanent line of Moscow starts from the youngest son of Nevsky, Daniel, of whom it is recorded that he treacherously seized on Kolomna and annexed it. Moscow was in a very good position for growing outwards. In the river system of central Russia we have flowing eastward first the Volga, then the Klyazma, then the Moskva, and more to the south the Oka, which joins the Volga at Nizhny Novgorod. By the Oka, Moscow had good communications with Kiev, from which, as will be remembered, much of its population had come. By the Istra and the Lama, Moscow was connected through an easy and familiar portage with the northern part of the old water road, the river Volkhov and Novgorod. It communicated easily with the Klyazma, and by the lower Oka it had a direct road to the Volga and the Caspian. As Russian colonization moved along the rivers, Moscow attracted settlers and, as time went on, a certain measure of trade, the dues of which were a valuable source of income. On the other hand, Moscow was less exposed than most of the neighbouring principalities. To the south of it lay Ryazan, which had always to bear the first brunt of Tartar invasions. If the Tartars reached further north they naturally followed the main line of the Volga, without turning aside to the tributary rivers. As time went on, this last circumstance became very important. Tartar raids made life on the Volga unbearable—as the attacks of the Polovtsy had done for the area around Kiev—and large numbers fled from the Volga southward, increasing the population of Moscow. St. Sergius, the founder of the Trinity Monastery, who had himself come from the north in this way to seek solitude, complains that the new immigrants "have spoilt the wilderness." The town of Tver, during the beginnings of the Tartar yoke, made premature attempts at liberation, and troops of John Moneybag of Moscow accompanied the avenging army of the Tartars. Many of the inhabitants of Tver then sought refuge in Moscow. John and his successors also ransomed Russian prisoners from the Tartar horde to augment their agricultural population.

Labour was at this time the only important source of wealth. Land was nothing unless it was cultivated. The population was fluid, and labour would go wherever it could obtain tranquillity and good conditions of work. Relying on a policy of peaceful absorption, the Moscow princes missed no chance of extending their domains, occasionally by open robbery, and regularly by economies and purchase. At first, no plan was visible in the acquisitions of Moscow. They formed a kind of mosaic, including distant towns far from the little city. But as time went on, geography itself suggested the direction of advance. Soon the princes possessed the whole of the little Moskva River, then they obtained the basin of the Klyazma, later, the whole of the Middle Volga, and only last of all the unhampered control of the Oka. The seizure of Nizhny Novgorod at the juncture of Oka and Volga in the reign of John Moneybag's great-grandson, Basil I, completed the absorption of this central block of territory. For the more distant future, Moscow's position was indeed imperial. It was almost at the junction of the two main zones of Russia, the forest zone of the north and the steppe zone of the south which were so necessary and complementary to each other. From its central watershed the stream of colonial advance would naturally carry it along the larger rivers which have already been mentioned: to the Baltic (Volkhov and Dvina), to the Black Sea (Dnieper and Don), to the Caspian (Volga), and to Siberia (Kama).

After Alexander Nevsky, the office of Grand Prince, though bestowed by the Khans, passed by a regular order of seniority to his younger brothers, Yaroslav of Tver (1263) and Basil of Kostroma (1272), and thence to the next generation. Much of the politics of these Grand Princes was taken up with Novgorod, which often managed to play off the next in succession against the reigning sovereign. As the minor principalities were dealt out roughly in their order of value, one can see that the towns on the Volga were at this period the most desired. Moscow, as at first hardly worth having, passed to junior princes, Khorobrit and Daniel. There followed a violent feud between the descendants of Yaroslav of Tver and of Daniel of Moscow, the office alternating between these two branches according to the favour of the Khan. Tver, however, as has been mentioned, was premature in its resistance. Prince Michael of Tver was called to account at the Golden Horde and there murdered, not by Tartar hands, but by his rival Yury of Moscow, at which the Tartars themselves expressed disgust (1319). Yury was in turn killed by a son of Michael, Dmitry Big-Eyes; Dmitry too was killed and another prince of Tver, Alexander, became Grand Prince (1326). This Alexander, however, soon found himself in much the same position as Michael. In 1327 Chol Khan, cousin and lieutenant of the Khan Uzbek, came with the usual Tartar arrogance and violence to collect tribute in Tver. The sturdy inhabitants rose and killed him with all his followers. John I of Moscow, brother and successor of Yury, went straight off to Uzbek and returned with a punitive expedition of 50,000 Tartars. Alexander fled to Pskov, and Tver was terribly ravaged. Uzbek appointed John Grand Prince and gave Alexander's brother, Constantine, an army to hunt him down. The princes and Novgorod urged Alexander to draw the vengeance on himself and surrender to Uzbek; but the men of Pskov begged him not to go and were prepared to share his fortunes. John now persuaded the Metropolitan to excommunicate both Alexander and Pskov. Alexander fled to Lithuania but returned later and for ten years ruled undisturbed in Pskov. In 1336, being homesick for Tver, he sent his son to appease the Khan and, receiving an encouraging report, went himself to Uzbek, who gave him back Tver; but John, by another visit to the Khan, got this decision reversed; Alexander was summoned again and killed. The dignity of Grand Prince was confirmed not only to John but to his sons after him, and never really passed out of his family.

Moscow received a further important accession of strength from the side of the Church. When there was no single political authority, there was still unity of the church administration under the Metropolitan. The Metropolitan Cyril in 1299 left the devastated city of Kiev with all his clergy; indeed, at that time nearly the whole remaining population of Kiev dispersed. The Metropolitans for a time dwelt at Vladimir, but here too through the struggle between rival lines there was no security, and the Metropolitan Peter came to make his home under the shelter of John I in Moscow. Peter, like Nevsky, made the courageous journey of propitiation to the Tartars; when he died he was accounted a saint, and miracles were reported at his tomb. His successor Theognost, therefore, remained in Moscow, which eventually became the permanent home of the heads of the Russian Church.

John I (1328–40) is known by the nickname of Kalita or Money-bag. The name is significant. John set his successors an example of able economy, of concentration of resources. While he had money he could propitiate the Khan; while he enjoyed the Khan's good will, he could secure for his small principality immunity from Tartar invasions. In spite of his servility the Church commends him, as having gained a breathing space of forty years. With security, John Moneybag could attract settlers, and the fluid population naturally streamed in his direction; with money, too, he could equip them for agriculture. With money, he could also extend his domains by well-considered purchases. It was only in the first generation of the Tartar bondage that the yoke was felt with its full weight. The Tartars found that they could entrust to so subservient a Grand Prince the collection of their tribute. This gave Moscow a powerful economic hold over the rival small principalities. The tribute was extremely heavy and a Tartar force could be called in, if necessary, to see that it was paid.

His son Simeon (1340–53) was not only confirmed as Grand Prince: the Khan "put all the other princes in his hands." From his interpretation of these powers he was called "the Proud." This was an absolutism at second hand; but it was still an absolutism; and Simeon was only continuing the heightened tone of authority which had distinguished the first notable princes of central Russia, Andrew and Vsevolod III. He is said to have explained that: "Rus was only strong and glorious when the princes obeyed the eldest without contradiction, and only by such unqualified obedience to himself could they free themselves from the Tartar yoke." The term "father" came to be substituted for "elder brother" in his relations with other princes.

Simeon was not proud to the Tartars; he described Russia as "your faithful province." Five times he had to make the difficult journey, but each time he came back "with honour." He married his sister to the Prince of Tver. Simeon perished in the Black Death that raged through Russia from 1352. That he had a sense of purpose, we feel from the words of his will. He exhorts his heirs to stand together and to listen to the boyars and the heads of the Church: "I write you this word that the memory of our fathers may not cease and that our candle may not go out." On his younger brother John II, who succeeded him (1353–59), the Khan confirmed a further right—that of justice over the other princes.

So far the Moscow princes had been extremely cautious; and their principal merit was sound good sense. The son of John II, Dmitry, breaks this sequence. Profound changes had taken place in the political factors. The Tartars had conquered Russia by their implicit obedience to their Khan; the Russians had lost it by their interminable divisions. Now the conditions were nearly reversed. The Golden Horde that ruled Russia had more or less detached itself from the main body of the Tartar Empire, and now its own Khans succeeded each other rapidly, sometimes by assassination. About the time of Dmitry's accession there were two rival Khans, Abdul and Murad, and the most powerful man at the Horde was the Vizier, Mamai. The Russians could utilize these dissensions. Around Moscow a generation had grown up in peace and quiet; it could not remember the Tartar terror. The gradual centralization of power had created at Moscow a class of loyal boyars who had no wish to exchange its service for any other. Moscow had also the special counsel and blessing of the Church.

Dmitry was a child of eleven, and his succession was challenged by Prince Dmitry of Suzdal, who obtained a *yarlyk*, or appointment as Grand Prince. But his own elder brother rebuked him for breaking the oath sworn to John II. Moscow obtained a *yarlyk* from Khan Murad. The boyars put their child-sovereign on horseback and set out for Vladimir to conquer the succession. Dmitry of Suzdal ultimately even refused the *yarlyk* when offered to him.

In a dispute for the principality of Nizhny Novgorod the boy-prince took a strong line, sending St. Sergius to close all the churches there until his settlement was accepted. "He brought all princes under his will," says the Chronicle. In this he was greatly helped by one of those brotherly associations so common in Russian history; there the Orestes often finds his Pylades. Dmitry's cousin Vladimir of Serpukhov made with him an agreement which was always observed on both sides and served as a model for the treaties which Dmitry later enforced on other princes. Neither was to interfere in the other's domain, but when the Grand Prince mounted his horse, his cousin was to follow him, and when the Grand Prince sent his cousin to war, he was to go.

This model treaty was soon required. Michael of Tver had a powerful son-in-law in Olgerd of Lithuania and was constantly challenging the authority of Dmitry. In the long struggle between them we are struck by many features: by the entire disregard of Dmitry for the *yarlyki* of the Khan; by the help which he receives from the junior princes and boyars of Tver itself, who evidently think that Tver's is a lost cause and seem to prefer the service of Moscow; by the striking unanimity an active support of the other princes, in many cases already due to actual dependence on Moscow, but also prompted by disgust for Michael's untimely appeal to the weakened and divided Horde; by the extreme caution of the great Olgerd who stands facing his enemy for days and withdraws without fighting, looking round him on all sides for possible dangers as he retreats; by the constant loyalty of Vladimir of Serpukhov, whose independent action sometimes decides the issue. Dmitry in the end imposes on Michael the friendly terms of his treaty with Vladimir. Tver is definitely a "younger brother"; Michael is to have no separate relations with the Khan; he is never to call in the Lithuanians (1373). In the next great struggle with the Tartars, the help of Tver is loyally given.

A series of skirmishes and actions led up to this struggle. The Russians no longer feared to face the Tartars in battle. In 1365 a raiding Tartar force was caught on its way back by the men of Ryazan and sharply defeated. In 1367 Pulad, attacking Nizhny, was driven over the Pyana with great slaughter. In 1373 Mamai himself laid waste Ryazan, and Dmitry waited for him all the summer on the Oka. In 1374 Mamai's envoys and 1500 Tartars were slaughtered in Nizhny Novgorod. In 1375 Nizhny is devastated, but next year Dmitry compels Kazan to pay him to retire. In 1377 a Russian force, taking things altogether too easily, is surprised and routed on the Pyana. In 1378 the Tartars surprise Nizhny and set fire to the town, and on August 17, Dmitry with a big force by three desperate counterattacks wins a victory on the Vozha. The Russians are now sending the Tartars only a reduced tribute.

Mamai is now himself Khan and collects a great army. All the Russian princes gather round Dmitry except Oleg of Ryazan. Yagailo of Lithuania has promised to join Mamai by September 1, but two of his brothers are with the army of Dmitry. Before starting, Dmitry seeks the blessing of St. Sergius, who predicts a hard-won victory and gives him two monks to fight at his side. His army is estimated variously as numbering between 150,000 and 400,000. Mamai demands the old tribute and is refused. The Oka is crossed on September 1 and the Don, after a new message of blessing from St. Sergius, on September 7. Next day the Tartars come down from the hills to give battle on the plain of Kulikovo. The clash is tremendous and the Russian infantry is overborne, but with a strong wind behind him Prince Vladimir makes an unexpected cavalry charge on the Tartar flank and the day is won. Dmitry was discovered half dead under a tree, with his armour all battered in.

Kulikovo marks an epoch but is not a decisive event. Dmitry had brought all his forces to bear and had only 40,000 men left; but the Tartars had plenty of reserves. Mamai was gathering a new army when he was attacked and overthrown by a rival Khan, Tokhtamysh. Tokhtamysh invades Muscovy and by stratagem surprises the Russian defences. Serpukhov he captures and, pillaging everywhere, appears before Moscow. Dmitry is away, hastening his levies, but the spirit of Moscow is warlike. Prayers continue day and night; the citizens will allow no one to leave; Dmitry has built a stone wall around the Kremlin and now possesses artillery; missiles of every kind and defiant taunts are hurled at the Tartars, who in three days fail to make any headway. Tokhtamysh arranges a parley and treacherously kills the leaders of the defence; but Prince Vladimir, with his detachment outside, defeats a Tartar force and Tokhtamysh withdraws of himself. Twenty thousand Russian dead were buried in Moscow.

Dmitry of the Don died in his prime in 1389. He was a tall, thickset man with dark hair, temperate in his life and devoted to religion. He could not read, the Chronicle tells us; "but he had the holy books in his heart." The reign of his son, Basil I (1389–1425) was less eventful. He completed the river domains of his House by annexing Nizhny Novgorod, and he only made one visit to the Horde, travelling with great pomp, in order to have this annexation confirmed. At one moment it seemed as if all the spadework of the preceding reigns might be undone. A new Mongolian world-conqueror had arisen, Timur or Tamerlane the Great, who by 1371 held everything from the Caspian to Manchuria. Tokhtamysh, who owed his crown to him, rebelled against him in 1395, was crushed on the Terek, and fled. Timur entered Russian territory and took Elets (near Orel). Basil, marching out to meet him, sent in haste to Vladimir for its famous icon and, on the day that it reached Moscow, came the news that Timur had passed on elsewhere. Edigei, the Vizier of the Golden Horde, following the new tactics of surprise, appeared before Moscow in 1405. He stayed there a month without attacking the city and accepted a large sum to withdraw at a moment when troubles at home anyhow compelled his return. It was Edigei who defeated Basil's father-in-law Vitovt in 1399 on the Vorskla, but even there the Tartars did not show fight until compelled by the extravagant demands of Vitovt. Basil could not prevent the seizure of Smolensk by Vitovt; he invaded Lithuania, and several of the malcontent Russian princes there took service with Moscow; this, if their domains were on the frontier, meant an extension of territory. A counter-offensive of Vitovt ended, without fighting, in the usual truce (1406); the same process was repeated in 1412; the frontier remained at the river Ugra, perilously near to Moscow.

On Basil's death broke out the one serious civil war in the princely family of Moscow. So far the younger brothers of the reigning prince had usually died before him, so that a succession from father to son had followed of itself. Now Prince Yury went to the weakened and discredited Horde to claim the throne from his young nephew Basil II (1431). A Moscow boyar Vsevolozhsky secured the confirmation of Basil, not by disputing the old order of succession from brother to brother, but by flattering the Khan with the thought that he could break through any custom. This did not end the matter. Basil had promised to marry Vsevolozhsky's daughter; but his mother, the proud daughter of Vitovt, arranged a higher match and at the wedding mortally insulted the two sons of Prince Yury. In the fighting which followed Basil was taken prisoner, and Yury now reigned in Moscow. According to that very tradition to which he had appealed for the throne, he had to give an appanage to his dethroned nephew. The boyars began to rally round Basil, and Yury found himself a foreigner in Moscow. He saw nothing for it but to yield the throne to Basil, but his sons, Basil Cross-Eye and Shemyaka, who clearly had no claim at all, renewed the struggle and continued it with fury even after the death of their father. The fortunes of war varied. Basil Cross-Eye seized the throne but was deserted by his brother Shemyaka, who recalled Basil II. The Cross-Eye was driven out and made submission, but again took up arms. Basil II, who had meanwhile quarrelled with Shemyaka, defeated the Cross-Eye, and captured and blinded him. In 1443 Basil II fell a prisoner to the Tartars while leading his men in action. He was released for a large ransom, which gave rise to discontent; and he made new enemies by bringing back with him some Tartar princes who had entered his service. While giving thanks for his deliverance at the Trinity Monastery, he was seized in church by Shemyaka and his followers, brought to Moscow and blinded. The Metropolitan Jona, like his predecessor Photius, backed Basil II throughout and secured his release. Again the country rallied to him. Moscow, where Shemyaka had found himself as much isolated as his father, was easily seized by Basil's followers and Shemyaka again made submission to him. Again he broke his engagement and was denounced by the Church, which throughout gave its authority to the new order of succession from father to son. He broke faith yet again and was deserted by his closest friends. Appealing to Kazimir IV for help, he raided Basil's domains from Novgorod and was ultimately poisoned by an agent sent from Moscow. His son was granted territory in South Russia by Kazimir.

It is striking that the Tartars could get so little profit out of this desperate struggle. In 1437 Ulu Mehmet, expelled from the Golden Horde, had founded the separate principality of Kazan, and it was he who took Basil II prisoner in 1445. The Tartars secured only temporary or partial successes and in 1451, when they appeared before Moscow, they were beaten off at all points and disappeared in a single night, leaving all their heavy baggage behind them. The complex story of this long civil war brings out impressively the strength of the new order. Moscow is an institution, and the men who serve in it are not going to see it destroyed. The Church well knows that only the growing authority of Moscow can finally deliver the country from the Tartar bondage, and it does not mean to let Moscow go the way of Kiev. But the great crowd which joins the sightless Basil after his liberation shows that there is a nation and that it knows on which side it stands. The question of the succession is settled finally. Basil ends his reign far stronger than he began it. He has annexed Mozhaisk and Serpukhov and he has a strong grip on Ryazan. From the five hundred square miles of Prince Daniel the actual domain of Moscow has grown to fifteen thousand.

Apart from this, the power of Moscow had been greatly strengthened by a habit which was peculiar to this branch of princes. All around, principalities were being split into more and more infinitesimal divisions. John Moneybag had left to the eldest of his five sons only one half of his domain, with no more than a senior joint right over Moscow. With each successive will of a Moscow prince (and the princes regarded their political power as property to be bequeathed like their territory) the proportion of the eldest son was increased until at the death of Basil II the heir received sixty-six towns out of ninety, with sole rights of coining and of justice, and the trade of Moscow was left entirely in his control. It was on this foundation that the Russian autocracy grew up; not, at the outset, by any theory of government, but by the mere fact that the eldest son could buy up all the rest; that he alone could appease the Golden Horde, or take up arms against it; that the rival princes by their constant subdivisions provided him with a number of separate preys which he could easily absorb piecemeal.

The reign of Basil II witnessed the completion of another process which was of great importance to the future. Side by side with the growing principality stood the merchant city of Novgorod the Great, with an empire that extended along the Middle Volga to the Ural Mountains. Novgorod depended on the control of the Middle Volga. But by now Moscow was so much stronger and her population so much increased and emboldened that it made its way in large masses across the Volga and northward into the jealously guarded northern hinterland of Novgorod, which by the end of the reign of Basil II was distributed between the two powers. It was the Church that led this colonization. Holy men, like St. Sergius, went into the forests for quiet and meditation; others gathered around them to learn from them; the community came to be a halting-place, an almshouse, a hospital, a market; peasants clustered round it; the princes gave large grants of land and special privileges. And now some true disciple of the austere founder would seek his way further afield into the wilderness of forests, break up new ground and found in time a new community. The great monasteries were the chief pioneers of a Christian culture of simple tillers of the soil. The principal lines of this colonization naturally followed the rivers; by these same roads travelled the marauding rovers of Novgorod. By the side of their unloved depots stood the outposts of this new people's colonization from Muscovy. There is no surer way of winning a country than to settle it. The jealous secrecy with which the Novgorod merchants guarded their precious hinterland broke down before the new facts. At a moment of agreement, an attempt was made to discriminate the frontiers, but the settlements of the two kinds were so interlaced that the task was impossible. Basil the Sightless dealt masterfully with Novgorod; in 1456 he imposed on it a fine of 10,000 roubles and demanded that the *Veche* should issue no documents without his consent and seal; Novgorod was to receive no princes who were hostile to him. He was with difficulty prevented by the Archbishop Jona from taking strong measures for the settlement of all issues.

We have seen the political division of Russia which had followed on the Tartar conquest, on the rise of Lithuania and on its union with Poland. During this period a similar split began to appear in the Russian Orthodox Church. The Metropolitan, Alexis of Moscow, backed Dmitry of the Don through thick and thin; he excommunicated princes not only for failing to send their contingents against the Tartars, but for helping Olgerd. Of this, Olgerd complained to the Patriarch of Constantinople, and in consequence a special Metropolitan, Cyprian, was appointed for West Russia. On the death of Alexis, Pimen was appointed for Moscow; but when Pimen died, Vitovt was at peace with his son-in-law Basil I, and Cyprian's authority was recognized both in Lithuania and Muscovy. War broke out again, and in 1415 Vitovt made the prelates of South Russia elect a separate Metropolitan, the Bulgarian Gregory Tsamblak. Photius of Moscow recovered the undivided authority. When he died, the prelates of Moscow chose Jona of Ryazan; but the Patriarch of Constantinople had already appointed the Greek Isidore. Isidore was at first accepted in Russia. But he attended the Council of Florence where, as a desperate means of saving Constantinople from the Turks, the Orthodox prelates agreed to union with the Latin Church under the supremacy of the Pope (July 6, 1439). Isidore had promised Basil II that he would remain true to Orthodoxy. Returning to Moscow as papal legate, he substituted the Pope's name for those of the Patriarchs in the liturgy, and read out the acceptance of the union of churches. He was arrested, but escaped. The Russian prelates again chose Jona, and did not think it necessary to send him for consecration to Constantinople. From this time there were always two Metropolitans in Russia; one in Moscow and another, for Lithuania, in Kiev.

All through Russian history from the very beginning there have been testimonies to the great numbers of the Slavs and the almost irresistible power which they might have if they were ever united; despotism can be built upon a passive and peaceable people better than on any other. We are surprised at the numbers of Russian troops mentioned by the early Western travellers to Moscow; they altogether exceed the proportions of Western armies. The future greatness of the Russians had been foretold by the Khazars. The future greatness of Moscow is said to have been foretold by the Metropolitan Peter, friend of John I, who predicted that "her hands will go forth over the shoulders of her enemies." In the reign of Basil II, the monk Michael Klopsky of Novgorod thus warned the Archbishop Euthimius: "Today there is great joy in Moscow; the Grand Prince of Moscow has a fair son; he will break the customs of the land of Novgorod and bring ruin on our town."

Basil the Sightless left his greatly strengthened throne to his son John III, sometimes called the Great (1462–1505). To eliminate all question as to the succession, he had had him crowned as co-ruler during his own lifetime.

The dazzling successes of John III were based on the laborious work of his predecessors. He is one of those rich heirs of history who are able to use freely the resources left to them, and find that instead of exhausting them they have vastly increased them. It should be borne in mind that he is the contemporary of the Tudors and of the rise of strong monarchies in other countries of Europe. But John himself had qualities which might ensure success. He was the last person to squander his accumulated resources in any kind of gamble. Always, by preference, he made two bites at a cherry. He kept within the limits of his own sense of power and thus, in general, he felt almost surprisingly sure of himself. Why did the slow moves of John's diplomacy—for he had little throughout to ask of his army—bring about such simple and complete triumphs? It was because his throne was grounded on a people united by long and painful sufferings, moulded together by a sense of imminent military danger from all sides, and devoted to its own special form of Christianity, which at this time was humbled and threatened at its fountainhead by the capture of Constantinople by the Turks (1453).

When John came to the throne, Muscovy extended like a great wedge northeastward from the city into a wilderness of forests; but the rival principality of Tver was no more than fifty miles from the capital, and the threatening frontiers of Tartary and of Lithuania were neither of them more than seventy miles off. Indeed at this time—for John was still a tributary of the Tartars—there was no part of Russia except Vyatka which enjoyed actual independence.

One of the most startling successes of John's reign was the comparatively easy absorption of Novgorod the Great with its immense territory, which was achieved by different stages between 1465 and 1488. In the time of Andrew of Vladimir a small Novgorod army could rout an immense force of Volga Russia. These conditions were now reversed. The selfishness of the ruling classes in Novgorod made the city depend more and more on levies which had no interest in fighting for her, and

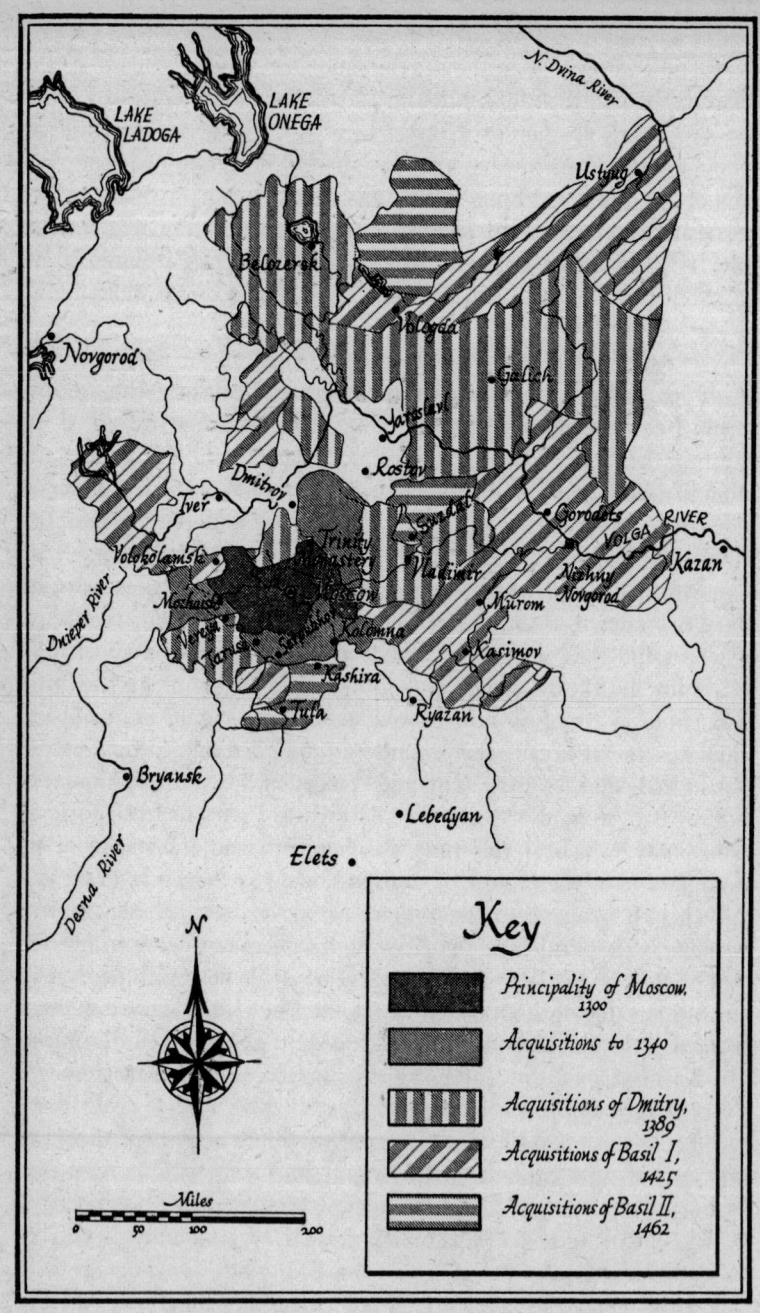

LAKE LADOGA

LAKE ONEGA

N. Dvina River

Ustyug

Novgorod

Belozersk

Vologda

Galich

Yaroslavl

Rostov

Dmitrov

Suzdal

Gorodets

VOLGA RIVER

Tver

Trinity Monastery

Vladimir

Nizhny Novgorod

Kazan

Volokolamsk

MOSCOW

Dnieper River

Mozhaisk

Vereya

Serpukhov

Kolomna

Murom

Kasimov

Kashira

Tula

Ryazan

Bryansk

Lebedyan

Desna River

Elets

N

Key

Principality of Moscow, 1300

Acquisitions to 1340

Acquisitions of Dmitry, 1389

Acquisitions of Basil I, 1425

Acquisitions of Basil II, 1462

Miles

0   50   100   200

GROWTH OF MOSCOW, 1300–1462

in the few combats which took place the Novgorod army was a disorderly rabble and was easily routed. Far more effective, however, was
the grip which the Grand Prince had on Novgorod's hinterland and
food supplies. There was no single great campaign, invading and conquering all the Novgorod territory. John himself had his allies within
the city. Of the ruling parties in Novgorod one, though led by magnates,
rested on the lower classes, and these could be brought to Moscow's side
almost at any time by the stoppage of supplies. Novgorod, it must be
remembered, had always continued to recognize some prince or other.
It was only a question, from which side the prince should be taken.
Now that Moscow had absorbed most of Great Russia, the only alternative to Moscow was the Grand Prince of Lithuania; and Novgorod, in
race and spirit an entirely Russian city, could not turn for help to that
side without feeling that she was giving herself to an alien. Far stronger
than the racial tie, in this respect, was that of the Orthodox Church, to
which both in Novgorod and in Muscovy any Lithuanian alliance was
regarded as treason. The last ruling oligarchs, the Boretskys, headed by
Martha, the widow of a *posadnik*, resolved on this dangerous step. As
had been foretold in Novgorod itself to those who made this choice, the
Grand Prince of Lithuania gave no effective help.

At the outset John warned the bishops against relations with outside
Church authorities: "You, our bedesman, had better take care." Novgorod had reoccupied land ceded to Basil II and had stopped couriers
from John's governor in Pskov. Pskov asked for a separate bishop which
John, "after hard thinking," correctly refused: the request was repeated
in 1468. Meanwhile an envoy from Novgorod in reply to John's grievances replied that on the questions raised he had no instructions.
"Amend yourself, my patrimony," is John's reply, and he now asks for
support from Pskov. In 1470 Novgorod turns for help to Kazimir IV,
who sends Prince Michael of Kiev with a large force. This displeases
the new Archbishop Theophilus and the Moscow party, and the *Veche*
is divided; but loud voices protest: "We are free: we are no patrimony."
A treaty is made by which Novgorod passes under the sovereignty of
Kazimir; freedom and Orthodoxy are guaranteed; no Catholic churches
are to be built; the viceroy's suite is limited; only one year's tax is offered;
yet Kazimir is to defend Novgorod against Moscow; Novgorod reclaims
its old supremacy over Pskov which, it must be remembered, lies between it and Lithuania.

John denounces Novgorod as turning from the true faith, and the
Metropolitan Philip holds up the fate of Constantinople. In May 1471,

John, with well thought-out dispositions, advances towards Novgorod; not a drop of rain falls this summer, and all the roads are practicable; the various forces concentrate, ravaging on their way. Tver and Pskov support John. Prince Michael and his men have left Novgorod in March; Kazimir does nothing. John stops at Torzhok while his armies win on Lake Ilmen and elsewhere; the Archbishop's cavalry refuses to fight against Moscow. A large Novgorod levy stands on the Shelon; John's army crosses the stream and with one charge routs it; among the captures, we are told, is a copy of the treaty with Lithuania. Inside the walls there is no rye left; the Moscow party prevails, and Theophilus is sent to make peace. This is accorded, and a treaty is concluded; Novgorod is the patrimony of John, but the men of Novgorod are free; no Lithuanian princes are to be admitted; the Archbishop has to be consecrated in Moscow.

John observes his terms, but there are great riots in Novgorod. In October 1475, John comes to Novgorod as a prince, in peace but with a large force. He demands the usual mixed court of prince and *posadnik*: "I want to look into the matter." Some of the more hostile boyars he seizes and sends to Moscow in chains.

Shortly afterwards, evidently by arrangement, two of the Moscow party come to John in Moscow and salute him as "Sovereign," instead of the old title of "Lord." [1] John asks whether it is the will of the people of Novgorod to accord him this title. In reply there is naturally a violent riot in the Veche and some of the Moscow party are killed. The answer sent is that Novgorod desires no new title and no new form of justice, and again appeal is made to Kazimir. John, after consulting with his family and with an unusually representative council, takes action; many of the Novgorod boyars enter his service; he stops at Torzhok and at ninety miles from Novgorod, holding the envoys sent to him; at thirty miles off, he orders up the men of Pskov on his flank with their artillery; at twenty miles he is met by the Archbishop and other envoys, who addresses him as "Sovereign Lord" and beg for clemency; he gives no answer and invites them to dinner; they ask for a negotiation with his boyars and terms are suggested, but John moves his troops up to the city and builds a wall round it; he has made all arrangements to stay there. In the city there are divisions. At last John gives his terms: "The sovereignty is to be the same in Novgorod as in Moscow." Fresh envoys offer anything short of this; the answer is: "As in Moscow." John adds:

[1] The first word (*gosudar*) implies ownership; the second (*gospodin*) is used of a master of free servants.

"There is to be no town bell in Novgorod, and no *posadnik*; all the sovereignty is to be ours." This, after six days, is accepted; John refuses further guarantees; details of the settlement are to be communicated later. These are found to include the loss of all subject towns and the precious hinterland of the Northern Dvina. Martha Boretsky and seven notable boyars are carried off, and the town bell is removed to the Kremlin. John enters the city twice to take measures against the plague which has broken out there (1476).

Next year John had trouble with his brothers, and the Tartars and Lithuanians aimed a joint attack on Moscow. Novgorod again appealed to Kazimir. John made a quick and secret march on the city, which he cannonaded. The gates were opened to him and he entered. He seized his principal enemies, tried them, and executed them. A hundred families he moved wholesale to the Middle Volga. In 1487 fifty of the leading merchant families were transported to Vladimir; the next year, on the report of a plot against John's governor, 7000 of the gentry were moved to the environs of Moscow; Moscow families, in the same wholesale way, were moved into the territory of Novgorod.

In 1472, before finishing with Novgorod, John had already made himself master of the vast region of Perm near the Urals. Vyatka was finally absorbed in 1485. A glance at the map (page 182) will show the full proportions of what had happened.

John was now able to absorb also some of the other remains of independence in north and central Russia. In 1463 he acquired what was left of the principality of Yaroslavl by the voluntary submission of all its princes. In 1485 he brought to a final conclusion the long struggle between Moscow and Tver. Here, too, he had plenty of friends in his enemy's camp. Two of his brothers' appanages he absorbed, one by death and one by confiscation. Verea, one of the last outstanding domains in the Moscow family, he annexed. Half of Ryazan came to him by bequest, and the other half was really in his hands through his sister Agrippina, grandmother of the infant prince.

In 1453, Constantinople, the mother church of Russia, had fallen into the hands of the Turks. Its last Emperor, Constantine Paleologus, died fighting on its walls. His niece Zoe became a ward of the Pope. John III was a widower. The political extinction of Constantinople seemed to Latin minds to offer an opportunity for the reunion of the churches, an idea which had been accepted in Constantinople during the last days of independence at the Council of Florence and even, as we remember, by the Greek Isidore as Metropolitan of Russia. The

hand of Zoe was now offered to John, and with it of course the renewed
suggestion of reunion. In 1472 John married Zoe, who took the name of
Sophia. She came to Russia under the escort of the Cardinal Antonio,
who at every town entered first, carrying the Latin cross. When the
party approached Moscow, the Metropolitan Philip said to John: "My
son, if you allow him to do this out of a wish to pay him honour, then
he comes into the city by one gate, and I, your father, am out of it by
another." The Cardinal yielded, and the Latin cross was packed away in
a sledge. Antonio, however, asked leave to debate the differences of the
two churches. This was granted, but we are told that he received such
a vigorous and exhaustive reply that he retired with the words, "I have
no books with me." The effect of this marriage was exactly the opposite
to what the Pope had contemplated. John took up the role of successor
of the Greek Emperors, the natural champion of the Orthodox Church
in its time of tribulation.

One of the early effects of Sophia's influence was that John finally
threw off the Tartar yoke (1480). The vigorous peasants of Vyatka had
even repaid a former raid by sacking the capital of the Golden Horde,
Saray. In 1472 the Khan Ahmed was on the Russian frontier, and after
a brave resistance took the little town of Alexin; but a Russian army
estimated at 180,000 men barred his way. In 1476 Ahmed summoned
John to the Horde and received a hostile reply. Sophia said: "My father
and I lost our patrimony sooner than submit." There is an unauthenti-
cated account of a second Tartar embassy which John received with in-
dignities, dashing on the ground the image of the Khan presented for
his homage and stamping on it. Anyhow, John took up a position of
open challenge and in 1480 Ahmed, having allied himself with Kazimir IV and knowing that John was in difficulty with his brothers, led a
large army on Moscow. Finding the Oka guarded, Ahmed threatened
Moscow from the side of the Ugra. John sent his wife towards Archangel, and himself made preparations for flight. Moscow was furious;
John was accused of drawing the Khan on Moscow and then turning
coward. The sturdy bishop of Rostov, Vassian, did not mince words with
him. He called him a runaway and a betrayer of Christ. "You are not
immortal," he said. "Fear you, too, shepherd! Will not God exact this
blood of your hands?" John's own son refused to leave the front. John
joined his army, only to leave it again and treat for peace. Twice he
made the army retreat, but on November 19 the Tartars suddenly departed of themselves. On the way back Ahmed was surprised and killed
in his sleep by the Nogays; his sons were overthrown by the recently

established Tartar Khanate of Crimea. It is just in such a slow and in-conspicuous way that other great decisions in Russian history have often come of themselves. But such settlements are sometimes more perma-nent than those achieved by a single brilliant victory.

Sophia brought with her to Moscow great pride, great political astuteness, a genius for intrigue, and a desire for the old Byzantine cere-monial, which could only place the sovereign much farther apart from his boyars and people. The apparatus of court ceremony, while isolating the sovereign, increased his prestige, and already John's methods of ac-tion harmonized well with the atmosphere of closed doors, of foregone decisions, and of a set purpose. Church authorities, high and low, did everything to enhance this new prestige. John took the title of Sovereign of All Russia, also that of Tsar or Cæsar, though this was at present mostly used in dealings with foreign states, especially the less powerful such as the Livonian Order of Knights. He also styled himself Samo-derzhets—a translation of the Greek word αὐτοκράτωρ, but meaning in its Slavonic form rather an independent sovereign, and referring to Rus-sia's liberation from the Tartar yoke. The two possible meanings of the word, however, merged into one; and John's reign is the time when Russia became, not only in fact but in principle, an autocracy. The Church later invented a legend according to which Vladimir Mono-makh, who only became Grand Prince of Kiev in 1113, was invited by his grandfather (the Greek Emperor Constantine Monomachus who died in 1054, more than fifty years earlier) to share with him the joint government of the Greek Empire. In token of this, so it was maintained, Constantine sent to Vladimir his own royal cap, sceptre, and mantle, which were identified with those preserved in the city of Vladimir. An-other legend traced the first Russian prince, Rurik, by a direct descent of fifteen generations, back to the Emperor Augustus, who was claimed to have had a son named Prus, the ancestor of the Lithuanian Prussians and thus of Rurik! Even the Greek Patriarch was induced to quote the first of these legends. Moscow claimed to be a third and last Rome. The first Rome and the second, it was said, had both fallen through heresies—the second Rome, that is Constantinople, through its renunciation of its independence at the above-named Council of Florence: "The third Rome, Moscow, stands, and a fourth there will not be." John in his life-time crowned first his grandson and then his son. The ceremony was performed with his grandson Dmitry (by his first wife) in 1598; and when Sophia's influence prevailed against the boyars, and secured the substitution of her own son Basil, it was repeated for him.

Around the Tsars of Moscow was already gathered a strong aristocracy. From the time of John Moneybag, princely families had one after another taken service with Moscow, and latterly these included families of the highest rank; such newcomers, especially those who transferred their allegiance from Lithuania, stipulated for the continuance of their local courts and local rights. On the other hand, boyars who had been for generations in the service of Moscow and had contributed to build up her power were equally jealous of their standing. From the reign of John onwards, official genealogies were compiled for the settlement of such disputes. But that was by no means the end of the matter. The Grand Princes themselves had never discriminated between their property and their political rights. John III, when he altered the succession in favour of Basil, asked why he should not do what he liked with his own property. Equally the princes and boyars regarded their rights of service as property, so that past records of appointments in the state service were also taken as a basis of seniority, which must somehow or other be brought into harmony with that of birth. Thus, for instance, in an army the commander of the main body was senior to that of the right wing; next came, equal, the vanguard and rear guard; and last, the left wing. A prince who was offered one of these commands would look up in the records of service the positions held in a previous generation by his own ancestors and those of the men with whom he was now asked to serve, and would entirely refuse to accept any lesser post than that which this comparison indicated. Even if he were willing to waive the question, his family would not allow him to do so and would claim that its honour as a whole had suffered loss. Such quarrels took up a great deal of the time of the Grand Princes; and the party judged to be the offender might be thrown into prison or subjected to some far more humiliating punishment. It goes without saying that the system was a denial of all common sense and entirely incompatible with the efficiency of the state service, but all the boyars old and new held on to it very tightly. Fortunately for the new autocrats, there was no strong corporate sense of class interests in the boyars as a whole, and they could easily be dealt with piecemeal by their masters. If their ambitions had taken a more corporate form, the fierce struggle between Tsars and boyars which was now to follow would have been even more severe.

In the last ten years of the century John's annexations proceeded in the same gradual, apparently indecisive, but effective manner on a new side, towards the southwest, and at the expense of the grand principality of Lithuania. Kazimir IV, whose royal powers were seriously circumscribed, was frequently taken up with the quarrels of Poland and Lithuania and with other preoccupations relating to Prussia, Bohemia, and Hungary. Hence his failure to give any effective help to Novgorod. In Lithuania there were still remnants of the princely family of the line of Chernigov, always in the old days hostile to the Monomakhs. Here too had taken refuge the descendents of Shemyaka. But these princes were glad enough now to gravitate toward Moscow. Lithuania had imposed on the local Russian princes only a loose control and had left them in possession of their domains; but now that Lithuania had fallen into the wake of Polish policy, religious pressure was being brought to bear on these Orthodox princes and their subjects, and those who were nearest to Moscow territory simply transferred themselves to the allegiance of John, which inevitably opened a whole series of wars with Lithuania and Poland.

John had the clearest instinct of the issues at stake. With his increased dignity and with a great nation behind him, he definitely considered it to be his mission to reunite all Russian territory. In 1494, after a war with Lithuania, he extorted from it a recognition of his newly claimed title "Sovereign of All Russia." Replying to an offer of the Emperor Frederick III to confer on him the title of King, he said: "We, by God's grace, are sovereigns in our land from the beginning, from our first forefathers, and our appointment we hold from God"; as to the Western title of King, he adds: "We have wanted it from no one, and do not want it now." It becomes the standard reply to such suggestions: "We have no need of recognition." In 1501, the King of Poland, backed by the support of Hungary and of the Pope, complains that John is seizing his patrimony; John replies: "But what do they call their patrimony? The land of Russia is often from our ancestors of old our patrimony"; and in 1503, on the repetition of the same complaint, he answers: "And do not I regret my patrimony, the Russian land which is in the hands of Lithuania—Kiev, Smolensk, and the other towns? . . . Why, not only that is our patrimony, the towns and districts which we now have, but all Russian land of old from our forefathers too." To his ally the Khan of Crimea John said plainly that with Poland there could be no permanent peace till all was restored, "only truces in order to draw breath." He himself waged two wars with Poland and Lithuania; his successor Basil III waged two; Helen, regent for John IV, waged one, and John IV was at war with Livonia or with Poland over a period of twenty years. Klyuchevsky reckons that for the forty years from 1492 to 1532 Russia was at war chiefly on this issue.

In this struggle John III had a valuable partner. In his father's reign the Tartar Edigei had formed a separate Tartar Horde in Crimea. Edigei's sons perished in civil wars, but were succeeded by Azi-Girei, the founder of a permanent dynasty. Azi's son Mengli-Girei allied himself with John. The Turkish sultan had made himself suzerain of Crimea, and Mengli was glad to have a powerful friend outside. Also, Mengli was engaged in a life and death struggle with the sons of Khan Ahmed and it was with John's help that he defeated the last of them, Shah Ahmed, and put an end to the famous Golden Horde. In 1487 John also made himself arbiter of the affairs of Kazan, driving out the Khan Alegam and replacing him by his own protégé, Mehmet Amin.

Kazimir IV confined himself to complaints on the subject of John's western annexations. Kazimir died in 1492, and Poland and Lithuania were for the time divided. John and his ally Mengli now invaded Lithuania; princes and towns hastened to join him. Lithuania begged for a peace and for a Moscow bride for the young Grand Prince Alexander. John insisted first on the cession of all that he had won and of the title "Sovereign of All Russia." In 1495 Alexander married John's daughter Helen, agreeing to leave her in the Orthodox faith with a chapel of her own. The terms were not kept, and meanwhile numbers of other princes were transferring their allegiance from Lithuania to Moscow. John accepted these new subjects and declared war in 1500. Twice he won signal victories, on the Vedrosha and at Mstislavl, and the Livonian knights, who joined Alexander, were also driven to retreat. Alexander, now succeeding to the crown of Poland, asked for peace. John granted a truce for six years, again on the basis of the cession of all that he had won. In 1496 John engaged in a war with Sweden, which led to no marked results. To please his ally the King of Denmark, who was a bitter enemy of the Hansa League, John seized all the German merchants at Novgorod with their goods, their warehouses and their chapel, and from this blow the trade of Novgorod never recovered.

In 1497, at John's orders, the clerk Gusev and others drew up a law code (*sudebnik*) which forbade judicial corruption and arranged for assessors to control the judges. His reign was disturbed by church controversy. Toward the end of the fourteenth century had arisen in Novgorod a sect known as *Strigolniki*, who believed that priests were unnecessary, that laymen might preach, and that prayers for the dead were of no avail. This sect did not last long. But during the last years of Novgorod's independence the prince Michael of Kiev, sent by King Kazimir to help the city, brought with him members of a new sect known as

Judaisers. These challenged the deity of Jesus Christ, the doctrines of the Incarnation and of the Trinity, the worship of saints, the use of icons, and the practice of monasticism. The exceptional piety and learning of some of the converts attracted the attention of John himself; the sect won many high adherents in Moscow, including even the Metropolitan Zozima. Joseph of Volokolamsk, one of the most notable churchmen of the time, fought the heresy with vigour and ruthlessness; and, supported by Grand Princess Sophia, he secured the condemnation and burning of its chief leaders (1504). He also succeeded in repulsing a strong attack on the altogether excessive wealth of the Church, led by one of the saintliest of Russian ascetics, Nil Sorsky.

These controversies continued into the next reign. Basil III (1505–33), as the son of Sophia, naturally leaned on her supporters; and he had need of their support, for it was only by the special indulgence of the Metropolitan Daniel that he was able to put away his childless wife Solomonida and espouse Helen Glinsky of Lithuania. Joseph died in 1515. He had been boldly opposed by Prince Patrikeyev, a pupil of Nil Sorsky who in monasticism was known as Vassian Cross-Eye. Vassian had for ally a Western scholar, Maxim the Greek, who had studied in Paris, Florence, and Venice; one of his teachers was Girolamo Savonarola. Maxim was brought to Russia to correct church books, and wrote against the superstitions which he found everywhere. Vassian and Maxim renewed the attack on the wealth of the Church. "Where in the traditions of the Gospels, Apostles and Fathers," says a pamphlet ascribed to Vassian, "are monks ordered to acquire populous villages and enslave peasants to the brotherhood? . . . We look into the hands of the rich, fawn slavishly, flatter them to get out of them some little village . . . We wrong and rob and sell Christians, our brothers. We torture them with scourges like wild beasts." Vassian and Maxim also criticized Basil III's divorce of Solomonida, and both were thrown into prison.

Basil III completed the work of his father. This son of Sophia was so autocratic that boyars looked back to John as more genial and accessible. He crushed the liberties of Pskov, which was too loyal to resist him (1510). He annexed the remainder of Ryazan. From Lithuania he rescued the Russian frontier city of Smolensk (1514). There was now one undisputed authority from Chernigov to the Gulf of Finland, to the White Sea, and to the Ural Mountains. The Russian Empire was as good as made.

Moscow

(1533–1682)

CHAPTER VI

John the Dread

[*1533–84*]

Basil III died in 1533, leaving the throne to an infant son three years old, John IV, who was to be known as John the Dread.

For the understanding of this deeply interesting and tragical reign we must again take account of Poland. We remember that Poland and Lithuania had been loosely united by the marriage of Yagailo and Jadzwiga in 1386. In its first period, it is true, this union was broken by several interruptions, but in the main, when Lithuania quarrelled with Moscow, Poland was behind Lithuania.

The kings of Poland suffered constant diminution of their powers. Great concessions had been extorted by the aristocracy in the past, and the temporary alliance between the King and the gentry during the reign of Kazimir IV only led in the long run to a substitution of magnates and gentry for magnates alone as the opposition to the throne. In this enlarged sense the *szlachta* or gentry came to dominate Poland entirely on the death of Kazimir IV in 1492.

Let us take some of these diminutions of the royal power. In 1374 under Louis the Great at the Sejm (or assembly) of Koszyce, the King was engaged to recover all lost territory, not to cede any; to levy not more than the most trifling dues from a given province. In 1422, after a camp riot in front of the enemy, Wladyslaw V (Yagailo) was precluded from confiscating estates or coining money without agreement of the barons and prelates. In 1430, the royal justice was restricted to trying and executing murderers or other serious criminals caught in the act. In 1454 at another camp riot, was initiated a movement which restricted the King (Kazimir IV) from leasing out the royal estates; the county magistrates were to be appointed from candidates chosen by the knights. Even small gentry obtained the right of justice over their own peasants. No new laws were to be made nor war waged without the assent of a general assembly of the gentry. Under Jan Albrecht (1492–1501) new

privileges were extorted by the *szlachta*. In 1496 it was given a monopoly
in the possession of country estates and in the conduct of export trade,
which finally arrested the growth of industrial classes in the towns. The
right of two sons in a peasant family to leave their district was restricted
to one, and later abolished. No time limit was to be set to the measures
taken by a master to recover a fugitive peasant. Under Alexander, who
acceded in 1501, the Senate claimed to govern the country, and no
obedience was to be rendered to a king who did not obey it. Under
Sigismund I (1506–48) the peasants were finally fastened to the soil
and were obliged to do one day's work a week for their master. In 1543
it was forbidden to redeem a peasant from his master. In 1520–1 the
posts of peasant local government were transferred from the peasants to
the master. By a law of 1518 the peasant was even precluded from
bringing any legal complaint against a master. The time of John the
Dread witnessed further concessions of the gravest kind. In 1537 by another refusal to fight, which is known as the "cocks' war," the King was
in the end compelled to exempt the gentry from the poll tax. In 1565 the
export of Polish manufactured articles was forbidden. On the extinction
of the line of Yagailo with the death of Sigismund Augustus in 1573,
the Polish gentry practically threw their throne open for auction, and
John the Dread himself at one time thought of being a candidate. Eventually they elected Henry of Valois, later Henry III of France, who engaged to call the Sejm every three years, to abstain from making any
war without the Senate, and to regain all lost territory. He accepted the
appointment of sixteen permanent councillors, who had the right to be
heard on all questions; in the event of his not listening to them, his
subjects were released from their obedience. By a further secret agreement, known as *Pacta Conventa*, he made other more extraordinary
concessions. He engaged always to be at peace with France, to procure
auxiliary French forces for the wars of Poland, to build a fleet at his own
cost, to refill the treasury, and to pay the debts of his predecessor.
Within a year Henry, who was already sick of his throne, escaped to
France to take up there the succession of his brother Charles IX. He
had succeeded in bringing to the point of ridicule the royal power in
Poland.

The Reformation at the outset won much ground in Poland. At
one time it commanded very general support among the *szlachta*, who
linked up this cause with that of their class immunities. This movement, however, was rudely repressed when Rome had recovered from
the shock of the attack and organized her counteroffensive under the

formidable lead of the Jesuits. In no country was the reaction more
violent than in Poland. The kings, who had at one time shown a tendency to liberalism, were driven back into docile service of the reaction.
This greatly affected the position of the Orthodox Russian subjects of
the Polish-Lithuanian State. In 1569 was brought about the Union of
Lublin, by which the two countries were definitely united under one
king, who was to be chosen in a common Sejm, of both countries. The
gentry might settle indiscriminately in either country, and Lithuania
rapidly came to be occupied by Poles. The Lithuanian officials were
largely Polish, and the Lithuanian gentry soon became Polonized. Old
Russian territories, Volhynia, Kiev, and Podolia, were transferred from
Lithuania to Poland. The Orthodox Russians of Lithuania were vigorously persecuted, especially the poorer classes, and it had been largely
this that drove into the arms of John III those Russian principalities
which adjoined his frontier.

John the Dread was born in 1530. At the age of three he had lost his
father and was Grand Prince of Moscow. Russia was ruled by his mother
Helen, a Russian of Lithuania whose family had only in the last reign
entered the service of Moscow. She was guided by her uncle Michael
Glinsky and by her lover Prince Obolensky, and her rule was arbitrary
and capricious. The uncles of the Grand Prince were alienated and
thrown into prison. Having to choose between her two advisors Helen
took the worst of them, Obolensky, and her uncle Michael was imprisoned till his death. An ineffective war was waged with Lithuania,
and in Kazan the Khan Enalei, friendly to Moscow, was replaced by
Safa Girei of the hostile Crimean dynasty, who with the Crimean Tartars ravaged Muscovy. It seemed as if the Tartars were reuniting their
empire.

In 1538 Helen suddenly died—as was suspected, by poisoning—and
her favourite Obolensky was at once overthrown by the exasperated
boyars. The regency was disputed between two princely houses, the
Shuiskys and the Belskys. Thrice the power changed hands and twice
the Metropolitans themselves were forcibly changed during the struggle,
one of them, Joseph, being done to death. The Shuiskys prevailed, and
three successive members of this family held power in turn. Their use
of it was entirely selfish, dictated not even by class interests but simply
by those of family and favour. John at the age of eight was deprived of
his nurse and at eleven of the boyar Vorontsov, to whom he was much
attached; the boy called in the Metropolitan but he too was insulted
and mishandled.

John had a remarkably quick and intuitive mind, extremely sub-
jective, retaining the smart of every insult or injury. He was a quick
reader and thoroughly mastered such literature as was accessible to
him. This consisted of some Greek historical records with loose accounts
of the history of peoples of the world, the Bible, and Russian Church
literature. John's mind brought everything that he read to bear on his
own position. He read of Tsars, Tsar David, Tsar Solomon, Tsars of
Constantinople and of the Golden Horde; his thoughts, taking refuge in
themselves from the reign of caprice and license all around him, dwelt
on every passage that magnified monarchical authority; it was not only
that he read, but that he assimilated and transformed all that he read;
his mind mobilized it for future use. In his palace he and his younger
brother Yury were treated with scorn, or at best complete neglect. He
records later how the boyar Andrew Shuisky lounged with his feet on
the bed of John's own father; he tells us that he was even short of food
and clothes. Meanwhile, for the reception of foreign envoys he was
dressed in full pomp of state; and the men who made so light of him
in private would fall on their faces before him and declare themselves
his slaves.

John felt that there was something in him, or rather something in
his office, which could command obedience. At the age of thirteen he
put this to the test. He suddenly handed over Andrew Shuisky to the
kennel-keepers of his palace, who imprisoned Shuisky and did him to
death. But his own rule was as wilful as that of the boyars. As a child,
he had tortured animals and thrown cats from the roof; and such tastes
had been encouraged in him by those who sought his favour. His assertion of will was followed by a number of arbitrary and cruel punishments.

At little more than sixteen John astonished his counsellors by his
decision to be crowned, and not as Grand Prince but as Tsar; he made
a careful study of precedents for this ceremony. At the same time he
decided to marry, and the seriousness with which he had thought out
all the bearings of this step were an astonishment to those around him.
He made an unexpected and opposite quotation from the saints and
explained that he had discarded the idea of a foreign match, because
mixed marriages did not turn out well. The young ladies of the realm
were paraded and John made a wise choice. It fell on Anastasia Romanov, of a family which had long since taken service in Moscow and
was deservedly popular among the poorer people. The marriage was
a most happy one.

In 1547 a great fire broke out in Moscow. Fires were frequent there, but this one was not likely to be forgotten; it was a whole series of fires through April and June, in the middle of which the belfry of John the Great fell down; and it culminated in a huge conflagration which burned down two of the oldest monasteries and most of the churches. The superstitious people, certainly urged on by the discontented boyars, declared that the fire was due to witchcraft. A mob demanded the death of John's uncle Yury Glinsky and of his grandmother. Yury tried to escape but was run to earth and dispatched, and a crowd of threatening petitioners made its way to the Sparrow Hills outside the city, where John had taken refuge. John at once ordered his men to attack them, and his boldness of front succeeded; the demonstrators were easily dispersed. But John passed at this time through a great internal crisis. He felt now that his office was a heavy and serious responsibility calling for the best that was in him, and that to control the boyars he must have the good will and support of his people as a whole. He picked advisers to whom he gave the name of the Chosen Council; the principal figures in it were the Metropolitan Makary (who was the compiler of the Lives of the Russian Saints), the court chaplain Sylvester, a man of great integrity and the author of a set of rules of conduct in life known in Russian literature as the *Domostroy*, and the chamberlain Adashev, who was of comparatively humble origin; thus, like his contemporaries the Tudors, John chose his chief helpers from the middle class. He allowed himself to be not only directed but restrained by the advice of the Chosen Council, even agreeing to do nothing without its approval. In the same year, 1547, he sent the Saxon Schlitte to Western Europe to bring back to Russia scholars and artisans.

Now followed the happiest period of John's reign. In 1550 he called together an assembly of the land (*Zemsky Sobor*). His grandfather John the Great had summoned a kind of general assembly after consulting his mother and his Council of Boyars, when he decided to risk his attack upon Novgorod, thereby possibly challenging a long war with Lithuania. But John the Dread went much further; the Zemsky Sobor of 1550 was intended to represent all classes. He opened the assembly with an eloquent speech—there is always something of an appeal in his speeches; he charged the boyars with seeking the power; by his own sins, and his orphanhood and youth many had perished in civil strife; he had grown up without instruction; he had been used to the evil devices and habits of the boyars, and from that time to this, "How I have sinned, and how many punishments has God sent against you! And I did not repent, and have myself persecuted poor Christians with every violence"; now he has asked pardon of the clergy and granted pardon to the princes and boyars; he has compassion on his subjects, whom he describes as "people of God and given me by God"; he will himself be their judge and defender; they need not fear the strong and the glorious. John summoned this assembly in order to inform himself of all abuses in his realm. Petitions had already been streaming in to Moscow against the selfishness and exactions of the local governors, and John gave an order to Adashev which later led to the establishment of a new *Prikaz*, or office, for the regular reception of petitions. He also instructed Adashev to take measures for appointing better judges—an initiative which, as we shall see, by no means remained on paper. Further, instructions were given to remodel the law code (*Sudebnik*) of John the Great, and this work, completed within the year, was presented for acceptance in 1551 to a great assembly of the Church at which the leading persons among the boyars and gentry were also present.

During John's minority, petitions had come from the provinces asking that the population should itself be allowed to organize the repression of crime, especially of murders and robberies, which the local governors had failed to effect; and at that time was authorized the election from all classes of special judicial authorities (*gubnye starosty*) for this purpose, who were given a free hand not only to judge but to execute. In 1552 John gave a notable further development to this beginning. Where the population was itself prepared to guarantee a fixed amount of state dues to the treasury, local (*zemskie*) officials on an elective basis were authorized to collect the local taxes in lieu of the old governors (*namestniki*), who in such places were abolished. Where governors remained, the population was allowed to elect assessors who had the responsibility of countersigning their judgments and were even authorized to impeach them where necessary. This right did not remain a dead letter. John, it may be remembered, was at this time twenty-one.

In 1552 his attention was claimed by external affairs. There had been a number of quick changes in Kazan. Safa Girei was displaced by a Russian nominee, Shah Ali; but the new ruler was very unpopular in Kazan; a message was sent to the Nogai Tartars of Sarai, near Astrakhan, asking for a substitute, and Ediger Mahmed was sent thence. This challenge to Moscow was taken up by John. In June 1552 he led a great expedition of over 100,000 men against Kazan. The Crimean Tartars at once invaded Muscovy and John was almost compelled to turn aside to save the town of Tula, which was besieged by them. Tula, however, held good, and in face of its brave resistance the Crimean hosts retreated. John went forward to settle with Kazan. The expedition presented many difficulties. Kazan was the one great Tartar fortress between Moscow and the Urals, and its picked garrison of 30,000 men made a magnificent resistance. John in every way gave the expedition the character of a crusade. He took with him the cross of Dmitry of the Don, and launched his troops with the words: "Lord, in Thy Name we go forward." His ships and stores were sunk, but he held on to his task, scouting day and night in person in the front line. In answer to his summons to surrender, the garrison killed many of their prisoners in front of the walls. John had 150 cannon; a German engineer blew up part of the wall and the Russians entered, only to be driven out. A great tower, built by the Russians to command the city walls, was nearly captured by the defenders; a Tartar force outside made vigorous attempts at relief; the Russians discovered and cut off the water supply. On Sunday, October 11, the order was given to storm the city. The Chief Mullah died fighting in front of the mosque; the garrison sent its prince, Ediger, for safety to the Russian camp with a message "We will come out to drink the last cup with you"; six thousand men, leaving their armour behind, fought their way into the midst of the Russian army and were cut to pieces. Kazan is situated almost at the junction of the greatest river of Europe, the Volga, and the greatest tributary in Europe, the Kama. On its fall it became evident, not only that the Tartar domination was finally broken but that the Russians now had a straight road of comparatively easy advancement eastward. If Russia had borne on her back the main brunt of the onslaught of Asia, it was natural that Russians should consider themselves entitled to be the advance guard in the counterstroke of Europe and of Christendom. In the very next year there came from Astrakhan, another of the three great Tartar centres, a request for a prince to be nominated by John, and though his tenure was for a time disturbed, Astrakhan was finally annexed without difficulty in 1566. In the same year Wisniowiecki, who was at the head of a large section of the Cossacks of South Russia, transferred his allegiance from the Polish-Lithuanian State to Moscow.

The annexation of Kazan and Astrakhan was an enormous gain to the empire. Muscovy now extended not only to the Urals but to the Caspian. The changed conditions were at once felt on the side of the Caucasus, where a number of smaller peoples, some of them Christian, were for the first time brought into contact with Moscow. This of itself threatened the security of the one remaining Tartar state in Russia, the Khanate of Crimea.

Eastward, however, the road was open. Before John died, Moscow had gained a firm footing beyond the Urals in Siberia. Large estates near the Urals had been given to the great merchant family of Stroganov with permission to work metals and salt, and to extend its domains beyond the mountains. Thus in September 1581, the Cossack Ermak, who was under sentence of death for rebellion, led a small host of similar free-booters, not more than 150 in number, against the Siberian prince Kuchum. Ermak was successful; in 1582 he already had a hold on the two mighty Siberian rivers, Irtysh and Obi. His conquest he lightly handed over to the Tsar, in return for a full pardon and some presents. The Russian march to the Pacific had begun. It was to be marked by singularly few armed conflicts, rather by the sheer force of flowing; and by 1643, with but little help from the government, Russian colonization had reached the Pacific. In those great waste spaces, communication was made comparatively simple by the magnificent rivers; and hardy men who defied all rigours of climate kept pushing forward, before all things, to find a place of greater freedom. The addition of almost half a con-tinent to the Russian Empire was to be the work of the Russian people.

Shortly after the fall of Kazan, John received visitors who opened up another perspective. English merchants, finding themselves faced with Dutch and other competition, after consultation with the famous explorer Sebastian Cabot, clubbed together to explore a new route east-ward through the Arctic Ocean. Three ships set sail in May 1553, under Willoughby and Chancellor, but Chancellor, after waiting in vain for a week at the rendezvous in the north of Norway, went forward alone; Willoughby's crew were found later, frozen to death. On September 2 Chancellor found himself in a bay and, seizing some fishermen, learned that he was in Russia. He asked for leave to visit Moscow and started even before it reached him. John received him in great state and with great favour.

In 1555 Chancellor returned as ambassador of Queen Mary. Before granting the trade privileges for which he asked, John consulted the Moscow merchants, and they unwillingly accepted the terms of the treaty. The English might trade in Russia without paying any dues; their goods could not be seized except for their own debts or crimes; they might engage, punish, and dismiss workmen, whose offences were not to be visited on their employers. The English were under the jurisdiction of their own chief factor, and their offences against Russian law were to be judged by the Tsar himself; their suits against Russians were to have speedy trial. Individually they could not be arrested for debt, if payment was guaranteed by the chief factor.

John well knew what a price he was paying for English friendship; he described it as "heavier than tribute." But he was one of the earliest and most far-sighted of Russian statesmen; and in the hereditary struggle with western enemies—the German Order, Poland, and Sweden—in which he was himself soon to be involved, he desired to develop his one free outlet to the West (through Archangel), by which alone he could make sure of obtaining those military and technical experts or materials which he needed to face his enemies on more equal terms, and he hoped to use this new friendship as a powerful counterpoise to them. He dispatched Nepey as his ambassador to England with Chancellor who, sharing to the full John's appreciation of this new connection, was drowned off Scotland in his zeal to secure the safety of the Russian envoy. Nepey was received with honour, and the English felt that they risked nothing in granting the Russian traders the same facilities in their own dominions; they were placed under the special jurisdiction of the Lord Chancellor. Nepey took back with him to Russia several experts, particularly in medicine and in mining, two specialties in which Russia continued to be mainly dependent on foreign supply.

In 1553 John had a very serious illness. He was anxious that his Council of Boyars should swear allegiance to his infant son Dmitry. This was opposed by his cousin, Prince Vladimir of Staritsa, who himself hoped for the throne. The Prince was supported by those of the boyars who were discontented, and the question became the occasion for a demonstration of great hostility to the Romanov family, who would naturally have the regency for John's infant son. The recent minorities of Russian sovereigns had been no argument for the succession of minors, and Sylvester and Adashev openly took the side of Prince Vladimir. John, lying on what was thought to be his deathbed, could hear the vehement discussions of the Council, and in particular the ill-will expressed against the family of his wife. He demanded that the oath be taken, and he was unwillingly obeyed, even by Prince Vladimir himself. John recovered, but he treasured his resentment in his heart. In the next year some of the boyars committed the offence of all offences; they were caught planning to escape to Lithuania.

In 1558, five years after John's illness, arose a question of the first importance, in which he was again at issue with his principal counsellors.

In this matter John has the judgment of history behind him. Sylvester was anxious that he should complete his triumph over the heathen by the conquest of Crimea. This would have been a direct challenge to Turkey on ground on which the full strength of Russia could not possibly at that time be brought to bear. Crimea was strong enough, in spite of incessant wars, to remain a thorn in the flesh of Moscow for more than two centuries. John had in view a quite different objective, in the choice of which he anticipated the most illustrious of his successors, Peter the Great.

It was clear that the days of the German crusading Orders on the coast of the Baltic were numbered. Vitovt, it will be remembered, had in 1410 broken the back of the Teutonic Order when he led against it his great Slavonic crusade and won the battle of Tannenberg. The Teutonic Order had since secularized itself as a duchy, accepting Protestantism as a good occasion for this change, and became the nucleus of modern Prussia. The question was, what would happen to the Knights of the Sword, who held that part of the Baltic coast which was economically and politically indispensable to an expanding Muscovy as an outlet for closer communication with Europe. The Knights of the Order realized their danger and even successfully memorialized the Emperor Charles V to prevent the passage to Moscow of European experts, scholars, and above all, military instructors. But it was anyhow only a question who should have the heritage of the Order. Russia had rivals in Sweden and in Poland, two countries which were later to serve as barriers between Russia and Europe up to the reign of Catherine the Great. John, knowing the weakness of the Order, decided to move first. At the outset he was successful. Marching with a large army into Livonia he speedily won Narva, Neuhaus, Dorpat, and other places.

He chafed greatly at the opposition of Sylvester and Adashev, and finally breaking with them, sent the priest to the Monastery of Solovetsk on the White Sea and the layman to a command in Livonia. Sylvester originally went off of himself. It is clear that, keeping the Tsar's conscience as his confessor, he had very much pressed his authority. John complains of his having treated him "as if we did not exist." He was told "how long to sleep, how to dress"; he was expected "to say nothing to his councillors and to let them say anything to him." "If I try to object, they shout at me that my soul is lost." Sylvester had even threatened him with the wrath of the Church for not taking up the crusade against Crimea. John cites the example of Aaron, who was not allowed "to mix in the government of men," and adds that "a kingdom ruled by a priest always comes to ruin." His austere mentor is not one of his victims; of him John writes: "I want to be judged with him in the next world before the Court of God." With Adashev he is more summary; he describes him as a dog whom he himself has taken from the dunghill. Soon afterward John lost his beloved first wife, and became convinced that she had been poisoned. He dwelt on the bitter opposition of the boyars to her family. "If you had not taken from me my young one," he writes later, "there would have been no sacrifice of blood."

The friends of Sylvester and Adashev among the boyars were not prepared to accept their dismissal, and resisted; John replied with several executions. The ablest of these boyars was Prince Kurbsky, a man of letters like John himself. Kurbsky, while holding a command in Livonia, abandoned his army and went over to Lithuania, from this time forward acting as the soul of a coalition against his former master. Kurbsky helped to stir up Poland to take action against John, and was later even responsible for an invasion of Moscow from the side of Crimea. Not content with this, Kurbsky wrote him four bitterly hostile and insulting letters, to which John replied in two letters of equal vehemence and bitterness. In this most interesting controversy is pictured the root question of John's reign, the question whether the Tsars or the boyars should predominate in Moscow. John had all the time before his eyes the example of Poland with its consistent diminutions of the royal authority to the point of sheer impotence. He well remembered the rule of the boyars during his minority. He was full of the instinct which had prompted his grandfather to challenge Poland and to champion her Orthodox Russian population. It was not personal arrogance—as he sometimes tried to show by extravagant humility—but a sense of all that depended on the triumph of authority in Moscow, that drove John further and further in this conflict. He resented anything that called in question his one obsessing idea—the divine character of his power and the mission that lay on him as the holder of it.

Both the letter-writers are expert controversialists; both make free and original use of the Scriptures. Kurbsky compares John to Rehoboam, refusing to listen to advice. The authorized advisers are the boyars, whose services and genealogies the writer recounts; but he finds also a place for his humbler allies, Sylvester and Adashev, "for the gift of the Spirit is not given by outward riches." He justifies his flight by the scriptural injunction: "When they persecute you in one country flee into another." He strikes surer when he reproaches John for his inhuman punishments, "reviling the image of the angel."

John in reply contrasts the courage of Kurbsky's servant in bringing the letter with that of his master in writing it. He states his whole position in a parenthesis: "When we, inspired by God, set about governing our own realm." "By the will of God we were born in this sovereignty." "Is that really sweet?" he asks, giving a picture of the boyars' rule; and pointing to the fall of Constantinople he adds: "Do you recommend that ruin for us too?" Most significant is his taunt to the whole class of boyars: "God is able of these stones to raise up children unto Abraham."

The war in Livonia continued to go favourably for John. The Grand Master Kettler could only put small bands in the field. The Order was breaking up. The Bishop of Oesel sold his island diocese to Frederick III of Denmark, who granted it to his brother Magnus. In 1561 Kettler made over Livonia to Poland, bargaining for himself a hereditary vassal dukedom of Kurland and Semigallia. Poland's participation in the war began with raids on both sides; but in 1563 John advanced with his artillery and took the old Russian town of Polotsk on the Dvina, all the more important for its water communication with Riga. The Poles won a striking success at Ivantsevo near Orsha; but Sigismund Augustus asked for peace and was prepared to cede all that John had won.

Meanwhile the tragedy of John's internal conflict reached another sharp crisis. Having broken with those whom he himself had elevated, bitterly mortified by their adhesion to his opponents the boyars, John did not know whom he could trust. It was in John's own fears that were grounded the tyranny and terror which he inflicted on others. He was firmly convinced of the sanctity of his office; yet he could see no friend around him. In December of 1564 he came to a strange decision. Suddenly the news spread that the Tsar had abandoned Moscow. Sledges had been seen drawn up in the Kremlin, and they had carried him away, with his family and all his belongings, his icons and his treasures. No one knew where he had gone. A month later arrived from the monastery of Alexandrovskoe two letters addressed to the Metropolitan; one bitterly accused the whole governing class, not only the boyars but the clergy, of trying to drown the imperial authority in a chaos of disorders; the other, which was also to be read out to the people, assured them as a whole that John was their friend, that he had no wrath against them, that he sought only to safeguard them from their oppressors. The letters were obediently read out, and the appeal they made was completely successful. Shops were closed, no songs were heard, the capital was as if in mourning. The people of Moscow entreated the Metropolitan with tears to ask the Tsar to return, to assure him that the people were faithful to him, that they themselves would if necessary rise and destroy his enemies, and to beg that he should "rule however he pleased." The merchants asked that he should rescue them from the hands of the powerful. With this mission the Metropolitan, accompanied by prelates and boyars, had to go to Alexandrovskoe. John made his conditions. No objection was to be raised to any executions or disgraces which he thought necessary. He intended to establish a new system of government.

John came back. It was noticed that he had passed through a terrible nervous crisis; his eyes were dim, his hair and beard were almost gone. He started at once with several executions, especially of the friends and supporters of Prince Kurbsky; but he did not stop at this. The new system which he set up was madness, but the madness of a genius. He had failed to find support in men of the middle class. He would now walk out of the whole system as it stood, leaving it in existence but taking with him all the resources of power. Let the boyars go on with the ordinary work of administration; he appointed two of them, of whom he had no reason to be afraid. But outside the normal State, as a kind of personal possession, or, if you like, as a kind of supreme police control, lay the *Oprichnina*, the Apart, the Peculium—the word was derived from the term used to describe a wife's or a widow's portion. Here John was supreme and unquestioned; the *Oprichniki* swore an oath that allowed neither God nor man to come before his commands. "Set apart" were to be any domains that John might care to claim; they amounted in the end to about half the realm; Moscow itself was divided between the two. In this reshuffling of all property, John astutely took for the *Oprichnina* those regions, especially in the north and centre, which still preserved nominal principalities of their own and rights of local jurisdiction. The *Oprichnina* had its own special court, its ministerial offices, its own army, its own special police—at first one thousand and later six thousand in number. The *Oprichnik* police rode on black horses and were clothed in black, carrying a dog's head at their saddlebow and a broom as the emblem that they were to clear the land of robbery. The *Zemshchina* (the other half of the country) was later mocked by John with a separate sovereign, and his choice fell upon a Tartar prince who had accepted Christianity, to whom John himself made a mock obeisance and gave the title of Prince of All Russia, contenting himself with the modest title of Prince of Moscow. John returned for a time to the armed suburb which he now established for himself in Moscow, but later lived in the Alexandrovskoe monastery, alternating between orgies of license and repentances half mocking and half sincere, in which, dressed as a monk, he would take part in the church services, read to his riotous company about the virtues of temperance as preface to a night of feasting and drunkenness, now delighting in torturing prisoners, now beating his head against the church floor in contrition, now praying for his thousands of victims: "whose names, O Lord, Thou Thyself knowest."

After three years full of violence and suffering, John called together a Zemsky Sobor to advise on the critical question whether or not to accept the peace proposals made to him by Sigismund Augustus. The representation was very well chosen though, according to the prevailing Russian system, it was based on the principle of groups. Church, boyars, military service men, merchants trading with western Europe, alike declared for war on the ground that the liberation of the Russian subjects of the Polish-Lithuanian State was a national cause. However, from this time onward everything went wrong. In this year a large army of Turks and Tartars tried to make its way through to Astrakhan, and though this failed, the Crimeans continued to give constant trouble. All John's enemies were uniting against him. In 1569, at Lublin as mentioned, a closer tie than ever before was established between Poland and Lithuania. The next year Moscow concluded a year's truce, and John attempted at least to secure that Estonia should become a Russian dependency, as Kurland had become a dependency of Poland. For vassal prince he chose Magnus, brother of the king of Denmark, and married him to his cousin. In 1571 the Crimeans brought against Moscow an army of 120,000 men. They captured and burned the capital destroying, it was said, 800,000 Russians and carrying away 130,000 prisoners. Two years later they came again but were stopped with difficulty at the river Lopasnya, some fifty miles from Moscow.

Meanwhile King Sigismund Augustus, the last of the Jagellons, died in Poland (1573) and, as has been mentioned, his place was filled for a short time by Henry of Anjou. John himself thought of being a candidate for the throne but he had nothing to offer the turbulent nobles of Poland. When Henry fled to Paris, John's candidacy or that of one of his sons was again suggested as a means of uniting the greater part of the Slavonic world. But the choice of the Poles fell upon Stephen Bathory of Transylvania, a man of notable military ability (1575). This same year John found himself at war with Sweden through his attempt to secure Estonia. In 1578 the Russians were badly beaten at Wenden; the next year they lost Polotsk, and a year later several other important towns. In 1581 Ostrov was lost and, while John was contemplating an offensive towards the sea, Stephen Bathory appeared in front of Pskov. This city, with its long record of military courage, was robustly defended by Ivan Shuisky, and the Polish successes here received a check. John lost in this same year not only his recent conquest of Narva, but the old Russian cities near the Gulf of Finland: Ivangorod, Yam, and Koporye.

By 1582 John was prepared to make peace. The Pope sent a mediator, the Jesuit Possevino, who put his influence on the side of Poland, seeing that John was quite unwilling to hear his plea for a reunion of Christendom. Possevino begged for leave to build a Catholic church in Moscow, threatening otherwise a trade blockade from the Catholic merchants; but he found John adamant. John expressed himself shocked that the Pope should be carried on high by his attendants. "The Pope is not Christ," he said, "his throne is not a cloud, and his bearers are not angels." A ten years' truce was concluded with Poland, and in the next year a three years' truce with Sweden, in which John reconciled himself to the sacrifice of all that he had lost. The first great Russian attempt to break through to the Baltic had failed. John despaired of success until he should have an army trained on the European model. It was at this time that he turned for alliance to England.

Queen Elizabeth had taken a close interest in the new relations with Russia, and a most interesting correspondence passed between her and John. In 1569 John, through Jenkinson, proposed a full offensive and defensive alliance, the more valuable to him because his outlet by the Gulf of Finland was then more blocked than ever. He wanted Elizabeth to forbid her subjects to trade with Poland; he wished for masters of shipbuilding and gunnery. What the importance of this help was to Russia, we can understand from enemy testimony. Sigismund Augustus of Poland wrote to Queen Elizabeth begging her to refuse it. "Up to now," he says, "we could conquer him only because he was a stranger to education and did not know the arts."

John proposed that either of them, if expelled from his own court, should take refuge with the other. Elizabeth put him off with vague assurances; she could not oblige him with a similar request for asylum; she wanted all the trade she could get, without the alliance. John reproached her with being governed by merchants, not like a sovereign, but "like a poor lady." Elizabeth made a spirited reply, but John was in the main right. What the English wanted in Russia was free transit trade down the Volga to Persia and to the untold riches of Siberia.

John in his later years proposed a marriage with Lady Mary Hastings (for which he would at that time have had to divorce his fifth wife). Negotiations with the lady were opened with great distinction by Pisemsky. Lady Mary was only frightened. Meanwhile Bowes was sent to Russia to press for the full trade monopoly (already French and Dutch ships were visiting northern ports of Russia). Bowes committed nearly every fault of diplomacy, including loss of temper, and the question was unsettled at the end of the reign.

John's wild orgy of terror became only wilder in his declining years. He was courageously rebuked by the Metropolitan Philip, who frequently interceded for the victims. John avoided him; but Philip courageously denounced his cruelties in church and, when ordered to keep silence, replied: "Our silence puts sin on your soul and brings death upon it." John was troubled; but in 1568 he had Philip deposed and dragged from church amid his weeping congregation. He was sent to the Otroch Monastery in Tver. Thither John sent later to demand a blessing, when on his way to wreck the city of Novgorod. "Only the good are blessed," replied Philip, and paid for his courage with his life.

Of John's vengeances one of the most savage was his attack on Novgorod. Suspecting negotiations with Poland, he marched on the city in January 1570, ravaging all the country and killing right and left in the city. Whole families were thrown into the river, and men in boats pushed them under; these horrors lasted for five weeks. John then addressed the chief citizens who remained: "Men of Novgorod who are left alive," he said, "pray God for our religious sovereign power, for victory over all visible and invisible foes." Many of his punishments were too horrible to be described. In 1569 he killed his cousin Prince Vladimir. The next year marked the executions of two of the chief *Oprichniks*, Basmanov and Skuratov. In 1581 he burst into the apartment of his son's wife and treated her with brutal violence; when his son protested John struck him with the pointed stick which he always carried with him, and the wound proved fatal. From this time he knew no more peace. He spoke of abdicating and becoming a monk. He could not keep his bed, and his howls were heard through the palace. On March 27, 1584, he died in a sudden access of passion. "And later," writes a contemporary, summing up the tragic end of this reign, "as it were, a terrible storm, come from afar, broke the repose of his good heart, and he became a rebel in his own realm."

CHAPTER VII

Muscovy [1]

Muscovy by now was created, and we must pause to consider the structure of this new colossal state. The internal changes which followed on its formation were no less far-reaching and critical than its external importance.

Klyuchevsky, speaking of the internal reforms of John the Dread, describes them as originating in "the idea of setting up a continuous inflow, controlled by law, of the healthy forces of the public into the governing class, which with us is at every turn trying to become a caste blocked off from the people, a growth poisonous to all the rest, infecting the body of the community." In this matter John was combating a tendency opposite to his own and far more powerful, a tendency which he himself in other matters served to strengthen. Ordinarily the government lay upon the people like a kind of upper stratum alien to it, and was often entirely regardless of it. But the Russian Empire itself is much more the work of the silent economic forces of the people than of the action of the government. There was now a people; the Moscow princes, by their work of unification, had broken down the barriers between its different territorial compartments, and in this sense their work was national. Russia already bid fair to be and has since become the largest national unit in Europe; and the oneness of its language, its instincts, its atmosphere, its aroma, is henceforward one of the cardinal factors in European history. A nation had been behind John the Great when he united the Great Russian territory, and it is this that gave greatness to a man who otherwise had little of it. He felt the nation and acted for it; he spoke for it in simple words which are singularly direct and convincing.

The Great Russian people was hammered out of peaceful, silent, pacific elements by constant and cruel blows from enemies on all sides,

[1] Founded mainly on Klyuchevsky (Lectures 31–40).

which implanted in the least intelligent of Russians an instinct of national defence and of the value of a national dictatorship. Russia lived in a state of constant war. On the west were forces determined to block her off from Europe, and with every fresh turn of history these forces seemed only to increase in power. On the Baltic coast, which to the genius of John the Dread had seemed to be so necessary to Russia's contact with Europe, the Livonian Order, as long as it lasted, out of a trembling instinct of self-preservation did what it could to prevent the civilizing and the Europeanizing of Russia. The scholars, artisans, and instructors whom John recruited in Europe through the Saxon Schlitte, were, on the urgent representation of the Order, prevented by the Emperor Charles V from coming through to Moscow. When the inevitable collapse of the Order came, in spite of John's bold bid its heritage was divided between two powerful neighbours, Poland and Sweden. Sweden, in the period which followed, was to make herself mistress of nearly all the Baltic coast. Lithuania, which had absorbed under its loose sovereignty so many Russians along the very nerve of old Russia, the water road, had by a trick of history carried over these Orthodox Russians into the orbit of Poland, between whom and Moscow from that time forward "any peace was but a truce to draw breath." Further south, the strong remaining bulwark of the Tartars, the Khanate of Crimea, had in 1475 been conquered by the Turkish Empire; and from this time forward, this last outpost of what had once been an eastern menace to Russia was now linked through Turkey with a system of obstacles that blocked Russia's communications with Europe.

On the west, in the course of ninety years which included the whole reign of John the Terrible, Moscow had forty years of war. From the south, from the side of Crimea, war was incessant. Frontier warfare had been continual, as Russia gradually pushed back the Tartars on the southeast. Muscovy had no frontiers; and at each halt in their advance the Russians constructed elementary lines of protection. The first frontier line was the Oka; the next ran from Nizhny Novgorod to Serpukhov, Tula, and Kozelsk. By the time of John the Dread, the line ran through Ryazhsk, Orel, and Putivl. Under his son Fedor it had reached Elets, Kursk, and Voronezh. By 1600 it touched the Donets; and fifteen years later it had progressed three hundred miles further southward. It consisted of a palisade, a trench, and an earthen rampart, but could not be continuous in these vast spaces. Giles Fletcher in his admirable *Russe Commonwealth*, published in 1591, tells of an enormous *gulay-gorod* or movable line of defence, two to seven miles long according to need, consisting of two loopholed walls of wood, three yards apart.

Every year the Tartars issued from their fastness in the Crimea, through the four-mile-wide Isthmus of Perekop to raid and ravish Russia. They had 30,000 picked cavalry, and their infantry, which accumulated reinforcements from all the other territory populated by Tartars eastward, numbered as many as 120,000 and sometimes rose to 200,000. If one compares these figures with those of European armies during the same period one will see how vast and how wholesale war still was in Russia—a survival of the time when people left their moorings and invaded other countries en masse. These invasions were such as to convince the dullest of peasants of the necessity of national defence and of national sacrifices. The Tartars, while on campaign, lived on mares' milk and on dried bread. They carried on their horses baskets in which to kidnap Russian children, particularly girls. They took with them leather thongs, with which to drag away with them Russian men-prisoners. These they sold in the market of Caffa to all parts of Asia Minor, to Africa, and even to some parts of Europe. These slaves were numbered by hundreds of thousands. In one of the Tartar raids on Moscow in the reign of John the Dread 130,000 prisoners were carried away. A Jewish merchant who sat at the entrance of Perekop had seen so many pass through that he asked whether there were any more people left in Russia.

This necessitated equally constant and regular measures of defence. Everywhere the frontier line was planted with military colonists. All life here was military; and to this part streamed from the interior the daring spirits who sought a breath of freedom and knew that here initiative would be valued and rewarded. Runaway peasants from all parts lived here on the basis of piece labour, by which they could control and command reward for their toil. They were ready for anything, for fighting, scouting, trading, as the occasion might demand. This was the origin of the Cossacks. The name, which originally meant a piece labourer, indicates not a race but a vocation. These rude frontier warriors of Christendom and of Europe were the true successors of the *bogatyri* of the earlier period, who tempered themselves in the constant warfare between Kiev and the Polovtsy. They possessed wonderful military resource and were masters at taking cover. They practically never parted with their horses and were trained riders from childhood. Their scouting tactics were those of the Russian army of today. Tall, lonely trees were used as observation posts (*vyshki*); different points at some distance from each other were garrisoned, and between them relays of individual Cossacks patrolled, never dismounting. The Tartars usually succeeded in keeping their dispositions secret and would suddenly appear with great enveloping forces at a given point, passing if possible over a watershed so as to avoid crossing rivers, and making use of the innumerable gullies of Russia; they had no fires by night. Messages were flashed by the patrols of the defence to the Russian main body, which was mobilized and concentrated every year in five sections, advance guard, main body, two wings, and rear.

To cultivate far afield would have been to ask for trouble; to cultivate behind the line was to ask for serfdom; but around the towns, which were far more fortresses than depots of trade, there was crown land tilled on peculiarly burdensome conditions; crown horses were supplied but no seed; no pay was given. Those who refused these terms would go forward far beyond the line to Razdory on the Don where they had a completely democratic government of their own, with very rough-and-ready methods, debating "in a circle" and electing their own chiefs. Cossacks on the frontier land could become "squires." Though possessing no peasant labour, poverty-stricken gentry also lived on the frontier under the same military conditions. The Plain, as this region was called, was the most disorderly part of Muscovy.

The measures of defence could not of course be confined to the frontier. Yearly some 65,000 recruits were expected to be ready for service by the end of March. The numbers, though it is difficult to fix them, were enormous. John the Dread led an expedition of over 100,000 against Kazan. In one of the Lithuanian wars we have mention of garrisons of 30,000, for instance in the siege of Pskov, and of a main body of 300,000. There were 1200 *Streltsy* armed with muskets, living in suburbs of their own and allowed to trade without dues, which of course prejudiced the regular, heavily taxed trade. The gentry supplied an enormous household cavalry. Fletcher speaks of 4300 Polish mercenaries; there were many Swedes and Scots; the contingent of Tartars and other aliens was very large. Thus in Russia numbers approaching those of modern mass warfare had to be maintained without any adequate national finance and on a basis suggestive of a kind of monstrous feudalism. It was this system of organization which dictated all the conditions of internal life in Russia.

It was quite impossible for the Tsars of Moscow to pay money alone for a standing army. There were indeed money wages, but these came to diminish rather than grow. They were paid yearly only to the highest officers, and to others sometimes not more often than once in four years. They were regarded as a supplement, to help toward the expenses of a campaign. The permanent remuneration had to be in land. Not only in Russia but in Poland, from the time when commerce gave way to agriculture, land was the ordinary means of reward, and large estates had been given to faithful servants of the prince as patrimony. Now provision was made on a much larger scale and on a different basis—that of the so-called *pomestya*, which appear about 1454. The *pomeshchik* received his land not as hereditary, only in recompense for, and for the period of, his military and other state service. This class, which became very numerous, was created more or less offhand out of the most various elements. Some were those who had served at the small courts of appanage princes. When Novgorod was subdued, the families which were transported to central Russia were settled there as farmers on a military tenure; those who came from Moscow to take their place in Novgorod were put on the same footing. Government Offices were springing up in Moscow, and land on military tenure was the ordinary reward for the government clerks and their families. There were always in Russia plenty of floating elements, successors of those called in earlier times *izgoi*, such as sons of priests who did not enter the priesthood. In 1585, 289 Cossacks were similarly incorporated offhand in this new gentry. In it were absorbed numbers of newcomers, such as 300 families who came from Lithuania to Moscow in the time of the regent Helen, or Tartars from Kazan who entered the Russian service. In 1550, a thousand persons picked from the provinces were planted round Moscow on this new tenure.

The conditions of tenure stated precisely the number of recruits who had to be placed in line. The allotment of land corresponded to this number and was graded carefully according to class, which was practically synonomous with military rank. Reviews were held at stated times, and young men who attained the military age of fifteen were expected to register without delay, after which estates might be granted to them. The system even took account of the daughters of these new service men who, if by the age of fifteen they married a man capable of military service, were entitled to a definite dowry in land.

The older hereditary estates (*votchiny*) and the new *pomestye* existed for a long time side by side, only to be equalized by Peter the Great. The patrimony estate had its influence on the *pomestye*. From 1674 the owner of a *pomestye* might sell it; quite early such estates could be alienated for forty years or bequeathed for four generations, and from

1600 they could be bequeathed outright. But on the whole the reverse influence was far greater; the patrimonies themselves were put under the same obligation of military service, and in fact all land in Russia came to be held only by the title of service to the Tsar.

As a system of agriculture, nothing could have been more unsound. The squire was firstly a fighter and only secondly a squire. His absences were frequent. His efficiency was rated only by his military service. He could be moved at will, which prevented him, at least at first, from acquiring any permanent interest in his peasants. The new gentry received certain elementary rights of class organization; for instance, they themselves elected those who were to allot estates and taxes; they also elected certain assessors to the central authorities and certain officials for municipal needs, such as fortification. Many of them were very poor; thus arose the class known as *odnodvortsy*, gentry who practically had no peasants at all.

The system weighed heavily on the growth of the towns; for each estate tried to supply itself with its own home artisans. Meanwhile the trading population, which had sprung up of itself, not only in towns but at various crossroads and points of river trade, was now brought under the same stern control of the State; trading too became a special form of state service, a monopoly and an obligation. The merchants were graded in the same way as the gentry, from the so-called *gosti* at the top to the lesser guilds electing their elders, lower down. Those town inhabitants who, as in Novgorod, were half artisans, half tillers, were crushed out of existence, as the State came to demand more and more that everyone of its subjects should be registered under a settled form of employment.

Very large areas had by this period come into the possession of the Church. The earlier monasteries of the Kiev period had been established mostly near towns and usually owed their foundation to the generosity of princes and boyars, though sometimes to that of a group of peasants. In the appanage period every small princely capital required a monastery at its gates. But as time went on, monasteries sprang up on a different basis, and more and more frequently in remote parts of the country. Typical is the origin, in the first half of the fourteenth century, of the famous Monastery of the Trinity.. St. Sergius, when the Volga was raided by Tartars, took refuge in the forest, where he soon found himself surrounded by a growing peasant community. Ascetics in some cases roamed for twenty or even fifty years about Russia before founding a monastery; St. Paul Obnorsky lived for three years in the trunk of a lime tree. Young disciples of large communities went afield to found others. St. Sergius was especially active in founding new communities. In this way arose a whole chain of monasteries, a whole network of pioneer colonization; by one line it advanced as far as the White Sea to Solovetsk (1429); St. Stephen of Perm led another advance to the Ural Mountains. These inroads upon the wilderness were looked upon as a holy work.

In time the Russian monasteries became proportionately as rich as those of Western Europe in the Middle Ages, and a blight of wealth fell upon the Russian Church. We read of a prior who lived in a small cell but extended the monastery domain for five miles on either side, with the result that the peasants burned down his church. Another monastery possessed twenty villages and exercised its own right of justice. The Monastery of St. Cyril by 1582 owned 70,000 acres, that of the Trinity, with 700 monks, had an income equivalent in volume to two million dollars of our money of the present day.

These acquisitions were obtained in various ways. Landowners would pledge their land to the monastery for mention in its prayers, and there came to be a precise tariff for all the various forms of mention, descending in dignity from mention at the altar to mention by the church wall. A monk demands ten roubles from a peasant for mentioning him, and says that it is too little. Some gave land to obtain the right of joining the community in old age. All these bargains were described as "settling one's soul." Sometimes they were very detailed agreements, stipulating, for instance, for the portion of a widow's daughter and for provision for a favourite servant.

It is not surprising that, even in backward Russia, criticism found a voice. Fletcher speaks of "the hypocrisy and uncleanness of that cloister brood." Before the fall of Novgorod, arose the interesting rationalist heresy of the so-called *strigolniki* (shavers), and later, also in Novgorod, the heresy of the "Judaisers." Each of these heresies was a protest against external forms of religion, passing in some cases to a denial of the Godhead and of the truth of the Holy Scriptures. From the Judaisers and from connections with Westernized Lithuania sprang later some faint flickers of Western Protestantism. Protests were raised against the wealth of the Church. The protests were led by St. Nil Sorsky, one of the holiest of all the saints of the Russian Church, who had passed through the discipline of Mount Athos and had founded the first of those peculiarly austere communities known as *Skity*. Nil was opposed by a typical ecclesiastical statesman of the time, Joseph, Prior of Volokolamsk, who pleaded that without rich monasteries educated persons would not become monks and the Church would be left without suitable chief dignitaries. The right of receiving estates by bequest was eventually limited to the smaller and more impoverished houses and later abolished altogether (1580).

From the various owners of land, we will turn to its cultivators, the peasants. The origins of the peasants' village community or *mir* are obscure and have been much debated. Though the clan association was largely lost in the early migration of Slavs from the Carpathians to the Dnieper, and though the village community had a broader basis than kinsmanship, there was probably a connection between the two; and though the towns along the Dnieper were trade depots independent of family or even tribal relations, communities of a kind can be traced far back in the hinterlands of west Russia. The peasants from very early times elected their village elders for the dividing of individual holdings. Communal land tenure was a stage of culture in practically all other countries of Europe. It answered the needs of a working population cultivating large areas with primitive implements.

During other subsequent migrations the peasantry again tended to break up into small units—of three or four households, or of one; but these units soon grew. A common relation of all to the local prince, who left them to settle how to divide up the common payment to himself, gave another occasion for corporate life; in this stage the prince was for the peasants chiefly an agent of land settlement, and they were largely left to themselves. The principalities were small and none of them possessed a powerful state organization. It was impossible to prevent the peasant from passing easily from one to another. As the soil was poor and his implements crude, the fertility of his holding gave out in a short time, and he would often move to a new field.

After the Tartar devastation in 1237–9, vast numbers of peasants were left houseless. These quartered themselves on the land of other peasants or more often on that of landowners, and would make an agreement by which a part of their crop would go to the owner. Most of such peasants had no stock or implements for starting farming, and these they would receive from the owner. The agreements as to mutual obligations were very precise, and this encouraged the peasant to keep the area which he leased in thorough culture. He had to build a house and farm buildings, he engaged to drain marshy land. For this he received loans and other assistance, and he bound himself not to go away without repayment.

There were other forms of engagement known as *kabaly*. A man of any class, in order to escape class obligations and to obtain a protector, might sell himself to a master; and his labour was regarded as only repaying the interest, not the capital of the price which he had originally received. Such arrangements were even made with only a fictitious purchase price, for the sake of protection.

The ordinary contracting peasant might, if he discharged all his obligations, leave his lot after the harvest in the week preceding and the week following St. George's Day, November 26. He might not go at any other time. Besides the *obrok*, or rent, which was paid largely in kind and was often closely defined, he also rendered, in lieu of interest on the loans which he had received, compulsory labour or *barshchina*, similar to the corvée of Western feudalism.

Peasants were divided into two classes. There were the registered peasants on crown property, united into a village community, and paying a lump sum from the community to the State. These peasants, who were sometimes very well-to-do, were able to discharge their obligations because, living in very large households, they had the help of other peasants who were not registered, and who were free to move about and make special agreements such as have been described. Relationship, not only for purposes of tax-paying, was taken to cover all who lived under the direction of the head of the house—for instance, those who served an apprenticeship under him and married his daughters; on the other hand, sons who left the family roof would be considered as separate. All the registered peasants were individually responsible for the taxes of the whole community; so they had every reason for wishing that none among them should go away; and later they showed great energy in recovering such fugitives. On the other hand Russia was advancing through the vast distances northward, eastward, and southeastward—especially in the latter direction, as soon as it was opened up, as the land here was very fertile; and the stream of migration to these parts, largely supplied by the extra hands in the great peasant households, gradually denuded the central districts. Many of the settlers were free lances who sought the careless fighting life of the frontiers. Others put themselves under the protection of the Church. Many more were invited by frontier landowners large and small, who could not discharge their military service unless they had labour.

This depletion of the centre made the burdens very much heavier for those who remained. We read, for instance, of increasing poverty, of six days' corvée in the week, and of constant evictions. The exactions

of the State became heavier and heavier with every progress of state organization. Fletcher speaks of some fifty villages between Archangel
and Moscow, half a mile or a mile long but completely deserted. We
read of holdings overgrown by the forest, of estates tilled by slaves, of
increasing loans, of impossibly heavy fines far beyond the capacity of the
peasant, and of hopelessly unpayable debts. Peasant property, says
Fletcher, was no more than "as passing from hand to mouth. The government officials come fresh and hungry upon them lightly every year
to pull and clip them all the year long."

Thus, by the nature of things, though still possessing the right to
migrate, most of the peasants could not use it. On the one side they
had no hope of repaying the loans which they had received. On another side, as we have seen, that of the peasants, the village community
itself was against their moving. On a third side, that of the State, there
was every argument for keeping the peasant to the spot on which he
lived. It was only so—by knowing where to find its subjects—that the
State could raise the needed taxes and recruits.

In the last half of the sixteenth century a further evil developed. The
richer landowners enticed the labour from the smaller estates, which of
course thereby became incapable of performing their duties of service.
How could you pay taxes, how could you raise recruits in a wilderness?
The peasant had little to gain by these transfers; but he might be attracted by the allurements held out to him by another employer. Bitter
conflicts, developing into open battles, took place in connection with
these transfers. The richer owners would kidnap peasants and carry them
away. Among a large number of migrating peasant families in the
province of Tver in 1580 Klyuchevsky reckons that only 17 per cent
moved in the normal way, whereas 60 per cent were transferred by
kidnapping; 21 per cent adopted the only real remedy left open to them,
which lay outside the law—they went away of themselves, abandoning
their homes. At the very end of the sixteenth century, legislation interfered and kidnapping was forbidden. The peasant was to stay with his
former owner, and was thereby already more or less fastened to the
soil. The period of five years originally allowed for hunting out a fugitive
peasant was later indefinitely extended.

. To meet the growing needs of state organization a new and complex
system was required and a great and cumbrous bureaucratic machinery
was developed. Princes, in the appanage period, had managed their
domains like private estates. There were house officials, such as the
major-domo, the steward, the cup-bearer, the chief huntsman, or the

falconer, to whom were confided not only definite tasks but definite sources of revenue and even definite domains. The Muscovite State was too large to be managed in this way, and the growth had come with astonishing rapidity before the old habits were dropped. The new Government Offices, or *Prikazy* (Commands), grew up in a haphazard manner, according to the exigencies of day-to-day requirements, and still continued to follow in the main the lines of a prince's household. From the major-domo's department developed the Big Treasury, which concerned itself particularly with the direct taxes but also had judicial functions. Of this a side-product was the *Bolshoy Prikhod,* or Big Revenue, which dealt with monopolies and indirect taxes such as that on salt. The sovereign gave orders as they occurred to him. Thus, John the Dread ordered Adashev to receive petitions, and there arose in consequence a Prikaz or Office for Petitions. Some of the Prikazy had a local significance. Annexed appanage principalities were for a time administered under this system, and later we still find a Prikaz of Kazan, administering not only the territory of the former Tartar Khanate, but Siberia. However, though palace needs were still a primary consideration there arose perforce a number of Prikazy which dealt with needs of state and had more the appearance of modern Ministries. Such came to be the Razryadny Prikaz, which served the purpose of a War Office, as it dealt with military appointments; it also made the allotment of estates granted for military service; out of the Razryadny Prikaz was later developed a special Prikaz for the last-named purpose (*Pomestny*). Other Prikazy dealt with different aspects of justice, such as the Robbers' Prikaz and the Slave Prikaz, the last of which watched very carefully any attempts to escape state service by accepting bondage to a given master. More modern was the new Posolsky, or Envoys' Prikaz, which served as the Foreign Office and for which a special palace was built. It required, of course, a supply of trained interpreters and played a part both in education and in the beginnings of printing in Russia. By 1600 there were thirty different Prikazy, often overlapping each other; it was frequently impossible to define to what competence a given matter belonged. Later on, we find over sixty Prikazy, of which thirteen relate to palace needs, fifteen to war, ten to economic questions, and only twelve to needs of the population. For trade, public health, charity, and public education, even in the beginning of the seventeenth century, there were no Prikazy at all. As Klyuchevsky truly says, all was asked of the people and nothing was done for them.

The Prince had always been surrounded with a Council or Duma (the word means counsel). This, in the appanage period, was a quite informal council of higher palace servants. This Duma of Boyars had necessarily developed under the new conditions. Its members were graded. There were the Duma boyars, next the *okolnichie*, or nobles of the second rank, and as time went on the Duma contained more and more Duma gentry, men who were required for their ability and as heads of departments of different Prikazy. There were also clerks of the Duma, even more necessary for their experience, but these had no right to vote and were expected to stand, unless the Tsar invited them to sit down. It was the habit in Muscovy for all big questions to pass through the Duma of Boyars, and, in his Sudebnik or law code of 1550, John the Dread even accepted the principle proposed by his Chosen Council that on big questions the Duma's assent was necessary. The formula for the issue of laws was: "The Sovereign has instructed (*ukazal*) and the boyars have given their consent"; yet ordinarily in practice all decisions were left to the Tsar. The Duma often sat all day, and it dealt not only with political affairs but also with judicial matters on appeal. The seats were very carefully allotted according to seniority.

During the reign of John the Dread very radical changes were made, especially in the field of local government. The local governors were both negligent of their duties, and despotic. In particular, they completely failed to preserve public security, which was one of the first requirements of the population. These governors were glorified palace servants sent down to the provinces to live upon them under a system known as *kormlenie*, or feeding. They were entitled to large and undefined dues on their entry into office, and at the three principal feasts of the year they exacted tribute of every sort, mostly in kind. They had little interest in doing their duty; if criminals remained at large this was even a source of income to them, as they were allowed to fine the whole district concerned. The population therefore asked that it should be allowed to keep order for itself.

Steps were taken in this direction during John's minority by the successive regents, the Shuiskys and Belskys. At the petition of certain districts, charters were issued to them, authorizing the election of elders (*gubnye starosty*) by all classes of the population, who were assisted in the work of police by subordinate elected officials (100th, 50th, and 10th men). These hunted up and tried and executed criminals, and exercised a supervision over vagrants. They were even entrusted with the disposal of the criminals' property. The governors were forbidden to interfere with these new courts, which elected their own clerks and reported direct to Moscow.

John himself carried these local rights much further. A local petition, complaining of the depredations of the governors, asked that the population should be allowed by elected persons of its own choice (*izlyublennye* or desired) to levy the local dues and send them to Moscow. This was granted not only to the petitioners but to any town or district which would pledge itself to levy the dues fixed. In case of default the sum, increased by way of fine, was levied direct from Moscow. These officials were sometimes called local elders (*zemskie starosty*), but from the expression used in the original petition their official title was the Desired. They controlled not only the collection of taxes, but civil suits and some criminal. Wide use was made of this benefit, and a subsequent petition speaks already of the system as applied everywhere. As a matter of fact, not every locality was ready to guarantee the dues or could find competent elective officials; so that the two systems, old and new, went on side by side. Where the elective officials were introduced, the governors were abolished. Where the governors were retained, the population was allowed to elect assessors who countersigned the governor's judgments and at the end of his term were even authorized to impeach him. Where both *gubnye* and *zemskie* elders were introduced, they appear to have been assimilated, but there were defects of coordination, and no one system was universally applied. The electoral basis of the *zemskie*, as compared with that of the *gubnye*, retained more of the principle of class divisions. In general, the new institutions were received with real gratitude by the public. It should be added that the work of these new local elective officials was definitely regarded as state service. They were mutually responsible for each other's conduct: and whereas bad service might lead to confiscation or death, good service led to remission of taxes.

In 1550 John took another striking initiative in calling together an assembly of the land (Zemsky Sobor). He desired to rest on the population as a whole, and he trusted to find in it a support in his life struggle with the great magnates who were trying to turn Russia into a second Poland. "Fear entered into my soul" he writes as he reviews the abuses practised on his subjects. It is then, after a solemn act of humiliation of himself and of all classes in the presence of the national Church, that he founds the Prikaz of Petitions and gives a similar order for the purification of local justice. He commands that the law code of his grandfather be brought up to date, a work which was immediately performed. He initiates the changes in local government which have already been mentioned. All this, though throughout the initiative is that of the sovereign himself, makes a great record for the first Russian national assembly. It was John who brought it to birth, and the Assembly only considered those questions which he presented to it. The nucleus of the Assembly consisted of representatives of all sections of the administration; and the Assembly itself was regarded as responsible for helping to carry out those decisions which the Tsar adopted on its advice. There was no established order of procedure. In 1566 John summoned the second Zemsky Sobor to consider, as already mentioned, the all-important issue of peace or war with Lithuania. It is significant that the eight different groups of the population represented at this Sobor in their different ways all made offers of hearty service for the continuance of the war, the clergy with their prayers, the nobles and gentry with their swords, and the merchants with their purses. This of itself shows to what extent the nation was engaged in the struggle with Lithuania. It was John himself who later signed the inevitable truce with Poland, this time without summoning his Sobor at all. The Zemsky Sobor continued to gain in importance in the next two reigns, and in the subsequent Time of Troubles its significance and its potentialities increased immensely.

The later rulers of Moscow had done much to beautify the city. The first stone church was the Cathedral of the Assumption, founded in 1326. In 1332 followed that of St. Michael the Archangel; Simeon the Proud did much to decorate the church walls. The first stone walls of the city were the work of Dmitry of the Don, but John the Great was at work for twenty-five years, further beautifying Moscow with walls, towers, gates, a palace, and new cathedrals and churches—work which was continued by Basil III. In 1588 Fletcher wrote that Moscow was even larger than London. Others report that it was twice the size of Florence or of Prague, and the French Captain Margeret declared that the circuit of the walls was more extensive than that of Paris.

CHAPTER VIII

The Time of Troubles

[*1584–1613*]

THE EVENTS which followed the death of John the Dread read like a sensational novel. But in Russia, as elsewhere, everything has a reason; and these events must be followed closely, because they give us a glimpse of what the Russian people were like without a Tsar, and shed light on similar convulsions of later date.

In Moscow, the sovereign was everything; hence the extraordinary persistence with which the popular imagination throughout this period fastened itself to the idea of a Tsar and followed this or that impersonator. But with the failure of the various claimants the State, or as it was called, the Sovereignty of Moscow, stood out more and more clearly with a distinct entity of its own.

Eastward, the conquest of Siberia continued. Ermak was surprised and killed on the Irtysh by the Siberian prince Kuchum in 1584; but Kuchum was defeated in a decisive battle where the combatants on both sides numbered only 900 men; he fled to the Nogai Tartars and was killed. Southeastward, Russia had already reached the Caucasus, and the Christian prince of Kakhetia put himself under her protection; but Abbas the Great of Persia barred further advance. Russia was herself now one of the greatest of Eastern powers, and only a no-man's land separated her from China. It was the West that now threatened her, and this period is the story of the great opportunity of Poland.

The gentry of Poland formed an aristocratic "republic" contemptuous of the monarchical power above them and of the peasant population which they ground into the soil beneath them. It will be remembered that when many of the ancestors of the Great Russian race migrated from Kiev northeastward to the neighbourhood of Moscow, there was a similar migration from Kiev westward greatly strengthening the principality of Galicia, which later fell under the rule of Poland. Now, on the contrary, the devastated country on the Lower Dnieper was being reoccupied from the west. Polish magnates received enormous grants of land on a military tenure. The comparative liberty of frontier conditions now tempted numbers of the Little Russian population of Lithuania and Poland to return to their earlier home. This movement, from about 1550 onwards, resulted in a recolonization of the Lower Dnieper by peasants or slaves from Poland. It was peculiarly a movement of the people, as was also the stream of fugitives gravitating in the same direction from Muscovy. The two streams joined, the two populations were close akin by race and by religion. The most adventurous spirits of both states combined to set up here a kind of people's refuge. This was a step in the formation of the modern Ukraine.

But the settlers from the side of Poland were soon followed by an influx of Polish gentry, and their first freedom was soon diminished. From 1569, the date of the union of Poland and Lithuania, the gentry of this part grew stronger and more arbitrary. There was already on the Dnieper a nucleus of Cossacks similar to those of Russia, and from 1600 they were feared on every coast of the Black Sea, including those of Asia Minor. They had long since established amid the rapids of the river the famous Zaporog Fastness, which acted as a focus for all the discontented. The fastness was on islands. No woman entered it; married Cossacks lived outside. It had a government of its own, entirely democratic, like that of the Cossacks of the Don. Every attempt was made by the Polish government to reduce its Cossacks to obedience. From 1570 onwards it sought in vain to restrict them to a given number, three hundred or five hundred. With the exception that the Cossacks were Orthodox, the conditions which had created them were alike in Poland and in Russia; and there was nothing essential to separate the interests of the Zaporog Cossacks and those of the Don. Cossacks of all parts were ready enough to join any enterprise which promised adventure and plunder.

The second son of John the Dread, Fedor, had grown up during his father's terrifying last years in an atmosphere of incessant fear. John had thought little of him, and spoke to him roughly and with contempt, asking him if he meant to be nothing better than a bell-ringer in a convent. Indeed, Fedor was far more fit for a monastery than for the throne. He had the slow, shuffling walk of a monk, a melancholy face and a feeble voice. He is described as playing like a child with his sceptre and globe, his face fixed in a continual foolish smile. Sometimes indeed he had flashes of that second sight which is so often to be found among Russia's wandering "fools of God." But he was devoid of all will. Fedor might be described as an eternal minor, who could never grow up. He had no children and seemed unlikely to have any. He had, indeed, one half-brother, son of John's last wife—Dmitry, who was a mere child. But this marriage of John, his fifth, was not recognized by the Church, and Dmitry was not prayed for among the family of the sovereign. Under these circumstances, there was full play for the intrigues of boyars, which were almost like preliminary skirmishes between possible new dynasties. The last favourite of John, the ambitious Belsky, wanted to substitute Dmitry for Fedor on the throne; but he had many enemies in Moscow. His attempt to raise a mob failed; he was sent into exile, and Fedor was duly crowned.

The House which in recent times had the most notable record of enterprise and ability was that of the Shuiskys, descended by direct line from Rurik; three Shuiskys had in succession been regents during the minority of John the Dread; another had greatly distinguished himself at the close of the reign by his courageous defence of Pskov. Two other families might compete for the precedence, less on the ground of birth than of close kinship with the throne. Nikita Romanov, one of the most openhanded and popular boyars of Moscow, came of a family which had entered its service in the reign of John I; he was the brother of Anastasia, first wife of John the Dread, who is described by the English envoy Horsey as having "ruled him with admirable affability and wisdom," and he was therefore the uncle of Tsar Fedor. For a few months he acted as regent, but then fell seriously ill and died two years later. There remained another boyar, Boris Godunov, of Tartar origin, one of the principal agents of John the Dread in his later years, whose sister Irene was married to Tsar Fedor.

On the illness of Nikita Romanov the regency passed to Boris Godunov. It is said that Romanov especially trusted his sons to the care of Godunov; the two families, as connected with the dynasty, were to face any opposition of the boyars together. The new regent met with opposition from Mstislavsky, the titular chief boyar, but he had no difficulty in overcoming it, and Mstislavsky was driven into a monastery. The Shuiskys still held out against him; they induced the Metropolitan Dionysius to raise the question of divorcing the childless Tsaritsa Irene from her husband. Boris managed to postpone this question and, seizing the leading members of the Shuisky family by night, scattered them over Russia in different prisons. He obtained the titles of Familiar Great Boyar and Viceroy of the realms of Kazan and Astrakhan, receiving the revenue from many towns and districts. He held at his own house the receptions of foreign envoys, and corresponded with the Western Emperor and with Queen Elizabeth of England, giving and receiving large presents.

Boris was unquestionably well qualified to govern. He had a handsome, gracious presence; he was particularly thoughtful of the poor; though not learned, he was of quick apprehension (Horsey), was a strong advocate of education, and had many of the instincts of a statesman. Horsey goes on to describe his rule thus: "Every man living in peace, enjoying and knowing his own, good officers placed, justice administered everywhere. Yet, God hath a great plague in store for this people"; and Fletcher finds Russia "so full of grudge and woeful hatred that it will not be quenched till it burn again into a civil flame."

The death of Bathory in 1586 again raised the question of the succession in Poland, where every fresh king had to be elected. Fedor was mentioned as a candidate and received much support from the Russian nobles of Lithuania. Orthodoxy, however, was a fatal bar; and the choice fell on another foreign prince, Sigismund of Sweden, who by his mother was a nephew of the last Jagellon. Two years later his father's death put him also on the throne of Sweden, but his arrogance and, still more, his fervent Catholicism, alienated the Protestant Swedes. He had seemed likely to unite the two principal enemies of Russia, but he was replaced in Sweden by his uncle Charles IX, and this led to a war in which Boris had the chance of making another bid for the Baltic coast. Boris never allied himself definitely either with Poland or with Sweden; he confined himself to small intrigues, and the opportunity passed. Russia was, however, able to recover some of the territory recently lost to Sweden.

In 1588, Jeremy, Patriarch of Constantinople, was in Moscow. Ever since the Turks won Constantinople, the Russian Church felt ashamed to be under the authority of a subject of the sultan. Jeremy was urged to remain in Russia, still holding the title of Patriarch. This he refused to do, but he consented in the next year (1589) to consecrate as special Patriarch of Russia, the Metropolitan Job. Thus was instituted the Russian Patriarchate on the very eve of those convulsions which were for a time to leave Russia without a Tsar, and the increased authority of the Church was to prove invaluable in carrying the country through this time of troubles.

In 1591 Moscow was aroused by the news that young Prince Dmitry, the only remaining heir to the throne, had been murdered in his appanage of Uglich. It seems that a band of hooligans entered the small town and dispatched Dmitry, whereupon the inhabitants rose in anger and killed the murderers. The regent Boris sent down to investigate the matter one of his intimates Kleshnin, who was commonly supposed to have planned the murder, and also Prince Basil Shuisky, a born intriguer with unlimited ambition. The investigators asked all the wrong questions, called none of the right witnesses, and declared that Dmitry had died in a fit of apoplexy by falling on a knife.[1] This version received the confirmation of the Patriarch Job, who was a devoted follower of Boris. In 1592 a daughter, Theodosia, was born to Fedor, but she died the following year. In January 1598 the reign of the weak Tsar came to an end.

Here some reports speak of a violent struggle between Boris and Fedor Romanov, who on the death of Dmitry is said to have rushed at Godunov to attack him. Yet Boris, who had held the power so long and had filled the State with his own officials, was the natural successor. He refused, however, to consider the question until he should be elected by a general assembly (Zemsky Sobor). Boris of course realized that, as a new Tsar, he would incur the enmity of all the rival boyar families, and that the old struggle for an oligarchy on the Polish model would be renewed; so he wished to rely on the body of the nation and to make his title as strong as possible. The Sobor, including elected representatives from the provinces, chose Boris as Tsar, and the election was confirmed by the crowd on the Red Square. Boris, however, still refused. The Patriarch Job led a religious procession to the monastery to which the Tsaritsa and her brother had retired, and was followed by an immense crowd which knelt down outside and moaned its petition that Boris should be Tsar; we are told that those who did not moan sufficiently loud, were struck until they did so. To this general appeal Boris gave his assent.

The new Tsar, already well acquainted with all the tasks of government, was active in his foreign relations. He wished to invite to Moscow European scholars, especially for the teaching of languages; and when this was resisted by the Church, he sent Russians for study abroad to Lübeck, England, France, and Austria, and formed a bodyguard of German troops from the Baltic provinces. In 1597 Boris, while still regent, had legislated against the kidnapping of peasants from the smaller estates to the larger, and now, as if to guarantee the still existing right of free movement, he reasserted this principle and allowed

[1] Platonov, the historian of the Time of Troubles, dissenting from Solovyev and Klyuchevsky, accepts the story of the knife.

peasants to move at least from one small estate to another. In this series of measures he showed consideration both for the peasants and for the smaller gentry. Boris again took a hand in the affairs of Livonia and wished to establish there a Danish prince under Russian suzerainty, but as before his policy was never resolute enough to be successful.

After all the trouble which he had taken to secure a national demand for his accession, the fault of Boris was still in his title; and in the Russia of the Tsars, as created by the two Johns, the title was everything. Nothing shows more strikingly how definitely John the Dread triumphed in his assertion of the divine right of the sovereign than the persistence with which, after his miserable end, Russia, deprived of a born Tsar, demanded what it could not now have. Boris, though able, was timid and suspicious. There is no reason to think him guilty of all the various crimes imputed to him: that he caused the invasion of the Crimean Tartars, that he killed Prince Dmitry, that he killed the infant daughter of Fedor, that he killed Tsar Fedor, and that he was responsible even for the burning of Moscow. For only one of these charges does there seem to be any foundation at all. Yet Boris had no confidence in himself, and, evidence or no evidence, Moscow mistrusted him—to quote the brilliant phrase of Klyuchevsky, "for faults of conscience unseen but felt." Boris lived in a constant state of fear. Belsky, to whom he confided the building of a fortress, made his commission the occasion for levying a small army, and was seized and deported. Boris encouraged retainers, or as they were called in Russia, slaves, to inform against their masters, the great boyars; and the reports of these spies were followed by executions and sudden and secret deportations. In 1601 the whole family of Romanov was crushed in this way. Fedor, the eldest of Nikita's five sons, was forced to become a monk, taking the name of Philaret, and his wife became a nun at the same time. This did not, however, prevent them both from being deported; and the other four brothers were at the same time sent to the most various and distant parts of the empire, ranging from the White Sea to Siberia, and were treated with such rigour that only one of them survived. Fedor's little son Michael was separated from his parents and sent into exile.

From 1601 to 1604 there were severe famines in Russia, and it was quite impossible for the boyars to maintain their large households. As a result, the discharged retainers streamed down towards the Cossack frontiers, greatly augmenting the disorderly elements which they found there. When Boris crushed the hostile boyars, he forbade their households to take service with anyone else and these too swelled the ranks of discontent. John the Dread had even decreed that those fugitives who could escape to the frontier might remain there. Now under stress of the famine they formed into great bands of robbers who often carried their raids almost to the gates of Moscow. Such was Hlopka Kosolap (Slave Crooked-Paw), who killed in battle a general of Boris, but was overpowered, captured, and hanged, while many of his followers were executed. But very soon afterwards arose a far more serious enemy. This was a young man, most probably Yury Otrepyev, son of a serving gentleman, who had entered the household of the eldest Romanov as a retainer. Forced to fly from the agents of Boris, he became a monk under the name of Gregory, and wandered from one monastery to another until he found himself clerk to the Patriarch. Here he spoke freely of a hope that he would some day rule in Moscow. Some indiscreet words made it necessary for him to fly again, only just in time; and making his way across the Lithuanian frontier he appears to have stayed for a while in a school, then sojourned with the Zaporog Cossacks, and later entered the service of a Polish magnate, Adam Wisniowiecki. Wisniowiecki's new retainer was taken ill and made a kind of deathbed avowal that he was the murdered Dmitry. Wisniowiecki took him to the Voevode of Sandomir, Mniszek, with whose daughter, Marina, "Dmitry" fell in love. He was already treated with royal honours by some of the Polish nobles, and was converted by a Franciscan monk to the Latin confession. In 1604 Mniszek took him to Cracow, and there he was presented by the Legate to King Sigismund. The King did not dare to risk an open conflict with Russia but gave him an allowance, permitted any Polish nobles to take up his cause, and encouraged Mniszek to direct the movement. "Dmitry" was affianced to Marina; the marriage was deferred till he should have recovered the throne of his ancestors.

Boris, on hearing of the appearance of the Pretender, denounced him vigorously in messages which he circulated as widely as possible, not only in Russia but on the Polish side of the frontier. The Patriarch Job added his anathema, and Shuisky denounced the imposture. But, for the discontented, the Pretender's name was exactly the flag that they sought. In the conditions of the time, and in particular in the obscurity that shrouded the murder of the real Dmitry, there was no chance of verifying or disproving the truth of this story. Everyone believed as he wished. "Dmitry" obtained very considerable support in Poland, and malcontents of every kind were waiting for him on the opposite side of the frontier. When he invaded Muscovy in October 1604, he at once made rapid progress and won several towns without difficulty. Only Novgorod

Seversk, defended by Basmanov, held out stoutly. Boris sent Prince F. Mstislavsky with an army to relieve the town, but Dmitry and his partisans defeated it outside the walls. To replace Mstislavsky, Boris sent Shuisky who in January, chiefly by his superiority in artillery, and in spite of desperate bravery on the part of the Pretender, completely defeated him. This made little difference, as very shortly he was joined by 40,000 Cossacks and established himself firmly in the town of Putivl. All accounts coming from the field of war spoke of the growing irresolution of the Russian forces. "It is hard to fight a born Tsarevich"; and again: "There were no hands for fighting."

It was at this moment of crisis, on April 13, that Boris suddenly died; and his death was interpreted as a judgment of God. His young son Fedor, for whom everyone had a word of praise, was quietly accepted in Moscow as his successor. But there was now still less chance of getting the Russian troops to resist the invader. On May 7 Basmanov, the trusted general of Boris, with some of the most notable boyars, the Golitsyns and M. Saltykov, declared to their troops that the Pretender was indeed Prince Dmitry. On June 1, Fedor Godunov was easily deposed in Moscow and brutally murdered; the Patriarch Job was also deposed. On June 19 the Pretender entered Moscow in triumph. He was gladly accepted as Tsar by the people of Moscow. It is very possible that many who supported him thought in their hearts that he was an impostor but were all the more ready to accept him as one of themselves.

This young man is an interesting figure. He was ugly, awkward, and red-haired, with a melancholy expression, but he was certainly possessed of great courage and of much ability. He almost compels one to think that he believed in his own authority. Immediately on his accession, he was informed by Basmanov that Basil Shuisky had secretly denounced him as an impostor. He gave over the latter for trial to a General Assembly of the land which was for the first time summoned on a more or less regular elective basis, including representatives from all classes. The Sobor decided that Shuisky was guilty, but the Pretender, in almost an excess of courage and magnanimity, reprieved him at the place of execution and even restored to him his former honours. It would seem as if he thought that by this he had morally killed Shuisky as an enemy, but it was not so. Shuisky set about conspiring again, only with greater wariness.

The Pretender now boldly challenged the test of a meeting with his presumed mother the Tsaritsa Maria Nagoy, now the nun Martha. She was brought to Moscow and the new Tsar met her in a tent in a village near by, and directly afterward, his escort and those present were allowed to witness the mutual exchanges of tenderness between the assumed mother and son. He was consistent in restoring to honour the expelled members of both families, the Nagoys and the Romanovs; Fedor Romanov, now the monk Philaret, was appointed Metropolitan of Rostov. Daily the young Tsar worked with his Council of Boyars, showing discrimination, good sense, and resource. He was widely informed, and commented perhaps too freely on the ignorance of the boyars, saying that he would make it possible for them to travel abroad. The boyars, who appear never to have believed in him, were disgusted with his abandonment of the old stiff etiquette and his disregard of all formalities. Whatever the Poles may have considered to be his obligations to them, he flatly refused any cession of territory, nor would he introduce in Moscow the Latin confession; for this he found a substitute in a proposal for a united Christian crusade against Turkey. The Poles had desired that the aggressive title of Tsar should be dropped; the Pretender assumed that of Emperor. Marina Mniszek was brought by her father to Moscow and, though remaining a Catholic, was crowned and married by the Russian rites, greatly to the dissatisfaction of the Russian prelates.

Shuisky now made overtures to the troops quartered outside Moscow; finding that the Pretender was very popular, he told them that they must save their Tsar from the Poles who wished to kill him. On May 17, 1606, before daybreak, Shuisky and other boyars with their followers, armed and on horseback, charged through the sacred gate of the Saviour into the Kremlin, and forced their way into the palace. Basmanov, who came out to stop them, was cut down. Seeing no safety but in flight, the Pretender jumped from a window. He was seriously injured in the fall, but the *Streltsy* standing sentinel outside were prepared to take his part. He himself asked that he should either be confronted with his mother or taken to the Red Square to speak to the people. Prince V. Golitsyn announced that Martha had now disowned him and declared that her true son was murdered in Uglich. The Pretender was struck down; his body and that of Basmanov, with masks on their faces, were exposed in the Red Square; his remains, it is said, were then burned, and the ashes fired from a cannon in the direction of Poland from which he came.

Shuisky was now the obvious candidate for the throne; yet he was no more than a weak intriguer, perhaps the least worthy of his family to ascend it. Like Boris, he had to retain some measure of independence of the boyars and to capture the good will of the people as a whole. Unlike Boris at this point, he chose the way of fear. As the Patriarch at such moments was expected to take the initiative, and the Pretender's Patriarch Ignaty had been deposed, a General Assembly was suggested; but Shuisky preferred to organize a mob on the Red Square which demanded his immediate election. Philaret was at first appointed Patriarch, but Shuisky had him replaced by the Metropolitan of Kazan, Hermogen, an old man of eighty. Little was known of him, but he was to prove one of the noblest figures in this time of distress.

Shuisky had not escaped his difficulties. The boyars compelled him to swear that none of them should be punished without trial by their peers, that punishments should not be extended to the families of offenders, and that informers, who had been the plague of the reign of Boris, should be punished for untrue accusations with the penalty belonging to the charge which they brought. This oath he tried to balance by another which he took without counsel of the boyars and, to their great annoyance, publicly in the Cathedral of the Assumption: that he would do nothing at all (that he would not punish anyone, whether boyars or others) without the approval of a Zemsky Sobor. As a precedent, for what it was worth, hardly any engagement could have taken Russia further towards a constitution.

Messages were dispatched over the country declaring that the late Tsar was a Pretender who had won the throne by magic. The country understood nothing from successive and conflicting messages on this subject. Impersonation of heirs to the throne was in the air. In the southeast arose another Pretender, this time a false Peter instead of a false Dmitry; no real Peter had existed; but the new legend was that Theodosia, the infant daughter of Tsar Fedor, had really been a boy with this name. An adventurer named Molchanov, who fled from the palace on the death of the first Pretender, made his way westward telling everyone that he was Dmitry, again escaped from his enemies. In the face of this multiplication of Dmitrys, Shuisky thought it best to lay the ghost by starting from the beginning. The body of the murdered infant prince was brought from Uglich to Moscow and borne through the streets by Shuisky himself, who extolled the virtues of the dead, and the body was buried beside the Tsars in the Cathedral of the Archangel where later convenient miracles were reported at the tomb. If Dmitry did miracles, he must be really dead.

Yet the disorders in the country only increased, especially in the southwest, in the region of Seversk, thronged with Cossacks and other malcontents where the Voevode, Prince Shakhovskoy, was in revolt. Another insurgent chief was Ivan Bolotnikov, a former slave. Bolotnikov raised the standard of an out-and-out class war; slaves were to kill their masters and take their wives and daughters; peasants were promised the possessions of their squires. Shakhovskoy was for a time in league with Bolotnikov; so were many of the poor gentry of the frontier, who were in their turn rising against the boyars. Such were Pashkov at Tula, and at Ryazan, one of the most notable figures of this troubled time, Prokofy Lyapunov, a very masterful service gentleman descended from a princely family, who was prepared in the universal anarchy to seek his fortune from any side that offered it. Bolotnikov marched on Moscow, where the mob eagerly awaited him. The weak Shuisky had a nephew, Prince Michael Skopin Shuisky, who was the promise of his family, with great gifts of mind and character, and marked political and military ability. Lyapunov and later Pashkov, when they found what kind of associate they had in Bolotnikov, separated from him and re-entered the service of Moscow, and Bolotnikov was routed by Shuisky's troops under Prince Skopin; but he escaped to Tula, where he prepared to stand siege. Meanwhile risings took place all along the east of Russia from Perm and Vyatka down the Volga to Astrakhan, and everywhere peasants, Cossacks and slaves threatened the country with complete social dissolution. In May 1607, Tsar Basil Shuisky himself, at the head of 100,000 men, marched to the siege of Tula. The false Peter had taken refuge there with Bolotnikov, but it was felt that some better Pretender was wanted, and above all one that commanded some stronger support. From Tula therefore a message was sent to the Poles begging for another impersonator of the original Dmitry. A second notable Pretender appeared (this was to be the answer to the miracles at the tomb), but not in time to save Tula, which was starved into surrender. Bolotnikov was drowned and the false Peter was hanged.

Of the new false Dmitry little is known. Around him were Polish adventurers led by Rozynski, Cossacks from the Zaporog Fastness, and Cossacks of the Don under their ruthless leader Zarutsky. In the spring of 1608, he defeated Tsar Basil's troops on the Volkhov and marched on Moscow. Envoys of Poland were still in Moscow, and Tsar Basil hastily concluded with them a truce of three years. Mniszek and Marina were allowed to leave Moscow on condition that all claims to the throne associated with the first Pretender were dropped, and that the Poles not only withdrew from Russia but also engaged to support no future claimants. These envoys, however, were not able to pledge either the Polish partisan leaders in Russia, or their own King Sigismund. The new Pretender and Rozynski, as soon as they knew that Mniszek and Marina had left Moscow, intercepted them and took them to their camp at Tushino. Nothing seems extraordinary in these strange times. Marina accepted the second Pretender as her husband (the first Pretender, whom he in no respect resembled) and, more than this, the nun Martha, mother of the original murdered prince, recognized the second Pretender, like the first, as her son.

From June the new Pretender and his host were permanently established at Tushino, which is close outside Moscow on the northwest side. Constant skirmishes and sometimes larger engagements took place. A pitched battle on the little river Hodynka remained indecisive. With the Pretender were two notable Polish partisan chiefs, Lisowski and Jan Sapieha, and these set siege to the famous Trinity Monastery north of Moscow. The monastery was walled, being almost a town in itself. It was stoutly defended by the Russian service gentry inside, inspired by the sanctity of the shrines which they were guarding and by the knowledge that if captured these would be sacked ruthlessly. The monks themselves took a sturdy part in the defence, and frequent sallies delayed the progress of the siege works. This was the one oasis in the district. The invaders sacked Rostov, whence they removed Philaret to Tushino and made him their Patriarch. The neighbouring towns fell into their hands, and Yaroslavl was deserted by its population. The Cossacks committed every kind of violence both in town and country. Shops were looted, peasants and wayfarers robbed and beaten. In all, the Pretender had now twenty-two towns in this area; and those of northeast Russia, perplexed by the quick changes which had taken place in Moscow, debated whether to acknowledge him.

Moscow itself was entirely demoralized. Tsar Basil had more support in the higher classes, while the Pretender was popular with the poorer of the people; but all alike, from princes downwards, were ready at any moment to change sides in pursuit of personal advantage. Families would meet at a meal and separate, some to go to the palace of Tsar Basil, others, in the language of the time, "to flit over to Tushino." There were persons who held rank and received pay in both camps. In Tushino there were drunken revels and constant riots; and in the spring of 1609 bands of adventurers, discarding all discipline, went pillaging on their own account through the country. Another pitched battle was fought on the Hodynka, but though Tushino seemed at first to be winning, Moscow saved the day and drove off the attack.

Meanwhile Prince Skopin Shuisky had gone north to Novgorod and opened negotiations with the Swedes. In return for the cession of Karelia, the Swedes lent him 5000 men under De la Gardie. Skopin gained one success after another, capturing several towns and important roads and winning two battles. As he advanced southward on Moscow, another force under Sheremetev, loyal to Tsar Basil, was recapturing towns and advancing from the east to the rescue of the capital.

At the same time a new and more serious competitor entered the field. King Sigismund of Poland, who had recently had to face a civil war at home, at last found himself free to intervene in Russia. The Polish nobles were willing that he should increase the kingdom by direct conquests of Moscow territory; and in September 1609 he appeared before Smolensk. This beautiful town, well defended by deep gullies and surrounded with magnificent walls by Boris Godunov, who called it "the precious necklace of Russia," was then and is now on the boundary of Great Russian population, and like Pskov had the strong patriotism of a frontier fortress. The garrison was led and inspired by a brave governor, Shein. Sigismund sent to Tushino to demand that all Polish bands should join him before Smolensk. Quarrels ensued at Tushino, and the Pretender, scorned and flouted by his Polish allies, fled by night, disguised as a peasant, to Kaluga.

His Russian partisans were persuaded by the Poles to appeal for protection to Sigismund; and in January 1610 their deputies reached Smolensk. These were Saltykov, an intriguing boyar, Andronov, an ambitious leather merchant, Gramotin, a clerk, and others. With Sigismund, whom they were ready to accept as sovereign, they concluded a very interesting treaty, indicative of the limits of Russian concession and showing the claims of other classes than the boyars. While safeguarding the rights of the Orthodox Church and those of the nobles, the treaty secured also that for other classes there should be no family punishments, no punishment without trial, and freedom of travel abroad without the penalty of confiscation. On the other hand, the treaty gave no rights to slaves; and peasants were not to be transferred, whether from Russia to Poland or between individual squires. In particular, while the King was to promise not to humble the high boyars, he was to engage also to promote suitable gentry and others according to their merits. The terms of the treaty were later to be further defined by a Zemsky Sobor, as were also the fundamental laws of the State. The ordinary work of legislation was to be entrusted to the Duma of Boyars. This treaty was almost equivalent to a constitution. After all, Sigismund possessed no stronger position as sovereign of Poland.

Rozynski and his Poles, who still stood out against their King, finally destroyed the camp and village of Tushino, and marched northward to Volokolamsk. Marina took refuge for a time with Sapieha at Dmitrov, and then returned to her supposed husband at Kaluga, to whom later she bore a son. The Trinity Monastery had held out successfully for more than a year, and the siege had now been abandoned. All this cleared the road for Prince Skopin in the north; and defeating Sapieha on his road, he made his way through to Moscow. This brilliant young man of twenty-four received from Lyapunov, who was always on the lookout for new chances, a letter in which he was saluted as Tsar. Skopin tore up the letter and at first arrested the messenger, but later let him go and did not report the incident to Moscow. He entered the city on March 21 with De la Gardie, who had urged him not to do so. Meanwhile Novgorod Seversk held out stoutly for Tsar Basil in the south; Rozynski retired from Volokolamsk, which left the Metropolitan Philaret free to come to Moscow; and the Tsar's troops pressed hard on the Pretender at Kaluga. Even King Sigismund now made advances to Tsar Basil, which were rebuffed.

The old, weak, and suspicious Tsar, and still more his intriguing brother Dmitry, were jealous of their nephew and deliverer. Skopin was asked to a banquet at which he suddenly fell ill, and two months later he was dead. Lyapunov, organizer of adventures, now made approaches to the Pretender, who had also the support of Prince Golitsyn. Tsar Basil's brother Dmitry, who was universally suspected of having poisoned Skopin, was put at the head of an army to fight the Poles, and on June 24 was thoroughly routed by one of the ablest generals of the time, Zolkiewski, who followed the flying troops towards Moscow. The Pretender had now appeared on another side, the south, and his emissaries were in the city, inflaming the mob against Tsar Basil; it was even feared that his friends inside would open the gates to him. In these circumstances Lyapunov and his brother Zakhar, who was in Moscow, planned to dethrone Tsar Basil. On July 17, boyars and representatives of every class met under arms on the Red Square, and later at the Serpukhov Gate. They called on Shuisky to descend from the throne where he had been the occasion of so much bloodshed and had won so little confidence. Shuisky made no resistance and retired to his private house; but two days later he was seized and compelled to become a monk.

The throne was now empty, and the Duma of Boyars with its weak president, Prince F. Mstislavsky, established a regency to find a new sovereign. The Patriarch Hermogen strongly urged that the Tsar should be a Russian and suggested two names: Prince V. Golitsyn and a boy of fourteen, Michael Romanov, born before his father, Philaret, took the vows. A Zemsky Sobor was summoned, but no one came. Zolkiewski at Mozhaisk and the Pretender at Kolomenskoe were both within a stone's throw of Moscow, and clearly a representative assembly was out of the question. The mob was for the Pretender; and the boyars in their fear invited Zolkiewski and his troops to advance to Moscow. Zolkiewski, who throughout behaved like a statesman, offered the same terms as had been accorded to the Tushino party at Smolensk in February. The boyars were prepared on these terms to swear allegiance not to Sigismund, but to Wladyslaw his son, and that only on the condition that he should at once accept Orthodoxy. Zolkiewski knew well that the King would never let his son, who was a minor, abjure Catholicism; but he communicated the message and on August 27 induced the boyars to swear allegiance to Wladyslaw. Two days later arrived strict instructions to Zolkiewski from Sigismund; he intended to have the throne for himself. Zolkiewski was well aware that Sigismund would never be accepted, and concealed his instructions. Fulfilling his own obligations to the boyars, he drove the Pretender from the neighbourhood of Moscow, and then urged that a special embassy should be sent to Sigismund to press their wishes. Partly through his management, the embassy included Prince V. Golitsyn and Philaret, the father of Michael; so that the two claimants suggested by the Patriarch Hermogen were practically removed from the scene. On September 20, in spite of the vigorous protests of the Patriarch, the boyars admitted Zolkiewski and his men by night into the city. Here Zolkiewski behaved with marked discretion, maintaining strict discipline and referring all disputes between Poles and Russians to a commission equally chosen from both sides. He also showed great respect for the Patriarch and consideration for the boyars. However, he took an early opportunity for resigning the command to Gosiewski and went off home, taking with him as a captive the deposed Tsar Basil with his brothers.

When the envoys reached Smolensk, Sigismund used every pretext to avoid sending his son to Moscow, and explained that he himself would first restore tranquillity in Russia. At the same time he demanded the surrender of Smolensk. This was entirely incompatible with the candidature of his son for the Moscow throne. The envoys were in Sigismund's hands. One of them, Tomila Lugovskoy, was roughly pressed to urge the townsmen of Smolensk to surrender. The growing instinct of intelligent patriotism was in his answer. "How can I do this," he replied, "and lay on myself a dreadful curse? Not only the Lord God and the people of the Moscow sovereignty will not suffer me for this; the earth itself will not carry me. I have been sent from the Moscow sovereignty as its petitioner, and is it for me to be the first to transgress? By the word of Christ, it is better for me to tie a millstone on me and throw myself into the sea. We are sent to the Royal Court not to care or ask for ourselves but for the whole Moscow State." Others were more pliable. Mstislavsky himself accepted from the King the title of groom of the palace, and many others sent in servile requests for office, honours, and estates.

Ultimately the boyars in Moscow settled that the King should act as regent until the Prince should come to Moscow. Sigismund dispatched thither Saltykov and the merchant Andronov, whom he raised to the rank of State Chancellor, and the two outdid each other in servility to him, sending many of the treasures of the Moscow Tsars from Russia to Poland. Saltykov went so far as to urge Sigismund to march on Moscow at once. To all this the Patriarch Hermogen opposed the most strenuous opposition. He laid it down that the only conditions on which Wladyslaw could be accepted as Tsar were that he should come at once, that he should accept Orthodoxy, and that he should secure the withdrawal of all Poles and Lithuanians from the country. In December the eastern towns were prepared to swear allegiance to the Pretender. On the 21st of that month he was killed by a Tartar, in vengeance for a murder which he had committed.

The death of the second Pretender brought a sharp turn in Russian opinion, and an atmosphere of general agreement that the whole country must join together to find a Russian sovereign and to drive out the Poles. Here again the first move came from Lyapunov; but the district which first sent a message to hearten Moscow was the occupied province of Smolensk, where the Poles, in spite of their professions of peace, had persecuted the Orthodox. The message of Smolensk was circulated from Moscow, and the Patriarch urged all to unite to save Russia. Zarutsky with his Don Cossacks, Trubetskoy from the southwest, were ready to act with Lyapunov. Town after town took up the summons, and a great host collected to march on Moscow. Saltykov urged the timid regency to instruct the Russian envoys in Sigismund's camp that they were to submit in everything to his wishes. Such a message was signed by the boyars; but Hermogen utterly refused to add his signature. "To depend on the King's will," he said, "is to swear to the King and not to the Prince, and I give no blessing to such letters. And to Prokofy Lyapunov I will write that, if the Prince will not come for the Moscow sovereignty, be baptized into the Orthodox Christian faith and take the Lithuanians out of the Moscow State, then I give my blessing to all who will come to Moscow and die for the Orthodox faith." The same unwillingness was shown by Philaret and Golitsyn, the envoys at Smolensk, on their receipt of the new instructions. Seeing that the Patriarch's name was missing, they said: "We were sent by the Patriarch, boyars and all people of the Moscow sovereignty and not by the boyars alone; now we have come to be without a sovereign, and the Patriarch is with us the first man; to take counsel now in so great a matter without the Patriarch is not fitting." This was all the more remarkable because Hermogen had replaced Philaret himself in the Patriarchate. Hermogen was arrested by the Poles in Moscow, and a month later Philaret and Golitsyn were seized by the King at Smolensk and sent to Marienburg as prisoners.

The Poles now gave orders in Moscow that no Russian was to bear arms. On March 18, 1611, the carters refused an order to transport a cannon; and as the crowd though unarmed looked threatening, the Poles and especially their German auxiliaries charged it and slaughtered 7000 persons. In the outer parts of the city the Russians had time to arm and organize, and the Poles had to confine themselves to the Kremlin and the inner town. To all else they set fire, and it burned almost to the ground. Within a week, Lyapunov and his colleagues with 100,000 men encamped outside the city. Meanwhile on June 3 Smolensk, after a heroic resistance, was taken by storm. The Poles had no interest in Sigismund's personal ambitions, and insisted that his army should be disbanded.

The national host outside Moscow contained also the germ of a national assembly. It ordained as follows: "Of the various lands of the Moscow sovereignty the princes, boyars, nobles, and all service men, who stand for the House of the most Holy Mother of God and for the Orthodox Christian faith, have approved and chosen by all the land boyars and voevodes, that they may set the land in order and provide for all affairs of the country and of the army: if they do not do this, then, by all the land, we shall be free, to change them and in their place choose others, speaking with all the land." The same corporate instinct breathes in the messages exchanged by the different towns. But everything was ruined by the arrogance of Lyapunov. Of lower rank than his colleagues Zarutsky and Trubetskoy, he claimed to decide all questions and receive all deputations. Gosiewski in the Kremlin was aware of the dissensions in the Russian camp and, releasing a Cossack prisoner, he sent across with him a forged document, written in the name of Lyapunov and calling for a massacre of Cossacks. The Cossacks in the Russian camp demanded that Lyapunov should come to them, showed him the document and, in spite of his disclaimers which were confirmed by others, cut him down. The Cossacks attacked other leaders of the gentry, so that many of these left the camp. To complete Russia's misfortunes the Swedish troops, helped by treachery, at this time entered the city of Novgorod, and a new Pretender appeared in Pskov, to whom later the Cossacks in the camp outside Moscow swore allegiance. For all that, the Polish general Chodkiewicz, marching on Moscow to relieve the Polish garrison, found himself unable to get through. Saltykov sent urgent messages from the Kremlin to Sigismund, begging him to come and help on his own terms.

After the failure of the first national host, the instinct that Russia must stand together became not weaker but far stronger. Letters in this sense were exchanged between the principal towns. Kazan and Perm, reporting the death of Lyapunov, whom they described as champion of the Christian faith, wrote: "But we have agreed to be all at one, to stand for the Moscow and Kazan sovereignty, to do no harm to each other, not to let the Cossacks come into the town, to stand firm on that till God shall give us a sovereign for the Moscow State, and that we will choose a sovereign by all the land; that, if the Cossacks choose a sovereign alone at their own will, we do not want such a sovereign." When deliverance was to come, it was not to be from the boyars but from the almost exclusively peasant population of the north and the northeast where there were very few squires, and elective peasants and municipal self-government remained in force. The plea for union and joint action was manfully urged in letters from the Patriarch Hermogen. Imprisoned by the Poles, he was taken by them to the Red Square and ordered to dissuade the people from resistance; what he said, was this: "Blessed be those who come to save the Moscow sovereignty; and you, traitors, be accursed." They were the last words he spoke in public. He was taken back to his cell, where on February 17 of the next year he died of starvation. Letters of much the same import were sent all over the country from the Trinity Monastery by its abbot Dionysius and the cellarer (treasurer) Abram Palitsyn. After the fire of Moscow, refugees of all kinds took shelter at the monastery, which became an enormous almshouse and at the same time the focus of Russian patriotism.

In October 1611 a letter of Hermogen, who had his own fearless messengers, reached Nizhny Novgorod. It was read out in the Cathedral and the Zemsky elder Cosmo Minin, a butcher, declared at once that he offered his property for the national cause, an example which was followed wholesale by the citizens. Minin insisted that the leader must come from the gentry; and Prince Dmitry Pozharsky, who had played an honourable part and been wounded fighting with the Poles, consented to lead, on the condition that Minin himself was appointed treasurer. The leaders then wrote to the other towns: "And you, too, sirs, should march as soon as possible on the men of Lithuania. When we are once in an assembly, we will take counsel by all the land."

By the end of March 1612, Pozharsky had moved with his growing army as far as Yaroslavl. Here there was a necessary delay for organization. The district was cleared of the Cossacks, and the Swedes were persuaded to remain neutral. The Cossacks at Moscow sent a man to kill Pozharsky; he failed, but it was not till August 10 that the second national host arrived outside the capital. It was just in time to anticipate the coming of Chodkiewicz on a second attempt to relieve the Polish garrison in the Kremlin. The Cossacks at first refused to fight, and on August 22 Chodkiewicz advanced almost to the western gates of Moscow. Palitsyn, however, persuaded the Cossacks to do their part; and on September 3, with the help of a daring attack by Minin, Chodkiewicz was driven off. On October 22 the Cossacks stormed the inner town (*Kitay gorod*). On November 27 the Kremlin itself was surrendered, and the boyars and young Michael Romanov recovered their liberty. The garrison had stood siege for a year and a half and had been driven to eat dead bodies.

Letters were now sent out to all towns requesting them to send representatives from the clergy, gentry, traders, artisans, and peasants to elect a new Tsar. The deputies were asked to "get a firm agreement, and to bring mandates from all classes of persons." The Assembly gathered in Moscow; and before it set to work, the city fasted for three days. The choice of a Tsar was a very difficult matter. There was no candidate with an evident claim. Mstislavsky was considered, but retired; Golitsyn was thought of, but he was at present a prisoner in Poland. Intrigues and parties were busy; and agreement could only be secured in favour of some name which had not been tainted in the Time of Troubles or, still better, had had no past at all. The question was settled by an unexpected move from the side of the Cossacks, who proposed a candidate already put forward by some of the gentry, Michael Romanov. It was in his favour that his candidature carried the blessing of the dead Patriarch Hermogen, and that he himself was the son of the patriot Metropolitan Philaret. But what really settled the matter was his connection by marriage with his great-uncle, John the Dread; here again, as throughout the Time of Troubles, the Russian instinct clutched at a hereditary connection with the old dynasty of Rurik. On February 21, 1613, Michael Romanov was elected unanimously by the Zemsky Sobor. The election was formally confirmed; and the crowd on the Red Square, when asked for their assent, shouted for Michael before his name was uttered.

Michael himself, after his release from the Kremlin, had gone with his mother to a monastery at Kostroma near the family domain. A band of Polish partisans, who were in the neighbourhood, decided to seize him and capturing a peasant, Ivan Susanin, demanded to know his hiding place. Susanin, who knew, refused to say, and died under torture without telling. On March 13, the delegates of the National Assembly presented themselves at Kostroma. In reply to the anxious questions of Michael's mother, the nun Martha, who urged that each of the preceding Tsars had found his subjects unfaithful, the envoys replied: "Now we have all been punished, and we have come to an agreement in all towns." Michael, the first Tsar of a new dynasty, was crowned in Moscow on July 11, 1613.

Poland had had her chance of putting a Polish prince on the throne of Moscow and uniting the Slavonic world, but the license and indiscipline of the partisan leaders who thought only of pillage, King Sigismund's eagerness to seize Russian territory for Poland, and his jealousy of his own son, had defeated all such hopes. The extent of the failure was put plainly to the Polish Diet on the eve of Michael's election in an eloquent speech by a far-seeing Polish statesman, Leo Sapieha, Chancellor of Lithuania. Sapieha attacks those "who not only alienated the Muscovites from His Grace the King's son, and from their friendship with the Polish people, when in time we might have brought about with them a union such as that which we have succeeded in making with the Lithuanians; but roused and provoked them, and by their own wrongdoing themselves compelled the Muscovites, although broken up into factions, to come to agreement and unity."

"And now," he proceeds, "we must expect and fear that, choosing for themselves some potentate as ruler, they will seek full vengeance for the sufferings we have inflicted on them, will demand and try to recover their own property, will exact compensation for the destruction we have caused, or even pay us back all that our people have done to them."

CHAPTER IX

Serfdom

[*1613–82*]

THE ROMANOV dynasty was borne to the throne by a wave of patriotic feeling among all the sounder elements of the population under the direction of the national Church. For a brief period we catch a glimpse of Russia as a people and not merely a state. Parts of the picture are anything but pretty; but there were notable beginnings of local initiative which promised much for the future. The Romanovs were to end as they began, in a chaos of social disruption; and the explanation of this co-incidence is to be seized here in the first period of their power. Under the new dynasty we are to have a history more and more restricted to the State alone; the life of the people is entirely suppressed. And the one cardinal fact, that the foundations of the State are rotting, though it will cause the convulsions which bring one sovereign after another to a violent death, will remain practically unchronicled. The explanation is in the period with which we have now to deal.

In the Time of Troubles the Moscow State, or Sovereignty as it was called, had to do the best that it could for itself without a sovereign; a fact which was clearly realized and expressed at the time. The force of events brought Russia quite near to what is called a constitution; in other words, state requirements and procedure had to be defined, at least for immediate needs, and that is the way in which every constitution begins. Boris Godunov was actually elected by a fairly representative Zemsky Sobor. The first Pretender entrusted to a yet more representative national assembly the trial of his accuser Shuisky, an issue which was essentially the question of the Pretender's own right to the throne. Shuisky evaded a Sobor, but on the one hand guaranteed to the boyars rights such as trial by their peers, and on the other hand made in the Uspensky Cathedral a disingenuous promise to do no harm to anyone without a Sobor, thus making the guarantee of justice general. Still more important were the negotiations of the Russian representatives with King Sigismund at Smolensk in February and again in August, 1610. Here are discussed the guarantees which a Polish prince is to give as conditions of his accession to the Russian throne, and we have something like the elements of a Magna Carta. The rights of the Orthodox Church are secured, the boyars reiterate the demands already mentioned, the gentry demand promotion by merit, the Duma of Boyars becomes a legislative body, and the Zemsky Sobor assumes the position of a constituent assembly, authoritative in filling any omissions in the guarantees which are now claimed. We find in the first of these negotiations the interesting claim for freedom to travel abroad without confiscation of estate. Only—and it is a big only—the peasants remain without relief, and peasant transfers not only between Russia and Poland but between private estates are forbidden.

It was the most representative of Zemsky Sobors that elected Michael Romanov to the throne, and their use by no means stopped with his accession. On the contrary, his mother, the nun Martha, before sanctioning his acceptance (the father, Philaret, was a prisoner in Poland) demanded a kind of guarantee of assistance from the country as a whole in the work of government; the National Assembly was often consulted in the first ten years of his reign and was summoned frequently during the first half of that of his son Alexis. It is probable that Michael on his accession was made to accept a private agreement to observe the rights of the boyars.

The Time of Troubles had unsettled all foundations of the State. Its termination was only due to a united national effort. It was impossible then that affairs in Russia should remain exactly as they had stood before. One of two things was likely to happen, either that the country would go forward on the lines already indicated, or that it would slide by the victory of sheer fatigue further and further back into the grooves from which for a time it had been forced to issue. The story that follows will tell us which of these two things happened.

The social chaos had produced all-round distrust. Everyone had betrayed everyone. To find a candidate untainted in this period the electors had had to fix on a mere boy, generally unknown. The accession of Michael was not the end of the fight with disorders. The Russian Cossack chief Zarutsky, taking with him Marina and her little son, went south and organized further rebellion, which had to be crushed by force. The Cossacks, whose unbridled license throughout the Troubles left an evil memory in men's minds for long afterwards, were not brought to some degree of order without a further struggle. The country as a whole was ravaged and impoverished. Large areas had gone out of cultivation; masses of the population had been carried from their moorings; and most estates were comparatively starved of labour. Above all there was unrest in men's minds. A number of new men had come to the fore. The new dynasty had yet to make its own tradition, and was not taken on trust.

If one looked abroad, the task was no less difficult. Smolensk, the sturdy frontier town, had been lost. Even Novgorod was for a time in the hands of the Swedes. In the long duel between Russia and Poland, Russia had lost much ground. On the other hand, just at this time when the resources of the State were almost exhausted, she was brought more closely into contact with a Europe in which modern civilization had built up powerful states, with strong monarchies able to rely on well trained public servants and on all sorts of new technical resources for peace or for war. The new Russian dynasty, for the very reason that its right was questioned, had to be even more careful of its dignity than the old; and in order to maintain its position, so far from being able to grant the country a time of quiet and ordinary development, it had to make further demands on the national resources than ever before.

To satisfy the state needs and to carry out the state service, the new dynasty had to rely on the great corps of civil and military service men created on the basis of land tenure under its predecessors. This numerous class of gentry was, like everyone else, impoverished. It was in the psychology of reaction, full of evil memories of the past and of fears for the future; it had learned nothing and forgotten nothing. Its wealth, as we remember, was its labour, and its labour had dispersed all over the realm. Much of it had gone down the new road of colonization which was fast developing along the Lower Volga; some of it had gone farther afield to Siberia. Here the Russian people continued to advance rapidly through the vast and almost empty forests. Soon after 1640 it had reached the Lena.

The gentry, then, made urgent demands for the restoration of their fugitive peasants. In the last reigns of the House of Rurik, enormous grants of crown land, that is of crown peasants, had been made to service gentry. These grants continued, reaching in 1678 a total which was more than half of the population. In 1597 Boris Godunov, as regent for Fedor, had forbidden the kidnapping of peasants from small estates but had fixed five years as the time limit in which owners might hunt out their fugitive peasants. In 1601-2 he again licensed the transfers of peasants between smaller estates, but this was not extended to estates of the Palace, the Church, and the higher ranks of service. Even the first Pretender, regarded as a champion of the peasants, ordered the return of fugitives who had taken their property with them; peasants without property were allowed to stay with those who had fed them during the preceding years of famine. Shuisky, the boyars' Tsar, issued in 1607 an interesting edict, of which the original is now lost, but which can be taken to be genuine, though it is very doubtful whether it had any effect; he extended the time limit for hunting out fugitives from five years to fifteen, with a penalty of ten roubles (very heavy at that time) on those who concealed or sheltered them. The local police and even the local priests are to take an active part in the search for fugitives. The edict contains some humane provisions for the children of slaves. The protest against peasant transfers made by the Russian envoys at Smolensk in 1610 has already been mentioned.

From 1621 onwards the gentry sent in reiterated demands for the extension of the old time limit from five years to ten. The first large landowner to secure this right was the Trinity Monastery. Others made their peasants sign away their own freedom, agreeing that if they escaped they might be forcibly detained or forcibly fetched back; or, that they must find substitutes before leaving. In 1637, gentry of Ukraine obtained the ten-year time limit, on the plea that service in Moscow made it difficult for them to look after their home interests. In 1641 the right was extended to all service gentry in Moscow. The gentry then pressed further and asked that the time limit should be abolished altogether, and on March 19, 1642, a ten-year limit was conceded to all. In the same year the limit was extended to fifteen years, and in 1646 the time limit was finally abolished. It had been the one last hope of legal escape for the peasant. With the rapid growth of state burdens and the constantly increasing impoverishment, this was the only relief left open to him. Now he was driven outside the law, if he was to find any escape from impossible conditions.

Practically, the decisive factor in this legislation was that from 1646 onward ownership was fixed by the government registers, in which all squires were required to enter the names of each of their peasants. Those registered in a given estate were henceforth regarded as legally attached to it, and this applied to "all who shall be born after the census . . . because their fathers are written in the census book." Serfdom thus becomes hereditary. At the same time, new punishments are found for owners who sell their slaves, register their peasants under the heading of slaves, or register cultivated land as waste. A time limit for outstanding suits is still maintained, but by 1649 this too is abolished.

In 1649 the youthful Tsar Alexis, under the strong influence of a rising which took place in Moscow in the preceding year, issued a new code of laws or statute (*Ulozhenie*). This finally confirms the establishment of serfdom, which henceforth becomes a state institution. The government of this time certainly did not regard itself as handing over the peasants as property to the gentry. It was actuated by the desire to re-establish order and, above all, to get the most possible out of the population for the public services. It did not even formally repeal peasant rights; it simply ignored them. But when it legalized serfdom, it created new habits and new conceptions, which in practice gradually turned the peasants into property. During the seventeenth and even the eighteenth century free cultivators continued to contract agreements, and some of these secured themselves the right of leaving; but this was guaranteed only to themselves, not to their children. Owners were compelled to register these extra peasants like the rest, and the mere fact that the registers were taken as the test equalized all such persons with serfs in the eyes of the government.

The peasants had long since reached the stage at which they had no surplus income whatever. The master was able to increase his claims at will, and the peasants saw little hope and had little opportunity of appealing to a law court. The gentry were expected to treat the peasants well, not to bring them to ruin by their exactions, and above all not to provoke them to flight. Such offences on their part could even be punished by the knout. The governors might, and occasionally did, investigate such cases; for instance, a squire was punished for forcing his peasants to work on a Sunday; but peasants were forbidden to complain to any outside authority.

The peasants came to be regarded more and more as chattels. A law as early as 1625 ordered anyone who kills someone else's peasant to give in his place "one of the best" of his own peasants with his family, whereas the wife and children of the murdered man were left with the former owner. This, by the way, was a repetition of an earlier law applying only to slaves, which of itself shows the change of attitude toward the peasant. The squire had that place which, among the crown peasants, belonged to the elder of the community. He was responsible to the government for all his serfs, and his power over them was practically absolute. By a law of 1628 debts of a squire might be recovered

from his slaves and peasants. In 1642 the right of a creditor to seize a
serf for his own debts was abolished on the ground that the serf's master
would be defrauded. The sale of land without the peasant who worked
on it was forbidden; but that was because the government depended
on the peasants to pay the dues on the land. The right of a master to
take a peasant from the land into his house as a servant was at first
limited to cases where he had not enough slaves for his house service.
For similar reasons the government forbade peasants to be moved from
a *pomestye* estate to a patrimony. For all that, the practice of selling
peasants without their land grew up of itself and was ultimately so general as to receive the sanction of law in 1675. Later, serfs were freely
given as presents, or exchanged, or offered in payment of debts. They
might easily be exchanged for slaves. Also in practice the master came
to be allowed to set a peasant free, which was quite incompatible with
the principle that the peasant was fastened to the soil only in order to
do his service to the state. The *Ulozhenie* itself sanctioned corporal
punishment of peasants, and forbade them to bring any charge against
their masters except that of state treason. The master therefore became
the peasants' magistrate, and even outsiders would sometimes bring to
his court their suits against his peasants. In every way the peasant tended
to be equalized with the slave; on the other hand, slavery as such was
being gradually abolished; no man was allowed to pledge himself as a
slave beyond the life of his original creditor. Masters freely settled slaves
on peasant land, and were then obliged to register them as peasants.
Peasants could still accept contracts to buy and sell; they were free to
lend money, to trade, and to acquire, rent, or lease land; but their property was at the mercy of their master.

The old large peasant households, sometimes with an abundance of
side-sources of income such as fishing, beekeeping, and forestry, were
now for the most part replaced by families living continually on the
verge of bankruptcy and famine. A bad crop or an epidemic was enough
to ruin them. As they had no legal means of escape from ruin, enormous
numbers had recourse to flight. Some would simply hide in the woods;
other would gather in large robber bands; many made their way to the
Cossacks, other to the less warlike frontier of the east; some even fled
the country. Peasant risings came to be a running chorus to the whole
history of the State. The only remedy which the government saw was
to make the gentry more absolute. The *Ulozhenie* imposed heavy fines
on those who fled and on those who received fugitives. In 1658 flight
was made a criminal offence, and runaways were to be knouted "for

their brigandage" in depriving their master of his property. From 1661, a squire who received a fugitive peasant had to return him at his own cost, together with one of his own peasant families as compensation. Elders of crown peasants had the knout for sheltering fugitives. In 1664 was ordered the first of a series of general state hunts for fugitives, which were to go on for the next hundred years; and the receiver was ordered to surrender as compensation, not one but four peasant families of his own. Flight only became more and more common, and the punishments harsher and harsher. Frequently peasants murdered their squires, sometimes with their whole families, or set fire to their houses. By a law of 1667 fugitive peasants who had become priests or monks were unfrocked and returned to their masters. The law demanding four peasants for one was repealed by Fedor II in 1681, but in deference to numberless petitions from the gentry it was restored the next year. A law of a year later substituted a fine of twenty roubles or the knout. Peter the Great in 1694 confirmed this last penalty for all squires who did not at once surrender their fugitives.

By thus driving the majority of the population out of any law-abiding life, the government produced a long series of public disorders, which from time to time culminated in dangerous risings. In 1648 administrative abuses associated with taxation led to a violent riot in Moscow, when the Tsar Alexis himself was flouted and only escaped by surrendering to the mob some of his financial administrators. The fire which followed the next day renewed these disorders. The Moscow riots were echoed over the country in one town after another, always directed against the administration and particularly the tax-gatherer, and always based on financial grievances. Such were the large riots at Solvychegodsk and Ustyug. In Novgorod, on the ground that grain was being sent out of the country to Sweden, there was an outbreak in which the Danish envoy was seized and belayed by the mob. Archbishop Nikon, who dared to excommunicate the rioters in the cathedral, was nearly beaten to death; and the Tsar's summons to surrender was received with open scorn. On the approach of troops, the rioters submitted; but similar disorders which had broken out in Pskov continued much longer, the city holding out for a three months' siege, and only surrendering on the terms of an amnesty.

Still greater were the disorders of 1667–71 in the southeast, where migration, especially of the malcontent, had flowed down the Volga and created a large and turbulent population. In 1667 a number of migrants came from Ukraine to the Don Cossacks and, finding no means of support there, organized themselves into a great pirate host under one of the Don Cossacks, Stephen Razin. He was prevented from attacking Azov, but was invited by other Cossacks to the Yaik (Ural) River, where he surprised the fortress, routed the government troops, and remained in possession during the winter. He was joined by elements of discontent of every kind, Cossacks, fugitive serfs, fugitive slaves, or large groups of the non-Russian population. He was believed to be invulnerable. In 1669 he equipped a fleet and sailed the Caspian, stopping and plundering Russian ships, defeating a Persian squadron and even raiding the north coast of Persia. On his return he was met by government forces outside Astrakhan, but was offered full pardon if he would restore the ships, the guns, and the gentry whom he had seized. Most of the local population were really on his side. He accepted the terms but did not fulfil them, and in 1670 sailed up the Volga collecting recruits of every kind, calling all to a class war against the boyars. Two considerable towns, Tsaritsyn and Kamyshin, opened their gates; a government force coming from Astrakhan went over to his side, surrendering its officers, and he was admitted into Astrakhan by the inhabitants. Here he killed squires, plundered churches, looted shops, and introduced mob rule; the Voevode was thrown from a church tower. At the end of July Razin again sailed up the Volga and took Saratov and Samara. His advance guard raided the provinces of Nizhny, Tambov, and Penza, everywhere preaching a class war. Following the traditional habit of impersonation, he declared that he had in his army the Tsar's son and the Patriarch Nikon. He was, however, checked in his triumphal march by a stout defence of the fortress of Simbirsk, and a relieving army routed him. He fled by night, wounded; his army fled too, but was caught and crushed. Samara and Saratov refused to receive him. Trying to raise new forces on the Don he was seized by the Ataman of the Don Cossacks and sent to Moscow, where he was executed on June 6, 1671. Roving bands continued to ravage the centre of Russia; peasants went on killing squires and officials, and Cossacks seized various towns. It was only by pitched battles that order was restored; it is calculated that one hundred thousand persons perished in the repression. Astrakhan, ruled by a deputy of Razin, made yet another raid up the Volga but was taken in November 1671. A little below Saratov stands a hill bearing the name of Razin and commemorated by one of the most beautiful of Russian revolutionary songs. Legend says that he who mounts the hill by night will learn Razin's secret. The secret was class war.

While the mass of the Russian people sank into serfdom, all the germs of liberty born in the last period likewise disappeared. The government, always strengthening the grip of the centre, was everywhere opposed to local initiative; indeed the Time of Troubles, with its wholesale disorders, had made even the population itself see the advantage of such a central control. John the Dread had made only a beginning in local self-government. The Gubnoy authorities, responsible for public security and elected by all classes, had never been fully coordinated with the Zemsky officials elected on a class basis and entrusted with a wider jurisdiction. Even before the Troubles, voevodes (governors) sent from Moscow to the frontier towns, had been given full powers in all affairs except those of the Church; and when the country was in chaos, such officials became equally necessary in the central provinces. They had no such free hand as the earlier governors, and were kept strictly under control by headquarters. As time went on, the local institutions were abolished, or simply passed out of use. The local law courts lost all meaning under serfdom and were continued only on palace and crown lands. Finance and economy were still dealt with by local officials; but the indirect taxes, which were now constantly increasing, had never been under their control. The Zemsky institution came to be little more than a convenience for the squire, who would send the elected elder to do his errands. Even the ancient *mir* or village assembly lost three quarters of its importance when composed of serfs under the absolute control of the squire. From the beginning of the new dynasty, the government preferred a new and larger territorial unit, the *Razryad*, purely official and based entirely on military requirements. This was a stage in a new process, that of militarizing the internal government of Russia.

As with the local self-government, so with the incipient national assembly. Zemsky Sobors were in use throughout the reign of Michael and half of that of Alexis. In fact, Michael and his father Philaret, who on his return from captivity in Marienburg became regent, could not have restored order without the cooperation of the Sobor. But the culminating point in its history was the election of the new dynasty in 1613, and as the central officials regained their grip, it tended to become less and less necessary. Similarly its representative character, which was complete in 1613, was continually whittled away. The Sobor of 1634 was summoned in a single day and was probably not representative of anything outside Moscow. The Sobor of 1642 was summoned largely on an elective basis, and that of 1648 was one of the most representative of all. It was to this body that was entrusted the important task of codification, and the result of its labours was the *Ulozhenie*. But this work, called for in a panic, was skimpily executed. As time went on, the government fell into the habit of summoning on a class basis only those representatives of which it stood most in need, for instance the merchants for the discussion of new taxes.

The Sobor had never evolved any fixed procedure. Generally the sovereign put to it certain questions at an initial plenary meeting; it then dispersed into class groups, each group produced written answers to the questions set, and these answers were once more considered in common. By the side of the Zemsky Sobor, there was always the Duma of Boyars, to which the actual drafting of legislation was left. The competence of the Sobor was never defined. In no way were its decisions obligatory on the sovereign. Thus it cannot be said that this beginning of a national assembly in Russia ever gained a permanent footing, and there was nothing to prevent it from vanishing in the same haphazard way that it had arisen.

We have Sobors in 1650 for the insurrection at Pskov already mentioned, and in 1653 for the affairs of Little Russia. From 1654 to 1682 there is no Sobor. One function of the Sobor, in form at least, lasted on beyond the others: that of voicing the people at a disputed accession. Michael was elected at a Sobor; the right of Alexis was confirmed by a Sobor, not only for himself but for his children. But in 1682, on the death of his oldest son Fedor, there were two possible heirs, the weakly John of sixteen and the sturdy Peter of ten, and the question was referred by the Patriarch to a crowd on the Red Square who declared, as no doubt they had been instructed, for Peter. To this casual crowd has dwindled the Assembly that elected the Romanovs. In 1698 there was one more Sobor, for the trial of Peter's sister Sophia. How, indeed, could a national assembly have had any real vitality in a country in which at this very period so large a proportion of the population were converted into serfs? What sort of independence was to be expected from an assembly mainly composed of serf-owners, bound by military service to accept with submission every order of an arbitrary sovereign?

Similar in its effect, as isolating the State from the body of the commonalty, was a very curious development which now took place in the life of the Church. The enslavement of Constantinople had made Moscow the political champion of the Orthodox Church. This, as we remember, led under the two Johns to the doctrine of the Third Rome and under Fedor I to the establishment of a Moscow Patriarchate. After the Time of Troubles, with Russia weakened and Poland triumphant, this responsibility became greater and more onerous; the more so because at

this very time the Orthodox Russians of Lithuania were hard pressed
to defend their faith against the Jesuits, who were using every means of
propaganda to bring them into the Latin fold. Put thus on its defence,
Moscow had to reply with the same weapons. The Russians in Lithuania
were beyond the arm of the Moscow autocracy, and it was only the
weapons of reason which could avail there. But this was exactly where
the armoury of Russia was most deficient; and in this matter, as in
others, her inferiority to the cultured West was pitifully manifest. The
subjugated Church of Constantinople and the Orthodox of the Turkish
Empire looked only to Moscow for protection; but the Greek Patriarchs
and other prelates who visited Moscow had a keen eye for the perver-
sions which in Russia had crept into the sacred books and church services. It was shortly before the Time of Troubles that printing began in
Moscow, and the first presses were those of the Church. This, together
with Greek criticisms, suggested a revision of the church books, as any
errors would become far more harmful from the moment when they
were widely circulated in print. The task of correction was undertaken,
and was at first assigned to the Abbot Dionysius, who had played so
great a part in the national recovery of 1612–13. Dionysius with a few
colleagues set to work. But ignorance and obscurantism were extreme
in Moscow, especially in the domain of church life. Dionysius was accused of heresy and thrown into prison, and it was only a visit of the
Patriarch of Jerusalem that brought about his release. Under the Patriarch Joseph, church books were printed in large numbers with only
the loosest correction, and these only served to stereotype the mistransla-
tions and other errors.

The matter was taken up again with great vigour by the Patriarch
Nikon. This remarkable man was born a peasant near Nizhny Novgorod in 1605. His childhood was passed in the disturbed conditions of
the Time of Troubles. He had a cruel stepmother, and grew up a harsh
man. At first a country priest, he later became a monk and in 1646,
meeting the young Tsar Alexis, made a great impression on him. He was
appointed abbot of a Moscow monastery and was weekly invited to the
palace, acting as a kind of unofficial almoner of the Tsar in the relief of
the distressed. Consecrated in 1648 Archbishop of Novgorod, where we
recall his courage in facing the popular rising, he was later transferred to
Moscow as Patriarch. The gentle Tsar treated him with special affection
and described him as "his intimate friend of soul and body." He was
even accorded the title of *Gosudar*, or sovereign, which by an anomaly
intelligible in the circumstances had been given to Philaret, not so much

as Patriarch but as father of the Tsar. Nikon governed during the absences of Alexis. Without much education, he yet was able and very energetic; but his methods of rule took no account of the feelings of those whom he governed. Sharp and arrogant, entirely lacking in self-restraint, he made enemies everywhere—in the family of the Tsar, among the boyars, and among the clergy, on whom he inflicted the harshest punishments.

It was a misfortune that the correction of the church books, in any case so delicate a matter in Russia, should have been taken up by such a man as Nikon. When one enters into the details of the questions involved, one may be surprised at the extraordinary passion which they aroused. But that will only be so if one forgets what loyalty to the written word is in religion, and if one forgets that all this happened at Moscow. Among the principal questions was the spelling of the sacred name of Jesus. By a slip, the translators from the Greek had written Isus instead of Iisus, and many people now absolutely refused to be corrected on such a point. Again, in Russia the habit had been introduced of giving the blessing with two fingers instead of with three and had even received sanction in the *Stoglav* or record of the decisions of the celebrated Church Assembly of John the Dread in 1551. Two fingers, so say the defenders of the custom, represent the dual nature, divine and human, which hung on the Cross; three fingers represent the Trinity, of which only one Person was on the Cross. There were other questions relating to the administration of the Sacraments, and yet others, grounded only on habit, such as the wearing of beards.

In 1654 a Church Assembly was held. It was decided to correct the books. Greek and Russian manuscripts were assiduously collected, and the liturgy was printed with the corrections. At once there was vigorous opposition, headed by Bishop Paul of Kolomna, associated with the issue of the previous editions, and by Avvakum and other eloquent preachers, who knew their congregations and could carry them with them. The opponents declared that the perversion of the faith had been prophesied as a sign of the last times, and that the corrected books were the work of Antichrist. Nikon's only reply was to punish. Avvakum has told his own story. "Then I wrote them a tale with great abuse," he says at one point; "and I cursed them back," at another. The kindly Tsar, he claims, was for him: "he walked round my prison, groaned and went away"; so too the Tsaritsa: "she stood for me, the nice one, and tried to beg me off." Brought up before the Patriarch in the Chudov Monastery, he defends himself by vigorous counterattacks: "Rome has fallen long since," he says, "and the Poles are ruined with them"; to the Greeks, who have not known how to save themselves from infidel rule, he shouts the taunt "Go on coming here to teach us!" He walks away from the judges and throws himself on the floor. "Sit on there," he says, "and I'll lie down a bit." While he is being publicly unfrocked, he spits in the Patriarch's face. "We are monsters for the sake of Christ," he writes later; "if God wills that I should die, I will not join the apostates"; for a vehement letter written in prison, he was sent to the stake. Whatever the causes, it was clear that a great part of the Russian Church had been thrown into bitter antagonism to its chiefs.

Nikon carried his point, but the struggle was the beginning of his ruin. His increased unpopularity led to a combination of all his enemies against him. He was too proud to defend himself or even explain himself to the Tsar. A coolness grew up between the two; the Tsar ceased to invite him to the palace, and avoided him at church ceremonies. In July, 1658, a message from the Tsar that he was not coming to mass that day in the Uspensky Cathedral, led to a bitter outburst from the Patriarch. He informed the congregation that he would no longer retain his office, and began unrobing in their presence. Disregarding a not unfriendly letter from Alexis, he left Moscow for the Monastery of New Jerusalem which he had founded. There he waited to be asked back. In February 1660 a Church Assembly debated the questions raised by this interregnum, together with the violent letters and outbursts of Nikon against all whom he regarded as his enemies, including the Tsar. An attempt to arrange a reconciliation came to nothing, and in 1666, in the presence of the Patriarchs of Alexandria and Antioch, Nikon was deposed.

The corrected books were retained; but the opposition to them only increased with time. Numerous priests and whole monasteries refused to accept them. In the famous Monastery of Solovetsk on the White Sea, the opposition was not appeased by a direct messenger from the Tsar; in this matter the monks refused to obey him and declared themselves ready to suffer any penalty. The Greek Church, they said, was now in bondage and the purity of its faith was therefore in question; they themselves could not give up the traditions which had wrought the salvation of the holy wonder-workers of their own monastery; for these, they said, they were ready to die. In a letter to the Tsar they described the corrected spelling of the sacred name as "fearful to them all." The garrison of the monastery went further in its resistance, denying all allegiance to the Tsar. An army had to be sent in 1668, and after years of hesitation the monastery was taken by assault in 1676, and the leaders of the rebellion were hanged.

The importance of this strange story seems to me to go far deeper than the questions with which it is concerned. It seems no mere coincidence that the siege of Solovetsk was in progress at the same time as Razin's rebellion. The opposition called themselves the "Old Believers" and claimed, not without some justice, that it was the Church which had departed from them and not they from the Church. Cut off from their source of authority and persecuted in every way, they inevitably broke up into various sects; some of them later secured the consecration of bishops from Austria; others lived without priests. But whatever the merits of their religious views, they acquired under persecution the characteristics of a militant church. These *Raskolniki* (a name given in common to all of them) had their own self-discipline; they were often thriftier and more industrious than others, and more moral. Meanwhile, *Raskolnik* communities always served to focus the popular discontent. They might be a church of the ignorant, of the fanatical, but they were a church of the people, in permanent opposition to the great of the land. When the son of Alexis, Peter the Great, challenged outright the whole psychology of Moscow, they were convinced that Antichrist had indeed come; and in nearly all the peasant rebellions we find their hand, notably in the greatest of all, that of Pugachev in the reign of Catherine II. The top stratum of the Church might be the more enlightened, but it had lost touch with the people at the very time when the people itself had been driven underground. Owing its victory only to the support of the secular power, the official Church lost heavily in spiritual values. If later we find Peter, himself deeply religious, parading the streets of Moscow with public mockeries of the official Church, we must realize that it had lost credit and influence with the government itself. The reign of Peter was to witness the abolition of the Patriarchate and the institution of a civil procurator of the Holy Synod, who converted the Church into a mouthpiece of officialdom and later an instrument of police and repression.

Thus, in different ways, the bulk of the Russian people descended into a kind of abyss, of which there is no history. Meanwhile, on the top of this foundation, increasingly rotten and perilous, was erected an increasingly ponderous and costly state edifice. Michael had no strength of character; up to the return of his father Philaret from captivity and again after Philaret's death, the government was in the hands of favourites. Of the first favourites, the Saltykovs, who came with an unclean record out of the Time of Troubles, contemporaries wrote that "the only thing they did was to enrich themselves and their relations, rob the country and do injustice in all affairs, taking trouble that by favour of the sovereign he should see no one except themselves." The Sobor, called together in 1642 to consider whether to accept the offer of the Cossacks to hand over Azov, is full of similar grievances. The gentry, on whose behalf the peasants have been enslaved, complain that the clerks and deputy clerks of the administration "getting salaries, estates and patrimonies, growing rich off bribes, have bought up large estates and have made themselves brick houses such as even the well-born used not to have before"; they say that they are ravaged worse than Turkish or Crimean Mussulmans by the unjust courts of Moscow. The merchants complain that they are ruined by their state service, by foreign competition in trade, and by the governors who pillage them.

The chief legislative act of this period, the *Ulozhenie*, stabilized the system of central control. It forbade all alienation of lands to the Church. Society is now tabulated according to various kinds of state service, in class compartments based on class obligations. The clergy pray, the gentry serve at war, the merchants collect and supply money, the peasants plough the fields. No room was left for gaps between these classes, while by the very nature of things increasing numbers forced their way without leave past the barriers, endangering the public order and even the existence of the State. The Prikazy were at this time unified and made more efficient. The townsfolk, like the peasants, were brought under the tightest control; death was the penalty for residing or even marrying outside one's ward.

The principal purpose of all this centralization was the maintenance of a large army. Owing to the great inferiority in training and equipment, two Russians were required to face one foreigner. The gentry with their rustic levies were but a disorderly host. There were some special regiments of archers (*streltsy*), originally the Tsar's bodyguard, and of gunners; but more and more use was made of foreign officers to train new units on the Western model; it was for her army that Russia first had recourse to the civilization of Western Europe. In twenty-five years of this period 75,000 additional men were levied. Foreign officers had to be paid far more than Russians, or they would not come. All these new expenses had to be met. The war of 1654–5 cost the same sum as the whole state revenue of twenty-five years later.

So far the Moscow government had relied chiefly on direct taxes, especially on the land. The land tax had been assessed by a standard area of cultivated land, but a good deal of this land had gone out of cultivation. The household was now therefore taken as the taxable unit —a step towards shifting the burden from the land to the worker. There were special taxes for special objects, such as the tax for ransom of prisoners, the tax for postal service, the tax for the upkeep of the *streltsy*; the direct taxes were ultimately united, to simplify their assessment. But the government paid increasing attention to indirect taxation. Already a number of monopolies had been farmed out. Monopolies were so much criticized that they were dropped for a time towards the end of Michael's reign, but later they were more and more generally used; the farming of taxes always led to enormous peculations over which there was practically no public control. Such were the monopoly of taverns, and the control of the customs. With the habit of smoking came the tobacco monopoly and, as in other countries, a favourite plaything of irresponsible financiers was the salt tax which, about 1650, was equal to six times the value of the salt. When the official Chistago was killed in the Moscow riot of 1648, his assassin shouted at him: "Traitor, that's for salt." In 1662 there were more riots, due to a fantastic manipulation of the coinage. It was decided to establish a forced currency of copper coins with the value of silver and issued at par, which led to a drastic depreciation and a huge rise in prices. Again the rioters demanded the surrender of those responsible, but they were suppressed by the *streltsy* with the usual sequel of tortures, executions, and exile to Siberia. Ultimately in 1663 the silver currency was restored, and the copper was called in at one per cent of its face value. These quick changes, however, were used to serve the interests of the Treasury, which made enormous profits by them.

CHAPTER X

Russia and Europe: Ukraine

[*1613–82*]

Wʜʏ was Russia driven underground? Why all this centralization, this large army, this increasing taxation, direct and indirect? The answer is to be found in this same period; but to have told the whole story together chronologically, would have been to leave the reader in complete confusion. Indeed the politician of the time must have been as much distracted by a succession of diverse and apparently unconnected events as would be the chairman of a council dealing with affairs of municipal government. The vast majority of the Russian people was driven underground because of the increasing difficulties, especially external, with which the government had to deal. We might ask why some period of tranquility and peaceful reconstruction was not given to the country after the Time of Troubles; but reconstruction itself was impossible without the settlement of external issues which no Russian government could refuse to face. One thing only went of itself, and that was the advance eastward through Siberia. Here, as elsewhere, Cossacks were the road breakers. Their manner of dealing with the various scattered groups of inhabitants which they encountered was rough and ready; and the advance, though proceeding regularly by the founding of towns and the settling of military colonies, was at times disturbed by disorders such as are incidental to frontier life, including among other things scandals in the field of religion and morality. But the Russians did not meet with any considerable or organized opposition. By the twenties they are founding the town of Eniseisk, halfway through Siberia; by the forties privileges are offered to settlers on the Lena, and before the end of this period Russia concludes with China her first treaty, for the restitution of territory close to the Pacific which had been more or less abandoned by China and settled by Russians.

All the difficulties of Russia are on the opposite side, the West. Here her advance is an uphill struggle, because she is breaking her way violently and with great sacrifices past peoples which possess a much superior degree of state organization, particularly military. Every step backward or forward alike proves to a Russian government the arrears in civilization of its own people, so long separated from the common life of Europe. This brings home the necessity of costly improvements which impose new burdens on the population.

Russia's struggles with the original obstacles that lay between her and Europe have only brought her face to face with more powerful foes. We have, for a long time to come, a struggle with Sweden in the north, Poland in the middle, and Turkey in the south; and already from the reign of John the Dread and through the Time of Troubles we have seen that each of these questions is constantly complicating the rest. Any success of Russia against one of her opponents tended to bring the two others into line against her; as Russia was potentially a far greater force than any of them, their fears tended to unite them, and it was only occasionally that she was able to play off one against another. This meant incessant wars and consequently incessant and ever increasing state burdens.

Yet in none of these three cases could the struggle well be refused. The Baltic coast, the principal objective of Russia's most enlightened statesmen, John the Dread, Ordyn-Nashchokin, and Peter the Great, was essentially necessary if Russia were to get close economic and political contact with Europe. The almost extravagant welcome which John had given to the English merchants was simply the measure of Russia's need of external allies, or at least of friends, to balance the combination of her near enemies. It was more than that. Archangel at first represented almost the only line by which Western civilization could make its way through to Russia to reinforce her for the struggle with her enemies. With Poland, the call to the conflict was nearer and more intelligible to all. On this side, it was the appeal both of nationality and of religion. The struggle with Turkey was only the sequel of Russia's own long struggle with Islam. While Alexis in Moscow listened eagerly to petitioners form the Orthodox population of Turkey, the Sultan in his turn was receiving in Constantinople petitioners from the large Mussulman population of the Volga.

Sweden, at the end of the Time of Troubles, was ruled by her greatest king and general, Gustav Adolf. As a fervent Protestant he was opposed to Sigismund of Poland, whom indeed his father had driven from the Swedish throne. Sweden had sent De la Gardie to help Prince Skopin clear the road to Moscow. But she put a price on her help, and her

troops entered Novgorod. Pozharsky, on his road to Moscow, felt it necessary to keep her quiet by dangling before her the possibility of the
election of a Swedish Tsar.

At the accession of Michael his title was in no way recognized by his
neighbours, and his country was overrun both by Swedes and by Poles,
as well as by Russian adventurers. While Zarutsky and his Don Cossacks
were being hunted down in the southeast, while other Cossacks were
beaten off on the southwest and still others were exterminated by the
peasants themselves in the north—Pozharsky had to be sent against the
famous Polish partisan Lisowski, who kept disorders alive in the west.
In 1615 a parley between the Polish and Russian governments came to
nothing because, in the words of a foreign mediator Handelius, "it was
like trying to reconcile fire and water." The war with Sweden dragged
on until February 1617, when after several futile attempts at agreement
peace was at last brought about at Stolbovo by the mediation of the
English merchant and diplomatist Sir John Mericke. The Swedish claim
to Novgorod was abandoned, but the oftentimes disputed Russian towns
on the Gulf of Finland—Ivangorod, Yam, Koporye, and Oreshek—were
lost to Russia, who also agreed to pay 20,000 roubles. The Poles invaded
in September 1617, under Prince Wladyslav; the Hetman Chodkiewicz
took Vyazma and besieged Kaluga and Mozhaisk, and in September
1618, the enemy was close to Moscow. Tsar Michael summoned the
Sobor, which made a vow to stand siege for the new dynasty. The Poles
were driven back at the Arbat and Tver gates and, passing northward,
for a time occupied Tushino. The Chief of the Dnieper Cossacks, Sa-
gaidachny, also took part in the attack on Moscow. Ultimately there
was concluded at Deulino near the Trinity Monastery, not a peace but
a truce. Wladyslav did not even resign his claim to the Moscow throne,
and Smolensk was of course left in the possession of Poland. The next
year there was an exchange of prisoners, which enabled Philaret, father
of the Tsar, to return and take over the government, and to remove the
favourites who had imposed on the weakness of his son.

In 1632 there was the habitual interregnum in Poland on the death
of King Sigismund and, partly at the suggestion of Turkey, the Russians
made an attempt to recover Smolensk. The army was commanded by
Shein, celebrated for his earlier defence of that city, but Wladyslaw, who
had at last been elected King, came up with an army and cut Shein's
retreat to Moscow. Epidemics broke out in the Russian force and it was
driven by famine to surrender. It was allowed to march out, but only
after paying military honours to the conqueror; Shein on his return was

beheaded. Ultimately on the river Polyanovka was concluded what was called a "lasting peace." The Russians cut their losses, surrendering the towns won by the Poles and paying 20,000 roubles; but Wladyslav this time resigned his claim to the Russian throne and recognized that of Michael.

In 1637, Don and Dnieper Cossacks on their own initiative attacked and captured the Turkish fortress of Azov. The Cossacks, who fought with extraordinary bravery, drove off not less than twenty-four assaults of an army of Sultan Ibrahim numbering 200,000. Urgently requiring support, they offered their acquisition to Tsar Michael. In January 1642 Michael summoned a Zemsky Sobor to consider the question; here any expressions in favour of acceptance were more than counterbalanced by emphatic protests from all sides against the ruinousness of the taxes and the tyranny and abuses of the Tsar's officials. Michael had already warmly disclaimed the action of the Cossacks in a letter to the Sultan in which he repeatedly describes them as brigands, and orders were now sent to the Cossacks to evacuate. They did so, not leaving stone on stone.

Michael Romanov died in 1645. He was an inconspicuous figure and after Philaret's death he was again in the hands of favourites. This meant more administrative abuses, and his son Alexis, who, like so many Russian sovereigns at their accession, was a minor, had early to face the riots of Moscow and elsewhere (1648–50) which have already been mentioned. He was at the same time faced with an acute crisis in the question of the Cossacks of Little Russia.

This region, populated mainly by peasants and by Cossacks was, it will be remembered, Orthodox. The Patriarch of Jerusalem had in 1589 appointed as Metropolitan of Kiev Michael Ragoza, a man of holy life but of little political firmness. The administrative direction of the Church the Patriarch had confided to Bishop Terlecki of Lutsk, of noble birth and a man of the world. At this time the Jesuits, who had succeeded in suppressing Protestantism in Poland, were trying to extirpate Orthodoxy too; and Terlecki, finding his position uncomfortable, thought of saving what was sometimes called the Eastern Rite, by bringing it into subjection to the Pope of Rome. In this he was backed by Bishop Pociey of Vladimir-Volynsk, who carried considerable moral weight. The most important lay-champion of Orthodoxy at that time, Constantin Ostrozhsky, was ready enough for a union of churches if it also embraced Orthodox Moscow, but was not prepared to follow Terlecki and Pociey. However, they secured the consent of the Metropolitan Ragoza, went to Rome, and offered the West Russian Church to the Pope. There were vigorous protests, and at the Church Assembly of Brest in 1596 the two parties met separately and excommunicated each other. The followers of Terlecki and Pociey were henceforward called Uniats. Accepting the headship of the Pope, they were allowed to continue in their worship the use of the church Slavonic language, and even their old ritual. They secured full exemption from persecution, which now raged all the more violently against those Orthodox who did not accept the Uniat compromise. It may be questioned whether the Pope gained anything by this bargain. Orthodoxy stood its ground against persecution, and Uniat peasants have been known to explain their position of allegiance to the Pope by the theory that the Pope, who after all had authorized their church language and ceremonies, had himself become Orthodox.

Those Orthodox who did not accept the Unia were only invigorated by the Polish persecution. There had earlier existed in Russia, especially in the west including Novgorod and Kiev, institutions called *bratstva* or brotherhoods. These were at first simply parish clubs. The members dined together on feast days, elected elders, made regular contributions, submitted to a special discipline and gave each other mutual help. They acted as friendly societies in the event of sickness, and the whole brotherhood followed a member to the grave; they also made some provision for education; particularly strong was the Brotherhood of Lvov, which had received a special charter from the Patriarch Joachim of Antioch. These brotherhoods now became the nucleus of resistance to persecution and were joined by many of the Orthodox gentry. The Jesuits were armed with all the modern weapons of propaganda; and the brotherhoods, which had the assistance of rich patrons such as Ostrozhsky in founding schools, now organized education as their chief weapon of defence. Particularly active was Peter Mogila (from 1631), at first abbot of the Pechersky Monastery near Kiev and later Metropolitan, who sent young scholars to Lvov and to Western Europe, including Rome. This vigorous organization of education in Little Russia was later of great service in raising the intellectual level of the Orthodox Church in Moscow.

Behind these brotherhoods stood the Cossacks of the Dnieper with their fastness among the rapids, by origin Little Russian and by religion Orthodox. They were absolutely fearless and, like the Don Cossacks of Muscovy, would sometimes compromise their Polish overlord by expeditions of adventure and invasion across the Black Sea. At the beginning of the seventeenth century, in consequence of the attempts of the Polish government to reduce their numbers, there were a number of risings of Cossacks in which they commanded the sympathy and the support of the oppressed peasants. These risings, marked by ruthlessness on both sides, were usually rudely suppressed, and in their suppression it was the peasants who suffered much more than the Cossacks. Roman Catholic Polish gentry sometimes handed over the Orthodox Church of their peasants to a Jewish usurer, who could then demand a fee for allowing an Orthodox baptism or funeral. In the wayward character of the Cossacks the one thing constant was a support of Orthodoxy and this, in the circumstances described, meant also the support of Russian nationality against Polish, and the support of the oppressed peasant against the gentry.

The Poles had succeeded in making the elected Cossack Elder subject to their Crown Hetman. In 1647 a Cossack chief, Bogdan Hmelnitsky, brave, able, and daring, was insulted by a Polish official and, obtaining no justice, fled to the fastness of the Zaporogs. Thence he went to the Crimean Tartars and returned with a Tartar army, which was joined not merely by Cossacks but by recruits from the oppressed Russian peasantry. In the spring of 1648 he completely defeated two Polish Hetmans sent against him at the Zheltya Vody and at Kherson; the two Polish leaders he took prisoner and sent to Crimea. Hereupon the peasants rose everywhere, incited by their Orthodox priests to a war of liberation, and everywhere Polish gentry were killed and their houses ruined. It was exactly at this time that King Wladyslaw died, and the usual interregnum followed. By the time his brother Jan Kazimir had been elected, he found all Ukraine arrayed in arms against him. Hmelnitsky had defeated the ablest and most ruthless of his antagonists, Jeremy Wisniowiecki, at Pilava, exacted a heavy ransom from the rich city of Lvov, and besieged Zamosce. Jan Kazimir ordered him to retreat, promising to send emissaries to conclude peace. Hmelnitsky did indeed retreat, but the vital condition of the peace proposed was that he should give up all his peasant allies. To this he replied: "The time has gone by for that. I will rescue the whole Russian people from Polish slavery. I am now fighting for the Orthodox faith. All the common folk will help me as far as Lublin and Cracow, and I will not abandon them." Bringing the Tartar Khan of Crimea to his help, he surrounded the King near Zborov; but by the promise of a large sum down and a yearly tribute Jan Kazimir persuaded the Khan to desert his ally, and Hmelnitsky had now to accept the terms imposed on him. There were to be 40,000 registered Cossacks; all others were to go back to serfdom; the Cossack Hetman was to have Chigirin as a capital; no Polish troops or Jews were to be allowed in towns assigned to the Cossacks, and no Jesuits where there were Russian schools; the Metropolitan of Kiev was to be given a seat in the Polish Senate. Hmelnitsky found it impossible to carry out these terms. He was expected even to execute those who disobeyed them, and he was himself attacked by his own supporters. He called in the Khan again, but was again deserted by him in front of the enemy and was defeated. A new treaty was concluded at Belaya Tserkov (White Church); the number of registered Cossacks was reduced to 20,000. Meanwhile hosts of Little Russians had crossed the Dnieper to take refuge in Russian territory. Bogdan had sent message on message to the young Tsar Alexis begging for help, and he now sent an urgent appeal to him.

Alexis was thus implored to succour a numerous people, Russian and Orthodox, oppressed by a Polish aristocracy. The Romanov dynasty had not courted this appeal, for the sense of its penury and weakness was always kept before it by constant signs of exhaustion in Russia. Michael, we remember, when offered Azov by the Don Cossacks, had apologized for them to the Sultan and ordered them to march out. But a new dynasty in Russia could not be less careful than the old, of that mission of reuniting the Russians which had been so vividly before the minds of the two Johns and of the spokesmen of opinion of their time. Alexis had his own grievance against the Poles; though they now acknowledged the title of the new dynasty to the Russian throne, they were constantly throwing slurs upon it. Hmelnitsky had begged the Tsar to send envoys to Poland to mediate for him. Envoys were dispatched in the summer of 1653. They first demanded that anyone in Poland who disparaged the Tsar's title to his throne should be severely punished; this was refused. Next they demanded that Orthodoxy should no longer be persecuted, that the Unia should be abolished, and that Hmelnitsky should be granted the terms of peace which had been given to him at Zborov; this too was refused. Hmelnitsky had offered to Alexis the allegiance of Little Russia. To have his nation behind him, Alexis referred the question to a Zemsky Sobor (October 1), and obtaining its approval, he dispatched Buturlin to receive the homage of all Little Russia. On January 8, 1654, a Rada or general assembly of the Cossacks met at Pereaslavl. Hmelnitsky, in a blunt simple speech, asked it to choose a sovereign from Poland, Turkey, Crimea, or Russia. The Rada declared unanimously for Russia, and homage was thereupon sworn. The Tsar agreed that the Cossacks should number 60,000 and should elect their own Hetman; the rights of the gentry and of the towns were to remain as before, but the Cossacks were to administer the country and collect the taxes. The Hetman might receive envoys, letting the Tsar know; but he must not communicate with Poland or Turkey without orders from the Tsar.

This of course meant war with Poland, a second round in the long struggle, which was to modify profoundly the positions of the two antagonists. The causes of Russia's comparative success are to be found in Poland's decline. The cause of this decline was the strange Constitution which had by now taken final shape in Poland.

The Polish peasants were almost in a worse condition than the Russian; they were at the full discretion of the gentry; not only could they appeal to no other court than their master's—the master was not bound by any regular procedure, and was free even to kill a peasant. The master's rights included full control over the peasants' labour, and no limit was set to his exactions. Beyond the regular corvée, he could parade them for extra work whenever he desired. They might not accept a contract, such as carting, for any other employer. They had to buy at his shop, to sell on his market, to repair their tools in his smithy, to grind their corn in his mill; he fixed without control the remuneration of their labour; they might not own any more cattle or make for themselves any more cloth than he prescribed. On crown estates, which only the gentry might lease, the tenant master's rights were practically the same as elsewhere. The gentry had a monopoly of the sale of corn and of export. Only they were admissible to the national and local assemblies, to any administrative post or to any of the higher dignities of the Church.

All legislation and administration was subject to the Sejm or National Assembly. It was preceded by a number of local Sejmiki or assemblies at which the deputies, or as they were correctly called, envoys to the general Sejm, were bound hand and foot by definite instructions. Of the two houses in the National Assembly, the lower, or house of country envoys, was dominant. Sejms were summoned with six months' preliminary notice, and ordinarily sat for six weeks. First were read out the *Pacta Conventa*, or constitutional limitations of the royal authority. All decisions had to be unanimous. Deputies corresponded with their local assemblies, at whose demand they would maintain an uncompromising dissent from the decisions of the general Sejm. In this case (*liberum veto*), the general decisions were not obligatory on them or their constituents. As has been truly said, Poland was not a single

republic but a confederation of an enormous number of diminutive
local republics; in other words, the State was constantly separating into
its constituent atoms. To meet such cases, it was lawful for either majority or minority to form confederations with the object of enforcing
their will on each other—a legalized form of civil war.

The office of King was elective. During the regular interregnum
established by the Constitution, the Archbishop of Gniezno was "inter-
rex." He summoned first a convocation assembly of the Sejm, followed
later by an election assembly. This last met on the plain of Wola, south
of Warsaw, in an entrenched camp. All members of the gentry had a
right to attend this Sejm, and came armed; a special court had to sit,
to deal with the disorders always incident to the election. The promises
of various candidates and often the communications of foreign governments in their support, were read out. Election had to be ultimately
unanimous. The elected candidate had then to take in person or through
his agent an oath to the *Pacta Conventa*. A further coronation assembly
was then called in Cracow, and only this put an end to the interregnum.
Even when elected and crowned, the King was no more than a chief
magistrate, hardly more than an honorary official.

In May 1654 Alexis marched on Smolensk. From the first, news came
in that several towns had accepted the Tsar as sovereign, and that others
had been captured. On September 10, after a two months' siege,
Smolensk itself surrendered. In the summer of 1655 Prince Cherkassky
defeated the Lithuanian Hetman Radziwill and won Vilna, Kovno, and
Grodno. Another Russian force, acting with Hmelnitsky, captured
Lublin. These enormous Russian successes met with an unexpected
complication. Charles X of Sweden, the brilliant nephew of Gustav
Adolf, was no less successful, attacking Poland from another side and
capturing the three chief cities of the kingdom: Poznan (Posen), Warsaw, and Cracow. Poland was nearly all occupied by one enemy or the
other. Charles already had about half of Livonia and Estonia; he now
intended to conquer Lithuania, where Alexis had been so successful.
The Cossacks, insubordinate to any sovereign, were always changing
their allegiance whenever they saw a hope of an easier or more distant
master, and Hmelnitsky opened negotiations with Charles. Sweden was
now much more dangerous to Russia than Poland; so, breaking off the
Polish war, Alexis turned against the Swedes. The Poles were glad
enough to make peace, and even promised to recognize Alexis as successor to the Polish throne, thus reviving the idea of a united Slavonic
world.

In July 1656 Alexis marched into Livonia and captured Dünaburg, Kokenhausen, and Dorpat; but he failed entirely in an attack on the strong fortress of Riga, and also against the small towns on the Gulf of Finland. The Swedish war dragged along, and on the whole the Swedes prevailed. At the end of 1659 Russia, greatly exhausted by her efforts, concluded a twenty years' peace at Valiesar, which was later confirmed without time limit, in 1661 at Kardis. Russia gave up all that she had gained from Sweden.

Alexis was driven to this conclusion both by the exhaustion of his country and by new complications. In 1662, in the riots caused by the depreciation of the copper currency, he himself was treated with as scanty respect as in 1648. Faced at Kolomenskoe with an angry mob which demanded vengeance on some of the officials, he was saved only by the ruthless action of his guard, by which some 7000 persons perished. Meanwhile, the Cossacks of Little Russia were giving more trouble. In 1667 Hmelnitsky died. His successor Vygovsky attacked the leading friends of Russia among the Cossacks, and treated with Poland. There was war between the two parties, and Vygovsky called in the Khan of Crimea. However, the Khan deserted as usual, and Vygovsky fled to Poland; Yury Hmelnitsky was elected Hetman and swore homage to the Tsar.

This renewed the war between Russia and Poland; but the conditions were now very different. A brilliant Polish general Czarniecki had by now recovered his country from the Swedes, and in 1660 beat a Russian army soundly not very far from Moscow. A joint expedition of Russians and Cossacks marching on Lvov was surrounded by Poles and Tartars. The young Hmelnitsky went over to the Poles and the Russian commander, Sheremetev, was forced to surrender and was carried as a slave to Crimea. The Russians lost in turn most of their acquisitions, Vilna, Grodno, and Mogilev. Hmelnitsky resigned and became a monk; and the new Hetman, Teterya, was sworn to Poland. However, the left bank of the Dnieper still held to Moscow and elected as Hetman the Ataman of the Zaporogs, Bryukhovetsky. The Polish king Jan Kazimir, after regaining the right bank of the Dnieper, crossed the river and won notable successes on the left bank, but was at last brought to a halt. A revolt against him had broken out in Poland: and the Cossack Doroshenko, who had succeeded Teterya as Hetman of the right or western bank, offered his allegiance to Turkey. This changed everything and gave Russia and Poland a common enemy. In 1667 the able Russian statesman Ordyn-Nashchokin concluded peace with Poland for thirty and one half years at Andrusovo near Smolensk. Russia ceded Lithuania but kept Smolensk and the left bank of the Dnieper. Kiev on the right bank was also conceded to Russia for two years.

This treaty marked an epoch in the relations between Russia and Poland. Nashchokin represents a new policy. Poland, he saw, was on the decline and was threatened by other enemies, Sweden and Turkey, who were also enemies of Russia. From this time onwards it was the policy of Russia rather to support Poland, of whom she was no longer afraid, against these other enemies. Thus to neutralize the central obstacle which lay on Russia's western frontier, was a policy which made it much easier to deal with her other difficulties; and this was the course to be followed by Peter the Great.

Ukraine continued to give Moscow unceasing trouble, and helped to bring more actively upon the scene the third great antagonist of Russia, the Sultan of Turkey. In 1665 Bryukhovetsky came with a very ill-advised deputation to the capital to ask that the administration of Ukraine should be in the hands of governors, troops, and tax collectors sent from Moscow. This may have met the wishes of the peaceful population, which suffered greatly from Cossack caprice and violence, but it was sure to make trouble with the Cossacks themselves. The request was granted and the deputation rewarded; but there was vehement opposition in Ukraine—especially from the Church, as it was proposed to transfer the Metropolitan of Kiev from the ecclesiastical jurisdiction of Constantinople to that of Moscow. In 1667 the Zaporogs killed a Russian envoy on his way to Crimea, which brought a sharp reproof from the Tsar. Doroshenko, Hetman of the right bank, offered to resign in favour of Bryukhovetsky if he would expel the Moscow governors and bring the left bank into allegiance to the Sultan. In January 1668 the two Hetmans agreed on this course and a number of Great Russians in Ukraine were massacred. Doroshenko now had Bryukhovetsky murdered and declared himself Hetman of both banks. The left bank, however, turned again to Moscow, and in 1669 elected a Hetman favourable to the Tsar. It was agreed that Russian governors should be appointed only for a few of the largest towns, and should not interfere in local affairs; the collection of the taxes was again left to the Ukrainians themselves. However, the Sultan Mahomet IV now claimed to be Lord of all the Cossacks, and in 1672 invaded Ukraine. Poland was torn by great internal dissensions. The Khan of Crimea and Doroshenko joined the Sultan, who took Kamenets in Podolia and turned its churches into mosques. Jan Kazimir had been succeeded as king by a Polish noble,

Michael Wisniowiecki, who made a disgraceful treaty with Turkey, ceding Kamenets and the Ukraine, and promising a yearly tribute. This treaty the Polish Sejm refused to ratify, the more so as the most famous of Polish generals, Jan Sobieski, was already checking the Turkish advance. On the death of King Michael, after some consideration of Tsar Alexis himself as a candidate, the Poles elected Sobieski. In 1673 Mahomet IV returned to the attack, and the Russians who had crossed the river were driven over to the left bank, which they managed to retain. Alexis died in 1676; and during the reign of his son Fedor II, the Cossack capital Chigirin was besieged by 14,000 Turks (1677). It made a stout defence and was ultimately relieved, but in 1678 a new Turkish army of 80,000 undermined and destroyed the fortress. In 1681 a truce of twenty years was concluded between Russia and Turkey.

Fedor II, son of Alexis by his first marriage, had a short reign (1676–82). It is notable for the final abolition of the system of precedence among the nobles based on a mingled calculation of birth and service, as described earlier. The young Tsar found universal support of his condemnation of this ridiculous system, which he described as "hateful to God, hateful to brotherhood, and destructive of love." Most of the old books of precedence were publicly burned. Fedor II also established the first college in Moscow. It had the pretentious name of the Slavonic, Greek, and Latin Academy. Its chief object was to train learned champions of the cause of Orthodoxy, and only Russians and Greeks were eligible as teachers. It was given rights of censorship over books, and the supervision of foreigners who had entered the Russian service; but its curriculum included languages and other secular subjects. In establishing it the young Tsar described wisdom as "the mother of kingly duties, the inventor and perfector of all blessings."

Throughout the whole of this period there was a steady pressure of facts themselves which forced the Russians to understand the imperative need of education. This was not identically understood in all quarters, but the need itself was too manifest to be disregarded. The Russian Church could not possibly support its role of the champion of Orthodoxy and of oppressed Russians beyond the frontiers without cleaning up its spiritual armour and defending its faith by those weapons which only education could supply. Claims of freedom of thought had been put forward in Russia itself as long ago as the heresies of the Strigolniki and the Judaisers, and once the faith was challenged it had to call in intellect to its defence. During this period there lived in Russia a notable Croatian scholar Yury Krizhanich, a man with a mission of uniting the

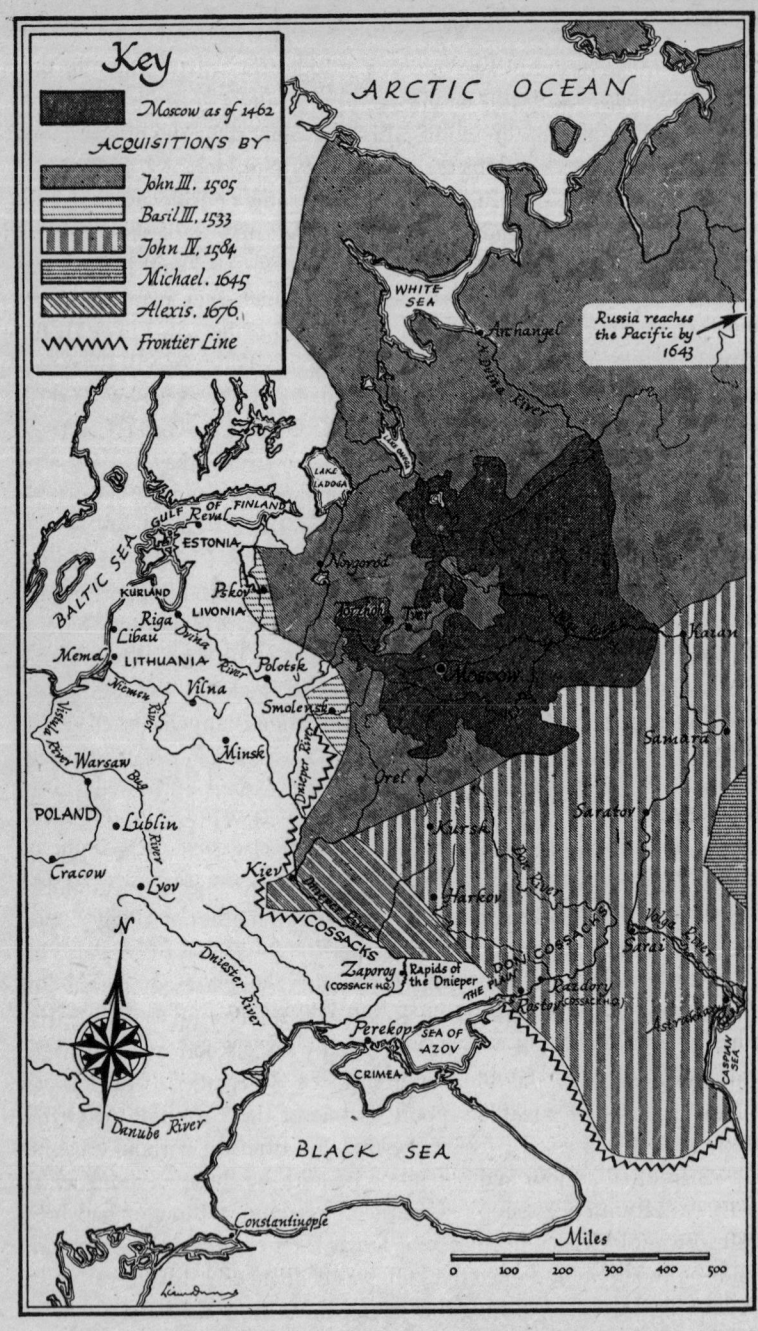

Key

	Moscow as of 1462

ACQUISITIONS BY

	John III. 1505
	Basil III. 1533
	John IV. 1584
	Michael. 1645
	Alexis. 1676
∧∧∧∧∧	Frontier Line

ARCTIC OCEAN

Russia reaches the Pacific by 1643

WHITE SEA

Archangel

N. Dvina River

LAKE LADOGA

GULF OF FINLAND

Revel

BALTIC SEA

ESTONIA

KURLAND

Riga

LIVONIA

Libau

Dvina River

Memel

LITHUANIA

Niemen River

Vilna

Vistula River

Warsaw

Bug River

Minsk

POLAND

Lublin

Cracow

Lvov

Dniester River

Danube River

Pskov

Polotsk

Smolensk

Dnieper River

Orel

Kiev

Bug River

COSSACKS

Zaporog (COSSACK HQ)

Rapids of the Dnieper

Perekop

CRIMEA

SEA OF AZOV

Novgorod

Torzhok

Tver

Moscow

Kursk

Harkov

THE PLAIN

DON COSSACKS

Don River

Razdory

Rostov (COSSACK HQ)

BLACK SEA

Constantinople

Kazan

Samara

Saratov

Volga River

Saraï

Astrakhan

CASPIAN SEA

Miles

0   100   200   300   400   500

GROWTH OF MOSCOW, 1462–1682

Slavs, who on coming to Russia in 1659 declared: "I have come to the Tsar of my race, and to my own people." He rendered great services to Russian culture, especially by his studies in language, which is the one great bond between all Slavonic peoples; and he urged everywhere such a training as would give to the Orthodox Russian more character and more self-reliance so that he could stand his own ground amid the general ignorance and servility which had made Russians so easy a prey to the Westerner. Kotoshikhin, who was insulted by a Moscow boyar and fled to Poland and Sweden, where he wrote a striking book on the Russia of his time, speaks bitterly of the complete unrestraint, suspiciousness, and above all ignorance of Russian society, of its indifference to any serious work and of the lack of any training for the state service.

But it was by self-evident state requirements, beginning with the army, that Russia was made more generally conscious of her need of the West. Boris Godunov had a German bodyguard; John the Dread had settled Germans in Moscow. Under Michael a Scot, Colonel Leslie, was sent in 1631 to levy 5000 infantry in Sweden. A year later six regiments were raised in Moscow and put under foreign military instructors. In 1647 a Western system of drill was printed. Gradually the habit of levying foreign troops offhand gave way to the practice of securing Western military instructors to train the Russian troops in Western tactics.

The question of arms and equipment raised that of research into the existing resources of the country. In 1632, 16,000 muskets and 6000 swords were bought from Sweden. In 1634 copper experts were brought from Saxony, and the mineral wealth of Russia now began to be investigated as far as Solikamsk (on the Kama), the Yugorsky Shar at the very north of the Urals, and Eniseisk, halfway through Siberia, a district which is one of the greatest treasuries of metals in the world. In 1632 a commercial company under the Dutchman Vinius was established at Tula, and this was the beginning of the principal state ordnance factory. In 1644 the Hamburg merchant Marsalis established a similar company in Russia. Though the first needs of the government were military, many other requirements were felt and satisfied at the same time. Articles of comfort and luxury were to be found in the so-called German suburb, now firmly established in Moscow, and possessing its own churches, school, and theatre. Velvet came into fashion; clocks had for Russians the fascination of a new toy; pictures and ornaments came to decorate the interior of Russian houses; the Court purchased comfortable Western carriages; painted glass and gold cloth were sought for;

stone houses became much more common. Investigation was extended into other fields than the military, such as Russia's forest wealth and her salt and alabaster. Harbours, as necessary for communication with the outside world, also received attention, and that of Archangel developed rapidly from 1670. Russia was a sleeping treasure house waiting for the magic touch of the technical sciences of Western Europe.

Russia began by asking Europe for the finished products of Western civilization, to meet the requirements of her state service. It was not in this offhand way that Europe had been able to produce these finished products, which had behind them a whole background of civilization. Gradually the Russian customer himself was driven backwards to a fuller and closer appreciation of what he really lacked. He began by asking for weapons and went on to ask for military training. He began by asking for clocks or any other fascinating machinery and went on to ask for technical science. He began by asking for ready-made books on given subjects, and went on to ask for education. He began by asking for knowledge and inevitably, however slowly, he was compelled to recognize the need for that training of character which can alone produce competent, self-respecting, and honest servants of the State. But this was an inversion of the natural order of sequence. He began by asking for the end, and went on with infinite inner conflicts and searchings of heart to ask for the beginnings. At each step his conception of his own requirements had to be painfully revised; and he would at times come to a dead stop, in fear that he was going too far, that he was losing whatever individuality he possessed. Further, all these things so necessary to him were to come from the outside, from the foreigner, and even then not for the people but for the State, for the top layer, thence only gradually filtering down to the middle and lower ranks of state service. The foreigner who came into Russia had, as a matter of course, to be treated far better than there was any need to treat a home-bred clerk or officer. He had to have a higher salary, European conditions of personal freedom, and a guarantee of free exit. This of itself provoked an instinctive patriotic revulsion. We have already the antithesis of Europe and Russia, of the Westernizers who wish to bring in wholesale what is so obviously better, and the Slavophils who fear to lose their souls in whole-'e imitation of the foreigner.

It is in this period, and during the process which we are now describing, that this antithesis becomes far more articulate; and it is to continue to the end of our story. Slavonic scholars who come like Yury

Krizhanich, to serve the cause of Russia and of Orthodoxy, tend to strengthen the Slavophil instinct of wounded pride and patriotism. "They fool us," writes Krizhanich, of the foreigner in Russia, "they lead us by the nose, sit on our backs and ride on us, calling us pigs and hounds, think that they are like gods and we like fools." And of the Russians he writes that "They don't want to help themselves till they are forced to, and are cheated mercilessly all the time by foreigners," that they are too easygoing, that they have no pride or spirit or sense of personal worth. That is what he wishes to see implanted in them—and every friend of Russia since his time has wished the same.

Krizhanich, putting the training of character before all else, emphasizes three guiding principles in his program—the authority of the Tsar, political rights, and technical instruction. The character of the reigning Tsar was perhaps more favourable to such a program than that of any other before or since. Alexis was a man of most lovable character, who would have made a most excellent constitutional monarch. His great desire, simply and plainly expressed, was "that we, great sovereign, and you, boyars, with us, may in one mind govern this people in the world justly and equally for all." He showed the greatest consideration for those who served him—for instance, where he writes to a father who has lost a child: "Of course you must grieve and mourn, but do not mourn too much," adding as a postscript the words "Don't be too sad." The grace and beauty of his character stand out in a remarkable letter which he sent to his Minister Ordyn-Nashchokin. Nashchokin, like Adashev, was of the gentry; his promotion was solely due to his ability; he was constantly attacked by the older families, whom he irritated both by his superiority and by his plainness of speech. At this time he was Governor on the frontier. He heard that his own son had committed the cardinal offence of flying to Poland. At once he wrote to tell the Tsar, begging to be relieved of his office. Alexis prefixed to his reply a long and affectionate form of address full of the most generous praise, which could leave Nashchokin in no doubt of his master's continued confidence, even before he got to the body of the letter. Having thus assured his servant of his favour, he says everything that he can to comfort him and his wife. As to the resignation, "What made you think of it?" he writes: "I think it must have been excessive grief. It is no harm to fall down; the harm is not to rise again briskly from the fall. God is really with you and will be always. Your son is a young man; so he will remember his nest and will soon return to it." To Tsar Alexis good Slavophils have not ceased to look back, as typical of the moment in Russia's consciousness which she has got to regain before she can make any steady and orderly progress.

The old and the new were not yet in desperate conflict. Alexis himself, without any sense of contradiction, stood between the two. He was sincerely religious, and he was sincerely enlightened. He invited as tutor for the children of his first marriage the learned White Russian monk, Simon Polotsky, who gave them such an education as no Tsar's family had ever received. Fedor II knew Latin and Polish, and Sophia shared the benefits of Polotsky's teaching. Three other scholar monks from Little Russia, Slavinetsky, Satanovsky, and Ptitsky, dealt in their published works not only with theology and philosophy, but with cosmography and anatomy. The sainted Fedor Rtishchev, friend and chamberlain of Alexis, founded in the Andreyevsky Monastery a school for the study of Greek, Latin, Slavonic, rhetoric, and philosophy, in which he himself spent much of his time. The School of St. John, founded in 1667, taught the same subjects with "other free studies." Other schools were the Spassky, founded on the Nikolskaya in Moscow for Greek and Slavonic, and the Slavonic, Greek, and Latin Academy. Matveyev, the friend and counsellor of Alexis at the end of his reign, knew Latin and Greek. Matveyev kept open house for a circle of enlightened friends; here the lady of the house entertained, and subjects of current public interest were frankly discussed. It was here that the Tsar met his second wife, Natalia Naryshkin, the ward of Matveyev and later the mother of Peter the Great. Matveyev also maintained a troop of actors, and Biblical plays were presented on the stage.

That these beginnings were anything but inconsiderable is shown by the fact that this period produced Ordyn-Nashchokin. We have in him a first-class modern statesman, as he was indeed recognized by foreign judges of his time to be; Klyuchevsky reckons him as the one statesman-minister of Russian history with the possible exception of Speransky. But what is most surprising is that his type is not that of the autocratic Chancellor, like Richelieu or Mazarin or Bismarck, but that of the liberal constitutional Minister, such as Cavour.

Coming of the gentry of Pskov, which always had a more liberal tradition than the rest of Russia, he rendered notable service during the rebellion of his native city in 1650. He was employed both in war and negotiations in the conflicts with the Swedes and Poles, gaining a good knowledge of their institutions and an intimate understanding of frontier questions. In 1665 as Governor of the frontier possessions, he set himself a task which seems almost an anachronism in this still medieval Russia, namely that of combating the German monopoly of Russian trade. He organized the Russian frontier merchants on a basis of mutual support and responsibility, which not only enabled them to hold their own against German competition, but gave them very valuable elements of self-government; such a system he later wished to extend to other parts of Russia. Foreigners, unless specially licensed, were only to trade with the local merchants of the frontier; they might not trade with each other, nor offer commissions to Russians, nor sell in retail; goods bought in Russia were freed of export duty; a commercial superintendent not dependent on the Governor was established at Archangel. In 1667 it was the statesmanship of Nashchokin that brought about peace with Poland at Andrusovo, and fixed the foreign policy of Peter the Great. This peace, he saw, would simplify all conflicts with Turkey; it made it much easier to protect the Russian Orthodox in Poland; he even hoped by this means to free the Christians of Turkey. He also followed John the Dread and anticipated Peter, when he urged that Russia's main attention should be given to securing an outlet on the Baltic. The Swede he described as the obvious enemy and the chief hindrance to foreign trade. Put at the head of the Posolsky Prikaz, the Foreign Office of that time, Nashchokin became for a period the principal adviser of Alexis in all affairs. The burning question between the incipient Slavophils and Westernizers he settled in the simplest and most incontrovertible way by his maxim "There is no shame in borrowing what is good, even from your enemies"; "With us," he says, pathetically enough, for his and later generations, "they like or hate a thing according to the man who is doing it." Everywhere he brought intelligence into the work of administration. He was opposed entirely to any deadening government routine which crushed out initiative and deprived the State of any chance of having intelligent servants. "They must not," he said, "be always waiting for a decree from the sovereign. Matters have to be settled by common sense, and often without interference from above," and again: "where the eye can see and the ear can hear, there one must make one's plan without delay." The competent servant for him was worth any number of incompetent ones; he says, for instance: "It is better to sell half your army and buy a military organizer." He, like his master, showed the greatest consideration for all who served with him.

He was the first to understand that it was not enough for the State to take from the traders and peasants whatever it might happen to require for its own needs, but that it must pay that attention to their welfare and needs which would enable them to produce. He was also one of the first to see the possible profit of Russian trade relations with Persia. It was this consideration that led him to make a beginning of a fleet, with the construction of a fine vessel christened *The Eagle*, which was unfortunately destroyed during the Razin rebellion.

Nashchokin dissented sharply from his sovereign when Alexis, keenly feeling the pull of Russian nationality and of Orthodoxy, insisted on retaining Kiev, in violation of the treaty of Andrusovo. On this issue the two parted company, and Nashchokin became a monk in a monastery near Pskov. He left behind him beginnings in every field of state policy, out of which was to be evolved the program of Peter the Great.

The type of Ordyn-Nashchokin was not to be repeated. That of Alexis was repeated perhaps more than once, but not under conditions which allowed play for its partly negative merits. Even in his own time, it was not a force but a phenomenon. Far stronger than the enlightenment of Polotsky and Rtishchev was the stolid obscurantism of the Muscovite Church, exemplified by the bishop who exclaimed: "Abhorred of God is any who loves geometry; it is a spiritual sin." Out of such profound conservatism it will take more than the gentle Alexis to shake Russia; and the hand that can do that will be no moulder of Russian constitutionalism. For the purely practical ruler, state needs will again assume sole importance.

And still there remains the yawning contrast between the two aspects of Russia's history described in this chapter and the last. Underneath, there is growing barbarism. Krizhanich asks for political rights just at the time when both political and civil rights have been taken away. The basis for peaceful progress does not exist. The Russia whose upper class is just beginning to open its eyes on Europe, is a Russia which, precisely in the interest of this upper class, has just legalized serfdom.

Certainly the contrast was felt from the outset. The Time of Troubles, the accession of a new dynasty, had set some minds at work, and there was a spirit of criticism in the air. Khvorostinin, a young noble of the reign of Michael, was one of the first Russian freethinkers and, though he ended in submission to the Church, is claimed as one of their first ancestors by the modern intelligentsia. Kotoshikhin continued this new tradition of criticism. And by simpler souls too the contrast between enlightenment and serfdom was painfully felt. Rtishchev made some beggars whom he found on the road mount into his carriage; one of his estates he gave away; in selling another, he diminished the price in return for an engagement of the purchaser to treat the peasants humanely; he set free many of his own serfs, and in his will, his one instruction to his heirs, was that they should be good to their peasants "because they are our brothers." From the beginning of legalized serfdom, we have the type of the "conscience-stricken gentleman"; and the sense of guilt for this standing iniquity, only the stronger for the conscious cowardice that dare not apply the remedy, is to grow into an obsession which takes the central place in the minds of the best of the gentry and of the best of their rulers.

St. Petersburg

(1682–1796)

CHAPTER XI

Peter the Great

[*1682–1725*]

Tsar Alexis had two families. By his first wife, who was a Miloslavsky, he had two surviving sons: Fedor II, who succeeded him in 1671, and John, who was evidently unqualified to take a part in public affairs. There were also several daughters who, in contrast with the two gentle-minded sons, possessed vigour and ability. Of these, Sophia was the most capable, but Martha and Maria were by no means without character. Alexis took as his second wife Natalia Naryshkin, the ward of Matveyev. The Naryshkins were a vigorous and fine-grown family. By this marriage Alexis had three children, a boy Peter born in 1672, and two daughters. Russia's recent acquisitions from Europe, especially in the form of military instructors, had greatly strengthened the German suburb on the east of Moscow, which had close contact with the Court. Alexis, who was all for instruction, had given the children of his first marriage a really good education, but Peter was too young to profit by it, though Polotsky wrote at his birth a court address containing the words: "The conqueror has come." Tsar Fedor gave him as his first teacher a Russian of little character or intelligence, Zotov, who was later to play the part of a court fool; but Zotov had only to teach him the elements of language, history, and geography.

Peter was only ten when Fedor died, but in mind and stature he looked more like a boy of sixteen years, the age of his incompetent step-brother John. The Patriarch Joachim and the principal boyars decided that as John seemed likely to remain incompetent, Peter should be the Tsar. The Zemsky Sobor as we know had dwindled to nothing; the Patriarch put the choice to a chance crowd on the Red Square, and Peter was proclaimed Tsar.

This, however, meant an inevitable contest between the families of the two successive Tsaritsas. Natalia became regent; but Sophia, who foresaw the nunnery as her fate, was in no way prepared to accept this

decision. She was a well educated woman and was one of the first of
those who broke through the seclusion ordinarily forced upon her sex.
She had friends among the *Streltsy*, or Palace Guard, officered and
partly manned by Russian nobles and possessing many privileges. With
the help of one of their officers, Hovansky, Sophia was able in May to
inspire a riot of the *Streltsy*. The Guards came to the palace declaring
that Natalia was ill-treating the boy John. Natalia spiritedly stood out on
the Red staircase with John and Peter by her side, and John told the
crowd that he was well looked after. Matveyev, who had been exiled under Fedor, but had now been recalled, calmed the *Streltsy* and came
back to tell the regent that all was well. Unfortunately some rough
words from their commander Prince Dolgoruky renewed the trouble,
and the *Streltsy* not only killed Dolgoruky but stormed into the palace,
killed Matveyev, and after a three days' hunt found one of the regent's
brothers whom they also dispatched. These events took place before
the eyes of the boy Peter, who maintained a wonderful coolness throughout but never forgot them. On May 23 a council decided that both boys,
John and Peter, should reign together, and the regency passed to Sophia.
There still remains the double throne with two small seats and a curtain, from behind which the regent could prompt a decision.

Sophia proved an able and enlightened regent. Hovansky, presuming
on his services to her, headed a disorderly movement among the *Streltsy*
in favour of the Old Believers (*Raskolniks*). These with their noisy
controversies disturbed the public; Sophia insisted that they should be
heard only in the palace, and they debated with her there amid scenes
of disorder. Sophia, however, acted with energy and arrested and punished the chief leaders. Hovansky now developed an attack on the
boyars in general, appealing to all disorderly elements; but Sophia completely outmanœuvred him. She went to the Trinity Monastery, summoned him to her and had him executed.

Sophia's principal Minister, Prince Basil Golitsyn, was one of the
most cultivated men of his time, and even wished to raise the question
of the emancipation of the serfs. Sophia's legislation made several improvements in the cruel laws dealing with beggars and with women.
In 1686 she concluded a treaty with King Sobieski of Poland, the saviour
of Vienna in 1683, by which Russia joined in a crusade of Christendom
against Turkey on the condition that Kiev, the mother of Russian
towns, which at Andrusovo had been ceded by Poland to Russia for two
years only and had never been given back, should permanently remain
Russian. Golitsyn twice led an expedition against the Sultan's vassal

the Tartar Khan of Crimea, and though the enormous difficulty of moving a medieval army through the steppes prevented any real success, he was at least the first to have carried the Russian attack across them to the isthmus of Perekop. In 1689 Sophia concluded with China at Nerchinsk the first Russo-Chinese treaty, by which the Russian settlers retired from territory which they had occupied on the Amur.

Meanwhile Peter lived with his mother under constant suspicion at the village of Preobrazhenskoe, near Moscow (the name of the village means Transfiguration). He was fine-grown in body and mind; even thus early he had an uncontrollable energy which kept him in constant movement. His mother left him in no doubt as to his position, and it was natural that the child's thoughts should centre around the idea of forming a kind of bodyguard. Since the Moscow princes had the right to be surrounded by large numbers of playmates of their own age taken from the nobler families, and could ask for such playthings as the palace was able to provide, Peter was often sending to Moscow for such things; but his playthings from the start had to do with war. He was from the first a born technician, a true son of that mercantile period of European history in which his life was cast. He could not get a piece of machinery into his hands without taking it to pieces and working it himself, and later during his visits to Europe he could usually tell at sight, from the look of an instrument, what was its probable use. Cut off, like John the Dread, from all education except that which he could give himself, Peter broke easily enough with all the old traditions of the Moscow palace. His training was from the first practical; most of it he found for himself on the streets and in the fields around the village. Constantly increasing his band of playmates, he drilled them into a little army, and formed among them many of the closest associations of his life. He was not far from the German suburb and soon became acquainted with some of its leading men: the Swiss Lefort, a man of remarkable versatility and charm, the dour Scottish soldier of fortune Gordon, the Dutchman Timmerman who acquainted him with the use of the astrolabe. In 1689 his mother married him to Eudokia Lopukhin, but the marriage in no way altered the course of his life and was foredoomed to failure by all his character and habits.

Sophia was now at last alarmed. One of her counsellors, Shaklovitov, urged her to kill not Peter but his mother; and five *Streltsy* were suborned by him for this purpose. Two other *Streltsy*, however, hastened to Preobrazhenskoe to warn Peter. Awakened in the night, he left the house on horseback, having his clothes brought to him in a neighbouring wood, and made across country on horseback straight for the Trinity Monastery, as Sophia herself had done when threatened by Hovansky. Sophia had already taken the title of autocrat, and had wished to be crowned with her brothers; in this, however, the *Streltsy*, whom she had sternly reduced to order, gave her no support. Peter was joined by one after another of the leading boyars, one of whom, Prince Boris Golitsyn, directed his cause with great discretion and ability. No woman had yet reigned in Russia, and Sophia's claim could not in the public mind compete with Peter's. John was cleverly kept out of the question. Peter had only to remain at the monastery and, one regiment after another, the troops joined him there, soon including all the foreign soldiers from the German suburb. Sophia herself tried to go to the Trinity, but was sent back. Then she sent the Patriarch, but the Patriarch did not return. Then Peter boldly sent an order to two regiments of the *Streltsy* under Colonel Tsykler, to come to him, which after much debate they obeyed. Next he felt strong enough to demand Shaklovitov, who was surrendered to him; from Shaklovitov, by the customary process of torture, were discovered all the details of his plot, and he was executed. Now Peter summoned the rest of the *Streltsy*, and they too left Sophia. There was nothing for her to do but to await his coming to Moscow. He arrived on September 12, and relegated her to the convent which she had so much feared.

Peter did not at once assume the power. He left the regency in the hands of his mother, who was much less competent than Sophia and was guided by inferior advisers. Peter continued with his sports, which were becoming ever more serious. He had discovered among the possessions of a great-uncle an old English boat which could sail against the wind. It was no fanciful instinct that took his thoughts to the sea. It was only by the sea that Russia could get direct contact with that European civilization that was so necessary to her, if she were to become a modern state; here he was only following in the footsteps of both John the Dread and Ordyn-Nashchokin. Peter set to work with this boat until he had made himself the master of its construction; before his death he was recognized as the best ship's carpenter in Russia. To get more room for sailing, he next built a little fleet on the lake of Pereaslavl, and finding that even here he was restricted he went in 1693 to Archangel, where he revelled in the open water and took lessons from the English and Dutch skippers who visited that port, at present the only one that gave a direct road to Europe. Next year his mother, to whom he was greatly attached, died. Peter was now sole ruler; but he did not change his habits or live in Moscow, nor did he displace his brother John the nominal co-Tsar. Peter himself returned to Archangel.

His first naval experiments however were to be on another side. Sophia's war with Turkey was not ended. On this side, too, Peter wished to get to the open water; and in 1695 he conducted a campaign against the Turkish fortress of Azov, which blocked the mouth of the Don. His flotilla proceeded down the Volga, and the expedition then passed over on to the Don. This suggested to Peter an enterprise which he never lived to complete, but on which he later expended much work: the making of a canal between the Volga and the Don at the point where the two rivers are closest to each other. Against Azov Peter brought both troops of the old formation and those which were developing out of his corps of playmates; the two villages of Preobrazhenskoe and Semenovskoe were to give their names to the two first regiments of the Russian Guard; he also made use of the Cossacks. He found, however, that he could not take Azov unless he could threaten its sea communications with Turkey. In the following year, after months of laborious preparatory work at his new wharves at Voronezh on the Don, Peter made his second attempt at Azov; and this time, by a vigorous blend of all methods and a healthy competition between his various forces, he was able to take it by storm. He at once set about constructing harbours on the neighbouring coast and launched a gigantic program by which the various classes and institutions of the country had to supply given numbers of ships.

His brother had died in this year, leaving three daughters; and Peter was now sole Tsar. His next step was to carry out a suggestion often made to him by Lefort, that he should himself go on a journey of education to Europe. An embassy was formed, with Lefort at its head, to visit European courts and concert measures for the crusade against Turkey, which was still contemplated. To this embassy Peter attached himself under the name of Peter Mikhailov. His real object was to study Europe and bring back to Russia teachers of all those arts of which his country was most in need; the crest of the mission bore the words, "I am among the pupils, and seek those who can teach me."

The start was delayed by the discovery of a plot among the *Streltsy*; the chief conspirator was Colonel Tsykler who had done so much to help Peter in the crisis of 1689, but was now piqued at not having more influence with him. By the aid of torture the various accomplices were discovered, and five of the conspirators were condemned to death.

Peter was now able to start on his journey. At Riga he pushed his way into the secrets of the fortress and received a rude rebuff from the Swedish governor, which he did not forget. He had a better reception in Kurland and Prussia. The friendship which he made with the Elector of Brandenburg was to become almost hereditary between the two Houses. This strange young man of enormous stature (he rose a head above any ordinary crowd) with quick and convulsive gestures, always in ceaseless movement, a barbarian in his habits, direct and practical in his insistence on knowing everything that was to be learned, and with that kind of genius which consists in extraordinary quickness of thought, left the strongest impression on all who met him. "He is very bad and very good," wrote the Electress of Hanover. He hurried on to Holland, where, outdistancing the official embassy, he took up his quarters at Zaandam, living in a cottage and working as a common shipwright on the wharves. His incognito was discovered, and the attentions of the street boys drove him to Amsterdam. From this centre he visited works and factories, picture galleries, anatomical theatres, commercial and other institutions, with the result that he enlisted nearly a thousand experts of various kinds for the service of Russia. Being told that the theory of shipbuilding was better understood in England, he passed over to London. He was assigned quarters in Deptford, which he and his companions left in a terrible condition as the result of their stormy revels. In London, as in Holland, his object was to see and learn everything, and engage experts in those subjects which the given country could best teach.

From London he went on in 1698 to Vienna, whence he hoped to visit Venice; but here he heard that the *Streltsy* in his absence had risen against him. Some regiments had been kept long at work at the new entrenchments in and near Azov; thence, in consequence of a threat of war they were brought back, without visiting their homes in Moscow, to the western border. Some of them went to Moscow and got into communication with Sophia and her sister Martha; the *Streltsy* certainly intended to depose Peter and restore Sophia to power. They were vigorously confronted by Shein and others of Peter's lieutenants, and when attacked proved to be no more than a disorderly mob. All danger of the rising was over by July.

Peter, returning on July 25, decided that in the *Streltsy* he would make an example of all opponents of reform. With the *Streltsy* he connected the Raskolniks, who were numerous in their ranks. The signal of reaction was for him the Russian beard; and he at once shaved with his own hands five of his principal lieutenants, and ordered that none should enter his presence with beards, on which he put a tax. The beard was only a symbol. Another symbol was the old Russian costume, which Peter replaced, especially in his army, with the European pattern. All this was only the preface of a series of terrible executions, sometimes of hundreds in one day, in which Peter struck down the first five of the condemned rebels and compelled his principal lieutenants each to kill a given number. The executions were preceded by prolonged torture. There was evidence enough to have gone to the end with Sophia, but she was allowed to live out her life under the strictest watch in a more distant nunnery. Martha and Peter's wife Eudokia, whose sympathies were also with the insurgents, were at this time compelled to take the veil.

In 1699 Peter travelled down the Don to the Black Sea. He was still occupied with the Turkish war, but already his thoughts were travelling in another direction. For him, as for John the Dread and Ordyn-Nashchokin, the most important of outlets was to the Baltic. This was no national cause; there were no Russians to reunite, no Slavs to liberate. The outlet was sought as an economic necessity and to make Russia European. At this time the Baltic coast was almost all in the possession of Sweden, which owned not only Finland but Ingermanland, where St. Petersburg now stands, Estonia with Reval, Livonia with Riga, and also Pomerania in Germany. This coast empire had been won by a succession of brilliant monarchs, backed by perhaps the finest army in Europe. After the triumphs of Gustav Adolf in the Thirty Years' War, and later of Charles X in Poland, Sweden had had a period of recuperation under the able rule of Charles XI, who had now just died, leaving on the Swedish throne a boy of seventeen, Charles XII.

This young man's boyhood passed in riotous practical jokes with night frays on the streets, smashing the shop windows, and even having calves and sheep driven into his palace to be cut down in bloody play by him and his brother-in-law and boon companion, the young Duke of Holstein. The governing was left to his grandmother, who meant to retain it as long as possible. The position of Sweden was a challenge to all her discontented neighbours. Denmark, which had claims on the semi-independent duchy of Holstein, resented its close friendship with Sweden. Pomerania, the fruit of Swedish victories in the Thirty Years' War, was an inset in the middle of Germany, distasteful alike to Hanover and to Prussia. Livonia and Estonia blocked off from the Baltic both Poland and Russia. To this explosive position the match was set by an able and enterprising Livonian noble, Patkul. Charles XI, wishing to enforce the royal authority in Livonia, had taken into possession of the crown a great proportion of the baronial lands. Patkul was the spokesman of the barons' resistance. Summoned to Stockholm, he saw his life in danger and, making a daring escape, carried his grievance over to the continent. It was he who instigated a coalition against Sweden. The initiative was taken by the King of Poland, August II, who was also Elector of Saxony. Denmark willingly joined. Peter, though equally willing, deferred his open adherence, and deceived the Swedes with a show of friendship till the moment when he was able to end his war with Turkey in July 1700. The news of the treaty reached him on August 18, and he declared war against Sweden the next day.

Meanwhile the other allies had already taken the field. Charles, on learning the danger, put an abrupt end to his amusements, returned to Stockholm, asserted his authority, organized his military resources, and invading Denmark and advancing to Copenhagen, forced the king without delay to an ignominious treaty at Travendal, by which Denmark retired from the coalition; this peace was concluded on August 18, the day before Peter declared war. Charles had now to deal with Poland and Russia. Taking Russia first and using his military position, which gave him a base almost everywhere on the south coast of the Baltic, he appeared in Livonia. Peter meanwhile was besieging the town of Narva. He had destroyed the *Streltsy*, and his program of reorganizing the Russian army on the European model was still only at its beginning. The covering Russian force was under a foreigner, the Duc of Croy, who had been lent to Russia from Vienna. The foreign generals had not the confidence of their Russian troops; the old medieval militia of Moscow was no match for Western opponents; supply, transport, and the medical service were chaotic or nonexistent; units failed to appear or even to materialize at all, and there was always a constant flow of desertions. The Russians were encamped without any regular military positions, and on November 19 in the midst of a snowstorm the fearless young king was upon them. The Russians had an overwhelming superiority in numbers, but once the Swedes had cut into them, nothing but isolated resistances were possible. Sheremetev, in command of the cavalry, could have enveloped them, but instead retreated as best he could across the Narva; a bridge which collapsed drowned numbers of Russians under the eyes of their enemies. Medals were struck for the victorious king, one side showing the flying Tsar, and bearing the legend "Tres uno contudit ictu" (he brought down three at one blow).

Nothing in Peter's career was more admirable than his bearing un-

der this defeat. Charles was not so much a general as a soldier in every
fibre; Peter was less of a general than Charles; he was by speciality a
military organizer. Indeed he could organize anything; but military
necessities he put before all others. Through all this period of his reign
the central executive was detached from Moscow; Peter's capital, for
the time, was the place where his headquarters stood. He could turn
his unbounded vigour to any immediate need which lay before him, not
losing sight of any problem connected with it, whether of near or of
remote importance. Reading his letters one finds little that is brilliant or
out of the way, but an absolute directness, a terseness which dispenses
with all delays in the process of thought and comes at once to conclusions which lesser men might have taken days or months to reach.
Peter was no theorist but an opportunist; each of his actions was dictated by a present necessity. All this vigour he threw into the work of
military organization. His tremendous will which, in spite of his absences, could not be challenged without open revolt, was applied with
the same nervous impact to every detail of military preparation, the
levying of recruits, the difficulties of pay, the collection of stores, the details of transport. Fortunately for Peter, Charles, after a short hesitation,
thinking that he could finish with the Russians at any time, turned aside
to follow into his lair the first of all his enemies, August of Poland.
Poland at this stage of her decline was something like a political quick-
sand. Polish nobles could be won over by honours or bribes, and a
Polish king elected from outside the country might be driven from his
throne. Charles had little difficulty in triumphing over August, or in
quartering his victorious army on Poland, on whose resources it lived
for several years; but it was more difficult to reach a definite conclusion,
to eradicate finally the party of August, and to finish with him, not only
in Poland but in his hereditary stronghold of Saxony.

While Charles was thus engaged, Peter spent the whole of 1701 in
skirmishes with minor detachments of Swedes, which were invaluable
in the experience which they gave to the Russian troops. If Charles'
Baltic coastline enabled him to leap out on each of his enemies in turn,
it was also an impossible frontier to defend in its entirety. It was the
coastline that had suggested the coalition; and Peter, though routed at
Narva, could in his enemy's absence set about conquering that part of
it which he destined for himself. The very difficulties of his allies left him
a free hand. He therefore sent Sheremetev into Ingermanland, Estonia,
and Livonia. At the end of 1701 Sheremetev won at Eristfer his first
pitched battle against a considerable Swedish force, and in the summer

of 1702 was again victorious at Hummelshof. In Livonia the Swedes by now held no more than the fortresses, and Peter resorted to the brutal but effective expedient of introducing Bashkirs, Kalmyks, and other Asiatic nomads and so devastating the province that it could not for a long time serve as a base for any Swedish attack. This process he next repeated in Estonia. Called aside for a time to Archangel by a threat of a Swedish attack, which proved groundless, Peter next attacked Ingermanland. Here on October 11 he stormed Nöteborg, the key position of the Swedes, at the point where the Neva leaves Lake Ladoga, on the site of the old Russian town Oreshek; this fortress he renamed Schlüsselburg. Proceeding down the Neva to its mouth, on May 1, 1703, he captured the small fort of Nyenschantz on the north of the river and renamed it St. Petersburg. Peter was very thorough in military matters; for the defence of his new town, which from the outset he intended to be his capital, he built without delay a fortress on an island at the mouth of the Neva, to which he gave the name of Kronstadt, and completed this part of his program by establishing a foundry in the province of Olonets, which was also to reflect his name, Petrozavodsk (Peter's Works). In the same year he reconquered along the south shore of the Gulf of Finland the two old towns lost to the Swedes during the Time of Troubles, Koporye and Yam; and in 1704 he was able to capture the university city of Dorpat in Estonia, built on the site of a Russian town founded by Yaroslav I under the name of Yuriev, and at last took the fortress of Narva. A Swedish flotilla attacked his new city of St. Petersburg, and Peter himself, serving under Apraxin in his own advance guard, took part in the capture of several of the attacking vessels. There are few instances of such firmness of purpose as Peter showed when he founded his new capital on Swedish soil in the interlude allowed him by his conqueror.

After triumphing over the Poles in the field, Charles, in spite of difficulties caused chiefly by his own masterfulness, succeeded in forming a Swedish party and summoning a Sejm, which deposed August and elected as king Stanislaw Leszczynski. Peter meanwhile in the spring of 1705 took the offensive with an army of 34,000 men. He conquered Kurland, Vilna the old capital of Lithuania, and Grodno at which the Polish Diets were often held. Charles made a forced march to meet him in the sharpest winter frosts; and in the spring of 1706 Peter only just had time to extract his army from Grodno, much of his artillery having to be thrown into the river Niemen. In September of the same year Charles, who had followed August into Saxony and quartered his army there, forced him at Alt Ranstadt near Leipzig to make peace and to recognize his own dethronement in Poland. August had made constant demands to Peter for money and help, and a Russian army under Menshikov was at this very time with him. He did not dare to tell Menshikov of the treaty, and even remained with the Russian troops when on October 18 they defeated the Swedish general Mardefeld at Kalisz; but the treaty was soon made public. By one of its provisions August had to surrender Charles' inveterate enemy Patkul, who was at that time serving as Peter's diplomatic agent in Poland; Charles had him broken on the wheel.

Charles was now free to turn against Peter. Leaving 10,000 men in Poland, he advanced with an army of 33,000, excellently trained, equipped, and provided. He made straight for the river gate of Russia between the Dvina and the Dnieper, while from his northern base in Livonia, Lewenhaupt with 18,000 was to descend southward bringing large supplies. Charles, leading his advance guard, entered Grodno before the Russian rear guard had left; the Russians devastated the country as they retired.

Peter tried hard to get his enemy to treat for peace. He was in the greatest difficulties. In this critical period he was faced with no less than four revolts. The Bashkirs, who had ample complaints against Moscow, rose in rebellion and threw the Middle Volga into confusion. A *strelets* Stephen raised Astrakhan in a class war against all boyars, officers, and Germans, on the cry that Russians were ordered to worship idols and that all the girls were to be married to Germans; to avoid this, a hundred marriages were made in one day, and the town rose on July 30, 1705, and sent to the Cossacks to ask for help; but Field Marshal Sheremetev after fierce fighting stormed it on March 17, 1706.

As usual, large numbers fled from the heavy taxation and levies of recruits to the Cossacks of the Don. At the end of 1707 Peter sent Prince Y. Dolgoruky to hunt them out and bring them back. This was a direct challenge to the principle to which the Cossacks owed their very existence; Dolgoruky captured 3000 fugitives, but the Cossack leaders sent out a general summons to resist; and Bulavin, of Bakhmut, putting himself at the head of the rising, surprised Dolgoruky at night and slaughtered him and his men. He was himself defeated by a loyal Ataman, Maximov, and fled to the Zaporogs of the Dnieper, whence he returned in the spring of 1708, spreading the same class war cry as Stephen of Astrakhan. He beat a government force and seized Cherkassk, the chief town of the Don Cossacks, where he executed Maximov. Other leaders followed his example and sacked Saratov, Tsaritsyn, and

Kamyshin. One Goly (the Naked) called "all the naked and barefoot" against the boyars. The rising spread northward as far as Tambov; but there was no discipline, and the government troops began to prevail. The brother of the slaughtered Dolgoruky approached Cherkassk, Bulavin's own followers rose against him, and he shot himself (July 1708). The revolt went on till November, and 2000 Cossacks escaped to take service with the Khan of Crimea. The repression was as ruthless as the rising.

Such was the position when Charles defeated the Russians at Golovchina and occupied Mogilev on the Dnieper. He had rejected suggestions of peace, saying that he would dictate his own terms to Moscow. From the Dnieper he was advancing towards the province of Smolensk when he was checked by a Russian force under Prince N. Golitsyn at Dobroe. Instead of forcing his way forward, he now took a decision which had a decisive effect on the campaign. The Dnieper Cossacks were even more turbulent than those of the Don, and had had a much shorter connection with Russia. Their Hetman Mazeppa, who had first met Peter at the Trinity Monastery while he was still in conflict with Sophia, was an old man of great ability and astuteness. Peter had trusted him through thick and thin. As late as this summer two notables of the Dniper Cossacks, Kochubey and Iskra, had warned Peter that Mazeppa was about to betray him. Peter summoned them, refused to believe their story and had them tortured and executed. The Cossacks were always in search of the easiest possible of sovereigns. They had turned from Poland to Russia, and had even at one time sworn fealty to Turkey. Mazeppa was prepared to join Charles against Peter. For this reason Charles turned aside from the direct road to Moscow and descended the Dnieper southward, at each step travelling further and further from his base. He expected to be reinforced by large Cossack forces; these were the most fertile provinces in Russia, and from this new base he would advance against Moscow in the spring.

On October 26 Mazeppa openly declared against Peter, and three days later joined Charles; but he brought only an insignificant force with him. Menshikov, with the Russian troops which had fought in Poland, stormed the Cossack fortress, Baturin, and most of the leading Cossacks declared for Peter. Even Mazeppa made overtures to him and Peter, hard pressed all around, was ready to forget the betrayal and even to retain Mazeppa in his former dignity; but Mazeppa after some wavering ultimately declared for Charles. In May 1709 Peter's troops had to take by storm the famous Fastness of the Zaporog Cossacks; they could hardly have succeeded, but that the Zaporogs took a detachment of

Peter's for a friendly force come to their relief, and sallied forth to join it.

When Charles turned southward, his lieutenant, General Lewenhaupt, who was bringing him reinforcements, guns, and stores from Livonia, was left exposed to the Russians. On September 28 they attacked him with vigour at Lesnaya. Though for the first time the numbers were almost equal, Lewenhaupt was completely defeated and lost two thirds of his army, with all his guns and stores. With the relics of his force he managed to join Charles on the Lower Dnieper. The Swedes, losing connection with their own base, found no recompense in the help of Mazeppa. They lived through one of the hardest winters recorded, and Charles, whose habits even in peace were those of a soldier on campaign, stood the hardships better than any one else; but by the spring of 1709 he had only a very small force left, ill-fed and short of equipment, to face the large army which Peter's efforts had now collected against him. Charles, however, advanced to besiege Poltava. When his chancellor Piper warned him that his demands passed the limits of human forces he answered: "If an angel were to descend from Heaven and tell me to go back, I would not." By July, in spite of a most courageous defence, the fortress was on the point of surrender. Peter now crossed the river Vorskla, which separated the two armies (June 27). The battle began at four in the morning and was over at eleven. A gallant Swedish charge threw disorder into the Russian right wing, but the left under Menshikov then enveloped the small Swedish force. Charles, who had been wounded before the battle, drove along the line exposing himself freely. When a shell shattered his carriage, he was carried by soldiers on two crossed spikes. His army was disappearing under his eyes, but he was almost the last to leave the field. The Swedish rear guard, hotly pursued to the Dnieper by the victorious Russians, was compelled to surrender; Charles and Mazeppa with hardly any escort, crossed the river by boats and escaped to Turkey. On the night of the battle Peter entertained the captured Swedish generals. "I drink," he said, "to my teachers in the art of war." "It is well," replied Rehnskold, "that you have paid us for our lesson." From the field of Poltava Peter wrote: "Now the first stone for the foundation of St. Petersburg is laid with the help of God."

The war lasted another twelve years after Poltava. The last years were mainly devoted to driving the Swedes from their last foothold in Germany. In 1710 Peter had little difficulty in conquering Estonia and Livonia and capturing the fortresses of Riga, Dünamünde (renamed Dvinsk), Pernau, and Reval. Thus he gained his long-desired outlet to the sea, with two valuable harbours. To the semi-independent Duke of Kurland he married his niece Anne, daughter of his brother John. In the same year he entered Finland and captured Viborg and Keksholm. Charles, who remained in Turkey, at last succeeded in stirring up the Sultan to declare war on Russia. Peter with an army of 40,000 advanced into the Danubian provinces but was surrounded by a Turkish force five times as large on the river Pruth. He only escaped surrender by the ability of his diplomatists, and as the price of peace, to his great vexation, he had to surrender his first conquest, the fortress of Azov. Charles could not get the Sultan to renew the war and was at last ordered to leave Turkey. When his house was approached by Turkish troops, he and his few companions entrenched themselves and gave battle, and he was only taken prisoner after exploits which cost him four of his fingers and other wounds; the Turks were glad to see the last of him.

Peter had meanwhile easily re-established his client August II on the throne of Poland; the old alliance was re-formed and the years 1712 and 1713 were spent in driving the Swedes from Pomerania. Here in the middle of Germany appeared a Russian force under Menshikov, to which was left the bulk of the fighting. Meanwhile, in 1713, Peter advanced further into Finland, conquering the two principal towns Helsingfors and Abo, and defeating the Swedes decisively at Tammerfors. In August 1714 the young Russian fleet, with Peter on board, won a signal naval victory over the Swedes at Hangö-Udd and captured the isle of Aland, which was only a short distance from Stockholm. Charles in this same year arrived from Turkey at Stralsund, but was not able to save the fortress. Stralsund fell in 1715, and the next year by the loss of Wismar the Swedes were deprived of their last footing on the south coast of the Baltic.

The next years were taken up rather with diplomacy than with war. Peter had in 1716 married another niece, Catherine, to the Grand Duke of Mecklenburg, Karl Leopold; and the marriage treaty contained provisions which were bound to alarm several courts in Germany and in Europe. Wismar and Warnemünde were to be annexed, not by Peter's western allies but by the Duke of Mecklenburg, who engaged on his side to put his country entirely at the disposal of the Russian army and to accept Peter's protection from his own nobles. In the division of the spoils Peter also favoured neutral Prussia at the expense of his allies Denmark and Hanover; and the landing expedition which the Danes were planning against Sweden naturally lost all its interest for them.

The diplomacy of the Europe of the new monarchies from its first evangelist, Machiavelli, was unscrupulous enough; and Peter, whose first resource against a hostile minister was to try and buy him, was entirely without scruple; but he lacked also something that was perhaps more essential; he had no sense of restraint, and this became more evident as he plunged further westward with his schemes. Sweden was mortified at the loss of her continental possessions. The Treaty of Utrecht, concluded in 1713, had left other malcontents, in particular Spain; for it had adjusted the claims of France and her enemies by a partition of the Spanish Empire. Goertz, Minister of Holstein, a restless and versatile schemer, passed into the service of Sweden and conceived the idea of uniting all the malcontents. Sweden was to seek compensation for her lost territory on the side of Norway, that is at the expense of Peter's ally Denmark. At the end of 1716 Peter and Menshikov were in communication with Goertz. Peter, without yet committing himself to Goertz's ideas, visited Paris in 1717, hoping to marry his daughter Elizabeth to the boy-king Louis XV, and perhaps to detach France from the Treaty of Utrecht. He had already begun to quarrel with Hanover; and it was part of Goertz's scheme to work for the expulsion of the new Hanoverian dynasty from England. The French regent, however, Philip of Orleans, between whom and the throne stood only a sickly child, was as interested as England in the maintenance of the recent settlement, and Peter's marriage project had no success. Returning to Holland, he had several talks with Goertz, and in 1718 plenipotentiaries of Sweden and Russia met at Lofö on the island of Aland. Charles XII invaded Norway; but he was killed by a chance shot, while inspecting his advance siege works before the small fortress of Friedrichshall. The Swedish nobles, who had so often tried to limit the power of the crown, were adverse to new adventures; they set on the throne not Charles' elder sister, married to his friend the Duke of Holstein, but the younger, Ulrica Eleonore, with her husband Friedrich Adolf of Hesse. This put a sudden end to the negotiations with Russia; Goertz was recalled from Aland and executed, and Sweden went on with the war as best she could.

The next year (1719) the Russian navy dominated the Gulf of Bothnia and a Russian army landed close to Stockholm, sacking two towns and burning over a hundred villages. In 1720 Russian forces landed again; and at last on August 30, 1721, peace was finally concluded at Nystadt. Livonia, which at the beginning of the coalition was destined for Poland, passed into the permanent possession of Russia and with it Estonia and Ingermanland, on which stood Peter's new capital. Russia obtained also part of Karelia and part of Finland. Peter never intended to retain the whole of Finland, and had conquered it in order to have something to bargain with.

The conclusion of the treaty was followed by a series of celebrations in St. Petersburg, accompanied by the usual great drinking bouts of which Peter and his companions were so fond. In November, on the initiative of Bishop Theophan Prokopovich, one of the few churchmen who had supported Peter throughout, he was hailed by the name of Peter the Great; and the title of Emperor (Imperator) was conferred on him and his successors.

In the long struggle Peter had proved completely victorious. He had secured his "window on Europe," and he had driven the Swedes from the continent. Russia had now no political obstacle in her way to prevent her from getting direct contact with Western Europe and becoming a modern European state.

CHAPTER XII

Peter and Russia

[*1689–1725*]

THE WORK of Peter the Great in the reorganization of Russia was not based on theory; only in a business sense was it logical; it was defined by his character and methods and by the conditions of his time.

Peter lived fifty-three years and was Tsar for forty-three. From the beginning to the end he was bursting with inexhaustible and almost intolerable energy. His extraordinarily powerful frame was instinct with movement. He could bend a silver piece in his hand; he could cut through a piece of cloth waving in the air. His long arms swung as he moved, and his handsome but threatening face sometimes twitched with convulsions; he was like a moving thunderbolt.

He hated Moscow, and left it almost for ever before he came to power; it was only at the end of his reign that he had a new capital in St. Petersburg. He moved rapidly all over the empire and visited in the course of his life Germany, Denmark, Holland, England, France, and Austria. Whether at home or abroad, every stay on his march had a purpose, often several purposes. On his visits, though they were so often prescribed by military needs, he did not lose sight of any economic question which affected the region in which he was. At home, if he can be said to have had a home, he preferred simple quarters and lived in the simplest clothes, patched by his second wife and her daughters; in the wilds of Russia, whatever humble cottage in which he might stop became the Palace. The peasants said of him: "He works harder than any muzhik."

His helpers were not distinguished by brilliance, still less by independence of character; they were the men who could most effectively carry out his orders. His letters to them were very human; he always recognized that a good agent must be given a free hand according to the circumstances with which he had to deal. His will was for them so absolute, that he could afford to fill his racy correspondence with mocking allusions to past drinking bouts, to address Prince Romodanovsky as his

king, and to sign himself with pseudonyms or with some depreciatory
diminutive of his Christian name. There was no question whether he
would be obeyed. Menshikov, to whom he delegated his most important
commissions of all, he would strike roughly in the face. When he was
furious, a sentry would be placed at the door to prevent anyone from
approaching, while his wife Catherine, the only person who could calm
him, would sit stroking his shaking head, and his courtiers waited with
terror for the moment when they could speak to him with safety. The
complaint of his unhappy son Alexis was that it was impossible for his
father to sit doing nothing.

Peter was first of all a mechanician. His first toys were pieces of machinery. He not only shaved his courtiers' beards; he was his own court
dentist and kept in a little bag the teeth which he had extracted; but
the object to which he applied all his technical knowledge was the possession and extension of power. For success he needed not only an army
in the field; he must take infinite care over every detail of training, equipment, clothing, commissariat, transport, stores, recruiting, finance, and
administration. To the subject of stores he would apply the same tremendous vigour and severity of purpose as to the conduct of his armies.
Having himself the fewest of needs, he was a ruthless economist.

It would be a great mistake to think that his reforms were in any
sense doctrinaire. On the contrary, with his genius for affairs, he was essentially an opportunist, and his drastic changes were dictated and modified from time to time by the various pressing necessities which he had
to face. He did not jump at conclusions; it is true, he arrived at them at
a pace not possible for lesser men; but for all that all his reforms were
born of experience. It was his signal quality to get to the root of a matter
at once. He sees at once what is needed and does all that is needed to
get it done.

Up to the battle of Poltava in 1709, he was absorbed in the immediate demands of his struggle against Charles XII. One forgets that
the war itself went on for twelve years after that, while Peter was pushing home his victory to the full; and after the Treaty of Nystadt, he engaged in a war with Persia which brought him some new territory; in all
during his long reign there were not two years of peace. But in these last
years he had time to think under less urgent pressure; Prince V. Dolgoruky urged on him the importance of reform at home; and Peter dates
his active attention to internal questions from the end of the feasts
which were held to celebrate the victory of Poltava. Nearly all his great
reforms were made in this period and the majority of them in the last

half of it, say between 1717 and 1725. At this time it was as if his mind travelled backwards to origins and causes, as if his hand gradually felt itself in to the root of each question with which he had had to deal. Measures of expediency adopted during the war gradually filled out, as it were, into precise and systematic legislation; matters attended to so far by patching were now put into final order.

Reform, like every other activity of Peter the Great, grew out of the needs of his army. The army he needed to hold his own against the superior civilization of Europe and to win him the outlet which would enable him to repair his inferiority. Peter found a disorderly medieval levy, of which the provisioning was left practically to chance. As wars were incessant, it had the evils of a standing army without its organization. It was almost worthless against European troops; it had no commissariat, very inadequate artillery, and no medical service. The élite of the army had been the *Streltsy*, and these regiments were violently destroyed by Peter only two years before his rout at Narva. He already had many foreign officers; and several units had been trained by foreigners, including the regiments of his "playmates." In the course of his reign the whole army was put on the territorial basis of modern conscription. Every province had to recruit, clothe, quarter, and pay for such military units as were assigned to it. Peter had thought much about demobilization, but found no better basis for a peace footing than to quarter the army permanently on the population. This was an enormous new burden. The old national militia had at least had strong local ties; with Peter the new regular army became more and more professional. It loomed large in the life of the provinces, helping to extinguish individual and local spirit. The crushing impositions of Peter's reign drove ever larger numbers into opposition and lawlessness; throughout there were strong bands of robbers well organized and equipped, who made open attacks on towns and seized government funds, sometimes killing squires and officials. It was natural, often inevitable, that the regular army should be employed to preserve public order; and the local commander came to have a territorial authority even in times of peace. Squires evaded the order to provide quarters by handing over to the troops the dwellings of their peasants; in every way the new army lay like a dead weight on the population.

Especially heavy was the burden of recruiting. During the war Peter scraped up every man that he could, using any and every means. His officers recruited peasant cultivators and servants of squires. Volunteers were accepted from both of these classes, though later the squire was allowed to send a substitute for a peasant who was wanted for the land. The army was doubled and even trebled. Thirty thousand recruits were taken yearly throughout the war. In particular, Peter laid his heavy hand on all that social ooze which one way or another escaped classification, for instance, sons of priests, the remainder of the old classes of house slaves or retainers, peasants who had been set free by their masters and, above all, fugitives from their masters' estates. It can be imagined what kind of material he had for the first years of the war. At the front there was ordinarily a terrible leakage by casualties, epidemics and, most of all, by desertions. But the elements of a regular army were at last obtained, and it was trained throughout on the new model.

Putting all these new obligations on the working classes, Peter was no less rigorous with the gentry. It will be remembered that most of the old books of precedence, which made birth pre-eminent over efficiency, were publicly burned under his step-brother and predecessor Fedor II. Peter now went to the opposite extreme. In future birth was to count for absolutely nothing, rank was to be given according to efficiency, and rank alone was to define a man's status in society. All officers became gentry. Peter completed the formation of a huge and motley service class of various origins swamping the remains of the old nobility. It was a vast new corporation, not dissimilar to that which much earlier had become the ruling class in Poland, and it is significant that the name of that class—*szlachta*—was in Peter's time used to describe the gentry of Russia. State service was compulsory for all. A table of ranks was drawn up in three parallel columns representing respectively the military, the civil, and the court services, in which the grades corresponded throughout. Those in the first eight grades automatically became gentry. Peter had his hand on the children of the gentry from the age of ten, when their names had to be reported; and the adult gentry were required to present themselves for periodical reviews. The punishment for absence was the loss of all civil rights; defaulters could not invoke government protection against robbery.

The gentry were required not only to serve but also to train themselves for service. Education became obligatory for the whole class. This does not mean that education was provided for all. By Peter's orders, schools were to be established in all the chief provincial towns; the curriculum was modern and utilitarian; it included reading, writing, arithmetic, geometry, and fortification. It was only by incessant threats that even a beginning in this program could be achieved. Where the schools did exist, the gentry evaded in every way sending their children to them.

In more than one case students fled from school wholesale; but Peter
was inexorable. For marriages of the gentry a certificate of education
was made compulsory. Meanwhile Peter throughout his reign, while im-
porting wholesale his experts of every kind from Europe, was sending
young Russians abroad to study every subject from philosophy to
cookery. As his pet interest was his infant navy, a particularly large proportion of these scholars were trained in Holland, England, and Venice
in shipbuilding and navigation, but there was hardly a country in Europe
to which Peter did not send some of them; some were even sent to
Turkey. To stabilize the country estates, which were further subdivided
with each new generation, Peter introduced the principle that one son
should be the sole owner. This son did not need to be the eldest; the
parent was free to choose. While the favourite son received the real
property, the movables were divided between all. The juniors were thus
compelled to seek some career in the public service. This law of Peter
was ill defined, led to many family quarrels, and did not long outlive
him.

For the merchant class the changes made by Peter were not so precise. Under Moscow, the merchants had been regarded as peculiarly
responsible for the financing of the State; and representatives of this
class had charge of the collection of taxes. Peter demanded everywhere
respect for the trading class. Except for Ordyn-Nashchokin, he was
practically the first Russian to understand that while the State so enormously increased the burdens which it put upon the population, it was
imperative to take every possible step to increase the productivity of the
country. He himself had a thorough and far-sighted understanding of
economic questions.

The works for the Volga-Don canal had to be abandoned because
of the great natural difficulties; but toward the end of his reign Peter
was successful in giving an excellent start to the canal system of Russia,
a task in which he himself took the most intimate part. He sent scientific
commissions to study the resources of different areas, and at the end of
his reign explorers sent by him investigated the far corners of the empire, as far as the Bering Straits. He was peculiarly careful of the uses
to which by-products could be put; measures of his dealt with the exploitation of peat and potash. Peter was the founder of Russian industry.
He conceived it as a national need and pushed it forward with all the
authority and initiative of the State. For a given state need, for instance
army cloth or—even more essential—the exploitation of metals, he
would form offhand a ready-made company composed of men of all

classes, Russians or foreigners, would grant them a subsidy, give them a government loan, exempt them for so many years from taxation and supply them with free labour by the simple expedient of making them absolute masters of all the peasants in a given area. The peasants were not consulted in the matter, and were left at the unfettered disposal of their new employers. For the employers themselves this was a state service which they were not allowed to escape or to question.

In his ardour for the development of Russian industry, Peter thought it essential to give some measure of self-government to the merchant class. He made in succession several experiments. In 1699 he instituted *burmistry* (burgomasters) elected from the merchants and holding office two months at a time. He then established at Moscow a Ratusha, or Rathaus, an assembly with something of an elective basis, possessing jurisdiction both administrative and judicial over local affairs. In the smaller towns he introduced *burmistry* and, applying the principles of the well-known Magdeburg Right, which had passed from medieval Germany into Poland and Lithuania, he exempted the elected town authorities from the jurisdiction of the provincial voevode. His new institutions in the capital he replaced later by a *Magistrat* (Magistracy) centred in St. Petersburg, which was to serve as the parent body of a whole system of smaller magistracies throughout Russia; but this *Magistrat* had already much less of the elective principle, and tended to become a merchant aristocracy on a basis of co-option; it was abolished soon after his death, and nothing more was done for local self-government till Catherine II. Peter gave a further measure of organization to the merchant guilds. By a property rating he distinguished from each other two guilds; each possessed rights of internal administration and justice.

In the government of the provinces Peter made many changes. The old *gubnoy* elective system of local government had now only a formal existence, and Peter abolished it. He wished to make use of the elective principle for the local gentry, and when introducing his new state division into *gubernii* he provided that *landräte*, or counsellors to his new governors, should be chosen by them. But most of the gentry, especially in the middle ages of government service, had been absorbed into the army and the central administration, and those that remained showed no interest in the right that was offered them, so that the *landräte* became nothing more than superfluous officials at the cost of the State. For all that, we must recognize that they were a beginning of that corporate organization of the gentry which was to be carried so much further by Catherine II.

Peter divided Russia into eight, and later into ten, *gubernii*. His reason was that in his travels he had found no local initiative; the authorities were always awaiting orders from Moscow; he himself mobilized all resources for the time on to the local problem with which he was dealing, and he desired to make this easier in future by establishing strong local representatives of the central government. The new *gubernii* were huge in extent; each included several of the older provinces; these last remained under the old authority of the voevode. In *gubernii* near the frontier, authority was vested in a governor general, while in the interior the title was that of governor. Peter had another administrative unit which obtained for financial purposes and which tended to cut across other divisions; it was that of the *dolya* or portion, reckoned always as a certain number of households (5524) and therefore varying enormously in extent according to the density of the population: these divisions were based on means of communication and the requirements of the government. Later the number of the *gubernii* came to be greatly extended; and the smaller units contained in them were known officially by a name employed more vaguely in earlier times—*uyezd* (district). At the outset one *landrat* was to control each district; and two *landräte* were always on service with the governor to act as a check upon him; the governor acted only as their chairman, with a double vote. Soon, however, authority came to be vested in the governor alone. Peter saw more clearly than his predecessors the necessity of separating the administrative authority from the judicial, but he did not achieve this object. For two separate staffs of officials his means were too limited; and, in particular, his stock of capable officials was too small. By the force of things, the administration continued to have a complete hold over local justice.

Peter also made a complete transformation in the central institutions. From the earliest times the Grand Princes and the Tsars of Moscow had been surrounded by a Duma or Council of Boyars, in which seniority was very closely defined; there were magnates; there were intermediate nobles; there were gentry whose services had merited this promotion; and there were also, although not entitled to vote, trained clerks who exercised great influence over the proceedings. Hating Moscow and nearly always absent from it, having comparatively nothing in common with his boyars, Peter while on campaign at first did all the business of state through a small commission appointed out of the Duma which he called the "Intimate Chancellery." This was no more than an office for carrying into effect the various commands which Peter sent from his place of work, usually of a purely practical kind. In course of time Peter found it necessary to organize a regular standing office in the capital. This was called the Senate. Composed at first of ten members, it was no more than a clearing house. It had no state authority except as representative of the sovereign; it was not at first regarded by him as consultative; and its business, like that of the Intimate Chancellery, was purely practical. But with the development of Peter's requirements, and especially from the time when he began to give closer attention to home affairs, the Senate increased in importance and authority. Where a permanent law had to be devised, Peter would sometimes in his terse instructions himself raise the question as to the lines which this law had better follow, and ask for the Senate's opinion. The Senate thus came to be not only the authority for drafting, but sometimes for deciding the form and even the purpose of a law, and it was collectively responsible for its execution. One function of great importance, which remained in its competence in spite of the many changes which took place after Peter's death, was that of expounding and interpreting the laws already promulgated. Judicial cases of first-class importance might also be referred to the Senate, which thus ultimately became the supreme court of appeal. With this extension of its powers, however, the Senate did not gain any kind of right to challenge the will of the sovereign. Peter treated the Senate throughout with scant ceremony. He fined senators for not doing their work; he put a sentry on guard in their chamber to see that they did it; he had an hourglass to measure their industry; he demanded answers to given questions within short limits of time; he appointed one official after another to control the Senate, first an *Ober-Revizor* and later a General Procuror, who could report the Senate to the sovereign, or veto its measures, in which case after a given delay the sovereign would decide.

Peter inherited from Moscow the old Prikazy, offices set up in a most haphazard way to satisfy administrative requirements as they arose, and often overlapping each other. In Peter's time there were already ministries in countries of Western Europe, but he did not introduce them into Russia. After consulting the philosopher Leibniz, he decided for the Swedish model of ministerial colleges in which no single person had an absolute control and responsibility; and he obtained from Baron Fick a project along these lines. Peter had very few, if any, lieutenants on whose ability and honesty he could rely; and he had to fit into his scheme the foreign experts whom Russian ignorance made indispensable. Each college had a president; two vice-presidents, one of whom was a foreigner;

four councillors, of whom one was a foreigner; four assessors; and two secretaries, one a foreigner. All had to sign the decisions adopted, and take responsibility for them. At one time the presidents of colleges were expected to sit in the Senate; but this was found to hinder their work, and later the Senate kept touch with the colleges through their ex-presidents. In their jurisdiction and competence these new colleges were a great advance on the old Prikazy. The departments responsible for war indeed increased in number, but they were regularized; special branches were instituted for artillery, supply, and transport, and a college was created for the young navy. Other colleges dealt with foreign affairs, revenue, and audit; and entirely new organs of government were created in the colleges of commerce, of mines, of manufactures, and of justice.

On the same lines, those of collective responsibility, Peter completely reorganized the administration of the Church. The Patriarchate of Moscow had been founded with the full approval of the Patriarch of Constantinople. This independent church authority had proved invaluable during the Time of Troubles in restoring Russia's political independence. A Patriarch was father of the first Romanov sovereign, and another Patriarch, Nikon, was for some time the counsellor of Tsar Alexis. It was the Patriarch Joachim who had insisted in 1682 on the accession of Peter himself. Peter was a religious man; he enjoyed singing in the church choir; in his last illness he had a small church improvised in his cottage. But the Church was full of his opponents. The reactionary Raskolniks were of course among his bitterest antagonists; but even among the more liberal churchmen, such as Stephen Yavorsky, who boldly preached against his system of *Fiscals* as demoralizing to the whole population, few were in sympathy with his drastic changes. When still hardly more than a boy, Peter had been unable to prevent the election as Patriarch of the reactionary Adrian who denounced the shaving of the beard as heresy. When Adrian died (1700) Peter declared that the choice of a successor was so important that it must be deferred for full consideration. No appointment was ever made; and in 1721 he issued an ordinance by which the government of the Church was put into commission. It was to be governed in future by a Holy Synod, composed of the principal hierarchs; the Synod, like the Senate, bore the title of regent; it replaced the Patriarch. As the Senate, during the Tsar's absence or minority, was to have the regency of the State, so was the Synod to act permanently in affairs of the Church. To the Synod Peter attached an office held by a layman, that of *Ober-Procuror*, whom Peter himself described as the "Tsar's eye"—he was there to see that the Synod did nothing displeasing to the sovereign. Thus began a secularization of the church authority, which was to have fatal results later. That resistance was not more pronounced, that public opinion did not condemn Peter even more than it did, was largely due to the deadness which was creeping over the Church itself. Peter in his drinking bouts openly made mockery of church ritual; at the marriage of the court fool Zotov, he and his courtiers went in procession through the streets of Moscow attired in church vestments and drawn over the snow in sledges harnessed to bears, goats, and pigs. The glorious ceremony and ritual of the Orthodox Church indeed remained; so did the sense of a spiritual church, especially among the peasants and, no doubt, among many others. But from the time when the official Church was enabled, by the lay authority alone, to triumph over and persecute the Old Believers, it had no longer the same hold over the life of the people. The substitution of Synod and Procuror for Patriarch carried further this process of demoralization.

Peter had established a whole network of new institutions which were very burdensome to the people. The collegiate principle of itself meant many officials to do the work of one; and each was costly. If the whole gentry as a class were to serve, they too had to be put at the charge of the producing part of the community of which the vast majority, the peasants, were deprived of a legal status. Unquestioning submission to the monarch is not a school of character; and the morality of the time was at the lowest ebb. Peter, whose own expenses were absurdly modest, used the utmost vigilance to impose honesty on his servants. With this object he created the *Ober-Fiscal* at the head of a whole system of *Fiscals* or government agents, who were to detect any financial abuse. The widest use was made of informers; delation was in every way encouraged; the informer was entitled to a quarter of the property of the person against whom he informed; in some cases he was given the right to the domains, rank, and legal status of his victim; the old law, which ordered that a false informer should suffer the penalty that he had wished to inflict on another, was thus entirely reversed. Even at the top of the system, the General Procuror of the Senate could not be punished for any unfounded charge which he brought against the Senate. The *Fiscals* filled the country with spies and demoralized public life, making subservience the first of its virtues; but for the repression of corruption all was in vain. The *Ober-Fiscal* Nesterov, a promoted slave (or retainer) who had high officials executed and hanged the Governor of Siberia, was himself in the end broken on the wheel for corruption.

Peter's endless repetition of laws on this subject made no difference, for the laws were not obeyed. As Prince Dolgoruky said to him, "In the end you will have no subjects at all, for we are all thieving." It may be added that the use of bribes abroad, which under Peter was one of the principal weapons of Russian diplomacy, was a not inconsiderable addition to the expenses of the State.

To meet all these burdens Peter imposed innumerable taxes and employed a number of financial improvisers, mostly of low origin, of whom the most eminent was the ex-slave Kurbatov, to find new devices of taxation. Among the objects taxed Klyuchevsky reckons stamps (an invention of Kurbatov), inns, mills, land, weights, hats, shoes, coffins, private loans (of which the government took 10 per cent), leather, baths, leases, cellars, troughs, stovepipes, scythes, fuel, sale of meat, melons, cucumbers, boats, and to close the list, religious belief (in the case of the Old Believers), beards and whiskers, marriage, and even birth. The arrears of these taxes were ordinarily more than half the sum demanded, and in some cases much more.

The financial burdens fell with particular weight upon the peasantry. Peter was far closer to the Russian peasant than any Tsar before him or since. Many of them saw him at close quarters and were familiar with his rough-and-ready clothes, his axe, and his pipe. No Tsar had had so clear an instinct of the good of the community as a whole; it shines through all his words and letters. Peter liked the peasants, he enjoyed being with them; he was a humane man when he had time to be humane; he was too able not to see the evils of the system which had been bequeathed to him. But a life's furious energy was hardly enough to do the task which he had set himself. His autocracy he never allowed to be in question, because by no other weapon could he force a torpid and hostile country to imitate Europe; serfdom he recognized as something which he could not replace. Therefore, with all his changes, he did nothing for the peasants. Much worse than that, all his new creations put upon them a burden which could not be borne. "The weight imposed," writes Engelmann, the historian of serfdom, "made the foundations sink deep into the ground." Take, for instance, the making of St. Petersburg. By order of the sovereign, no stone house was to be built in the rest of the empire till a certain number had been set up in the new capital. Yet St. Petersburg was built on a marsh. Piles had to be driven in for months before there was any foundation for the city. In this task all were employed, even nobles; but the main burden fell on the peasants. They were taken by forcible recruitment from their squires.

When they were used up, they were set free—in most cases to look after themselves. It was the same with other big public works.

The law which fastened the peasant to the soil also particularly forbade the squire to expel him from it. By a new law squires were free to take into their houses any peasants whom they wished to have as servants, and the connection between land and service was thus destroyed. By Peter's system of closely defined duties and rights for each class, peasants were forbidden to engage in trades. Crown peasants were not allowed to take government contracts, for fear of infringing on the rights of the merchant class. A peasant's property became practically that of his squire, and could be borrowed at will. The squire's court came in practice to be the only one to which a peasant could appeal; his steward saw to it that this was observed. The squire would have the village elder flogged if there were delays in paying taxes.

Most burdensome of all was Peter's new poll tax. So far, taxation had been assessed by land, originally by acres and later by farm buildings. This at least took account of riches and poverty; for land that went out of cultivation the peasant would not be required to pay. The tax was evaded in various ways; for instance, a number of households would surround themselves with a single fence, in order to count as one. Peter shifted the tax on to the person; his poll tax was a levy on each individual head. In order to levy it, Peter ordered a general census, which was carried out with the greatest rigour but met with such obstacles that it was hardly completed before he died. The tax on the person had at least one good effect. It made it the interest of each individual worker to cultivate as much land as he possibly could; and the area of cultivation was very considerably extended in the succeeding years. But all the visits of officials and punitive expeditions incidental to the levy were a great vexation to peasants who were trying against odds to pay their way.

In his determination to label all the undefined sections of the population lying between the interstices of the class system, Peter deprived of liberty the free cultivators of the vast northern provinces, such as Archangel and Vyatka, where, in the main, there had never been squires or serfdom; and these were all swept into the net of bondage. What they would have paid to squires, they were made to pay to the State.

The constant outflow of thousands and thousands who found life too hard to be borne was from this time perpetually on the increase. Peasants not registered in the census were regarded as fugitives, and fugitives were treated as criminals. Peter forbade the peasant to leave his squire's estate without a written permission which, if he went further than twenty miles outside the district in which he lived, had to be shown to a government authority and countersigned. Members of a peasant family had no right to travel except with the head of the family, who was alone entitled to a passport; persons without passports were regarded as fugitives. The most frequent of all subjects of legislation were the regulations for man hunts to recover such fugitives. They were ordained from year to year and were backed with the full government authority. Elders sheltering fugitives were knouted, and squires were subjected to fines so heavy that they could never be collected. Squires, on their side, defended themselves against the visits of government officials with arms in their hands at the head of their peasantry. Bands of robbers became more and more common, especially in the turbulent provinces of the southeast.

It is easy to imagine how numerous were the elements of opposition and how instinctive was the deep resentment which Peter aroused by his changes. The attitude of the clergy has already been mentioned. Both in the clergy and in the rest of the community one must distinguish, as far as one can, between the vast majority who were fully permeated with hostility and obscurantism, and that more enlightened section of the public which was all in favour of learning from the West but would have been happy if the slow growth of education had been continued under Peter on the same amiable lines as under Alexis and Fedor II. But this last section was almost as much opposed to Peter as the rest. It included many of the best of the boyars who saw their class drowned in a new motley ocean of so-called gentry, in most cases men from nowhere. It is true—as one of these boyars, Prince M. Shcherbatov, writes later—that if Peter had not bullied Russia into civilization the work which he did would have taken a hundred years, and would almost certainly have led to such civil strife as would have put the country at the mercy of some invading power. The question was, how much that was good was destroyed by this levelling hand. "Superstition has decreased," wrote Shcherbatov, "but so has faith," and again "how could there remain any manliness and firmness in those who in their youth trembled before the rod of their superiors, and who could not win any honours except by servility?" It was not so much what Peter did that gave the shock to the Russian consciousness, but the way in which he did it and the pace at which it was done. By racing against the wind, as Klyuchevsky puts it, Peter increased the velocity of the wind against him. The quiet man was everywhere affronted.

This instinctive opposition generally remained without open expression. In Peter's reign, it is true, there were four open risings, but mostly of Cossacks on the frontiers; there were three distinct plots, including that of the *Streltsy*, all of which were suppressed. But there was yet a danger, far more formidable, that threatened the permanence of Peter's work. How long after his death would Russia submit to his changes? Peter would die, and would have a successor. His heir was his son Alexis, the very type of the instinctive resentment of those who wished to be left in peace; and all the advantages of time were on the side of Alexis. In this deeply tragical story we get the closest picture of Peter's ideals and difficulties and of the passive opposition of the old Russia.

Peter's first wife, Eudokia Lopukhin, picked for him by a counsellor of his mother and married to him when he was seventeen, had nothing to distinguish her from the boyar's daughter of the time, and Peter's constant travels made ordinary domestic life for him impossible. His son Alexis, born in 1690, was left to his mother's care and nurtured on her grievances. After the revolt of the *Streltsy*, finding that in their wish to replace him they had thought among other things of his wife and child, Peter compelled Eudokia to take the veil and gave the charge of his son to his sister Natalia, whom the boy never liked. Eudokia herself, as was later discovered, threw off the veil, and though she could not leave the nunnery, had a love affair with another man. Peter, who was constantly in the German suburb, at first fell under the influence of a dashing young German, Anna Mons, but later formed a much more serious attachment for Catherine Skavronsky, of Lithuanian origin, who had at one time been a servant in the house of Pastor Glück of Marienburg, and later came into intimate relations with Menshikov. Peter married Catherine, who shared all his interests and some of his hardships, notably in the unfortunate campaign on the Pruth. Catherine set herself to act as a lightning conductor for Peter's outbursts of anger; not only Menshikov but many others made use of her good offices; she extended them to the family of Peter's brother John and even to the Tsarevich Alexis, of whom she appears to have won the sincere good will.

Alexis was not stupid. In disposition he seems to have resembled his grandfather Tsar Alexis and his step-brother Fedor; he learned foreign languages and read books. But his was a mild nature; any excessive activity was a burden to him; and he was entirely out of sympathy with the radical changes made by his father, especially those relating to the Church. Peter, who examined him in his studies and set him laborious tasks connected with transport and shipbuilding, demanded that he should throw himself into his father's interests, and tried to make him into something which the Prince could not possibly become, a successor to himself. Alexis, keeping his resentment secret, submitted to his father's orders, but in reply to his reproaches openly described himself as "your useless son." When Peter insisted that Alexis should marry a German princess whose sister was espoused to the Emperor Charles VI, Alexis only asked that he might choose among several princesses and soon reconciled himself to the choice of Peter (1711). He appears to have lived with his wife not unhappily; but she died after bearing him a daughter Natalia and a son who was given the name of his grandfather, Peter. It was at this point that Peter, in an "announcement to my son" (1715), ordered him to choose whether he would throw himself into his father's work or resign the throne and enter a monastery. Alexis wished to resign and live in the country, but Peter would not tolerate any indefinite position. Alexis at first expressed himself as willing to take the vows. As his counsellor Kikin said to him, "The cowl will not be nailed to your head." When he avowed to his confessor that he sometimes wished his father's death, the confessor replied: "Why, so do we all." Peter left some months for his decision and then wrote from Holland, demanding an immediate reply. Alexis was either to name the date at which he would leave Russia to join his father or name the date and place of taking the vows. Consulting with Kikin, Alexis decided to use the opportunity to escape from Russia but not to join his father, and when he had passed the frontier he made his way to Vienna and asked for the protection of the Emperor Charles VI (November 1716).

Charles behaved with great consideration. He realized that Peter would be furious at this exposure of his domestic troubles before all Europe, but he did not give up Alexis. He kept his presence in Vienna quiet and smuggled him away to the Castle of Ehrenberg in Tyrol. Here he was run to ground by Peter's agents, and when the Emperor had him moved to the Castle of St. Elmo at Naples, his pursuers tracked him thither. Peter meanwhile almost threatened the Emperor with war, but Charles would only agree to Alexis' return if it were by his own consent. Tolstoy, admitted to the fortress, executed Peter's commission pitilessly and with great ability, assuring the Prince that Peter would make war to recover him, and using other means to frighten or perplex him. Alexis agreed to return on two conditions: he asked leave to marry a peasant girl Afrosyna, who had followed him on his wanderings, and to live in the country; the throne he was perfectly willing to renounce. Peter agreed to these terms, and Alexis returned to Russia. Here he made a solemn renunciation in the Cathedral of the Assumption at Moscow, and publicly received Peter's pardon (February 13, 1718). But an examination of the accomplices of his flight, in particular of Kikin, began to make it clear that the question went much deeper than any inefficiency or unwillingness on the part of Alexis. The Tsarevich had become the centre of hope for all the disaffected, and the confessions of his friends put a more and more serious complexion on his own conduct. Ultimately he himself confessed that he had expected to be summoned to Mecklenburg during a mutiny of the Russian troops and would perhaps have been prepared to go there if the mutineers had killed Peter, or had proved strong enough to resist him. In further avowals he confessed his intention to resume his right to the throne, move the capital back to Moscow, discontinue the new Russian fleet, and restore things to the condition in which Peter had first found them. He even spoke of having tried to stir up a mutiny through the Metropolitan of Kiev and of having been ready to take the side of the Emperor Charles against the interests of Russia. Peter, who was often liable to fits of fury, some of which he expended on his son, was sobered by the gravity of this new aspect of the question. In a letter full of restraint but very human, saying that no man could doctor his own disease, he committed the decision to the highest ecclesiastics and administrators in the country, including some who were by no means hostile to Alexis. The clergy spoke of the beauty of pardon without directly recommending it. The civil commission investigated the matter to the end, which only helped to show up its extreme gravity, and they declared for a death sentence on the Tsarevich. Next day Peter with the principal lay commissioners entered the prison of the Tsarevich, and a day later it was announced that he was no more (November 1718).

The succession was thus left open. Peter had by Catherine two daughters, Anne and Elizabeth; he had also had two infant sons named Peter, and one named Paul, who all died in early childhood. For him the question of the permanence of his reforms preceded every other interest. He therefore took an extraordinary step which was to cause endless trouble after him. In a decree of February 1721, he declared that the sovereign in future had the right to choose his successor, thus reducing the Russian Empire to the situation which prevailed in Rome during its decline and fall. Having claimed this power, he never made use of it. Continuing his vigorous spadework to the last, at the end of 1724 he contracted a severe chill while engaged in saving the lives of some drowning sailors. This was aggravated by his attendance at the ceremony of blessing the waters in January 1725. His powers left him very suddenly. While he was writing his last instructions, pen and paper dropped from his hand. His daughter Anne was sent for to take them by word of mouth, but all he could say was: "Give all to—." The succession was left to be disputed by force.

Peter's work was complete as far as one lifetime could make it so. There was no department in which he did not make the beginnings of Russia's new civilization. He himself corrected and simplified the Russian alphabet which was in use after him. He was himself the editor of the first public newspaper in Russia. He prescribed the translation of books on all subjects into Russian, and flooded the Russian language with new unintelligible German titles and words. Under his direction was brought out the first textbook on social behaviour, in which his subjects were ordered to be amiable, modest, and respectful, to learn languages, to look people in the face, take off their hats, not to dance in boots, or to spit on the floor, or sing too loud, put the finger in the nose, rub the lips with the hand, lean on the table, swing the legs, lick the fingers, gnaw a bone when at dinner, scratch one's head, talk with one's mouth full; and his assemblies or social gatherings, at which he made attendance compulsory, were the first crude school of European conventions. Russia was to be Europeanized by the knout, a process which could only take effect on the thin upper stratum of the Russian community. The rest of it regarded Peter as Antichrist. All sorts of legends described him as a son substituted for a daughter, as a bastard of Lefort, as an imposter taking the place of the real Tsar, who was declared to be imprisoned in Stockholm. The methods of Peter's lifework, far more than the work itself, violently rebuffed all the native instincts of this backward and isolated country. Yet among a series of talentless, vulgar, and mostly foreign successors, the will of Peter held good. By his will, Russians continued to live in an unhealthy marsh that lay outside Russia, and the structure of the State as he left it was in substance to remain until the Revolution of 1917.

CHAPTER XIII

Peter's Successors and Russia

[*1725–62*]

WHAT we have now to study is Peter's new Russia without Peter.

Peter, by his tremendous will power, had shaped at least the framework of a new Russia. It is true that he sought ready-made results, that he worked throughout for the State, that with him the form was made before the substance. Yet the existence of the forms led towards the creation of those realities which the forms were meant to represent. It was an inverted and painful process; and the great wonder is, that Peter's reforms should have endured at all after his death. Into this question we must now inquire.

Mirabeau, during the expropriation of church lands in the French Revolution, uttered a phrase which is applicable to other epochs: "Let us create," he said, "the army of the vested interests of the Revolution!" Peter had made a revolution, and he had formed his army of vested interests, a new governing class, taken from anywhere and everywhere, with promotion according to service. Creating this new class, he destroyed by inference the old aristocracy. The boyars, or magnates, had made their fight against John the Dread, and had failed; they failed again now. New families, though sometimes of old blood, had come to the fore during the first two Romanovs. Remnants of the old class remained even long after Peter, and they again had an opportunity during the comparative interregnum that followed under Peter's first successors; but already they were almost swamped by the new elements. Something like this had happened at a much earlier period in the history of Poland, when Kazimir IV relied on a new mixed class of gentry to resist the great magnates. But the class of service gentry rested in Russia from the outset on an opposite basis, not on personal or local rights but on service to the autocrat of the State. Peter went much further in this direction; and the universal obligation of state service accompanied and was supposed to justify the rights which the gentry of Russia possessed over the subject population below them.

In Peter's aristocracy there were very mixed elements. Side by side with the Dolgorukys of the line of Rurik, a family which had been prominent since Tsar Michael, and the Golitsyns of the line of Gedimin, who had distinguished themselves much earlier, stood Prince Menshikov, son of a groom and himself formerly a pieman, with other new men who owed their elevation entirely to Peter, and foreigners, especially Germans—such as Ostermann, a man of humble origin with a genius for intrigue, and the capable military organizer General Münnich. The balance of numbers and power was with the new men; for beneath these notables was a mass of officials whose very posts had not existed before Peter. He had turned the whole class of serving gentry into a governing caste. On the plea of state service, he had almost emancipated this class from taxation; and he had laid it as an unbearable weight on the producing forces of the country. He had, moreover, incorporated and legalized its predominance in a vast network of new institutions in which, by the collegiate principle, there were often five or more persons to do work which might have been done by one. Such, in a measure, was the Senate itself, which like the Senate later created for similar reasons by Napoleon, became in principle the regent when by the absence of the sovereign the supreme power had, so to speak, to be put into commission. Such also were the colleges; such were the innumerable branch offices of government institutions throughout the country. The principal officials outside the Senate came to be described by a new foreign name, "the Generality," as those highest in all three tables of rank bore the title of General. There even came to be something like a regular procedure in the many palace revolutions which followed on Peter's preposterous edict abolishing the regular succession to the throne. When some body of troops had installed a new sovereign, the Senate and Generality would be called together to give their sanction to the change.

The basis of power in this regime lay in the army; but the Guard itself was like an incarnation of the élite of the new gentry class, whose very rights were based principally on military service. The lower ranks in the Guard were largely filled by gentry. In a regime which left everything to force, the Guard, as the cream of the gentry, and stationed in the capital, became the usual arbiter of power. As time went on, changes of sovereign due to nothing better than the ambition of some adventurous politician or officer came to be varied by transfers of power which were at least connected with some political idea. For practical purposes, the Guard was a kind of repository of the political thought of the ruling gentry class. More than once the signal for a revolution was some order to the Guard to abandon this privileged position and to disperse its gentlemen privates as officers among the regiments in the provinces.

Behind the Guard, and naturally following its lead, stood the mass of the enormous new army, trained on the foreign model largely by foreign officers, equipped with modern weapons and dressed in uniforms of German cut. This standing army of something like 300,000 men sucked the last resources out of the working population and crushed all provincial initiative; it was the custom for the gentry to send refractory peasants to it as a punishment. It was only the army that could hope to collect the extravagant taxes, more than trebled since the accession of Peter, overlapping each other and touching every function of ordinary life.

This then is the period *par excellence* of a state without a people; and the one thing which gave distinction to the state, namely Peter himself, had disappeared. Ignoble palace revolutions, more like brawls than political events, succeeded each other through this miserable period. The State, conceived merely as an instrument of power, counted for everything; the people counted for nothing. The State itself was chiefly interested not in Russia but in Europe, in foreign politics, in the prestige or territory which it could win abroad. Occasional explosions, due to old sores left without attention and to new burdens never made bearable, seemed to the sordid or mediocre rulers of that time as troublesome interruptions, to be terminated by force and to be forgotten as soon as possible. The ruling class, which became more and more detached from its responsibilities to the vast peasantry beneath it, was dragged from its estates first perhaps for study in Europe and then for unlimited state service in the army or elsewhere; cripples and old men were left to sustain the role of the gentry in the country.

The eyes of the official Russia were set upon Europe. Peter in his last years had entered on a daring program of intrigue abroad which, after alarming many politicians in Europe, might seem to have ended with his death. It was not so, however, at least as far as concerned the reaction of European factors upon Russia itself. Peter had married his niece Anne to one of the last of the Kettlers, Dukes of Kurland, certainly with the hope of bringing this province within the orbit of Russia. Further westward he had married another niece, Catherine, to the Grand Duke of Mecklenburg, well in the middle of Germany; and the marriage treaty included the extraordinary provision that Mecklenburg was to support a Russian military force, which was to help the Grand Duke to repress his insubordinate barons. Further westward still, Peter betrothed his eldest daughter Anne to the young Duke of Holstein. The Duke's mother was the elder sister of Charles XII of Sweden and the natural heir to his throne, and Peter certainly had this consideration in view. Further still to the west, Peter had tried to marry his youngest daughter Elizabeth to King Louis XV of France. Those of these foreign commitments which he was able to realize tied Russia faster to Europe. They meant a considerable additional charge on the Russian people, through the occasions they offered for Russia's intervention in European affairs. But they also meant something much more serious, of which Peter apparently had no time to think. As he himself annihilated his son Alexis and as his other sons died in infancy, the Russian throne itself in this succeeding period was to be bandied about between the various heirs of these foreign marriages; and the monarchical power, which under Peter became dominant even to the extinction of every other force in the country, was thus put in the hands of persons who had either lost all contact with Russia or had been educated from the start in the traditions of petty princely courts in Germany.

Here a single glance will show the violent oscillations of the succession between the various claimants. Peter is succeeded by his second wife Catherine, originally a Lithuanian servant with no right whatsoever to the throne and raised to it by Menshikov and his lieutenants precisely for that reason. From Peter's second wife the throne passes two years later to the son of the unhappy Alexis (Peter's offspring by his first wife), Peter II. When in 1730 Peter II dies at the age of fifteen, the throne passes to Anne of Kurland, daughter of Peter's step-brother, the puppet Tsar John V. On the death of Anne the crown goes to her grand-nephew John VI, not yet one year old. Hardly a year later John is dethroned, and the succession reverts to his step-great-aunt Elizabeth, daughter of Peter the Great. From Elizabeth in 1761 it goes to Peter III, son of Anne of Holstein, at one time regarded as presumptive heir to the throne of Sweden. Not a year later Peter is ousted and finally disposed of by his own wife Catherine, actually Princess Sophia of Anhalt-Zerbst, a German wife of a German-bred Tsar, with no right whatsoever to the Russian throne, who nonetheless by the will of history proved to be the only continuator that Peter's policy was ever to find, and the only Russian sovereign to compare with him in glory.

By Peter's decree of 1721, not only he but every successive Emperor was to name his own successor. Dying suddenly, Peter made no use of this power. Before he had breathed his last Menshikov, deadly anxious for his own position, took Peter's second wife to the Guard, secured their support, and brought a detachment of them to the Senate, which was now debating the succession. The older boyars were all for the son of Alexis, Peter II, the rightful heir to the throne. The Guards knew Catherine well; she had accompanied them on campaign. Some of their officers came boldly into the Senate, and roughly interrupted the speeches, protesting at any consideration of the young Peter. The troops outside beat their drums and the Senate was forced to proclaim Catherine. She announced her determination to adhere to Peter's changes; nor could she do otherwise, as but for them she was without any significance. The first Russian woman to mount the Russian throne was thus a foreigner, and an ex-servant; the peasants in Moscow suggested that it should be their wives who should swear to Catherine I, not they. The power was in the hands of Menshikov, but a Supreme Secret Council of six persons, with Catherine as president, exercised the sovereign prerogative. Catherine, in the second of her two years of sovereignty, wasted colossal sums on her personal expenses. Even in this reign, the highest officials themselves, such as Yaguzhinsky and Menshikov, had to urge that the peasants' burdens were intolerable, and that they were simply dying out. Menshikov found a telling way of bringing this conclusion home: "The peasants and the army," he said, "are like soul and body; without the one you cannot have the other." "You will have no subjects," was the comment of another high official. In consequence the poll tax was lessened and some of the irrecoverable arrears were struck off. The Academy of Sciences, projected by Peter, was opened in this reign.

In 1727 when Catherine was approaching death, the dispute as to the succession broke out again. Many claims were discussed; but this time the older boyars won over to the cause of the rightful heir even Menshikov himself, who saw that it was not to be resisted and wished to secure his own position. To do this more effectively Menshikov betrothed his daughter, a girl of sixteen, to Peter, who was twelve; he even wrote to him as his "father." Peter succeeded to the throne, but very quickly became disgusted with Menshikov and with his bride. Ostermann, who was tutor to the boy, found him very unruly and resigned his post. The deputy tutor, Prince Alexis Dolgoruky, gave the young Tsar his own son for companion, and the two boys became fast friends. Suddenly Peter ordered the arrest of Menshikov and, as nothing followed, dismissed him to his estates, depriving him of all rank, office, and decorations; soon he was sent off to Siberia.

The Dolgorukys now had the boy in their own hands. He was betrothed to the daughter of Prince Alexis, also his senior, for whom he had no more liking than for his earlier fiancée. He disliked St. Petersburg and moved his capital to Moscow; there, though he declared himself to be of age, he took no part in public business, and spent all his time in hunting. He appears to have wanted to shake himself free of the Dolgorukys, when he suddenly died of a severe chill at the age of fifteen, on the very day which had been fixed for his wedding.

The throne was again empty. Moscow was full of representatives of the service gentry who had arrived for the wedding. The power was in the hands of the Supreme Secret Council; under Peter II it had been filled with Dolgorukys and Golitsyns, who represented the political tendencies of the older boyars. The ablest member of the Council was Prince Dmitry Golitsyn. Dispatched by Peter the Great in 1697 to Italy for the study of political conditions, he had become a European scholar with a special interest in political economy and in foreign constitutions, of which he most admired those of Venice and England. We must remember that we are now in that period when England, under the Hanoverian dynasty, was ruled by the great Whig aristocracy. Golitsyn had an excellent library containing many books on his favourite subject, among which were no less than ten on the English constitution. Always in favour of Europeanizing Russia, he believed that Peter the Great had gone much too fast. The civilization of Russia, what there was of it, had rested largely on the culture of the boyars, and these were now submerged in a mob of new men. Golitsyn hoped to do in Russia what the Swedes had done on the death of Charles XII in 1718. The Swedish nobles, who had a long tradition of constitutional resistance to the sovereign, at that time enforced an aristocratic constitution.

As soon as the boy Peter died, the Supreme Secret Council, co-opting two more members of the Dolgoruky and Golitsyn families, drew up a series of conditions to impose on the new sovereign. Again all the various claims were discussed, including even that of Peter's divorced wife Eudokia. On the well-known constitutional principle that a bad title makes a good king, the choice fell not on any descendant of Peter but on his niece Anne, the widowed Duchess of Kurland, who was without children. The Council dispatched that night to Anne at Mitau the conditions under which it was prepared to raise her to the Russian throne. Without the consent of the Supreme Council she was not to marry, to name her successor, to declare war or peace, to raise any new taxes, to create any new boyars, to condemn any of the old without trial, to exercise any control of the Guard, to make any military appointment above the rank of colonel, or to spend anything beyond the civil list which the Council would fix for her. Yaguzhinsky, who was not a member of the Council, learned of these conditions and dispatched simultaneously to Mitau a message assuring Anne that they did not carry any real authority. Anne accepted both the offer and the conditions without demur, and within three days set out for Moscow.

She halted outside, to acquaint herself with the situation before entering. In the interval, the Supreme Council had been subjected to a fire of criticism. Apart from the Council's program, there were two other tendencies. The gentry in no way desired to be controlled by a council of magnates, which they described as "ten Tsars instead of one"; some among them would have liked to secure a more democratic constitution, but the majority preferred to leave things as they were, and to return to the familiar grooves of autocracy. As soon as the Council let its plan be known, those who opposed it, including many of the older boyars, and even members of the Dolgoruky and Golitsyn families, demanded that other proposals should be considered. For a moment we seem almost to be living in a Russia of later days, with an orgy of talk, innumerable party groups, and none of the elements of a common agreement; such is the impression conveyed by the reports of more than one ambassador then in Moscow. Golitsyn was compelled to modify his first scheme. He now proposed that the Council should consist of twelve nobles, the Empress having two votes; there would be a Senate of thirty-six members to draft all laws; a chamber of the gentry numbering two hundred; and a lower house of merchants, which would also represent the poorer classes. Class privileges were to remain as they were, but compulsory state service was to be abolished. Nothing was said in favour of the serfs; on the contrary, peasants who held government posts were to be dismissed from them. The gentry on their side were no less selfish. All their claims were for class privilege.

Advised by Ostermann and others, Anne first declared herself Colonel of the Preobrazhensky Regiment, entertaining her soldiers with drinks as Catherine I had done before her and as Elizabeth and Catherine II were to do after her. Then she entered Moscow. The Senate petitioned for a commission to examine the rival constitutional projects, and to this she agreed. But while she was dining with the Supreme Council, some of the Guards, no doubt with her knowledge, broke into the room and kneeling before her begged her to resume the autocratic power. Hereupon she turned to the members of the Supreme Council asking why she had not been told that they alone were responsible for the conditions which they had imposed on her, and demonstratively tore them up before their eyes. Homage was sworn to her as autocratic sovereign. The Supreme Council was disbanded, and in the course of time the principal members were punished with death, prison, or exile. Anne, by her marriage, had been semi-Europeanized; and it was not surprising that she moved the court back to St. Petersburg.

The ten years of Anne's reign (1730–40) are the gloomiest part of all this period. Anne was a dull, coarse, fat woman, harsh and spiteful. Her conceptions of the pleasures and also of the responsibilities of sovereignty were drawn from the poky little half-German court of Mitau. Her friends, who now became the arbiters of Russia, also came from Mitau. The most intimate was Biren, a man of polished manners but of no ability whatever in politics and no interest in them except in so far as they contributed to his income. Others, such as the gambler Loewenwold, were even inferior to him. Under this higher circle of favourites were other foreigners, who at least had some administrative past in Russia: in particular the astute diplomatist Ostermann, and the able General Münnich. To these, under the orders of the Court, was entrusted the actual administration of the country. After disbanding the Supreme Council, Anne created another inner council of her own significantly called her Cabinet, of which the members bore the misleading title of Cabinet Ministers. The Cabinet was a return to the old proprietary days of the early Russian princes; Russia was treated as if it were a farm; and the ordinary state business was hopelessly entangled with the requirements of the Court. These requirements were enormous; the Court was five times more costly to the nation than it had been under Peter the Great. The agents of the German favourites and ministers were also in large part German; and Russia had an experience of German rule which left a lasting impression; it was remembered as a time of drunken court revels when the people were "treated like dogs." In this reign great storms swept over Russia; vast famines, particularly that of 1733 when the starving peasants came in crowds to beg in the towns, were followed by widespread epidemics; great fires broke out. Meanwhile the country was traversed by punitive columns trying in vain to levy the enormous arrears of impossibly heavy taxes. One of their methods was to chain up the local Voevode or to leave squires or village elders starving in prison till some payment was made. The squires, in turn, could only satisfy the officials by seizing any movable property of the peasants that they could lay hands on. Peasant elders were knouted, and peasant farmers were sold up wholesale. Meanwhile the Secret Chancellery, a product of Peter I's "fiscal system," spread over the country a network of spies and informers, whose delations brought misery to masses of the population. Any charge was welcomed; torture was freely used. As many as 20,000 persons were at one swoop expelled to Siberia, of whom 5000 were lost on the road without further trace or further attention on the part of the government. Much of the country was passing out of culture. Even Anne herself was forced to inveigh against the widespread iniquities of her own officials.

As control lapsed and the Court became more absorbed in itself, the gentry systematically extended their rights, which were less and less hampered by any kind of responsibility. Already in 1727 it was calculated that two thirds of them were on leave; and in 1736 their obligations of service were defined anew. Service was to last not more than twenty-five years; where there were two sons, one would be excused from it. Yet even in this black reign, when so much of Peter's policy was allowed to drop, the educational part of his program was adhered to as rigidly as ever. Children were to be entered in the government registers at seven and to present themselves for examination at the ages of twelve, sixteen, and twenty. Even the son excused from service was required to attain the educational qualification for a civil post. In 1731 Anne founded for the gentry a privileged Cadet Corps. In the same year Peter's law, by which one son at the choice of the father held a monopoly of inheritance of the real estate, was abolished. It had led to family quarrels ending in parricide and to all sorts of evasions—the father, for instance, selling his estate in order to provide for all his sons equally.

In this reign the foreign commitments of Russia were continued and increased. Following the so-called system of Peter the Great, Russia strengthened her ties of friendship with Austria. In 1733 Peter's protégé King August the Strong of Poland died; to contest the throne with his son August, there reappeared the former protégé of Charles XII, Stanislaw Leszczynski, with the support of Louis XV of France, who had married his daughter. Russia threw an army of 50,000 men under Lacey into Poland, and Stanislaw was beseiged in Danzig. As the siege dragged, Münnich himself took over the command and, though at a heavy price, brought it to a conclusion. Leszczynski fled to France, and August III was established as King. The war had spread into Europe in general, and at one point Lacey was even sent to the Rhine to succour the Austrians against the French.

In 1735 Russia, Austria, and Persia, to whom had been restored the conquests of Peter the Great, made war on Turkey. Russia's objective was Crimea, which was thrice invaded and devastated by Münnich and

Lacey. Azov and Ochakov were captured and Münnich won a notable victory over the Turks close to the Pruth of evil memory, at Stavuchany; here he took a strongly fortified camp with small loss. In these earliest recorded engagements of the modern Russian army we are stuck from the outset by the enthusiasm of the tributes which one general after another pays to the fighting qualities of the troops, a verdict soon to be confirmed by their opponents at Zorndorf and Künersdorf. "Our men," wrote Münnich, "showed unspeakable keenness for battle." The Russians won Hotin and Jassy. A flotilla was to descend the Dnieper and sail for Constantinople, and it was hoped that the Christians of the Balkans would rise to join the Russians; this was the first attempt to put to military use the ties of race and religion there. As was usual, the Russian army moved through the steppe without any adequate services of transport and supply, and the wastage was enormous. Through the incompetency or dishonesty of contractors, the river flotilla never started. The troops in Moldavia, owing to their indiscipline and excesses, made more enemies than friends. Austria, meanwhile, having been less successful, concluded peace at Belgrade in 1739; and all that Russia got out of the war was a patch of territory in the steppe and the agreement of the Turks to dismantle the fortress of Azov.

Anne died before her time in 1740. Three years earlier, on the extinction of the Kettler dynasty, with the use of Russian troops she had forced Biren as Duke on the unwilling nobles of Kurland, who had earlier refused to recognize him even as a noble. She had also married her niece Anne, a daughter of her sister Catherine of Mecklenburg, to the incapable Anton Ulrich of Brunswick-Lüneburg; and in August 1740 a son was born of this marriage, who was christened John. Before her death on October 17, Anne named this baby as her successor and Biren as regent. As favourite, Biren had freely exploited Russia; but he was quite incapable of bearing the responsibility of power. An attempt at open protest, led by a colonel of the Guard, was suppressed; but shortly afterwards General Münnich, after inviting Biren to dinner to allay his suspicions, had him seized the same night. Men of the Preobrazhensky Regiment threw a sheet over him and later a soldier's greatcoat, and carried him off without resistance to their guardhouse, from which he was sent by stages to Pelym in Siberia.

The Princess Anne became regent. This lady spent most of her time indoors in almost complete *déshabille*, talking gossip to her German friend Countess Mengden; the rest was taken up with quarrels with her insignificant husband. In March 1741 Münnich, who was at first all-powerful, resigned—probably in order to leave the sinking ship. The gentry, with their almost complete monopoly of legal rights, had been gaining in class consciousness; and in the recent reign they had been deeply mortified at the rule of unscrupulous and often incapable foreigners. There was a feeling of bitter antagonism against the Germans. Hopes were centered in Elizabeth, the younger daughter of Peter the Great. Sweden, which now entertained hopes of recovering the conquests of Peter, had declared war on Russia, championing at least in name the claims of Elizabeth to the throne. The Guard, who by all their traditions were attached to the line of Peter, were ordered to Finland. Elizabeth was in danger of arrest. On November 25, on the eve of their departure, a few soldiers came to her at night and begged her to move. Wearing a cuirass and holding a cross, she betook herself to the Preobrazhensky Regiment, which swore to follow her. She led a company into the Winter Palace, where she awoke the regent Anne with the words, "Time to get up, sister." Münnich and Ostermann were seized, also the helpless Anton, and Elizabeth installed herself in power. The babe John was imprisoned in the fortress of Schlüsselburg, and his mother and family were sent to the provinces.

Elizabeth, who reigned from 1741 to 1761, at least brought a breath of relief after foreign rule. She took as her motto the program of her father. The Swedes were quickly driven back, and the frontier of Russia in Finland was advanced further westward. Elizabeth herself was a curious blend of the old and the new. With a large frame, an easygoing nature and a lively disposition, living in apartments which were always untidy, possessing as many as fifteen thousand dresses, seeking her pleasures in the simplest company such as old peasant women, very Russian and assiduously Orthodox, she at the same time left her mark on Russian history by an edict abolishing forever the death penalty, though it was retained later for military and sometimes for political offences. Choosing as one of her principal advisers Count Ivan Shuvalov, a man of high integrity and great enlightenment, she helped him to carry through a notable program of education. This included the foundation of the first Russian university, that of Moscow, in 1755. In Elizabeth's reign Russia began to find better models for culture than the petty stilted German courts, and to feel the influence of Western culture as represented at that time by French literature and thought. The best of the Russian nobility, such as Count Ivan Shuvalov, felt that Russia needed something more than mere technical knowledge for the performance of state service—that a true education must go deeper and begin with the training of character.

This reign saw the beginning of modern Russian literature in the person of Lomonosov, a peasant of Archangel who obtained what education he could in Moscow, was sent abroad for study and at one time was conscripted for the Prussian army. He broke ground for his country in studies of the most various kinds, philological, historical, economic, and scientific, and he was also the first notable poet of the new Russia. His language was stiff and often pompous; several of his compositions were court odes; with him was initiated that pseudo-classical period of Russian literature which was to blossom in the artificial atmosphere of the Court of Catherine II, but his powerful intellect and his robust patriotism in the field of learning rendered services of the first order to Russian scholarship.

Elizabeth's principal minister was another Shuvalov, Count Peter, a modern statesman of great resource and versatility. His chief task was of course to find money for the treasury; for this he debased the coinage with the easy explanation that the money being lighter would thus be easier to carry; he also taxed vodka with the comforting reflection that even in times of distress and poverty people would still want to get drunk. Like some of the financial improvisers of Peter I, he paid great attention to the sources of indirect taxation; he urged with reason that it would affect all classes alike, and thereby tend to relieve the burden of the direct taxes, which lay exclusively on the peasantry. Peculation was always rampant, and in 1742 there was a mistake of one million roubles in the budget; in this year the arrears amounted to three millions, and in 1761 to eight. Shuvalov, like Menshikov and Yaguzhinsky before him, pointed out that the ruin of the peasants was the ruin of the State, of which the peasantry were the "chief strength." Elizabeth herself published a bitter complaint at the end of her reign: "The laws," she wrote, "are not carried out because of common enemies inside, who prefer their lawless gains to their oath, duty and honour; the insatiable pursuit of gain has gone so far, that some of the courts established for justice have become a mockery." Mass flights to the frontier and peasant uprisings went on almost uninterruptedly. Yet Elizabeth built for herself the Winter Palace at a cost of ten million roubles; her floor was littered with unpaid bills, and her French milliner refused to give her further credit.

In 1756 Russia for the first time joined in an all-European coalition, including France and Austria, of which the object was to dismember the small and almost frontierless kingdom of Fredetick the Great of Prussia. When the death of Charles VI of Austria without a male heir raised questions of the succession both to the Empire and to the Habsburg dominions, Frederick had seized the opportunity to invade and annex Silesia. France under the direction of Choiseul then drew closer to Austria. It was some searching remarks of Frederick on the personal life of Elizabeth that helped to bring Russia into the coalition. Frederick's only support came from England, then under the direction of the first William Pitt.

In 1757 a Russian army of 83,000 men under Apraxin entered East Prussia and completely defeated the small detachment of Prussian troops under Marshal Lehwaldt which had been left to defend this province. The Russians, following their usual tactics, devastated it thoroughly. Isolated as it was from the other domains of Frederick, East Prussia was retained by the Russians till the end of the war, and the blow was for Frederick's a grievous one. Apraxin did not follow up his successes; this led to complaints from France and Austria, and to the fall of Elizabeth's Chancellor Bestuzhev-Ryumin, who was not in sympathy with the war. Next year the Russians, under Fermor, marched on Berlin. Frederick had brilliantly defeated the French at Rossbach by a flank cavalry attack led by Seidlitz (November 5, 1757) [1] and the Austrians at Leuthen by an advance in oblique formation (December 5). He had not yet met the Russians in person, and was now in Austria pushing home his successes, but by a rapid march he relieved Küstrin and separated the two Russian armies of Fermor and Rumyantzev. Fermor formed his men in square, according to the tradition of Münnich, on a well-chosen position near Zorndorf. Here Frederick attacked on August 25, 1758. The Prussians advanced on the Russian right, which was reinforced and held firm; the Russian cavalry charged and took 26 Prussian guns, but was driven in confusion on to the second Russian line which fired upon it by mistake. Seidlitz counter-charged, and a hand-to-hand fight followed, in which the Russian infantry held its ground although all its ammunition was expended; but many of the men took to drinking and orders were not obeyed. Frederick wished to finish the battle and launched his tired troops against the Russian left. This attack was driven off, and the Prussians were flying, when Seidlitz again restored the position with a cavalry charge. Neither side had more ammunition; a murderous fight

---

[1] From this point onward, all dates are given in the New Style, which was adopted in England on September 3/14, 1752. The Old Style was retained in Russia till after the Revolutions of 1917.

with swords and bayonets continued until dusk. Both armies camped on their positions, and the next day Fermor led his men away in good order without being molested. Frederick also withdrew.

The Russians were able to carry out their original intention of marching to Pomerania. They had lost 20,000 men at Zorndorf and the Prussians 12,000—which they could much less afford. Zorndorf was a kind of Malplaquet. It was not by such drawn battles that Frederick could hold good against the overwhelming superiority of his enemies. On the Russian side, all the defects of provision and of command had been repaired by the stubbornness of the Russian infantry.

In 1759 the Russians again advanced under Saltykov, a general more to the soldiers' taste. On August 3 they drove off five desperate attacks of a Prussian force, and pursued the enemy; Saltykov attributed his success entirely to the "prowess of his indomitable army." In spite of miserable supply, with transport in unrepair, Saltykov made his junction with the able Austrian general Laudon, and the two were attacked by Frederick on August 23 outside Frankfurt-on-the-Oder, on the rolling downs of Künersdorf. The Russians bore all the brunt of the attack, which began before dawn. Frederick was feeling for a weak point in the Russian defences. Finding their right impregnable, he made a flank attack on their left preceded by a very heavy cannonade. Here he was able to drive in a wedge behind the Russian front line, but it still held firm, and Laudon gave effective support. At 5 p.m., after a terrible day's fighting, the Moscow regiment charged the Prussians out of the ground won by them, and saved the Russian batteries. The Prussian cuirassiers of the Guard were routed by the Cossacks. The allied forces pursued Frederick's flying army, which broke up in disorder. The Prussians lost in killed alone 7000, the Russians 2500, and the Austrians 1400. The captured spoil included 28 flags and 172 guns. Frederick wrote to Berlin that out of 48,000 men he had only 3000 still in hand. He added: "I have no more authority over the army. They will do well in Berlin to think of their safety. It is a cruel misfortune. I will not survive it. I have no resources left, and to tell the truth, I count everything lost. I shall not survive the ruin of my country. Farewell for ever." However, this success, due like Zorndorf to the Russian private soldier, was so squandered by the allied commanders that he was able to continue the struggle.

In 1760 a Russian force of Cossacks and Kalmyks actually raided Berlin, and we learn from Frederick himself that it was a long time before he ceased to dream of that moment. Small events sometimes leave big memories, and the traditional alarm with which the Germans have later contemplated an advance of Russian hordes upon Germany and Europe may be dated from this time. Frederick was now at the end of his strength, and it was only the death of Elizabeth on January 5, 1762 (in the old style December 25, 1761), that saved him from ruin. In November 1762 England and France treated for a separate peace, which was concluded at Paris on February 10, 1763. These two Powers thus paired out of the war; and Maria Theresa of Austria was now left alone to do that which she had failed to do when helped by France and Russia.

Elizabeth soon after her accession had summoned to St. Petersburg her nephew Peter, the son of her sister Anne, Duchess of Holstein. This Peter had been brought up by a Swedish tutor in the Lutheran religion. He was a person of the feeblest intellect and contemptible character, childish, brainless, obstinate, and deceitful. His ideas were those of the new Prussian militarism; he continued to play with toy soldiers even after his marriage.

In 1744 he had been married by Elizabeth, on the suggestion of Frederick the Great, to Princess Sophia Augusta of Anhalt-Zerbst, whose father rose to be a field marshal in the Prussian army. Her mother had served as one of Frederick's political agents and had spent most of her life in wanderings over Europe. The Princess was brought up under a rough discipline, and being very gifted sought her enlightenment in her own way. She was successively instructed in four forms of Christianity— the Catholic, the Calvinistic, the Lutheran, and later the Orthodox. It was Orthodoxy that appealed to her most; she describes it as a great oak, with roots deep down in the ground. Her principal study was men and women, and her chief art was to make herself agreeable and useful to all, while committing herself to no one. She came to Russia at the age of fourteen with three dresses, bought out of the travelling allowance sent by the Empress Elizabeth; and received in Orthodoxy the name of Catherine. She was already mature in body and mind. She soon made herself independent of her mother, whose indiscretions nearly resulted in both being sent out of Russia. On her marriage she early recognized that her husband was an idiot. He neglected her entirely, living openly with mistresses. Her ambition was from the start unbounded. She records that she knew that somehow or other she would become "autocratic Empress of Russia," and she says that though she would have been glad to part with her husband at any time, she could not part with the Russian crown.

On succeeding Elizabeth in 1762, Peter III at once proceeded to show his complete futility. It is true, at the instance of his minister Shuvalov, he abolished the Secret Chancellery of Anne in an edict which announced the end of all delation. In May 1762, probably on the same advice, he issued another edict by which the gentry were in future relieved from the obligation of state service, and this decree was received by them with rapture. In future they were only required to undergo a short military training; residence abroad could be counted as state service; only the educational part of the program of Peter I was retained. On the other hand, Peter's own actions were a constant affront to every Russian instinct. During the war he had acted almost as a Prussian spy in Russia. He now not only concluded peace but alliance with Frederick, ordering his army to pass from one side to the other. He also planned a new war against Denmark purely for the interests of his native Holstein, and ordered a movement of troops in that direction. He publicly kissed the bust of Frederick and knelt before his portrait. He surrounded himself with a bodyguard of Holsteiners. He introduced the exhausting Prussian drill into the Russian army, and he put his troops into the new Prussian uniform. Meanwhile he gave orders that the icons were to be removed from the churches, and that the Russian priests were to dress like German pastors; he would talk loudly during the services or put out his tongue at the priests. His wife Catherine he threatened to divorce and send to a nunnery, and he publicly insulted her at a ceremonial dinner.

Catherine very carefully refrained from leading any movement of open opposition. Her friends, who were many and able, were particularly strong among the Guards. Four different groups of supporters acted for her, independently but in the same general direction, and forty officers, who could answer for ten thousand soldiers, were soon enlisted on her side. It was just now that Peter proposed his new war against Denmark and issued a further edict on church affairs, by which he declared that all forms of religion had equal privileges in Russia, that fasts were in future to be voluntary, and that all church lands reverted to the State. Catherine still held back; she was behind the scenes, aware of everything, but waiting for others to come to her. One of the conspirators was arrested, which compelled the rest to hasten their plans. Alexis Orlov went down to Peterhof and brought Catherine to St. Petersburg. Here he took her to the Ismailovsky and Semenovsky regiments, which came out in her favour. Fourteen thousand troops gathered around the Winter Palace. Catherine issued a manifesto, in which she claimed to stand for the defence of Orthodoxy and the glory and public security of the country. Peter, who was at the suburb of Oranienbaum, was lost in a confusion of conflicting suggestions. Now he would march on Kronstadt, but was told that the fortress would fire on him; next he thought of flying to his army abroad; next he asked Catherine if she would share the power with him; and finally, when her troops reached him, he made a humiliating abdication, asking only to retain his fiddle and his dog, his negro slave and his mistress. He was removed to the village of Ropsha, where on July 17 he died in a scuffle during dinner, of which Alexis Orlov, entrusted with his custody by Catherine, wrote: "We cannot ourselves remember what we did." Catherine in a second manifesto declared that she had accepted the throne to save the country, and added that autocracy without the necessary qualities in the ruler is very dangerous.

Who would take this miserable record as the history of a people? Not any serious historian. Of the six immediate successors of Peter I, three are women, one a boy of twelve, one a babe of one, and one an idiot. Through the barrack capital of St. Petersburg, situated outside Russian soil and cut off from the life of the Russian people, brainless or squalid adventurers succeed each other. And where, except in the Russian army, are there signs of Russia? From 1719 to 1727, one hundred thousand peasants took flight; some to the nomad Bashkirs, some to Poland and Moldavia. Under Catherine I the troops were moved from the country to the outskirts of the towns, and the collection of taxes became more and more difficult; punitive columns were constantly sent down to the villages, and had often to suppress peasant risings. In 1734 an honest man, Anisim Maslov, who was *Ober-Procuror* of the Senate, when asked by the Empress Anne to study the question of taxation, discovered an old order to the Senate to find some way of collecting taxes without arrears and for that purpose to define the obligations of the peasants, the measure for which they were always asking. This order had been evaded. Maslov fearlessly pressed the question, but died a year later; and on his project Anne wrote the word "Wait." Taxes were collected now by the army, next by the squires, then again by the army, then again by the squires; but all methods were found to be ineffective.

In 1734, after the great famine, the squires were at least reminded of their earlier obligations by a command to them to feed their starving peasants. But throughout this period the powers of the squires over the peasants were extended. The squire might himself fix the punishment of a fugitive (1736); he obtained the formal right of controlling even the conduct of his peasants (1754); he might send a peasant to forced labour in Siberia (1765). In spite of Peter I's edict on the subject, in which he had condemned the practice as non-Christian, serfs were now freely sold piecemeal, away from their land and the other members of their family. The journals of Elizabeth's capital contained advertisements of serfs for sale, especially girls.

Two tendencies in the question of serf ownership were in conflict throughout this period. The government was always trying to make someone responsible for each worker's poll tax, and therefore allotted peasants to others than squires, for instance in 1743; so that serfs came to be the property of merchants, townsfolk, servants, or even crown peasants. The new gentry, however, whose rights were increasing as their responsibilities diminished, managed to defeat this tendency; and ultimately only those who were entered on the gentry register were allowed to possess serfs. When a criminal code was drafted in 1754 it contained no separate section on the peasantry, who were treated only under the heading of property of the gentry. It allowed to the gentry "full power without exception" over the peasant, excluding only torture and manslaughter; the master was free to move his serfs about "for his own best advantage." Thus in the interval between the first census completed about 1725 and the second completed about 1742, we find that while the crown peasants increased by 42 per cent, the owners' serfs showed an increase of only 12 per cent.

The edict issued by Peter III in May 1762 emancipated the gentry from state service and, completing the process by which this service class became an ordinary aristocracy, it ought logically to have been followed by a personal emancipation of the peasants from the squires. So strongly was this felt among the peasantry that at the accession of Catherine II about two hundred thousand were in open rebellion, and were only reduced to submission by armed force and in some cases by the use of artillery. The peasants, who had originally been reduced to serfdom in order to enable the squires to discharge their state service, had to wait another hundred years for their own emancipation.

How then can we sum up the history of the Russian people in this period? On the positive side, there is the steady emancipation of the gentry from the duties which gave them their state rights over the bodies of their peasants, and their transformation for the first time into something like an aristocracy of Western Europe. They gradually came to represent almost exclusively the *pays légal*. Negatively, and almost as if only by inference, we have arrived at a position in which the peasant, though legally he still had some remains of state rights, had in practice lost them entirely. He no longer counted—not even for the chronicler, except incidentally. And the innumerable changes in the succession finally lodged on the perilous throne a foreigner who, however exceptional in her intelligence, was practically precluded from dealing with the threatening danger to the State without challenging its whole social system and in particular the class which had elevated her and maintained her in power.

CHAPTER XIV

Catherine the Great

[*1762–96*]

Catherine, on her accession, even retained for a while her predecessor's principal minister, Shuvalov, and showed no animosity to those who had taken her husband's side to the last.

She was more than abreast of the highest culture of her time. As she tells us herself, she became serious in her reading from the moment when a book of Voltaire's fell into her hands; from that time onwards she had a keen appetite for anything that was good; she enjoyed and digested Blackstone's *Commentaries* on law; Buffon's *Natural History* she describes as a relaxation. Toward the end of her reign, after collecting the early annals of Russian history, she set about writing a history of Russia, and the task was evidently a delight to her. She took a special interest in making cameos and engravings, and she could also sculpture and paint. A figure that gave distinction to her Court was the poet Derzhavin, who was employed by her in several high offices. He was a court poet, but in a better sense than his contemporaries of the pseudo-classical school; for he genuinely reflects the culture of a small privileged class, living from day to day and enjoying life as it finds it, while not forgetful of its limitations; and there is a true inspiration in some of his work.

Catherine's own numerous literary works are of no great merit, but her letters are of a high order; full of freshness, they are also full of intellect. Her métier, as she herself said, was administration and affairs, but the side of administration in which she excelled was diplomacy. Those who enjoy watching the adjustment of policy to the situation with which it has to deal, will rate Catherine as a political genius. It is this rare political ability that is revealed in her letters. She wrote frequently to Frederick the Great, Joseph the Second, Voltaire, D'Alembert, Falconnet, and her own administrators and generals, especially Potemkin; but most often of all to her friend the encyclopædist scholar Grimm. Catherine was not merely a patron of the French encyclopædists; she was herself one of them, and not by any means the least. Grimm tells us that after talking with her in her palace, he would walk in his room for hours before he could go to sleep. He describes her brilliance as like a fountain showering down in sparks.

Catherine rose at five, lit her own fire at six, and often worked fifteen hours a day; she was particularly considerate to her servants. Her methods of work were Russian, not German: great bouts at a given task, leaving many gaps—but full of interest and enthusiasm while they lasted.

With separate tables assigned to different subjects, working with four secretaries, she left her mark in many fields of administration. Though not like Peter always on the highroads, she at different times travelled widely in her huge empire, and, as with Peter so with Catherine, each journey was planned and utilized as a course of self-education. She travelled down the Volga as far as Simbirsk; she journeyed along the tract of the new canal which was to unite the Volga to the Neva and, toward the end of her reign, she made the most brilliant but the least instructive of her journeys through the new fairy domain which Potemkin had staged for her in South Russia. She would turn to any interest suggested by the place which she was visiting; from the Volga, in her own words, she brought back ideas to last her ten years.

Catherine's Court and her paladins were of much greater brilliance than those of Peter I; but it was Catherine herself who made them brilliant. She not only selected their tasks, but she literally made their reputations, and for this purpose she made the cleverest use of her correspondence with sovereigns, scholars, and publicists in Western Europe. It was Catherine herself, coming after the most sordid period in the history of the country, who first gave style to Russia. Some of her best helpers were also her favourites, but in practically every case her favourites were also her friends. Taking only the principal among the long list of her lovers, there were some, like Lanskoy and Mamonov, who were her house pets, persons much younger than herself, pleasing to her by their grace of manner, sometimes treated by her almost as children and sincerely mourned when they died. Others, like Gregory Orlov and Potemkin, were by character or ability among the foremost figures of her reign; with Orlov and Potemkin one may suppose that for Catherine the principal charm lay in their manliness and strength of will, the more attractive to a woman who was herself full of courage and who perhaps saw courage in a courtier who was not afraid to make love to his sovereign. Of Potemkin she writes: "Bold mind, bold spirit, bold heart," and

complains at his death, which was long after their most intimate relations had ceased, that she has no one left to lean on. "He is cleverer
than I," she said. Toward the end of his life, during the second Turkish
war, when Potemkin despairs of success, it is she who puts heart into
him, reminding him that earlier it was he who had to do the same for
her. Their letters might almost be those of man to man, with the difference by which Catherine herself characteristically explained her
amours, that "one of the two friends was a very attractive woman."

The story of Catherine's reign is speckled from end to end with plots
or risings against her, and no wonder. She had no title whatsoever to the
throne, though she was pleased to say that she owed it to "God and the
choice of her subjects." She had won it by the removal and ultimately
the murder of her husband. For the whole of her long reign she was keeping out the rightful heir, her own son Paul, whom Elizabeth had even
thought of substituting for his father. Besides Paul there was another
legitimate claimant in the person of that unhappy young man, who as
a child of one had reigned for a year as John VI. He was now a prisoner
in the fortress of Schlüsselburg, under the strictest guard, in a cell unknown to almost everyone but his jailor, who had had precise instructions from Elizabeth to kill him if there was any danger of his rescue. At
the very outset of Catherine's reign adventurers or malcontents in the
Guards, who had been accustomed to set up any sovereign they pleased
and who had set up Catherine, plotted small mutinies which were suppressed. Catherine showed the greatest coolness in all these matters.
Her chief anxiety was to prevent them from becoming fully known; for
as she truly said, it would only take a spark to upset St. Petersburg. Thus
she takes a close part in each investigation. At the same time she systematically discountenances and forbids any excited ill-considered vengeances, any extension of the blame to the innocent, and any use of torture. A young adventurer in the Guards, Mirovich, gambler and debtor,
ignorant and eccentric, makes a plot to rescue John VI, and he and his
confederate Ushakov even have the prayers for the dead read over them
in advance. Mirovich intends to bring John to St. Petersburg, seize the
fortress of St. Peter and Paul, picket the bridges, fire on the palace,
summon the Senate and colleges, and send Catherine and Paul to
prison, very much as was done with Peter III only two years before. In
July 1764 he enters the fortress of Schlüsselburg by night with forty-five
men, and overpowering the small garrison of thirty, arrests the governor
and makes his way into the prison. He is at first driven back, and meanwhile the jailors kill the unfortunate prisoner. Mirovich, when he gets

to him, finds him dead, and makes the characteristic comment: "Now there is no help for it. They are right and we are wrong." John was buried in Schlüsselburg with the utmost secrecy. Mirovich, who gave bold answers at his trial, was executed.

Another pretender to the throne was the so-called Princess Tarakanova, who claimed to be the daughter of the unmarried Empress Elizabeth. This lady, very pretty and quick-witted, was an adventuress with many aliases, Italian, German, and even Turkish, familiar with several European languages and with the fringes of society in London and Paris. In order to arrest her, Alexis Orlov, in command of a Russian fleet in the Mediterranean (as will be explained in the next chapter), even shelled the town of Ragusa and as that failed, had to feign himself her lover and lure her on board. She was brought to Russia and imprisoned, first at Kronstadt and then in St. Peter and Paul. Here she died of consumption after writing humble letters to Catherine, but with the signature "Elizabeth." The flood which has given rise to a celebrated legend took place two years after her death.

By the side of these were numberless other plotters and rebels, who are really of much more general significance. Following Russian tradition which attaches all importance to the identity of the sovereign, these pretenders, with a regularity that borders on monotony, took the names now of Catherine's murdered husband Peter III, now of the murdered John, now of the deprived heir to the throne Paul, and sometimes of some imaginary prince who had no real existence. It would be weary work to enumerate them. It was enough that any deserted soldier or Cossack or peasant should be stirred by some individual wrong and find some nucleus of general discontent, that he should take one of these names or sometimes, even better, announce the coming of the given "rightful heir." The Cossack or peasant would easily get a priest of the Old Believers to serve mass in his honour. Some of these adventurers were chiefs of the great robber bands which infested the country. In such cases the immediate and perhaps the only object was looting. Other leaders came from the gentry.

Catherine's ordinary punishment for all these pretenders was to send them to Siberia, especially to the mines of Nerchinsk, sometimes after parading them through the villages in which they had boasted their claims. Some were knouted or even branded; some were reprieved and successfully reduced to insignificance. Some went on plotting in Siberia and carried their pretensions as far as Japan. Pretenders to the Russian throne appeared in Albania and in Montenegro; their program was to realize the great dream of Alexis and Nashchokin by uniting all the Slavs. These disorders were the only possible form of expression left to the masses, to articulate the profound social discontent which, with only too good reasons, pervaded the country during this reign.

Among the rebels stands out the Archbishop of Rostov, Arseny Matseyevich, a man of much learning and of harsh and fearless character. One of the last acts of Peter III was to appropriate the domains of the Church, which were administered by the State under the name of "economic lands." Catherine had seemed likely for a moment to reverse this measure. When she confirmed it, Matseyevich anathematized her, protested to the Synod, and even wrote twice to the ex-Minister Bestuzhev. When he was tried by the Synod, Catherine was present and stopped her ears not to hear his fearless abuse. He was unfrocked and sent to a monastery; but there, conversing with the soldiers who guarded him, he boldly impugned her right to the throne and denounced the murder of John VI. Tried again in 1767, he was removed to a prison at Reval, where he lived cut off from all human intercourse under the name which Catherine gave him—Andrew the Babbler. No one was allowed to speak to him or to quote a single word uttered by him; even his confessor and doctor at the time of his death were made to swear this oath. Matseyevich had said that the Church had been plundered worse than in Turkey; the merchant Smolin in 1771 made the same protest, and in a letter to the Empress denounced "your unjust government, Catherine." All these individual voices were the rumbles before the tremendous storm of the rebellion of Pugachev.

By a continuous process since the death of Peter the Great, the new and motley class of gentry, in which it gradually became less easy to distinguish the vanishing remains of the old Moscow nobility, had been steadily emancipating itself from those obligations of service which had been the sole origin and justification of its class privileges. The two kinds of estates, the old patrimonies and the later *pomestya*, held temporarily as pay for military service, had by Peter been finally merged into one. Under him all estates were hereditary, and all were held on the condition of service. But no sooner was he dead than the disappearance of a strong and directing hand at headquarters made it comparatively easy for obligations to be escaped even though the law remained the same. A succession of chance sovereigns was not likely to be able to restrain this new service aristocracy; and new liberties of this class, appropriated at first only in practice, were gradually sanctioned and confirmed by such legislation as dealt with them. This process was completed in 1762, exactly on the eve of Catherine's accession, by the edict of Peter III which formally released the gentry from the obligations of state service. This, of itself, established a paradoxical position. Those claims of the State which had induced it to give the gentry increasing authority over the peasants, had disappeared; on the other hand this authority was now hereditary and the rights which it carried, so far from being withdrawn or even diminished, were made more and more absolute. It is, then, at this point that the State itself for the first time treated the peasant as the personal property of his master. Now it was the gentry class that had carried Catherine to power. With the exception of the merchants, who had certain privileges, the gentry had a monopoly of civil rights in the country. For Catherine, a foreign adventuress, it was practically impossible to quarrel with them.

Other circumstances enhanced the already wide gap that separated the gentry from the peasantry. I would suggest that a man's view of life is more or less fixed by his view of the world as he first sees it at the age when he opens his eyes on public affairs; he takes the world as he then finds it, and generally reads any later changes into this picture of it only by way of corrections. It was something like this that now happened to Russia. This is the moment when Russia began to give herself some intelligent account of Europe. It was only the gentry who could know Europe. Their travels, which at first had to be enforced by Peter the Great, had become not only voluntary but very agreeable, and had now begun to bear fruit. Under Elizabeth, the purely technical student of Peter's time gave place to young folk anxious to pose as connoisseurs of the contemporary school of manners in Europe. Under Catherine a further stage of education was reached by the gentry. They began to swallow wholesale the political and social ideas which were in vogue at the time. Now this was a very peculiar period in the life of Europe. The movement for the free development of the individual, which had begun in Italy in the Renaissance and had passed into the special field of religion in the German Reformation, had later transformed itself into a creed of political and social thought first in the English Revolution, then in those English thinkers who summed up its lessons, such as Hobbes and Locke, and now in the brilliant group of French writers headed by Voltaire, who led an ardent campaign against the remains of feudalism and the religious intolerance of later Roman Catholic policy under the direction of the Jesuits. Now in Russia there had never been European feudalism and the Roman Catholic Church had no authority. What was for Europe, and for France in particular, a phase, what the

French discussed with all sorts of reticences that did not need to be expressed, was for Russians a school of thought to be followed out to its logical conclusions. Now Catherine herself was a foreigner. It was not merely that she was not a Russian: she was something else very distinctive, a European of this period and phase, herself a pupil and product of the French humanitarians. Brilliant as were her abilities, she was not profound or sincere enough to detach herself from this environment; she led the gentry in a movement which she and it believed to be self-education, a movement which separated it still further from all its native roots, which accustomed it to despise what was Russian—for instance, in some of the schools of this period the utterance of a Russian word was punished by caning the hand—to feed on the generalizations so popular at the time, and even, as so easily happens with formulas, to find in them an excuse for shaping no thoughts of one's own.

Nor was Catherine, in this respect, in any way an exception among contemporary sovereigns. In Europe this was the period of Benevolent Despotism, seldom sufficiently studied in England or America. England, since the English Revolution, was for once the political model of advanced minds in Europe and paid little attention to a movement which seemed to fall so far short of her own achievement. Europe, on the contrary, was still in that period of transition which was so soon to lead up to the French Revolution. During this period, unconscious of what was to come, sovereigns took a pride in being intellectually in advance of their subjects and in pressing on them reforms which would be good for them. Such were Frederick the Great in Prussia (1740–86) and Joseph II in Austria (Emperor from 1765 to 1790), Charles of Naples (1735–59) with his reforming Minister Tanucci, who later followed the same Liberal program as Charles III in Spain (1759–88) with his Ministers d'Aranda and Florida Blanca, Joseph in Portugal (1750–57) with his Minister Pombal, "the Great Marquis," and other lesser sovereigns elsewhere.

These are features of Catherine and of Catherine's Russia which conditioned everything, and help to explain her political action. One task had lain unfinished since the time of Alexis. A new law code was urgently required, and in every subsequent reign commissions had been appointed, sometimes with experts, sometimes even with representatives elected from the provinces; but just because the government lived from hand to mouth and this task was a serious one, it had never been seriously faced. Catherine saw an opportunity of giving a striking example of her allegiance to the humanitarian school. For a year and a half she worked hard at an *Instruction* (*Nakaz*) designed for delegates to a great national commission, to lay down the principles of the new law code. This *Instruction* she twice showed to her principal advisers, and in each case allowed them to exclude a good half of it. Her original draft was very daring, at least intellectually daring; and even with the many corrections which she accepted from her counsellors, though they deleted the most drastic pronouncements in her own draft, the *Instruction* is a very striking manifesto. Of the five hundred-odd paragraphs, two hundred and fifty are borrowed straight from Montesquieu's admirable and suggestive book *The Spirit of Law* (*L'Esprit des Lois*), and one hundred from the no less important work of the Italian Beccaria on *Crimes and Punishments*. Catherine makes it no secret that her own contribution would cover only a few sheets. The first paragraph says that the Christian religion teaches us to do all the good to each other that we can; Clause 35 lays down the principle of equality before the law; the object of administration should be not so much punishment as the prevention of crime (241); it is dangerous for a country to be divided into a few large estates (417); sovereigns are meant to serve their people (520); freedom is the permission to do all that is not forbidden by the law (16); serfdom ought to be rare, and can only be excused by interests of State (253); on the other hand it would be dangerous to free all the serfs at once (260); agriculture cannot prosper where there is no property; capital punishment should be limited and torture abolished; education is better than punishment. The omitted sections include the following principles: Serfdom, if allowable, should exist mainly for the interests of agriculture; each peasant must have food and raiment; squires should only be allowed to punish as masters and not as judges; it would be well to have peasant judges and a system of jury; in Rome the laws could not rely on the slaves because the slaves could not rely on the laws; serfs ought to be enabled to buy their freedom; freed men should not again be reduced to slavery.[1]

The *Instruction* (*Nakaz*) was, in Catherine's own words, meant to be a kind of alphabet. Its publication was forbidden in France; but Frederick the Great, to whom she sent a copy, made her a member of the Berlin Academy; the British Ambassador Macartney declared that it was "better than a pitched battle." The *Nakaz* was the first of those long philosophical preambles, with a review of the various principles of legislation followed all over the world, that since then have habitually been prefixed to acts of legislation in Russia. But it would be a mistake

[1] See Brückner, *History of Catherine II*, pp. 532 *et seq.*

to judge the *Nakaz* solely by the limits of Catherine's application of the principles which it contained. The *Nakaz* is a flag, a program. Catherine, however honest or dishonest, here states that these are the principles which should underline her legislation. When the government itself says: the way in which things should be done is entirely opposite to the way in which we are doing them, it does at least one great thing: it encourages all its subjects to think for themselves and to criticize freely. That is the value, unfortunately the sole value, of Catherine's *Nakaz*.

This *Instruction* completed, Catherine summoned to Moscow in December 1766 a Great Commission from the whole empire, elected from all classes and from all nationalities. It contained five hundred and sixty-four members; of these, according to the analysis of Brückner, twenty-seven were high officials; one hundred and fifty were gentry; there was one representative from each of the two hundred towns, elected, unlike the rest, without any class distinction; fifty were delegates of the crown peasants, soldiers, and farmers; seventy were from the frontiers, especially from the Cossacks; and fifty were delegates of the non-Russian nationalities, excluding those which were nomadic. There had never been such elections; it was long since there had been anything like them, and the population did not understand them. In some places it obediently chose the officials, who had to explain that it was not at all themselves who were wanted. In the end Catherine succeeded in getting a good representation of the country, with the very important omission of the squires' peasants.

The delegates were to bring with them written instructions from their electors, expounding the needs of each locality or class. Of these the peasant deputy Chuprov from the province of Archangel received no less than one hundred and ninety-five, which is evidence of the crown peasants' interest in the election. Some districts even asked their delegates to report daily on the work of the Commission. The principal refrains of these instructions were the intolerable conditions of class antagonism, the absence of any definite rights, the miserably bad provision of justice, the uncontrolled arbitrariness of government officials, their corruption, and the hopelessly overpowering burden of taxation. One note can be traced throughout most of these electoral instructions: however variously it was understood, nearly all stood for an extension of local self-government. The gentry thought only of their own class, and as will be seen, were able to secure considerable advantages; but this claim one way or another was almost universal. It was more than intelligible; for, since the time of John the Dread, except for rare occasions nothing had been done to satisfy it, and the overwhelming centralization was bound to produce this demand. In a word, with all regard for the conditions of the time, these instructions may be described as a claim for decentralization and for personal rights.

The Great Commission sat for a year and a half. It was a very picturesque assembly, and in general there was an atmosphere of brotherhood; for instance, a fine was imposed on a delegate of the gentry who spoke abusively of the peasants. The Grand Marshal Bibikov was not a competent chairman and the procedure was cumbrous in the extreme, matters passing from one sub-commission to another with an unnecessary multiplicity of cogs in the wheel. But the assembly as a whole, both on the introduction of each main question and at the conclusion of the debates on it, had full opportunities of discussion. The Russian conception of such an assembly was the same as Catherine's own. It was regarded as a vast forum, an opportunity for ventilating the requirements of the population through representatives of each category of class or of locality, leaving all final decisions to the autocratic sovereign. Catherine followed the debates closely throughout, in some cases gave useful directions, and was herself responsible for the ventilation of the question of serfdom by the mouth of a young delegate of the Tambov gentry, Korobin.

The main subjects debated were all of great current interest. The older noble families, of whom the most enlightened representatives wished that Peter had not hurried the gradual education of Russia into a storm of violent change, and still more resented his creation of the new motley class of serving gentry in which they felt themselves swamped, continued the tradition of Prince Dmitry Golitsyn in favour of a restricted but regularized constitution on the model of Sweden or England. They only proposed that a distinction should be made between them and the serving gentry. In this matter, after a long debate, things were left as they stood.

The merchants were next prominent, with the claim that their monopoly of trade should be respected. The gentry had their own serf industry on their estates, and thus not only deprived the town trade of customers, but also faced it with serious rivals. As a result, the towns remained stagnant, and their population since the death of Peter had not advanced from its insignificant proportion of 3 per cent of the whole, which was only to be increased to 4 per cent under Catherine. The enlightened conservative, Prince M. Shcherbatov, charged the merchants with having entirely failed to respond to the call which Peter had made to them, to send their sons to be educated abroad and to develop trade consulates and other connections there. This debate reached no definite conclusion.

Far the most important subject discussed was serfdom. Catherine's desire was at least to free the squires' serfs wherever an estate was sold. She had encouraged the Free Economic Society, which she had founded, to offer a prize for an essay on the conditions of the peasantry; and the prize-winner declared for peasant proprietorship; but in spite of Catherine, the Society decided against publishing his essay. A number of peasant petitions had reached her, though forbidden by law. Her spokesman on the Commission, Korobin, spoke with spirit, eloquently quoting the *Instruction* in his support. He denounced the squires' habitual seizure of the earnings of the peasants, predicting the ruin of the State from the injustice of present conditions, and moved that the squires' rights should be defined. The gentry met him with jeers and abuse as a traitor to his class. In debate he more than held his own. "How can a peasant be good and virtuous," he asked, "when no means of paying us are left to him? If he drinks, it is not from self-indulgence but from despair." Shcherbatov, who had already denounced the ill-treatment of factory serfs, made an eloquent appeal for the peasantry. "We are men," he said, "and those who are under us are like us. All my blood rises in me." The peasant Chuprov, only following in the steps of the notable peasant writer of the time of Peter, Pososhkov, went to the root of the matter by laying down the principle that each class had its state duties and that therefore obligations must be defined for all, including the serfs of the squires. Korobin's motion, however, was not even put to the vote, and the debate had no effective sequel. The vested rights of the gentry were too strong to be touched.

The assembly supported Catherine in her demand for the further extension of centralization, at the expense of the local liberties guaranteed by the government at the time of annexation in the Baltics and in Ukraine; and this tendency, as will be seen, had later fatal results for the peasants of Ukraine. Other subjects discussed were justice, economics, and finance. It was asked that taxation should be levied in money, not in kind, and that the trade taxes should be defined. Catherine used the Commission to develop an interest in questions of public health.

The sittings were interrupted by the outbreak of war with Turkey, which called for the services of many of the members; and in June 1768 the Commission was prorogued. Large sub-commissions appointed by it, however, continued to sit in St. Petersburg till 1774. Of these, that which dealt with the class system discussed an important project of the Baltic baron Ungern-Sternberg. He proposed that peasants should have the right of complaint to government institutions, and that peasant justice should be organized in courts of three instances: elders chosen by the peasants, the squires' court, and the government court of the district; also that punishments prejudicial to health should become illegal; that in matters of justice the stewards should not act on their own authority; that husbands should not be parted from their wives or from their minor children; that peasants transferred to another estate should receive land there; that the squires' dues and corvées should be defined by law; and that peasant marriages should be freed from control. His opponents succeeded in emasculating this project, which was not carried further. Peasant elections, they said, would lead to riots; the squires were not worse than other judges, and anyhow would answer at the court of God; peasants if allowed to have property would squander it, especially on drink.

The Great Commission certainly, as Catherine herself said, gave her invaluable materials, but the use made of them was altogether too trifling. She was able to make a certain reconstruction of the higher institutions of government. The Senate, which had an overwhelming mass of business, was divided into six departments. The reign of favourites made the better of the nobles anxious that there should be a regular and authoritative Supreme Council of the sovereign. Catherine I and Peter II had had their Supreme Secret Council, Anne her Cabinet, Elizabeth her Conference, Peter III his Legislative Council. Catherine thought of instituting a properly defined Council of State, consisting of authorized advisers of the sovereign. She even nominated the members, but then reverted to the old plan of councils summoned at haphazard and nominated for the occasion according to her own preferences at the time.

In the field of local government, however, she created some new institutions which in substance were to survive as long as the monarchy. Peter the Great's division of the empire into large administrative units (*gubernii*) was much in need of further regulation. Beginning, in his opportunist but significant way, with his new acquisition Ingermanland which contained St. Petersburg (1702), he instituted by 1710 eight *gubernii* and extended the number to eleven in 1719, which included secondary units (*provintsii*) under the charge of voevodes. Most of the auxiliary posts or institutions which he established were abolished after his death. Catherine issued in 1764 general instructions to the governors, by which they were made "heads and masters" of their *gubernii*. In 1775 and 1780 she further systematized the provincial administration. Still allowing for the secondary unit, *provintsia*, by way of exception, she divided the empire into fifty *gubernii* (which we will henceforth describe as provinces) each subdivided into *uyezdy* or districts, a term which had previously had a much less definite significance. Larger areas were placed under viceroys or governors general. The *gubernia* was directed by a governor, who was left a free initiative except in the presence of his superior, but was assisted by assessors and a systematized office, the Provincial Administration, with defined responsibilities. Other institutions were the Civil Law Chamber, the Criminal Law Chamber, the Court of Conscience; the Treasury Chamber under the presidency of the vice-governor; and the Office of Public Welfare. The institutions of the district were on an elective basis; a District Court, a Lower County Court, and for the crown peasants a Lower Justice (*rasprava*). An Upper County Court and an Upper Justice, also based on election, acted as superior instances within the *gubernia*. Thus, in general, the local authority was to a certain extent subdivided, and in the smaller units the principle of local initiative was extended, in which the role of the gentry was predominant. The collegiate principle was maintained both in administration and in justice. At last justice and finance were discriminated from pure administration. The gentry also elected for the district an administrative official, the *ispravnik* (or corrector), who was not only in charge of the police but was generally responsible for the local well-being and for any provision of charity.

This tendency towards a local initiative of the gentry (*dvoryanstvo*) was specially developed in the legislation affecting their class and gave them general responsibilities which went much beyond its limits. We have noticed the peculiarities in the origin of the Russian gentry: the patrimony by the side of the *pomestya*, the remains of the old boyars gradually drowned in an ocean of service men. This mixed character of the gentry, which Peter I inherited from the Tsars of Moscow, was mixed and diluted infinitely further by his Table of Ranks, which based all official status on state service. Creating a huge corporation of officialized state gentry Peter, as has been said, created a greaty "body" which, with its special obligations of education and its practical monopoly of contact with educated Europe, was sure to get some soul of its own. In fact, its corporate consciousness makes itself very evident in the years succeeding his death. The period between Peter I and Catherine I is marked, as we have seen, by its constant endeavour on the one hand to evade its obligations, and on the other to acquire further privileges, and this movement is crowned by the edict of Peter III emancipating it from the duty of state service. It was on the support of this class that Catherine's imaginary title to the throne was bound to rest; and her reign is, essentially, the period of the *dvoryanstvo*. It has been said that she gave them their soul; certainly, she gave them their style. Following Montesquieu, she desired some such broad base for her authority, an idea which she expressed in her *Nakaz*. She withstood the claim of the older aristocracy put forward in the Great Commission to limit the access to the *dvoryanstvo*, but in her Charter of the Gentry (May 2, 1785) she greatly extended its class rights. The gentry could escape state service or enter it under privileged conditions; they retained their exemption from personal taxation; they obtained exemption from corporal punishment; they could not lose their rank, estates or life except by judgment of their peers, and in the case of deprivation of rank the sentence had to be confirmed by the sovereign. Only hereditary gentry could own serf villages; they were relieved of all the restrictions imposed by Peter on the sale or exploitation of their estates, which could not be confiscated out of the family; they were still responsible for the care of their serfs. The gentry were ordered to choose district marshals of their class (1766). In 1775 they were locally organized with provincial and district marshals, and assemblies of deputies which met every three years. These assemblies elected the marshals and also the assessors of the upper provincial law courts, and judges and officials for the districts; the governor might refer questions for their discussion: they might represent their needs to the governor or to the sovereign; they might collect funds for their common needs, and it was they who had to recommend personal exclusion from their class.

At the same time Catherine attempted to develop further the beginnings of self-government in the towns. They were given definite town property in land (1766); town justice was reorganized on a class basis, and courts were established for the protection of orphans and widows (1775). In 1785 was issued a charter for towns (May 2). The town magistracies, which had been restored, had the right of appealing to the sovereign at the institution of any new state burdens. Various categories of town dwellers were established, based on various qualifications of capital, membership of guilds or corporations, and professional and educational status. The town was to choose a mayor and a town council (or *duma*) based on these categories, which appointed a standing com-

mittee of six members (one from each category). The council was to
meet once in every three years. The town was thus expected to manage
its own financial affairs, reporting to the governor of the province. But
this system remained for the most part on paper. As these town *dumy*
received no powers of rating or authority over the police and had to
subsist on voluntary contributions, they were quite unable to do anything very effective for the provision of public health and of charity.

At the instigation of her able adviser Sievers, Governor of Novgorod,
Catherine had founded the Free Economic Society to investigate the
conditions of agriculture. She took a special interest in roads and canals,
and wished to develop Russian trade with Asia. She founded in 1763 a
great Foundlings Hospital in Moscow and in 1773 a similar one in St.
Petersburg. In 1764 she founded the Smolny Educational Institute for
girls of good family. She was also founder of the Public Library at St.
Petersburg. Prince Cherkasov helped her to make a beginning of medical
provision; in 1763 she founded a College of Medicine, and five years
later herself set the example of inoculation against smallpox. For the
rest, Catherine's achievements mostly remained on paper. She claimed to
have founded 144 towns, but when the poet Derzhavin, as Governor of
Archangel, went to the formal opening of the town of Kem, he found
that no such town existed. On a much larger scale the same thing happened with the city which was to commemorate Catherine's reign—
Ekaterinoslav (Glory of Catherine). Enormous sums were poured into
its construction, but before much had been achieved the work had to
stop for want of funds.

In 1771 a grievous plague, brought from the Turkish front, after taking many victims in southwest Russia, broke out in Moscow. Strong
measures of quarantine were imposed and Catherine sent Eropkin with
full powers, which he used with courage and ability. But the toll of the
plague was a thousand daily, and the Governor of Moscow, Saltykov,
losing his head, left the city. In September a mob murdered the Archbishop Ambrose for forbidding the kissing of icons, and wanted to kill
all doctors and gentry and stop all medical measures of prevention;
Eropkin suppressed the riot only by the use of cannon. Catherine, who
showed courage when all around her were in dismay, was only with
difficulty stopped from going to Moscow herself. Gregory Orlov, whom
she sent as dictator, took prompt measures; and in the winter the plague
died out after killing, according to Catherine, 100,000 persons. While
avowing this figure to Grimm, in her foreign correspondence she generally dismissed the whole affair as an incident.

In May 1773, the innumerable elements of discontent massed together into a storm of revolt, which at one time covered almost all east and southeast Russia, under a Don Cossack, Emelian Pugachev. A Cossack at eighteen, Pugachev served as a private in the Seven Years' War and was marked for distinction. Knouted several times for his independence, and sent home ill from the Turkish front, he helped a kinsman to fly from arrest. He himself had therefore to fly to Ukraine where, in a monastery of the Old Believers, he was given money and encouraged to lead a rebellion. Thence he travelled to the Ural River, where he was seized and taken to Kazan. He escaped again and appeared on the Irgiz as Peter III, returned from travels in Poland, Egypt, and Jerusalem. Marrying a Cossack girl, he appointed maids of honour and surrounded himself with bogus courtiers, actually bearing the names of Orlov, Vorontsev, and Panin; he even produced later a sham Paul. A clever adventurer from the gentry, Shvanvich, served as his Secretary of State. Two of his forts he named Moscow and St. Petersburg, and appeared at parades as Emperor.

In the autumn of 1773 Pugachev took several forts and besieged Orenburg. His army was joined by Cossacks from the Don and the Dnieper, and by non-Russians such as Tartars, Kirghiz, Bashkirs, Mordvins, Chuvashes, and Votyaks, all the Tartar and Finnish tribes which remained in this part of Russia; the Bashkirs had kept the memory of their insurrection under Peter the Great, and of the subsequent seizure of their land by the government. Equally accustomed to a camping life were the numerous exiles and convicts, who during their long halts on the road to Siberia had found it easy to escape from their escorts; of these alone there were 4000 in Kazan. Pugachev declared that he would shut up Catherine in a nunnery, and wherever he went he killed the gentry and seized their estates. The price set on his head rose from 500 to 28,000 roubles. His name filled all conversations in Moscow and in St. Petersburg, where the gentry were in a panic, and the mob, including the innumerable house servants, was only waiting to rise.

The first general sent against him, Carr, proved quite incapable. Catherine who refused to despond and took pleasure in comparing her difficulties with those of Peter the Great, sent one of her best lieutenants, Bibikov, with full powers. Bibikov was appalled by the entire absence of ability and courage in the gentry, on whom he could not even count for loyalty. His soldiers were all predisposed to the brigand chief. Bibikov did succeed in raising a local militia out of the Kazan gentry, but confessed himself powerless in face of "the quiet, almost universal movement of the mob." "It is not Pugachev that matters," he wrote, "but the general indignation." He blamed "the blindness and ignorance, the incompetent and dishonest officials, the weak and stupid officers." He declared that the people had just grievances which must be satisfied. Catherine on her side ordered that there should be no punishment exceeding "due strictness," and described the rising to Grimm as a farce.

Pugachev captured town after town on the Volga and in the Urals, and in December was master of Samara. Golitsyn defeated him in March 1774, relieved Orenburg, and defeated him again. Pugachev, however, now transferred the centre of the rising to the Middle Volga and even westward toward Moscow. The rebellion, at first a revolt of Cossacks and nomads, began to turn into a peasant war. Pugachev hanged five hundred priests and officers in three months, roused the peasants everywhere, and was expected in Moscow at any minute. It is to Catherine's credit that she still urged humanity on her lieutenants. Energetic action by Count Peter Panin and Michelson at last began to take effect. In August Michelson defeated the rebels, inflicting a loss of 2000; near Tsaritsyn, which had only held out under the greatest difficulties, he captured 8000 more. Panin was equally effective on the side of Penza. At this point a famine on the Volga had a great effect on the rising, and it gradually died down. Again defeated by Michelson, Pugachev, with what was left of his great chaotic host, fled to the Urals. Suvorov, fresh from his astonishing victory over the Turks at Kozludji, starting on his new command in the literal words of Catherine, "with no other luggage than his zeal in service," was following the rebel chief with 300 mounted infantry at the pace of sixty miles a day, when Pugachev was surrendered by his last adherents. He was brought in an iron cage to Moscow; even at his trial Catherine strictly forbade any use of torture; Pugachev was executed in Moscow in January 1775.

Terrified at the time by this tremendous explosion, the gentry now rejoiced at their undeserved triumph. Many of them came to gloat over Pugachev's execution. All thought of reform was dismissed. The lot of the peasants became even worse than before; and, whatever Catherine's professions and desires, her reign was the culmination of serfdom. In an edict punishing a cruel proprietor, she used the ironical words: "Be so good as to call your peasants cattle"; and she plainly predicted that the existing state of things was leading straight to a huge social cataclysm. Her able and honest administrator Sievers never ceased to press for measures of reform, especially for the fixing of the peasants' obligations in rent and in work; he declared that "the payments of dues passed all belief." Yet the number of serfs was vastly increased under Catherine. The frequent and enormous grants of land which she made to her lieutenants on any court occasion, were grants of new-made serfs out of that diminishing section of the peasantry which still remained comparatively free, the crown peasants. Catherine, who finally destroyed the Zaporog Fastness, also extended serfdom to the great area of Ukraine. In 1763 Ukrainian peasants had been forbidden to leave their estates without permission of the squire, and in 1783 most of them were definitely fastened to the soil. This act, like the original fastening in Great Russia, was carried out without even any mention of serfdom; each was simply ordered "to remain in his place and calling." It was purely a fiscal measure, and part of the general program of centralization for equalizing conditions all over Russia. In January 1797 Paul was to extend the same measure to Ekaterinoslav, Crimea, and the Caucasus.

Russian squires were now allowed to send serfs as convicts to Siberia without any restrictions, and to fetch them back when they pleased; Sievers complained that the army lost thousands of men yearly by these regulations. All petitions, whether to the Empress or to government offices, were declared illegal and punished with knout and life exile. Public sales of serfs by auction were forbidden in 1771 but were allowed in 1773, so long as no hammer was used at the auction.

The economic effects of these conditions on the country were ruinous. The gentry might have been expected, on their relief from compulsory service, to settle in the country and manage their estates. On the contrary, they gravitated more and more to the towns and around the Court, especially during and after the insurrection of Pugachev, and left all administration to their stewards, living on their revenues as absentee landlords. Instead of utilizing their rights over peasant labour on the spot, which would at least have shown them the limits of what could be expected of it, they preferred to lease their land to their peasants at arbitrary rents, against which the peasant had no appeal whatever. Though in this reign the rouble sank one quarter, the rents demanded rose from two roubles in the sixties to four in the eighties, and five at the end of the reign. On the other hand, there were estates where the peasant was compelled to work six days a week for his master, with no time left for attention to his own land. The number of house servants, which should have diminished enormously as soon as the gentry were no longer obliged to appear with their local troops on service, on the contrary increased. There was no control at all over the squires' chastisements; peasants were chained up, whipped, or caned for any supposed misdemeanour: for instance, five hundred strokes of the rod were given for absence from the holy communion; there were squires who had regular tariffs of punishment. Another unnoticed effect of serfdom was that the peasants were prevented from gravitating, as they otherwise must have done, from the barren soil of the north-centre to the now liberated territories on the black soil of the south. The government itself greatly increased the poll tax during this reign.

All that now counted in Russia was the new gentry class, relieved of former state burdens and absolute in its authority over the peasants. The stunted towns could not develop any considerable industry; the bulk of trade was in the hands of foreigners, who got the main advantage out of it. Meanwhile the pampered gentry, depending on the toil of others for their material needs, equally, in the brilliant comparison of Klyuchevsky, lived intellectually on the labour of others, swallowing ready-made formulas from Europe, derived from a world that had nothing in common with their own conditions. The Russian gentry in ever larger numbers became familiar with the charms of western travel; and their chief preoccupation was to be taken as finished products of European culture. They showed a wonderful proficiency in their imitation of everything European. French judges declared that many home-educated Russians were far quicker to assimilate the latest French ideas than, for instance, the students of Germany. Technical education had given way to general culture. Even in the two naval academies the course now included the fine arts, with acting and dancing. At provincial schools for the gentry, dances were held twice a week. The new romantic literature of Europe, from Rousseau onwards, was absorbed more whole-heartedly in Russia than anywhere else, though it did not prevent the sentimental readers from inflicting monstrous punishments on their house servants, in some cases for nothing else than their own distraction. The Russian gentleman came to be more and more estranged from all the realities of his own country: "a stranger at home, he tried to be at home among strangers, and in European society succeeded only in seeming a kind of foundling." [1] As everything French was in fashion, especially French tutors, some recognized no limit in their adoption of the revolutionary ideas which were at that time permeating France. The republican Romme was the tutor and friend of young Count Stroganov, later one of the intimate counsellors of Alexander I; and the children of Count Saltykov were entrusted to the care of the brother of Marat, also a republican. It was the republican encyclopædist Laharpe to whom

[1] Klyuchevsky, Lecture 87, Vol. V, p. 147.

Catherine committed the education of Alexander I himself. Entire inaction while on their estates, succeeded by intense boredom, had first been solaced by floods of sentimental literature, but led in the end to a more serious study of Western political thought. It is in Catherine's reign that we find the origins of that peculiar psychology which was later to stamp the Russian intelligentsia.

Catherine had herself encouraged her educated subjects to criticize; she had even tried to teach them by example. She did not feel happy unless she had written something every day, and besides her real masterpieces, her letters, and besides the textbooks which she drew up for the education of her grandsons, she wrote plays aimed against her unlucky contemporary, Gustav of Sweden, against Cagliostro the charlatan of Paris, and against the foibles of the society of her time. Though under a *nom de plume*, she took a leading part in the direction of the first satirical journal Vsyakaya Vsyachina (*A Little of Everything*) founded in 1772, which very soon had several imitators.

Catherine had a mental attitude characteristic of sovereigns; she wanted everyone around her to be smiling. Being herself a woman of broad nature and vigorous intellect, she found satire an enjoyment. The whole history of her reign, that is, of her brilliant Court and her loyal gentry, is a sort of hypnosis of admirably manufactured mirth; the shameless story of her foreign diplomacy is another such hypnosis; with such a program, and with such an environment in the Europe which she tried so closely to reproduce in Russia, it was inevitable that she should succeed too well. We have seen that she succeeded in creating the beginnings of a corporate and independent spirit in the gentry. There were many who would stop where she did. But there were a few, at first of course only a few scattered individuals, who would take seriously the all too vital questions which she raised, and replace her satire for entertainment with a satire which came from the heart. Such was the playwright Von Vizin who, while he joined Catherine in showing up the laziness and obscurantism of Russian society, passed on to speak in terms of manly indignation of the radical evil of the community, serfdom. Up till now there had been individual critics, sometimes a small band of friends who were critics. Now began, still on a very small scale, the formation of a whole group which was later to lead to the creation of a highly critical public opinion.

The man who may be said to have begun the formation of such a group of critical thinkers was N. Novikov. Son of a squire and official, himself an ex-Guardsman, he availed himself of Catherine's example to found in succession three satirical journals, *The Drone* (1769–70), *The Painter* (1772–3), and *The Purse* (1774). *The Drone* satirized less people than abuses, for instance, the court service which "demands better pretence than an actor's," the "young Russian pigling," who comes back from his education in Europe "a perfect swine," and most of all, serfdom and the mentality of the serf-master, whose view was that "only cruelty can keep these beasts in order." Catherine called on her rival journalists to be "charitable," and it was her disapproval that caused the changes of title in Novikov's journals. The second of these, *The Painter*, he boldly dedicated to her as the anonymous author of the play *What a Time!* and became more outspoken as he went on. *The Purse* was stopped in September 1774, and Novikov, renting the university press of Moscow, devoted himself to the publication of educative literature. He was also one of the earliest of Russian Free Masons. Among those who were associated with him was the liberal customs official Radishchev.

CHAPTER XV

Catherine, Poland, and Europe

[*1762–96*]

Underneath the glamour of a European Court, a glamour all the more picturesque from the admixture of the strange and varied resources of a great Eastern empire, the economic and moral life of the country was going from bad to worse. Yet meanwhile Russia went on adding enormously to her commitments and expenditure by an extravagant forward policy in Europe. With Catherine we go a great step further in the glaring contrast between Russia at home and Russia abroad, a contrast which led and was meant to lead to a complete mystification of Europe as to realities in Russia. It is the monstrously unequal march of a great giant, whose one leg is sinking further and further in the morass created by serfdom, while the other stretches further and further afield to cover new territory and to meet new problems with which the Russian government is increasingly incompetent to deal. Russia's advance eastward was natural, and justified itself: there the Russian was an agent of civilization; that is why it went of itself and is little chronicled. In every advance of Russia westward she was kicking against the pricks, she was undertaking the responsibility of government over peoples which, if smaller, were considerably more civilized than herself. We shall see what further complications were introduced into this process by the great European event at the end of this reign, the French Revolution.

Catherine herself said that her métier was government. The special field of administration of which she was a consummate master was diplomacy. Catherine was throughout really her own Foreign Minister. In the two main periods of her foreign policy—the so-called northern system of alliances with Count Nikita Panin and later the Austrian alliance with Bezborodko and others, her ministers were men not without distinction, often with ideas, but they were merely her executants; the ruling, guiding, directing mind throughout was hers. These were the worst and most shameless days of what is called the old diplomacy. Brilliant sovereigns, sharing to the full in the new enlightenment which

France was spreading over Europe, directed the affairs of vast states by personal correspondence between themselves, all the more convenient because the secrecy made disavowal easy.

Catherine was in constant correspondence with her contemporaries Frederick the Great and Joseph II of Austria; she corresponded with Stanislaw Poniatowski of Poland and even with her enemy, Gustav III of Sweden. To Frederick the Great she wrote something like 180 letters lasting over twenty years (1761–81). She herself did not go abroad, and found it more convenient to make her correspondents come to her. She entertained in Russia Prince Henry of Prussia in 1770 and 1776, Joseph II in 1777 and 1780, and Gustav of Sweden in 1777 and 1783. Her letters are written in a free and lively style, discursive and with much natural charm. In them Catherine shows throughout the very high faculty of seizing the exact opportunities of the moment and shading to them her own aims. All the transitions in her friendships—and she was always ready to change her friends according to circumstances—were gradual almost to the point of being unnoticeable. She made the fullest use of the extra civility which might be reasonably claimed by a woman. Also, in spite of her remarkable foresight and brilliant ability and statecraft, there is something of the rich woman in the easy, sometimes almost happy-go-lucky, way in which she pledges the resources of a great empire to realize her own fancies. It seems as if it is all being done in a drawing room, where it would be indecent to emphasize to her the seriousness of the vast propositions which she entertains. At the same time, among elect minds she stands out as one who can entirely hold her own. Europe might be beguiled into the belief that Russia's strength was colossal; but Catherine was not unconscious of Russian realities, and of her own constant insecurity on a throne to which she had no kind of right except ability. She was her own agent of propaganda. This work, in the conditions of the time, could be done ideally through her correspondence with the French thinkers or with prominent persons in Paris society, and the use which she made of these intermediaries was consummately clever. But also in the actual tussle of widely conflicting interests she was more than a match for Joseph of Austria, and was fully on equal terms with Frederick the Great, though the main idea of the period, the partition of Poland between the three Eastern monarchies, was his suggestion and was by no means in the real interest of Russia. In the long detail of their relations, she several times seems almost to be playing him like a fish on a hook. It is even more so with others.

The Europe of this time offered her this opportunity, if she were able to use it. Frederick himself owes his salvation in the Seven Years' War to the death of Elizabeth of Russia; his country is entirely exhausted and he knows it; peace is to him a necessity, peace and economic organization. Maria Teresa has in this same Seven Years' War failed, even with the help of France and Russia, to right the wrong which was done her by Frederick's seizure of Silesia; the Holy Roman Empire is already little more than a name; Germany itself is from now onward either a dualism or something even more plural. The France of Louis XV and later of Louis XVI is in decline; the French Revolution is seen by many to be looming on the horizon. Italy has no political unity, is ruled largely by foreigners and, in the interest of the balance of Europe, is expected to provide consolation prizes for those who have lost something elsewhere. Spain, in spite of a short galvanic revival, is also on the decline. Even England, which enters this period as for the first time conscious of her world empire, is to suffer during Catherine's reign the severest blow which that empire ever received, in the severance of her American dominions, a blow which for a time many continental judges believed to be fatal to her.

But the Western states were for Catherine in the main only onlookers and possible arbiters. She had to deal principally with her nearer neighbours, with whom Russia's past relations are already familiar to us: Sweden, Poland, and Turkey. This was the heritage left to Catherine in the long story of Russia's gradual approach to Europe. Doubly, they were obstacles to her; they were territorial barriers, and also they blocked Russia off from that contact with Europe which was necessary to make her a modern State.

The question between Russia and Sweden was that of the possession of the southern coast of the Baltic, which ethnographically was neither Swedish nor Russian; it was a purely economic question. It was settled by Peter the Great, who took the risk of introducing a very considerable German population into the Russian State. Sweden was on the decline after her immense exertions in the sixteenth and seventeenth centuries, and only wars of reprisal were to be expected from her, at moments when Russia's hands were filled with other difficulties.

The central obstacle was Poland. Ordyn-Nashchokin had found it possible to immobilize her, and even to go into alliance with her. With Peter I the alliance had practically become a Russian protectorate. Catherine was to reap the fruits of this process. The outstanding question between Russia and Poland was that of the religious dissidents, which concerned the Orthodox Russian population under Polish rule. To bring this population into the Russian Empire was a legitimate aim; it was only a continuation of the policy of John III, who had declared that no peace with Poland could be permanent until this was achieved.

Against Turkey the issue was at once national, religious, and economic; national, because Russia only escaped from the Tartar yoke after the Turks took Constantinople; religious, because it was a struggle between the Cross and the Crescent; economic, because the last rampart of Tartar conquest, Crimea, had passed under the sovereignty of Turkey, which prevented Russia from utilizing the fruitful steppes of the south and cut her off from the shores of the Black Sea.

The start was like an overture. Catherine had to tune her orchestra for what was to follow. The conditions did not seem promising. Elizabeth had been allied with Austria against Prussia; Peter III had changed sides. But Catherine saw at once the advantages which might be drawn from a policy which committed her to no one; while assuring Frederick of her alliance, she withdrew her army; it gave him, however, a moral support which was very valuable to him in his impending operations against the Austrians. In St. Petersburg, Catherine, anxious to escape any association with her husband's policy, pronounced strongly against Prussia; meanwhile she urged Frederick to end the war and offered her mediation, and at the same time urged peace on Austria too, much to the surprise and indignation of Austria. Ultimately Frederick himself asked for Catherine's mediation, and Austria hastened to make direct peace with him at Hubertusburg (February 5, 1763).

At the same time began an exchange of opinions between Frederick and Catherine on the subject of Poland. It was with an outlying part of the Polish question that Catherine first had to deal. Kurland, originally territory of the Livonian Knights, had long been a duchy under Polish suzerainty held by the Kettler family, whose last descendant was succeeded, in the reign of Anne, by her favourite Biren. Biren remained in St. Petersburg to rule Russia even after Anne's death, and when deprived of his regency was exiled to Siberia. In 1758, August III of Saxony, who was King of Poland, desired to obtain Kurland for his son Charles, and to this Elizabeth of Russia had consented; even at the time Catherine had opposed this concession. Catherine saw that she could do what she liked with Poland. "There is there," she wrote, "a happy anarchy which we can work at will." She forced on Kurland the returned exile Biren; she bribed numerous members of the Polish Diet; she threatened Brühl the Polish Foreign Minister; she sent troops into

Kurland on the pretext of repressing disorders; eventually Charles had to abandon the struggle and leave the Duchy (April 1763). To the protests of Poland Catherine replied that she was defending the Polish Constitution, of which she claimed to be guarantor; that is, she was preventing a foreign elected King of Poland from securing a hereditary domination in the country for his son. When Polish troops were to be sent to Kurland, Catherine defended the anarchical right of the Polish Diet, which made any mobilization without its consent illegal.

In October 1763, August III died. Of sixty senators forty-eight supported the candidature of his son Charles, and these also wished to drive Biren out of Kurland. Catherine threatened to send the Polish envoy in Moscow out of Russia and to "populate Siberia with her enemies." Frederick had already written to her suggesting joint action at the new election. "We will give a king to Poland," quietly writes Catherine, and the two speak plainly of their "intentions." Russian troops were moved into Poland, Russian bribes were freely distributed, and the candidate sponsored by Frederick and Catherine, Stanislaw Poniatowski, was elected on September 6, 1764. France had been willing that her former ally, Saxony, should lose hold of Poland if one of the greater Polish nobles were chosen, but Poniatowski had no such standing and neither riches nor strength of character; he was a puppet king, and in fact was one of Catherine's discarded lovers. Catherine writes freely about the "king we have made," but to one of her French correspondents she writes, "we do not know how it happened." In this year Russia and Prussia concluded a treaty for common policy in the affairs of Poland.

Poland was now in the most critical stage of her existence. The election of foreign candidates as kings invited foreign intervention; the elected kings themselves had only a temporary interest in Poland. The elections of Sigismund III, August II, and Stanislaw Leszczynski had been accompanied by great disorders; that of the successor of Jan Kazimir had led to five years of legalized civil war. The Sejm, talked out or blocked by the free veto of individual members, often dispersed without a decision; this happened to thirteen out of twenty-six successive Sejms; in such cases the local *Sejmiki* settled things for themselves. The sharpest religious intolerance kept alive the question of the dissident or non-Catholic population; no new churches of their confessions might be built, and those not authorized were pulled down; the dissidents were excluded from political rights and official posts, in despite of a treaty concluded with Russia in their favour in 1719. Justice was demoralized; public spirit was at its lowest ebb. "What can I do with you, poor

State?" said the eloquent preacher, Skarga, at the beginning of the seventeenth century; and again, "it will fall when you do not expect it and crush you all in its ruins; you will be poor exiles, despised vagabonds."

But a remarkable awakening had now set in. The movement of French thought led to a wave of enthusiasm for education which carried even the Jesuits with it. Colleges, observatories, libraries were founded; public debates were held on scientific subjects. Several notable authors, including Konarski and Leszczynski himself, pointed to the urgent necessity of reform. They urged that all classes must share the burden of taxation, the administration must be purified, the army strengthened, trade and industry developed; voices called for emancipation of the peasants. The powerful Czartoryski family led the movement for reform; the reformers were determined that the *liberum veto* should be abolished and decisions taken in future by a simple majority. In spite of the strong opposition of the Russian and Prussian ambassadors, much was done. The procedure of the Sejm was simplified and made independent of the instructions of the *Sejmiki*; the veto was abolished; commissions were set up for financial, economic, and military reform; the towns were freed from the jurisdiction of the gentry (1764).

Russia had now a grip over the whole of Poland. The Russian Ambassador in Warsaw, Repnin, whose every step was guided by Catherine, was almost ruler of the country. The Russian troops introduced at the election of King Stanislaw had not withdrawn; Polish foreign policy was almost entirely conducted from St. Petersburg. It might have seemed that Catherine had in her own hands the disposal of Poland. Had she wished only to detach the Russian and Orthodox population, it would have been comparatively easy. Repnin was instructed to protest against the violations of the Russo-Polish treaties of 1686 and 1719, by which Poland had engaged not to persecute the Orthodox; he demanded the return of monasteries and churches which had been expropriated. At this time there was very strong religious feeling in Poland; here the Jesuits had almost as great an influence as ever, and the bishops of Cracow and Vilna aroused the Poles against Russian aggression. The Sejm refused equal rights to dissidents. The opponents of all political reform now appealed to Repnin. He prompted two confederations, or armed leagues of opposition, in Thorn and Slutsk. He forced the summons of an extraordinary Sejm in October 1767; he made it accept a special commission, chosen from its members but nominated by himself; he seized leading reformers and deported them to Russia; he then restored the "liberties" of the evil old constitution and had them incorporated by the Sejm in a treaty which he made it conclude with Russia (February 1768).

However at Bar, close to the Turkish frontier, under the lead of Pulawski, a number of patriotic nobles availed themselves of the right of confederation to oppose the domination of Russia. There followed a partisan war in which the Russian troops, claiming to stand for the old constitution, were usually able to overcome any resistance in the towns, but had the greatest difficulty in reducing opposition in the country.

It was now that the greatest of Russian generals was first employed in an independent command. Alexander Suvorov belonged to a gentry family of Novgorod. He was so puny a child that his father would not enter him for military service. This, however, was the boy's one enthusiasm; and before he was fifteen he had given himself an education of his own, by studying all the books he could get about the great captains of war. When at last allowed to join the army, he had to enter it at the bottom, and it was by his own choice that he long remained first a private and then a sergeant, accepting every duty of these ranks and learning intimately all the needs and instincts of the Russian soldier. As a staff officer at the battle of Künersdorf he saw nothing but irresolution, quarrels of commanders, delays, and incompetence, and during a two years' peace command of the Suzdal regiment he knit his men into a closely united community, whose every need and thought was known to its commander; Suvorov was himself its teacher of religion and mathematics; he even showed his men how to mend their uniforms. This work of organization he continued throughout life, and extended it to every section of the Russian army which he commanded. The corporate spirit which he thus created was the foundation of all his future successes. This little wiry man with the quaint mobile face whose every word was a flash of thought, never happy except in a soldier's shirt, going into action with a cane and insisting on directing his bayonet attacks in person, was able to get more out of his clever "children" than any Russian general before or after him. In action he depended on mobilizing the product of this training on to a single quickly chosen and quickly executed decision. "Intuition, rapidity, impact"—these were the three articles of his creed, and he put them into simple words in a "soldier's catechism" which he made up for his men: "The head of the army does not wait for the tail. The bullet is a fool, the bayonet is a sportsman; fortune goes past like a flash of lightning; seize her by the hair:

she will never come back to you." The wiseacres laughed at such words and credited his luck with his successes, for in his long life he was never fairly and squarely beaten. "Luck today and luck yesterday," said Suvorov; "allow a little bit for mind."

In Poland Suvorov had to move a small force rapidly, usually at night, through a hostile country, facing and countering each danger as soon as it arose and appearing as the deciding factor at one point after another; it was he who defeated the French general Dumouriez, sent by Choiseul with arms and money to assist the confederates; later he outgeneralled Dumouriez's successor and captured Cracow; it was Suvorov who reduced the most formidable of the partisan bands, led by Oginski.

But the war in Poland was soon complicated by another. In 1762 Turkey had promised help to Poland. The unfortunate confederates were pressed toward the Turkish frontier, and there a Cossack rising broke out against them. Poles and Jews were massacred wholesale in the frontier township Balta; reprisals came from Galta on the Turkish side and the Cossacks, crossing the brook which marked the frontier, ravaged Galta. The Poles demanded the withdrawal of the Cossacks from Balta; this led to war, and the Tartars of Crimea thereupon invaded Russia (1768).

Catherine looked forward to this war with pleasure and built, as she said, "all kinds of castles in Spain." In 1769 Prince A. Golitsyn beat the Turks and took Hotin, but was replaced by Rumyantsev. This distinguished general, who was of senior rank to Suvorov, had already attained a high reputation. A godson of Catherine I, he was in 1740 reported from the Russian Embassy in Berlin for refusal to study, nightly brawls, smashing furniture, throwing his clothes out of the window, and keeping company with soldiers and lackeys; he wanted to exchange the civil career for the military where, according to the Ambassador, he was "not wanted." In the Seven Years' War he reappears as saving the situation by a daring charge through a wood at Gross Jägersdorf, and is recognized by his opponents as at that time the best trained military theorist in the Russian army. Catherine described him as "the Russian Turenne."

Rumyantsev advancing into Moldavia took Jassy, where the inhabitants swore homage to Catherine. He had very small forces (40,000) and was in constant difficulties for supplies; there was plague in his army; the Turks attacked him at Fokshany, but were defeated after a fierce struggle. He had to retreat for stores to Podolia, and the enemy advanced with 200,000 men. In reply to his complaints, Catherine wrote: "Europe is looking at you; the Romans, when they had two or three legions, did not ask how many men the enemy had, but where he was." On July 29, 1770, Rumyantsev defeated a vastly superior force on the Larga, and on August 12, with 17,000 men, engaged the main Turkish army at Kagul; though enveloped and sorely pressed, the Russians won by the bayonet and captured the Turkish camp; Rumyantsev, in reporting this success of "my incomparable army," adroitly turned back on Catherine her reference to the Romans. Potemkin took Ismail; Repnin took Kilia; Igelström took Akkerman; and Count Peter Panin, with heavy loss, stormed Brailov. Azov and Taganrog, the old acquisitions of Peter the Great, were also regained, and Catherine already dreamed of a Russian fleet on the Black Sea and of conquests in the Caucasus.

Much the most striking success of the war must be credited to Catherine herself. The fleet in the Baltic had gone completely out of repair since Peter the Great; Catherine saw in it "only ships and men, not a fleet and sailors," and described it as only "fit to catch herrings." She had herself taken it in hand; now she sent it on a sensational voyage through the Sound, the North Sea, the English Channel, and the Atlantic to the Mediterranean. This great enterprise seems not to have alarmed England, though it caused anxiety in France; but it was to prove one of the most notable advertisements to Western Europe of the power and aggressive policy of Russia. The fleet, under the command of Alexis Orlov, reached the coast of Greece and there made an attempt to rouse the Orthodox population against the Sultan; it carried agitators, proclamations and arms, but not enough of the latter to be effective, and the plans for landing were muddled; there were risings in Morea, but these the Turks were able to put down. Orlov, however, blew up a fort at Navarino, won a naval fight off Chios on July 5, 1770, and two days later won the most signal of Russian naval victories, defeating and burning the Turkish fleet at Chesme Bay. Catherine wrote to Voltaire: "There is nothing one need despair of." However, a French officer, Baron Tott, helped the panic-stricken Turks to put the Dardanelles into a state of defence, and Orlov, who was to have followed up his success into the Black Sea, did not even menace Constantinople, contenting himself with occupying some twenty islands in the Ægean. Meanwhile, Dolgoruky entered Crimea, won Eupatoria and Kerch, captured some Turkish ships, and installed as Khan a Russian protégé, Shagin Girei.

Frederick the Great in his letters to Catherine wrote fulsome praise of the Russian victories, but he was extremely anxious. Before Navarino,

Catherine had even lightheartedly prepared a manifesto to the Corsicans to make them rise against the French. Austria was also alarmed, and drew nearer to Turkey. Frederick sent his heir Prince Frederick William to St. Petersburg. In his anxiety to "curb Russian ambition," the Prussian king had decided to make an extraordinary suggestion: that Catherine should in the main take the compensation for her victories against the Turks not from Turkey but from Poland.

The monarchical diplomacy of the period was utterly unscrupulous, and partitions had been in the air for a long time past. Patkul had proposed to Poland the partition of Sweden; the Spanish Empire had been partitioned by the Treaty of Utrecht; Frederick had himself seized part of the dominions of Maria Teresa; and Prussia in her turn had been the object of a scheme of partition in the Seven Years' War. As to Poland, the idea was of much longer standing. In the fourteenth century the German Order had discussed with Austria and Hungary the partition of Poland; at the end of the fifteenth, Russia and Austria contemplated a similar scheme; in 1657 the idea was taken up by Sweden, Prussia, and Austria; in 1661 King Jan Kazimir of Poland had foretold a division of his country between the three actual final partitioners, Russia, Prussia, and Austria; King August II, of Poland, had even himself proposed a partition.

In 1769 Austria had appropriated the small country of Zip; and Catherine had suggested that she and Frederick should imitate Austria. Frederick now submitted a detailed plan, and proposed to send Prussian troops into the country. Nothing could be more shameless than the details of these negotiations. Catherine suggests that "there must be archives in Berlin containing some claim on Poland"; and Frederick suggests to Austria—who must be brought into the deal to prevent her from assisting Turkey—to look in her archives for a claim on "some province that you would like." The confederate forces had been dispersed by Russian troops; the King of Poland, though at heart a Polish patriot, was in the pocket of Catherine. Maria Teresa could hardly forget that as late as 1683 her own capital had been saved from the Turks by Polish chivalry, and for some time she protested; but in the end she joined the others, and Frederick said of her that "the more she wept for Poland, the more she took of it." The King was kidnapped, but escaped from his captors. The three Powers concluded a treaty of partition on August 5, 1772. Of the 729,000 square kilometers of Polish territory, with a population of twelve million, the partners appropriated 201,000 with five million inhabitants. Russia seized 88,000 square kilometers of predominantly Russian territory around Polotsk, Vitebsk, and Minsk (White Russia); Austria got 78,000 on the side of Galicia; Prussia got 35,000 in Posen and Polish Pomerania; the three Powers claimed to justify their action by the anarchy in Poland. The country itself was exhausted by the Confederate War; villages had been ravaged and burned; land was uncultivated; there was no public order, and many Poles had gone abroad. A Sejm was summoned under the menace of Russian troops, Russian bribes were freely distributed, and on January 18, 1773, the seizure was confirmed.

The morality of the Partition requires no further comment. Catherine has been sharply criticized for sharing Polish territory with other Powers, when she was terminating the long dispute over a Russian population subject to Poland. She showed great unwillingness to do this, and she certainly departed from the dream of Alexis and Nashchokin to which, as we shall see, her grandson was to return. But here she was in no position to choose. Between 1771 and 1773 she had on her hands the Turkish War, the plague of Moscow, and the revolt of Pugachev. Gustav III of Sweden had prevailed over his nobles and restored the monarchical power, and he was watching for any opportunity of attacking Russia.

Rumyantsev had been unable to do anything effective in 1771–2. The Turks came to Fokshany to discuss peace in 1772, but the parleys had no result. In 1773 he was reinforced, and advanced to the Danube. Suvorov, who held a subordinate command, by a daring night attack seized Turtukay on the southern bank, from which he sent a rhyming message to Rumyantsev; but he was not supported and had to recross. Weissmann, however, crossed and won at Karas on June 18, and the main body followed; Rumyantsev won on June 18 and held out again at Kuchuk-Kainardji on July 14. Silistria resisted attack, and he had to recross for stores, but he returned to the attack, won again at Karas, and advanced on Varna and Shumla. At Hirsovo, with only 3000 men, Suvorov, attacked by 12,000 Turks, let them up to within range of grapeshot, routed them and pursued them for twenty miles (1774). On July 1, faced by 40,000 Turks at Kozludji, disobeying his superior officer, in an all-night series of advance guard actions with the bayonet he penetrated six miles through the Turkish front and stormed their camp in pouring rain. Zaborovsky had crossed the Balkans when the Turks sent to ask for peace, which was concluded on July 21 at Kuchuk-Kainardji. Crimea was declared independent; Russia obtained Kerch and Yenikale to the east of it, and Kinburn with all territory from the

Dnieper to the Bug westward; she thus succeeded in enveloping Crimea, and got access to the Black Sea; her acquisitions, which included Azov, Kuban, and Terek, reached almost to the foot of the Caucasus. On the Danube she obtained a protectorate over the Christian population of Moldavia, whose tribute to Turkey was limited and defined; a clause of the treaty gave Russia the right to a church in Constantinople, and the Sultan also made a general engagement not to persecute Christians; these clauses were in a later period interpreted by some to imply a Russian protectorate over the whole Christian population of Turkey.

We have now reached the middle of Catherine's reign and the point where she transfers her friendship from Prussia to Austria. The reason is clear. There is much more than she wants of Turkey; and Turkey, she well knows, will not even accept the situation as it stands; she cannot afford to raise all Europe against her, and Turkey has a powerful supporter in France. The "northern system" of diplomacy under Nikita Panin meant friendship with Prussia and England and antagonism to Austria and France; Russia must now have Austria's support against Turkey; besides, in her Polish policy, Catherine would now prefer to enhance Austria's importance as opposed to Prussia's. Catherine made the transition in the most masterly way. She knew that Prussia did not want war, but she managed to avoid anything which could give a foothold for active protest or bring about a break. In 1777, on the death of Max Joseph, Elector of Bavaria, Austria, who had contemplated an exchange of her distant dominions in the Netherlands for this province, claimed the succession. This was vigorously resisted by Frederick II, at the head of the minor princes of Germany. Concluding a new alliance with Russia in this year, he called Catherine to his support. Catherine showed no overwillingness, and the appeals of Frederick became more and more insistent. He reminded her that Germany was "her native country," and looked to her as even "the guarantor of the constitution of the German Empire." Both Prussia and Austria submitted their cases for Catherine's consideration and Kaunitz, the Austrian Minister, sent his son to Russia. In October 1778, Catherine invited a joint mediation of the chief Powers of Europe under her leadership, and ultimately a peaceful settlement was reached in March 1779, at Teschen. Frederick praised Catherine as "the most redoubtable rampart of Germany," and she on her side wrote that she was "tired of bothering about other peoples' affairs." It is easy to see how, in the quarrels of divided Germany, Russian prestige had gained by her action.

We must mention at this point another way in which Catherine extended the prestige of Russia. Like France and Spain she intervened in the American War of Independence, but not as a combatant. In 1780 she joined Sweden, Denmark, Austria, and Portugal in the Armed Neutrality, which challenged the arbitrary use that England made of her power on the seas. The Armed Neutrality demanded that neutral ships should have free communication with nations at war; that the neutral flag should cover enemy goods, except contraband of war; that only arms and munitions should be contraband; that blockades, to be recognized, should be effective; and that these principles should regulate the decisions of prize courts.

Continuing with the transfer of her favours from Prussia to Austria, Catherine next proceeds to invite Joseph II of Austria to visit her in Russia. He comes in 1780 under the name of Count Falkenstein, and in lengthy conversations at Mogilev and St. Petersburg the two make a project of joint attack against, and partition of, Turkey. Catherine declares that she "would not keep Constantinople" and puts forward her famous "Greek Plan," by which a buffer state is to be created under an Orthodox ruler; Austria at this time seizes Bukovina. In March 1779, the Turks had made a fresh treaty with Russia at Aimali Kavak, to regulate certain unsettled details; but their alarm was great when at the birth of Catherine's second grandson, he was given the name of Constantine and entrusted to a Greek nurse, medals being struck with a picture of St. Sophia. Joseph writes asking Catherine's conditions for what they have agreed to call a defensive alliance, adding that she will know best and that he is "willing to carry out her wishes." According to Catherine's reply (September 21, 1782), Dacia (present-day Roumania) is to be independent under an Orthodox prince; and Russia will annex the territory from the Bug to the Dniester, and receive an island in the Ægean; if the war leads to the expulsion of the Turks from Constantinople, the city should be independent under her grandson Constantine. To Austria she offers rather vaguely "some Danubian provinces and Mediterranean ports." Crimea she leaves out of the question; she intends to annex it, and is not prepared to accept any outside interference. Joseph, replying on November 24, asks for part of Wallachia, and for territory on both sides of the Danube including Belgrade; also for annexations southwestward to the Adriatic; Venice, the present owner of Dalmatia, is to be compensated with Morea, Crete, and Cyprus. Austria also asks for freedom of trade on the Danube and on the Dardanelles. Catherine, writing on January 15, 1783, says that "she is not prepared to accept the Venetian part of the program," which makes Joseph so angry that he declares himself to have been deceived, but later contents himself with saying that, as Turkey is ready to negotiate for a settlement of immediate questions, no war is needed.

The correspondence was thus interrupted; and Catherine was not sorry, as it left her free to finish off by herself the question of Crimea. Various Khans had succeeded each other rapidly on that throne before Shagin, and he was in turn deposed; but he was restored to power by Suvorov, who carefully guarded against any Turkish intervention. Shagin, throughout the puppet of Russia, in April 1783 made over his dominion to Catherine, who did not delay to annex it. She now writes to Joseph that Russia is strong enough to settle her own differences with Turkey. To her friends she says: "When the pie is cooked, they will all have an appetite." It is now that she makes her triumphal visit to Crimea, taking with her all the foreign ambassadors, and inviting Joseph II to see what she calls *"mon petit ménage."* Potemkin as Viceroy has staged a fairyland, less for Catherine, who is almost one of the conspirators, than for her foreign guests. To each foreign envoy a separate palace is assigned in Kiev with furniture, porcelain, and wines complete; there is a succession of feasts, public welcomes, and deputations even from the wild Nogays, Kalmyks, and Khirgiz; Suvorov and his men are sent past at the charge exactly as in battle; gazing at the Black Sea, for which Potemkin is now constructing a Russian fleet, Catherine chaffs Joseph on the shortness of the journey to Constantinople—no more than two days.

The Turks almost interrupted these celebrations, and did indeed prevent the visit of the two sovereigns to Kinburn. "We have lost our doors," they said; and it is indeed from now that we must date the direct menace of Russia against Constantinople. Russian consuls were intriguing furiously at Alexandria and Smyrna. Heraclius, ruler of Georgia, had put himself under the protection of Catherine. All these provocations produced in July 1787 an appeal of the Sultan to the patriotism of his people, and an ultimatum to Russia demanding the withdrawal of Catherine's protection from Heraclius, the restoration of Crimea, and indeed the reversal of the Treaty of Kuchuk-Kainardji; the Russian ambassador Bulgakov was thrown into the Castle of the Seven Towers.

The war which followed witnessed one of those military revivals of energy and enthusiasm which so often arrest the progress of Turkish decline. The Russian army destined for the Danube was entrusted to Rumyantsev, the Black Sea army to Potemkin who had no military habits, experience, or ability, with Suvorov to do the hard work for him.

The Turkish army and fleet had both been reorganized. Things went none too well for Catherine. The Turks threatened Kinburn; after two attacks Suvorov allowed them to land on the headland outside and, repeating his manœuvre of Hirsovo, let them up to two hundred yards' distance before firing; he was wounded and driven back, and the enemy celebrated their success with thanksgiving; but next day Suvorov drove them from all sides into a narrow circle and, though again wounded, he led his troops to a complete victory and held his own thanksgiving service. Hassan Pasha, reorganizer of the Turkish fleet, attacked on June 18, but of his ships three were lost and eighteen were damaged; on the other hand, many of the new Russian vessels were destroyed in a storm. The Turks retreated to Ochakov. Here they were vigorously besieged by Suvorov, who was twice more badly wounded. In his absence the troops, who were suffering from a frost of twenty degrees, themselves asked to be led to the attack and at an enormous loss stormed the fortress on December 17, 1788.

Catherine again planned to send her fleet to the Mediterranean but this was prevented by a new embarrassment, an attack from Sweden. Russia had for some time past prosecuted the same unscrupulous tactics of corruption in Sweden as in Poland, stirring up the nobles against the King. Catherine openly expressed her contempt for Gustav III and even wrote a play about him; on his side, he aimed at recovering all that Sweden had lost to Russia. The Turkish War gave him his opportunity, and he was supported by England and Prussia. Gustav was much hampered by his Diet and believed that the war would strengthen his authority; at first, it proved otherwise; two Swedes, Sprengtporten and Egerhorn, intrigued with Russia; and the officers at the front, in the camp of Anjala, openly mutinied and even sent a deputation to Catherine. Denmark, being allied with Russia, sent an army into Sweden. The King was threatened all round, but this brought public sympathies to his side. He was more than once able to threaten St. Petersburg, but the Russian fleet held good. The war continued with alternate successes, each side winning a notable naval victory; and peace was at last concluded at Verela on August 14, 1790, confirming the position which existed before the war.

At last Suvorov, transferred to the army of Rumyantsev, was able to win decisive successes in the Balkans. At Fokshany, cooperating with the Austrian general Koburg, he repeated the tactics of Kozludji; flanking his Russian force with the Austrians, he plunged for the centre of the enemy's position, and in a ten hours' battle won a signal victory (Au-

perish at the most alarming rate from the time when he crossed the frontier. Another thing which he could not carry with him was roads; a series of thunderstorms broke up the superficial tracks at the very outset, and all movements were thereby delayed. The Grand Army included soldiers of many nations: some of them, like the Prussians, most unwilling allies. Discipline began to go to pieces from the start, and large numbers deserted into the nowhere surrounding the lines of advance and lived by looting. Napoleon's losses before he reached Vilna were a very large fraction of the whole.

Following his plan and utilizing the dissensions of the Russian generals, Napoleon marched on the adventurous Bagration and tried to cut him both from Barclay and from his line of retreat. The outflanking movement was entrusted to Davoust at the head of the First Corps, to which he had given a splendid discipline. Davoust brought Bagration to bay at Mogilev, and if only Junot, entrusted with the frontal attack, had been at all as prompt, the plan might have succeeded; but Junot was hopelessly late, and thus it was Davoust who came to be in danger. Bagration, after a hard fight, retreated on Smolensk.

Napoleon now turned against the northern Russian army under Barclay. He was entering the zone between the two great rivers flowing to the Baltic and the Black Sea, the Dvina and the Dnieper. Barclay was at Vitebsk on the Dvina, but only intended to delay the French. Napoleon could not bring him to action; but if he again turned southward and anticipated Barclay at Smolensk, he could take from him his only good road to Moscow. He therefore hurried on against Bagration, sending Murat and Ney across the Dnieper. Here they touched the great road made by Catherine II leading from Poland to Moscow, surrounded by a double line of birch trees and still known as the Big One. A reserve division under Neverovsky alone stood in their way; but utilizing the trees to delay the French cavalry, and halting at one point after another, it fought a fine delaying action as far as Smolensk. This town lies between gullies descending from a plateau to the south bank of the Dnieper. The main road approaches by the plateau but crosses to the north bank at this point. The French encircled Smolensk and attacked on all sides. The Poles under Poniatowski on the east side and Ney on the west had to fight their way through deep ravines, while Davoust attacked from the south. Dokhturov, who was in a high fever, chose the exposed chapel over the gate as the point from which to direct the defence. The Russians made a stout resistance for a day and a half, and only retreated when the town was in flames at many points (August 17-18).

Most of Barclay's army had thus been given time to make its way by crossroads to the Moscow road east of Smolensk; but Napoleon still had time to cut off a considerable part of it. The retreating army set up a screen northeast of Smolensk against which Napoleon hurled Murat and Ney. Junot was to cross the Dnieper and turn this position from the south, but again failed; and after obstinate fighting, very costly to both sides, Barclay was able to get his whole army away.

At Vitebsk and again at Smolensk Napoleon half thought of stopping, but again pushed on to reach a decision at Moscow. Barclay had been sharply criticized in St. Petersburg, and popular clamour demanded a Russian general. The command was given to Kutuzov, trained in the school of Suvorov and, if not a first-class general, a very shrewd one; Napoleon called him "the old fox of the north," and he was very proud of the name. He began by halting as if for battle, and then resumed Barclay's policy of retreat; but he felt bound to stand before Moscow, and at Borodino he awaited the French attack. Kutuzov had taken up his position south of the main road and parallel to it, with his left or western flank turning sharply southward. One can understand why a Russian general might expect his enemy to keep to the main road. But it was a hot summer and Napoleon, engaging the hooked line south of the road, tried to turn it by the opposite flank, that is, southward, and dispatched Poniatowski and his Poles on a circuit through the forest. Poniatowski was held up by Tuchkov, posted on this side, who fought to a finish, being one of three brothers who died in action in this war; his men then retreated, still fighting, towards the main body. Meanwhile a tremendous fight was in process in the centre, with terrible losses on both sides; at one moment it was only the personal courage of Murat and Ney that prevented a Russian breakthrough, but ultimately these generals could guess from the confusion opposite them that something threatened the Russian rear, and they urged Napoleon in repeated messages to launch his reserves and complete the frontal onset. Napoleon has said that no general—of course, under the conditions of his time—could effectively command more than 100,000 men, and here he had 144,000. Whereas in his other battles he could nearly always see the whole field of action, here there was no point from which he could see more than one third of it, and even that was only a long way behind the line. His communications were already dangerously extended, and he refused to launch the Guard so many miles from France. The battle therefore broke up into a series of heroic episodes, with desperate courage on both sides, and desperate slaughter; each side lost 40,000 men and some forty generals fell, including Bagration (September 7). The Russian army was almost broken up, but in the next few days numbers of stragglers rejoined their colours. Kutuzov retreated on Moscow; outside, at Fili, he called a council to discuss whether to make one more stand, but dissolved it without asking for any decision and himself quietly issued the order to continue the retreat. The event proved that he was right in putting the further existence of his army even before the safety of Moscow.

Napoleon entered the city without resistance. The Governor Rostopchin, a strong Conservative, had made lively appeals to the patriotism of the people, even putting emancipation from serfdom as the reward of their efforts. When retreat was not to be avoided, he set free a number of criminals, took away with him the fire engines, and circulated instructions for setting fire to the city. Fires broke out soon after the French entered. The ammunition of their army was housed in the Kremlin, and with a strange persistence the wind in its changes often blew from that quarter in which the fire was then at its strongest; Napoleon had to leave the Kremlin for the Petrovsky Castle outside the city. The French, in their march through Russia, had suffered increasingly from their sense of isolation. The thought which had sustained them was Moscow, and discipline rapidly slackened on their arrival. Moscow was an enormous repository of stores of the most varied kind, but not necessarily of those which the army most required. Beyond Moscow there was nothing. Napoleon now awaited peace, but though there was great depression in St. Petersburg, Alexander stood firmer than ever. "It is I or Napoleon," he said as early as the receipt of the news of Borodino; "I or he; we can't both reign together"; and on learning of the fire of Moscow, "After this wound all others are trifling"; as to the thought of peace: "I would sooner let my beard grow and live on potatoes in Siberia; if I have not one soldier left, I will stand at the head of my dear gentry and my good peasants and will sacrifice all the resources of my empire"; and again: "I and the people at whose head I have the honour to be, are determined to stand firm." "Oh this splendid people," said his mother; "it has shown plainly what it really is." Everyone at this point understood that Russia's destinies were in the hands of her people.

For Napoleon, peace was imperative. At one time he proposed to march on St. Petersburg, a suggestion which his officers received with consternation, and ultimately he sent Lauriston with instructions to bring back "*la paix à tout prix.*" Kutuzov was ordered to refuse all negotiations, and Alexander sent no reply. Meanwhile Kutuzov marched by the light of burning Moscow to a point southward, near the road to Tula, whence he could menace the French communications, and took the offensive with marked effect; the first snowstorm presaging an early winter did the rest, and Napoleon decided to evacuate Moscow.

At least he hoped to take a different direction for his retreat, in order to keep up the impression of an offensive. The French army marched out in a southwesterly direction; some units were like a rabble; there were soldiers who pushed wheelbarrows containing their spoils from Moscow. At Malo-Yaroslavets Kutuzov already blocked the road, which climbs a steep slope to the little town. The French and Italians attacked as they came up, and the town changed hands many times. Napoleon, who was in the rear, was told that he could not break through; amid the rival arguments and quarrels of his generals, he decided almost without decision to return to the old wasted road northward; Kutuzov, who was not at all for forcing a decision of all issues, had at this very time retired also.

The long return march, which emphasised at every point the completeness of the defeat, was for the French a crescendo of misery. Napoleon realized his disaster quicker than anyone else, and was at first completely prostrated. Davoust saw his rear guard melting away under his eyes. The peasants were entirely hostile; the march was constantly interrupted by attacks of Cossacks and of partisan bands under daring leaders—Orlov-Denisov and Seslavin. The road lay over the battlefield of Borodino, where nothing had been done to remove the wounded. The French were attacked while crossing the Vop, and arrived at Smolensk in great disorder. The cold was becoming more intense, and many of the men had neither great coats nor boots.

By Smolensk, Napoleon was again himself. After restoring some order, he divided his army into six columns which were to leave Smolensk on successive days. Traversing the scene of Neverovsky's action, the two first columns arrived safely at Krasny; the third under Napoleon was stopped eastward of the gully of the Losmina, some four hundred feet deep; Napoleon dismounted, and leading his Guard in person, made his way across the gully; stopping beyond it, he facilitated the passage of Prince Eugene and of Davoust. To wait for Ney, who commanded the rear guard, seemed hopeless.

Ney, on reaching the Losmina near midnight with 5000 men and 10,000 stragglers, charged up the further slope and even captured two Russian guns; but by now a Russian army of 50,000 men was between him and Napoleon. Of this he was informed by the chivalrous Russian general Miloradovich, who in asking for his surrender offered the full honours of war; it was here that Ney replied: "A Marshal of France never surrenders." Marching back eastward, he found a small stream which ran northward to the Dnieper and following it to the river, he and his men crossed the ice on all fours; making their way along the comparatively unoccupied north side of the Dnieper, they rejoined Napoleon at Orsha (November 17–20).

Kutuzov now lagged behind. To the British attaché Wilson, who was constantly spurring him to further efforts, he replied: "I don't want to reach the frontier like a pack of vagabonds." The allies might wish him to fight Napoleon to a finish in Russia, but he realized that from here to the frontier he could count on no support of the population, and was only too glad for the enemy to go away without fighting; he therefore followed at a distance. But, for the French, the danger was now greater than ever. On the north side they were threatened by the Russian army of St. Petersburg, under Wittgenstein, pressing hard on the remains of Victor's force. On the west, Chichagov was returning with his army from the Danube, and he occupied the bridgehead of Borisov, blocking the main road westward at the river Berezina. Napoleon seemed caught in a trap. It was here, however, that he showed his greatest resource. He engaged guides to lead him to a ford in the river southward and, trusting to their carrying his intention to Chichagov, meanwhile himself marched northward of the main road to the village of Studyanka. Chichagov was deceived and withdrew his northern detachment, which enabled Napoleon to make a lodgement beyond the river; but this momentary respite was followed by a joint attack by Chichagov on the one side and Wittgenstein on the other, the French being between the two. Still, they succeeded in crossing the river, leaving behind them vast numbers of stragglers but hardly any unit which retained its efficiency (November 26–9).

At Smorgony Napoleon decided to return to France. He fully justified his departure by the new army of a million men which he put into the field for the campaign of 1813. On his arrival in Warsaw he constantly repeated: "It is only one step from the sublime to the ridiculous," a proper summary of a campaign whose one object had been to win back Alexander.

The French army struggled on to the frontier in the most intense cold, which sometimes drove the men to throw themselves into burning houses. The Cossacks continued to infest their march at point after point. Arrived at Kovno, the place where the invading army had entered Russia, its remains made their way over the ice after a combat in which Ney and Gerard themselves used muskets; and when Ney that night announced himself to Mathieu Dumas with the words: "I am the rear guard of the Grand Army," he stated no more than a fact. Of the 600,000 men who had entered Russia near Kovno, some 50,000 came out by the same road.

We have entered into the detail of this campaign because it had far more than a military significance. It set a tone for many years to come, to the mood, rather than the thoughts, both of Russia and of Europe. Who had won the campaign of 1812? Alexander had not treated, and the last and bravest of French soldiers had been glad to leave Russian territory. Yet on no field of battle had the Russians tactically prevailed; at Malo-Yaroslavets both sides retreated; and even on the Berezina Napoleon achieved his object, which was to get out. In actual fact Napoleon was his own conqueror; he attempted a task which, in the conditions of Russia, exhausted the powers of organization. If anyone defeated him, it was the country itself and the climate. The people had their share in it, but that of the Russian commanders was much less. Yet the triumph of Russia was evident and complete. Simple human nature had this time proved greater than any organization; endurance under reverses showed itself more powerful than genius. From this, for the overpowered intellect, it was an easy step to the inference that no plan was better than a plan, and this was almost taken to be the lesson of the struggle not only by Russia but by Europe; not only both Russians and French who took part in the campaign, but even historians on both sides, as they approach these events, undergo the domination of the mystical; it is so even with the businesslike Thiers. Russia was taken to possess something that made her stronger than the empire of Napoleon. From this followed in Europe an altogether extravagant estimate of her power.

Alexander on reaching the frontier, crossed it, in order to liberate Europe (January 15, 1813). This step, which was in keeping with all the part he had played, was quite as full of import for Europe and for Russia as Napoleon's passage of the Niemen. Kutuzov was opposed to it, but died directly afterwards; the few Russian Liberals were, curiously enough, almost its only supporters. But what passed into Europe was not Russia as a nation, but Alexander. From now onward he completely overshadowed his country which had saved him. It was his personality, and not Russia, that reaped the prestige of the victory, and his army was no more than the instrument of his policy and the support of his predominance.

The Prussian general York, on learning the condition of the Grand Army, had taken the courageous step of allowing himself to be caught by the Russians and concluding with them the Convention of Tauroggen (December 30, 1812). The Prussian patriot Stein, who had helped throughout the Moscow campaign to hearten Alexander, was dispatched by him to East Prussia and raised this province against the French. The movement spread to Berlin, and King Frederick William III after some hesitation issued an appeal to his people and joined Alexander in Silesia, concluding an alliance with him at Kalisz on February 27, 1813. Napoleon reappeared with a large, new army, but consisting mostly of recruits and sadly lacking in cavalry. The allied sovereigns passed Leipzig and attacked him at Lützen (May 2), but he won a hard-fought victory and they retreated to Silesia. At Bautzen (May 21) Napoleon won again but took no trophies, and soon afterwards he concluded an armistice at Parschwitz (June 6).

Napoleon, whose new army sorely needed further organization, counted on making better use of the interval than his enemies, but they were now joined by Austria (August 10). This accession of strength was to turn the balance, and also to rob the war of its character of liberation. The allies resolved to retire before Napoleon but to fall on his lieutenants. While Napoleon was defeating Blücher, Schwarzenberg tried to surprise Dresden in his rear; but Napoleon returned and won one of his most brilliant triumphs in front of the city (August 26–7). However, his lieutenants were defeated at Grossbeeren (August 23) and on the Katzbach (August 26), so that he could not follow up his success; and Vandamme, sent to cut off Schwarzenberg, not being supported by a frontal attack, was compelled to surrender at Kulm (August 30). In October the allies closed around Napoleon at Leipzig, and in three days of fierce fighting overwhelmed him with numbers and broke up his new army (October 16–19, 1813).

Alexander was regarded as the soul of the coalition, the sovereign among sovereigns, the "Agamemnon," the "new sun." It was he, single-handed except for the support of Blücher, who compelled the allies to follow up their victory into France (December 1813). "Only the sword," he said "can and must decide the course of events"; "I can't be coming four hundred leagues each time to your help." He stood out wholeheartedly for the deposition of Napoleon. He was opposed to the abortive negotiations of Châtillon where, encouraged by temporary successes, Napoleon asked too much (February 17–March 15, 1814). He would take around the latest dispatches at night to the fat Schwarzenberg and read them to him, sitting on his bed; he was indignant at every delay, was always for keeping the army together and marching on Paris, and when Napoleon made his last desperate move, threatening the allied rear, he declared that he was still going forward, even if alone. A message from Talleyrand in Paris encouraged him to do so; he carried his allies with him and Paris, exhausted and alienated from Napoleon, made no great resistance. It was to Alexander's summons that it surrendered, and he entered in triumph on March 31, 1814.

In Paris, where he lived in Talleyrand's house, he kept his troops under a martinet discipline, thereby making many of his officers feel ashamed before the French and the allies. He had throughout declared his friendship for the French nation. While refusing to intervene in internal affairs, he supported a provisional government formed by Talleyrand, which deposed Napoleon and after some delay obtained his unqualified abdication; it was Alexander who saved him from some such prison as St. Helena, and obtained for him the retention of the title of Emperor, and the sovereignty of little Elba. He paid visits of sympathy to the Empress Josephine and to Queen Hortense; he walked the streets without escort; the French were charmed with him and put all their hopes in him; Parisians asked that he should "either stay or give them a sovereign like himself." He insisted successfully that France herself should not be diminished in territory, and that there should be no war contribution; she was even allowed to keep all the art treasures seized from other countries. He declared for "strong and liberal institutions as answering to the degree of public instruction" in the country. When it was clear that there was no alternative to the Bourbons, he gave a plain warning in this sense to the returning Louis XVIII and opposed his entry at Paris until he should guarantee a constitution. The departure of the allies was deferred till a Charter was issued on June 14. He paid a public tribute to Kosciuszko; he dispatched the Polish officers of Napoleon to Poland to assist in organizing the national army. To Lafayette he said publicly: "With God's help, serfdom will be abolished in my reign." It was all admirably done. In the person of the liberal autocrat of Russia, Europe saw at once her arbiter and her liberator.

At Vilna, the capital of Lithuania, on his way back to St. Petersburg, addressing the Poles, he said: "Gentlemen, yet a little patience, and you will be more than satisfied with me." On his way to Vienna he was the guest of his friend Czartoryski in Poland, and expressed the same hope. At the congress of all the powers where the spoils were to be divided and the boundaries of states fixed, Alexander was again the commanding figure. But the people's war against Napoleon had been spoilt from the time when Austria joined in it, and at Vienna the reactionary Austrian minister Metternich was able to assert himself with effect. His views were entirely anti-national, and such was the character of Austria herself. In the settlement of Vienna, those princes who had backed Napoleon too long were among the chief sufferers; but the cause of peoples suffered still more. Italy, repartitioned, was handed back in the main to Austrian rule. All hope of Germany unity was lost in the jealousies of Austria and Prussia.

Alexander's claims were at least based on an idea—the reunion of Poland. Now was the time for Czartoryski's dream of making him the restorer of Polish integrity, **with a** constitution under his personal sovereignty. But Prussia had **to be** compensated; and as Saxony had backed Napoleon almost to the end, Alexander proposed that it should be given to Prussia. This project was defeated by Talleyrand, who at the Congress represented the restored French monarchy. Talleyrand's work at Vienna was a veritable masterpiece. Starting under the disadvantages of the representative of the defeated country, he first made France the champion of all the smaller states; he next contrived to win for her an equal voice with the other Great Powers; next, he drove a wedge between the allies. Alexander quite forgot his diplomacy, was extremely overbearing, claimed to rule the decisions by the promises he had made in advance, wanted to fight a duel with Metternich, and played right into the hands of Talleyrand. The opposition of Austria and England to the claims of Russia and Prussia was so strong that Talleyrand had even succeeded in forming an alliance of these Powers with France to resist them with force (January 3, 1815), when Napoleon spoilt everything by returning from Elba and re-establishing himself at Paris (February 26–March 20). Napoleon, finding this treaty in the cabinet of Louis XVIII, sent it to Alexander. Alexander showed it to Metternich, who had helped to negotiate it, and tore it up in his presence with the words: "Metternich, while we are alive, we must never speak of this matter." Unity was thus restored and the allies declared Napoleon an outlaw; but we can imagine the effect of this experience on Alexander.

In the last act of the "Hundred Days" and Waterloo, the Russian army was too far off to take a part. The allies, after their object lesson of the dangers of disunion, came to an agreement. Prussia was given half of Saxony: and Alexander, resigning his claim to the rest of Poland, received the bulk of the Grand Duchy of Warsaw, so that Poland was again partitioned after all. Alexander offered to grant a Polish constitution; and a similar though much vaguer agreement applying also to Austria and Prussia was inserted in the decisions of the Congress. Russia, Prussia, Austria, and Britain concluded a quadruple alliance against revolution in France (November 20). It was settled that another congress should be called in three years, and that the victorious sovereigns and their ministers should remain in communication with each other to secure the tranquillity of Europe.

It was now that the Tsar put forward his remarkable scheme for a Holy Alliance. While Napoleon was in Moscow, Alexander had surprised his wife by asking for her Bible. As he said later to the German pastor, Eilert, "The fire of Moscow lit up my soul; then I got to know God and became another man"; he became convinced that "nothing can be done by human efforts." From that time he studied the Bible twice a day, marking with his friend Admiral Shishkov the passages which seemed to apply to his situation; the Ninetieth Psalm had a special attraction for him. On the retreat after Bautzen, he and Frederick William III pledged themselves to a special "act of adoration" if victory should be granted to them. In Paris, in 1814, Alexander held a great military thanksgiving on the Place de la Concorde. He had visited the mystic Stilling and during the Hundred Days he saw much of Baroness Juliana Krüdener, who described herself as a repentant sinner and believed she had a mission to tell him his duty; for a time he fell completely under her influence; in this period he loved to receive Quakers and to pray with them. It was a natural reaction from war, which has repeated itself in our own time. Alexander's Holy Alliance was a monarchs' League of Nations. While in Paris in 1815, unable to sleep in his anxiety to prevent further wars, he rose from his bed and wrote down the draft of it, which he showed to Baroness Krüdener. It was a personal engagement between sovereigns that they would exhort their subjects to religion, treat them as their children, hold together as brothers among themselves and settle everything in peace. It excited much amusement among some statesmen. Frederick William of Prussia readily signed the pledge; so, after cracking a joke with Metternich, did the Emperor Francis of Austria. The Prince Regent, debarred by the

British Constitution from such an engagement, wrote to say that Alexander had just expressed his views; the witty Louis XVIII of France, the worthless Ferdinand of Spain and the restored monarchs of Naples and Sardinia were other recruits. Two sovereigns were left out of the Holy Alliance—the Sultan and the Pope. Alexander at this stage resented its association with politics; there were some, he said to Eilert, who could not distinguish the sacred from the profane. For Metternich, its only significance lay in a league of sovereigns against peoples; and though it never became a formal treaty, it helped to breathe a mystic spirit into a general policy of repression (September 26, 1815).

Alexander loyally performed his promise to give a constitution to Poland. The models used included the abortive plan of Speransky, Napoleon's Polish constitution and the Charter of Louis XVIII; the aged revolutionary, Carnot, who was in Warsaw at the time, thought it more liberal than the French Charter. The sovereign himself was to take the oath to the constitution. Two chambers were established on a reasonable franchise; the Diet was to meet for a month in every two years; the State Council was to draft all laws, but the Diet might make petitions and interpellations. Polish was the official tongue, and all posts were to be held by Polish subjects. Freedom of press and person were guaranteed. Above all, Poland was allowed to possess her own army of 40,000 men. Alexander confirmed this constitution, and made a triumphal entry amidst extraordinary enthusiasm. As Governor he appointed Zajaczek, formerly a republican, and a general of Napoleon. He even discussed with Prince Oginski the possibility of restoring the White Russian provinces to the new Poland, which much irritated the prominent writer and statesman Karamzin and even many of the Russian Liberals.

Another reform which helped to give the impression that Alexander's liberalism was mostly for the non-Russian parts of his empire was the emancipation of the Lettish and Estonian serfs of the Baltic provinces. In 1804–5 these had been given facilities for acquiring freedom with land: a solution not satisfactory to the German barons of these provinces. In 1811 the proprietors in Estonia proposed to free all their peasants without land, and this solution was adopted by Alexander in 1816 for Estonia, in 1818 for Kurland, and in 1819 for Livonia. It necessarily created a large proletariat. The more industrious set themselves to acquire property, and became expert farmers; the less competent became paid labourers.

The Liberals worked hard to popularize this measure in Russia. In 1818 two plans were put forward. That of Kankrin, a very competent and honest administrator of German origin with no Liberal predilections, was the first businesslike attempt to deal with the subject, and aimed at creating in the course of sixty years a class of cultivator proprietors; the other plan, that of Alexander's Conservative watchdog Arakcheyev, was drafted at the order of Alexander himself who, however, prescribed that the interests of the squires were not to suffer and that no compulsion was to be used; Arakacheyev asked to be assigned five million roubles a year, with which the State would buy from squires the freedom of their serfs together with part of their land. The plan was approved by Alexander, but again as so often before, political unrest in Europe prevented it from being carried out. In 1820 Alexander received a project from the Liberal N. Turgenev; it proposed the foundation of a society to improve the lot of the peasants and to lead up to their emancipation; Alexander was again favourable, but again revolution in Europe induced him to drop the idea. In 1819 on the apparent initiative of some district gentry, the government formed a commission to follow out in certain neighbouring parts of Russia the settlement adopted in the Baltic provinces, but it failed to conquer the local opposition. Alexander's attitude was anything but consequent. The sale of individual peasants was again challenged and discussed, and though again morally condemned by Alexander, was allowed to continue. The rights of squires in the punishment of their peasants were restricted in 1811, but were again restored in full in 1822. Flights and man hunts continued as before. From 1812, when the government in its war proclamations had practically promised emancipation, the peasants' discontent was greater than ever.

What they did receive for their sacrifices in the war was something very different. Perplexed with the problem of demobilization and burdened with the care of all Europe, Alexander founded military colonies which would allow him to mobilize troops more quickly; after all it was the Russian army that was the base of Alexander's own dominating position in Europe. This project, initiated in 1816 and entrusted to Arakcheyev, was carried out on the most undesirable lines at a large cost to the State. The whole population of these villages, including the children, were put under a rigorous drill and supervision which they detested; all the men and even the children had to wear uniforms; the women were registered; marriages were prescribed. These colonies were quickly and widely extended, and in 1825 included ninety battalions around Novgorod and thirty-six with forty-nine cavalry squadrons in South Russia. The peasants detested them, especially the uniform as the badge of military bondage. They were willing, they said, to give two sons from every family, but not all; or to be moved to the steppe or Siberia, if only they were left in peace. As it was, whole village communities were moved, and the hours spent on the goose step left too little time for agriculture. In 1817 some sent deputies to appeal to the Empress Mother; these were arrested by Arakcheyev; others begged on their knees to the Grand Dukes Constantine and Nicholas. In 1819 a great movement of protest involving 9000 peasants broke out at Chuguyev, and submission was only obtained by flogging batch after batch of them. Arakcheyev described this scene with gusto to the Emperor. This old drill sergeant of Paul now almost monopolized the confidence of Alexander; in the end, practically all state business passed through his hands; his letters to his master are full of sickening protestations of devotion, but to all others he made the most challenging display of his power and took a constant pride in his ignorance. Meanwhile a policy of thoroughgoing reaction prevailed in education. In 1817 Alexander combined the control of religion and education under a single ministry entrusted to the bigoted Prince A. Golitsyn.

In 1818 Alexander still championed France against the bitter hostility of Metternich at the European conference at Aix-la-Chapelle; in the same year he opened the Polish Diet with a remarkable speech, in which he declared that "free institutions were not a dangerous dream, but confirmed the well-being of nations." He added: "I hope to extend them to all countries entrusted to my care, and am glad of the opportunity of showing my own country what I have long been preparing for it." The Polish Diet accepted most of the measures proposed to it; where it dissented, Alexander congratulated it on its independence.

We have reached the point where we must study the reaction of Russia's triumphs abroad upon opinion in Russia. Russians were told everywhere in Europe that Russia, more than any other country, had achieved the defeat of Napoleon. Alexander, when he mobilized Russia's material forces to assert his own predominance in Europe, had challenged a great recoil. Béranger, the French singer of this period, opposes to the Holy Alliance of monarchs a Holy Alliance of peoples, and calls on France, conquered in the field, to take up the torch and teach the world; he takes comfort in that spiritual power of France which had always been so strongly felt in Russia:

> *Nous vient un joli refrain,*
> *Et voilà le monde en train.*

From this time onward, the ideas preached in the French Revolution and carried over Europe as far as Moscow by the armies of Napoleon, were to make their great counterstroke against the material conqueror.

In 1790, a year after the fall of the Bastille, appeared the *Letters of a Russian Traveller*, by Karamzin. With the works of this writer, the great wave of genuine feeling which was pervading Europe and did so much to cause the French Revolution, entered Russia and conquered everywhere, putting an abrupt end to the pseudo-classic period. Karamzin was no Liberal but stood for old traditions and gradual progress; he was the author of a *History of Russia*, which was a record of its sovereigns, and he encouraged his readers to accept the world as they found it. But he spoke in simple and genuine Russian, and his sentimental letters and tales appealed to everybody. The poet Zhukovsky, feeding the fast-growing literary public of Russia with translations of works of the German romantics, often commonplace and often fantastic, continued the development of this new democratic literature, which interested itself in the personal joys and sorrows of the ordinary individual; and from Zhukovsky we pass straight to the greatest figure in the history of Russian letters, the poet Pushkin. Born in 1799, he grew up during the epic period of the struggle with Napoleon, when Russia was living a common life with all Europe; though he was intensely patriotic, his culture and his genius were cosmopolitan. This was the Europe of the romantic school, and Pushkin at this stage had many affinities with Byron. There was now a thinking Russia, though as yet it was in the main confined to the younger generation of the aristocracy; the fresh Russian mind, at last taking its place in European civilization, was in kind keenly critical.

All the palace revolutions of the eighteenth century were the work of the Guard, which was the corporate essence of the Russian nobility. This was the class which before the wars had a monopoly of Russia's contact with Europe. The war of 1812 compelled everyone to take an interest in politics. The Russian army after 1812 spent whole years in Germany and in France, where a section of it remained as part of the army of occupation. In talks round camp fires, the conditions produced in France by the Revolution were constantly contrasted with the absence of personal liberty in Russia. The hero of the war of 1812 was the Russian peasant soldier; was it not he that had conquered the Grand Army? Yet the French peasant was a man, and was treated as such. The young officer, Küchelbecker, wrote: "When I look at the brilliant qualities with which God has gifted the Russian people, first in the world for glory and power, for its strong melodious language which has not its like in Europe, for the cordiality, kindheartedness and quickness of mind that are peculiar to it above all others, it grieves me to think that this is all crushed, withering, and perhaps dying out without bearing any fruit in the moral world." Another future Decembrist, Pestel, a brilliant staff officer, dates year by year his rapid progress from loyalty to the throne to a republicanism which in some ways even anticipated the Bolsheviks.

In 1816 a number of young Liberal officers of the Guard used to meet under the chairmanship of Prince Trubetskoy, Colonel of the Preobrazhensky Regiment, and at the beginning of 1817 there was founded a "Society of Salvation." This was kept secret from the public, but was well known to the Emperor, who was familiar with many of its members and even read memoirs which they wrote. The prevailing tendencies in the Society were three: Nikita Muravyev, a high staff officer, was in favour of an English constitution, with a House of Lords to act as a restraint upon the sovereign. Nicholas Turgenev, an eminent authority on taxation, in which field he strongly advocated the principles of Liberalism and Free Trade, had one absorbing interest, which for him dominated all others—the emancipation of the serfs. This he believed could best be achieved by the autocracy; but if the reform were not made from above, he was ready to work with those who sought other ways to it. Paul Pestel will always be an interesting study. At the point which he reached in his rapid political evolution, he stood for a Jacobin conspiracy to overthrow the autocracy, with the murder of the sovereign and reigning family. But this was only to be the preface to a gigantic social reform. The peasants were to be freed, all class distinctions abolished, a central government established with all the instruments of power, including spies and censorship to prevent a counter-revolution; half the land was to be divided in shares between the whole population, and half was to remain at the disposal of private enterprise.

The Society of Salvation was from the start agreed that a political *coup d'état* was required. But the differences in the views of its members were always evident. The increasing reaction in the government, and the need of propaganda work for obtaining much wider support in the public, induced them to abolish the society and to substitute for it a Society of Welfare, with a much more modest program and four different sections, in which the principal immediate problems of reform were to be studied in detail. Alexander, in his remarkable liberal speech to the Polish Diet in 1818, had drawn a distinction between "the holy principles of liberal institutions" and "destructive teaching, which threatens a calamitous attack on the social order." At Aix-la-Chapelle he had asked: "Does not the morbid state of France make it a duty for the European Powers to keep off the infection?" Yet he had successfully opposed Metternich's desire to isolate France from the Concert of Europe. He instructed Novosiltsev to draft a constitution for the Russian Empire; he recalled Speransky and spoke of giving him an important task. On the other hand there was noticed in him an increasing asperity and dislike for company; he was more and more taken up with military parades.

Alexander had ordered the circulation of an attack on the German universities as a hotbed of revolution, and in March 1819 a German student Sand murdered the author Kotzebue, who had served Paul and was now acting as an agent of Alexander in Germany. In March 1820, a popular movement restored the Constitution of 1812 in Spain, and the people of Naples imposed this same constitution on their King in July. Metternich summoned a congress to Troppau to discuss these movements. On his way thither, Alexander opened the Second Polish Diet (September 12, 1820). The government had in several matters not respected the constitution, and the Grand Duke Constantine by his military harshness had driven the Polish officers to despair and even to suicide; in consequence nearly every bill presented by the government to the Diet was refused, practically without discussion.

At Troppau (October 1820), Alexander got news of a mutiny of his own old regiment, the Semenovsky; the men had risen for purely military grievances in protest against the extreme harshness of their commander, Colonel Schwarz, and the officers had tried to restrain them; but Metternich made excellent use of his opportunity, and got from Alexander a renunciation of his Liberal ideas. Russia, Prussia, and Austria signed a treaty "not to allow changes made by illegal means" in Europe and to use force where necessary to prevent them. Austria was commissioned to abolish the constitution in Naples, and next year Alexander offered his troops to put down a similar movement in Piedmont.

Alexander's repentant submission to Metternich put him in a quite impossible position when the general movement for liberation spread to Greece, which had always been taught to look to Russia as the champion of the Orthodox Church. The Greek revolutionary society, the Hetæria, even claimed Alexander as a member. The Greek movement began from the Danubian provinces, where Russian influence was predominant in consequence of her protectorate of the Christian population, and it was led by a former officer of the Russian army, Ypsilanti. More than this, Alexander's acting Foreign Minister at this time, Capodistrias, who was with him at Troppau and Laybach, was a Greek and was later to become the first elected president of independent Greece. How was Alexander to interpret under the principles of the Holy Alliance a national war for the liberation of Greece? He kept to his new agreement with Metternich. He disavowed and censured Ypsilanti. But Morea now rose in revolt. The Patriarch Gregory was murdered in his pontifical robes at Easter in Constantinople and his body was brought to Odessa, where he was buried as a martyr. The archbishops of Adrianople, Salonica, and Trnovo were also murdered, and there were wholesale massacres of Christians in Turkey. Russian ships were searched and seized, and the Russian Ambassador, after vain protests, left Constantinople. Meanwhile central Greece rose and was invaded; the Sultan called in Ibrahim, son of the powerful Satrap of Egypt, Mehmet Ali, to reduce Morea; the Great Powers could agree upon nothing. On his return to Russia, Alexander received from Count Benckendorff, chief of staff of the Guard, a complete and accurate account of the secret societies; Benckendorff advised that they should be watched closely but that no sharp action should be taken. Many of the conspirators were personally known to Alexander. To Vasilchikov he said: "You know that I have shared and encouraged these illusions and errors"; he added after a pause: "*Ce n'est pas à moi à sévir.*" But he was now almost completely isolated from his people, and his policy was one of pure reaction.

In 1820 a "converted" freethinker, the courtier Magnitsky, now the most extravagant of pietists, was sent as commissioner to inspect Kazan University. He proposed to abolish it altogether, but Alexander preferred a reconstruction. Magnitsky therefore ordered the professors to "conform their teaching to the ideas expressed in the Holy Alliance," for which they were given the most minute instructions. History and philosophy were to be based on the statements of the Bible and the Fathers; the Biblical view, whatever that meant, was made obligatory in the teaching of physics and medicine; professors of mathematics were ordered to show in the triangle a symbol of the Trinity. All this was accompanied by punishments and exclusions. There was similar repression of the press, though at present of a casual kind, dependent on the whim of the censors. Baroness Krüdener came to St. Petersburg to preach a Greek crusade, but was requested to leave the city. Alexander now regarded her as an *"ignis fatuus."* But he fell under the influence of one of those strange "holy men" that Russia produces, one Photius, who wrote in the third person a life of himself, describing in detail his midnight combats with devils. To this pass had come the Prince Charming of 1801, the champion of enlightenment and liberty. In October 1822 Alexander attended the Congress of Verona where he offered his army to suppress the constitutional movement in Spain, and he actually moved troops for that purpose. He received a warning from Laharpe, with whom he now ceased to correspond.

Meanwhile the divisions in the Society of Welfare and the appointment of Pestel to military duty in South Russia had led to the disbandment of the society. It only disappeared under ground. There remained two societies representing its different tendencies, a Northern Union in St. Petersburg standing for a constitutional monarchy, in which the leading figure was the poet Ryleyev, and a Southern Union, practically under the dictatorship of Pestel, working for a republic. Pestel's Union entered into contact with Polish malcontents. The organization of the whole movement was quite incoherent. As Pestel put it later, few if any of the members held to the same view throughout; nor, with irregular meetings and communications, was it at all possible to say what had been decided. There were various grades of members, and the outside grades were never told anything of the objects of the movement, while the inside grades were never agreed on the subject. Two irresponsible hotheads, Yakubovich and Kakhovsky, wanted to be allowed to kill the Emperor, and another member, Yakushkin, was at one time quite irregularly authorized for the purpose. There was talk of killing the whole imperial family, or transporting it abroad. It was enough for a few of the disgraced Semenovsky soldiers to be in a given corps, for the conspirators to assume that the corps as a whole was already at their disposal; there was similar loose talk of the fleet. Ryleyev was for a federative system of government; Pestel was a born centralist. Ryleyev religiously left all final settlements to an elected constituent assembly; Pestel wanted to settle everything himself.

After unconstitutionally postponing the Polish Diet, Alexander summoned it in February 1825, and expressed himself as satisfied with it. On September 13 he left St. Petersburg for Taganrog where the Empress, from whom he had long been estranged, was trying to recover her health. They lived very simply there and in great affection, Alexander showing her every kind of attention. He had frequently spoken of abdicating, and now more than ever recurred to this idea. He was quite worn out, and a chill which he contracted led to gastric fever. After a long drawn-out illness, of which every detail is recorded by two doctors, by the Empress and by Count Volkonsky, refusing almost till the last to follow his doctors' instructions, he is recorded to have died on December 18, 1825; the Empress closed his eyes; his body was embalmed and brought with every care to St. Petersburg.[1]

The news of his death was long in reaching St. Petersburg. Alexander's next brother Constantine had abdicated his right to the throne in January 1822. Alexander had accepted the abdication; a statement to this effect had been deposited in three copies in St. Petersburg and Moscow, to be opened only on his death. In so delicate a matter this was not nearly enough. Alexander's next brother, Nicholas, who was very much younger than his two elders, had never been properly prepared. Alexander had spoken to him more than once (and on one occasion impressively) of the probability that he would be called upon to mount the throne; but he was left in ignorance of Constantine's act of abdication. He therefore proclaimed Constantine in St. Petersburg, while Constantine, who was Viceroy of Poland, proclaimed Nicholas in Warsaw. There followed a long and vexatious correspondence in which Constantine, instead of coming, as Nicholas asked him, to St. Petersburg to make a formal abdication, threatened to leave the Russian Empire altogether, if he were further troubled about the matter. This was the occasion seized by the conspirators to make their *coup d'état*. On December 26 two thousand soldiers of the Guard formed in square outside the Council of State shouting for "Constantine and Constitution," which latter many of the soldiers took for the name of Constantine's wife. Nicholas showed the greatest reluctance to use force. Miloradovich, the Governor General of St. Petersburg, was sent to speak to the leaders of the insurgents but had no success, and as he turned to retire he was mortally wounded from behind by the conspirator Kakhovsky. Nicholas at last gave the order for cannon to be brought up, and after a blank discharge two volleys of grape cleared the square.

The rising of the Decembrists was almost the first attempt of the Guard at a palace revolution that did not succeed. It was almost the first that had anything like a political program. It was unsuccessful, mainly because none of the ideas which it represented had as yet any general support in Russia. Of the palace revolutions it was the last, and with it ceased for ever the dominant role of the Russian gentry; from

---

[1] There are four parallel records of his illness and death. In spite of this, there is a persistent legend that he lived for many years after as a peasant in Siberia.

now onward the bureaucracy governs in Russia. But the Decembrist rising is much more important as a preface. Though the insurgents were not at all agreed as to what they would do if they succeeded, their various ideas were to act as a leaven. They were later widely regarded as martyrs; their rising is the first act in the Russian Revolution.

CHAPTER XVIII

The Reign of Nicholas I

[*1825–55*]

THE REIGN of Nicholas I is at first sight one of those periods which lie like cushions between epochs of greater force, vitality and importance. But it is this period, which seems entirely stagnant and marked by few events and those of secondary value, that gives birth to forces which fix the direction of the future.

Nicholas himself has no such interesting and enigmatic personality as his elder brother Alexander. There are figures which not only fill the stage in their own time, but in a way mortgage in advance the inheritance of their next successors, leaving them with a number of inconvenient legacies which make their lifework nearly negative. Such was Catherine the Great for Paul; and such was Alexander for Nicholas. Paul's family, by a long interval in age, falls into two parts. Nicholas was nineteen years younger than Alexander and was completely overshadowed by him; he was born in 1796, the year of the death of Catherine the Great, and for him there was no brilliant grandmother as educator and of course no Laharpe; the French Revolution had spent its fury, and there was reaction in France itself. In the Napoleonic wars Nicholas' first appearance was similarly belated. Sixteen years old at the time of the Moscow campaign, he had no part in it or in those which followed; he was only in time for the military parades of sovereigns, triumphant, rescued, or restored. When he first visited western Europe, among those whom he met prevailed a state of mind best characterized by the sigh of relief of one of the restored sovereigns, "We have had a bad dream"; or by the petty German prince who ordered that all his officials should return to the rank and duties which they had held at the time of his flight long years before. Nicholas' adolescence was passed under the growing mysticism and reaction of Alexander.

Nicholas' character is simple. Possessed, like Alexander, of that fine stature which was common in his mother's family, absorbed in those

details of the parade ground which so attracted successive Russian emperors, he was honest, very limited in mind, but full of a sense of duty;
his self-chosen preparation for responsibility consisted of frequent conversations on the current business of the empire with those who awaited
their turn to report in his brother's antechambers. He was not lacking in
nobility, and could make others feel the prestige of his dignity. Take
the memorable scene during the cholera in St. Petersburg in 1831. A
panic-stricken mob attacked the hospitals and defied the authorities.
Nicholas drove at a slow pace to the Haymarket. He told the mob to
come nearer to him. "On your knees," he said. "Come nearer! I am
afraid of no one. Cross yourselves! Pray God for pardon!" and he was
obeyed. His mind did not rove like Alexander's from one impression to
another; he had very few ideas but what he said, he meant; and though
reserved and distrustful of others and therefore disliked, in some fields
he introduced more real improvements than his brilliant brother.

Nicholas' first awkward legacy from Alexander was the Decembrist
rising, which spoiled the very beginning of his reign. The Decembrists
were some of his natural associates, men who might have been mounting guard in his palace. He treated the matter in a peculiarly personal
way, taking the closest part in the investigation. On their side, the principal conspirators wrote to him from their prisons letters of the frankest
kind, and were not afraid to explain in full their projects and aspirations.
The letters were very diverse. Pestel, the would-be dictator, the man
who held so many threads, turned craven. He gave away every name he
could think of, even names he had only heard once, even the friend
who had charge of his papers; he racked his brains to think what more
he could tell. Ryleyev showed much more dignity; while regretting the
rising, he claimed the main responsibility for it, and Nicholas later
made himself the guardian of his family. Nicholas faced this investigation as a necessary means to discover the causes of unrest, and made use
of some of the suggestions contained in these letters. Five of the conspirators were hanged; the other principal Decembrists were exiled to
Siberia or sent away for life service in the ranks of the army. There had
been no death sentence under Alexander, and the execution of the
Decembrist leaders made a great impression.

The reforms of Nicholas, all matters of detail with nothing showy
in them, were devoted in the main to improving the bureaucratic machine of government. This period is *par excellence* the reign of officialdom. Nicholas was a careful steward of his estate and was ably served by
his honest Minister of Finance Count Kankrin, who had a wide ad-

ministrative experience and acted as a watchdog of the resources of the State. One feature of Nicholas' reign was the great importance which he gave to his personal chancellery. One section of it (the Second), under Speransky, was entrusted with the codification of the laws; to another (the famous Third Section) was given the control of the political police. It is strange to hear Nicholas say at the end of his reign: "I have no police; I dislike it"; never was police rule so organized or so oppressive as in this reign. The bureaucracy itself was submerged in a mass of superfluous papers; once ten wagons-full, dealing with a single case of fraud in a contract, were sent from Moscow to St. Petersburg, and wagons and papers all disappeared unaccountably on the road; the government was itself compelled to hold commissions for the diminution of unnecessary correspondence. Even the reforms of Nicholas, for instance in the peasant question, were prejudiced from the outset, because the work was wholly entrusted to the bureaucracy and kept secret from the population, whose support was therefore never enlisted.

Alexander also left to Nicholas several legacies in foreign policy. When Alexander died, we shall remember that he escaped the awkward decision of making war for the Greeks against Turkey. Nicholas had never pretended to be a Liberal. "As to the Greeks, I call them rebels," he said, and he thought they should have been made to submit to the Sultan. On the other hand, Russia could not allow that the championship of Greece should be left to others, and in January 1824 Alexander had himself proposed joint intervention of the Powers. After a visit of Wellington to St. Petersburg in April 1826 England presented to the Porte a joint Anglo-Russian demand that Greece should receive full autonomy, though still paying tribute to Turkey. Even the reactionary Charles X of France was for a crusade against Turkey; in July 1827, in spite of the indignation of Metternich and the abstention of Prussia, three Powers—Russia, England, and France—took joint action; on October 20 their combined fleet destroyed the Egyptian fleet of Ibrahim at Navarino. With the death of Canning, Russo-British cooperation came to an end, and fear of Russia led the British government to describe the battle in Parliament as an untoward incident. Russia, however, did not give up the Greeks. When all Christians were expelled from Constantinople, she declared war on Turkey (April 26, 1828). The Russians occupied Moldavia and Wallachia, and passed the Danube. After initial reverses, they captured Silistria; and Diebitsch, crossing the Balkans, won Adrianople (August 19) and threatened Constantinople; the Russian fleet had already made a diversion south of the Balkans. By the treaty of Adrianople (September 14) the Roumanian Governors (*Hospodars*) were to be appointed for life and to be free of Turkish interference in internal affairs; the Straits and the Black Sea were to be open. As to Greece, it was curiously enough England that now, out of fear of Russia, wished to diminish the liberated territory. Capodistrias, Alexander's former minister, became the first President.

One thing Nicholas did, which his successors from the time of Peter I had practically all promised but failed to do. Since the Statute (*Ulozhenie*) of Alexis, commission after commission had met to bring the laws up to date, but without effect. Nicholas entrusted Speransky with this task. Speransky, who chose able assistants, did not make a new law code, but he did render the great service of tabulating all existing laws in forty-five volumes with an index. Law on paper in Russia has always been a very different thing to law in practice; it was still more so, as long as the laws themselves were totally unknown to many of those who were called to administer them.

In local government Nicholas, returning to the ideas of his father Paul, systematically restricted the independent part played by the gentry under Catherine. It was not that the gentry were excluded from service; on the contrary they were brought more than before into the direct service of the State, and the marshals elected by them served as a kind of nursery for the supply of governors; the change consisted in bringing them under the rigorous direction of headquarters in the bureaucratic work of the empire, instead of encouraging them as a class to assert an independent initiative in local affairs.

But the chief of all the preoccupations of Nicholas was the peasantry. In this connection he at one time plainly said that he did not wish to leave to his son problems which he ought himself to solve. As early as 1826 he instituted his first commission for the study of practical reforms. It was followed in the course of his reign by five others, which of itself is evidence both of the Emperor's insistence and of the opposition of his nearest counsellors. In 1834 he took the matter into his own hands, choosing a worthy executant of his intentions in Kisilev, whom he asked to serve as his chief of staff to carry them out. For what concerned the crown peasants he instituted a new Ministry, that of Imperial Domains, which he also entrusted to Kisilev. Arakcheyev's unhappy experiment of military colonies under Alexander shows up pitifully enough by the side of Kisilev's achievements. The economic wellbeing of the crown peasants was very considerably advanced; they were withdrawn from the jurisdiction of the local police, who had been a great source of vexation, and were put under the care of new officials of a higher status and morale; schools and other institutions were established for them. The only fair criticism which suggested itself was that Kisilev's jurisdiction was too much like a state within a state, artificially fostered by the special favour of the government; but Kisilev himself always wished to extend the benefits of the crown peasants to the squires' serfs as well; and this was also the wish of his sovereign.

Nicholas made more than one attempt to give further effect to Alexander's law of 1803 authorizing and regulating agreements between squires and their peasants, by which the serfs obtained freedom with land. Unfortunately the bureaucracy here outdid itself. On the plea of making sure that such agreements were entirely free on the part of the peasants, was established such a system of verification, mounting even to the Minister of the Interior himself, as could only delay any agreements of this kind. On the other hand much was done to regulate the position of the serfs; and toward the end of the reign, under the direction of Bibikov, inventories were enforced in South Russia fixing the dues and duties which they owed to their squires; Nicholas wished to apply the same system in the Lithuanian provinces.

Indirectly the work of Speransky in tabulating the laws had a great value for the peasants; it recalled to memory the conditions under which serfdom was legalized—that is, not at all as a simple privilege to the squires but as a means to enable them to discharge duties to the State, from which they had since been set free; least of all was it then contemplated that the peasants should simply become chattels of the squires. But beyond this, definite acts of legislation were brought to light which the government itself had entirely forgotten; for instance, squires were not allowed to endanger life in the punishments which they inflicted; now these punishments were put under a supervision strict at least in principle. For ordinary crimes peasants were now under the usual criminal courts; in any major punishment, the squire had to act with the knowledge and assistance of government institutions. Nicholas himself throughout his reign constantly insisted to the gentry on their obligations to their peasants, and this was no mere advice. Only toward the end of the reign did peasants obtain even a partial right to present petitions to government authorities; otherwise, the police were expected to find out abuses for themselves; but where instances of tyranny were established, the Emperor demanded severe punishment of the squires concerned. Another important advance was that the peasant secured a legal right to property of his own; till then, even in theory as well as in practice, the squire could lay his hands on anything which the peasant possessed.

In his measures for the welfare of the peasants Nicholas met with continuous resistance, which even went so far as the omission from new editions of such statutes as established peasant rights. He himself, too, repeatedly reasserted the rights of the gentry, even declaring toward the end of his reign that all the land was their property. By then, rumours of impending emancipation were frequent among the peasants; and in large areas in the southeast, numbers of them made their way into the provincial towns declaring that they wished to join the militia for the Crimean War which was then in progress, and on the supposed authority of the Emperor claimed their freedom in return. The government used armed force to suppress this movement.

The reign of Nicholas was divided into periods, not by Russian events but by events in France—a convincing proof of the counterstroke of French ideas in Russian politics both external and internal. In July 1830, Charles X, friend of autocratic Russia, who was at that time closely collaborating with Nicholas in foreign policy, was overthrown by a peaceful revolution. There was little bloodshed, no guillotining. The King, who like James II of England had thought the time was come to reassert the full royal authority, found the ground gone from beneath him and was glad to escape of himself from the country. The new government in France was not revolutionary, but bourgeois "liberal." It was a constitutional monarchy under a junior branch of Bourbons, the Orleans family, in the person of Louis Philippe, son of Louis "Égalité," and himself at one time active in the service of the Republic during the first French Revolution. He was given the title of King of the French—a mark that the people which made him King could also unmake him. Nicholas detested him as a usurper. Up till now all the continental governments had stood for autocracy, and England, isolated from the rest, could only check the general reaction in the field of Spanish South America; henceforward there was cooperation between England and France and Europe was divided into two camps, the autocratic East and the constitutional West. The events in France found an echo in constitutional movements in Baden and in Italy and above all in Belgium, which after the fall of Napoleon had been unnaturally united to Holland in spite of differences of race and religion, for no other reason than to create a fairly strong buffer state on the frontier of France. The Belgians now rose against the Dutch and achieved their independence in the new Kingdom of the Belgians.

The news from Paris had a similar echo in the east, in Poland. Alexander, after giving a constitution to that limited Poland which he received at the Congress of Vienna, had shown in many ways that the union of two crowns, the autocratic crown of a strong Russia and the constitutional crown of a weak Poland, was incompatible, especially on the head of a sovereign who, whatever his professions, showed by his actions that he was at heart an autocrat; Russians also felt keenly the contradiction of the grant to Poland of rights which were not yet given to Russia. In practice Alexander made several substantial breaches in the Polish Constitution. He appointed Novosiltsev to act as his deputy over the head of the official Viceroy, the Pole Zajaczek. Dissatisfied with the Diet since it refused the measures which he proposed, he had summoned it irregularly; and when the public showed its dissatisfaction, the constitutional liberty of press and person was not respected. It must be remembered that Napoleon, when, within the limits of the Grand Duchy of Warsaw, he gave independence to 2.5 millions of Poles, had introduced the *Code Napoléon,* making all equal before the law, and had abolished serfdom; it was in the revolutionary and Napoleonic campaigns that Poland had been able to create the nucleus of a modern national army.

Nicholas had considered himself bound by his obligations and was crowned in Warsaw, though with the Russian crown. The Poles continued to claim the western provinces annexed to Russia in the partitions of Catherine, where the great majority of the population was unquestionably Russian. In contrast with Alexander, who had said much to encourage this claim, Nicholas from the outset declared that he could not reconcile it with his position as a Russian. He had resumed the summoning of the Diet; and in 1830 it threw out a law for the restriction of civil divorces as allowed by the code of Napoleon. Pestel's group of the Decembrists had negotiated with a conspirative Polish society, as Nicholas discovered in his investigation of the Russian conspiracy.

On the night of November 28, 1830, a band of Poles broke into the Belvedere palace of the viceroy, the Grand Duke Constantine, and killed a general whom they mistook for him. The Grand Duke apparently might easily have put down the rising, as he was urged to do even by some generals of the Polish army. Instead of this, he lost his head and withdrew from Warsaw. In the city there were many different shades of political opinion which, beginning with the more moderate, succeeded each other rapidly in the leadership of the movement. Two moderates, Prince Lubiecki and Count Jezerski, went to St. Petersburg to obtain clemency and concessions for their country from Nicholas, but he insisted that submission should precede conciliation, and threatened the destruction of Poland in case of resistance. The Diet in Warsaw now deposed him (January 25, 1831) and, with vain hopes of French support, faced a war with Russia.

Many of the older officers stood aloof from the movement. The peasants, who at first gave it support, drew aside when it became clear that the bourgeois authorities in Warsaw were not in favour of a settlement of peasant grievances. One government succeeded another, and the command of the Polish forces changed hands with lightning rapidity. Most fatal of all—the Poles from the outset tried to make good their claims to Volhynia and Lithuania, provinces where the population could not be expected to support them. Diebitsch, sent into Poland with a trained army of 150,000, himself died of cholera; but his successor Paskevich, with the support of Austria and Prussia who barred their frontiers to the Polish insurgents, was soon able to defeat the Polish armies, and closed in on Warsaw. Passing the Vistula, he stormed the suburb of Wola on the western side and levelled his guns on the city, and nothing was left to the insurgents but surrender.

The Polish Constitution was replaced by an Organic Statute (March 1832), which abolished the Polish Diet and army and practically repealed the constitutional liberties, though guaranteeing freedom of person and property and retaining at least a separate administration for the affairs of Poland. However, this statute was never really put into execution, for which excuse enough was found in the continued agitation of Polish emigrants abroad and the recurrence of isolated outbreaks of protest or insurrection inside the country. Poland fell entirely under Russian bureaucratic government. The universities of Warsaw and Vilna were closed, and the Russian language was introduced not only in secondary but even in primary schools. In Lithuania and White Russia, where the Polish minority had introduced their own culture and had formed a large Polish oasis around Vilna, every attempt was made to Russify institutions, and the Roman Catholic religion was an object of constant attack. Russian institutions were even introduced wholesale in Poland proper; it was divided into *gubernii* (provinces) in 1837, and marshals of the gentry were instituted in 1852. Hardly any of the national resources were spent on public needs. In 1839 Poland became an educational district of Russia, which meant that education was discouraged in every possible way; study abroad was prohibited; no books on history or social studies might be published; the works of the best writers, such as the great national poets Mickiewicz and Slowacki and the historian Lelewel, who had played an active part in the insurrection, could not be printed; the result was that the public sank into apathy; it was as if Russia could only hold Poland by uncivilizing it. It was no wonder that the various groups of emigrants abroad devoted their best energies to education; on one other point they were all agreed —as to the necessity of another armed rising.

In the long period from 1831 to 1848 which forms the major part of the reign of Nicholas, there was enforced silence both in Russia and in Europe. In this dismal period Russia, for Europe, is the Russian government and Nicholas; and Nicholas stands as the most secure and powerful protagonist of throne and altar against all movements of discontented peoples; this was a position forced upon him by Alexander's premier role in Europe. For Europe this was a period of permanent unrest, not least in France, where the bourgeois regarded the monarchy of Louis Philippe as their own creation and property. The rapid industrialization of France was raising acute social questions. There had been beginnings of socialist thought in the later period of the first French Revolution, especially during the administration of the Commune in Paris by Chaumette and Hébert and again directly after the fall of Robespierre; these beginnings were followed up by several social theorists, from Saint Simon and Fourier to Louis Blanc. In 1832 there was street fighting in Paris, roughly suppressed, and in April 1834 a strike at Lyons developed into an insurrection, with similar movements of unrest in other large towns. At one moment a Republic was proclaimed in Paris. The failure of the plot of Fieschi in 1835 was followed by more repression and more unrest. Political discontent was chronic in West Germany and in Italy.

All this drew the three autocratic sovereigns of the East closer together. Nicholas met the Emperor Francis II of Austria at Münschengrätz in 1833. On his arrival Metternich made a profession that he was "not finessing," and the blunt Nicholas gave the delightful answer: "Prince, I know you." Nicholas had come to propose an alliance of Russia, Prussia, and Austria against revolution, directed of course against France and England, and Prussia's adherence he obtained in his subsequent visit to Berlin (October 16). Russia and Prussia gave each other a mutual guarantee of their Polish possessions; Russia and Austria agreed each to allow the other's troops to pass through her territory. The old Austrian Emperor Francis II was so much impressed by Nicholas that he left an instruction to his successor to do nothing without his advice. Nicholas became definitely the head of the reactionary camp in European politics. Switzerland was forced to refuse asylum to political refugees, who could now only find safety in England and America. Nicholas did not play so aggressive a part in European affairs as Alexander, but he found himself intervening in the affairs of Portugal and Spain, where he counselled moderation to the champions of absolutism.

In Russia Nicholas continued with his efforts for peasant reform up to 1848; but for educated society this period was one of complete repression of all thought and initiative. In 1826 Nicholas confirmed a statute of the censorship proposed by the old reactionary Admiral Shishkov, whose object was "to make printing harmless"; the Minister of the Interior might prohibit any publication, and all editors so prohibited were for a time deprived of the right of editing, whether alone or with others. Every ministry received by this statute practically a separate censorship of its own, and the Liberal censor Nikitenko declares that at one time there were more censorships than books published in the year. Except for school textbooks, all works on logic and philosophy were forbidden. Writers were forbidden to leave spaces marked with dots; they might even later be called to account for anything which had passed a negligent censor. In 1828 this statute was completely remodelled; but the government continued to issue innumerable circulars; books on anatomy and physiology were forbidden to include anything which might "offend the instinct of decency." Nicholas himself played the part of censor and "recommended to Mr. Pushkin" that he should reissue *Boris Godunov*, the greatest of Russian tragedies, "with an elimination of superfluous material, as a novel after the manner of Walter Scott." He announced his special approval of the most servile writer of this period, Bulgarin.

While the censorship crippled thought and the bureaucracy pounded out its innumerable regulations, the public lay in a state of torpor. Nothing is more striking than the abasement of so many even of the most independent minds before the authority of the supreme drillmaster. One finds it in many of the letters of the Decembrists while under trial and also in Chaadayev. If it was so with the few elect, what of the ordinary individual? Very few had the courage and individuality required to live in this dense fog. Nearly everyone was directly or indirectly an official and therefore at the mercy of his superiors, so that servility was the rule everywhere. There have been in other countries periods of stifling convention; but the conventions were often a tyranny of society itself, the outcome of its own narrowness and supineness; in this case they were the gospel of a purely reactionary government, at a time when all Europe was thinking hard and when Russians were beginning to think more than ever before; they were imposed by the will of one extremely limited man, Nicholas. In these conditions the very qualities of loyalty and service took a character of degradation. "Obey without discussion" was the actual demand of Nicholas; "moderation and accuracy" became the ideal of what was expected both of the official world and of unquestioning subjects in general. Banality reigned supreme, stifling the individual thinker, who could find nowhere a school of responsibility and initiative and perished like a flicker of light in isolation from his fellows, with no hope that he would leave the world any better for those who followed him.

In this long period of repression and gloom stand out the towering figures of the two greatest poets of Russian literature, Pushkin and Lermontov. Pushkin had no strong political views, and it is therefore not surprising that he was not marked with any particular political courage. The failure of the Decembrists closed a book in his life; he himself had henceforward no great faith in Liberalism. Yet this was the moment, as he himself felt and said, when he felt his powers to be most completely developed. He turned them all to the task which was really his: he concentrated them on the perfection of his art, but equally on the assertion of his independent individuality. He held firm to his own integrity at a time when character was everywhere crushed around him, and he well knew that the victory was his for all time. The lines in which he expressed this confidence were later chosen for inscription on his statue.

In 1837 a trained dueller was put up to make aspersions on his wife, such as, in Russian social conditions, made a duel inevitable; Pushkin, of course, had to call him out, and was killed. When Pushkin was hounded to death by the society of which he was a part, stinging verses, showing up vividly the ignominy of the social plot that killed him, announced the accession of his brilliant successor Lermontov, like Pushkin a poet at fifteen, who was to perish in a duel at an even earlier age; Lermontov is the most striking and convincing of the Russian Romantics. His scorn was not merely, like that of Pushkin, for the banality and servility of his own social world, but for the baseness of life itself in Russia during this period.

It was no chance that Pushkin, on the occasion of Napoleon's death in 1821, and Lermontov ten years later, wrote as poets and not as politicians, two of the most remarkable expressions in literature of that intimate connection which was to bind the French Revolution to the Russian. "All hail!" writes Pushkin in 1821. "To the Russian people he showed a great destiny, and from the gloom of exile bequeathed lasting freedom." Lermontov saw clearer and farther, and his extraordinary *Prophecy* is a precise and detailed description of the chaos and bloodshed that were to overwhelm Russia in 1918.

Around Pushkin, who is the central figure in Russian classical literature, stood several notable poets. Two other authors, though both very great artists, yet mark the coming of the tendency which was to substitute criticism and sociology for pure art. Griboyedov, who died young as Minister in Persia when a Teheran crowd attacked the Legation, satirized the servility of the period in his brilliant play *The Mischief of Being Clever*, which could never be performed in public during his lifetime. Old Krylov continued the fables which he had been publishing from time to time since 1809, and was able to carry the approval of Nicholas himself while showing up the whole official world of his time in his subtle pictures of beasts of prey.

Gogol, one of the greatest writers of Russian prose, reveals as sharply as his contemporary Dickens and with a boldness of outline which is equally near to caricature, the savagery, hypocrisy, and corruption of the period. His *Revisor* (*Government Inspector*) is not, as some superficial foreign readers have taken it, a comedy, an amusing sketch; it is a bitter and poignant description not of exceptions but of the average, and Nicholas himself was man enough to realize this and to tell the author so; his *Dead Souls* is, among other things, the final expression of contempt for the condemned system of serfdom. But Gogol himself, as soon as he turned from describing and tried to preach some lesson, lost his footing and fell into an obscurity of mysticism.

So perished in isolation the great Russian authors, because they were alien to all their surroundings, and a critical thinking public had yet to be created. The typical writers of this time were those who accepted it. Bulgarin with his *Northern Bee*, and Grech with his *Son of the Fatherland* limited themselves to supplying what they imagined to be asked for. Bulgarin hopes "by a pleasant path-strewed with flowers to lead the fair sex to the temple of virtue"; and he writes in 1831: "Whenever His Majesty the Emperor may be pleased to use my pen for political articles, I will endeavour accurately and zealously to execute His Majesty's will." Count Alexis Tolstoy anonymously parodied the current servility in the works of "Kuzma Prutkov," with his endless maxims, which recall and outdo anything that was achieved by the

banality of Martin Tupper. One great writer did not quarrel with his generation. This was the novelist Goncharov, the creator in literature of the aimless, likeable man without backbone and without enemies, the idealization of all the weaknesses in the Russian character, for which Goncharov himself evidently had a tender feeling, and to which, to judge by his diary, he was himself by no means alien. Scattered among the mass of servile officials and submissive citizens, we have also the fitful personalities of the so-called "superfluous men," who have no place in this period, but lack the strength of character or of mind to create anything better. Such are the *Eugene Onegin* of Pushkin, the Pechorin of Lermontov (the book is entitled *A Hero of Our Time*), and, best of all, the *Rudin* of Ivan Turgenev. Rudin indeed has plenty of mind and is full of high ideals; he talks so well that it is almost impossible to disagree with him; yet the author breaks him ruthless over the first real test of character with which he faces him, and Rudin turns away to a life of disillusionment which he ends by dying in a flash of secondhand heroism on a barricade in Paris. The superfluous man wraps himself in the shawl of Byron and, at least too good to sink in the marsh of banality, seeks pleasure in the consciousness that he is unlike others and that he is therefore deeply unhappy.

Yet it is in this marsh that the Russian reading-public is created, though not by any means by the frogs of the marsh. When the staff of the Decembrists were swept off the scene, there was for a time silence; but both in St. Petersburg and Moscow a few elect thinkers were turning eagerly to the study of contemporary thought in Europe. Where else was there for them to turn? Russia at this time could offer them little or no material toward the formation of a tradition of their own. Their main interest was sociology, and in this field a number of masters, Kant, Fichte, Schelling, Hegel, followed each other in succession in Germany. The most notable of these Russian thinkers was Vissarion Belinsky, of humble origin, frail and consumptive but with an all-conquering intellectual courage, living in a backyard in Moscow under foul sanitary conditions as a struggling student of the University. His grandfather was an austere and saintly village priest; his father a clever drunken country surgeon, mated to a stupid wife; the child grew up as a critic. He was excluded from school for non-attendance and from the University for "incompetence"; he directed his own studies and, as a child, fascinated a visiting inspector by the hawklike keenness with which he pounced on anything that interested him; of one of his teachers he made a friend, and turned all his lessons into tutorial classes on literary criticism. He had to possess his own soul. "By my life, at the cost of tears, weepings of the soul, I made these ideas my own." He sought for himself "a peace and harmony such as outside life cannot give you or take from you." "You will be not in the world, but the whole world will be in you." "Our lot puts the cowl on us. We must suffer, that life may be easier for our grandchildren. We must renounce all happiness, because destiny is cruel to its instruments."

The superfluous man flowered and withered without effect in Russia because, while there were individual thinkers, there was no school of thought. This was what Belinsky was to found. Around Professor Stankevich gathered a group of brilliantly able and honest thinkers, who were later to become the leaders of the most various directions of political thought. Constantine Aksakov, theologian and poet, son of a writer of tales of peasant life, was, with his brother Ivan, to be a leading exponent of the Slavophil theory of the religious and intellectual mission of Russia in Europe; Michael Katkov, the youngest and in a way the spoilt child of the group, was later to be the best independent apologist of government policy; Michael Bakunin of the gentry of Tver, a rapid and brilliant explorer of the German philosophy of the time, was to be the fountainhead of Russian anarchism. It is most remarkable that these young men were all fellow-students in Moscow University and that they were close personal friends. Somewhat apart from them, but in intimate contact, stood Alexander Hertzen, an older man, who had earlier been expelled from the University and exiled, but was now allowed to return. Belinsky, not Stankevich, was the real centre of the group. Though absolutely fearless in the independence of his opinions, and tolerating no compromise of convention, he was able to secure the affection of all in a remarkable degree; yet it would be impossible to identify him with any single tendency of thought, and this was really due to his transparent intellectual honesty.

The new Russian intelligentsia, of which these men were the kernel, was not in time to know Kant except by later study; and indeed from all the German thinkers, the Russians take only what they want and can never be regarded as exponents of the systems in question. For them the first great contemporary German philosopher was Schelling, whose theory of intuitive contemplation of and absorption in the absolute met the cravings of isolated individual thinkers in a society which had so little to offer them in the way of standards, æsthetic or ethical. But it was hardly more than a year before Bakunin, who was generally the advance skirmisher, made Belinsky transfer his enthusiasm to Fichte, who had helped to create the morale that inspired the youths of Germany in the War of Liberation in 1813. From Fichte, with equal rapidity and with the same guide, namely Bakunin, Belinsky passed on to Hegel, who remained his teacher for a somewhat longer period; but nothing is more characteristic than Belinsky's ultimate break with Hegel, nor the lively personal colour of the language in which he expresses it. He cannot make any slavish submission of his independent personality to a "World Spirit" or to any doctrinaire system, and he reassumes his full liberty.

This is not the place to follow in detail the many turns of direction in Belinsky's thought. His significance is that his keen critical mind fought its way from nowhere, namely the Russia of his time, with enthusiasm for any guide who could show him a part of his road, through a thicket of abstract theories to a consciousness of his own, in which he realized both the inviolable integrity of individual personality and the impossibility of any individual personality worth having without constant contact with all the human interests that surround it. Individualism and socialism, properly understood, are necessary to each other. If Belinsky had been less wholehearted and less fearless, he must almost certainly have stopped thinking at one or another stage in his restless progress. That he was perfectly ready to dismiss any dogma the moment that it proved insufficient to him, is the secret of his achievement. In this mental wrestle to find his own soul, Belinsky was meanwhile the creator of a school of literary criticism with the same intellectual honesty and the same exacting standards.

During the forties, Russian political thought, already strong and vigorous, was divided between two schools—Westernizers and Slavophils. The preface to this discussion was a private letter of Peter Chaadayev, published without his knowledge in 1836 in the *Telescope* of Professor Nadezhdin. Chaadayev had been a friend but not a fellow-thinker of some of the Decembrists. His turn of thought was essentially religious. He believed at this stage that Russia must return to union with the great body of European civilization and with the Roman Catholic Church. In his letter, which was one of a series, he drew a merciless picture of Russia's own moral poverty; she had, he urged, no past worth the name, no present, and no future. "We are not of the West or of the East," he wrote, "and we have the traditions of neither." "Life," he says, "is constantly putting to Russians the question: 'Where are you?' " He finds "no regular movement of the spirit, no good habits, no rule for anything, nothing individual to rest our thought upon."

"Each of us has to take up for himself the thread broken in the family." "With us, new ideas sweep away the old because they do not spring out of them." Like Belinsky he is seeking a school, a morale. The *Telescope* was stopped, and Nicholas on his own imperial authority declared Chaadayev to be insane. Chaadayev published later another letter under the title *L'apologie d'un fou*, but it does not have the interest of the first.

The question to which Chaadayev directed attention was the finding of a meaning for Russian history, and this study led up to the debate between the two groups of thinkers known as Westernizers and Slavophils. The Westernizers, not from any religious point of view, wished Russia to form part of Western civilization. The Slavophils, equally condemning the miserable want of content in the bureaucratic Russia of the time, turned away from the West in a spirit of patriotic contempt and resentment, to seek out in Russia herself the elements of a civilization of her own. The Castor and Pollux of Slavophilism were two brilliant thinkers, Kireyevsky and Homyakov. Ivan Kireyevsky was at one time a pupil of Hegel; later he followed him no further than to seek an answer to his question as to what was Russia's contribution to the world spirit of civilization. For this answer he relied on the old Greek Fathers, particularly on Isaac the Syrian, and the doctrine which he preached is of real importance to world thought. Kireyevsky and the Slavophils specially interested themselves in the yoking together of intuition and instinct, a line of enquiry followed out in our time much in the Slavophil spirit by Bergson. Logic, so Kireyevsky holds, is not the sole function of the intellect, still less of the personality. The object of thought is not to know but to be, and the whole man can only exist where reason and intuition each performs its proper task. Alexis Homyakov, theologian, philosopher, and poet, was the debater of the school, and with him Slavophilism has a more distinctively Russian tinge. The Slavophils sought in their past those elements which inspired the instinct of Christian brotherhood, among the first of which they set the village community and the wage-sharing associations of workmen. They believed that Russia possessed enough culture of her own to pursue an independent course. The dispute is one which might go on for ever; it reflects alternating tendencies which are to be found throughout the whole of Russian history and to which attention has already been called. On the other hand, the solution is there; but it is not in logic— it is in flesh and blood. Every Russian has in him, at least potentially, the instincts both of the Slavophil and of the Westernizer, and this often comes out in very striking contrasts between theory and instinct. This is particularly noticeable in Hertzen, the founder of that school of thought which saw in the Russian peasant the hope both of Russia and of Europe. Hertzen gets rid of his intellectual difficulties much more summarily and less thoroughly than Belinsky. In 1848 he left Russia because he could not live in compulsory stagnation; but reaching Paris on the eve of a new revolution, he was quickly disillusioned in the bourgeois civilization of the West as a ground on which anything spiritual could grow.

In February 1848, events in France again marked a period in Russian history. Louis Philippe, whose government had been discredited by its selfishness and corruption, was overthrown in what has been described as a revolution of contempt. This time, the echoes in the rest of Europe were far louder than in 1830. Metternich, for twenty-four years the policeman-in-chief of central Europe, was overthrown with equal ease in Vienna (March). Italy, united in a league of princes under the headship of a "Liberal" Pope, rose against Austrian rule. Revolution ensued all over Europe. In the course of the next two years the Emperor of Austria had to fly twice from his capital, and the King of Prussia once. Hungary broke away from Austria and ultimately, deposing the dynasty of the Habsburgs, declared her independence; it was clearly impossible for what remained of Austria to reduce her to obedience. At Frankfort met a preliminary German Parliament, which drew up a declaration of rights and tried to draft a new constitution for all German-speaking territory. The King of Prussia, Frederick Wilhelm IV, was for a time content to figure as the hope of German Liberalism; and it was only when he was definitely invited to become Emperor of Germany that he drew back in fear of war with Austria. 1848 is the year of large, loose, and optimistic confederations of the most various and conflicting interests in the name of Liberalism. 1849 is the year of desperate isolated resistances of those who remain faithful to their watchwords of 1848 in spite of the conquering reaction.

Only two European thrones were unshaken throughout this storm, those of Victoria and Nicholas. Throughout, the revolutionaries turned for moral or even for material support to England and Palmerston, and the monarchs to Russia and Nicholas. Nicholas made his attitude clear from the outset in a fiery memorandum of March 27, 1848, declaring that Russia was threatened and ending with the words: "Give heed, ye peoples, and submit yourselves, for God is with us." It was now that he declared that "all the land without exception belongs to the landowning gentry." While censuring Frederick William IV for his Liberalism, he wrote that if a Republic were introduced, he would find it his duty to come and restore the old Prussia. It was Nicholas who reduced Hungary to the allegiance of the Habsburgs; a Russian army under Paskevich surrounded the Hungarians at Vilagos and forced them to surrender (August 13, 1849). It was Nicholas who decided Frederick William IV against accepting the crown of a democratic Emperor of Germany; at Warsaw he mediated in the disputes of Austria and Prussia, and decided in favour of Austria. Meanwhile a short-lived Second Republic in France led up to the Presidency (December 10, 1848) and later the Empire of Napoleon III (December 2, 1852).

The last period in the reign of Nicholas, from 1848 to 1855, was, at home, one of complete suffocation. The university chairs of philosophy and divinity were united in one; metaphysics and moral philosophy were withdrawn from the curriculum; all articles on the subject of these changes, whether for or against, were forbidden. The Slavophils, the patriots of Russian thought, were put under "not secret but public police inspection." Newspapers were forbidden even to commend new inventions until they had been officially declared to be useful; in 1851 a commission was appointed to examine all music for the discovery of possible conspirative ciphers. As Nikitenko wrote in 1850: "If they play tricks in Europe, the Russian gets a hit on the back." "Every movement in the West," writes Granovsky, "is reflected here by some measure of repression." Papers now came out publishing bare news without any comment. Where anything further was attempted, to quote the words of Ivan Aksakov, "the writer, as if he were a thief, used any artifice to get his thought through to the public between the lines; the written word tore itself away from the censor's hands and entered God's world crumpled, ruffled, and mutilated, and was welcomed by the public as a token of victory, or keenly relished as a forbidden, secret, and tempting fruit." Count S. Uvarov, himself the reactionary Minister of Public Instruction from 1833 to 1849, was not allowed to use the word *demos* in his book on Greek antiquities, nor might he say that Roman emperors were killed, only that "they perished." From a scientific work the censor removed the expression "forces of nature." Nikitenko, himself a censor, was called upon to explain what he meant by using the term "the movement of minds." The censor Akhmatov stopped a book on arithmetic because between the figures of a problem he saw a row of dots. The socialist Petrashevsky, who had held innocuous meetings for discussion, was arrested with thirty-two of his friends, of whom twenty-one were actually condemned to death, and brought out for execution before they were sent to Siberia, among them one of the greatest of Russian writers, the epileptic Dostoyevsky. The police were on their way to arrest Belinsky when he escaped them by dying. The novelist Ivan Turgenev was arrested in 1852, and one of the leading Slavophils, Samarin, was imprisoned for criticizing the administration of the Baltic provinces. Russian literature was compared to a plant trying to grow on the edge of a crater. All foreign travel was prohibited.

In spite of all this repression, the year 1848 was to have its sequel in Russia; but the *dénouement* of the despotism of Nicholas was to come in an indirect way. Two main issues divided the two leading Powers in Europe, Russia and England. There was an irreconcilable contrast in all conceptions of government, and there was also the rivalry of two empires in the East. The Near Eastern question had been twice raised in a critical form during the reign of Nicholas. Mehmet Ali, Turkish Governor of Egypt, whose vigorous son Ibrahim had tried to suppress the insurrection in Greece, twice quarrelled with the Sultan, and seemed likely to capture Constantinople. In 1831–3 Ibrahim, invading Syria, inflicted severe defeats on the Sultan's forces. The policy of Nicholas was to support the Sultan, whose weakness now made him almost entirely dependent on Russia and therefore a useful instrument. England was also against any change in Turkey as that was likely to lead to European complications, and it was only France who supported Mehmet Ali. Nicholas made good use of his opportunities. At Unkiar Skelessi Russia and Turkey concluded a defensive alliance for eight years, and the Sultan agreed to close the Dardanelles to all other Powers when Russia should be at war, though Russian ships might freely enter the Mediterranean (July, 1833). The second conflict between Mehmet Ali and the Sultan took place in 1839, and the Egyptian troops were again everywhere successful; the Turkish fleet revolted to Mehmet. France was for supporting him; but ultimately, after a short period of great excitement, she gave way to the other Powers. Mehmet received Palestine for life, and his governorship of Egypt was made hereditary. On July 13, 1841, all the five Powers agreed that the Dardanelles should be closed to all warships as of old, except when Turkey herself was at war.

Mehmet Ali, if left alone by Europe, would almost certainly have been successful. Nicholas therefore made repeated and sincere attempts to come to an agreement with England as to the future of Turkey, and at the same time to detach her from her friendship with the France of Louis Philippe. During the second Egyptian crisis he dispatched Brünnow to London, and this time the two governments acted together (1840). He showed several signs of friendship for Queen Victoria, and sent his son and brother to visit England. In 1843 he concluded a Navigation Convention. To the ambassador Bloomfield he spoke of alliance and a common understanding. In May 1844, he himself visited England; Queen Victoria described him as "extraordinarily polite," but found him rather terrifying. He had conversations, very frank on his side, with Aberdeen and Palmerston. "Turkey," he said, "is a dying man; we can try to keep him alive, but he will and must die. I am afraid of no one about it except France. With so many tons of gunpowder close to the fire, how can we prevent the sparks from catching? We should consider it reasonably, and try to get an upright and honest understanding." There followed an exchange of letters in which the English statement was less definite than the Russian; but Aberdeen talked to Brünnow of an alliance. The two governments were at variance throughout the revolutionary period of 1848-9, which Nicholas made it a point of honour not to utilize. For all that, in 1849, when Kossuth and other Hungarian leaders were given asylum in Turkey, Austria and Russia demanded their extradition, and as England and France supported Turkey and sent their fleets to the Dardanelles, a crisis was only averted with difficulty.

Nicholas anticipated a period of European wars from the establishment of the Second Empire in France in 1852. Napoleon III, having no sound basis of power, was always seeking some way of enlisting support and increasing his prestige. To please Catholic opinion, he had come forward as the champion of the Roman Catholic Church in a conflict over the Holy Places at Jerusalem, a dispute between Orthodox and Catholic priests, which could not have endangered peace if there had been no other causes of war. In a striking conversation with the British ambassador, Sir H. Seymour, Nicholas again proposed an understanding with England. If everything were left to chance, he said, he might have to occupy Constantinople, but neither Russia nor England should possess it (January 1853). On February 21 he proposed an eventual scheme of partition; Russia was to retain rights over Moldavia and Wallachia; Serbia and Bulgaria were to be free; England might have Egypt, and Crete, "if the island suits you." To judge by his words, he evidently believed that he could count on the complete agreement of Austria, which he had saved four years before.

To deal with all issues, Nicholas dispatched Menshikov to Constantinople with very precise instructions, which were accurately followed. Menshikov had two claims to make—for the Orthodox rights in the Holy Places and for general guarantees as to the Orthodox population of Turkey. Arriving on February 28, he demanded to deal with the Sultan direct. As to the Holy Places, after much debate an agreement was reached. No acceptable formula could be found on Menshikov's other demand. England and France were entirely opposed to any general protectorate of Russia over the Christian subjects of the Sultan. The British and French ambassadors acted more and more closely together, and rival Turkish influences were enlisted on either side. On May 21, after twice proposing to Turkey an offensive and defensive alliance, Menshikov, acting on his instructions, left Constantinople.

The protection of the British fleet had been promised to the Sultan. Nicholas gave a time limit for the submission of Turkey to his demands, and the two Western Powers encouraged Turkey to refuse submission. On July 3 Nicholas sent troops into the Danubian provinces, which it will be remembered were tributary to Turkey but under Russian protection, declaring at the same time that this was not an act of war. A solution proposed by all the four other Great Powers at Vienna was accepted by Nicholas but refused by Turkey (August 19). Further attempts to reach a settlement failed. The British and French fleets were instructed to pass the Dardanelles (October 22). On October 27 Omar Pasha crossed the Danube, and on November 1 Russia declared that she would resist any attack. On November 4 the Russians were beaten at Oltenitsa, and on November 30 they destroyed the Turkish fleet at Sinope. On February 27, 1854, France and England demanded the evacuation of the Danubian provinces; on March 12 they concluded an alliance, and on March 28 they declared war on Russia. Austria, without going to this length, had given strong diplomatic support to France and England throughout this crisis and joined them in presenting four demands to Russia; the Danubian provinces and Serbia were to be under a collective guarantee of Europe instead of under a Russian protectorate; the navigation of the Danube was to be free; the convention of London of July 13, 1841, was to be revised; and Russia was to renounce any general protectorate over Orthodox subjects of the Turkish Empire.

The Russian army met with no success in its invasion of Turkey, and when the French and British forces reached Varna, it abandoned the siege of Silistria (June 26) and recrossed the Danube and Pruth. Austrian troops occupied the Danubian provinces. The danger to Turkey was therefore already averted; but to give a further lesson to Nicholas the allies, once they were mobilized, decided to push home their success by an invasion of Crimea. They landed successfully at Eupatoria on September 14, 1854, with 56,000 men and, defeating the Russians on the Alma (September 20), they could probably have entered Sevastopol without delay; but opinions were divided and they halted. This gave time to General Todleben to put the fortress in a proper state of defence.

In the siege which followed no other military reputation was made except Todleben's. The Russians sank their fleet in the harbour, and a relieving army under Menshikov more than once tried to break the allied lines. Great courage was shown on both sides, for instance, at Balaklava in the famous charge of the Light Brigade, which repulsed a Russian attack on the English base (October 25), and in the soldiers' battle at Inkerman where a night surprise was driven off by the allies (November 5). There were unnecessarily large losses on both sides throughout the campaign owing to faulty military organization, but the balance of loss was overwhelmingly on the side of the Russians. Frauds of contractors were common, and supplies failed to arrive, though numberless horses were worn out in the work of transport; a reinforcement to the allies could travel from the west of Europe to the Crimea quicker even than Russian reinforcements from Moscow, south of which there was as yet no railway system. For the Russian nation the war was an object lesson in the corruption and incompetence of the bureaucracy and the fine courage of the private soldier, which has been commemorated by one of the combatants, Count Leo Tolstoy.

Nicholas had placed his hopes in "General January" and "General February," that is to say in the severity of a Russian winter. The month of February was fatal to himself. He had already dismissed the notorious Buturlin committee appointed to inspect and control the censorship itself. On December 2, 1854, Austria after treating with France and England, demanded Nicholas' compliance with the four points; Austria was to be free to act if they were not accepted by January 1, 1855; Prussia now supported the demand; on January 7 Russia admitted the points as a basis for discussion. On January 26 Piedmont, then under the direction of Cavour, joined the allies in the war. Invaded in his own territory, seeing his system crumbling around him, Nicholas declared: "My successor must do as he pleases; for myself I cannot change." Stricken with a severe chill he did not take ordinary precautions, and only realized his grave condition the day before his death. Nicholas expired on March 2, 1855, and with him fell in ruins the system of which his personality was everywhere regarded as the incarnation. The European predominance of St. Petersburg, built up by Catherine II and strengthened by Alexander I, had come to an end; but Russia, in some measure at least, was to become the Russia of the Russian people.

CHAPTER XIX

The Great Reforms

[*1855–74*]

THE NEW sovereign, Alexander II, had had his political training under
the oppressive and reactionary regime of his father, to whom he was
greatly attached and entirely loyal. As a young man he had been educated by the eminent poet and translator Zhukovsky, who was an ad-
mirer of the German Romantic school. Zhukovsky was by instinct and
temperament conservative and a supporter of the autocracy; thus he
carried forward on two sides the tradition of the Romantic and absolutist historian Karamzin, who had played an important part during the
embarrassing beginnings of the reign of Nicholas. Nicholas was absorbed in details of military organization and drill, and Zhukovsky, with
some support from the Empress, had tried to turn his pupil to more
intellectual interests; but Alexander himself fully shared the military
tastes of his father. Nicholas did not repeat with his son the mistake
which had been committed in his own case; he initiated Alexander
early in public affairs, with the result that he obtained a firm supporter
for his drill-sergeant system of government. In the most reactionary
period of the reign, after 1848, Alexander was almost prepared to go
farther than Nicholas. He took a part in the repressive censorship committee of Buturlin; he stood more strongly than Nicholas for the rights
of the gentry; he opposed the inventories which defined peasant obligations in the southwest, and when these were confirmed by Nicholas in
December 1852, it was Alexander who prevented their application to
Lithuania. His accession was therefore regarded with anything but hope
by the Liberals, an impression which was confirmed by the fact that
Bibikov, the Minister of the Interior, who was the author of the inventories, was now the first to lose his post.

This impression of Alexander, however, was erroneous; and when it
disappeared, its place was taken by an equally wrong conception, so that
the character of this sovereign has been little understood. Alexander was

an honest Conservative, forced by the overwhelming logic of facts to put in the forefront of his program the liberation of the serfs. Once he had accepted this task, he avoided no material or moral sacrifice in carrying it through. From the time when serfdom reached its culmination in the reign of Catherine II, there had been a long succession of avowals from those who were most concerned with the government of Russia, that this radical evil threatened the collapse of the State, a fear which was forced on them by the constant process of peasant exhaustion and the endless series of peasant disorders. The government could best appreciate these evils when they affected the army, on which it depended entirely for its prestige not only abroad but at home. This was the lesson of the Crimean War. The military strength of Russia had been greatly exaggerated. And now the autocrat was humiliated at home, by foreign forces not at all formidable in numbers and only indifferently led. Russia herself had thrown many more men into the war, but the wastage was enormous. The transport inflicted an enormous burden upon the population, only to achieve a small result; the medical service was as usual almost negligible, and epidemics were rampant; wholesale peculation was at work in the rear; thus supplies at the front were short, and equipment inadequate. The Russian infantry fought splendidly, but their commanders were often incompetent. Above all, there was shown up in the front line, where there was every demand for intelligence and initiative, the standing contrast between the status of the Russian serf and that of the free man of Western Europe; and it made serfdom look absurd as a basis of military power.

Nicholas himself had had to recognize the bankruptcy of his system and Alexander, on mounting the throne, continued his negotiations with the enemy Powers. At a conference with France, England, and Austria at Vienna (March 1855), where Prince A. Gorchakov represented Russia, it was agreed that she should resign all claim to a protectorate over the Danubian provinces and over Serbia, and that the Danube navigation should be free. Gorchakov was willing to admit foreign warships to the Black Sea, but not to take all Russian warships off it. Austria did not here identify herself with the full claims of France and England, and returned to a neutral position. These negotiations therefore came to nothing, and the allies proceeded with their attack on Sevastopol. Napoleon III expressed his intention of coming with reinforcements to complete the siege on the southeastern side. As the Russian relieving army was gaining ground, Canrobert sent a French force in the direction of Azov, but this was countermanded by Napoleon. Marshal Pélissier, replacing Canrobert, concentrated his efforts on the siege. An assault was launched against the Malakov redoubt, but was driven off by the besieged. On June 16, the British commander, Lord Raglan, died and was succeeded by General Simpson. The Russian relieving army attacked the allies on August 16 on the river Chernaya, but was checked by the French and Piedmontese troops; the latter, more recently arrived, gave a very creditable account of themselves. On September 8 the French with great bravery stormed the Malakov redoubt and held it in spite of all efforts to recover it; the Redan resisted the British attack. The garrison now blew up what was left of its defences and retreated to a strong position north of the great harbour, in which it might have continued its resistance almost indefinitely. The town was won after a siege of 336 days, which cost the allies in all something like 100,000 men. The Russian losses are estimated at about 300,-000. On November 28 the Russians obtained some consolation from the capture of Kars in the Caucasus.

In this war, then, the military events were not decisive. The burden of military organization and, still more, the economic results, in which all alike were losers, pointed the moral of its futility. Both Napoleon and France were tired of it. The British fleet had had no success in the Baltic, and the British military administration had led to public scandals. England was prepared to go on. But Russia was able to persuade Austria to make joint approaches to France, of which the British government was not at first informed. Four points, based on the previous negotiations, were put forward by Austria, to which Palmerston when informed later added a fifth, demanding that the Aland Islands should remain unfortified. These were presented to Russia, as well as an ultimatum from the side of Austria, giving Russia a time limit to January 16. The Russian Ministers were unanimously for ending the war, and in spite of the objections of Gorchakov, the young Emperor decided for peace.

Consequently, representatives of the Powers met in conference at Paris on February 25, 1856, and Russia and France cooperated against the persistence of England. The Peace, which was concluded on March 30, declared the Black Sea to be neutral; no warships were to sail on it, and no arsenal was to be constructed on its shores; thus were annulled Russia's naval efforts on this side from the time of Catherine and Potemkin. Navigation of the Danube was to be free under a commission appointed by the Powers. Russia lost a portion of Bessarabia. Turkey was placed under a joint guarantee of all the Powers and admitted to the Concert of Europe. A firman was arranged giving guarantees to the Christian subjects of Turkey, but no right of interference was allowed to foreign Powers. The Danubian provinces of Moldavia and Wallachia received an accession of territory from the side of Bessarabia and remained under Turkish suzerainty, all their existing rights being put under a common guarantee of the Great Powers in place of the abolished Russian protectorate. England at the same time gave up the right of seizing neutral property, except in case of neutral ships carrying actual contraband of war or of neutral goods conveyed on an enemy ship; privateering was declared to be abolished.

Alexander described this Peace as worth the terms which had to be given for it. For some time there was disagreement among the Powers, as to whether the two Danubian provinces, Wallachia and Moldavia, should be allowed to unite. England, in her support of Turkey, opposed the union; France and, of course, Russia, supported it; Austria, seeing that a united Roumania would inevitably in the long run lay claim to Transylvania, joined with England. The Turks carried out in their own fashion elections in Moldavia, which were declared to have pronounced against the union of the two provinces; France and Russia threatened to break off relations unless the population were given a free hand. In October 1857, both provinces pronounced almost unanimously for union. In 1858 a Conference in Paris decided that each should be governed by a *Hospodar* (Governor) appointed for life and have its separate assembly, but that a central Commission should be allowed to propose measures common to both provinces. In the next year both the assemblies chose the same candidate as *Hospodar*, Prince Alexander Cuza; and three years later the Powers recognized the unity of the new Roumanian State, with a single ministry and assembly. In 1866 Cuza was expelled; he was succeeded by Prince Charles of Hohenzollern, who was recognized by all the Great Powers. That the question of Turkey's internal administration had been in no way settled, was shown in 1861 by risings in Bosnia and Herzegovina; and in 1863 Serbia was finally able to get rid of the Turkish garrisons. In 1871, during the Franco-German War, Russia seized the occasion to disavow the clause of the treaty forbidding Russian arsenals and warships on the Black Sea, and Sevastopol was then restored.

For Russia, as soon as the Treaty of Paris was signed, the question of reform superseded all others. As the first step to any reform, serfdom had evidently got to be abolished. Alexander had faced this courageously; it did not necessarily involve political reform; the Tsar was the only possible trustee of the peasants, and did not need to be a Liberal in order to appreciate their first essential requirements and their economic importance to the country. But the Crimean War had been a general breakdown of the system of Nicholas, and the breath of reform was in the air. Alexander gave permission for travel abroad, and abolished the obscurantist restrictions introduced in the universities since 1848. These acts of the Tsar were enough to start a new epoch.

Without any change in the laws, the censorship ceased, in the main, to obstruct the press, which used its liberty to impeach the wholesale incompetence of the administrative system. Every kind of abuse was shown up; it became a reproach to be an official. Lacking any training in independent iniative and accustomed always to look to headquarters for instructions and for protection, the officials made no stand against this campaign and seemed as ashamed of themselves as everyone else was of them. The war itself gave plentiful material for administrative exposures, and criticism went on to attack the civil branches of the government. Public opinion was ripe for expression, and new and important reviews appeared, such as the *Russian Conversation* (*Beseda*) of Koshelev and Filippov, and the *Russian Messenger* (*Vestnik*) of Katkov, moderately Liberal and edited with great ability. Newspapers also were founded, though in a country with the distances and poor communications of Russia magazines played a more important part; the Slavophil Kireyevsky founded *The Voice* (*Golos*) in St. Petersburg, and Katkov took over the *Moscow Gazette* (*Vedomosti*). This was also the time when a whole number of specialist magazines were established for engineers, doctors, educationalists, economists, and businessmen. The new press liberty was very precarious. The censorship acted without system, and while it sometimes allowed much licence, at others it forbade the discussion of given questions. However, the new opportunities were daringly utilized; and it was now, in this general atmosphere of condemnation of the government, that Russian public opinion had a chance of forming itself. Hardly less important was the new and free access to the universities, of which great numbers took advantage. The later character of the Russian universities, so very democratic and so very critical, defined itself in the main at this time; and we shall see how soon this new generation of students took an active part in politics.

The leaders of public thought were at first not very definite in their demands. Alexander's first liberal measures were greeted with the greatest enthusiasm, but the public, which had not recovered from the pressure of the police regime of Nicholas, waited more or less passively for benefits to be thrown to it. There was no great disagreement between the pronouncements of Granovsky, who died in October 1855, and those of the future Radical Chernyshevsky in the *Contemporary*, or those of the Liberal Socialist Hertzen; yet Hertzen could write with absolute freedom in his famous *Kolokol* (*The Bell*), published in London, which found its way into the cabinets of ministers in Russia. Granovsky, in a private memorandum published later by Hertzen, had asked for the gradual abolition of serfdom without upsetting the economic system of the country. Chernyshevsky called for a program of education, more railways, and "a rational distribution of economic forces," which of course meant emancipation of the serfs. Hertzen, in the first number (1855) of his new magazine *The Polar Star*, addressed an open letter to Alexander asking for the abolition of serfdom, of corporal punishment and of the censorship. But no one had yet claimed a constitution. If for the Emperor himself questions of constitutionalism were quite distinct from that of serfdom, it was the same with many Liberal and revolutionary thinkers. Such in general was the state of public opinion when Alexander, announcing the conclusion of peace, directed all thoughts to reform with these significant concluding words: "May Russia's internal welfare be established and perfected; may justice and mercy reign in her law courts; may the desire for instruction and all useful work grow everywhere with new strength; and may everyone enjoy in peace the fruits of honest labour under the shelter of laws equally just to all, equally protecting all."

This pronouncement was greeted with rapture by the public in general and raised the greatest alarm among the more conservative of the gentry. Consequently Count Zakrevsky, Governor General of Moscow, begged Alexander to say something to reassure them. Alexander in reply said that he would not abolish serfdom by a stroke of the pen, but that it was impossible to go on as at present. "Better," he said, "to abolish serfdom from above than to wait till it begins to abolish itself from below," and he called on the gentry to "think of the proper way in which this can be done." These words of themselves mark an epoch in Russian history. Lanskoy, the new Minister of the Interior, who was a Liberal, could hardly believe his eyes when he read them, but Alexander on his return to St. Petersburg confirmed them and added that he in no way regretted them. In an autocratic country no one can so effectively launch a movement of reform as the sovereign himself.

Lanskoy had probably been a member of the Decembrists' looser and more innocent organization, the Society of Welfare; and though he had issued in 1855 a circular which mentioned "the sacred rights of the gentry granted by the crown," he was for emancipation. As Deputy Minister to superintend this task, he chose a cautious Liberal official, Levshin, who was instructed to collect former projects and various opinions. In Russia, the sovereign had sometimes been not unwilling to consider the views of well-known writers presented in the form of memoranda or privately circulated; but so far the whole question of emancipation was kept out of the press.

The principal lines of settlement now advocated in such memoranda were as follows. The serfs might be set free by decree without obtaining any land; such had been the settlement in the Baltic provinces in the reign of Alexander I, and it had resulted in the formation of a proletariat. The peasant, while receiving his personal liberty, might also retain occupation of the land, redeeming it slowly by payments, and in this case the State should indemnify the gentry at once; for this course there was no ready money; the government had made large paper issues during the war, and could hardly expect to obtain from abroad any loan which would cover this enormous expense. A third course was suggested by the lines followed at first in the Baltics (in 1804) and also during the previous reign by Count Kiselev when in charge of Roumania during the Russian occupation, and by Bibikov in southwestern Russia. This was to extend the establishment of so-called obligatory peasants, who were under definite obligations to their masters until they had succeeded in redeeming their land.

Recent precedent at first gave the preference to this last course. Further questions of detail, however, inevitably arose. In north Russia the poor clay soil had almost lost its value; the peasants here lived chiefly off side earnings, and it was from this source that they paid their dues to their masters; here, to give the peasant his personal liberty was to ruin his master, and the squire's retention of the land would not compensate him for his loss. In central and south Russia, on the other hand, the wonderful black soil could be made capable of much better culture; the large peasant population exceeded the labour requirements of the gentry and had few side earnings; and here, if the gentry retained the land, it was the peasants who would be ruined. Clearly no one solution would apply everywhere.

The step that was next necessary was to force the gentry to move, and this only the sovereign could do. No marshal of the gentry yet dared suggest a plan, for fear his initiative might be used against the interests of his class. Alexander encouraged conferences of gentry for discussion of the subject. Throughout he was much helped by his aunt the Grand Duchess Helen, a Princess of Würtemberg, now widow of the Grand Duke Michael, who took a keen interest in cultural and economic questions. With the assistance of two enlightened men, N. Milyutin and Kavelin, she had already drawn up a plan of emancipation for the peasants on her estate of Karlovka, which she submitted to the Emperor, asking for further instructions and suggesting local conferences of landowners.

In January, 1857, a number of ex-ministers and others were privately but collectively consulted on the projects which were so far before the government and became the Emperor's Private Committee for the purpose; but its chairman, Orlov, was a reactionary and chose several reactionary colleagues, and they tried in various ways to shelve the question. In August this committee forwarded to Alexander proposals of Levshin for giving the peasant his house and garden and a small plot and establishing an "obligatory" stage; the scheme was to cost the State nothing. Alexander consulted Kisilev, while abroad, saying "I am more determined than ever." He added to the committee his Liberal brother, Constantine. Meanwhile the reactionary members assured the gentry that nothing would come of it all. One Posen had put in a memorandum suggesting that it should be left to gentry and peasants to make free agreements, which would of course have blocked the whole reform. In September, the committee proposed to divide the process of emancipation into three periods, the first without time limit, and the second to last ten years. Orlov declared that he would cut off his hand before agreeing to emancipation with land.

It will be remembered that Alexander himself had prevented the application of Bibikov's inventories to Lithuania. There, as in southwest Russia where these inventories had been applied, very many of the gentry were Poles. Seeing Alexander's present intentions, these were now disposed to help him; by taking a hand in the matter they could best look after their own interests. In November, the Governor General of Lithuania, Nazimov, brought to St. Petersburg suggestions for an emancipation on the Baltic model, that is, without land. In December these proposals were approved by the Private Committee. Alexander, however, demanded some better plan.

The proposals at least gave him what he most wanted, an initiative of the gentry themselves. He therefore issued a rescript appointing district and provincial committees in Lithuania, with elected and nominated members, to draft details; house and garden were to be redeemed by the peasants, and they were to occupy other land in return for defined obligations of rent and labour. Lanskoy, as Minister, added to this rescript a circular of a distinctly Liberal direction; it stood for a division of the estate between squire and peasants, for regular payment of day labourers, and for the transference of peasant justice and of the appointment of recruits from the squire to the peasant community. Alexander ordered the rescript to be sent to all other governors and marshals of the gentry; Lanskoy sent off his circular with it.

Even in the last reign the gentry of St. Petersburg, who included several Liberals, had asked leave to move in the matter. They now repeated their request. In this case the Private Committee managed to substitute for Lanskoy's circular one of a less Liberal kind. The gentry of the southwest now followed the example of Lithuania; even the Russian provinces of Chernigov and Poltava were ready to move. In December 1857, support came from Nizhny Novgorod; here the Governor, A. N. Muravyev, who had belonged to the Decembrist Society of Salvation in 1817, persuaded many of the provincial gentry to send a deputation to the capital. His opponents sent a counter deputation, but before it arrived the request of the first for provincial committees had been granted. At last, finding the Emperor determined, the gentry of Moscow and other Russian provinces came to the same conclusion as the Poles—that they had much better not let the question be settled without them. A committee was established in every province. The nominees of the government were usually Liberals and represented the peasants' interest in the matter.

A very important initiative came from the provincial committee of Tver; the Liberal marshal of the gentry, Unkovsky, urged the redemption by the government of all rights over the peasants and their retention of undiminished allotments; this would provide adequate compensation for the gentry of this northern province; all police relations between squires and peasants should cease.

In January 1858, the Private Committee was renamed the Main Committee. The Grand Duke Constantine had already demanded publicity, and the question was now brought into the open. Chernyshevsky, writing in the *Contemporary*, placed Alexander higher than Peter the Great. Hertzen, on learning of Alexander's rescript on Lithuania, headed the next number of his *Bell* with the words: "Thou hast conquered, O Galilean!" At a banquet in Moscow men of learning and letters with others of Liberal views paid homage before the Emperor's portrait. He indeed required the support of the public against the opposition of the gentry. But one effect of the publicity was to show up the manœuvres of those who still resisted the reform tooth and nail, and to emphasize any concessions which the government made to them. This, the burning question of all questions, on which the Russian intelligentsia had been bred from Rtischev to Belinsky, was to be the school in which Russian political parties were to be formed. The publicity itself was insecure; and in August 1858 even the judicious Katkov was compelled to stop the special supplement which he devoted to the subject.

In April 1858 the government instituted an official department for the emancipation. The reactionaries of the Main Committee, on their summer holidays, spoke freely against the reform; they were rebuked by Alexander. He too travelled over the country and his journey was decisive in its effect on the opposition. In Tver he promised that representatives of the gentry should be summoned for consultation to St. Petersburg before the law was issued. In August this was announced by decree.

Alexander, relying on his sovereign power, had been searching for the men who could best carry out his intentions. He had now found them, and two men were henceforward especially prominent. One was Rostovtsev, from the first a member of the Private Committee. His grandfather was a workman, his father a merchant. Though not a very cultivated man, he possessed a quick common sense and a sound judgment which brought him into the service of the Grand Duke Michael, and raised him to the post of director of military education. During the Decembrist conspiracy he had taken a course which showed great moral courage; after telling the conspirators that he would do so, he warned the Emperor Nicholas against the plot, not mentioning any names; he had Alexander's entire confidence. Of the peasant question Rostovtsev at the outset knew nothing, but he was very quick to learn. Studying it while on a holiday in Germany, he wrote the Emperor four letters, which show of themselves how quickly his mind was moving. Though still vague as to the details, he became convinced of the justice of the view put forward by Unkovsky—that the peasants must have not only freedom but land, that they must retain the allotments which they already occupied, that the gentry must be compensated not only for the land but for the labour, and that there was no way for the State to escape the financial burden which all this involved. Alexander ordered that these letters should be printed for the Main Committee. Their chief principles were accepted, though the government still stood for a period of the "obligatory" kind. In February 1859, at the request of Rostovtsev, were established two committees, later combined into one, to draft the actual laws required; Rostovtsev himself was appointed chairman, with the right to choose other members and to settle the procedure. He associated as full participants in the discussions, with equal rights with the officials whom he selected, experts of the peasant question taken from the provincial committees. His committee worked in three sections, judicial, administrative, and economic. In May Alexander appointed a financial committee which also worked with the drafting committee. The whole body thus included thirty-six members, of whom eight were invited experts. It began its sittings on March 28, and decided to print its proceedings in 3000 copies for the use of the government and the provincial committees.

Alexander's other notable helper was Nicholas Milyutin. In his youth Milyutin was reproached by his mother for keeping the coachman fifteen hours in the cold during an improvised dance, and it was then that he began thinking of peasant emancipation. An official of the Ministry of the Interior before he was twenty, he was discovered by the minister Count A. G. Stroganov, and wrote some of the speeches of his successor Perovsky. He was put in the economic department, and at twenty-six wrote an excellent memorandum on famines; it was left to him to prompt the intervention of the government with tyrannical squires. He was associated with Nicholas I's efforts for peasant reform. In 1846 Nicholas thought of a reconstruction of the practically obsolete City Council (or Duma) of St. Petersburg. Milyutin took a leading part in this work, and ultimately his courage drew on him the anger of the reactionaries, with the result that he was dismissed in 1858 and was regarded by Alexander as a dangerous man. On the other hand, he had the confidence and warm friendship of his chief, Lanskoy, who was nearly seventy and constantly relied on him for help. Also he had firm friends in the Grand Duchess Helen and the Grand Duke Constantine. He was put on the special emancipation department of the Ministry, and was then appointed in the place of Levshin as Assistant Minister specially entrusted with this task. He was that not too common thing, a thoroughly conscientious and enlightened permanent official, and he had at his fingers' ends exactly all that special knowledge which Rostovtsev lacked. It was in the close cooperation of these two men that lay the hope of a successful settlement. Rostovtsev let Milyutin suggest several members of the drafting committee, and Milyutin was thus enabled to bring into this work two of his own closest friends, Yury Samarin and Prince Cherkassky, both ardent, enlightened, and courageous Slavophils commanding the respect of public opinion. The reactionaries continued their fight in the drafting committee, always attempting to cripple or nullify the reform; but Alexander backed the reformers throughout. The "obligatory" period, though retained, was limited to twelve years.

Another contest was going on between the Ministry of the Interior and the gentry. Outright opposition had indeed died out, and the Ministry in every way spurred the activity of the provincial committees, supporting Liberal minorities wherever possible. Tver was allowed to put forward its proposal for a state financial operation, though the Ministry, as a state organ, was still opposed to this. The other gentry were coming round to this view, as it meant ready money for the payment of their very large debts. But both Liberal and Conservative gentry were opposed to the dictation of the Ministry and to any features of the reform which might put the peasants more directly under the bureaucracy. On the other hand the Ministry, as guarding the interests of the peasants, had good reason to fear the class selfishness of the gentry as a whole. Some of the gentry demanded to vote on the whole question in their class assemblies, but this was forbidden. It was in this atmosphere of conflict that the first delegation of gentry, elected from the northern provinces, was summoned to St. Petersburg in September 1859; in spite of all the manipulations of the government only a minority were Liberal. Even these were to be disappointed. The delegation expected to discuss the defects and abuses of the administration. These too were not even to hold any official conference of their own and were only to be consulted on local questions. They only stayed one month in St. Petersburg. An address which they sent to the Emperor was not received, but they were allowed to hold private meetings and their desires were communicated to Alexander by Rostovtsev. All of them condemned bureaucratic control of the peasants. An address of eighteen members, asking for the right of criticism, was answered with a reprimand. Another address of Unkovsky and four other Liberals asked for elective self-government without class distinctions, independent law courts with jurisdiction over officials, and freedom of press on the defects and abuses of the administration. These too were reprimanded and put under police inspection, and on the receipt of a further address from Tver, Unkovsky was deported (February 1860). The second delegation, representing the southern provinces, was much more conservative and hoped to keep all the land; it got an even less favourable reception.

The drafting committee had to hurry throughout, and generally dealt with each point as it came before it. Among the peasants there was a notable calm and cessation of crime when discussion became public, but the tension had been long and disorders were feared. Count Rostovtsev was worn out, but only worked the harder; confined to his room, he held the meetings there and reported to the Emperor to the last; he died in February 1860; his last words were an encouragement to his sovereign to go on. To everyone's surprise, Alexander appointed as his successor a Conservative, Count Panin. "Panin has no opinion except to carry out my orders," he replied to the Grand Duchess Helen's apprehensions, and in the main so it proved. The southern delegation, which had made the same mistake, got nothing out of Panin. But Alexander was forcing his reform past a powerful opposition, and it still fought hard for any concessions. On November 3 the scheme, as amended, passed the drafting committee. It had now to go to the Main Committee; the reactionary chairman, Orlov, was then ill, and Alexander replaced him by his brother Constantine. This ensured its passage, without very serious changes (February 7, 1861); the allotments were slightly diminished and the rents somewhat increased. Next the scheme passed to the Council of State. The Emperor ordered an early decision and fixed a time limit, with the words: "This I desire, I demand, I command"; the main principles were not to be touched. He himself presided at the first meeting (February 9). A deputation of gentry was refused a hearing. With daily sittings, the work was completed by March 11. The emancipating edict was drafted by Samarin and re-written by Philaret, the Metropolitan of Moscow. It was signed on March 3 (February 19), read in the Senate on March 14, published on March 17, and read out in all the churches of the empire.

The opposition had secured some last successes. In the Council of State one important amendment was accepted; peasants who wished to escape all payments, were allowed to accept their liberty with one quarter of the normal allotment in full liquidation; these allotments were later known as "poverty lots." After the Act was announced, both Lanskoy and Milyutin were relieved of their offices, which was frankly recognized by Milyutin and his friends as a "semi-disgrace."

Sixteen Acts dealt with the various aspects of the settlement. The peasants were entirely emancipated from the gentry. As a class, they still remained separate from the rest of the population. Their collective responsibility for taxes and their old passport system still made them as individuals dependent on their village community, which they could not leave without its permission. The community was adopted as a new and, in a measure, autonomous unit of the administration, to replace the old control exercised through the gentry; according to the old custom, it distributed among its members its own land and its own taxes; it could levy rates for religious education or for social needs. On the other hand, it became the lowest rung of the local police system, and retained certain obligations of service to the State which, as a class burden, had lost their sense with the Emancipation.

In general, it may be said that the peasant retained about half of the cultivated land; and this had to be redeemed by payments to the State extending over forty-nine years; the State was to pay compensation at once to the gentry. The principles of division proposed by the gentry were not accepted. The amounts of peasant holdings varied in different provinces; they were less in the north, and greater in the centre and south; the actual existing peasant lots, always reckoned as in a sense peasant property, were much less diminished than might be thought, because the peasants had been working a good deal of extra land, often twice as much. Peasants could now take land on lease and could hire out their labour; they did not ultimately own the land; it became, when redeemed, the property of their village community as a whole; indeed, in order to protect the peasants, the government later forbade the selling of peasants' land to persons of any other class. Under the permission to lease, however, the peasants now took up more and more land for actually the Emancipation left them with less to cultivate than before. This put them at the mercy of the gentry, who could fix their own price. Many of these, having failed to make a profit on their estates when in control of the whole and also of unpaid peasant labor, on receiving their compensation from the State, sold out the remainder and left the country for the capitals. The actual allotment between gentry and peasants was entrusted to Arbitrators of the Peace picked with great care and discrimination, who are admitted to have carried out their work with great consideration for the peasants; that did not however prevent injustice in certain places, where, for instance, the squire might secure a central position with the best land and a practical monopoly of forest or water.

The government had greatly feared peasant disturbances as soon as the change should be announced. There were indeed risings in certain places, where the decree was declared to be forgery; and these had to be put down by martial law. At Bezdna in the province of Penza, the peasants under Anton Petrov, one of their number who claimed to be

the Emperor, broke out into open revolt and were fired on by order of
the government. In the main, this capital act of government policy, so
far the central event in the history of the Russian people, was received
with real gratitude. Samarin and Cherkassky were two of the best of
the Arbitrators. "The people," wrote Cherkassky to his friend Milyutin,
"are without any exaggeration transfigured from head to foot"; the
former serf, he said, had now more of the instincts of a citizen than the
crown peasant. "We have not at all built on the sand," wrote Samarin;
"we have got down to the rock. The Statute has done its work. The
people is erect and transformed; the look, the walk, the speech, everything is changed. That is won; that can't be suppressed; and that is the
chief thing." Of the Arbitrators he wrote: "This crop too has come up
as we hoped."

It must not be supposed that this far-reaching reform was carried
out all at once. The peasants obtained their personal liberty by the Act
of Emancipation, but the final settlement between the squires and their
serfs entailed a succession of agrarian measures. The Act of 1861, subject to further agreement, fixed approximately the amount of arable
land which, together with their homesteads, the former serfs were to retain in permanent use; for this they were to pay a fixed rent to the
owner of the estate. After 1863, if the peasants desired, all work, service,
and dues were to be commuted to money payments. After thus obtaining the legal recognition of the fixity of their tenure and also fixity of
rent, the serfs could with the assistance of the State Treasury buy out
the squire even without his consent, as regarded the homestead, which
became family property, and with his consent the allotment assigned
to them by the Act.

The actual process of this redemption based on agreement, moved
only slowly. In 1880 fifteen per cent of the peasants still remained outside the redemption scheme. The government bonds issued as an indemnity to the squires, sank to very much below par—77 per cent and
less. The peasants were seldom able to pay down the required one fifth
of the price as earnest money; survey and valuation were not faultless.
Hence, to put an end to the inevitable friction between the squire and
his former serfs, Alexander III on December 28, 1881, limited the
amount of the redemption payments; he also decreed the obligatory
redemption of both homesteads and allotments, which came into operation on January 13, 1883. Further, he made the redemption of tenanted land compulsory for the crown peasants. Government action in
the matter was completed in December 1893, by a law which established

that no land held as peasant's land could be mortgaged or alienated to anyone outside the village community.[1] Already, by the exclusion of the squire from its affairs, the community's authority was greatly increased. The new legislation adopted it as the administrative unit, making it the lowest rung in a ladder which mounted to the Ministry of the Interior. The permanent appropriation of all peasant land to the community as a whole gave it an economic authority over each individual member which was in practice overwhelming.

The effects and at the same time the defects of the Emancipation we shall trace through the whole remainder of our story. For the moment the cardinal point for us is this: it was on the question of the emancipation of the peasants that Russian public opinion was formed. Its leaders are familiar to us from the reign of Nicholas, but it is only now that they find their public, and it is some time before they even determine their various directions of thought. We have dwelt on the detail of the drafting of this reform, because only so can be understood the deciding factors in the shaping of the Russian intelligentsia at this critical stage of its formation. We here enter a period in the history of Russian public thought which is to last up to the Revolution of 1917.

Alexander had faced the abolition of serfdom as imperative to the well-being of his country. But in emancipating the serfs he had also destroyed the whole foundation of the administrative system; and, as a matter of practical necessity, the bureaucracy could not avoid the task of reconstructing this system from the bottom. Here was the widest field for disagreement. The bureaucracy was thoroughly fatigued by the distance which it had already travelled from its old moorings; Rostovtsev, we know, had died under the strain; Milyutin was early to succumb to paralysis; and Alexander himself, who was certainly no Liberal, has been compared to a man who reaches with great effort the top of a hill and is only too ready to glide down the other side.

Meanwhile, the new generation created in the universities, during the first years of the reign, asked for far more than had yet been given, for a new era of wholesale political experiment. With them, bureaucratic tradition had no influence and patriotic and conservative thinkers, such as the Slavophils, hardly any; the question was only between Liberals and revolutionaries, the choice between gradual and precipitate change. It could scarcely have been otherwise. In the stifling atmosphere of Nicholas, life offered no school of free initiative, conscience, and re-

---

[1] This account of the settlement and in particular of the immediate sequels in peasant legislation, has been valuably supplemented by Baron A. F. Meyendorff, formerly lecturer in Peasant Land Law in the University of St. Petersburg.

sponsibility. Thus it was left to theorists and students to carry the flag of free individual development. Meanwhile, with serfdom had disappeared the whole substructure of the State so that the field was open for, and demanded, discussion. Even for the squires the rights of property had never been sufficiently defined in detail. The Emancipation Act itself recognized that the peasantry were entitled to half the land. Why half? And if so, had half really been given? And were the peasants to pay too high for it? The reform was not, on the side of the government itself, a movement of political or constitutional beliefs; it was a social revolution. The autocracy itself was built not on individualist but collectivist principles. It had itself, in the Emancipation, opened the whole field of socialist ideas. It had allowed discussion, but only half-discussion; here too there was no law, no accepted principle.

As late as February 1858, Hertzen and Chernyshevsky were joining their voices to the universal homage to Alexander. But on Chernyshevsky, who was to become the first leader of the new Radicals, the intrigues and delays which at times blocked the progress of emancipation had a decisive effect. His colleague on the *Contemporary*, Dobrolyubov, a brilliant literary critic only twenty years old, was even more impatient; and in the absence of any real school of public service, it was only in literature and in literary criticism that the great economic questions of the time could be discussed. The Slavophils, so invaluable as connecting Russia's past with her future, at this very time lost their public and even their organs in the press. Chernyshevsky began to write bitterly of the greed of the gentry and to demand more drastic solutions. Chernyshevsky was a theoretical economist, as many less studious and capable thinkers were at that time. In No. 4 of the *Contemporary*, 1858, he attacked the proposed redemption dues of the peasants as excessive. Under the title *The Russian at the Rendez-Vous* he impugned the weakness of the liberals. Dobrolyubov, taking as his text Goncharov's famous sketch of the weak-kneed Oblomov, showed up the Liberal gentry as useless and effete and asked for a new and more radical spirit. Hertzen, who belonged by age to the older generation, still defended the Liberals. Katkov, though a former member of the Belinsky group, from a Liberal gradually became almost an official publicist, not lacking in independence but patriotically defending the government. Chernyshevsky, to avert a rupture, visited Hertzen in London; the meeting only convinced both men that the break between Liberals and Radicals had got to come. Hertzen, without malice, condemned the precipitateness of the "new men" in two articles: *Very Dangerous* and *The Superfluous*

Persons and the Men with a Grudge. They struck him as conceited and arrogant; he struck them as obsolete.

Meanwhile the government was alarmed by the appearance of a Liberal program published by Hertzen, which demanded "as the natural consequence of the Emancipation" civil equality, independent justice with trial by jury, reform of the police, responsibility of ministers, financial control by the public, public control over legislation, free conscience, free press, and free trade. The new Minister of the Interior, Valuyev, was a sheer opportunist and secretly a friend of reaction. He early began attacking the Arbitrators of the Peace, whom he wished to make dependent on official instructions.

It will be seen then that a new period had set in; and it was now that Alexander's government had to complete the inevitable task of reform with failing energy, with growing indisposition, and constantly interrupted by agitating symptoms of hostility.

From 1861 onward were appearing in *The Russian Word* (*Russkoe Slovo*) the daring theories of a remarkable young man of twenty, Pisarev, who violently attacked the old Liberals and stood for a sheer negation of authority, whether in politics or in literature. It was about these new "Nihilists" that the Liberal, Ivan Turgenev, wrote at this time his novel *Fathers and Children*; it was he who first dubbed them with the name Nihilist, and he was himself the object of some of the most vehement attacks of the "new men." Pisarev was for an insurrectionary freedom from all authority and convention. Science was his enthusiasm, as the one instrument which could better the lot of the peasant population; for art he professed indifference and contempt. Pisarev was a glaring individualist, not a socialist at all; but for his early death by drowning, he would almost certainly have developed out of this stage of youthful impertinence; his action was in the field of literature, and he cared but little about politics. But literature, as has been explained, was the only mirror in which the Russian public could get to know itself, and Pisarev and his admirers succeeded in thoroughly frightening the government. Meanwhile the conservative gentry were offended in all their deepest instincts by the Emancipation and longed to recover their power; and it was the gentry that surrounded the throne.

From Tver in 1862 came Liberal demands for responsible finance, for public and independent law courts, for publicity of acts of the administration, and even for a national assembly, and the same views were expressed by Chernyshevsky in his *Unaddressed Letters*. Fly sheets began to appear, calling for terrorist acts against the government—such as that addressed *To Young Russia* in 1862, in which even the murder of the Emperor was advocated. About this time fires broke out in St. Petersburg and were attributed either to revolutionaries or to Poles. This stiffened the reactionary mood. Chernyshevsky was tried and, on loose evidence, sent for twenty-four years to Siberia; Pisarev was sentenced to two years' imprisonment. Both their magazines were suspended.

Alexander had declared on his accession that "the happiness of Poland is to be found in complete fusion with the peoples of my Empire"; he allowed "repentant" emigrants to return. Prince M. Gorchakov (from 1856) proved a kindly Viceroy. In 1857 Count Zamoyski was allowed to found an Agricultural Society, which aimed at improving the lot of the peasants and served generally as a centre of culture and public spirit. A series of religious and patriotic demonstrations commemorated notable anniversaries. On February 27, 1861, a procession with crosses was attacked by Cossacks and fired upon. For this Gorchakov gave an apology. A prominent Pole, Marquis Wielopolski, came forward with a program of conciliation, in which he never had any wide support. He was for turning Polish sympathies toward Russia, as opposed to Prussia and Austria. Gorchakov invited his help, and he suggested what he considered to be the essential reforms. On March 26 the old Polish Council of State was restored to deal with the budget, petitions, and other public matters; local consultative councils were also established. Wielopolski himself, however, said that he would not have "a state within a state." The demonstrations continued, and on April 8 a great crowd was dispersed by rifle and bayonet with many casualties. On Gorchakov's death in May 1861, viceroys with various policies followed each other in quick succession. The demonstrations grew more imposing than ever. Count Lambert forbade them but then gave way on this point, and consequently had to fight a duel with the Governor General, Hertzenstein. Lüders, who succeeded Lambert, set up martial law. Alexander now sent his brother Constantine as Viceroy, putting Wielopolski at the head of the civil administration. Secret societies had sprung up, and Constantine was shot at (April 1862). The Poles still put forward their claim to Lithuania.

The inevitable rising was precipitated by a measure of Wielopolski who, restricting the levy of recruits to the towns, tried to use it as a means of seizing all those associated with the secret societies. On the night of January 22, 1863, simultaneous attacks were made at ten different points on Russian detachments. The rising never took the form of a regular war. Thousands went to the forest and conducted a fitful guerilla. Mieroslawski arrived with a few officers from Paris to head the movement, was twice defeated and recrossed the frontier. His successor Langiewicz was caught in Galicia (March). The peasants remained indifferent. Risings of the Polish gentry in Lithuania and Podolia only extended the operations and prejudiced success. England, France, and Austria sent notes urging an amnesty and the restoration of the Constitution of 1815; but Bismarck made a convention with Russia guaranteeing joint military measures (February 8). Austria turned against the Poles. Traugott, the last Polish dictator, tried to coordinate the efforts of the insurgents and to win the peasants with the offer of land, but he was caught with his staff and hanged in the citadel of Warsaw in April, 1864. General M. Muravyev, the ruthless Russian dictator at Vilna, eradicated all resistance there.

The government stood firm against foreign intervention, and public opinion rallied to it. Slavophils such as I. Aksakov, who had so far been not unfavourable to the Poles, now turned sharply against them. Hertzen, deserted by the Radicals, whose voices at this time were hushed, offended the Liberals by his Polish sympathies, and from this time forward lost his influence. Katkov by his patriotic articles captured the leadership of opinion. Loyal addresses streamed in to the Emperor from the most various sides.

Alexander now sent Nicholas Milyutin to Warsaw, to study the conditions and perhaps find some better policy than sheer repression. Milyutin's advice was to transfer land in Poland from the gentry to the peasants, and he was instructed to carry out this policy. As the Russian government had no love for the Polish gentry, the Polish peasant received very much more of his master's land than the peasants had received in Russia; the arrangements for the compensation of the gentry were hastily planned and obviously inadequate. Certain incidental causes of contention between squires and peasants were left untouched, it would seem deliberately, to promote friction between the two classes (March 1864). Milyutin's other intentions were not carried out, and sheer repression prevailed. In Lithuania every effort was made to destroy the Polish nationality; a 10 per cent contribution was imposed on Polish estates; the Polish language was prohibited; churches and monasteries were seized. The Uniats, against their will, were officially reunited to the Russian Orthodox Church (1874). The Polish Council of State was again abolished (1867), and all institutions in Poland were systematically Russified; this included Warsaw University (1869); in the secondary schools all subjects except the Polish language and literature were taught to Poles in Russian.

For all these interruptions, reform had to be continued in Russia. The reform of finance was in the able hands of Tatarinov, who had made a study of the financial systems of other countries. The Ministry of Finance was freed of certain complications with the jurisdictions of other Ministries, and was put under the inspection of the State Comptroller or Auditor; public budgets were to be presented annually for all expenditures; the State Bank was erected to centralize credit and finance (1866); by a decree of 1863, a new and reformed system of excise was established.

The revolutionary spirit was nowhere so strong as among the students. On February 21, 1861, a students' meeting developed into a riot and was charged by the Cossacks. In June, students' clubs with their uniforms were forbidden; the numerous bursaries for poor students were withdrawn, and meetings were only to be held by special permission. In the autumn there were serious riots, followed by mass expulsions, street processions of the students and attacks of the troops; three hundred students were imprisoned. Alexander was disturbed at this. He already had before him an admirable scheme of educational reform and now sent Kavelin abroad to study university administration; free discussion of the question was allowed in the press. The result was the law of June 30, 1863, passed in due form through the Council of State, which restored all the academic freedom granted in 1804; the universities were to be governed by councils elected from the various faculties; but student organizations were not legalized. On June 26, 1864, special local councils were appointed to promote education, on which the elective authorities of local self-government were to be represented.

These new authorities of self-government (*Zemstva*) were the creation of another reform of 1864, second in importance only to the Emancipation itself. The Act of Emancipation had among other things disturbed all the foundations of local government. N. Milyutin, at the head of a commission for local administrative reform, had investigated the question. It was possible to develop further the precedent of the provincial committees which took part in the abolition of serfdom; but Milyutin was for abolishing the class principle in local government; when Valuyev succeeded to the Ministry, he wished to modify Milyutin's project by increasing the representation of the gentry but he was defeated. There was another precedent of which more use was made,

Speransky's project of 1811. But Speransky, anticipating even the Bolshevik system of Soviets, had allowed for four Dumy or Councils, that of the Circuit, that of the District, that of the Province, and that of the Empire, each of the first three electing its local executive and also its delegates to the higher assembly. The reform of 1864 took only the two middle units, the District and the Province. Zemstva (or County Councils) were established. The District Zemstvo elected a permanent governing board and also representatives to the Provincial Zemstvo, which in its turn elected its own governing board. The marshals of the gentry presided *ex officio* at the Zemstvo meetings, but were not at the head of the executive. Yearly sessions were held both of district and provincial Zemstva. The Zemstva could levy rates for local needs. They were directly under the Senate, the highest legal organ of the State; the provincial governors were to restrict themselves to securing the observance of the law. The original competence of the Zemstva included roads, hospitals, and food; but to these, at the suggestion of Baron Korff, were added education, medical aid, veterinary service, and public welfare in general. The law instituting the Zemstva was announced on January 1 (13), 1864, and Zemstva from 1865 onward were gradually set up in thirty-three provinces.

This institution gave rise to the greatest hopes. It is to be noted that the unit taken for this important experiment in self-government was not the town but the country, and that the Zemstva were for a long time restricted to the purely Russian provinces of the empire. What Turgot had wished to give to France on the eve of the Revolution was given to Russia by this law, namely a school of administration directly responsible through the principle of election to the public itself. Many of the best public men in the country, who were too proud or independent to seek employment in the hack work of administration with all its intrigue and corruption, were glad to enter this new service. The competence of the Zemstva governed, it is true, subjects to which the central government had so far practically given no attention, but they included none the less the most urgent needs of the population, public health, and education. The very fact that the central government reserved to itself all police and military authority tended to make the Zemstva more popular, and to put them in the position of authorized spokesmen of the population and critics of the central machine. The Zemstva were a school of responsible administration, not only for their elected members but for those public servants whom they employed. From the outset was visible to all the standing contrast between the application of the elective principle in local government and the re-tention of absolutist control at headquarters; and in the accepted phrase of the time, many asked when "the building would be crowned," that is, when besides elective local councils there would be an elected national assembly.

The next capital measure was the reform of the law courts, which introduced trial by jury. If the squire had been the local administrator, he had also been the local magistrate; and therefore the creation of lower courts was now inevitable. But reform was no less necessary in the higher courts. Nothing at all had been done to improve them since the time of Catherine II, and in the words of Ivan Aksakov, one's hair stood up at the thought of what one saw there. To this question also much attention had already been given. If Speransky was the real initiator both of the Zemstva and of the future Imperial Duma, he had taken no less pains with the reform of justice, which was his special sphere. But the opposition of the gentry had prevented any serious reform. There was a jangle of conflicting instances of jurisdiction, founded on class privileges. Procedure was secret, without advocates; judges were ill-paid and untrained. An eminent lawyer, Zamyatnin, as Minister of Justice, had charge of the reform and was assisted by a committee of able jurists, which included the future Procurator of the Holy Synod, Pobedo-nostsev; in 1862 Alexander gave his consent to the principles adopted. The courts were made free of all class distinctions and independent of the administrative officials; the judges were properly remunerated, and were irremovable; the trials were to be held in public, with oral procedure and trained advocates, whether crown lawyers or private barristers; law fees were regulated. Most important was the introduction of the jury on the English model. Appeals could only be based on alleged irregularities of procedure, and were addressed direct to the Senate, as the highest Court of Appeal. Such was the law of December 6, 1864. For the local courts were instituted Justices of the Peace, elected by the Zemstva.

We shall see that in the period of reaction which followed, curtailments of all sorts mutilated this and other reforms, till in the end one might almost ask whether exceptional legislation did not supersede all ordinary procedure. Yet the law itself—which, unlike the temporary rules which curtailed it, had passed through the Council of State—was not repealed; and it stood as a standard of what the government deemed justice in its essence to be. All were surprised that so many able and disinterested men were found to fill the new posts of judges; and the

Bar of St. Petersburg and Moscow, starting with the great tradition of gross abuses fearlessly abolished, continued in times of reaction to keep alive the principle of judicial independence.

Far less successful was the so-called press reform of 1865. Here there were the greatest hesitations in the official world. The drafting of the law was entrusted to an able legislator, Golovnin; but at this very time the government was in arms against the new temper shown in the press, so that Valuyev was able to emasculate the reform. It appeared in 1865, in the form of temporary rules only, which as a matter of fact lasted for forty years; in the case of serious publications and newspapers of the two capitals, it was no longer necessary to present the proposed material to the censor in advance. The preliminary censorship was replaced by the punitive censorship, such as exists in all countries; but the punitive system is no alleviation unless all punishment is entrusted to the law courts, and Valuyev secured that this enormous power should be in the hands of the administrative authorities.

It remains to speak of two other important reforms which were completed only during the period of reaction. On June 28, 1870, were instituted the reformed Town Councils. Town Dumy or Councils had been nominally established by Catherine II; Paul had abolished this institution and Alexander I had restored it, but it never really existed except on paper even in the capitals. No registers of voters had been kept; often the Duma was not elected, and the services of public welfare within its competence were left to the police; at best, the Town Duma had no power of rating and could only ask for contributions. Here again Nicholas Milyutin had done distinguished work, when he was asked in the reign of Nicholas to examine the working of town government; he had been assisted by other notable political thinkers, such as the Slavophils Yury Samarin and Ivan Aksakov; their labours had resulted in a law (1846) which applied only to St. Petersburg and was itself seriously curtailed a few years later. Town reform was thus at first further ahead than country reform; then came the liberal Zemstvo Law of 1864; and it was only in 1870, when reaction had again set in, that the Town Statute for the empire was completed. Drafted in 1864, it was first presented to the Council of State in 1866, at the very moment when the revolutionary Karakozov had just fired a shot at the Emperor; the discussion was adjourned for two years, and the new Town Councils (or Dumy), when sanctioned, were based on a system of curiæ which gave marked predominance to the wealthy and tended to destroy their representative character. The rest of the provisions were similar to those of the Zemstvo law which, however, was already becoming an object of criticism and attack from the side of the reactionaries.

Different was the fate of the last first-class measure of this period, the army reform of January 1 (13), 1874. Whatever else in the new regime was now brought in question, the military bankruptcy of the Crimean War was as plain as ever, and the sovereign's interest in the army was not complicated by any political hesitations. This task was in the excellent hands of Dmitry Milyutin, brother of Nicholas, who remained Minister of War after his other Liberal colleagues had disappeared, and retained to the end the full personal confidence of the Emperor. The Tsars of Moscow had created an irregular levy, based on land-tenure but made to perform almost the functions of a standing army; Peter the Great had created a huge standing army based on compulsory service and, ultimately, on serfdom. Milyutin, after an expert examination of the modern systems of conscription in Western Europe, carried through a reform in which the Liberals themselves found nothing to blame.

There was of course no question whether Russia could abandon the principle of conscription; military service, though regarded by the peasant as a personal bondage, was accepted by him as a self-evident obligation, and he only asked that the burden should be fairly distributed. By the new law, it was declared to be an equal obligation for all classes. The years of service were from 20 to 26 in the active army, from 26 to 35 in the reserve, and from 35 to 40 in the militia,—a great reduction of the old terms. Only sons, only grandsons, or breadwinners on whom depended the support of younger brothers and sisters, obtained what was called the first exemption. The second exemption was granted to those who had brothers under eighteen years of age; the third exemption was given to the next in age after a brother who had already been called. Such was the definition of those liable for service, and from them the customary proportion was selected by lot. In case of national danger the exempted might be called up, but only in reverse order, i. e., first all those of the third exemption, then those of the second exemption and only last those of the first, in which case a special summons of the Emperor was required to legalize the call. If there were no exemptions by class, account was taken of education. University students had to serve only for half a year, those who had passed through secondary schools only for two years, scholars from the so-called town or district schools only for three, and from primary schools for four. Any student or scholar who without waiting for the lot volunteered for service, would only serve half an ordinary term.

The work of Dmitry Milyutin for the army did not end here. He reorganized the whole system of training and, above all, of army education, so that in the ranks the number of literates advanced more regularly and rapidly than in any other section of the population. It was in the army that most Russian peasants learned how to read and write.

CHAPTER XX

End of Alexander II

[*1866–81*]

IN 1861 the serfs were set free; in 1866 a shot was fired at the emancipating Emperor; in 1881 he was murdered. What will explain this sequence of events?

It is now that we are first face to face with the modern Russian intelligentsia. The tragedy of the Emancipation was that it came late; it was only now that the government had made a real attempt to satisfy the first need of the majority of the population. Meanwhile, from Catherine II onward, Russian educated society had been intellectually Europeanized from the top layer downward. In the enforced silence of the reign of Nicholas, and under the influence of the French Revolution, thought and criticism had reached down to the growing middle class, which at present had no recognized place in the State; and Belinsky and his contemporaries had fought their way to a morale of their own, which owed nothing to the government. The young men admitted in large numbers to the universities, very often as government scholars, realized that the charge of their education really lay on the peasants. The peasants were the absorbing subject of public interest during their period of study. The Act of Emancipation entirely changed the whole structure of the State. Anyhow a new world had to be created, and all were free to form their own idea as to what kind of a world it should be. Russian thought naturally concentrated on political and economic theory, and the thinkers pursued their theories to their logical extremes.

Thus, when opinion did first show itself in the press, it was such as the government could not like. Pisarev would have been an incident in some other countries; his Nihilism would have been discounted as an amusing literary pose. But now, numbers of young persons of both sexes, narrower and more serious than Pisarev, repeated his maxim that one would make no mistake if one scrapped the existing system wholesale, with all its conventions of morality and religion; and their numbers, their enthusiasm, their narrow-mindedness, their distinctiveness in a world of ignorance, egoism, and passivity, became a great danger. The government had already begun to whittle away what it had given. In 1864 schools were divided into classical and modern, and only students of the former could go to the universities; little had been done to advance women's education, and the local town schools were to be founded not by the State, but from voluntary contributions. Primary schools were almost nonexistent, and the projected parish schools remained on paper. From 1859 onward, many students had engaged in teaching in Sunday schools organized by Professor Pavlov and others, and teaching often became propaganda; consequently all these schools were closed. The University Statute itself had been the outcome of student riots.

On April 16, 1866, a young man, Karakozov, fired point-blank on Alexander II as he was entering his carriage after a walk in the Summer Garden. Karakozov had been connected with a Communist group of students; the murder of the Emperor had been discussed in it, but dismissed; Karakozov was recognized by his fellow-members to be quite unbalanced, and his act was entirely his own. From this time the government lived in suspicion of the students. The Liberal Golovnin was replaced as Minister of Education by Count Dmitry Tolstoy, who had even opposed the Emancipation. The *Contemporary* and the *Russian Word* were finally forbidden by an Imperial Rescript of May 23, which inveighed against "encroaching aspirations directed against all belief, family, property, and authority." The kindly Governor General of Petrograd, Prince Suvorov, was replaced by a police martinet, General F. Trepov. The publicist Katkov asked for more repression.

The two principal fields in which the growing reaction developed were education and the press. Count Tolstoy discovered a strange means of limiting the spread of education, and at the same time bolstering up the gentry class. He derived his idea from Katkov who, still retaining a sympathy for British institutions, pointed attention to the part played by the classics in English education. The young Nihilists, in their renunciation of all tradition, included the classics wholesale. Science was for them the only subject worthy of stury; Büchner's *Stoff und Kraft* was their typical popular textbook; out of superficial economic theories they constructed ready systems for their new world. Tolstoy decided to use the classics to counteract Nihilism; he founded a philological institute and invited Slavonic philologists from Austria. His Liberal opponents pointed out that it was at this very time that England was beginning to develop more modern education; the Council of State there-fore rejected his proposals, but the Emperor confirmed them. By a new law of May 1871, in the gymnasia or classical schools forty-seven hours were now to be given weekly to Latin and thirty-six to Greek; special attention was to be concentrated on grammar. This meant much less study of Russian. Natural science, history, and geography were excluded, and the teaching of modern languages reduced. The sting of the law lay in the fact that, as the gymnasia alone qualified for entry into the university and as poorer scholars lacking the necessary preparation in classics could not enter the gymnasia, the universities would tend to be-come preserves of the well-to-do classes. At the same time strict school discipline was introduced; a severe system of inspection of students was established, the inspectors being mostly chosen from the classical teach-ers; to report on the conduct of one's fellow scholars was declared to be a merit. The original Real Gymnasia or superior modern schools were at the same time replaced by schools of a more modest kind. The move-ment for women's education had made very great progress during this reign and Tolstoy did what he could to block it, for instance interdicting to them the study of medicine, with the result that a number of Russian women went to study in Switzerland, which became the headquarters of the Russian revolutionaries. This policy was carried through to an ac-companiment of student disorders, for instance in 1874 and 1878. Tolstoy extended his system of ministerial inspectors to primary edu-cation; they were required to control all school appointments; he wished to go much further in this direction and to get the schools as far as possible out of the hands of the Zemstva, but here the opposition of the Council of State was supported by the Emperor. With the Zemstva Tolstoy's inspectors were in chronic war.

In this period of reaction some of the principal reforms of this reign were curtailed and others were stillborn. Such, as already described, was the press reform, which though it freed writers from the preliminary censorship, subjected them to post-factum penalties arbitrarily imposed by the administrative authorities. The town reform of 1870 was very inferior to the Zemstvo reform of 1864, and the Zemstva now began to suffer from all sorts of restrictions. Public-spirited men of the most various views had gladly taken up zemstvo work. The Zemstva collected nine million roubles to found almshouses and the same amount for relief work; in the first ten years of their work their budgets were in-creased sixfold; but as hardly anything had been done earlier for the satisfaction of local needs, they still felt cramped for lack of money. By a law of 1868 their power of rating was restricted. They were compelled first to meet all obligatory expenses imposed upon them by the government, which sometimes took as much as 82 per cent of their budget, leaving only 8 per cent for public health and 5 per cent for education; from 1866 the publicity of their debates was restricted and put under the control of the local governors. A good many of the best Zemstvo members lost interest and dropped out of the work, and this again tended to leave the leadership in reform in the hands of their juniors.

Similar curtailments took place in the field of justice. Attempts were made from the outset to postpone the operation of the great reform of December 1864. But here, even after Karakozov's attack, Alexander held firm. The new law courts were so successful as to draw tributes from many who had been critical toward them; Katkov regarded them as marking an epoch in the history of the country.

Some acquittals in censorship and other cases irritated the minister Valuyev, and in one case the Emperor thought of removing the judge concerned. Zamyatnin, the Liberal Minister of Justice, was able to persuade him that this would be a breach of his own recent law, but this was his last success. He was replaced by a police administrator, Count Pahlen. The government found ways of evading the principle that local magistrates were irremovable; and crown lawyers were brought under closer ministerial control. Administrative punishments were retained in practice; press cases were in 1866 withdrawn from the ordinary court of assize; in 1871 preliminary inquiries into state offences were transferred from the magistrates to the gendarmes and crown lawyers; in 1874 political cases were withdrawn from the ordinary court, and in 1878, by no means without reason, they were handed over to courts-martial.

Similar was the fate of the press, which was constantly being subjected to new restrictions; for instance, certain papers could only be sold to their regular subscribers (1868); magazines had to be submitted four days in advance to a preliminary censor (1871); the Minister of the Interior could forbid the discussion of given questions of state for three months (1873). Even Slavophils were compelled to publish their works abroad, and their organs were crushed by frequent punishments; yet the Slavophils were the patriotic party. A frank pronouncement of theirs, adopted by the Moscow Town Council, which expressed a hope for "greater freedom of press and conscience, and for a moral revival with more national consciousness and self-respect," was described by the Minister of the Interior as "impossible." The revolutionary opponents of the government knew better than to be so outspoken, and more and more of the political literature of the country was circulated illegally.

Meanwhile the peasantry continued to engage the attention of all. The appanage and crown peasants had been emancipated in 1863 and 1866 respectively on better conditions than those of the squires, receiving larger allotments of land. Peasants took up more and more land from the gentry; serfs attached to factories on receiving their freedom went elsewhere, so that several of those works closed; but so much labour set free to find its own price made for a great advance of industry, and this was one of the questions with which the government had to deal.

The financial position, after the expenses of the war and of the Act of Emancipation, was extremely difficult; and the renewed permission to travel had resulted in a good deal of money being taken out of the country. The able Finance Minister, Reutern, appointed in 1862, aimed at recovering the metal standard for the rouble; but his operations were hampered by the action of profiteers. The Polish insurrection added further expenses, and the gold reserve had very much shrunk. One part of Reutern's policy was to develop railways, and this led up to a fever of speculation such as accompanied the beginnings of railway construction in other countries. The government also assisted the foundation of private banks, and it was now, as a direct effect of the Emancipation, that Russia began to pass into a period of capitalism. By his ability and economies Reutern was able to avoid a deficit in 1873; in 1875 he was even able to add to the gold reserve. This of itself served to justify the great reforms; Reutern had nailed his flag to them in a notable memorandum of 1866, declaring that a return to the past was impossible, and that the reforms of the law courts and the Zemstva must in the long run promote an honest administration of the country.

The provision brought into the Act of Emancipation at the last moment by the reactionaries, allowing peasants who wished to escape payment for their land to content themselves with beggarly allotments, was bound to produce some impoverishment. All the lots in central Russia were ordinarily very small, so that many peasants had either to lease them out or to rent more land in order to make ends meet. Russia was at this time greatly increasing her grain export in consequence of the repeal of the Corn Laws in England and the rapid growth of big cities in western Europe, and the amount of land brought under culture was rapidly increasing especially in the south and on the Volga. The raised standard of life brought a rise in prices, and a good many of the gentry either mortgaged their land or sold out. Peasant land-tenure extended rapidly, so that rents could be raised by even three or four times. The redemption dues were a heavy burden. Of the direct taxes, which amounted to 208 million roubles, all but 13 million roubles came from the peasants; the poll tax, amounting to 42 million roubles, rested exclusively on them. Former squires' peasants found their obligations three times as heavy as state peasantry. There were bad failures of the crop in Smolensk in 1867, and on the Volga from 1870 to 1873. Many households had to work their land without the help of a horse, and there were very few indeed which had more than one. Distress among the peasants had all the more effect now that attention was focussed on them. Even some of the more capable administrators brought prominently before the public the details of peasant distress.

But no section of the public took the lot of the peasant so much to heart as the new intelligentsia of the universities. The students had almost a crushing sense of their debt to the peasants. On the one hand, to every student who himself came of peasant stock, taught by the whole history of his country and its institutions to regard the peasants as a separate caste, class loyalty was an instinct; on the other, sons of gentry were now thoroughly awakened to the iniquity of the long history of serfdom which had been the support of their own class privileges. The public read with ardent sympathy the works of writers who described the cares and difficulties of peasant life. The riots of the students in 1861 had originated in their interest in the peasant question; the punishments and exclusions which followed only made a larger number of willing martyrs. Hertzen, in a notable article in the *Bell*, addressed to the excluded students, gave a watchword which was soon to be followed by hundreds. He spoke of the groan rising from the people as the first roar of the impending storm. "To the people!" he wrote. "This is your place, exiles of knowledge, soldiers of the Russian people." After the Polish rising, with the comparative slump in radicalism which accompanied it, the restrictions introduced into the universities by Count Tolstoy in 1867 restored the students' enthusiasm for the service of the people, which was also greatly increased by the famine of Smolensk in 1868. In that year and the next there were further students' riots followed by the usual wholesale exclusions. The young folk were greatly influenced by the *Historical Letters* of Colonel Lavrov, a moral teacher who helped to carry the young generation beyond the meagre egoism of Pisarev and found in the service of the people the motive which could justify and ennoble the Radical cult of individuality and independence.

This lesson, with the more powerful thinker Mikhailovsky, was developed further into a broad and consistent view of life, which armed the opposition with a creed of its own and helped to carry it beyond the first stage of mere isolated and individual endeavours.

Lavrov taught that the world was to be changed by education and persuasion. More violent was the remedy proposed by Michael Bakunin, one of the most remarkable of Belinsky's group of fellow-students in Moscow University and since then the apostle of intellectual revolt. He made a dramatic escape from Siberia in 1862, and from 1868, writing in exile at Geneva in his *Cause of the People (Delo Naroda)*, he called on all to free themselves first and foremost from religion, but also from all traditions of hereditary property and the family; the state, he said, had to be destroyed. Bakunin's creed was anarchism; the future society was to be based on a number of free local communities; the means of production were to be controlled. Bakunin called for an armed rising. "It is not difficult," so he lightly wrote, "to raise any village"; and his appeal was to many more attractive than the milder methods advocated by Lavrov. Nechayev, a young school teacher with a masterful personality, set about organizing a great conspiracy against the government. He initiated a number of small groups over which he himself retained absolute control. He worked in the name of a purely imaginary committee; he was dictatorial and unscrupulous, and even ordered the murder of one of the conspirators with whom he was dissatisfied. This brought the whole conspiracy to light, and eighty-seven persons were put on trial; of these, thirty-seven were sentenced to imprisonment, and others were exiled by administrative order (1871).

The Radical students were divided into two main groups; the propagandists who followed Lavrov and the insurrectionists who followed Bakunin. All were alike in their wholehearted opposition to the government and their entire devotion to the service of the peasants; they would therefore continue to work together long after the fundamental difference in their choice of methods would naturally have made their cooperation impossible. A single small group of student friends would contain adherents of both views, and it depended chiefly on the course of public events, that is, on the action of the government, whether a given student would not from a propagandist become an insurrectionist. Among the notable propagandist workers were Nicholas Chaikovsky and his followers, including Prince Peter Kropotkin, trained in the aristocratic Corps of Pages, liberal thinker and student, traveller in

Siberia and China, converted to anarchism during a visit to Europe in
1871–2. They conducted propagandist education in St. Petersburg, especially where possible among the workmen, and circulated their favourite
literature of economic theory. They came to the conclusion that to help
the peasants one must live and dress like a peasant; and students, men
and women, began taking up by hundreds any posts in the country;
some were teachers and village clerks; some were blacksmiths or nurses;
some kept inns or shops which served as depots for their literature. This
was mostly of the pamphlet kind; but in 1872 the first volume of Marx's
Capital was translated into Russian. Between Marx and Bakunin there
was a sharp controversy, Marx urging that the machinery of state should
be captured in order to create a better world, and Bakunin that the state
itself should be abolished.

The educational work of Chaikovsky and his friends was forbidden.
This only stimulated their activity. Through the government printer
Myshkin they could print secretly in Moscow. By 1873 they had an
accession of new members, including factory workers, among whom
laboured a young lady of high family, Sophia Perovsky. Branches were
formed in the provinces, for instance by Kravchinsky (Stepnyak) who
went log-cutting in Tver, by Axelrod in Kiev, and by the peasant workman Zhelyabov in Odessa. In 1872–3 the movement to the people attracted numbers of young and generous spirits. The best settled down
to regular work for the peasants, especially as school teachers. S. Perovsky was a vaccinator on the Kama. K. Breshko-Breshkovsky, wife of
a provincial judge, won such devotion that the peasants spoke of her
as "the Empress." They circulated accounts of the peasant risings of
Razin and Pugachev, or exposures of the injustices of taxation (*A Clever
Machinery*) or of land-tenure (*How Our Land Came To Be Not Ours*).
A *Golden Charter*, which claimed to be the true land law and was
printed in gilt letters, was circulated in Ukraine. One propagandist,
relying on the Bible, visited the Dissenters with great success. In 1874–5
there were groups in nearly every province, especially in the restless areas
of the Lower Volga and Dnieper. In all, between two and three thousand persons, of whom a large proportion were women, took part in this
work. In 1874 the government made a police inquiry which resulted in
the trial of 193 persons and several sentences of imprisonment. In the
course of a year some 770 persons were arrested and 215 were sent to
prison; many more were punished by administrative order.

In their mission to the peasants these *Narodniki* (or men of the people) were quite unsuccessful. Persons with strange views were far more conspicuous in a country district than they would be in a town. The peasants themselves were confused at this new phenomenon and did not know what to make of it. They would ask the priest to explain the novel literature which was handed to them. Sometimes they themselves fettered the agitators and handed them over to the police. This failure, in the minds of the *Narodniki*, conduced to the triumph of Bakunin's simple theory of force over Lavrov's slower road of propaganda. On the other hand, only in one instance (that of Stefanovich and Deutsch at Chigirin in 1877), were the agitators able to produce a peasant rising, and that only by circulating the report that the Tsar himself had sent them and wished for a revolt against the gentry; this device led to a futile local movement followed by repression, and discouraged not only the peasants concerned but also the other *Narodniki*, who condemned this stratagem. One of the lessons of the failure was that the peasants could only be interested in land, not in politics; even socialism, in general, fell dead flat.

All this tended to widen the gap between the propagandists, working by persuasion among the peasants to make them desire a more just distribution of wealth and therefore remaining comparatively unorganized, and the insurrectionists, who found there was nothing more to do in the country and gravitated towards action not through the people but for the people, by means demanding the closest kind of political organization. Embittered by their failure, these now concentrated in the poorer parts of the large cities, where they lived without passports and waged a systematic war on the police. On the other hand, the various groups continued to cooperate; and the provincial settlements were regarded as useful footholds for the support of an organized attack. The acts of the insurrectionists always helped to bring down the thunder of the government, not only on the propagandists but on wholesale categories of the general public; in 1877 fifty members of a peaceable group in Moscow were put on trial.

By now M. Nathanson and others had founded in St. Petersburg an organized society under the name of Land and Liberty. Its object was to bring about an economic revolution from below by militant methods. It had a closely systematized staff, which was to produce strikes and riots wherever possible and was also to conduct propaganda. Its "heavenly chancellery" manufactured false passports, and its "disorganization department" planned acts of terrorism. A demonstration of December 1876, in front of the Kazan Cathedral, where the chief speaker was the propagandist Plekhanov, led to further arrests and sentences. Among the revolutionaries the tide flowed even stronger in the direction of terrorism.

The general disaffection was increased by the oppression which the government at this time meted out to non-Russian nationalities of the empire. The Ukrainians speak a kind of Russian which philologists themselves have not yet determined whether to regard as a separate language or as a dialect; Nicholas I had taken measures against its use and after 1863 Alexander II resumed this policy, which was associated with his repression of everything Polish. In 1875 the branch of the Imperial Geographical Society engaged in the study of Little Russian (Ukrainian) poetry was suppressed; the Ukrainian speech was not to be printed or presented on the stage; leaders in these studies were expelled from university posts.

Alexander's reign had begun with a severe rebuff from the side of Europe in the Treaty of Paris. As at other times, failure of Russia on the side of Europe was followed by great advance on the line of least resistance in Asia, with enormous accessions of territory. When this advance had been left to Cossacks and peasants, the line which it followed had passed due eastward, north of the centres of Asiatic population, to the Pacific. A glance at the map which gives the dates of the progress through Siberia, will show, for instance, that the Russians were on the Pacific at the Sea of Okhotsk before they were in Irkutsk, only about halfway across but further south. At the Treaty of Nerchinsk in 1689, Russia had actually retired from comparatively unoccupied territory which she had begun to settle on the Amur. Now she proceeded to complete her advance on this side. In 1858 Count Nicholas Muravyev was able to annex the whole left bank of the Amur and a great tract on the right bank reaching to the Pacific at Vladivostok; this territory was formally ceded by China to Russia in 1860. The Russian outflow of colonization, passing, as has been said, through the north of Siberia, had extended across the Bering Straits into America and made its way down the coast about as far as the present northern frontier of the United States. Thus three peoples, the Spanish, the Russian, and the Anglo-Saxon, have found an unexpected contact in that far part of the world, which is only a foretaste of the time when the Pacific will wake to life with these three civilizations encircling its western shores. In 1869 Russia sold to the United States the province of Alaska.

But in this reign takes place a purely military advance in another quarter, central Asia, in character quite unlike the penetration of Siberia, except in so far as the independent initiative of Russian generals might distantly recall the unfettered enterprise of the Cossacks. The way was cleared in 1859 by the surrender after a gallant resistance of the priest-prince Shamil, which brought to a close the long struggle against the gallant mountaineers of the Caucasus. The Russians established themselves on the Syr-Daria and Amu-Daria, erecting the fort of Verny on the Ili. Counter-raids from Kokand led up to the capture of Ali-Ata by Cherniayev and of the town of Turkestan by Verevkin (1863); the two generals then stormed Chemkend. After a critical check Cherniayev stormed Tashkend, receiving instructions to desist but only opening them when he had won the city (1864). In February 1865, Turkestan was constituted into a Russian province and attached to western Siberia.

Simultaneously Russia advanced at the expense of the two Khanates of Khiva and Bukhara. With Bukhara there were incessant conflicts. Here, after a check received by Cherniayev in 1866, the Bukharans were routed at Irjai, and Khodjend was captured. After a further advance, Turkestan was constituted into a separate area under a Governor General at Tashkend (1867). On May 24, 1868, Kaufmann captured the sacred city of Samarkand containing the tomb of Timur the Great. The town revolted and the Russian garrison had to stand siege, but Kaufmann relieved it and gratified his troops with four days of pillage. Khiva was stormed on June 10, 1873, and half of its territory was annexed. A civil war in Kokand was made the occasion for an invasion led by Kaufmann and Skobelev; and on March 20, 1876, Kokand was annexed to the Russian Empire under the name of Fergana. The Khanates of Bukhara and Khiva were henceforward vassals of Russia.

These annexations had been justified in 1863 by a circular of Prince A. Gorchakov (November 16) in which he maintained that the constant raids of lawless tribes made advance unavoidable until the frontiers of a well-ordered state were reached; the same plea has been made for the advance of other empires. In 1866 the Russians entered Kuldja in Chinese territory, "to pacify the country"; the frontier was fixed by a treaty of April 1881, which gave the lower Ili to Russia. The British Viceroy of India, Lord Mayo, had urged Lord Clarendon to negotiate for respective spheres of influence, and Gorchakov pronounced for intermediate buffer states, but the negotiations did not lead to an agreement. Lord Lytton, who was Viceroy in 1876, stood for a forward British policy. In 1878 Colonel Stoletov made a treaty at Kabul by which Russia took Afghanistan under her protection. The war between England and Afghanistan that followed led to a check of the Russian forward policy on this side.

From 1874 onward, the Russian forces in Transcaspia were at issue with the wild Tekkes of Akkal and Merv, who had often molested Russian caravans. In 1879 an abortive Russian attempt to storm Darjil Teppe led to a general rising, but next year a force of 8000 under the daring Skobelev advanced on Geok Teppe which, after a fine defence, was stormed on January 24, 1881.

All the friction with England caused by the Russian advance greatly helps to explain the British attitude toward Russia, when critical events took place on another side. Just when the Emperor was being more and more separated from a large section of the thinking public in Russia, events forced on him a new war on the side of Europe. While Russia was absorbed in the East, a change of profound importance had taken place in Europe, which had entirely altered her European position. This was the establishment in 1871 of the German Empire, which possessed in Bismarck a first-class statesman. Russia could no longer count on mediating between hostile powers in central Europe. On the contrary, she was now faced on this side with the strong and aggressive frontier of a powerful and united people. To turn the tables in this way without any notice or objection from Russia, Bismarck, who had been Ambassador in Russia, made a masterly use of the hereditary friendship between the two dynasties. In his wars of unification in 1864, 1866 and 1870–1, he secured Russian neutrality by his support of the Russian government, first against the insurgent Poles in 1863 and later on Russia's denunciation of her obligations in the Black Sea. Kaiser William I visited St. Petersburg to thank his nephew Alexander II for this neutrality. For the next few years, Bismarck based his diplomacy on friendship and, wherever possible, on cooperation between the three autocratic empires of central and eastern Europe, and in 1872 the three sovereigns met to discuss among other things the dangers of socialism. This grouping looked like a revival of the associations of the Holy Alliance, but the initiative in it had passed entirely out of Russian hands. The Franco-German War had been followed in 1871 by the outbreak of communism in Paris, which was for a time triumphant and was witnessed by the German troops. The first published translation of Karl Marx was in Russian, and of Alexander's difficulties with the revolutionaries we already know. Bismarck's view was that Russia should close the door on Europe and turn eastward. This policy of autocracy and eastern expansion for Russia would mean a sustained renunciation of the traditional Russian interest in the Slavonic and Orthodox peoples of the Balkans, that is, of the one foreign policy which appealed to all sections of the Russian people.

If the Balkan question came up again, the interests of Russia and Austria were so conflicting that Bismarck would be compelled to choose between the two. Ultimately, though this was not seen at present, there could be little doubt which he would choose. Bismarck had seen the internal weaknesses of Russia and had conceived a contempt for the Russians as "a female people." On the other hand, when he drove Austria out of Germany in 1866, he inflicted no harder terms on her than the surrender of her German allies, and from this time forward Austria, of whose population about half were Slavs, became more and more an advance guard of Germany for driving a wedge into the Slav world of the Balkans.

In the summer of 1875 there was a rising in Bosnia, with armed conflicts between the Christian and Moslem populations; Serbia and Montenegro secretly helped the insurgents. Austria was troubled by this disturbance near her frontier; and on January 31, 1876, the three Eastern empires with the support of England and France launched a joint note to Turkey, demanding religious freedom for the Christians and that the local taxes should be applied only to local needs; also that a joint commission of Christians and Moslems should be appointed to execute these reforms. Turkey acceded to these requests, but the insurgents demanded further guarantees and would not disband. In Turkey, feeling ran high; a Prussian and a French Consul were murdered at Salonika, and there were strong Mahometan demonstrations in Smyrna and Constantinople. On May 13, when Alexander was in Berlin, the three Emperors demanded an armistice and the immediate appointment of the commission, with a Christian as president; also that the reforms should be carried out under European supervision. England did not join in this step; and when the other powers sent ships to Salonika, England sent hers to Besika Bay. On May 29 the Turkish Sultan Abdul Aziz was deposed and murdered, and Midhad came into power with a program of reform. In June the Turks committed terrible massacres in Bulgaria, which aroused the indignation of Gladstone and generally of British public opinion. Serbia and Montenegro declared war upon Turkey.

Since 1874, Disraeli had been in power in England; following an imperialist policy, he had acquired the Suez Canal and had made Queen Victoria Empress of India; he showed the traditional British jealousy of Russia's advance eastward; he was entirely unwilling to join in coercing the Sultan of Turkey. British opinion, which had quite missed the significance of the great reforms in Russia and continued to regard Alexander as it had regarded Nicholas, suspected another scheme of

dynastic advance. Personally Alexander had every interest in peace and
ardently desired it, and he was more than ready to cooperate with
Europe in questions of Turkish reform. But the cry of oppressed Christians of Slavonic blood in Bosnia and in Bulgaria and the pluck of
Serbia and Montenegro in coming to their relief, aroused in Russia an
indignation and enthusiasm so universal as to make inaction on his side
impossible.

On July 8, Alexander and Francis Joseph, meeting at Reichstadt,
agreed not to intervene unless necessary, but also that if intervention
and territorial changes must come, Bosnia and Herzegovina should pass
to Austria. Thousands of volunteers, such as General Cherniayev of
Asiatic reputation and the future Liberal politician F. Rodichev, joined
the Serbian army. The Serbs were poorly equipped and suffered several
reverses. England at this time negotiated separately with Turkey to
secure for Bulgaria, Bosnia, and Herzegovina the same autonomy as
Serbia already possessed, but the Turks expected no real pressure from
this side and found less difficulty in refusing the demands of England
than those of Russia. In September, Belgrade lay open to the enemy,
and on October 30 Russia intervened with an ultimatum demanding an
armistice of two months, which was accepted.

In November Alexander told the British Ambassador that he desired
no annexations, would in any case only occupy Bulgaria, and would in
no event annex Constantinople; he wished to work with the English to
secure peace and reform in Turkey, but he would be prepared to act
alone, if Europe's demands were refused. The British Foreign Minister,
Lord Derby, thanked him for this statement and invited the Powers to
a conference at Constantinople on the basis that none of them desired
any separate gains and that they were ready to guarantee the integrity
of Turkey; meanwhile Disraeli, now Lord Beaconsfield, made a vigorous
war speech at the Guildhall. Midhat surprised the Conference by suddenly announcing the establishment of a Turkish Constitution. This
was generally regarded as a move in the game. The Conference came to
an agreement by which Serbia and Montenegro should obtain accessions of territory, and Bulgaria, Bosnia, and Herzegovina should receive
autonomy under Christian governors appointed for five years and approved by the Powers; an international commission officered by Swiss
and Belgians was to control the execution of the reforms, and the
Turkish troops were to be withdrawn to their fortresses. The Turks proclaimed their Constitution, and during the actual sittings of the Conference their Great Council unanimously refused to have any commis-

sion or appointment of Christian governors. The Conference could therefore only disperse. England attempted to postpone any further steps; but on a visit of Count Ignatyev to the western capitals, a protocol was drawn up in London on March 31, 1877, approved by all the Powers; it declared that they would keep a watch over the question, and concert means to secure peace and to guarantee the rights of Christians in Turkey; Russia engaged to disarm. Turkey refused even this formula, and pointed to the Treaty of Paris as making her absolutely independent of outside intervention. The feeling in Russia was by now at boiling point. The Minister of Finance urged the danger of bankruptcy, but the Emperor and the other Ministers were for war, which was declared on April 24, 1877.

It was some time before the war brought any success. The army reform of 1874 had had no time to take effect. Publicity, the essential guarantee against administrative abuses, was hampered by the recrudescence of the censorship. The Chief of Staff was incapable; peculation in army contracts raged as in previous wars. Roumania gave passage to the Russian troops. Crossing the Danube near Sistova at the end of June, they advanced on the Balkans; while the fortresses of Rustchuk on the east and Nicopolis on the west were invested, Gurko in the centre pushed his way over the Shipka Pass, where he was only two days' march from Adrianople. But Osman Pasha, coming up rapidly from Widin with 35,000 men, threw himself into Plevna, which became a breakwater in the middle of the Russian advance. Osman drove off an attack on July 20, and recovered the fortress of Lovats. In a further unsuccessful attack on July 30, the Russians lost one fifth of their forces engaged; in August Gurko, who had returned to the southern slope of the Balkans, was vehemently attacked for several days (August 20–3) by the Turkish general Suleiman, but a small reinforcement enabled him to hold his ground.

Roumania now joined Russia in the war, and Prince Charles took over the command in front of Plevna. Here on September 11 the allies stormed the fort of Grivitsa, and the impetuous Skobelev got a footing within the Turkish lines at a cost of 12,000 men; next day, a vigorous counterattack of the Turks nearly destroyed the remnants of his force. The allies now contented themselves with investing the fortress, and General Todleben, the hero of Sevastopol, was brought up to direct the siege. Suleiman, with the relieving army, failed to do anything and in December Osman, who had no food left, made a last desperate sally, in which he was surrounded and forced to surrender (December 10). In spite of winter hardships, Gurko captured Sofia; and two columns, crossing the Balkans and turning the large Turkish force stationed in front of the pass, compelled it to surrender after a hard fight. By this turning movement the Russians were also able to cut the remaining Turks from Adrianople; and Suleiman was driven back with his army to the shores of the Ægean. On January 20 the Russians were in Adrianople, and soon afterwards their advance guard reached the Sea of Marmora at Rodosto.

In October the Turks had already asked for mediation. In the eastern theatre Kars had fallen, and the Russians had even captured the forts of Erzerum. The Serbians and Montenegrins were again taking the offensive, and the Greek government was thinking of joining in the war. At this point Abdul Hamid made an appeal to Queen Victoria, and the Queen telegraphed to Alexander asking him to stop: an incident which for a generation in Russia made "the English woman" the symbol of hostility to any Russian approach to the sea. Alexander agreed to stop if so requested by the Turks, and on January 31, 1878, an armistice was concluded at Adrianople and peace preliminaries were signed.

England was not prepared to see any other Power in Constantinople or to accept any change as to the position in the Dardanelles. Gorchakov repeated his sovereign's disclaimer of any wish to annex Constantinople. On January 23 Admiral Hornby was ordered to pass the Dardanelles; Lord Derby had this order reversed by threatening to resign; and Count Shuvalov communicated the terms which Russia proposed to impose on Turkey. On a report that Russian troops were advancing on Constantinople, the British fleet was ordered to proceed thither—as Lord Derby explained, to protect the British who were in the city; to this Gorchakov replied that he was prepared to protect all Christians there and that, if the British fleet came, the Russians would enter the city for this purpose. The British fleet stopped in the Sea of Marmora with decks cleared for action, and this situation lasted for some weeks.

On March 3 Russia and Turkey signed the Treaty of San Stefano, based in the main on the conditions of the armistice of Adrianople. Serbia and Montenegro were to have full independence and increased territory; Roumania was to become fully independent; there was to be a large Bulgaria on both sides of the Balkans; it was to extend to the Midia line north of Adrianople; thence the frontier was to run to the Ægean, along the coast to the neighbourhood of Salonika, and from that point to the confines of Albania. This new Bulgaria was to have autonomy under a Christian Prince supported by a national militia, but was to pay tribute to Turkey; the Prince was to be elected by the Bulgarians, and to be confirmed by Turkey and the other Powers; a Russian commissioner, supported by an army of fifty thousand Russians, was for two years to safeguard and superintend the beginnings of Bulgarian autonomy. Bosnia and Herzegovina received the concessions claimed by the Conference of the Powers before the war: to be modified if necessary on agreement between Turkey, Russia, and Austria. The organic law of 1863 was to be carried out in Crete, and similar provisions drafted by local commissions were to be applied to Epirus and Thessaly. To the Armenians Turkey guaranteed reforms and protection from the Kurds and Circassians. Turkey was declared to owe a war indemnity of one hundred and forty million pounds, of which only thirty million were to be paid up, while for the remainder the Dobrudscha, Ardahan, Kars, and Bayazid were to be taken as satisfaction; the Dobrudscha was to be given to Roumania in exchange for her part of Bessarabia, which she would cede to Russia.

Russia had from the first admitted the right of the other Powers to be consulted as to questions affecting Europe as a whole, though Gorchakov's view was that she might herself settle which part of the treaty was referred for common consent. On Bismarck's proposal a Congress was to meet in Berlin, and meanwhile Beaconsfield continued his preparations for war. Lord Salisbury at this time took the place of Lord Derby, and issued a circular note emphasizing the control which Russia could now exercise over Turkey. Shuvalov, the Russian Ambassador in London, did his best to ascertain the British desires; Salisbury claimed that the liberated territory of Bulgaria should be much smaller and should be divided into two provinces, of which Eastern Rumelia, south of the Balkans, should still be directly under Turkish rule: Bayazid must be restored; the other Powers must take their part in the questions relating to Epirus, Thessaly, and Crete. With these claims, Shuvalov went to St. Petersburg and secured their acceptance there. On June 4 England and Turkey concluded a defensive alliance guaranteeing the remains of the Turkish possessions in Asia, the Turks making a new promise of reform; Cyprus was to be occupied by the British, so long as Russia retained her conquests in Asiatic Turkey.

In June the Congress met, and by June 13 looked like breaking down; but on July 13 a final treaty was concluded.

Bulgaria was diminished and cut off from the Ægean; the ceded territory was divided into two provinces of which the southern, Eastern Rumelia, was to receive some measure of autonomous administration, but to remain for military purposes under Turkish rule; Bosnia and Herzegovina were to be occupied (not annexed) by Austria. The territory ceded to Serbia and Montenegro was so arranged that a corridor of Austrian occupation was made to separate the two kindred states from each other; Bayazid was left to Turkey; the Sultan was advised to cede Thessaly and part of Epirus to Greece, but no definite provision was made for these areas. Otherwise the terms of San Stefano were in the main retained.

This settlement, as we shall see, was soon challenged as far as Eastern Rumelia was concerned by the action of the inhabitants, exactly as had happened in the case of Roumania after the Treaty of Paris. These parcellings of national territory to allay the mutual suspicions of European states, gave no guarantee of a permanent settlement. Russia, apart from some of her conquests in Asia, obtained in territory only part of Bessarabia, and even this arrangement tended to embroil her with her ally Roumania. The transfer of Bosnia and Herzegovina to Austrian rule, though previously accepted by Alexander when Russia and Austria were acting together, was a severe disappointment to Russian public opinion, which had regarded the war as a Slav crusade for the complete liberation of the Orthodox Christians of the Balkans. It was Russia who had liberated Bulgaria, but even the moral authority which she might now expect to have there received a mortifying check in the provision that put Bulgaria under a joint guarantee of all the Powers, directed as much against Russia as against Turkey.

Gorchakov described the signing of the Treaty of Berlin as the most painful act of his life. Even in a Russia subject to a severe censorship, the national mortification found its voice. None were so mortified as the Slavophils, the party of religion and patriotism. In a speech to the Slavonic Society in Moscow, Ivan Aksakov violently upbraided the government. The liberation of the Balkans had been spoiled, he said; Russia had been outwitted by German and Austrian treachery; the government had lost terribly in prestige; the public, he asserted, was furious with it, and the Tsar, who had failed to keep his promise to carry the liberation through "to the end," was now separated from his people. Such words, from such a quarter, were at this moment positively dangerous, and Aksakov was exiled from Moscow.

Alexander was indeed deprived of his last support in public opinion at the time when he most needed it. The revolutionary movement had been more or less silenced by the general mood of patriotism during the war. Now, at the moment of general disillusionment, it broke out again at once, with the added strength of organization. Bakunin had died at Berne (July 13, 1876), but Tkachev in his *Tocsin* and *Anarchy of Thought*, who had not been listened to after the failure of Nechayev, preached from Switzerland a revolution led by an organized minority with terrorism as the means, and to such a movement everything was tending. In Kiev there was a group of twenty-five insurrectionists well equipped with arms; it was two of this group that organized the peasant rising at Chigirin. Alexander Mikhailov had travelled through east and southeast Russia organizing revolutionary colonies and bringing them under the control of the headquarters of Land and Liberty in St. Petersburg, where he directed the movement from April 1878. Kropotkin made a remarkable escape from prison. The Kiev group organized a still more ingenious enterprise of this kind; one of them became a turnkey and was promoted to be chief jailor, when he let all his comrades out. Big trials only served to advertise the movement, especially that of 193 persons in St. Petersburg, where Myshkin compared his judges to prostitutes, and a scuffle took place while the court was being cleared of the public. General F. Trepov ordered a prisoner, Bogolepov, to be flogged for insubordination; and a young well-born lady, Vera Zasulich, fired at him point-blank. The case was referred to a jury (April 13, 1878) which, though the facts were evident, acquitted. The police tried to rearrest the accused outside the court, but she was rescued by revolutionaries and escaped abroad, to become one of their most untiring leaders in later times. A kind of rising in Odessa led to the execution of Kovalsky. In broad daylight on a street in St. Petersburg Kravchinsky, better known as Stepnyak, shot General Mezentsev, the Chief of Gendarmes, and escaping to England, published a glorification of his deed (August 15). At St. Petersburg and Harkov, the prisoners, most of whom were still awaiting trial, organized hunger strikes. On May 21, the government decided to dispense with a jury in all cases of offences against officials, and on August 21 all attacks on them were referred to courts-martial.

The Emperor now appealed for the support of the loyal elements in the public. In Kiev and Harkov the Zemstvo Liberals met in conference, and pointed out that while all guarantees of individual liberty were violated by the police, and while the demands of the public were persistently ignored, it was thereby precluded from giving any effective support to the throne. One leading young Liberal, Ivan Petrunkevich, tried to get the revolutionaries to desist from terrorist acts while the Liberals should attempt to secure concessions from the Emperor. In the

Zemstvo of Chernigov he made a drastic criticism of the government's hostility towards education, which could not fail to provoke the students, and urged that free speech and freedom of the press were the only weapons by which the public in general could effectively help the government. He was silenced by the presiding marshal and exiled from the province. The Zemstvo of Tver, on the initiative of Rodichev and others, asked the Emperor to grant to his loyal subjects that which he had already given to Bulgaria, namely, constitutional liberty, as the only means of achieving the Tsar's desire of "gradual, peaceful, and law-abiding development." At other more secret but more general conferences of Liberals, the same demands were put forward.

Meanwhile acts of terrorism only became more common. The object of attack was now the Emperor himself. Karakozov's attempt of 1866 had been imitated in April 1873 by Solovyev, who fired five shots at Alexander. Now his murder was becoming part of an organized campaign. The government appointed six governors general with full powers. An able police officer Sudeikin arrested all the Kiev group, and its leader Osinsky was hanged. The leaders of Land and Liberty summoned their followers to a meeting at Voronezh; while the moderates from the country settlements were waiting there, the extremists held a preliminary meeting at Lipetsk at which, at the instance of Zhelyabov, they decided to take the initiative (June 29–30, 1879). Even though many of the members had by now left Voronezh, they were not in a majority there, but extremists and moderates agreed to act independently, though still cooperating for common purposes. The moderates under Plekhanov continued their propagandist work under the title of the Black Partition, which was the name of their organ. The extremists under the name of the Will of the People pursued more vigorously than ever their attacks on the life of the Emperor. On September 7 they published his death sentence.

The conspirators were not more than a few hundred in number. Their weapon was the bomb. While they fought the Russian police the public remained passive, but the sympathies of many were certainly, if anything, rather with the revolutionaries, who thus were often able to obtain indirect help or shelter. They were organized in sections and worked efficiently; and they had good information as to the Emperor's movements. They made more than one attempt to blow up the Imperial train. On February 17, 1880, a workman, Halturin, who had for weeks introduced dynamite in small quantities into the Winter Palace where he was employed in repairs, blew up the Imperial dining room;

the Emperor was expecting Prince Alexander of Battenberg, who was half an hour late—otherwise he would have been destroyed. The government was now thoroughly alarmed. A Supreme Commission of administration was established, with control even over ministers. At the head of it was put a man who might have carried the country through this crisis, General Loris-Melikov. He had rendered distinguished service during the war in the Caucasus and during the plague at Astrakhan and, as Governor at Harkov, had shown that he could win the confidence of Zemstvo men. At the outset he had to meet an attack on his life from a revolutionary, Mlodetsky, whom he arrested with his own hands. On his appointment, he declared that he regarded the support of the public as the principal means of restoring normal conditions. Loris-Melikov was not a constitutionalist. He had not the intention of introducing a regular system of representative institutions; he meant to cleanse the administration and to carry the great reforms of the beginning of the reign to their proper completion. In this task he was willing and anxious to have the help and advice of representatives of the public. The notorious Third Section established by Nicholas I was abolished, and the police were placed under the direct control of the Minister of the Interior; Dmitry Tolstoy was replaced as Minister of Education by a Liberal of high character, Saburov. The reactionary Minister of Finance, Admiral Greig, had to give way to a Liberal, Abaza. Melikov at once gave the press a good deal of freedom; he himself told the editors that they could freely discuss political subjects, if they did not raise the question of a constitution. After six months' dictatorship, Melikov was himself able to recommend that the Commission should be closed as no longer necessary, and he became Minister of the Interior. He referred to the Zemstva for free discussion the question of a reform of the peasant administration, and he also wished to reform peasant taxation and the peasant system of justice. The Zemstvo of Tver, probably the most Liberal in Russia, declared that Melikov had justified the hopes of the public and brought honesty and good will into the relations of the government with the people; Melikov, it said, had wisely recognized the lawful needs and desires of the public, and it looked forward to a "happy future opening up for our beloved country."

Nothing frightened the revolutionaries so much as that Melikov should have captured the confidence of the Liberals. Many of them were but little interested in constitutions, and could hope for no realization of their Utopias without a wholesale social upheaval. The Governor

General of Harkov had been killed in 1879 by the revolutionary Golden-berg, who had later informed on all the details of the revolutionary or-ganization. Melikov was thus able to immobilize the conspirators almost completely. Now fearing, as they confessed, that Melikov would cut them off from the public, they feverishly renewed their activity.

On February 9, 1881, Melikov submitted to the Emperor a scheme for associating elective representatives of the public with the govern-ment in legislative work. Two government commissions would be ap-pointed: one to reform the administration, the other to reform the national finance. Their plans would be submitted to a General Commis-sion, which would include experts elected by the Zemstva and Town Councils. Fifteen of these elected persons would be associated with the Council of State in its final discussion of these reforms.

The revolutionaries had undermined several streets in St. Petersburg; one mine under the Police Bridge, designed to kill Alexander when he was starting for a journey to Poland, remained there for more than a year. Zhelyabov had organized small units of ten persons each, which co-opted their own members and had recognized leaders. Instruction and practice in the use of bombs were given them by the revolutionary expert Kibalchich. Zhelyabov even conducted a kind of bomb review, but he was arrested directly afterwards. Sophia Perovsky, who was his chief lieutenant, now hurried on the climax. On March 13 Alexander had already signed the project of Melikov, which he believed would bring satisfaction to his people. After assisting at a review, and dining at the palace of his aunt the Grand Duchess Helen, he was driving along the Catherine Canal when at the signal of Perovsky's kerchief a young Nihilist Rysakov threw a bomb at his carriage. The Emperor was not touched, and dismounted to speak to some of the Cossacks of his suite who were wounded. He even spoke not unkindly of the criminal, who had been arrested. At this moment a second assassin, Grínevetsky, with the words "It is too early to thank God," threw a second bomb between his feet. His legs were crushed, his stomach torn open and his face ter-ribly mutilated. He could only say: "Home to the Palace, to die there," and passed away unconscious an hour and a half later. The bomb that killed Alexander put an end to the faint beginnings of Russian consti-tutionalism.

Contemporary Russia

(1881–1947)

CHAPTER XXI

Industrialism, Socialism, and Liberalism

[*1881–1904*]

THE MURDER of Alexander II had in Russia the effect of a railway collision. With the bureaucracy even Liberalism stood condemned, and repression seemed the one road of salvation; the murder of the Tsar Liberator filled the Slavophils with devotion to the throne; the Liberals were shocked at the outcome of a movement in which they had almost looked upon the revolutionaries as colleagues; the Radicals if anything gravitated closer to the revolutionaries; several addresses of Zemstva on this occasion show the general bewilderment and confusion.

Yet reaction did not come all at once. It was widely hoped that the last concession of Alexander II to public wishes might still take effect; the ministers stood committed to it; all depended on the new sovereign. Alexander III was a man of giant physique, so strong that he could bend a horseshoe in his hand. Unlike his father, all his tastes were for the pleasures of home. He was quite honest, very laborious, very clear in his views, but by mind and education extremely limited in his outlook. He had no lack of courage. He had opposed the Liberal policy of the last months of the reign, and for him the murder of his father was a convincing proof of its failure. Yet family loyalty was so strong with him that he might have been willing to publish Melikov's scheme as his father's last legacy. This was vigorously opposed by Constantine Pobedonostsev, who had been his tutor. The regicides on their side not only avowed their act but threatened the same fate to the new Tsar. They themselves had no constructive policy, and their futility is best shown in their demands to the new sovereign, for which they simply borrowed the Liberal program. Kaiser William I advised against any concessions. Katkov protested that Liberalism was not a national movement, and Ivan Aksakov spoke strongly against Western democracy. This strengthened Pobedonostsev; he was instructed to draft the accession manifesto, which contained the words "with faith in the power and the right of autocracy." Melikov, who had not been consulted, resigned and with him Abaza and Dmitry Milyutin—the first instance in Russia of a joint resignation of ministers on a question of political principle.

The plot against Alexander II had to be cleared up. The task was confided to Plehve, a law officer who had served as head of the police under Melikov. Plehve made a very clean job of it. Those directly associated with the plot were rounded up. Zhelyabov, Perovsky, Kibalchich, Rysakov, and T. Mikhailov were executed; Grinevetsky had perished in his own explosion. The rest of the conspirators were imprisoned or sent to Siberia. The revolutionary organizations were practically destroyed, and those of the leaders who escaped, themselves testified that they could find in the public no basis of sympathy for their attempts.

There were further isolated acts of terrorism, such as Skankovsky's attempt on General Cherevin, the murder of Strelnikov in Kiev, and that of Sudeikin in St. Petersburg by Degayev, a former revolutionary who had acted in collusion with Sudeikin and was now compelled by his old associates to make this atonement. In 1884 was discovered a plot of Vera Filippov. In 1886 an attempt to kill Alexander III by derailing his train at Borki failed of its object but destroyed twenty-one persons.

Loris-Melikov was succeeded not by a reactionary but by a Slavophil, Count Ignatyev, who wished to strengthen the throne by the moral support of a consultative national assembly after the model of the old Zemsky Sobor; the new Minister of Finance, Bunge, was a man of approved honesty, industry and foresight, all for intelligent administrative reforms in the interest of the peasants; the new Minister of Education, Baron Nikolay, was Liberal. Ignatyev pronounced for cooperation with the people, for maintaining the rights of the Zemstva and town councils and for inviting the advice of local public men, not necessarily on the basis of election. Experts chosen by the government itself took part in the discussion of the redemption dues, of migration and of the liquor trade; the redemption dues were reduced and considerable sums were assigned to the Zemstva for the relief of local distress. Bunge abolished the detested poll tax at a loss of forty million roubles to the State (1883–6), and instituted tax inspectors to find what burdens the population could bear. He founded a Peasants' Bank, to give credit to those who wanted to take up more land.

But it was not long before this limited consultation of the public was dropped. Alexander himself asked "whether it was any longer necessary," and Ignatyev was replaced by the strong man of the reaction,

Count Dmitry Tolstoy, who remained Minister of the Interior till 1889. Of ministers tolerant of the public only Bunge remained. Reactionaries who regarded the Emancipation as almost premature and the Zemstva as dangerous were the only counsellors who received attention. Of these the most notable was Pazukhin, soon promoted to an important post in the Chancellery of the Ministry of the Interior. Under his direction a new Zemstvo Law was issued in 1889, introducing a rigorous class basis into the electoral system, with an artificial predominance of the gentry class; the Zemstva were forbidden to increase their budget by more than 5 per cent in a given year, so that backward Zemstva were condemned to remain backward; the Governor might, within a given time limit, strike out any item. Still worse was Pazukhin's law of 1890 establishing the Land Captains. These were officials chosen from the poorer gentry and put under the direct control of the Minister of the Interior, with the duty of supervising every detail of peasant life; by the peasants they were regarded as a partial revival of serfdom. In the system of local justice the Land Captains, who had no legal training, replaced the Justices of the Peace; under their direction were the peasant judges, who were guided not by common law but by peasant custom. The administrative and judicial functions combined in the person of the Land Captain were a source of confusion and vexation.

These changes were the outcome of a definite program of reaction, of which the outstanding prophet was Pobedonostsev. He was a man of fine mind and unimpeachable honour, but his theory was based on a profound mistrust of human intellect and of human nature. It is brilliantly summarized in his book, *Moscow Conversations*. Western democracy is rotten; only the Russian patriarchal system is still sound. The press is suspect because it has sometimes been misused; it does not represent public opinion; therefore let there be silence. Elections and parliaments have been associated with corruption; therefore let him who holds the power remain absolute. As others were forbidden to talk, these views had free scope and could meet with little criticism.

Pobedonostsev was throughout this period Procurator of the Holy Synod, "the Tsar's eye" to control the Church. Preachers who expressed themselves at all freely were ordered to send their sermons in advance to an ecclesiastical censorship. Village priests were expected to report to the police authorities those of their parishioners who were "politically untrustworthy." Every form of dissent was to be proscribed; for instance, the Stundists, who resembled our Baptists, the Dukhobors, who like our Quakers refused military service, and the peasant and other followers of

Count Leo Tolstoy's doctrine of nonresistance. In 1894 Stundist meetings were forbidden. Not long afterwards a number of Dukhobors escaped to Canada. In 1897 a church congress in Kazan asked for the condemnation of Tolstoyans as "particularly dangerous to Church and State." In spite of an eloquent plea for religious toleration from M. Stakhovich, Count Leo Tolstoy himself was excommunicated. The non-Orthodox and non-Christian communities were all persecuted in the same period.

But the principal fields of repression were education and the press. In 1882 Baron Nikolay was replaced as Minister of Education by a former Liberal, now reactionary, Delyanov, who remained in office till 1898. In 1884 the University Statute of Alexander II was replaced by another which took all autonomy from the universities; student clubs were again forbidden, on pain of service in the ranks of the army. A ministerial circular instructed that children of the lower classes should be excluded from secondary schools. Pobedonostsev attempted to transfer the primary schools from the Zemstva to the Church. Most of the priests were too ignorant for these duties; the Zemstva made a sturdy resistance and, as they found the money for the schools, the government ultimately left the work in their hands. Student troubles broke out in 1882 at the Universities of Kazan and St. Petersburg, and in 1887 at those of Moscow, Odessa, Harkov, and Kazan. Troops were used to suppress them, and the usual exclusions and exiles followed. Political trustworthiness was made the chief test in the appointment to bursaries. Only one university was founded in this period, but the government promoted technical schools of all kinds; institutes were established for experimental medicine, pedagogy, forestry, agriculture, and commercial and industrial studies. In 1896 the students of St. Petersburg were forbidden to keep their usual anniversary, and those of Moscow coming out to demonstrate their sympathy were driven in by Cossacks. The disturbances went on next day and as the students would not disperse, 400 were imprisoned, of whom 150 were sent into exile and 26 excluded. In 1898 Delyanov was succeeded by a reactionary professor, Bogolepov. Next year the Rector of St. Petersburg was hissed for severe criticism of the students, and a riot broke out in which the Cossacks used their whips. This disturbance spread to Moscow, and in all 13,000 students came out on strike; orders were given to enlist them in the army. In 1900 a meeting of 1000 students in Kiev was surrounded by Cossacks; 500 were arrested, of whom 183 were sent to the army and the rest expelled; troubles broke out again in Moscow, Harkov, and St. Petersburg. Bogolepov was murdered on February 27, 1901, by a revolutionary, Karpovich; but this was the beginning of a new period.

The press offers a sombre picture during the whole of this period. The temporary rules of 1865 were reinforced by further additions in 1882. Papers warned three times and suspended could only start again under a preliminary censorship. Four Ministers, those of the Interior, Education, Justice, and the Procurator of the Synod, could conjointly forbid a given person to engage in editorial work. By forbidding the printing of advertisements or sale on the streets, the government could always ruin a paper when it chose. Only the *Messenger of Europe*, a monthly edited with circumspection and dignity by the Liberal Arsenyev, was able to give any real reflection of public thought in this period. The *Novoe Vremya*, a miracle of astuteness and versatility conducted by Suvorin, managed somehow to wriggle through to the end of it between the Scylla and Charybdis of Russian editors—indifference of the public if one did not print anything interesting, and persecution by the government if one did.

The law courts fell more and more under control, and judicial independence could only be sustained by personal sacrifices. The government even codified its system of exceptional or abnormal law of which there were three grades, distinguished as exceptional protection, increased protection, and martial law. It was not for very long that a province was immune from one or other of these forms.

But while the government tried in every way to maintain a "public calm," or in other words a public silence, life was growing up of itself. The Emancipation had set going important processes of many kinds. The peasants took up more and more land. They received at the Emancipation about half the cultivated land, though soon subject to the restrictions of communal ownership. To escape these restrictions, enterprising peasants rented from the gentry, until on the eve of the great Revolution something like three quarters of the cultivated land was in peasant hands. As the gentry mortgaged or sold their land and went off to the towns, it became increasingly impossible to have a system of government tutelage based on the privileges of this class. The government, being opposed to individual peasant property, would sell land of the gentry not to individuals but only to village communities, or, which was a slight alleviation, to associations formed for the purpose; so that individual enterprise had for the present to content itself with leasing.

Some went far afield for new land, and the movement towards

Siberia grew throughout this period. There too the pioneer was faced with the opposition of the law. No individual could leave his commune without its formal agreement. This, however, would be given if he would bear his share of the village taxes, as the collective responsibility of village taxpayers was still in force. Some made almost incredibly long and difficult journeys as *hodoki* or scouters to find suitable land and, if successful, would be followed by numbers of their fellow-villagers; thus the peasant, in spite of the law, continued that process which peopled the Russian Empire.

Many more, now that they were free to move, went off to some great town, in particular to St. Petersburg or Moscow. By this process St. Petersburg gradually tended to become more and more a Russian city. The peasant did not come as an isolated adventurer. He would come from a given village, to a given quarter of a given town, where there were already several of his fellow-villagers, for assured employment in a given trade or handicraft, such as cabmen, carpenters, gardeners or, in increasing numbers, factory workers. The link maintained with the community had its value; there were villages whose prosperity depended mainly on these town earnings. The outgoing peasant preserved his potential right to an allotment of the village land, and would return as the years advanced, introducing a son or nephew into the place which he had held in the town. Thus the village community served as a substitute for poor-law provision. In some cases peasants did not have to go far to obtain factory wages. In the province of Vladimir, some worked in a country factory but lived at home and continued to cultivate their village holdings. Many engaged in cottage industries, which toward the end of this period were promoted with great energy and judgment by the Zemstva; these local industries were often of ancient origin and produced very beautiful work.

Russia was becoming an industrial country. The old methods of exchange, such as the fair of Nizhny Novgorod, progressively lost their importance as she gradually approached the conditions of modern Europe.

Mining became especially important, not only because of the enormous unworked mineral resources of Russia, but because the conditions of the country made it easier to develop these than some other forms of industry. Vast deposits of coal and iron were found in South Russia on the Donets, and from 1886 the output of pig iron showed a huge increase. Workers, now free to sell their labour, gravitated from all sides to the Donets. Foreign enterprise and capital greatly contributed to the

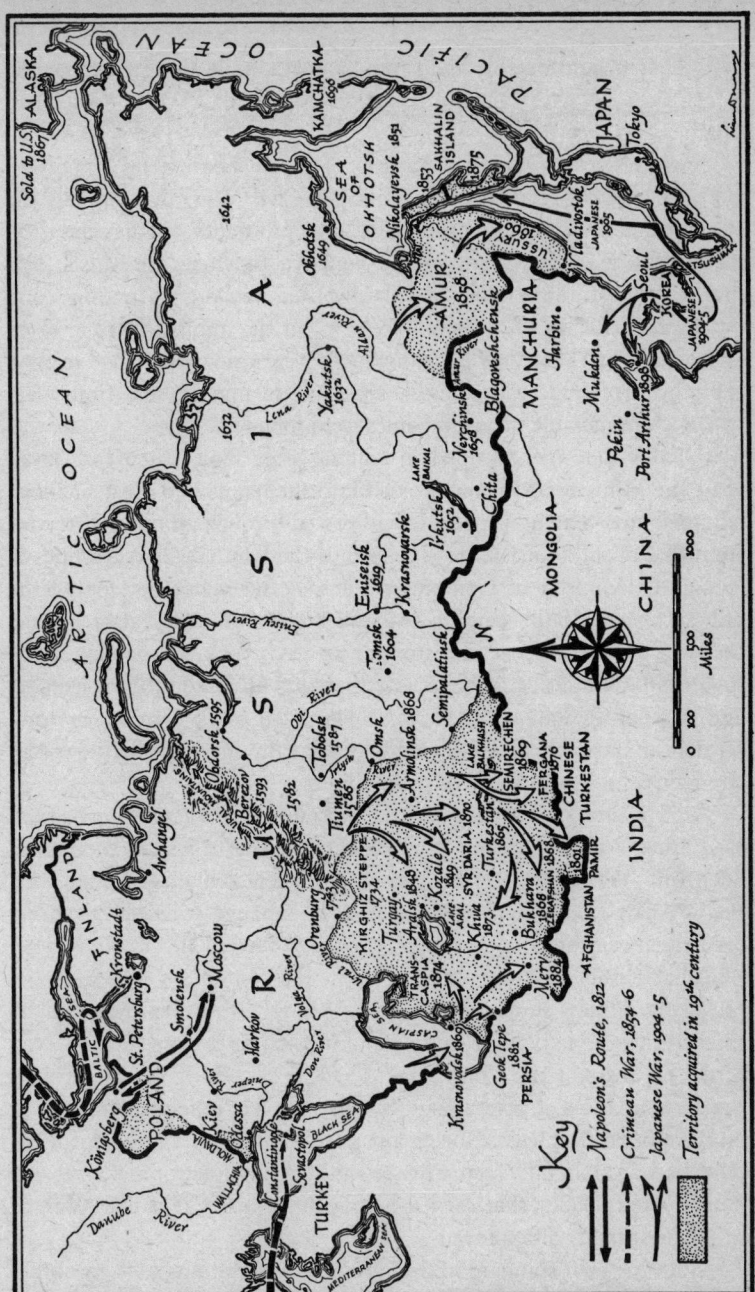

RUSSIAN EMPIRE IN THE NINETEENTH CENTURY

growth of a considerable industrial population in this part, and the large town of Yuzovo commemorates the work of the Welshman Hughes.

Factories also progressed rapidly. Moscow became an important centre of textile industry; the American Civil War, by stopping the American cotton import, contributed to its prosperity; the flax industry, almost the most important in the northern provinces of Russia, also grew rapidly. In 1850 there had hardly been any private trading companies in Russia; by 1873 there were 227, but the number had increased enormously by 1889. Very large dividends were paid. From 1898 to 1899 the growth of trade was colossal, especially in mining, and from 1896 to 1899 innumerable new companies were founded.

All this movement gained in volume after 1892, when for eleven years the Ministry of Finance passed into the hands of a great financial administrator, Sergius Witte. He had passed through all ranks of service from that of stationmaster to the head of the South Western Railways. Appointed Minister of Communications, he set about developing the railway system of the empire, and continued this policy after he succeeded Vyshnegradsky as Minister of Finance (1892). Russia now added to her railway mileage more rapidly than any other country in Europe; and, though new private companies continued to be formed, the proportion of state-owned railways was continually increased by new constructions and the purchase of private lines.

As Minister of Finance Witte, in spite of wholesale opposition, established a gold standard, thus enabling Russia to win financial confidence in Western countries and to hold her own in exchange with them. Apart from those who opposed any change whatsoever, strong influences were brought to bear at Court to force a silver standard on him, but without success. In this, as in the rest of his policy, he received the firmest support from Alexander III, who was himself most careful with the national economy and insisted on a close revision even of the expenses of the Court. Witte had to back his gold standard by the accumulation of a very large gold reserve. He defended this policy on the ground that Russia, being an agricultural country and dependent on the crop, could only secure her credit in this burdensome way. It was only Witte's finance that carried Russia through the Japanese War, of which he strongly disapproved.

With his gold standard and his gold reserve, he was able to obtain a large influx of foreign capital. It was a principle of Russian finance that foreign capital should be persuaded to come and spend itself in

Russia; and Witte was ready to help those who were willing to set up works in the country. He was always glad to support a sound concern by a government concession or even by a government subsidy and by large government orders. One of the chief achievements of this time was the construction of the Trans-Siberian Railway, and the orders for rails were of great service to the metal firms working on the Donets. Witte was criticized for committing the government credit to the boom in trade. It was now that the Russian market came to reflect regularly the booms and slumps of those of Western Europe, showing conclusively that Russia had finally passed out of the period of industrial isolation. But so utterly inadequate had been the development of her resources that hardly any boom could go so fast as to make up the arrears of the past. New developments created new markets and new demands; the more was done, the more there was to be done; and the country rode triumphantly through slumps which elsewhere might have been disastrous. As time went on, the incidence of taxation shifted slowly but surely from agriculture toward trade.

The tariff policy of Russia had always been in the main protectionist, though the measure of protection varied at different times; and Witte raised the duties on anything which he hoped that Russia herself could produce. Certain classes of heavy machinery, such as Russia could not yet construct, were admitted on easy terms; also agricultural implements. Cotton duties were used to encourage the culture of the vast fields now accessible in Turkestan, and though they were raised in 1887–91 they did not stop the increase of cotton mills. In 1894 Russia concluded a tariff treaty with Germany for ten years. This was preceded by a tariff war. Russia had in mind the needs of Russian industry and Germany the needs of German agriculture, which were always present to the Prussian gentry. Witte had to win his treaty by producing an alternative fighting tariff, and at one time trade relations between the two countries became almost impossible. Witte, however, was backed throughout by Alexander III; and in the end Caprivi conceded terms favourable to Russia in spite of the Junkers, by whom he was shortly driven from office.

In spite of opposition, Witte also carried through a state monopoly of vodka. Russian policy had so far fluctuated between the systems of monopoly, of farming out, and of excise. Witte's measure, which was ably carried out, aimed ostensibly at reducing drunkenness; it cannot claim to have had that effect; it only controlled places of sale, and at once illicit stills sprang up everywhere, usually with the connivance of the police who, as agents of the often hostile Minister of the Interior, were not under Witte's authority. The liquor monopoly, however, brought a very great profit to the treasury.

The rapid growth of Russian industry created the beginnings of a factory class. Most of the workers were peasants, still bound by certain ties to their villages. For many reasons the new conditions required regulation. The new industrialists were as crude as the new workers. Moscow, where there were vast supplies of labour, employed large numbers of hands at the most insignificant pay. The workmen were ignorant and incompetent; ordinarily it took three or more hands to do work which in other countries would be done by one; long hours did not necessarily mean serious work; women workers ordinarily took their children with them into the workshop. St. Petersburg, where labour was scarcer, took pains to treat it better and demanded of it greater efficiency. Bunge made important factory laws in 1882–6; but all reform had to reckon with Moscow obscurantism. By the law of 1882, children between twelve and fifteen might not work more than eight hours; minors were forbidden night work; employers were required to allow children free time for education. Bunge also established factory inspectors, to protect the interests of the workers. A law of June 1884 demanded education for minors, and ministerial regulations required that in some trades no workers should be admitted under fifteen. A law of 1885 forbade night work for women, or for those under seventeen in textile factories. Decrees of 1886 provided for the regular observance of these laws; the factory inspectors received extensive powers; no schedule of fines was valid without their sanction; the workman's terms of contract were regulated and protected.

These factory laws were essentially paternal in character, and in January 1887 Bunge was driven from office on the charge of "socialism." Certainly state socialism as opposed to individualism was the character not only of these laws but of the paternal autocracy as a whole. Now, under pressure from the employers, there was a revulsion in the direction of *laissez faire*. A law of May 1890 authorized the government or the factory inspectors to license night work for children; even those between ten and twelve years of age might be employed temporarily, on permission of the Ministers of Finance and the Interior. Employers used every kind of artifice to evade the rules laid down for them; payments in kind were counted as cash payments; wrong totals were entered, to allow for the taking of arbitrary fines; where possible they compelled their workers to buy all their provisions from the factory shop. In 1893 the new rules themselves were modified in the interests of the employers. In 1897, however, after two serious strikes, the hours of work for adults were limited to eleven and a half, or to ten if including night work. Even the employers themselves asked for this, as the tired workmen did bad work. In Volhynia some had introduced an eight-hour day with three relief gangs, with the result that their output increased by 25 per cent. The example was followed in Tver; in St. Petersburg and the great Polish industrial field of Lodz, the proportion of workers engaged in day work only were respectively 83 and 80 per cent; Moscow, however, remained at 31 per cent.

Though there was a notable rise in pay from 1883 to 1896—10 to 15 per cent, and in the south nearly 100 per cent—the growth of a labour population brought with it large strikes such as those of May 1896, January 1897, and June 1897, the last two of which were the occasion for the law of that year. However, a circular of the Minister of Finance in March 1898 allowed the addition of extra hours without limit.

Passing into European capitalism, Russia also became more nearly acquainted with the ideas of Western socialism, which Karl Marx had formulated into a systematic creed. Though the first translation of Marx's first volume was into Russian, the book was its own preventive against an extensive circulation. This, combined with the extreme conditions of censorship in Russia, meant that while a few Russian thinkers were among the most thorough students of Marx, the public and especially the still almost illiterate factory workers made their acquaintance with him only through popular pamphlets, interpreting his much debated propositions according to the bias of the writer. When Land and Liberty had split up at the conference at Lipetsk in 1879, the more moderate section led by Gregory Plekhanov, renouncing politics as "a bourgeois prejudice," had devoted itself to the study of economic questions. This group too had become more political by 1882, when the failure of the militant Will of the People had become obvious. Unlike that section, and supporting Marx as against Bakunin, Plekhanov's group desired to work through the State and not to destroy it. It gave its attention not to the peasants but to the workmen. It was prepared to cooperate with the middle class in winning a democratic constitution, which would make it much easier to educate the workers in Marxism; and it incorporated in its program the demands of the Liberals for liberty of conscience, speech, press, meeting, and association. Plekhanov and his few fellow-thinkers founded small groups for the study of Marx from 1883 to 1894; and from 1889 they succeeded in interesting factory workers. In 1891 there was an abortive attempt to organize a movement including both Liberals and Socialists, and a sketch of a constitution was even drawn up, but the movement came to nothing. The Socialists continued to organize by themselves. In 1898 at a Congress in South Russia, delegates of their various local groups and also of the Jewish socialist organization, the Bund, united and appointed a central committee, taking the title of the Social Democratic Workmen's Party.

From the outset there was a disagreement between those who, like the groups of St. Petersburg and Voronezh, aimed at a workers' movement for economic grievances, with freedom of action for each group, and those who wished for a central authority and organized political action. The whole movement was at present in its infancy. In 1900 was founded a conspirative organ, the *Spark* (*Iskra*), edited by Plekhanov, Axelrod, Vera Zasulich, Lenin (Ulyanov), and Martov, to organize propaganda not only among factory workers and students but also among peasants and in the army; it hoped even to win the more Radical members of the Zemstva, and was ready to join in any opposition to the government. So far Plekhanov had prevailed, but in December 1902 a committee was set up in Kiev to organize a second Congress, which was to revise the program and centralize the work; and at this Congress, which was held in July 1903, in London, the extremist and centralist section of Lenin prevailed, his followers taking henceforward the name of Bolsheviks (men of the majority). Lenin stood for the dictatorship of a small group of theorists with clear convictions, and not for a mass movement by persuasion. Congresses were to be summoned every two years.

In 1904 the Mensheviks, or followers of Plekhanov, prevailed in the *Spark* and drove the Bolsheviks from the central committee. Lenin now started a rival organ, V*pered* (*Forward*), and set up a bureau of the "Committee of the Majority." An effort was made for reunion in July 1904, by the Social Democrats of Odessa; and conferences took place in March and in May (1905), when a new phase of Russian history had already begun; the Mensheviks did not attend the second of these conferences, and the Bolsheviks chose the central committee.

But the prevailing tendency in Russia in this period was not Socialism but Liberalism. The Liberal movement under Alexander II had been tragically cut short by his death. It was now resumed on a broader basis, with the advantage of the new school of responsibility and experience created by the Zemstvo. The years 1891 to 1893 were marked by severe famines in the grain-growing provinces in the south and on the Volga.

The stagnant government was quite incapable of giving adequate relief. The famine brought home the needs of the peasants more strongly than ever before. A great voluntary relief organization was formed, and drew into it not only all the best zemstvo men but the best of the professional class. The government was divided between the urgent pressure of the need and its fear of any contact between the liberal professions and the peasantry; but this only added to the missionary character of the work.

From the famine onward, the work of the Zemstva gathered new enthusiasm and great energy; and as in the seventies, numbers of students again streamed down to the country for the service of the people, with the difference that they now sought permanent practical work in the Zemstvo service. The best Zemstvo members were Liberals; the best Zemstvo employees were revolutionaries; and the union of these two elements in practical tasks was educative for both.

Though the government did everything to prevent cooperation between different Zemstva, a common spirit naturally produced a common program. In the forefront was rightly put statistical work. It is hard for foreigners to conceive how difficult it was in the Russia of this period to obtain statistics which could be trusted. The government itself was like an ostrich hiding itself from the facts; and the censorship was entirely in the hands of the government. Directed by two notable Moscow professors, Chuprov and Muromtsev, a host of volunteer researchers obtained data which furnished a sound basis for Zemstvo work.

The two most important items of every Zemstvo budget were schools and hospitals. The Zemstvo had to defend its schools against the attacks of the Minister of Education, of Pobedonostsev, and of the local governors and inspectors; but it could rely on the ardent desire of the peasants for instruction; in some parts of the province of Moscow the school was brought to within three miles of every village. The medical work had the same missionary character. There were practically no local hospitals; the writer was acquainted with a district of the size of an English county served only by two doctors. Hospitals were founded in the various districts, and the provincial Zemstvo completed the system by taking care of the outlying parts. The hospitals sent up country first-aid points under *felshers*, or medical assistants, with a small but carefully picked stock of instruments for the more common needs. Here it was not at first easy to win the peasants' confidence, but the rapidly growing attendance of out-patients at the hospitals testified to the progress made; and ultimately these young doctors or school teachers of both sexes, especially the women, became trusted advisers of those whom they served. Medical work had first of all to aim at the prevention of infant mortality; next the peasants had to be taught to observe ordinary precautions of health; only after that could attention be given to special problems. As time went on, epidemics were combated by bacteriological stations in remote parts of the country; and frequently the Zemstvo would send its doctors to Europe, for instance to the Pasteur Institute at Paris, for the study of problems which had a local importance. The Zemstvo of Samara, in a campaign lasting many years and marked at times by great reverses, ultimately succeeded in almost entirely driving out a number of epidemics which entered from neighbouring Asia. The Zemstvo of Tver founded the first "open door" hospital for lunatics, depending on a regime of kindness from which the patients would never wish to escape; so successful was this experiment that the same principle was introduced in a large asylum at the gates of Moscow. The Zemstvo of Vyatka, a province with an almost exclusively peasant population, was one of the most successful in Russia. Tver was the first to introduce agricultural experts to advise the peasants how to make the best use of their holdings: this item of the Zemstvo budget was cancelled by the Governor of Tver, and on the protest of the Zemstvo concerned, its executive was replaced by one nominated by the crown.

Close to the very beginning of this movement Alexander III died (November 1, 1894). This marks a division in the period which we are considering. The difference was not in any change of government policy; it was that something which had been present during the life of Alexander III now dropped out. An autocracy, to be real, presupposes will power in the sovereign. Alexander was a narrow, obstinate man, but he had purpose and the will to carry things through. Nicholas II had been brought up in fear and respect of his father; and a monopoly of will in the sovereign is not the best way to train will power in his heir. Nicholas had a conquering personal charm, the source of which was an extreme delicacy of thought, almost feminine in kind; but he was hopelessly weak. The plan of his education was of his father's making, and was practical; but one of his tutors, Pobedonostsev, complained that he could know little of his pupil's ability because he was not expected to put him any questions. In 1890 he was sent on a journey of education to Greece, Egypt, India, Indo-China, and Japan, returning through Siberia; this gave him a bias towards imperial expansion eastward; Prince Ukhtomsky, who accompanied him, wrote a book in which he developed this idea into a whole creed. In May 1891, Nicholas was nearly killed by a Japanese fanatic, and was only saved by his cousin, Prince George of Greece. In Vladivostok he laid the first stone of the terminus of the Trans-Siberian Railway. Alexander III, rebuffed in Europe, had done everything to develop Russia's Asiatic power, and this was a heritage which he left to his son.

Nicholas had fallen in love with Princess Alix of Hesse Darmstadt, whose eldest sister Elizabeth was already married to his uncle, the Grand Duke Sergius. The Princess, who was deeply religious and even mystical, refused to go through a purely nominal conversion to the Orthodox Church, but on examination adopted it not only with sincerity but with fervour. This delay deferred the marriage; but Alexander III, when on his deathbed, persuaded her to come to Livadia; her first appearance before the Russian people was in his funeral procession. The marriage took place on December 7, 1894.

Nicholas on his accession declared that he would "follow his father in everything." In January 1895, among the congratulatory addresses from all public bodies on his marriage, he received one from the Zemstvo of Tver drafted under the influence of F. Rodichev. "At the beginning of his service to the welfare of his people," it dared to "hope that the voice of the people and the expression of its desires would be listened to," "that the law will henceforward be respected and obeyed not only by the nation, but also by the representatives of the authority that rules it," and that law would stand "above the changing views of the individual instruments of the supreme power." Nicholas did not at once see any harm in this pronouncement, but he was strongly taken in hand by Pobedonostsev, and in his reply he spoke of "senseless dreams as to the participation of the Zemstva in the general direction of the internal affairs of the State," and he declared for "an unswerving adherence to the principle of autocracy." Rodichev was not admitted to the reception, and was forbidden to live in St. Petersburg.

This was taken by revolutionaries abroad as a direct challenge, and from this date they worked with greater activity. Some of those who derived from the militant group of the Will of the People set about the organization of a Socialist Revolutionary Party, quite distinct from the Social Democrats and more in consonance with the earlier traditions of the opposition to the government. The S. R.'s, as they were called to distinguish them from the S. D.'s, concentrated their attention not on the workmen but on the peasantry, from contact with whom they derived as much as they gave, including a strong impress of Russian, as distinct from international, patriotism. The S. R.'s, who were soon far more numerous than the S. D.'s, and were much less hampered by central instructions and organization, found abundant opportunities for spreading their views in posts in the service of the Zemstva. They soon became *par excellence* the peasants' Revolutionary Party, and their socialism amounted to little more than the claim that all the land should belong to the peasantry. As the conditions of their work demanded, most of them were individualists of ready resource; and their mentality, though more daring and unscrupulous, was closely akin to that of advanced English Radicals.

Nicholas II was almost entirely deficient in will. Alexander had been his own Prime Minister; Nicholas had no Prime Minister at all. He was by no means deficient in personal courage, but his courage was that of a fatalist. He lived and died in an atmosphere of fatality. At his coronation the chain of one of the oldest Orders of the Empire fell broken to the ground. The distribution of kerchiefs, cups, and roubles arranged on the Hodynka field outside Moscow, where 300,000 persons were collected, owing to incompetent management by conflicting authorities, resulted in a crush in which probably a thousand persons perished. The inquiry which followed was a signal for the beginning of an endless war of intrigues which was to last through the whole reign.

Alexander had conscientiously chosen his own ministers. Nicholas often took them from the recommendation of the last person who had been in his cabinet. When he intended to dismiss them, he did not dare to hurt their feelings by telling them so; and they often received their *congé* unexpectedly by messenger or post, or even through the newspapers, just when their last audience had convinced them that they were securely in power. This weakness and duplicity threw the door open to every kind of ministerial or extra-ministerial manœuvre.

His two first Foreign Ministers, Count Lobanov-Rostovsky and Count Muravyev, were both unexpected appointments. To the Interior he appointed Goremykin, who at an earlier time had had slightly Liberal leanings. Witte was retained for Finance, but his lack of principle and his vulgarity, coupled with his frankness, soon obtained for him the strong dislike of the Emperor and the bitter hostility of the Empress. Goremykin, in view of the new Zemstvo movement, proposed to extend this elective institution to the western provinces where at present the Zemstva were nominated by the government, and Witte, seeing in this measure a dangerous Liberalism, succeeded in driving Goremykin from office. Witte at this time wrote an interesting memorandum in which he put the alternative that either the Zemstva must be crushed or a national assembly would become inevitable. He was able to put in his own candidate, a reactionary, Sipyagin, in place of Goremykin; but his unpopularity at Court gave openings to the opportunist Plehve and, upon Sipyagin's assassination in 1902, Plehve succeeded to the post of Minister of the Interior.

Alexander III had throughout been sincerely interested in the welfare of the peasantry. Nicholas shortly after his accession had to deal with the question of migration to Siberia. This was brought before him by Goremykin, who desired to put a check on the movement. Nicholas pertinently asked for figures, and on seeing in what numbers the peasants were going to Siberia said that it was evidently a natural process and ought not to be hampered but assisted. From this time, then, the government did as much to foster migration as it had previously done to prevent it. Free passes for the journey were given to *hodoki* and even to emigrating parties; agents helped to establish them in their new homes; temporary remissions of taxes were granted to them. But the government had no sooner put its hand to this work than it spoilt it. Earlier it took men of stout hearts and strong constitutions to make their way past the law to Siberia; now any loafer was glad to avail himself of the government's favours.

In general, the condition of the peasants was such as to inspire the greatest anxieties. The impoverishment was greatest of all at the very centre of European Russia, where they had no side earnings and little enterprise to utilize their small allotments. Various government commissions investigated the question between 1896 and 1902, such as the semiofficial congress on agriculture under Prince Shcherbatov in 1894, and others on the decay of cottage industries and the prevalence of fires. These served indirectly as an occasion for organizing cooperation between different Zemstva, an object which, as we know, was deeply suspect to the government. The chairman of the Executive of the Moscow Zemstvo, Dmitry Shipov, assisted by able helpers of various shades of political thought, had made Moscow a model for other Zemstva. Zemstvo chairmen were summoned to the semiofficial congresses which have just been mentioned, and Shipov arranged private conferences between them, so that at the congresses they should come out for a common program on economic needs. His conference of June 1902 was attended by some sixty chairmen. This conference, without raising any specific political proposals, already passed beyond the limits of purely economic needs. It called attention to the inequalities of civil rights, the hindrances to education, the limitations imposed upon the Zemstva, the defects of the financial policy and the need of a free press. In May 1903 the Zemstvo men agreed that all laws on local questions ought first to be submitted for discussion to the Zemstva, and that representatives elected by them ought to take part in the drafting of such laws.

Witte, hard put to it in his contest with Plehve, decided to court the support of the Zemstva. As Minister of Finance, he arranged for local conferences everywhere on "the needs of the agricultural industry," by which he of course encroached on the domains of other ministers. In Witte's official conferences the Zemstva, as such, were called to play an important part: sometimes the members of their Executive, and in some districts the whole of the Zemstvo Assembly. A common program recommended by Shipov's private conference was circulated in manuscript, and in one Zemstvo after another the same criticisms were made and the same demands were put forward. Plehve sent stern instructions to the official presidents of the conferences; in some places free discussion was prevented and in others the proceedings were hushed up. Yet in the end, while 180 committees were prepared to mark time, 181 declared for enlightened if conservative reform, and 418 pronounced for more drastic changes in the existing system; many committees asked for freedom of the press, inviolability of person, and a national assembly; outspoken protests against administrative abuses came from Kostroma, Tambov, Harkov, Sudzha, and especially Voronezh. Witte tried to use these results against the Minister of the Interior, but Plevhe proved too strong for him. Witte had also lost ground with the Emperor by his opposition to the policy of aggression in the Far East. He was suddenly deprived of the Ministry of Finance, and appointed to the more or less honorary post of President of the Committee of Ministers (August 29, 1903). Plehve soon brought Witte's committees to a stop. The leaders of the Zemstva, even the wise Conservative Count Heyden, received the Emperor's formal reprimand. When Shipov was again re-elected as chairman of the Moscow Zemstvo Executive, Plehve arbitrarily cancelled his election.

The Liberal movement now went beyond the limits of the Zemstva, and was becoming both more political and more definite. A group of young men of high birth, known as a *Beseda* (*Conversation*) gave a lead in political discussion, and several notable professional men were in close touch with the older Zemstvo Liberals—in particular Professor Paul Milyukov, an energetic political tactician, and Professor Peter

Struve, a brilliant political thinker, who beginning as a Marxist soon became the principal spokesman of intelligent Liberalism. Struve edited, first in Stuttgart and then in Paris, a periodical entitled *Osvobozhdenie*, which was smuggled into Russia and widely read. The supporters of this magazine included many prominent men who were known as Liberators, and established small but influential groups in several provinces.

Plehve was now in almost unlimited power. His devotion to the cause of reaction does not seem to have sprung from any conviction, but it was none the less complete. He was the true author of the innumerable regulations of this period directed against the Jews; he was almost openly the authorizer of pogroms (or armed attacks) upon them. Acute peasant disturbances had broken out in the south, and when the Governor of Harkov was criticized for ordering unruly peasants to be flogged, Plehve paid him a special visit of approval. He also supported the mischievous policy of oppression of the Armenians in the Caucasus. The strangest part of his program was associated with the name of Zuvatov. This was a police officer at Moscow; he formed the peculiar design of securing the support of the factory workers for the government by organizing them under police protection against the interests of their employers. Deluded by Zubatov, certain professors of Moscow University took part in educational work under his auspices, and clubs, savings banks, and other institutions were founded for the workers, who were glad enough to utilize any machinery which would enable them to meet each other. This strange intrigue became serious when Dr. Shayevich, an agent of Zubatov, organized a great strike at Odessa. As the workers' movement developed, it passed out of the control of the police and under that of socialist propagandists. One of the principal agents of Zubatov was Father Gapon.

In Plehve's time black reaction reigned everywhere. A group of students were not allowed to walk down the street together. Espionage raged everywhere in the universities and the schools. To invite any more than the smallest party to their houses, dwellers in St. Petersburg had to ask the written permission of the police. Witte told his successful rival that his assassination was inevitable. Plehve declared that the country was on the verge of revolution, and that the one way to avert it was a "small victorious war."

CHAPTER XXII

Far East Policy and Japanese War

[*1881–1905*]

We must return to the beginning of the period covered in the last chapter and trace its foreign policy. It has the same mentality as the home policy, and the same fatal break in the middle when on the accession of Nicholas the most vital public affairs become the sport of ministerial intrigue and of casual adventurers. The home policy and the foreign policy are part and parcel of each other.

Rebuffed in Europe after a victorious war by an ignominious treaty enforced by noncombatant powers, Russia under Alexander III sulked. This headstrong man, faced by a hostile Europe and a revolutionary Russia, put the greatest restraint on himself to recover absolute authority at home and to nurse the enormous potential resources of his State into a condition in which it could be indifferent to European hostility. This sulking attitude, in the official creed of Pobedonostsev, became a theory of Russia's apartness from the rest of the world, of her mission in Asia, of the inward rottenness of Western civilization and political ideas, and of the danger for Russia of any contact with them. This conception, we remember, was endorsed by the greatest statesman of the time, Bismarck, who had every interest in seeing Russia turn her back upon Europe and in particular upon the Balkans. "Russia," he said, "has nothing to do in the West; she only contracts Nihilism and other diseases; her mission is in Asia; there she stands for civilization."

In Pobedonostsev's sphere, that of religious affairs, everything was done in this period to enforce the official Orthodoxy, not merely on Russian priests or on thinkers such as Leo Tolstoy, not only on dissentients like the Uniats, but on the Lutherans in the Baltics, on the Jews, and even on the Mussulmans. Uniat persecution had been practised under Alexander II, with the result that families which had for generations held firm to the essence of the Orthodox faith and ceremonies, leaving to the Pope no more fruit of the bargain of the Unia than a nominal recognition of his headship, were now driven into the Latin confession. Their marriages in Roman Catholic churches were not recognized by the Russian government as marriages at all. In the reign of Nicholas II, the church property of the Armenian Christians was confiscated by the government. The Kalmyks of the frontiers of Asia and the Buryats at the extremity of Siberia saw their places of worship closed. It was the same with the Mussulmans in general, of whom missionaries with the government backing attempted what was practically a forcible conversion.

This unifying policy weighed equally heavily on nationality. The distinctiveness of the Ukraine had been an object of attack in the reactionary period of the reign of Alexander II; but here the government was dealing with little more than a literary movement. At this time, its principal significance was that it suggested to German politicians a weapon for disintegrating the Russian power. Poland, after the rising of 1863 had· been suppressed, long remained under severe repression, which aimed at hardly anything short of the extirpation of Polish nationality. Warsaw University had been completely Russianized, and Poles were taught their own literature in Russian; in 1885 Russian was introduced into primary schools as the language of teaching; Polish railway servants were sent to serve in other parts of the empire; in 1885 Poles were forbidden to buy land in Lithuania or Volhynia, where they had constituted the majority of the gentry; in 1887 foreigners were forbidden to acquire land in the frontier provinces, and on the death of foreign landowners their estates were to be forcibly sold; this was a measure of precaution against German penetration. Nicholas II was not personally hostile to the Poles. He paid a visit to Warsaw in 1896, was well received, and made a friendly speech on Polish loyalty. The Poles in his reign had certain ties with the Russian Court, and some of the greater gentry were for a policy of conciliation. However, in its substantial details the iniquitous regime of repression remained.

After the failure of the rising of 1863 Polish public thought underwent profound changes. Romanticism gave place to positivism, and a notable thinker, Swietochowski, called for spadework, to recreate from the bottom the bases of Polish nationality, whatever might be the political conditions imposed by superior force. Later, between those who sought to conciliate the Russian government and the champions of socialism, grew up the Party of National Democrats organized with remarkable political ability by a man of humble origin, Roman Dmowski. It was Dmowski's motto that, though Poland was divided, the

Polish people was indivisible; his program was based on the tenacity of the Polish language and of Polish peasant land-tenure (despite such persistent attacks as were now made on it by Prussian legislation), and he and his fellow-thinkers were able to give expression to the persistent vitality of his nation, not only in Russian Poland but in the partitionments of Germany and Austria. Also the beginnings of a big industry in Poland, marked by the growth of a greater Warsaw and the mushroom-like rise of the cotton factories of Lodz, began to supply that middle class which had been so painfully lacking in Polish history, and strongly predisposed the public mind toward application, caution, and common sense. In Poland, as in Russia during this period, the central interest of literature was the peasantry. Assisted by regular seasonal migrations to neighbouring Prussia, or even permanently to America, it made remarkable progress. Industrially the position of Russian Poland inside the Russian Empire was very advantageous, with a Chinese wall of protectionism separating it from the competition of central and western Europe and a huge hinterland of agricultural markets extending as far as the Pacific; and the keen activity of Polish technicians tended to give them inside this empire a position not unlike that of the Scots in the empire of Great Britain. Meanwhile, that the national spirit was anything but dead was testified not only by the National Democrats, but by the party of Polish Socialists, which was marked by a very strong tinge of patriotism.

Under Alexander III the German barons of the Baltic were a special object of attack. This was one of the most civilized parts of the empire; the ground of offence was that its civilization was German. On the foundation of the German Empire in 1871, irresponsible voices in Germany began to ask for these "lost provinces." In reply, from 1882 Russian propagandists, backed by the government, excited the native population of Ests and Letts against their German masters. Manors were attacked and forests were burned, but the Russian government gave no protection and spoke only of "fusion between the provinces of our common country." The government even favoured the revival of the Estonian and Lettish languages. This, however, was only to pave the way for the introduction of Russian, which from 1885 was imposed for all official acts and from 1889 was the spoken language of the administration. The permission of Pobedonostsev was required for the opening of each new Lutheran church; from 1885 persons were forbidden to leave the Orthodox Church, while priests were rewarded with official Russian decorations for conversions of Lutherans. From 1886 all the schools were put under the direct control of the repressive Russian Ministry of Education; in 1887 Russian was introduced as the language of teaching into the German University of Dorpat, and later into primary schools. In 1888 sixty Lutheran pastors were removed for trying to reconvert those who had been brought into the Orthodox Church. The special law courts of these provinces were abolished; the mayors were nominated by the government; and the press was put under the Russian censorship. The accession of Nicholas here too brought relief. In 1895 he received a petition for the restoration of the German church schools and language and showed himself not at all unfriendly to the German barons, who thus recovered much of their influence at Court.

Much heavier sufferers were the Jews. In the first years of Alexander III, Count Ignatyev was even lax towards pogroms, and a thousand Jewish houses were sacked in Balta with eight killed and two hundred wounded. Count D. Tolstoy was correct in this matter, but legislation against the Jews proceeded apace. The majority of the Jewish population of the empire was in Poland and the western provinces. From 1881 these were declared to be the place of Jewish settlement; and Jews, except under special regulations, were not allowed to live elsewhere. In 1888 a brutal government order demanded that all Jews should return to the villages in which they had lived six years earlier. Jews needed police permission to employ Christians; Jews were dismissed in 1886 from the judicial service and were excluded from all administrative posts and from many of the professions; only 10 per cent of Jews were allowed even in the universities of their area, and only 5 per cent in St. Petersburg and Moscow; in 1887 the same restriction was applied to secondary schools; in 1888 all Jews in receipt of government bursaries were registered as Orthodox. Special taxes, for instance, on the synagogue and on Jewish meat, were imposed for the upkeep of special schools for the Jews, but by no means all of this money reached its destination. Jews were forbidden to trade on Sunday. Children were baptized against the wishes of their parents; Jews who became Orthodox were given at request a free divorce.

These regulations in every case did not pass through the Council of State, which even in this period would have subjected them to frank criticism. They were adopted as temporary rules by the Committee of Ministers, or even only issued as dispositions of a given Minister. They offended world opinion, and in particular complicated all relations of the Russian government with the United States of America. They could not possibly achieve their purpose: as Witte, who was always consistent on this subject, put it, it was impossible to drown all the Jews. What they did achieve, was entirely to corrupt the police who had to administer them. In the phrase of the time, water could not be stopped from flowing, and Jews were always succeeding in evading the rules, which could easily be overridden by bribing the police and obtaining the necessary license.

For the Jews no remission came with the accession of Nicholas, whose attitude to them was throughout one of extreme dislike. The Jewish pale of settlement was therefore restricted; the number of Jews admitted to schools and universities was reduced; Jews might not acquire any real estate outside towns, and were thus precluded from engaging in agriculture except by leasing. The bitterest oppressor of the Jews was Plehve; in 1903 he promoted a pogrom in Kishinev, with the result that the next Governor, Prince Urusov, protested and resigned. Military authorities also complained of the demoralizing effect on their troops of witnessing armed attacks on the Jews without being allowed by the civil authorities to intervene.

Finland did not suffer under Alexander III. The original "Constitutions" guaranteed to the Finns on their annexation in 1809 were confirmed in 1872 and again by Alexander III on his accession in 1881. For him the question was one not of agreement but of honour; and the Finns on their side had behaved very correctly. Their rights were extensive; they had their own flag, army, navy, customs, posts, and railways. They had a great measure of local government: their own Senate (or Cabinet), their Diet with four Estates, their own budget, public debt, law courts, schools, and university. The Emperor had here the title of Grand Duke, and their contribution was a yearly payment of 250,000 marks made to him.

These rights were anything but agreeable to a reactionary Russian government. The Finnish frontier began at a trifling distance from St. Petersburg; and the Finnish Gulf had the greatest strategical importance for the defence of the Russian capital. The Finnish rights were also a challenge to Russians, who felt themselves to be politically in an inferior position: so that Finland tended to become a kind of barometer of Liberalism in Russia, and Finnish rights were always in danger in a period of Russian reaction. Meanwhile the Finns, in a period when small nations were everywhere working for self-determination, expected these rights to be not diminished but extended; there was now a strong movement for the development of the Finnish language and of Finnish culture.

Alexander III asked only for a union of currency, customs, and postal service, which the Diet was unwilling to grant. The Finns' turn for repression came under Nicholas II. They were hostile to the use of the Russian language in schools and administration, and wished that all the officers in their militia should be Finns. On the other hand, the Russian War Minister Kuropatkin demanded a closer military union. He wished to send the Finnish recruits to serve in Russian regiments, and to extend their period of service from five years to eighteen. In 1899 an ordinance of the Emperor gave to the Russian government a supervision of all laws of any interest to both countries; this the Finnish official journal refused to publish, and the Senate claimed the exclusion of matters reserved by the Finnish Constitution. A new form of oath for Finns was met with passive resistance; a big delegation, sent to Nicholas, was not received. The Finns now worked hard to arouse interest in their cause throughout Europe. The Governor General Bobrikov went on with his unifying policy, and was assassinated in 1904.

Under Nicholas II, the mountaineer population of the Caucasus also suffered from severe repression. Here the viceroy Prince G. Golitysn, a man of little judgment or ability, tried to gratify the reactionary forces prevailing at the Russian Court by extensive interference with local rights and with religion, which led to an attempt on his life. He was superseded by Count Vorontsov-Dashkov, a wise administrator who was successful in restoring harmony among the various races of the Caucasus and reconciling them to Russian rule.

This wholesale campaign against subject nationalities raised an effective barrier between Russia and Europe. Two foreign policies were possible to Russia: either the defence of Slavonic interests in the Balkans or imperial advance through Asia. The first of these had the sympathies of all sections of the Russian people and could not be achieved without them; it was not a mere coincidence that the reforming Emperor Alexander II had also attempted the emancipation of the Balkans; on the other hand any rebuff on the side of Europe, such as that of the Crimean War, had led to an extension of Russian power in Asia.

The ideals of nationality, which were so important a product of the French Revolution, were by this time taking effect in national movements in Bohemia and in Jugoslavia. The Balkan States by a gradual process, interrupted by the conflicts of European jealousies, were obtaining their emancipation from Turkey; and as they did so, they became more and more jealous of domination from any other side and determined to work out their own salvation. Bulgaria owed her liberation directly to Russian arms. But the Treaty of San Stefano which was to give her access to the Ægean had been upset by Europe, and Russia's triumph had been made the occasion of her humiliation. The policy of Alexander III towards Bulgaria was that of a bear with a sore head. The new Prince of Bulgaria, Alexander of Battenberg, had to deal with incessant Russian intrigues aiming at a complete domination of his country, in spite of the European guarantees against any Russian protectorate. In 1881 he dissolved his Chamber, and at the new elections obtained an emphatic approval of his independence; he dismissed the Russian officers in his army. In 1884, by speedy action, Eastern Rumelia was united to Bulgaria. Turkey took no steps to resist this, but the Serbs, egged on by Austria, entered Bulgaria. The Prince, though at first repulsed, routed them at Slivitsa and followed them into Serbia. The Sultan appointed him Governor General of Eastern Rumelia (1885). Russian hostility and intrigues continued; and in August 1886, the Prince was seized in his palace, forced to abdicate, and conveyed through Russia to Austria. A new government was set up under direct Russian influence, but was overthrown by the army; and the Prince was begged to return. He arrived on August 29, but in face of the relentless hostility of the Tsar he abdicated finally. Stambulov, who was the chief force in the regency, continued to deal vigorously with Russian plots. On Austrian advice, he established Ferdinand of Koburg on the throne. Russian influence prevented Turkey from recognizing Ferdinand, and continued to foment plots and assassinations ending with the public murder of Stambulov in 1895. Ferdinand took no vengeance on the conspirators, and made his peace with Nicholas II. Roumania, unpleasantly close to Russia, gravitated toward the Central Powers. Austrian influence prevailed with King Milan in Serbia, and after his abdication (1889), scandals, domestic and political, led to the assassination of his son Alexander in 1903. At one time Alexander III described the Prince of Montenegro as his only friend in Europe.

Thus in the Balkans the Tsar's angry and reckless conduct not only greatly increased the suspicions of Europe, but prevented any kind of confidence of the Balkan Slavs in Russia's good intentions. This, combined with the way in which the Russian government was treating the Poles, made any Slavonic policy impossible for Russia. Under Nicholas II the Russian government relaxed all interest on this side. There was one last strange episode, only little known. Witte tells how, when the question of Crete led to war between Greece and Turkey, Nicholas II sanctioned a mad intrigue by which his ambassador Nelidov was to create an "incident" in Constantinople; Nelidov was then to send a conspirative telegram through London, on the receipt of which in Russia a flotilla with troops was to sail from Odessa and attempt to seize the Straits. Witte and Pobedonostsev strenuously opposed this plan and Nicholas was induced to change his mind, but the episode throws a lurid light on the inconsequence, the dishonesty, and the futility of Russian policy during his reign.

On one important side Alexander, and Nicholas after him, opened a new era of Russian policy in Europe, though with many reticences and reservations. The foundation of the Third French Republic in 1870 did not please the Russian government, and there were incidents connected with Russian revolutionaries in France which made relations difficult. However, Russia was smarting from the Treaty of Berlin, and Bismarck was helping to advance Austrian influence in the Balkans. Relations with Germany were more than strained by the question of the Turkish frontier at Novi-Bazar, and a sharp exchange of dispatches seems to have led Bismarck to speak of a German mobilization; in 1879–80 he allied his country separately both with Austria and with Russia, keeping both alliances secret. Alexander II visited William I in 1881, and though Todleben was sent to develop the defences of Russian Poland, the alliance of the three Emperors was renewed for three years in 1884; Alexander refused to accept a clause by which the third Power was to remain neutral if the two others were at war with an outside Power. In January 1883 was founded the Triple Alliance of Germany, Austria, and Italy, which was renewed on March 13, 1887. In the same month Austria promoted the accession of Ferdinand of Koburg in Bulgaria. Bismarck's attitude toward France had become provocative in the extreme, and during the frontier incident of Schnaebelé provoked in turn a letter of remonstrance from Alexander to William I (April 1887). Throughout this period the Russian military preparations, which were of a defensive character, were directed against Germany. In 1887 France took up with alacrity a loan of 500 million francs to Russia; this was followed by several other large loans in 1889–91; the subscriptions were covered with enthusiasm by the French public. In 1890 the French and Russian military staffs conferred on questions of defence. In July 1891, Alexander III welcomed a French fleet at Kronstadt; the Russian fleet was rapturously received at Cherbourg and Toulon (1892–3). A commercial treaty was signed in June 1893; its significance was accentuated by the tariff war proceeding at this very time between

Russia and Germany. Russia's need of capital gave a strong argument
to the French government, and at the close of 1893, an alliance was
secretly concluded between the two countries. Nicholas II and President
Faure exchanged visits (1896–7), and for the first time, the existence
of the alliance was openly acknowledged (August 22, 1897). Though
Nicholas was too unstable to maintain all the reservations of Alexander
III, the alliance was still on both sides very circumspect in character,
especially in view of the sharp contrast between the two systems of government; it represented little more than a commercial entente and a
mutual insurance against common dangers.

William II of Germany strained every effort to counteract Russia's
friendship with France. The exchange of personal military attachés between the two Emperors enabled them to communicate regularly, apart
from their respective foreign offices, and of this William took full advantage. Nicholas, who was well aware of his own weakness, resented
though he often did not resist, the persistent efforts of William to exploit it. Nicholas was vain and easily captivated by any scheme which
was facile and grandiose. It was the constant policy of William to
flatter him by encouraging him to resist any limitation of his autocratic
power, and by offering him the dazzling perspective of empire in the
East; visiting the Russian naval manœuvres in 1902, he flashed the farewell message: "The Admiral of the Atlantic greets the Admiral of the
Pacific." Witte was early courted by William II, who expounded to him
a scheme by which the greater continental powers should draw closer
together and America should be isolated from Europe; on Witte's dissent, he proposed as the common object the isolation of England; on
this footing the two men agreed.

In 1898 the War Minister Kuropatkin learned that Austria was improving her artillery at a moment when Russia was unable to follow her
example. Witte, who was all for peace, suggested an initiative for the
stopping of armaments all round. This was adopted by Nicholas in his
invitation to a general Conference. The Conference met at the Hague
on August 24, 1898, and at least concentrated European attention on
the dangers which threatened peace. Detailed proposals were agreed
upon, with the object of limiting the horrors of war, and a permanent
court of arbitration was set up.

What we have seen, in Russia's European policy, is muddle and
intrigue followed by negation. The Balkans are at last left to themselves;
Russia has a somewhat hesitating alliance with France, of which the
realities are commerce and loans; but she has by no means passed out

of the orbit of German influence. On the German side, policy is inspired by a clear enough idea—that Russia should remain autocratic and turn eastward.

Mention has been made of the vast acquisitions of Russia in central Asia under Alexander II; under Alexander III a filibusterer, Ashinov, nearly disturbed relations with France by a reckless raid on Abyssinia, and this adventure was later continued in the intrigues of a charlatan, Leontyev. In July 1882, England established a protectorate over Egypt, and in 1885 conquered Burma. In 1884 Merv, which was 140 miles from Herat, did homage to Russia, and Persia ceded Serakhs. Katkov spoke of the Indus and Himalayas as the final British frontier; an expedition of Komarov on the northwest frontier of Afghanistan led to a mixed frontier commission, at which, however, the Russians did not appear; Afghan troops occupied Penjdeh, commanding Komarov's camp; they attacked him on March 30, 1885, but were routed with the loss of their guns; Gladstone demanded a war credit from Parliament, but Penjdeh and the Zulfikar Pass were ultimately allowed to pass into the possession of Russia; further Russian claims were conceded by England in 1887. In 1888 disputes took place between the two countries as to the navigation of the river Karun in Persia. In 1891 a Russian expedition appeared on the Pamir, claiming that it came on the invitation of the mountaineers; Afghan troops were defeated. Meanwhile General Annenkov ably constructed a Transcaspian Railway to Bukhara, Samarkand, and ultimately to Tashkend, and Transcaspia was annexed to the Governorship-General of Turkestan.

A similar post was established for the administration of the Amur. Migration to Siberia, as already mentioned, was throughout proceeding apace, and from the accession of Nicholas was fostered by the government. The Trans-Siberian Railway, begun in 1891, constructed in sections and at first with only a single line, ultimately brought the Pacific to within eight days' journey of Moscow. It passed along the south of Siberia through Omsk, Krasnoyarsk, and Irkutsk, but a great detour was necessary to make the circuit round Manchuria and reach Vladivostok; this of itself suggested a forward policy on this side. Siberia ceased to be known chiefly as a place of deportation for Russian prisoners, where distance alone made escape difficult.

Russia was all the time drawing nearer to one of the great storehouses of the world's population, the Chinese Empire. During the reactionary period of Alexander III and Nicholas II, more and more attention was given to this advance. Prince Ukhtomsky, who accompanied

Nicholas on his far eastern journey, pointed to the East as the proper sphere for Russian domination and called on young men of enterprise, instead of fuddling their heads with European constitutions, to come out into Asia and rule the world; this imperial advance of Russia was definitely adopted as a substitute for reform at home. Russia, in going eastward, was herself abandoning the West and trying to become more and more Eastern; the last of the great medieval autocracies tried to forget Europe by plunging into Asia. It was at this very time that an Asiatic power, Japan, was doing exactly the opposite—setting itself in every way to learn from Europe. The conflict between Russia and Japan, which with Russia's advance became more and more inevitable, was one in which Russia represented Asia and Japan the political ideals and principles of Europe.

To understand this contrast, it is only necessary to cite the oath taken by the Mikado in 1868 and to add that from that time forward Japan never departed from the principles which it contained. They were: "that a deliberate assembly shall be summoned and all measures shall be decided by public opinion; that high and low shall be of one mind in the conduct of the administration; that matters shall be so arranged that not only the government officials and Samurai (the aristocracy), but also common people may be able to obtain the objects of their desire, and the national mind may be completely satisfied; that the vicious and uncivilized customs of antiquity shall be broken through, and that the great principles of impartiality and justice . . . shall be the basis of action; that intellect and learning shall be sought out for the purpose of firmly establishing the foundations of the Empire." In a much more drastic form, it is the Tver address of 1895, described by Nicholas at his accession as "senseless dreams."

While Japan was still a closed country, the greatest of her future statesmen, Ito, worked his way to England on the *Pegasus* and made a study of European conditions; several times Prime Minister, he was able to realize his entire program. Class distinctions and disabilities were abolished; all offices and occupations were thrown open; both military service and education were made compulsory for all. After a great embassy to Western Europe in 1871, military instructors were introduced from France and naval instructors from England; educationalists were also sought for; Japan took from every country the best that it had to give. After great difficulties had been surmounted, treaties on a footing of equality were concluded with Mexico in 1888, with Portugal in 1892, with Great Britain in 1894, and with other countries by

June 1899. In 1869 was established a consultative national council drawn from the Samurai class; elective local councils were later introduced, and in 1880 the Emperor promised a Parliament; in 1885 was introduced a Cabinet of ten ministers; an edict of February 11, 1889, created a Constitution; elections took place next year; and in 1891 the promised Parliament assembled. It claimed constantly that the ministers should be responsible to itself, and the government frequently prorogued it and dissolved it; often it rejected the government's budgets; yet its first essays were satisfactory; all opposition to the government ceased at every time of national crisis.

The neighbouring kingdom of Korea had long remained closed to outside influences. China and Japan now contended for the predominance there, Japan standing for Western reforms and China opposing them. Crises arose between Japan and Korea in 1882, 1884, and 1894. The third of these led to war between China and Japan (1894–5). In this war the Japanese easily prevailed. They captured Seoul, took Assan and Ping Yeng, thoroughly defeated the Chinese fleet off the Yalu, and captured Kinchow, Talienwan, and ultimately Port Arthur; by a naval victory Ito captured Weh-Hai-Wei. The able Chinese statesman, Li-Hung Chang, was sent to treat at Shimonoseki; and on April 17, 1895, China ceded to Japan the Peninsula of Liao-Tung on which Port Arthur stands, with Formosa, the Pescadores, and a large indemnity; Weh-Hai-Wei was to be held till the treaty was carried out.

On the initiative of Nicholas II, Russia, Germany, and France did to the Treaty of Shimonoseki that which Europe had done to the Treaty of San Stefano in 1878; the Chinese indemnity was increased, but Japan was made to renounce all cessions of territory on the mainland. Here was the first realization of a "bloc" of the continental Powers of Europe, excluding England. At the same time Russia concluded a secret agreement by which she guaranteed China's territory on the mainland and obtained a concession to construct a railway through Manchuria to the coast. For the signature of this treaty, Witte secured a flying visit from Li-Hung Chang to Moscow during the coronation of Nicholas II (May 1895). The charlatan doctor, Badmayev, urged Nicholas to demand a railway to Pekin, but this project Witte defeated. The new East China Railway was to be entrusted not to the Russian government direct, but to a Bank created by it for the purpose; a special Russian police service was to administer the railway, and the property along the line might be acquired and controlled by the Company. Li-Hung Chang earnestly advised Witte never to push Russian influence further south of the main Siberian Railway. Russia obtained for China a loan which enabled her to pay her war indemnity.

In Korea, after the Sino-Japanese War, Russia took the place of China as the supporter of the reactionary party. The murder of the Queen, who acted with that party (October 8, 1895), led to a crisis between Russia and Japan, which ended by their both agreeing to maintain the independence of Korea (July 29). In 1898 was concluded a further agreement to make a fair division of the direction of commercial affairs and to keep there only an equal number of troops under the name of gendarmes (February 24). Shortly afterward Russia persuaded Korea to accept from her financial advisers and military instructors: the railway gauge of Korea was to be like the Russian; but she then agreed with Japan that each should act only in full consultation with the other (April 25, 1899).

By the treaty of 1896 (October 25 and December 29) China confirmed the concession of the East China Railway, together with a lease of a port in Shantung for fifteen years and the right to keep warships in the ports of the Lia-Tung Peninsula, a right which the Russians had already usurped. A new period opened for the unhappy Chinese in 1897. Feeling in China was at this time running very high against foreigners. This was in part due to the claims of Catholic missionaries, and in November 1897 two German missionaries were killed at a village in Shantung. Shortly before this William II had visited Nicholas and, while out on a drive, had asked him not to object to a German seizure of Kiao-Chow, and Nicholas against his better judgment had agreed. The Germans now entered Kiao-Chow, and imposed on China a treaty by which they obtained a ninety-nine years' lease of it, with mining and railway rights as well as a large indemnity (March 6, 1898). Nicholas, in spite of vigorous opposition from Witte and despite his own treaty guaranteeing the integrity of China, decided to occupy Port Arthur, demanding a similar lease of ninety-nine years. The Dowager Empress of China had put such a value on the Treaty of Integrity that she kept it in her bedroom; Chinese exasperation was extreme. By bribing Li-Hung Chang, Witte, though opposed to the whole of this policy, secured the signature of the cession of Port Arthur for twenty-five years on March 27, 1898. England followed suit by demanding a lease of Weh-Hai-Wei. France obtained a sphere of influence in Kwang Chow; Italy made similar demands but was rebuffed.

Li-Hung Chang and others concerned with this second Russo-Chinese Treaty were ruined politically by it. The Emperor of China since the Japanese War had been in favour of reform, but the Dowager Empress assumed the power in 1898, and the Emperor was compelled to reverse his liberal decrees. A patriotic society of Boxers, which drilled volunteers, organized a vehement movement against all "foreign devils." Christians were massacred and Boxer influence prevailed in Pekin itself, the government in the end openly supporting it (May 1900). To relieve the foreigners in Pekin, in June Admiral Seymour marched up with a mixed force from the coast, but had to retire to Tientsin. The Chinese troops joined the Boxers, and the foreign legations in Pekin were besieged. The European Powers and Japan now joined hands in a second relief expedition. In July 1900 a Russian and Japanese force took Tientsin, and in August the allies entered Pekin, where the Russians distinguished themselves by disgraceful looting. The cession of Port Arthur was prolonged to a term of ninety-nine years. The town was connected by rail with the Trans-Siberian.

All this time the situation of the Russians in Manchuria was a difficult one. In 1901 Chichagov in command on the frontier at Blagoveschchensk could find no better safeguard for his security than to drive 4000 Chinese with bayonets into the river Amur. Russia continued to send more and more troops into Manchuria.

Russian policy was at this time directed by an adventurer Bezobrazov who, to the amazement of the ministers, was ultimately appointed Secretary of State and kept the control of Far Eastern policy in his hands. Bezobrazov's scheme was to disturb the existing agreement as to Korea by driving a wedge of Russian concessions into the country. The Russian Court, under cover of a cry of "Russia for the Russians," took an intimate part in the manipulation of trade, and other adventurers even worse than Bezobrazov obtained timber concessions on the Yalu. Admiral Alexeyev, a courtier without military or political experience, was appointed Viceroy of the Far East (July 1903). In April 1902, Russia had engaged to remove her troops from Manchuria, withdrawing them in two detachments with an interval of six months. The first detachment was withdrawn in October; but in April 1903 further withdrawals were deferred unless new Russian demands were complied with. China, however, supported by England, America, and Japan, refused; and Russia decided to compensate herself by further advance on the side of Korea.

Japanese diplomacy made every effort to come to an agreement. This was quite possible, if Russia would either evacuate Manchuria or leave Japan a similar free hand in Korea. In November 1901 Ito himself was sent to St. Petersburg. He was treated with indifference; answers to his communications were sometimes delayed a week on the most trifling pretext, and ultimately he left Russia in despair. Japan, to preclude any repetition of Shimonoseki, at once concluded an alliance on January 13, 1902, with England, by which, in the event of war between Russia and Japan, the entry of any third party on the side of Russia would be followed by that of England on the side of Japan. The Japanese continued to press for the evacuation of Manchuria according to treaty. Count Lamsdorf, the Russian Foreign Minister, was opposed to the policy of provocation and was supported by Witte; but Lamsdorf himself was kept in the dark, and it was rarely that any of the dispatches passed through his hands; Witte was dismissed from his Ministry in August 1903, largely because of his dissent from the Emperor's Far Eastern policy. The Japanese Minister Kurino gave a last and earnest warning, and left St. Petersburg on February 3, 1904. Three days later Japan, without declaration, began war.

On the Japanese side, army and navy had been kept in the closest contact with the progress of the diplomatic debate. Japan inevitably had at the outset a great military preponderance. She could put 150,000 men in line at once, and all gaps could be filled without delay. East of Lake Baikal, Russia had in all only 80,000 field troops with 23,000 garrison and 30,000 railway frontier guards. The Trans-Siberian, with its single line, which was not constructed for heavy traffic such as guns, had a gap of a hundred miles around the mountainous southern end of Lake Baikal; so that till April troops and stores had to cross the lake by sledges. The naval forces were more equal; Russia even had a preponderance of one man-of-war, though she was much weaker in the smaller craft.

For Japan it was essential to seize the command of the sea and to fight the war on the mainland; she therefore attacked at once at Chemulpho on February 8 and at Port Arthur on February 9. At Chemulpho, Admiral Uriu, after summoning the Russian cruisers *Koriets* and *Varyaga* which steamed out of harbour to meet his superior force, sent both of them to the bottom (February 9). By this he secured freedom for Japanese troops to disembark at a point well to the north of Korea, so that the possession of Korea, one of the chief objects in dispute, was at the outset decided in favour of Japan. So exact had been the Japanese calculations, both of diplomacy and of war, that these troops arrived at the very earliest moment after the breakup of the ice. They speedily marched northward to the Korean frontier on the river

Yalu, and the very first engagements on this side were fought with Korea as already the Japanese base. At Port Arthur Admiral Togo, launching his torpedo boats against the Russian fleet, damaged two men-of-war and one first-class cruiser. With reinforcements of the attack on the Japanese side, four more Russian ships were damaged, and all this at a cost of six killed and forty-five wounded. By subsequent attacks Togo tried to block the mouth of the harbour. The most distinguished admiral of Russia, Makarov, a man of humble origin with great qualities of vision and energy, was now in charge of the defence; but on April 13 in a bold sortie he was sunk with his flagship, the *Petropavlovsk*, just outside the harbour.

The First Japanese Army under Kuroki advanced on May 1 against the positions of General Zasulich west of the Yalu. Zasulich tried to hold a long extended line; and Kuroki, after a feint to the south of it near the sea, crossed the river in a mist higher up, thereby threatening to turn the Russians by their left wing and to cut off their retreat. Zasulich, who had had orders not to await an engagement, managed with difficulty to extricate his rear guard and retired northward into Manchuria. This first victory on land gave great confidence to the Japanese, and also helped them to obtain foreign loans.

The sea being for the present in Japanese hands, a Second Japanese Army under Oku, consisting of three divisions, was sent to invest Port Arthur. Oku took eight days landing on the peninsula some distance to the east of the fortress, against which he advanced on May 21. On the 26th he attacked General Fock, at the strongly entrenched neck of the Peninsula of Kwang-Tung; Fock, if he had made use of his resources, might have kept him at a distance; but only a portion of the Russian force was engaged, and a Japanese division, wading through water, threatened its left flank and brought it to retreat. On May 29 Oku had possession of Talien-wan (Dalny).

With Korea occupied and Port Arthur neutralized, the Japanese were now able to deal with the Russian main army under Kuropatkin. They advanced upon him from the coast northward in three columns: Kuroki came with his First Army from Korea; Oku advanced from Port Arthur, leaving Nogi with two divisions to continue the siege; and Kamamura in the middle with a single division helped to connect the two wings. As Minister of War, Kuropatkin had played an ambiguous part in the events leading up to the conflict. He had been all for the acquisition of Manchuria, in spite of the Integrity Treaty; he had always thrown in more and more troops, yet never enough for a war with Japan;

he was not one of the inner circle that backed the intrigue of Besobra-
zov; in fact, Plehve alone of the ministers was in that group. At the
beginning of the war, which Nicholas evidently thought he would win
easily, Admiral Alexeyev was made Commander-in-Chief, but as he had
no reputation whatever, was no soldier and only nominally a sailor, a
public outcry demanded Kuropatkin. Kuropatkin never had a complete
control; Witte seriously advised him to arrest Alexeyev; the Admiral had
far more influence at the Court, and his advice constantly ran counter
to Kuropatkin's. Like the rest of the infatuated group who expected to
dictate peace at once in Tokyo, he was for fighting the deciding battles
on the sea coast. This, as Kuropatkin knew, was out of the question. He
intended to retreat till the railway had given his army the superiority;
but his orders for retirement from the Yalu onward were often disobeyed, and his instructions were overruled from St. Petersburg. Nicholas II, with whom remained such control as there was, hesitated throughout and was never frank either with Kuropatkin or with Alexeyev.

Kuropatkin had wished to retreat to Harbin, but was overruled. He
waited therefore at Liao-Yang, the point of junction of various roads
coming from the south. As these roads were far apart and ran through
mountainous country, the Russians had the opportunity, if they advanced, of beating the Japanese in detail. Stackelberg was sent forward
to get in touch with Oku on the Japanese left, but was defeated by him
at Telissu and driven back on the main body; Keller on the eastern flank
made a good effort to delay Kuroki. On July 24 Oku attacked the Russian right, which withdrew, Kuroki meanwhile forcing back Keller.
Kuropatkin had by now superior forces and could have acted against
the comparatively weak Japanese centre, but he overrated its strength
and awaited an engagement at Liao-Yang. Here was fought a ten-day
battle (August 24 to September 3). Kuroki pushed in the Russian left,
and by August 31 had penetrated the Russian line. More than once
Kuropatkin sent reserves to this side, and ultimately made a good retreat, with hard fighting to the end; the Japanese losses greatly exceeded
the Russian.

Retreating behind the Sha-Ho, Kuropatkin had now 220,000 men
as against the Japanese 160,000, and on October 2 he announced an
offensive. He intended to hold the Japanese left and centre, and crush
Kuroki by an attack entrusted to Stackelberg; but after initial successes
the Russian left was again forced back, and Stackelberg like the rest fell
back to the Sha-Ho. Here, in a deadly struggle between the two in-
fantries, One Tree Hill was captured and recaptured and ultimately

held by the Russians. In this battle the Russian loss (32,300) greatly exceeded the Japanese.

Meanwhile the Japanese were besieging Port Arthur. Its commander Stössel was not only grossly incompetent but a peculator and later actually a traitor; but a heroic officer, Kondratenko, was in command of the engineers. Stössel, when ordered by Kuropatkin to leave Port Arthur, suppressed the order and remained; it was he who ordered the untimely retreat of Fock, before the Japanese had succeeded in investing the fortress. Two Japanese battleships were destroyed by mines. On June 12 the Russian squadron at Vladivostok came out, sank three Japanese transports and successfully returned to harbour. On the 23rd Witthoft, now in command of the fleet at Port Arthur, came out of harbour but speedily retired. On the 26th, Nogi took some of the outposts; he had captured the fortress in the Chinese War and was anxious to save time, in order to secure as soon as possible the base of the Japanese advance into Manchuria; on July 26, in a two days' attack, he turned the Russian line, and on August 6 he captured two small forts on the eastern side. On the 10th Witthoft came out again, and had nearly passed the Japanese line when he was killed and his ship damaged; with severe losses the Russians were driven back to harbour. On August 30 Nogi, after shelling for two days, started a general assault which was marked by the greatest bravery on both sides, but a sacrifice of 15,000 men gave him only two small forts; on September 19 the Japanese again attacked on the northern side, and from October 26 to 30 they made a general attack on the east.

The Baltic fleet of Russia was now dispatched under Admiral Rozhdestvensky to recover the naval preponderance. The Russian Admiralty was in great disorder, and no one who was in a position to judge anticipated any success from this expedition. On October 21 the Russians fired at night on the English fishing fleet on the Dogger Bank and proceeded down channel without stopping; the news aroused great anger in England, and it was only by the immediate and thorough satisfaction offered by the Russian Ambassador, Count Benckendorff, that the crisis was surmounted.

On November 26 Nogi again attacked Port Arthur on the east side without success. The next day he attacked a commanding hill on the northwest, which the Japanese won on December 5 with a loss of 9000 men. They now possessed a view of the harbour and town; they had undermined the eastern forts and were close to the western. On December 15 Kondratenko, the most vigorous defender of the fortress, died. In an assault which lasted from December 18 to 28, two of the eastern forts were taken; and on January 1 Stössel, without consulting a council of war, sent a white flag and surrendered the fortress; it still contained stores for three months and over two million rounds of ammunition. Port Arthur had cost the Russians half their garrison or 28,200 men, and the Japanese 57,780.

The fall of Port Arthur set 100,000 Japanese free to join the main army in Manchuria. The Russian transport, which throughout the war had been administered more efficiently than any other department, could not feed in winter any more Russian troops than were already gathered in Manchuria; and the Russian government, in view of the temper of the people, had preferred where possible to send to the front battalions of reservists. Kuropatkin had now 250,000 men divided into three armies under Grippenberg on the right, Kaulbars in the centre, and Linevich on the left; Oyama, in command of the Japanese armies, could muster 185,000. Kuropatkin, to delay the advance of Nogi from Port Arthur, sent Mishchenko with 6000 Cossacks to harass the Japanese rear. Mishchenko successfully turned the Japanese left, on January 12 approached Ying-Kow, and returned after destroying some part of the railway. Following on this move, Grippenberg on January 24 crossed the Hun-Ho on the ice and captured at Kokutai a point in the Japanese lines. Two days later he took but abandoned Sandepu, and continued next day to push Oku further back. Oku, however, was reinforced; and Grippenberg, in spite of his protests, could get no further help. He retired on the main body and, expressing his annoyance freely, was dismissed.

Kuropatkin again awaited the Japanese at Mukden and here followed a battle with fourteen days of fighting. The Russian left was attacked first, and Kuropatkin continued to send his reserves to that side; but on the other flank Nogi, with his troops from Port Arthur, crossed the Hun-Ho and threatened to envelop the Russian right wing. Kuropatkin reinforced his right, but began a retreat which he was only with difficulty able to carry out. Each side in this battle lost over 70,000 men. Kuropatkin resigned the command and was replaced by Linevich (February 23–March 14, 1905).

At last the Baltic fleet under Rozhdestvensky was nearing the seat of war. It had awaited at Madagascar the very ill-equipped and ill-manned squadron of Nebogatov, and on May 9 it appeared in the Sea of China. On paper the two fleets did not look very unequal, but there was every difference in their efficiency. Togo waited at Masampho till the Russians appeared on the early morning of May 27. Battle was joined at two o'clock off Tsushima. The Japanese, at a range of 7000 yards, steamed across the leading Russian ships and in three quarters of an hour put most of them out of action. The Russian fleet broke up; at night the Japanese sent out torpedo boats. The next day was taken up with the chase, and of the whole Russian force only two protected cruisers and two destroyers escaped to Vladivostok.

Japan had now secured the command of the sea, the possession of Korea and also a large part of Manchuria, so that all the original objects of the war were achieved. Militarily, Russia had everything to gain by its continuance. The Japanese had come near the end of their reserves both of men and money; an advance into the middle of Asia would have been without purpose. On the other hand, every Russian reverse had marked a new progress in the tide of indignation against the government which was swelling up in Russia, where the country was rapidly getting out of hand of the authorities. Nicholas II was persuaded to listen to a suggestion of peace coming from President Theodore Roosevelt, and unwillingly dispatched Witte to America to make the best terms that he could, excluding always the payment of any indemnity. Operations meanwhile continued; Japanese troops in northeast Korea threatened Vladivostok, while others occupied the island of Sakhalin and the mouth of the Amur. Witte conducted the negotiations with great skill; after three weeks he had secured a good deal of moral support in America, and this made it difficult for the Japanese to obtain further loans there for the continuance of the war. On August 29 Komura at last waived the question of indemnity and the Treaty of Portsmouth was concluded. Korea was to be a sphere of Japanese influence; Russia was to leave the Liao-Tung Peninsula and southern Manchuria, and to surrender half the island of Sakhalin.

Thus ended the Far Eastern adventure, which aimed at nothing less than establishing a Russian hegemony over Asia, including, as one of its authors, Prince Ukhtomsky, avowed, the expulsion of the British from India. Instead of this, an Asiatic power, only recently possessing a serious army, had robbed Russia of her ice-free port on the Pacific. The chief explanation of this contrast was given in the farewell message of Kuropatkin to his troops; he complained that men of independence, initiative and ability received no encouragement in the Russian army. "Japan has been victorious," wrote a foreign military critic, "because she has learned that war is a business, not merely of the soldier or of the sailor, but of the nation as a whole." The lesson of the Japanese War is to be read in the liberation movement in Russia. "The Japanese," said a Russian Liberal, "will not enter the Kremlin, but the Russians will." The triumph of the Japanese was the victory of a people against a government; and the shock which it gave, was to send a wave of national protest rolling back as far as the western frontier of Russia.

CHAPTER XXIII

The Liberation Movement

[*1904–12*]

THE JAPANESE WAR even from the start was distasteful to the great majority of Russians; the Zemstvo Liberals, however, who had thought of making a demonstration at this time, felt that the public mood would not be favourable to it. On July 28, 1904, Plehve, on his way to the Baltic station in Petrograd, was assassinated by a bomb thrown by a Socialist Revolutionary, Sazonov.

It was at this time that the Imperial couple had at last an answer to their incessant prayers, in the birth of a male heir to the throne, the Tsarevich Alexis. It was early discovered that he was subject to the hæmophilic tendency inherent in his mother's family. This meant that even a trivial incident might set up internal bleeding, which there was no known means of stopping.

The Emperor's choice of a successor to the reactionary Plehve was Prince Svyatopolk-Mirsky, who, as Governor of Vilna and in other posts, had won wide respect for his liberal attitude. Prince Mirsky without delay gave an audience to leading editors of the capital, in which he asked for the confidence of the public. This brought him a reprimand from the Emperor but a most enthusiastic response from the public; it led to a mood of general optimism and cordiality. On November 2 even the time-serving *Novoe Vremya* asked for civil freedom and an unfettered press. At a meeting in Paris in October, Liberals, Socialist Revolutionaries, and Poles discussed the possibilities of a forward movement. It would best be headed by the one elected authority in the country, the Zemstvo. Shipov was therefore urged to call a more representative and public conference, at which political as well as economic questions should be frankly discussed. Shipov was no advanced Liberal and his leadership was a guarantee of restraint and loyalty to the throne. On his side Prince Mirsky assented to the holding of a private conference, and even himself communicated its resolutions to the Emperor.

The Zemstvo Conference of November 19–22, 1904, unanimously asked for freedom of person, of conscience, of speech, of meeting, of press, of association, for equal civil rights for all independent of distinctions of class nationality or religion, for elective local government not based on any system of classes, for a wider Zemstvo franchise, for freedom of education, and in particular set out the reforms required for the peasants and the factory workers. On one point only, the eleventh, there was division of opinion. All agreed that an elective national assembly should be called without delay, but the majority required that this assembly should have a legislative authority, while Shipov with the minority would have been content that it should be consultative only.

The Emperor, after consultation with Witte and others, issued two pronouncements together. In one he called on the Zemstvo men to mind their own business and not to discuss political questions; in the other, he expressed his own intention of granting reforms, which were to be drafted in the various ministries; the request for a national assembly was not granted. Hereupon the professional class came forward in vigorous support of the Zemstva. Professional men, though precluded from political meetings, were ordinarily allowed to gather for discussion of questions relating to their respective professions. Authors (December 3), lawyers, professors and journalists (December 18), doctors (December 31), successively organized banquets and meetings at which the Zemstvo program was adopted in its entirety, always with the claim for a legislative national assembly and sometimes with still further demands. In the course of the next few months, each of these professions organized itself into a union—these were the first trade unions in Russia—for the realization of this program.

The fall of Port Arthur on January 1, 1905, with the humiliating details which later became known, further discredited the government. On January 19, at a religious ceremony a gun in the fortress of St. Peter and Paul fired a shot toward the Winter Palace; the Emperor from this time ceased to live in the capital. The Zemstvo Liberals and the professional classes were now to be joined in the demand for reform by the factory workers. It will be remembered that Zubatov had been encouraged by Plehve to organize a workers' movement under the guidance of the police. Zubatov's principal lieutenant in St. Petersburg was Father Gapon, a man of unbalanced and electric personality, with great powers of organization. He had established a system of representation of workers, so many from each factory, and it played a prominent part in a great strike of the Putilov Metal Works, which took place at this time. Gapon decided to lead his followers to the Winter Palace, to put their demands to the Emperor in person. The government had no decided policy to meet the emergency, but when the various processions were on their way carrying icons and singing religious or patriotic songs, troops posted at several points were ordered to stop them, and fired upon them, killing many persons (January 22).

Prince Mirsky was dismissed and replaced by a bureaucratic nonentity, Bulygin. At the same time General D. Trepov, city prefect of Moscow, a fearless officer but with no experience beyond police work, was put in control of the capital; not long afterwards his police authority was made to extend over the whole country. One of his first steps was to expel those who had taken part in the procession; this foolish measure spread all over the empire the distressing news of January 22 and started a whole epidemic of strikes which, in the following months, embraced practically every trade and profession, and even students and schoolboys. This general movement of wholesale opposition to the government, when it extended to the non-Russian provinces of the empire, particularly Poland, assumed a threatening character not far removed from open separatism. Thirteen railway lines stopped work; isolated police officials were murdered all over the country, the assailants almost invariably escaping. The government attempted a commission on labour conditions with participation of the employees, but entirely failed to gain their confidence.

On February 17 the Emperor's uncle, the Grand Duke Sergius, Governor General of Moscow, was killed in broad daylight in the Kremlin by a bomb thrown by the Socialist Revolutionary Kaliayev. The Grand Duke had irritated nearly every section of the public in Moscow by his uniform roughness to merchants, professional men, students, and, in particular, Jews. Kaliayev made no attempt to escape, and kept the secret of his accomplices to himself; he refused an offer of the Grand Duchess Elizabeth to appeal for his life. The Minister of Agriculture Ermolov, who shared the views of Prince Mirsky, appeared in tears before the Emperor begging him to rally the loyal elements of the public by reasonable concessions before it was too late.

The result was a new series of pronouncements issued on March 3. In a manifesto the Emperor declared his intention to maintain the autocracy. In a rescript to Bulygin he ordered that a scheme should be drawn up by which "the worthiest persons should be elected to share in the drafting and discussing of laws." In an edict he ordered the Ministry to take account of such suggestions on this subject as might be sent to it. This edict was taken by the public as an invitation to organize parties for drawing up political programs. The various professional unions came to be united in a central Union of Unions, which claimed to represent the whole professional class, under the presidency of Professor Milyukov. The government announced certain preliminary reforms; on April 30, religious teaching was declared to be free; on June 29, some remission was given to the Jews; measures were taken to deal with peasant distress.

The reformers were tending to split up into parties. In April a conference of Zemstvo Liberals pronounced for an advanced program; in June Shipov and the moderates held a separate conference; in April and May a number of conferences of professional unions took place, declaring always for a radical program; meanwhile the Social Democrats held their third party congress. But there was a return of unanimity on the crushing news of the annihilation of the Russian fleet at Tsushima on May 27–8. In this case the full force of the disaster was felt at once; no one could hope any longer for ultimate success in the war. On June 6 the rival parties of Zemstvo men held a joint conference in Moscow, in which representatives of the Town Councils also took part. At the same time the Union of Unions demanded that the war should be stopped. This demand was shortly followed by the arrest of Milyukov; but on June 19 a joint deputation of the Zemstva and Town Councils was received by the Emperor. It was headed by a non-party man of distinguished character, Prince S. Trubetskoy. To his wise words of warning the Emperor unexpectedly replied with a firm promise to call together the promised national assembly as soon as possible, inviting the cooperation of the general public to initiate the new regime.

Thus encouraged, the reformers held a great congress in Moscow on July 19, in which the Liberals predominated more than ever. A grand remonstrance was drawn up, and a draft constitution was passed "at the first reading." On August 19 appeared the government's law instituting the Imperial Duma, which was wholly unsatisfactory to the public. The elections were to be held in four stages. All but formal class elements, for instance the country teachers and doctors, professional men in towns, and factory workers, were excluded from the franchise; the Duma was to sit yearly in four separate sections, and was only to be consultative. On August 29 Witte, entrusted with the negotiations with Japan, succeeded in ending the war; and all attention was now concentrated on home affairs.

Open discontent, disorder, and opposition continued all over the empire. In the late summer the battleship *Potemkin* was seized by revolutionaries; it withdrew from its consorts, and terrorized the Black Sea until necessity compelled it to seek internment in Roumania. On September 25 began another Zemstvo congress, at which for the first time there were representatives of Poland, the Cossacks, the Caucasus, and Siberia; it decided to accept the Duma in order to turn it into something better; it supported compulsory expropriation of squires' land at a fair market price. On September 5 the universities again received self-government, and the police were prohibited from interference with them. The result was that all the public meetings which were forbidden outside now took place in the universities. This induced the government on October 25 to licence meetings under severe restrictions in other places. On October 28 the police thought it necessary to intervene in Moscow University.

Meanwhile public excitement had penetrated to the peasants. The S. R.'s, who did practically all the revolutionary work among them, had by now realized that to stir up the peasants they had better drop the question of forms of government, in which they met with little sympathy and much opposition, and concentrate on one battle cry: "All the land for the peasants." This watchword met with immediate and complete success. On the analogy of the other professional unions was formed a Peasant Union with this program. The agitators told the peasants that the question of ownership of the land would now be settled by the Duma, and the restlessness caused by this announcement took shape everywhere in agrarian riots, which were peculiarly acute in the grain-growing provinces of the Lower Volga. In one district after another, estates were invaded and ransacked; attacks on human life were rare, but in several cases horses and cattle were crippled; often the landowner was quietly escorted to the nearest railway station. In many parts, particularly in the south and southeast, the police, feeling themselves powerless, withdrew; and the peasants, left to manage their own affairs, initiated small republics, which were only meant to have a local significance and involved neither any idea of separatism nor any definite political program; this stage of comparative agrarian independence developed during the late autumn and early winter. Something of almost the same kind was proceeding in the non-Russian provinces; and in Poland the Party of National Democrats, headed by gentry but followed by the peasantry, almost took charge of public life; in the field of education a free society known as the *Polska Macierz* did remarkable work. In October there were large meetings of protest in Kiev and Odessa.

One of the strongest of the new professional unions was that of the

railway men. On October 20 it was reported that the whole Congress
of this Union had been arrested. Nearly all the railways now went on
strike, and this forced most of the factories to stop work also. This
general strike came of itself without any controlling organization, but
the watchword put forward everywhere by the strikers was the demand
for a constituent assembly based on universal suffrage. In St. Petersburg,
where the strike was especially effective, the Ministers had to go by
water from the capital to Peterhof. General Trepov found no better
remedy than to order his troops "not to spare their cartridges." All the
Unions had now joined in the strike, and practically all work had
stopped. Electric light was turned off; newspapers did not appear;
schools closed of themselves. On October 27, following the lines of
Gapon's organization of factories, the socialist parties instituted a Soviet
or council of elected delegates, which at once took the lead in the movement and was followed by the Union of Unions. The President of the
Soviet was Khrustalev and the Vice-President, Trotsky. The Soviet
threatened to wreck all works which did not close of themselves. Milyukov had left the Union of Unions, and he had now succeeded in
uniting many of the Liberals of the Zemstva and the more moderate
professional men in a party which took the name of Constitutional
Democrats, very soon abridged by the public into "Cadets." The initial
congress of this party was now meeting in Moscow.

Witte had returned from America with the laurels of a successful
peacemaker. Already dominant in foreign affairs, he was the Emperor's
obvious adviser in some affairs also. He was at heart a strong Conservative; but he was now convinced that some kind of constitution was
inevitable. He addressed a strong memorandum to the Emperor in this
sense; after much consultation of others and in particular of the Grand
Duke Nicholas, who was insistent for reform, this brought the sovereign
to a decision. Witte's honorary post of President of the Committee of
Ministers was turned into that of President of the Council of Ministers
with a responsibility for general policy and control over his colleagues—
the first actual introduction of the cabinet system into Russia. On October 30 was issued a manifesto, promising all those reforms which had
been put forward at the Congress of Zemstvo men in November 1904,
under the presidency of Shipov. It further promised a wide extension
of the franchise for the new Duma, and gave it a legislative character;
without the Duma no law was to be passed; it was also to control the
action of the officials.

Witte had to meet the greatest difficulties in his new task. To start with, the reactionaries, who had practically complete control of the police, used them to organize armed attacks upon Jews all over the country, in particular in Odessa, a town closely associated with the career of the new Prime Minister. Witte's constant denunciation of anti-Jewish legislation and anti-Jewish hooliganism was known to all, and these pogroms were a demonstration of disobedience on the part of the administrative officials; the leaflets inciting them were actually circulated from the headquarters of the police in St. Petersburg by one Komisarov. The more moderate of the reformers, now that their program was adopted by the government, might have been expected to support Witte. He conferred with them, but in vain; he insisted on appointing as Minister of the Interior a reactionary with a discredited past, P. Durnovo. As the Minister of the Interior had control of the police, Shipov and his friends refused to serve with him; some of them, however, began to organize a Union of October 30 in support of the new manifesto, which was the germ of the future Octobrist Party. With the Cadets or Liberals, Witte was even less successful. They asked for concessions which he could not give, and he proposed to outbid them by issuing his own law of expropriation, a project which he had to drop in view of the fierce opposition of the reactionaries. Witte conferred with some other groups, for instance, the Poles and Mussulmans; but nowhere could he win confidence. His immediate difficulties were with the Soviet. On November 1, it put an end to the strike but only in order to organize further resistance to the government, and it declared for a democratic republic. On November 8 the rights of Finland were formally restored and a strike, which was in process there also, came to an end; the Diet was called on the basis of universal suffrage with proportional representation. On November 5 took place a great procession in Warsaw where the old emblem of Poland, the White Eagle, was openly displayed; next day the leading Polish party, the National Democrats, publicly demanded autonomy and arranged a congress of peasants from twelve hundred parishes; Witte replied on November 10 with martial law for all Poland. On November 8 a mutiny broke out in Kronstadt.

The Soviet believed that it could at any time renew the general strike, to force further concessions. On November 11 it gave orders to strike work for an eight-hour day; this strike had but little effect. The workers were also ordered to strike for the wrongs of Poland and because of severe repression of the Kronstadt mutiny; this strike came to an end on November 20. On December 8 a new law defined and limited the rights of the press under the guise of declaring its freedom; on November 16 Witte made a bid for the support of the peasants, reducing their redemption dues by half for the next year, after which they would be abolished altogether. Riots were going on all over the empire; in the Baltic provinces; in Siberia among the returning troops; in Sevastopol, where there was a mutiny of the fleet; and in many parts of southern Russia. On November 19 was held the last Congress of Zemstvo men, at which the Octobrists already attracted attention under the leadership of Guchkov; this Congress declared for correct constitutionalism and wished to support Witte, but it was overshadowed by the growing importance of the Cadet Party.

The Soviet had not shown itself capable of directing a revolution. Moreover, by the inconvenience which it caused to the ordinary inhabitant, it had produced a mood of reaction. Durnovo, inside the Ministry, and Trepov, now commandant of the Imperial Police, took full advantage of this change of mood to undermine Witte with the Emperor. On November 28 the Committee of the Peasant Union was arrested by the government. People had long been asking whether Khrustalev would arrest Witte or Witte, Khrustalev; on December 5 Khrustalev was arrested, and a week later martial law was declared in St. Petersburg, especially against the meetings of the railway men. The Soviet called on its supporters to withdraw their money from the savings banks and to refuse all taxes; Witte punished those newspapers which printed its appeal. On December 14 the servants of the Post and Telegraph struck work; two days later the government arrested the bulk of the Soviet—190 members. An attempt was made to call a third general strike. It was unsuccessful in St. Petersburg, but led to a movement of open conflict with the government in Moscow (December 22–January 1). Here a small number of revolutionaries led a by no means large number of workmen to an attack on the authorities; but the insurgents never secured control of the Nicholas Railway Station, and troops brought in from the northwest suppressed the rising with great severity. One of its principal effects was further to alienate the sympathy of those who took little interest in politics. Disturbances followed all over the south, at Saratov, Rostov on the Don, Novorossiisk, Ekaterinburg, Sochi, and Sukhum; but the movement of revolution was really at an end.

On December 24, Witte, frightened at the Moscow rising, made his last opportunist bid to the Liberals. He issued a regulation making the franchise to all intents and purposes universal; it was to include all taxpayers and nearly all lodgers and factory workers; preliminary electoral meetings were to be allowed, and the Duma was to control the verification of its own elections. For this edict Witte was never afterwards forgiven by the Court. It was thought to have been unnecessary. Durnovo, now that public opinion was turning against the revolutionaries, had no difficulty in suppressing them. Punitive columns, which sometimes burned whole villages, reduced the peasantry to obedience, though agrarian riots continued sporadically much later. The last of the movements of violence was a savage rising of the Letts and Ests of the Baltic provinces against their German masters, marked by many acts of brutality and by ruthless reprisals from the authorities.

It was in this atmosphere that the first Duma was elected. Both reactionaries and revolutionaries were discredited with public opinion. The only party which had any clear conception of parliamentary tactics was the Cadets (Liberals); they had studied European constitutions, and understood the working of the government's new electoral law much better than it did itself. As a result, they captured over 150 seats. Late in the elections an able organizer Aladin created a Labour group of 90. The other parties were insignificant. The Social Democrats at first boycotted the elections and, when they found the country was everywhere taking part in them, they were too late to make up lost ground.

Meanwhile the government spent the first three months of 1906 in hedging itself round with new barriers against the attack of the Duma. It seized the opportunity still left to it, of fixing the precise form of the concessions contained in the manifesto of October 30. By certain additions to the fundamental laws drawn up largely under the influence of Witte, the Duma was declared to have no competence on these laws or on others derived from them. Parts of the budget were "ironclad" and exempted from public criticism; loans and currency were put under the uncontrolled jurisdiction of the Minister of Finance; the army and navy, with all that related to them, were retained as prerogatives of the crown. The Council of State, so far nominated by the sovereign, was now strengthened for legislative purposes by an equal number of persons elected from the higher institutions of the country, including stock exchanges, universities, and Zemstva. It became the Upper House and received the same legislative rights as the Duma; if the two Houses disagreed as to the budget, the government might choose whichever of the two figures it preferred; if no budget were passed, the government might take the estimates of the preceding year. Witte, rapidly returning to the service of the autocracy, did not confine himself to the fundamental laws. He succeeded, largely through his personal credit, in obtaining an enormous loan from France before the Duma met, with the purpose, later avowed, of making the government financially independent of the Duma. As soon as he had rendered this service and arranged with much ability the return of the demoralized army from the Far East, the Emperor, who was long since disgusted with him, replaced him by Goremykin; the new Ministry included the able Kokovtsev as Minister of Finance, several leading reactionaries in other high posts and an entirely new man, Peter Stolypin, as Minister of the Interior. Stolypin, who had never served his way up through a government office in St. Petersburg, had proved to be almost the only provincial governor, in the last stormy months of 1905, who could keep a hold on his province and win respect even from adversaries of the government, freely risking his life, now to restrain a reactionary mob of hooligans, now to secure without bloodshed the submission of a revolutionized village.

On May 10, 1906, the first Duma was received in the Winter Palace, and then began its sittings in the Tauris Palace of Catherine's minister, Potemkin. Its first President, Muromtsev, drew up admirable rules of procedure, which subsequent party changes did not materially alter, and in his conduct of the debates he was throughout a model of dignity and fairness. The business of the House was practically in the hands of the Cadets. The government meant the Duma to be at least no more than the German Reichstag; but the Cadets intended to make of it a Parliament like that of England. Following the British analogy, as the Emperor's speech had contained no political program, the Duma put its own program into its answering Address to the Throne. Owing to the ability of the Cadets—in particular of the Cadet leader, V. Nabokov—and to the instinct of cooperation which inspired the First Duma as a whole, this answer, which contained definite and on the whole not extravagant proposals for the reform of practically every field of public life, was accepted by the Duma almost unanimously. There was at first a doubt whether the Emperor would receive it; and ultimately the Prime Minister Goremykin attended by his colleagues came down to the Duma, and in a tense silence announced to the House that its principal proposals were "inadmissible." The Cadet Nabokov at once mounted the tribune and proposed a vote of censure. In the debate which followed every abuse of the government was exposed and the ministers, with the exception of Stolypin, found no way of meeting this attack but to leave the House.

The vote of censure was passed unanimously; but the Duma had no weapon which could compel the government to resign. By the recently added regulations it was formally forbidden to make any appeal to the country. There was a deadlock during which the two camps of reaction and reform stood looking at each other. During this interval, Prince Urusov, as a member of the Duma, delivered a telling indictment of the part played by the police in the pogroms. The Cadets marked time by passing through a number of measures which they well knew could at present take no effect, and ultimately made a bid for the more active support of the public by raising the land question. Two bills were brought in by the Cadets and the Labour Party, and the Duma proposed to establish commissions of its own all over the country to investigate the details on the spot. Goremykin's Ministry now brought forward counter proposals by which large tracts of land would at a cheap price be put at the disposal of the peasants, and in public announcements it warned the country not to trust in the promises of the Duma. Such a position could not long endure. The Duma replied to the government by deciding to publish an appeal to the country, and that was the signal for its dissolution. On July 21, without any preliminary notice to its President, Professor Muromtsev, was posted the announcement that the Duma was dissolved. That night some 200 members, including practically the whole of the Cadet and Labour Parties, made their way to Viborg in Finland and there drew up an appeal for passive resistance until the Duma was restored. Till then, the country was asked to refuse to pay taxes or to send recruits to the army, and to disclaim responsibility for all foreign loans concluded without the Duma. Nothing had been done to organize a response from the country, and the Viborg appeal fell quite flat.

For the dissolution of the Duma the post of Premier had been committed to Stolypin. Basing himself on the fundamental laws, Stolypin claimed to be a constitutionalist but not a parliamentarist. In dissolving the First Duma he called another, within the legal time limit, for March 1907. He set himself on the one hand to crush revolution everywhere and on the other to carry through moderate reforms in which, he insisted, the government ought itself to take the initiative. One of the recent articles of the fundamental laws, No. 89, allowed the government to issue by exceptional decree during the vacation of the Duma such laws as might be urgently required. Of this article, which was borrowed from the Austrian Constitution and was supposed to cover only measures of detail that brooked no delay, Stolypin made the most extended use. On September 1 he set up field courts-martial which dealt drastically with revolutionary crime, the whole of the proceedings being ordinarily completed in four days. The usual sentence of these courts was death, and 600 persons were executed. On August 25 Stolypin made available for sale to the peasants large tracts of appanage and cabinet lands; on October 2 he made the peasants free to leave their village communes or to join others and to divide their family property as they pleased; he also removed restrictions on their elections to the Zemstvo; on October 18 peasants became eligible for any rank in the government service.

On November 22 a still more important edict dealt with the land question to which Stolypin, like the Duma, assigned the first place. Peasants were now allowed to claim their allotment in permanent property and to ask that, instead of being divided up in strips all over the village holding, it should be assigned to them in one place. For this drastic change the technical provisions were quite inadequate; the hated land captains were to be the arbiters between the village community and the outgoing peasant; but it was a great declaration of principle. Among the Russian parties practically not one supported Stolypin. Reactionaries and revolutionaries, for opposite reasons, desired to maintain the old collective ownership of land by the whole village community. The Liberals, though many of them opposed this principle, did not venture at this time to dissent from the Socialists, whose support they so greatly needed against the government. On the other hand, Stolypin found his justification in a process which, beginning in Great Britain and Holstein in the eighteenth century, had in the course of time triumphed almost everywhere in Europe and had now become popular in many parts of Russia among the peasants themselves, who had for several years past been dividing up their own landed property by common consent.

Everything was done by the government to influence the new elections. Stolypin, once he had successfully dissolved the Duma, was exposed at Court to the attacks of men of much more reactionary views, who had much greater influence than himself there; provincial governors, relying on their court connections, often defied his control; he needed a Duma which would support him. The Senate, by arbitrary interpretations of the electoral law, struck out of the franchise large and important categories such as those peasants who, though registered in peasant communities, lived mostly in the towns; the police detained voting papers, fixed impossible dates for polling, and in particular did all that they could to exclude Jews or Liberals. In face of these abuses of the administration, the attitude of the peasant electorate was very remarkable. In one place they refused to elect because the presiding official persisted in refusing fair play; in another they watched the voting urns all night to see that there was no tampering with them; in another they three times re-elected Aladin, excluded from the list of candidates by the government. The country, in particular the peasants, entirely refused to approve of Stolypin's dissolution of the First Duma. Those who signed the protest at Viborg had all been excluded from participation in the next Duma and they were replaced by outspoken revolutionaries, of whom a very large proportion had suffered for their opinions, generally by administrative arrest without trial. As a result, the Cadets' representation sank to 123, that of Labour rose to 201, and the two frankly revolutionary parties, the Socialist Revolutionaries and the Social Democrats, entered the Second Duma in force, the former with 35 members and the latter with 54. There were 32 Octobrists, 34 High Tories, and 12 pure reactionaries led by a speaker of brilliant parts and hysterical energy, Purishkevich. But for parliamentary ability the most notable group in the Duma was that of the Poles led by Roman Dmowski, whose tactics were to hold the balance between the Russian parties and by a mixture of daring and restraint to win whatever was possible for Poland.

While electing revolutionaries as the men who could best voice a national protest, the electors, and in particular the peasants, impressed upon them that they should try to make the Duma last as long as possible, if only for its great value as a national tribune, and leave the responsibility for a rupture to the government. The Second Duma met on March 5, 1907, in an atmosphere of police supervision, spies, and barriers which did not succeed in excluding the public. From the outset the reactionaries, well knowing that their group was prevailing over the more moderate views of Stolypin at Court, and that the country was too tired to attempt any armed protest, set themselves to discredit the Duma and secure its dissolution, if not its abolition. Every debate on practical questions was whenever possible diverted by them into a discussion of revolutionary terrorism. On May 30, in spite of great restraint both of the Cadets and of the Labour group, they succeeded in bringing about a full-dress debate on this subject, in which the inferiority of the depleted Second Duma to the First in political experience was made painfully clear. Nine party formulas were put forward, and all were rejected in turn. The only one that could have passed, was the admirable definition proposed by the Poles: "Terrorism is incompatible with parliamentary institutions"—which, it was well known, the reactionaries wished to destroy; but this was defeated by the jealousy of the Cadets, though their view was practically the same as that of the Poles.

The Duma was left without a formula on a burning question, and the reactionaries quickly followed up their success. It was announced in the Duma that the Emperor had barely escaped assassination by conspirators of the Socialist Revolutionary Party. The so-called plot when investigated proved to be merely a matter of police provocation, and it was well known that both Socialist parties had discountenanced all plots while the Duma was in session. Shortly afterwards the Social Democrats were also accused of a plot and Stolypin, who had made every effort to secure a working agreement with a moderate majority in the Duma, was compelled on June 14 at a suddenly announced secret sitting to demand the exclusion of all members of the Social Democratic Party. The Duma refused to grant this without making an investigation; but while the government materials were being examined, it was dissolved on the early morning of June 16 with no more ceremony than its predecessor.

An Imperial manifesto announced that there was a plot in the Duma, that the members were not representative of the needs and wishes of the population and that the Emperor would therefore change the electoral law—an evident breach of that clause of the government's own Constitution, by which no changes relating to the statute of the Duma were to take place without its consideration and assent. The new electoral law, which was published immediately and had manifestly been prepared in advance, legalized all the arbitrary restrictions of the franchise which preceded the second elections, but it also went further. The great majority of the towns lost their individual representation and were merged in the provinces; in the few which still possessed members of their own, these were divided equally between two different curiæ, of which the higher included a quite insignificant proportion of voters qualified by a large property franchise. In the provinces, where indirect election was necessary, the lists of "electors" chosen to select the actual members of the Duma was so manipulated that a complete predominance was assured to the by no means numerous class of country gentry, who were even able to decide which of the candidates chosen by the peasants should enter the Duma.

The law disfranchised central Asia entirely. In other parts of the empire, where a non-Russian population predominated, similar manipulation secured a predominance to the Cossacks or other Russian colonists. The representation of Poland was cut down from 36 votes to 14. In fixing the various arbitrary lists of categories by which the franchise was manipulated, the local governors were given complete control, with appeal only to the Minister of the Interior: another manifest breach of the amended fundamental laws.

Thirty-one Social Democrat members, including their leader Tsereteli, were sent to Siberia. Those who had signed the protest of Viborg were permanently deprived of civil rights. For the next two years the government continued a series of trials for political activities dating from 1905. It issued obligatory ordinances by which the administrative authorities might fine newspapers at will for a hostile attitude to the government; the provincial press was crushed. Along with the major political punishments went wholesale expulsions; meanwhile, those who had taken part in armed attacks on the Jews were now amnestied. A peasant, summing up the process of thought during the last five years, described the attitude of the public toward the government as follows: "Five years ago there was belief and fear; now the belief is gone, and only the fear remains."

After the dissolution of the Second Duma followed at first a period of deep disillusionment and prostration, which showed itself partly in a general outbreak of licence and a consequent failure of administrative control. Bands of robbers, especially in the east and south, traversed wide areas and held up the communications of the government. As control was re-established, came a mood of general egoism. Deceived in their public aspirations, men set about attending to their own material interests. Thus began a prolonged period in which the distinguishing marks were economic spadework, modest political claims, and steady persistence to make the most of those acquisitions of the liberation movement which were still left to the nation, in particular of what remained of the Duma. The Cadets set themselves to the tasks of a regular parliamentary Opposition. In a remarkable volume entitled *Landmarks* (*Vekhi*) several notable political thinkers, headed by Peter Struve, the chief standard-bearer of Russian Liberalism, asked for a severe and critical self-examination in which all the accepted values of the Russian intelligentsia were called up for judgment. Later in an article under the title "A Great Russia," Struve gave a reasoned exposition of all the main articles of a creed of Liberal patriotism.

It was in this atmosphere that the Third Duma, elected under the restrictions of the new electoral law, met in November 1907. It contained 50 reactionaries, 89 Nationalists or country Tories, who followed Stolypin, 153 Octobrists, 18 Poles, 23 Progressivists, 54 Cadets, 13 Labour men, and 20 Social Democrats. The Cadets, who would again have been the majority in any freely elected Duma, had now to surrender the leadership of the debates to the Octobrists, who, numbering about a third of all the members, sat in the middle of the House. Of these the most notable politician was their leader A. I. Guchkov, grandson of a serf and son of a Moscow merchant. His restless public career had included relief work in the great famines of 1891–3, travels in Armenia and Macedonia, participation in the Boer War against England, a journey along the Great Wall of China, activity in Manchuria during the Boxers' revolution, direction of Red Cross work in the Japanese War, where as in the Boer War he was taken prisoner, and a vigorous opposition to the Cadet program in the last of the Zemstvo Congresses of 1905. The rest of the Octobrists were mostly enlightened country gentry; many of them had risen high in the administrative work of the government, especially in the domains of finance, agriculture, and education, and had also been prominent in their provincial Zemstva; several, but for their liberal principles, might easily have already been in occupation of ministerial posts. Here was an Opposition which was capable of detailed and telling criticism of the government.

The Octobrist group was not described as a party but as an association. In principle it left much more freedom than the Cadets to personal initiative and opinions, but in the course of the first session of the Third Duma Guchkov was able to mould it into an effective force. Throughout, the work of the Duma had been largely done in commissions. These commissions, by the rigid instinct of equity which governed Muromtsev's rules of procedure, were always composed in proportion to the numbers of the various parties, each of which was therefore able to send its best experts in the given subject. Most important of all was the budget commission under Professor Alexeyenko, one of the first authorities on financial law in the country, who had no wish to become Minister of Finance and much preferred to be a permanent critic of successive Ministers. No change had been made in the Duma's competence, and it retained the right to examine the greater part of the budget. Every Minister, therefore, who desired to pass his estimates through the Duma, was bound to seek its good will. It will be noticed that both the first two Dumas had been dissolved before they got to the examination of the budget, so that they had never utilized this great power.

By a general understanding the prevailing party, the Octobrists, had pledged themselves individually against taking office until they could form a government themselves. But Guchkov was anxious in every way to support Stolypin against the reactionaries, who were at present the only possible alternative Ministry; and both Stolypin and Guchkov were anxious for close cooperation between the Ministry and the Duma. Stolypin did not choose all his own colleagues, and some of them did not share his views. These differences were cleverly utilized by Guchkov to enhance the moral authority of the Duma. The Duma would be ready to pass the estimates of a Minister with whose program it agreed, and thus its approval came to be a valuable support to Liberal ministers, not only in the public but even at Court. Each commission of the Duma had its elected spokesman; and as each commission was a microcosm of the whole House, the spokesman could speak for the Duma as a whole; these men, pledged against taking office, defended the independence of the Duma, and the ministers found that they had to deal with the Duma through them. The Duma had the right to ask full explanations from the ministers on all matters submitted to it; and thus, behind closed doors, began a process of mutual education, the Duma members acquainting themselves with the framework of the machinery of government, and the ministers compelled to learn to listen to intelligent criticism.

The first fruits of this process were seen in June 1908, in the public discussion in the Duma on the budget estimates. Army and navy were still prerogatives of the sovereign, but many naval and military estimates had to be submitted to the Duma. On the naval estimates Guchkov came out with the most scathing criticism of those numberless abuses which had caused the national humiliation in the Japanese War. This opportunity had been missed by the Cadets; it gave the Duma the chance of showing itself to be more patriotic than the government. On June 9 Guchkov made another telling speech on the army estimates; he spoke of "our buried military glory," and put the blame not on the army but on the government; calling for efficiency everywhere, he boldly appealed to the various Grand Dukes who held higher posts in the army administration to resign on patriotic grounds. The speech had a tremendous effect on the public, as showing that the Duma counted after all; it was followed up by others equally critical on the whole government policy in other fields, especially in that of education.

This was the turning point in the life of the Third Duma. It began to rally the confidence and support of the public. Though the law of June 1907 entirely prevented it from being an adequate representation of the country, the mere fact that the Duma could voice the country gradually brought the two more and more closely together. These were days of small things, and it was felt that the Octobrists were gaining all the ground which could at present be gained. At Court the Duma, by the restraint and competence of its criticisms, grew in authority. Abroad it was beginning to win respect; and this, with the constant dependence of the government on foreign loans, was in itself an asset to constitutionalism in Russia. The Duma was becoming a school in which its members learned the important lesson of mutual tolerance, of cooperation for objects on which agreement could be obtained; it was acquiring the atmosphere and instincts of parliamentary life.

The Third Duma lived out its full term of five years and the Fourth Duma, elected in 1912, was composed practically of the same personnel. The life of the Third Duma coincided with a period of remarkable economic prosperity. With several good crops, the government revenue rose steadily, and the estimates could thus be largely increased. Their distribution was in the main at the disposal of the Duma. Education was made accessible for all, and the salaries of teachers were raised considerably. During the Third Duma the railway administration, which was a subject of constant criticism, was so much improved that the railways for the first time gave a profit. In military reform, during its first years, the Third Duma had the hearty cooperation of the War Office, which sent General Polivanov to assist as far as possible the work of Guchkov and the Duma Committee of Imperial Defence; in cases where it could feel assured that the money would be well spent, the Duma not only passed the proposed estimates but increased them.

Most important of all was the cooperation of Stolypin and the Duma in the field of land settlement. Stolypin, it will be remembered, had in November 1906 made it possible for a peasant to claim his holding as personal property, united in one place. In default of the necessary machinery for carrying out this law, it led to conflicts between the outgoing peasant and their village communities, in which very often the latter burned down the farm of the former. On the other hand Stolypin had struck home when he assumed that the peasants' main desire was for property in land. Curiously enough it was those peasants who had led the agrarian riots of 1905, that now took the lead in persuading their fellow-villagers to make use of his reform. These men saw that the only course for a peasant who wished to divide off his land, was to persuade the whole village to divide up all the village holding at the same time. By the existing law, village communities could re-divide their property wherever a two-thirds majority should require. In village after village this majority was obtained, and the whole of the land was divided up into personal property. There were of course many individual hardships;

a peasant with five small boys would be counted as one "soul," and when they grew up they would suffer greatly from the new system. But in general, the new land settlement, which was much improved in its course through the Duma, produced most beneficent results. Whole areas of land far distant from the village and therefore left uncultivated, when divided up among the peasants, became prosperous farms; the villages themselves tended to become depots of industry for these farms. Cattle greatly improved in quality. Most interesting of all, Cooperation, which had remained a dream so long as the village community was joint owner of all property, began to spring up of itself everywhere as soon as the individual peasant had something of his own to cooperate with—especially in dairy produce and marketing of farm products. A further result was that a large number of peasants sold their new property and came to the towns with money in their pockets to start work there.

The economic growth of Russia went forward of itself. Just when the Duma was created, the men at the head of the leading trades and industries of Russia had federated themselves to secure an intelligent commercial policy and freedom of trade initiative. They held their own industrial parliament during the sittings of the Duma, and sometimes their deliberations were the more important; they received more and more attention from the government. Foreign capital, obtaining a better knowledge of Russian trade conditions and greater confidence in Russian investments, was entering in ever increasing volume. This brought into greater prominence the question of Russia's foreign relations—a question in which the Duma was able for the first time to assert with authority the instincts and preferences of the Russian people.

Stolypin's position was meanwhile weakening. In the spring of 1910, backed by Witte who wished to make the Court forget his concessions of 1905, the reactionaries attacked him for allowing the Duma to take such an active part in the control of the army and navy, and represented to the sovereign that he was gradually losing this prerogative. Stolypin was compelled to separate himself from the Octobrists, and had to rely in the Duma chiefly on the Nationalists. He introduced a bill on Finland which put all Finnish affairs of any consequence under the jurisdiction of the Russian Ministry and the Duma, to which the Finns were to send members. The Cadets boycotted the bill; the Octobrists, left without their help, tried in vain to rid it of some of its most objectionable features. In 1911 Stolypin introduced a bill for instituting elective Zemstva in the so-called Western Provinces, where the gentry were in the main Polish. He intended to make these new Zemstva strongholds of Russian patriotism, and manipulated the elective curiæ to give the predominance to the Russian peasant population. This bill was such as to please no one. Stolypin was just able to pass it through the Duma; the Council of State threw it out at the instigation of the reactionaries, who alleged that they were acting on the wish of the sovereign. Stolypin resigned; both the Empresses came to St. Petersburg to beg him to resume office; he returned on definite conditions, after frank reproaches to the sovereign for his weakness. To pass his bill, he now again had recourse to Article 89; he created an artificial vacation by proroguing the two Houses, issued his law as a government decree, and then called the Houses back to work. He was being worn out by the intrigues of the capital, and was already in failing health. In the autumn, while attending a gala performance at Kiev with the Emperor and the Court, he was assassinated by a revolutionary Bogrov, under circumstances which pointed strongly to the connivance of the reactionaries (September 14, 1911). He was succeeded as Prime Minister by Kokovtsev. From now onward, the government policy, if there was a policy, was one of drift. Kokovtsev was quite intelligent enough to see that a whole program of practical reforms was still required, but he had no hold over the Court or over his colleagues and was dismissed in January 1914, because he had protested against the influence at Court of the religious quack Rasputin, whose shameless immorality had been the occasion of a striking debate in the Duma. On the other hand, the Duma had plainly come to stay; it had become a habit; the country stood more and more behind it, and the bureaucracy and even the Court had reconciled themselves to its existence. The constitutional issue was yet to be decided.

CHAPTER XXIV

War and Revolution

[*1905–17*]

THE ALLIANCE with France, initiated with caution by Alexander III in 1893–4 and at first practically confined to military anticipations and commercial interests, had been publicly announced in 1897, but it presented many contradictions. The obvious incompatibility between the principles of government of the two countries found expression at moments of fluctuation in Russian internal politics; and, while emphasizing his friendship with France, Nicholas was much less likely than his father to maintain his independence as regards Germany or indeed to follow any settled policy at all. The Russian public understood this well, and the alliance aroused at first no great enthusiasm; but when Russia began to find a voice of her own in the liberation movement, the French alliance became an asset in the struggle for liberty at home. Precluded from any effective organization in the country, the Cadets of the First Duma relied rather on moral pressure from the more Liberal states of Europe, especially in matters of finance, than on their own campaign of passive resistance.

A new factor entered into the question when King Edward VII and Lord Lansdowne were able to bring about a gradual understanding between France and England, based on a successful settlement of the main causes of disagreement. Practically all popular sympathies in Russia were with the Franco-British Entente. During the long period of reaction, individual Englishmen living in Russia had never failed to enjoy personal good will. The alliance of England with Japan led at the time of the Japanese War to an official outburst of attacks on England; but the war itself was so unpopular in Russia that these took very little effect; this alliance had at most been an insurance against a general war.

On the other hand, the Japanese War had led in Russia to great dissatisfaction with Germany, as much in government circles as elsewhere. All Russians were ready to believe, even without proofs, that Germany's encouragement of Nicholas in his Far Eastern policy was dictated by a desire to draw Russia away from Europe and to get a free hand to Germanize the Slavs of the Balkans. William II kept up a lively correspondence with Nicholas which, now that it has been published and accepted as genuine by such authorities as Izvolsky, makes it clear that these conjectures were well founded. What gratitude William might have won from Nicholas for the moral support of which he is always boasting in the letters, was entirely discounted by the price which Germany put upon it. Russia's reverses and embarrassments were utilized to impose in 1904 a revision of the tariff treaty of 1894 entirely unfavourable to Russian interests and most unwillingly accepted by Witte, who had to negotiate it, only at the command of his sovereign.

The Russian government when at war with its people had emphasized its imperial interests in the East, and this line of policy had met with a great reverse. For the ordinary educated Russian, the proper foreign policy of his country was before all things closer contact with Europe and advocacy of the interests of the Slavs and the Orthodox of the Balkans. Imperial Germany at this time was struggling for outlets, whether political, commercial, or both. There were three lines of advance, very different in character, between which she could choose. First there was the line of peaceful penetration of Russia. The Russian Empire contained a considerable German population, which—especially the barons of the Baltic—had an altogether disproportionate part in its administration and ordinarily a powerful influence at the Court. Germans were much more alert than others to understand the profound economic changes initiated by the emancipation of the peasantry, and proceeded to occupy in the new industrial Russia as many of the best strategical points as possible. But this line of German advance depended entirely on peace with Russia. Germany's second line lay through the Balkans; here she had recently, through Marschall von Bieberstein, secured the most substantial successes of her diplomacy, especially in the project of the Baghdad Railway. Germany's policy, since the time of Bismarck, was to use Austria as a quite unofficial *annexe* of German political and economic advance and to help her to absorb the largest possible number of Slavs. Across the road of this advance lay first the vigorous strivings for independence among the Czechs and, further south, Serbia, of which there was already a national nucleus enjoying independence. There was a third outlet, more popular with the Prussian officers and entirely military in character. It was the road by sea: past, and if necessary over England, to open waters and to the outside world.

In July 1905, William II made a great effort to regain his hold over Nicholas. On his yacht he paid him a surprise visit at Björkö on the coast of Finland with a ready-made draft of alliance, which in the absence of the Russian Foreign Minister, he persuaded his weak-minded neighbour to sign. France was to be invited to adhere to this alliance, which was evidently directed against England; each side was to help the other with all forces, and no separate peace was to be concluded (July 24). Witte, now on his way back from the Treaty of Portsmouth, refused an invitation to visit England but accepted one from William and broke his journey at the hunting box at Rominten where, however, the character of the Björkö Treaty was not made clear to him. On his return to Russia, he and the Foreign Minister Count Lamsdorf had no difficulty in persuading Nicholas that the Björkö alliance was a direct breach of the existing alliance of Russia with France. Russia shuffled out of the alliance as best she could, though William continued to write to Nicholas as "your ally."

Meanwhile in London the Russian Embassy, under Count Benckendorff, had for some time been engaged in promoting an understanding with England. Its success had been endangered by the incident of the Dogger Bank, but the movement went on and was supported by the Russian Minister in Copenhagen, Izvolsky, who was appointed Foreign Minister in May 1906. It is significant that Izvolsky was the most Liberal member of the Cabinet and did all that he could to avert the dissolution of the First Duma. In England, where the Liberals obtained a sweeping majority in 1906, the public had followed with great interest the liberation movement in Russia, and all sympathies were with the Duma; the news of its dissolution the English Prime Minister Sir H. Campbell Bannerman received with the words: "The Duma is dead; long live the Duma!"

With Russia as with France, England aimed at removing from the outset the substantial causes of disagreement; and on September 1, 1907, a convention between the two countries brought a settlement as to rival interests in Persia. The northern zone, where Russian trade predominated, was left to Russian influence, and the southern to England, with a middle zone between the two; both parties were pledged to the integrity of Persia. Tibet, which shortly before the Japanese War had been induced to ask for Russian protection, was declared to be outside European policy, and Afghanistan independent but within the British sphere of influence. Izvolsky followed this up with a well-planned settlement of outstanding questions with Japan (1907 and 1910).

Russian public opinion was now strongly set towards friendship with England as an essential part of a national foreign policy. In Struve's notable article "A Great Russia," friendship with England and France was intimately connected with the championship of the Balkan Slavs, a Liberal economic policy at home, and the removal of disabilities for the Poles and the Jews. During the Third Duma there was a strong Slavonic movement in Russia common to all parties but closely associated with Liberalism, and a number of conferences of members of Slavonic parliaments took place at Prague (July 1908), St. Petersburg (May 1909), Sofia (1910), and Belgrade (1911). In 1909 the President and the leaders of several parties in the Duma visited England and were most cordially received.

Meanwhile Austria was preparing a counter move. In February 1903, she had agreed with Russia as to a program of reforms in Macedonia; to amplify this agreement Nicholas II and Count Lamsdorf had visited Francis Joseph at Mürzsteg (October). Baron Aehrenthal, the Austrian Foreign Minister, wished to restore the alliance of the three Eastern Emperors, and in 1907 made overtures to Izvolsky which were unsuccessful. It will be remembered that before the Russo-Turkish War, while acting in concert with Austria, Alexander II had agreed at Reichstadt to a conditional annexation of Bosnia and Herzegovina by Austria, and that after Russia had been left to fight Turkey unaided the Congress of Berlin allowed Austria to occupy (not to annex) these provinces. It would appear that on two subsequent occasions Russia expressed her acquiescence if these provinces should pass finally under Austrian rule. Izvolsky was anxious to secure an agreement with Austria and the other Powers to annul the clause of the Treaty of Paris forbidding the passage of Russian warships through the Straits, and meeting Aehrenthal at Buchlau in September 1908, he gave his assent to the annexation as an equivalent. Meanwhile, in July the Young Turks, with a patriotic policy, took control of Turkey, and Izvolsky was not able to obtain the assent of England with regard to the Straits, so that this part of the bargain fell through. The assent of France and England as signatories of the Treaty of Berlin was equally necessary for the annexation of Bosnia and Herzegovina by Austria, so that Izvolsky considered the whole bargain as off. However, on October 5, 1908, it was suddenly announced that Austria had turned her occupation of the two provinces into a permanent annexation and that Bulgaria simultaneously repudiated the suzerainty of Turkey. The two provinces are peopled by Serbs; Serbia failed to obtain any compensation from Austria and was most reluctant to accept this decision, which had not been sanctioned by the other signatories of the Berlin Treaty. Serbia mobilized, Russia concentrated troops on her frontier, and on March 17, 1909, Austria called in her reserves. Germany announced plainly that she would support Austria if attacked. Russian feeling was extremely strong, and all parties were united in their protests against the Austrian annexation; but the government felt that Russia could not face a challenge so soon after the Japanese War, and Austria and Germany had their way (April 1909). From this time onward, however, it was generally assumed in Russia that another challenge would come from Austria and Germany, and that it must some day be accepted; the Kiev military district had orders to be ready to repel an invasion within forty-eight hours at any time. The Bosnian crisis brought to the fore the question of Poland. It was clear that Polish sympathies could not be on the side of Russia without a liberal Russian policy both at home and abroad.

The peace of Europe was in some danger in 1911 owing to the incident of Agadir. In October 1912, a League of Balkan States, including Bulgaria, Serbia, Montenegro, and Greece, made war on Turkey. To the general surprise the allies were successful. Radko Dmitriev, defeating the Turks at Lule Burgas, drove them on Chataldja and Gallipoli; the Serbs won at Kumanovo and Monastir. Turkey concluded an armistice on December 3 but resumed fighting on February 3, 1913. On March 26, Adrianople surrendered, and on April 16 Bulgaria made an armistice with Turkey. On April 23 Scutari fell.

The allies had settled in advance the difficult question of the division of liberated territory. Austria, however, intervened to forbid any Serbian outlet to the Adriatic even at the expense of Turkey, as it would have made Serbia much less dependent on Austrian policy. Serbia, thus deprived of a part of her share, asked of Bulgaria compensation on the side of Macedonia, and this led to a war between the allies, in which Bulgaria stood alone against the rest. Exhausted by her earlier sacrifices she was soon overpowered, especially as Roumania joined in against her. The Treaty of Bucarest (August 10, 1913) was satisfactory to no one; it has been said that nearly every transfer of territory made by it was contrary to racial interests. Austrian policy had succeeded in dividing the allies.

On June 28, 1914, the Archduke Francis Ferdinand was assassinated at Sarajevo, the capital of Bosnia. Heir to the Austrian throne, he had married a Czech and had favoured an admission of the Slavs of Austria into partnership with the Germans and Magyars in the direction of the empire; he had tried to arouse a distinctively Austrian patriotism among them, and this was the occasion of his visit to Sarajevo, on the very anniversary of the loss of Serbian independence at Kosovo in 1389. Austria dispatched an ultimatum demanding practically the complete control of Serbia (July 23). The Serbs were ready to make any concessions compatible with their independence and sought the direction and support of Russia. Germany at once made it clear that she was prepared to support Austria through thick and thin and would not tolerate the interference of any Power. Russia counselled the greatest moderation to Serbia; England sought any means of securing a peaceful settlement; but all attempts broke down against the refusal of Germany to allow any outside intervention. Austria had already begun war against Serbia on July 28 and Russia made a partial mobilization, originally toward her southwestern frontier. Germany regarded this as a challenge, and secretly both Russia and Germany mobilized their full forces. Russia had succeeded in renewing negotiations with Austria, when on July 29 Germany sent an ultimatum simultaneously both to Russia and to her ally France; when the very short time limit expired, Germany delivered to Russia a declaration of war, so worded as to exclude further negotiations even if Russia did not actually reject the ultimatum. Russia rejected it (August 1), and France also refused. The Germans immediately entered Belgium; and this violation of the treaty guaranteeing Belgian independence, to which Germany was a party, brought England into the war.

The Russian Cabinet was anything but united on the subject of this war. The Foreign Minister Sazonov and the majority of his colleagues were warmly for taking up the challenge. The War Minister Sukhomlinov and two other Ministers, N. Maklakov and Shcheglovitov, desired above all things peace with Germany, which was regarded by the Russian reactionaries as the chief support of autocracy in Europe. This division in foreign policy corresponded intimately with the views of the respective Ministers on home affairs. The Prime Minister, the aged Goremykin, was strongly Conservative, but at the same time patriotic. In the country educated opinion as a whole was enthusiastically for the war; German domination had been widely experienced throughout Russia through the economic hold which Germans had secured in many industries and by their tenure of various offices of authority; the watchword of defence of the Slavs and the Orthodox of the Balkans appealed to nearly all. The Emperor, coming out on to the balcony of the Winter Palace, was received with a warmth which some had thought impossible; most of the enormous crowd fell on their knees. Early in the war the German name of the capital was changed to Petrograd.

The field army at the front was enthusiastic for the war; but the War Office, in the hands of Sukhomlinov, was supine and unfriendly. Not only for this but for other reasons of long standing, the equipment was gravely inadequate. The Duma, from 1908 onward, had had a marked influence on army reform, especially on the supply of machine guns; but there were still huge gaps, especially in the provision of heavy guns and of shell, and the medical service was hopelessly insufficient, as also were the arrangements for transport and food supply.

The plan of the Central Powers for an eastern campaign had originally been that the two allies should simultaneously enter Russian Poland, the Germans from the north, the Austrians from the south, and that they should thus, so to speak, amputate Poland from Russia at the neck. It was not long before the war that Russia took any measures at all for securing Poland; many thought that it would have to be abandoned at the outset without a struggle. In Germany, in the event of a war on two fronts, military opinion was divided as to whether to strike first to east or to west; but Germany decided to strike first westward against France; the Austrians were still to invade toward Lublin from Galicia, but East Prussia was to remain on the defensive.

The first month of the war brought the Germans well on their way through northern France toward Paris; and at the earnest prayer of her allies Russia took the offensive against East Prussia. Rennenkampf advanced westward, and was successful, at unnecessary cost, at Stallupönen (August 17) and Gumbinnen (August 19). Meanwhile Samsonov at the head of another large army was to strike northward from Warsaw, thus threatening to cut off the defending forces from Germany. Samsonov had only one good road of advance through a country full of lakes and marshes. The veteran Hindenburg was hurriedly called up to command the German defence. Daring for the time to disregard Rennenkampf, who remained quite inactive, Hindenburg faced Samsonov near Tannenberg, bringing up heavy artillery from Königsberg. Many of his men had their homes just behind them, and close behind their homes the sea; they knew well how ruthlessly the Russians had already ravaged parts of East Prussia. Hindenburg gave his orders standing near the monument which commemorated the great triumph of the Slavs over the Germans under the command of Vitovt in 1410. He knew intimately the road system of this land of lakes and marshes, which he himself had earlier saved from being reclaimed in view of its value as a military frontier. The huge Russian masses floundered clumsily without any cohesion, General Artamonov even disregarding his direct instructions, and left gaps of which Hindenburg was not slow to avail himself. Assisted by perfect discipline, Hindenburg was able at two points to drive a wedge into the Russian army, ultimately securing a position in which his artillery enabled him to threaten a very large part of it with destruction. Samsonov shot himself, three corps were entirely routed, and a colossal number of Russians were taken prisoners, with huge stores and so much artillery that every battery in the army was reduced from six guns to four; the bulk of Russia's inadequate heavy artillery had been sent against Hindenburg (August 26–30). Turning on Rennenkampf, Hindenburg outflanked him from the south and, in a series of hard-fought engagements, drove him out of East Prussia (September 8–15).

The Austrians had meanwhile launched the best part of their field army, nearly a million strong, from Galicia into Russian Poland. The southwestern front of Russia had been entrusted to a group of generals formerly associated in the Kiev military district—Ivanov, Alexeyev, and Ruzsky. The Russian staff, relying on secret information, had expected the Austrians to concentrate near Cracow, but they were far east of this, and advanced in a convex formation toward Lublin. Thus the Russian right wing found itself much too far westwards, and a portion of it suffered a serious reverse. Reinforcements, however, were sent up on this side. Meanwhile the Russian left, under Brusilov and Ruzsky, advanced into Galicia with the greatest rapidity, and threatened the Austrian rear. On September 3 Brusilov was at Halicz and Ruzsky entered Lemberg. The Austrian centre reached Fazlawica close to Lublin, and Plehve, whose forces were necessarily scattered in connecting the two wings, was outnumbered and in danger of being broken. However, he handled his troops with consummate skill. The turning-point in the battle came by a courageous decision of the Grand Duke Nicholas. On the receipt of the disastrous news of Tannenberg, he at once sent orders for Plehve to hold his ground at all cost, and for both wings to attack everywhere with the utmost vigour. On September 10, Ruzsky, in a desperate struggle, decisively defeated the Austrian right centre at Rawa Ruska, and a large part of the fine Hungarian cavalry was destroyed. The central Austrian mass could do nothing but make the hastiest retreat possible. This took almost the form of a rout; arms and stores were left behind everywhere; it was only with difficulty that the army of Dankl escaped at all. On neither side was there much heavy artillery, as the Austrians had sent much of their own to the Western Front; consequently it was in the main bayonet fighting, in which the Russians showed themselves completely superior.

Hindenburg now concentrated a force in the neighbourhood of Posen and in September made a dash upon Warsaw, which was still inadequately defended. The Russian decision to hold Warsaw was taken only at the last moment. The Guard entered in a scene of great enthusiasm. At the outset of the war the Grand Duke Nicholas had issued a proclamation claiming the help of the Poles in the Slavonic cause, and promising that this war would lead to the grant of self-government; the Emperor, when questioned by Count Wielopolski, crossed himself and confirmed the promise of the Grand Duke, and from this time forward the autonomy of Poland was a part of the government program, though opposed by the Empress and persistently hindered and postponed by the more reactionary ministers. The Poles responded to the Grand Duke's appeal by wholehearted work for the cause of the Entente Powers. For them the fact that Russia had England and France on her side seemed the main guarantee for the fulfilment of the Russian promises; also a victory of Germany and Austria in alliance could not lead to the reunion of Poland. Hindenburg actually reached the suburbs of Warsaw (October 14); but Russian reinforcements, including an admirable Siberian Corps, drove him back; the Russians crossed the Vistula under fire south of Warsaw and in a great sweeping movement the enemy were pressed back on Silesia (October 18). In response to Allied pressure, the Grand Duke aimed at an invasion of Prussia, but was already seriously hampered by the shortage in the reserves of shell. Another more organized German attack followed in November and December. In a series of most complicated operations, starting in the neighbourhood of Lodz, Hindenburg at one time seemed to have broken a way through the Russian forces and to be able to cut off a section of them; but Ruzsky, who had been appointed to the command of the new western front, assisted by the brilliant work of General Plehve, so reversed the conditions, that it was the advancing German force that found itself almost surrounded. The Germans escaped, though with difficulty, by the negligence of Rennenkampf, who was now in command of a corps in this district.

The Russian advance in Galicia had continued, but during the hard fighting of November and December in Poland, when large Austrian reinforcements also advanced northward from the Carpathians, the southern Russian group for a long time drew back to the river San. Later the Russians were able to advance on this side as far as Cracow, retreating, however, when the winter position defined itself to the north of

them in Poland. In Galicia the war was for the Russians one of liberation. As far as the San the population is mainly Ukrainian, and the invading troops coming from the Kiev area were of the same blood. West
of the San begins Polish territory, and the Russian army was received
almost as well here as in Russian Poland.

In February there were further operations at the extreme north of
the front in Mazovia, where German forces, in some furious fighting
through the forest of Augustovo, drove the Russians back on Grodno;
the Russian infantry met them throughout with the most stubborn resistance and sometimes secured some partial successes.

So passed the winter of 1914 and the first months of the new year,
during which the Russians were slowly fighting their way through the
Carpathian Mountains, storming hill after hill with only very feeble
artillery support. In March the Austrians attempted a counter movement, but the Russians continued to go forward; they had surmounted
the crest of the Carpathians, and at some points had already secured a
footing in Hungary. The important fortress of Przemysl, in which an
army of 150,000 Austrians under Kumanek had taken shelter, though
invested by much inferior forces largely of reserve formations, surrendered on March 22. The surrender was partly due to the disaffection
of Slav troops in the garrison; Czech legions were being formed by the
Russians, whose front line was now not far from Moravia.

Count Tisza, the Hungarian Premier, whose country house was already in Russian hands, now urged strongly at Berlin a special concentration of forces on this side; Austria had already been driven to
think of discussing a separate peace. In May 1915, the enemy opened
a strong offensive under Mackensen against the salient of the Russian
front south of Tarnow where it turned eastward from the Dunajec along
the Carpathians. The offensive was supported by an overwhelming
superiority of artillery which practically annihilated everything opposed
to it. The Russians, with little but field artillery and with sometimes almost a complete absence of ammunition, made a splendid resistance
wherever the bayonet could be used; but they suffered tremendous losses
and the Third Russian Army, which was the most exposed, in a few
weeks lost three sevenths of its number (150,000 men). Other armies,
especially the Eighth under Brusilov, also suffered heavily, and at the
end of June the total Russian losses of ten months of war amounted to
3,800,000 men. Large drafts of untrained men of all ages, often without
arms, were rushed up to fill the gaps. With desperate rear-guard actions,
especially at night, the Russians retreated slowly from the Dunajec and

Carpathians to the San, and later across the frontier to Brest-Litovsk. The same artillery superiority enabled the rest of the German line to sweep forward; Warsaw had to be abandoned (August 4); the fortresses made no adequate resistance; Kovno fell on August 18, Novogeorgievsk on August 19 and Osovets, which had distinguished itself more than the others, on August 22; and the Russians were driven entirely out of Russian Poland. Vilna and Brest-Litovsk were also abandoned; the German advance was only held up finally in September along a front extending through the marshes of Pinsk. The last incident of the campaign was a daring German cavalry raid through the Russian front at Molodechno, threatening some of the most vital of the Russian railway communications; this attempt was defeated and was followed by a sturdy Russian counterstroke. An enormous area of territory had been lost; but it is interesting to note that as yet the Germans had not approached the scene of any one of the battles of Napoleon's campaign. To those present with the Russian army there was the strongest contrast between this great loss of ground and the splendid fighting spirit and the sense of superiority, at least among all Russian forces opposed to Austrian troops.

The Russian retreat was accompanied by a wholesale movement of refugees eastward. In Poland the absurd orders of the Russian government, hastily and badly executed, aiming at a complete evacuation of this cultivated country by its population, led to the most acute distress; in particular, these measures were ruthlessly applied in the case of the Jews. Whole communities were driven from their villages, losing all regular means of livelihood and parting company for many years with all their settled habits; many victims were swept off by epidemics.

The shortage of munitions had long since become evident; but the War Minister Sukhomlinov refused to be dragged out of his apathy and even declined offers of help from private factories. An officer in the Intelligence Service, Colonel Myasoyedov, detected in regular espionage before the war but saved from disgrace by a personal guarantee from Sukhomlinov, had in the operations of the winter battle in Mazovia sent systematic information by aeroplane to the Germans, which had largely contributed to the Russian defeat. Myasoyedov's new treachery was discovered, and in spite of Sukhomlinov and even of court connections, he was hanged as a spy.

Before the disasters of the Russians in Galicia, Lord Kitchener had done everything that he could to get knowledge of their needs and to help to supply them, although at the time there was a grave shortage of shell among all the Allies. Unable to obtain information from Sukh-omlinov, Kitchener addressed himself direct to the Grand Duke, who actually appointed him agent to procure munitions for the Russian army. Thus the character of the alliance deepened, and the question of munitions inevitably brought the Allies closer into matters of Russian administration and politics.

The Galician disaster led to indignant protests of Russian patriotism against the failure of the government. The intensity of the devotion of the public at that time to the army and its needs made the munition scandals seem all the more criminal. The Emperor, who was also devoted to his army, felt as his subjects did. At the outset of the war, this time with the encouragement of the government, had been revived the Zemstvo Union of Red Cross under Prince G. Lvov, which gathered together the work of all individual Zemstva and quickly made provision for a million wounded; later it rendered invaluable services in the establishment of food stations at the front, and in the organization of transport. Leading members of nearly all parties in the Duma served in the Red Cross; and Guchkov, who had devoted most of his political life to army reform and lived in the front line, had made himself familiar with the negligence of Sukhomlinov and its effects, and denounced him at a meeting of the Zemstvo Union. On June 25 the Emperor summoned his ministers to General Headquarters and there dismissed Sukhomlinov, at the same time summoning the Duma for August 1 and asking the country for a great effort in the war. The reactionary Ministers N. Maklakov, Shcheglovitov, and Sabler were also dismissed as not in sympathy with it. The dismissed ministers were replaced by men in touch with public opinion and with the Duma: at the War Office General Polivanov, at the Ministry of the Interior Prince Shcherbatov, at the Ministry of Justice Alexis Hvostov, and at the Holy Synod, one of the most distinguished of churchmen and Slavophils, Samarin, who was marshal of the Moscow gentry. The Duma, as soon as it met, voted by an overwhelming majority for the trial of Sukhomlinov, which was accorded. It also asked for the establishment of a central committee of war industries for the supply of munitions, which would include representatives of the two legislative chambers. This too was granted, and the leading members of the Duma and of the Zemstvo Union became active workers on this committee; with this committee would cooperate a public and unofficial munitions committee already initiated by the Zemstvo Red Cross (June 15), which concentrated the work of numerous local committees all over the country. In the Duma was now formed a Progressive bloc which was only the natural outcome of a long period of approximation of all the central parties, including almost all except reactionaries and socialists; this majority was in character and in authority the same kind of basis that existed at this time in France and England for national coalition governments. The Progressive bloc put forward a detailed and reasonable program of reforms, which carried the consent of all its members; it also asked for a uniform Ministry possessing the confidence of the country, that is of the Duma; it did not ask for ministerial responsibility to the Duma, to spare the scruples of the more conservative members (September 4). The leaders of the Progressive bloc got into contact with Sazonov and the other more Liberal ministers. It seemed that the long process, which since 1861 had led toward a Russian constitution, was about to culminate in its achievement.

Unhappily for Russia, the greatest enemy of any constitution was in the Emperor's own house, in the person of the Empress, as is abundantly clear from her letters throughout this period. Her political predilections were always strongly in favour of autocracy; but one does not trace any consistent program of activity on her part before the war. Though a Princess of Hesse Darmstadt, she was entirely Russian in her war sympathies and did indefatigable work for the Russian Red Cross; her education had been largely English, and she showed her English sympathies on several occasions during the war; her attitude to German policy and methods was very much that of an average Englishwoman of the time; but in Russian affairs she was a determined absolutist, and could not tolerate the idea that her son should come to the throne with his powers in any way restricted. She was a woman of the narrowest mind but with a very strong will; the Imperial couple were devotedly attached to each other. The Emperor, as we know, was a weak man, and though quite intelligent enough to understand realities, succumbed to her influence when he was with her; he himself had never faced the question, how far he had limited his own powers in the constitutional manifesto of October 30, 1905. Their only son Alexis lived literally in constant danger of sudden death. The Empress was a mystic; she was capable of prolonged religious meditation; she found her greatest pleasure in church; having no great intelligence, she easily fell under spiritualist influences. The French spiritualist Philippe of Lyons, who was prominent at the Russian Court during the Japanese War, was succeeded by Gregory Rasputin, a man of the foulest life, who, however, was credited by all who met him with powers of clairvoyance. His connection with the Imperial couple, who knew hardly anything about what was going on outside their narrow circle, was at first limited to his intervention at dangerous crises in the health of the heir to the throne. On two occasions during the war when the best doctors despaired of the child's life, Rasputin (in one case by telegram) risked the prophecy that he would recover, and in each case recovery set in from that time. The most circumstantial stories against him, by whomsoever they were told, the Empress flatly refused to believe: for her, he was "a Man of God," "Our Friend," "He." She had a special animosity against the Duma, and against Guchkov in particular, for the exposure which it had made of Rasputin before the war.

Rasputin was not necessarily the agent of any political group, but he was a violent opponent of any diminution of the autocracy: if the Emperor were ever bound to listen to constitutional advisers, there would be no place for Rasputin, who entered the narrow atmosphere of Tsarskoe Selo as the self-appointed spokesman of the loyal Russian peasantry. In July 1914 he had sent an impressive warning against the war which the Emperor disregarded. He had foretold defeat, and defeat had come. Now his influence became greater than ever. From July 11 the Emperor spent two months at Tsarskoe Selo, and the Empress engaged in a vigorous campaign to secure the removal of the Grand Duke Nicholas from the post of Commander-in-Chief, which he had occupied with great distinction at a most difficult time and with the strongest moral support from the public. On August 24 the ministers were summoned to Tsarskoe Selo and there informed that the Emperor had decided to take over the command. His real reason, or rather the Empress's, was that he might not be overshadowed by the Grand Duke in the public eye. Sazonov and others did all that they could do to dissuade him, but in vain. The decision was received by the public with consternation; one of its inferences, however, was entirely incorrect; the Emperor, as much as anyone in the country, was devoted to the war and determined to carry it to a triumphant end.

With the Emperor at Headquarters the Empress, at first tentatively and informally but later entirely, became the real ruler of the rear. Her extraordinary infatuation for the judgment of Rasputin induced her to take every instruction of his as binding. The first thing to do was to get rid of the liberal ministers. In September they addressed a joint memorial to the sovereign which, indirectly at least, supported the Duma's formula of a Ministry possessing the confidence of the country; they expressed their difficulty in serving under the premiership of the aged and by no means competent Goremykin; the Ministers of War and of

the Navy, though in sympathy with this memorial, abstained from signing it on grounds of service discipline. The Emperor in reply summoned
the ministers to Headquarters on September 29, and there told them
that he would permit of no revolt against Goremykin. He ordered them
to continue their work until dismissed by himself; the Empress' letters
are full of the details of the search for substitutes. On September 16 at
the urgent request of Goremykin the Duma was prorogued, and a meeting of the Zemstvo Union, again calling for a "Ministry of confidence,"
was silenced; the delegates whom it sent to plead with the Emperor
were refused an audience; nor would he receive the delegates of the
Moscow gentry.

We thus pass into the fatal period of Rasputin's rule over Russia.
One of the first public scandals concerned the Church. An adherent of
Rasputin's, Archbishop Varnava, against all church law announced on
his own initiative the canonization of a new saint. Samarin, as Procurator of the Holy Synod, sent Varnava and his supporters into reclu-
sion at monasteries; the Emperor, however, decided over the head of
the Synod in favour of Varnava; Samarin did his utmost to warn him,
and on October 9 both he and the Minister of the Interior, Shcherbatov, were dismissed. On November 9 the same fate befell the very capable Minister of Agriculture, Krivoshein. Rasputin had in the spring
visited some of the holy places in Moscow and, while there, had made
himself notorious by his disreputable behaviour in a public place; the
police record of the scene was sent to General Dzhunkovsky, a devoted
servant of the sovereign, who held a high post at court, and Dzhunkovsky handed it to the Emperor, with the result that on September 8 he
was dismissed from all court appointments. A similar protest from another of the oldest friends and servants of the Emperor, Prince Orlov,
had the same result (September 5). These incidents became well known
to the public. In nearly all the Empress's further recommendations of
candidates for ministries comes the consideration: "he venerates our
Friend," or "he does not like our Friend."

The new Minister of the Interior was Alexander Hvostov (not to
be confused with his uncle Alexis), recommended by the Empress as a
Conservative member of the Duma, who could therefore hold it in
check; he had distinguished himself by a violent speech against German
exploitation. It was not many months before he quarrelled with Rasputin, and the public was later entertained with the extraordinary details of a plot of a Minister of the Interior to murder the favourite; it
was not clear what part police provocation had played in this plot; it

was revealed by the Director of Police Beletsky, who had formerly co-operated with both men. Ultimately both Hvostov and Beletsky lost their posts (March 1916), though Beletsky was half restored to favour. The whole story was reminiscent of the Middle Ages.

Rasputin's rule affected every part of the administration of the country. He held levées at which he received any solicitation and forwarded it with a scribbled order to the Minister concerned. He promoted an enormous government loan; he constantly interfered in the food supply; he dictated drastic orders concerning the transport; he issued his directions and prophecies with regard to the movements at the front and demanded that the plans of operations and the intended times of their execution should be communicated to him in advance, so that he might assist them with his prayers; he even dictated messages to be sent by the sovereign to the kings of Serbia and Greece. He was surrounded by unclean influences, and financial adventurers found him an easy tool; he was quite opposed to the war.

As the time for the next meeting of the Duma approached, Goremykin, who had twice had it postponed and had received a robust written protest from its president, Rodzyanko, frankly feared to face it under the new conditions, and was called upon to resign; and on February 2, 1916, was appointed as Prime Minister a Master of Ceremonies at the Court, Stürmer, known chiefly to the public by large defalcations and as an obsequious follower of Rasputin, of whom he was only the puppet. When the Duma met on February 22, the Emperor, who was at the front, unexpectedly visited it for the first time, and for the first time addressed it as "representatives of the people." He was rapturously received, and on the same day returned to the front. Rasputin had originally suggested the visit as a blind, but deplored the way his pupil had carried it out. On April 2, however, the Empress was successful in securing the dismissal of Polivanov, who was directly informed that it was due to his too close cooperation with the public in the work of the Munitions Committee.

In July fell another heavy blow. Poland, lost to Russia, had now to be reconquered with the help of the Allies. The Emperor's promise of autonomy had at his command been worked into a detailed scheme by Sazonov. The scheme was just and generous; it conceded all that could be conceded without establishing a dual authority in the empire as a whole. The Emperor approved it and Sazonov went for a holiday; it was now (on July 21) that he received the news of his dismissal. Both Stürmer and the Empress had visited the Emperor at Headquarters to obtain this decision. The French and British Ambassadors made a joint effort to prevent Sazonov's fall, but without effect. The Ministry of Foreign Affairs like the Premiership was entrusted to Stürmer, that is, practically to Rasputin. After the dismissal of Alexander Hvostov in March, 1916, Stürmer had for a time been Minister of the Interior.

Disillusionment in those hopes of greater liberty at home, which had been the chief spur to enthusiasm in the war and were closely connected with the alliance, produced a pessimistic mood in Russia during the winter of 1915–16. Serbia, for whom Russia had taken up the challenge, was overrun and apparently conquered; Bulgaria, liberated by Russian arms, had joined the enemy. Poland was in German and Austrian hands.

All through this period there was a striking contrast but an increasing interaction between the front and the rear. The heroic army had made its first huge sacrifices, screened off as it were by a curtain from the public. Toward the end of 1914, its immense needs had begun to be known, and the heavy reverses and the munitions scandals of 1915 had not only blended front and rear, but had dictated a far closer cooperation between the Allies. Not only the Russian public, but France and England were making feverish efforts to arm the Russian soldier. The healthy breath of this cooperation had helped Polivanov to remarkable achievements both in training and equipment which made Hindenburg think his goal as far off as ever. The troops under fire if now, as in all other countries, of inferior quality, were sound, and successfully withstood the many direct attempts at propaganda made upon them from the German lines. In March and April a vigorous offensive around Lake Naroch met with early successes, but ended in the usual heavy losses. Lord Kitchener was himself on his way to Russia to help to complete the work of munitioning, when he was drowned on the *Hampshire*. The French government sent more than one authoritative mission with the same object. In May a deputation of the Duma, headed by its Vice-President Protopopov, at this time a keen worker for equipment, visited England and France. In June and July, Brusilov on the southwestern front, by enormous sacrifices which amazed even Hindenburg, succeeded in breaking the Austrian line, and this served as a signal for great masses of the Slavonic troops of Austria, especially Czechs, to come over to the Russian side. The Austrians were swept far back; the front was extended to Galicia, and the Russians again found themselves in the autumn taking hill after hill by storm in the Carpathians, this time on their eastern side.

These triumphs were very dearly bought and the Guard Army in particular, being badly handled, suffered grievous losses: indeed the success was as much political as military, for the vast numbers of prisoners were in the main Slavs of Austria who wanted to join the side of the Entente. But it induced Roumania, which had long been treating with the Allies and was now faced by Stürmer with a time limit for its decision, to hurry into the war (August 27). The Roumanian army, almost entirely dependent on foreign equipment, was utterly unready; and the cessation of Roumanian neutrality proved in the end to be more to the advantage of Germany than of her enemies. While an unwise and unprepared advance was made on Transylvania, Bulgarian troops crossed the Danube in September, and General Mackensen speedily succeeded in conquering Wallachia, thus doubling in width the corridor by which Germany could cooperate with her southern allies, Bulgaria and Turkey. The greatly extended front had at this stage to be defended almost entirely by the Russian army. It continued, however, to show a quite good spirit, and the position as to munitions was so much improved toward the end of the year that the struggle was now conducted almost on equal terms in this respect, and advance and victory were generally anticipated for the spring. The Emperor, who had practically ceased to direct affairs in the rear and was absorbed in the single aim of winning the war, shared this anticipation, and Hindenburg, estimating the chances for the new year, reckoned a Russian offensive as one of his chief dangers.

Meanwhile, the rear was being thoroughly poisoned by the Rasputin regime, and there were times when the poison crept up nearer to the front. Deprived of the best portion of her railway system by the loss of her western provinces, Russia was gravely embarrassed by a crisis in the food supply, which always depended on transport, especially in that corner of the empire which contained the capital. Partly through this same breakdown of transport, some portions of the country were slipping out of control, and sections of the army were compelled to forage for food as best they could. The domination of Rasputin was more complete than ever, and he was courted and surrounded by ill-savoured financial adventurers, of whom one, Manassein-Manuilov, was actually the secretary of his puppet Prime Minister, Stürmer. Rasputin dealt confidently with capital questions in every province of the administration, and there were outrageous financial scandals. His political aims were quite reactionary, and an enigma; but the dismissed pro-German Ministers, Shcheglovitov and N. Maklakov, were forming a peace group and again had access to the Empress. The Allies were hampered by concealment and deception, and the growing petulance felt for them in high quarters was openly expressed by the Grand Duke Boris. Protopopov, on his way back from England, paid a visit to a German diplomatist in Stockholm, and shortly afterwards, deserting his colleagues of the Duma, was on Rasputin's recommendation put in charge of the Ministry of the Interior (October 3). Again the Empress turned to a member of the Duma to suppress the Duma. The official munitions committee continued its work as best it could.

Serious signs of disaffection began to appear among the workmen and the drafts for the army. Most of the leaders of the Duma were very anxious that there should be no upheaval during the war, largely in order to satisfy the expressed wish of Russia's allies. The Socialist Revolutionaries and the Menshevik section of the Social Democrats gave a conditional support to the war; but the small Bolshevik section, whose leader Lenin was in Switzerland with his principal associates, desired before all things defeat and peace as a preface to a world revolution. This view Lenin had emphasized at the two Socialist conferences of Zimmerwald (September 1915) and Kienthal (April 1916), and the German government enabled him to circulate defeatist literature in its prisoners' camps. The work of his colleagues in Petrograd seems not, as yet, to have had any considerable effect; but the general discontent gave them every opportunity. In October a group of strikers was joined by the soldiers sent to disperse it.

The Duma was at last summoned on November 14. Stürmer and the ministers filed out immediately after the opening ceremony, but the full House and the crowded public listened with enthusiasm to a speech in which the Liberal leader Milyukov detailed the delinquencies of the government, asking after each: "Is this folly or treason?" The Conservative Shulgin and the reactionary leader Purishkevich followed with equally vigorous denunciations. Stürmer did not dare face the Duma again; he wanted to dissolve it and to arrest Milyukov, but Nicholas would not go to these lengths and dismissed him (November 23). This was Nicholas' last chance. Stürmer was replaced by the senior member of the Cabinet, the Transport Minister A. Trepov, a Conservative, not very efficient, but patriotic, loyal to the Allies, and no friend of Rasputin. His position was misunderstood in the Duma, and he too was hissed there. The offer of the Allies to incorporate in the common war aims the acquisition of Constantinople by Russia came too late in the war to arouse any enthusiasm. Trepov had from the outset insisted on the resignation of Protopopov. The Empress wrote hysterically again and again to the Emperor to save Protopopov, and ultimately took him down to Headquarters with her. Protopopov re-mained, and Trepov dragged on without power till January 9, when he was allowed to resign.

The ex-Premier Count Kokovtsev already anticipated a revolution, whether from above or below. The sovereigns remained isolated even from the Imperial family. Warning on warning came from every side. The Empress Dowager had long since given her advice in vain, but it was now supported by the Grand Duke Paul, who on December 16 asked the Emperor for a constitution, the Grand Dukes Dmitry, Nicho-las Mikhailovich, and Alexander Mikhailovich, the Empress's two sisters, the Ambassadors of England and France, the Emperor's old friend and servant Admiral Nilov, and several others. It was in the midst of these warnings that on December 30 Rasputin was assassinated by Prince Yusupov, husband of the Emperor's niece, and Purishkevich, one of the extremist Conservatives in the Duma. He was lured to Yusupov's house, and after a futile attempt to poison him he was twice shot. His body was recovered off one of the islands in the Neva. The Emperor returned from the army to Tsarkoe Selo to attend his funeral.

The Grand Duke Dmitry, who had been in Yusupov's house during the murder, was sent to Persia in spite of a joint memorandum from the Imperial family. The Emperor remained some weeks at the palace in complete apathy, turning a deaf ear to all warnings. There was open and noisy talk of a palace revolution to replace him on the throne by his son, with a regent; and a plan of General Krymov with this object had sympathizers in society and in the Duma. So far, all the chances seemed to point to a change of this kind. A Minister of the Interior had himself plotted to assassinate Rasputin; his death was the work of a Prince and a Conservative leader, who evidently sought to save the dynasty. The Grand Dukes had come into line with the public, and only visited the palace to warn the sovereign. A mysterious letter of Guchkov to Alexeyev seemed to suggest that the leading generals were being sounded. One thing is clear—that the Emperor had ceased to count and that the Empress was inflexible. Protopopov alone had her confidence and seems to have been almost her only political visitor. Even the con-servative Council of State declared for the program of the Duma, and at the Russian New Year (January 14, 1917) Shcheglovitov, a reaction-ary who was opposed to the war, was appointed its president. N. Makla-kov, who held the same views, was received by the Empress. In Petrograd at this time (the end of January) a Congress of the Allied Powers came and went in an atmosphere of complete unreality. Protopopov divided his time between plans of repression and spiritualist conversations reminiscent of Rasputin. Later admissions of his show that he meant to challenge an outbreak, and intended, after suppressing it, to allege internal difficulties as a plea for making a separate peace. At the same time progress was made by the revolutionary agitators in their work of propaganda in the factories and the barracks.

The meeting of the Duma had again been postponed to February 27. The members anticipated dissolution and were determined not to disperse. The Red Cross Union of Zemstva and Towns was ordered to close its provincial committees. The workman's group on the central public munitions committee, though consisting of the most loyal elements, was arrested (February 9), and a strike broke out in Petrograd. At the same time there was a stoppage of the food supply, which was put to the credit of the government. There was plenty of food in the capital, but its distribution was entirely incompetent. The Duma met on February 27. In the Council of State, Shcheglovitov burked discussion, with the result that a number of members left the House.

On March 8 long queues besieged the bakers' shops. On the 9th the police fired on the crowds. Next day all factories and schools stopped work and everyone was on the streets. Soldiers began to take the side of the people. Conflicts took place near the Town Hall and the Znamensky Square. The Emperor, on being informed at his distant Headquarters, ordered the immediate suppression of the disorders; and General Habalov, the military governor, announced that he would fire on demonstrations. March 11 was a Sunday. Huge crowds with flags paraded the streets and held meetings. Patrols of police passed through the centre; others posted with machine guns at points of vantage commanding the principal thoroughfares fired on the crowds, who were joined by more and more of the soldiers. The next morning (March 12) the Volhynian Regiment of the Guard joined the side of the people, and nearly the whole garrison followed its example. The session of the Duma had been postponed by order on the 11th; but the members remained, and throughout the day, on the instructions of Kerensky, troops kept arriving to offer their support. The crowds seized the Arsenal, distributed weapons, opened the prisons, and set fire to the headquarters of the political police. At midday a few government troops appeared on the streets but were powerless. As yet there was no direction of the movement, which, in the words of one of the leading revolutionaries, went of itself. At three o'clock the Duma appointed a Provisional Com-

mittee representative of nearly all parties, under its President, Rodzyanko; the Social Democrats were unwilling to join it. At seven o'clock
in the huge lobby of the Duma took place the first meeting of a Soviet
or Council of Delegates hastily elected from the factories and barracks.
In the evening the Provisional Committee of the Duma received a telephone message from the Grand Duke Cyril and the officers of the
Preobrazhensky Regiment of the Guard, asking it to assume the power
and putting themselves at its service. On March 11 Rodzyanko had
telegraphed to the Emperor repeating the old request for a Prime Minister who had the confidence of the country and strongly urging the
dangers of delay. On the 12th he telegraphed: "The last hour has come,
when the destiny of the country and the dynasty is being decided." No
answer had been received to either of these messages. To the request of
the Preobrazhentsy, Rodzyanko, strongly pressed by his colleagues, after
a short delay consented, and the committee named Commissioners
(Commissars) who set to work at once. On March 14, ministers of the
Provisional Government were appointed: Kerensky, a Socialist Revolutionary, who was both a member of the Duma and Vice-President of the
new Soviet, was offered the Ministry of Justice. The Soviet had forbidden any of its members to take office with the Duma, but Kerensky not
only assented but obtained the sanction of the Soviet (March 15).

On the evening of March 14, deputies of the Soviet visited the assembled ministers, and next day the Soviet agreed to give conditional
support to the new government. A Constituent Assembly was to be
summoned on universal suffrage, and all local governing bodies were to
be re-elected on the same franchise. All civil rights were to be shared by
soldiers, but discipline was to be maintained at the front. The garrison
of Petrograd was not to be moved. Of typical significance for the future
was a demand put forward by the Soviet that the new government
should countersign the draft of a new Army Order (No. 1), the effect
of which could only be to destroy the authority of the officers. It was
not countersigned by the government, and by agreement the compromise already mentioned above was adopted. But the order was nevertheless circulated everywhere in the army as coming from the new Revolutionary Government, and the dissolution of all morale and discipline set
in wherever it was received.

All that was known of the Emperor was that he was dispatching
General Ivanov to put down the Revolution with a small force of picked
men; this force was unable to get through to Petrograd. The Provisional
Government telegraphed for support to all the principal generals in com-

mand of the army and received their adherence to the demand for a Ministry responsible to the Duma. This was also approved by the principal Grand Dukes. Nicholas at last replied, sending for Rodzyanko; but by this time things had gone too far. He left Mogilev and tried to make his way to Tsarskoe Selo but found the line to the capital blocked and turned aside to Pskov, the headquarters of General Ruzsky. Here he learned that practically all the generals were agreed that he should abdicate. On the night of March 15 arrived two delegates of the Provisional Government, the Conservative Shulgin and the Octobrist Guchkov, bringing the same request. Nicholas made no opposition at all. Till that afternoon he had meant to resign the throne to his son, as was required by the law of succession and desired both by the Provisional Government and by the Grand Dukes; but on being told by his doctor that the boy's ailment was incurable, he abdicated in dignified language in favour of his brother, the Grand Duke Michael, at the same time confirming the new Ministry and asking all to support it in order to carry the country to victory (March 15). An appeal in the same sense which he addressed to the troops was not issued, and shortly afterwards he was placed under arrest.

The Soviet and the garrison of Petrograd were entirely unwilling to accept another Romanov. This view was vigorously urged, especially by Kerensky, on the Grand Duke Michael. Kerensky was strongly opposed by Guchkov and Milyukov; but the Grand Duke, after consulting Rodzyanko, decided not to accept the throne unless and until he should be asked to do so by the Constituent Assembly when it assembled (March 16).

This decision proved to be the fall of the Romanov dynasty. Its overthrow was not the work of the Duma, which had waited till the capital was in the hands of the mob; or of Lenin, who was in Switzerland; or of Trotsky, who was in New York; or of their small band of colleagues in Petrograd, who were still only at the stage of propaganda and had nothing like a majority in the Soviet. The dynasty fell by its own insufficiency, and the immediate occasion of its fall was the rule of the Empress and Rasputin. It fell at a moment least desired by the Duma, in the midst of a foreign war and of active propaganda by the enemy in the Russian rear, when the whole framework of administration had been thrown into chaos and stretched to breaking point by the war itself; and there was nothing ready to replace it.

The Provisional Government was recognized without delay by Russia's allies. Like the Tsar it was bent on helping its allies to win the war.

It was the same kind of national coalition as had been created by the war in Allied countries. But whereas party was at a discount in other countries, in Russia the Revolution brought the moment when party, so far always frowned on by the government, became itself the basis of government, and every citizen, to count in the affairs of his country, had to choose some political complexion. For every Russian the Revolution, however casually it had come, was a far greater event than the war itself: it was the beginning of everything new for his country. With the disappearance of the Tsar, much as in the earlier Time of Troubles, all the old props of administration crumbled. So far, all the existing officials had claimed authority only in his name. The Provisional Government was what the country had to offer in experience of government outside the administrative machine; but this amounted only to a few fairly competent critics, without authority, educated in a Duma which had hardly been listened to and was itself based on a preposterously artificial franchise. The immense arrears of home reform had at least produced a certain unity of program. Universal suffrage for both sexes at the age of eighteen was unquestioned and was applied at once. Even the immediate concession of complete independence to Poland met with no opposition, though of itself it raised the claims of all other races of the empire (March 30). In the general optimism and brotherhood, the Constituent Assembly was to be left a perfectly free hand to deal not only with all political but with all social questions; an assembly which was sure to be predominantly peasant was to decide the ownership of all land; indeed, something like four fifths of the cultivated land was already, one way or another, in peasant hands. To the Constituent Assembly was automatically transferred the passive allegiance to authority; by long habit, Russians were accustomed to expect all decisions from above; one village sent to Petrograd to ask for a portrait of the new sovereign "Revolutsia." The death penalty, even in the army, was abolished by acclamation in the midst of a world war; and in the general amnesty no exception was made against open defeatists working abroad in cooperation with official Germany.

The Provisional Government, though acknowledged as such for eight months, cannot be said to have actually ruled Russia. The initiative of the Revolution had been with the crowds on the streets which, from the moment when soldiers joined them, had seen the autocracy topple over of itself. After the Revolution the right of directing the country continued to be disputed, often in not unfriendly discussion, between the government and the Soviet. In the hectic weeks that followed, the Soviet never remedied the defects of its own hasty election; it was enormously large, and did not know its own mind; its decisions sometimes executed a *volte-face* on the most cardinal questions. Its basis was the street, and the street was constantly at each new crisis bubbling up into excited meetings in which the most contradictory views might be equally applauded. Meanwhile, though this was hardly noticed, at each new issue some fundamental support of the political structure of the country was not so much discarded as allowed to slip away of itself. The most essential support of the Provisional Government fell away from it at the outset. At the very first meeting of the new Cabinet, a delegation from the Soviet sitting in the same building had asked its approval for its Army Order No. 1, which abolished the military salute and practically released the troops from the authority of their officers. The order was designed in the first place for the Petrograd garrison whose officers the Soviet did not trust; but its authors not unwillingly made it of general application.

The Prime Minister, Prince G. Lvov, had the extraordinary idea of inviting local self-government to organize itself as it chose. The Provisional Governors of course disappeared with the Tsar; even the elected Zemstva practically sank into abeyance. The commissaries of the government had no power; the police had fired on the people and was abolished, the new "militia" was never in working order, and every subordinate authority dictated to the one above it. In a word, one was witnessing the breakup of a whole community, and it was imperative to put some new authority in that empty gap as soon as possible. The commanders of the army could not find their bearings in these new conditions; they had the vaguest ideas on political questions, in which they had always been forbidden to interest themselves, and did not discriminate between the various "delegates" whom they let through to the troops. The front line was not unsound till the emissaries of disorder reached it. They announced that the officers had no longer any authority, that peace was about to be signed in Stockholm, and that all had better return in time for a land-partition which was about to take place. Then, depleted of trained officers by the incessant casualties, and spread out over vast distances, the soldiers began deserting in huge numbers, though very seldom while they were in charge of the front trenches. Within two months there were two million deserters, who flooded the rear, adding to the disorder. Directly after the Revolution were instituted army committees, one for every unit; officers here had the same vote as privates. The commanders wished to restrict them to domestic matters, such as the canteens; but they discussed and voted on all questions—for instance, the form of government—and soon they insisted that their sanction was necessary every time that the troops were ordered to attack.

Hardly anyone in the army had regretted Nicholas II. No one said a word for him. But the Soviet had feared a march upon Petrograd and was not sorry to see the army disorganized. Lenin with Zinoviev, Kamenev, Radek, Lunacharsky, and others, by agreement with the German General Staff travelled through Germany in a sealed carriage, and appeared in Petrograd on April 16; Trotsky arrived from Canada a little later. The breakup of the Imperial army was essentially necessary to the success of their program of further revolution; and Lenin, to the alarm even of many of his own colleagues, preached daily to large audiences the duty of fraternization between the two fronts.

On May 3 and 4 the Bolsheviks organized a demonstration against two of the most prominent Ministers, Guchkov and Milyukov, both devoted to the Allied cause. A Bolshevik procession paraded the streets carrying arms. A much larger crowd demanded the arrest of Lenin, who was at the time regarded chiefly as an agent of Germany. Order was restored, but Guchkov resigned because his colleagues were not firm about the restoration of discipline in the army; and Milyukov also, whose interpretations of war aims were widely questioned, was forced to retire. Lvov, though he lingered on in office, was already finished as a leader, and was really replaced by Kerensky, who was now Minister of War. The centre of gravity shifted very perceptibly to the left; but Kerensky, who showed much statesmanship at this time, managed to secure patriotic support and collaboration in the Ministry from moderate elements in the Soviet. At the front he did all that could be done by eloquent speeches to persuade the tired troops into a revolutionary patriotism. The war had still a year and a half to run, and if the Germans won it, the Russian Revolution was more or less finished. But however great an appeal this might have for the educated, it had none for the masses, and least of all for the army. The Bolsheviks had two strong cards in their hands: they stood for an immediate separate peace and organized from May onward extensive fraternization along the front; and they stood also, not for a redistribution of land by the Constituent Assembly, but for an immediate seizure of the estates by the nearest peasants—this, too, with all authority demoralized, they were able to put in action without delay.

The first local election on the basis of universal suffrage gave a majority to the S.R.'s. The greatest social event of this time was the agrarian revolution, which took up the rest of the year. The peasants carried it through in their own way and without any regard for equality, but by December it was almost complete and there was hardly a squire left. On July 1, 1917, in response to strong pressure from the Allies, Kerensky in person launched an offensive on the southwestern front, which was at first successful; but this was mainly the work of the officers and of the Czech legions, and he could get no enthusiasm from the rank and file. The offensive was a mistake; it was followed almost at once by rout and only led to more complete demoralization.

Through the summer, the Bolsheviks, by their persistent spadework, had been driving the war interest out of the public mind and substituting the discussion of the ideas of Karl Marx, who had long made a strong, if vague, appeal to the factory workers. Their leaders were not of one mind as to their tactics, but on July 17 a crowd of sailors, soldiers, and workmen, carrying arms, tried to seize the capital. Their attempt, though the work of comparatively small forces, was nearly successful, but was defeated by the patriotism of the Preobrazhensky Regiment and the belated opposition of the Soviet. News of the disastrous rout at Tarnopol (July 15) also aroused patriotic mortification; evidence of the dealings between German agents and leading Bolsheviks was published, and for the next two weeks the Provisional Government would have been generally supported in any reasonable use which it had made of its victory. But just now most of the Cadet ministers had resigned in protest at what they regarded as the concession of too great a measure of independence to Ukraine; and, containing now a large proportion of Socialists, the government was itself in two minds between the war against Germany and the war on capitalism. Trotsky was arrested and Lenin had had to go into hiding, but the Bolsheviks worked at their organization harder than ever, especially trying to secure the predominance in the military committees which had now been established throughout the army.

Differences of opinion had arisen between the Commander-in-Chief, Kornilov, who had re-established the death penalty at the front, and Kerensky, who hesitated to restore it in the rear. These were not removed by an enormous representative public conference in Moscow, which only accentuated the impossibility of any common agreement (August 26–8). The multicoloured Soviet, since its moderates had joined the government, was passing more to the left. Kornilov and the Cadets wanted to dissolve it. At Headquarters a plan was made for troops to march on Petrograd. The chief question was the position of Kerensky. A former colleague in the Ministry, Vladimir Lvov, tried to secure his adhesion; but any chance of agreement was spoilt by a number of political adventurers who surrounded Kornilov and wanted all power for themselves. General Krymov on the northern front moved first (September 8); but his troops soon began to fraternize with those which Kerensky sent against them, and the whole movement broke down. Krymov, after frankly avowing his hostility to Kerensky, committed suicide; Kornilov was put under arrest. Then mutual reproaches followed, together with such efforts at whitewashing and mystification as left all concerned discredited in public opinion.

Kerensky's basis was gone, and expedients of all kinds—such as a Democratic Conference with 1500 members (September 27), and a Vor-Parlament (October 20)—failed to restore it. Caught between two fires, Kerensky had set free the arrested Bolsheviks. Lenin, their leader, in spite of the hesitations and even the disloyalty of two of his lieutenants, Kamenev and Zinoviev, knew his own mind and went his own way. Trotsky, till recently a Menshevik, gave him the most effective assistance, especially with the regimental committees. The war of words continued for some months; and when the Bolsheviks again attempted to seize the power, hardly anyone was left who thought it his business to defend it against them. The Vor-Parlament was driven out of the Palace of Mary. The fortress of Peter and Paul and the *Aurora* from Kronstadt shelled the Winter Palace and the Admiralty. The last defenders of the Provisional Government were a women's battalion. Most of the ministers were taken prisoner and lodged in the fortress (November 7). Kerensky tried in vain to rally some Cossack troops outside Petrograd. In Moscow there was a longer resistance; a small band of military cadets made a plucky defence of the Kremlin, but were overpowered (November 12–14). The Commander-in-Chief, Dukhonin, ordered by telephone to open negotiations for an armistice, refused; and on the arrival of the new Bolshevik commander, Lieutenant Krylenko, he was murdered and mutilated. Moscow was again reinstated as the capital of Russia.

CHAPTER XXV

Communist Rule

[*1917–29*]

Lᴇɴɪɴ was the conspirative name of Vladimir Ilyich Ulyanov, son of a minor government official; he is first known to us by the school reports of his headmaster at Simbirsk, who, curiously enough, was the father of his future rival Kerensky. His brother Alexander, to whom he was devoted, was an S.R., and was executed for his share in a plot to assassinate Alexander III. Lenin, from the start, chose a different course.

At the party meetings of leading Russian Marxists at Brussels and later in London in 1903 he had challenged their veteran leader, George Plekhanov, who wished to use a democratic regime for the propaganda of Marxism, and Lenin secured a majority (*bolshinstvo*), which gave the name to his party. Lenin was also for the most extensive propaganda and for the closest contact with the factory class and its grievances, but he was the first builder of a totalitarian party, a determined group of professional revolutionaries, acknowledging the sternest discipline. These were at first almost exclusively intellectuals, living abroad and scraping a precarious subsistence from their writings. Lenin was a scholar of the first order; *Imperialism the Last Stage of Capitalism*, in which he analyzes the development and omnipotence of financial cartels, apart from its conclusions, is a first-class piece of research. He foresaw the World War, which he attributed entirely to imperialism, and he anticipated that the common experience of the fighting men of all nations in the line would give an opportunity of converting it into a war between classes. He had returned to Russia during the short-lived "revolution" of 1905; but in this case peace with Japan came almost before the movement began and helped to guide it into other and more equable channels. He had stoutly preached his principles throughout the World War, at first with very little effect. On his return after the fall of Tsardom, he found exactly that bankruptcy of all that was traditional and that gap calling for a novel authority which gave him his chance. He took that chance with both hands and with an absolute courage which sometimes alarmed his lieutenants. He had a wonderful flexibility of tactics which qualified him for meeting any emergency without any real deviation from his path. His objective was, of course, a world revolution on Marxist lines, but for this he depended largely on the world mood created by the war. His assumption of control in the broken and dissolving Russian community was in itself a marvel of ability and strategy, and he must not be held responsible for all that took place while he was still engaged in establishing himself in power. Much of it was due to the conditions, first of national and then of civil war, together with foreign intervention. He has for instance put it on record that he would have considered state capitalism to be a satisfactory first achievement. The first thing which he had to do was to bring order out of chaos in Russia.

The other leading figure of the moment, Trotsky, was very different. He had been a vice-president of the first Soviet in 1905, and up to the revolution was a Menshevik. Wholly internationalist in his temper and his life record, which for the most part lay abroad, he belonged essentially to the pre-Revolution period. Brilliant linguist, writer, and orator, he was a typical intellectual and a typical demagogue, adept at swaying a mob with his scorching phrases, but he had also inexhaustible administrative energy and resource. He was distrusted by Lenin and his other new colleagues as a newcomer, as a lone spirit, egotist, and opportunist, and his bitter tongue made him many enemies. He had not that simplicity of spirit which enabled Lenin so easily to bridge the gap that separated the intellectual from the common man.

None of the Bolsheviks, with the exception of Krasin, an industrialist, had had any experience of the management of a business. The views and predictions of Marx himself were founded on a series of theoretical deductions, intended for industrial countries. They had never been tried out in practice except for a few weeks of turmoil and bloodshed in Paris in 1871, with the German troops still encircling the city. The Bolsheviks had to apply them to Russia, an agricultural country, where the factory population was only eleven and a half out of one hundred and seventy-five millions. For a short period the Bolsheviks were in uncertain alliance with a small group of extreme S.R.'s, whose theory, in opposition to Lenin, was that farming Russia could pass straight into socialism, avoiding the stage of capitalism altogether. The first Land decree of the new government reflected this alliance; it legalized the central doctrines of the S.R.'s and at the same time the peasant seizures of estates, by enacting that all the land went to those who worked on it (November 7, 1917).

The Bolsheviks did not at the outset dare to hope for any permanence of their power. Their aim, as with the Communists of Paris in 1871, was to give such object lessons of their principles as might promote imitation in industrial countries. Here the peculiar conditions created by the war might give them ground for hope. Apart from the growing disgust for it, the increasing prominence of its ugliest sides, and the claim that it made for the poor man's sacrifice, the war had itself abnormally centralized all public life, and it was possible to take over this machinery of central control and turn it to the uses of a very different set of ideas.

Abrogating universal suffrage, they transferred the power in principle to a system of elective councils with a franchise limited to manual labour. Here, except for this crucial restriction, they were doing no more than to complete the fourfold system of elective councils foreshadowed by Speransky in 1811, and already for the most part realized in 1864 and 1905. Of Speransky's four rungs of local election, the two middle stages —the Province and the District—were filled by the Zemstva, though from 1899 with an artificial franchise; the top rung, the Duma, had been introduced in 1905, though it, too, was based on a mutilated franchise from 1907; the bottom rung, the parish council, had been claimed by all reformers in 1904–5, and might almost be said to have come into being of itself on the abdication of the Tsar in March 1917. Indirect election, the only principle applicable in a country of ignorant peasant communities such as Russia, was a feature of all this legislation, and it continued to be so under the Bolsheviks.

On the other hand, the Bolshevist leaders kept their Party under a vigorous discipline, and at first neither claimed nor desired a membership of more than five hundred thousand, even when all the resources of patronage were at their disposal; and to this party were always secured a monopoly of political power and of publicity and an absolute predominance in the provincial and national councils. This they secured by the abolition of the ballot and by the terrorizing of opponents. The National Council elected the Ministers or Commissaries, of whom Lenin was President.

One immediate step was to conclude an armistice with the Central Powers and to treat for peace (December 14, 1917). Another was to dissolve the Constituent Assembly by force after one long sitting. The strongest party, the Socialist Revolutionaries, quite outnumbered the Bolsheviks, who had only 168 members out of 703; it chose the President, Victor Chernov. As it was obvious that the Constituent Assembly would be very critical of the government, machine guns were brought into the Tauris Palace, and the members were invited to disperse (January 18, 1918).

In accordance with Marxist principles, the factories were at once handed over to the control of the workers. In most cases the workers themselves seized this control, and Lenin, before confirming their act had vainly to ask whether they were sure they could direct the work. The attempt was made to manage it through general assemblies of the workers. The Marxian formula was at once applied: "From everyone according to his ability, and to everyone according to his need." In other words, pay was irrespective of work, which more or less ceased. Trade unionists in Russia and, in particular, the skilled workmen had generally sided with the Mensheviks against the Bolsheviks, but strikes were now declared to be as illegal as under the old regime, on the ground that "the people had now its own government." The workers' control resulted in the looting of plant and products; in particular the railway men developed a kind of syndicalism, regardless of any interests other than their own. The assurance of fixed wages independent of work brought the production down to one sixth, so that these principles were later abandoned and even replaced by conscription of labour, which could be justified as a measure of military defence during the civil war. The most fantastic of all these first experiments was the abolition by decree of private trade, and the compulsory closing of all shops without any real substitute to put in their place. This led inevitably and quickly to starvation in the towns.

Bank credits and banks themselves—with the exception, for some time, of the Cooperative Bank of Moscow—were abolished, and all the land was declared to be national property. Church property was confiscated with the rest. The new government declared itself hostile to all religion, and a quotation from Marx describing it as "opium for the people" was affixed to one of the oldest shrines in Moscow; but in face of opposition the crusade of militant atheism was for the time deferred, though in outlying districts many priests suffered even death. Houses were confiscated and used by the government to satisfy the housing needs of the population.

An attempt was at first made to base the peace negotiations on the self-determination of peoples—that is to say, on national frontiers and plebiscites; but the Central Powers insisted on applying this principle only to Russia, and not even to that part of the empire which they already occupied. General Hofmann cynically informed the Soviet representatives that they were as absolutist as their predecessors. Trotsky, who as Foreign Commissary at first conducted these negotiations, took a line which later had far-reaching effects and irritated even some of his colleagues. He hoped to carry a simultaneous world revolution in one great wave; he brandished this threat in the Germans' faces, and used the enormous publicity of the negotiations to make an appeal to all peoples over the heads of all governments; and, when this did not soften the German terms, he demonstratively departed from Brest-Litovsk, with the impotent formula "No war, no peace," which left the Germans free to do as they pleased. Without a disciplined army, the Bolsheviks were powerless; the Germans denounced the armistice without the stipulated notice and advanced further. There was great confusion in the Party, but Lenin saw quickly that resistance was hopeless and, anxious before all things to establish his new regime, he was for cutting his losses. His new representative, Sokolnikov, was instructed to accept the German terms. These involved the sacrifice of nearly all territory gained by Russia since the accession of Peter the Great, including those small racial groups, Estonians and Latvians, who lay at the gates of his new capital and gave him an open sea route to the rest of Europe (March 3, 1918). An accompanying economic treaty provided for the wholesale German exploitation of Russia. Another peace treaty was concluded by these Powers with Ukraine, where they had since the outbreak of the Revolution fomented a movement of separation (February 9); the separation of Ukraine, which meant economic ruin to Russia, had long been an aim entertained by Austrian and German policy. Roumania, deprived of her gold reserve, which had been sent for safety to Russia, and of all contact with her still faithful allies, was also at their mercy, and ruthless terms were imposed on her in the Treaty of Bucarest. At various points in Russia, especially in the Baltic provinces and in the south, the Germans appeared as masters and showed no scruples in their restoration of order or in their contemptuous attitude to the party which they had helped to put in power. Finland, which had declared her independence from Russia, was at this time torn by a civil war between Finnish "Whites" and "Reds." Russia was powerless; and the Whites under Mannerheim, receiving substantial help from Germany in training and troops, were victorious. Ludendorff was even preparing a German prince for Finland. This brought back the frontier of Russia from the western coast of Finland almost to within artillery range of the old Russian capital.

The Great War, protracted first by the cessation of hostilities in Russia and then by her defection, still hung in the balance. The defeated parties in Russia for the most part looked for salvation to the Western Powers; on its side, the Entente sought means of re-establishing an eastern front. Kornilov, who had escaped from arrest, organized with Alexeyev a centre of resistance in the south, to which gravitated escaped officers from central Russia. Socialist Revolutionary members of the dispersed Constituent Assembly, under the lead of Chernov, formed another such nucleus on the Lower Volga. Siberia, where nearly everybody was an S.R., had established an autonomous government hostile to the Bolsheviks. A daring monarchist filibusterer, Colonel Semenov, had torn from them Trans-Baikalia. In Manchuria, General Horvat, an old official of the highest rank, maintained another conservative government, and Socialist Revolutionaries prevailed in Vladivostok.

To these disconnected and generally conflicting efforts a measure of geographical unity was given by the remarkable exploit of the Czech prisoners of war. These had entered the ranks of the Allies and contributed largely to the initial success of Kerensky's offensive. In return they received permission to organize themselves as a separate unit—a work which was superintended in person by Professor Masaryk—and they continued to fight the Germans till the Bolsheviks made peace. They then obtained from Trotsky, as Foreign Minister of the Soviet government, leave to make their way through Siberia to the Western Front; but the agreement was broken when the first detachments surrendered thir arms. The few who had done so, when attacked, reconquered their weapons, and the Czech echelons, spread out along the railway from Simbirsk to Vladivostok, everywhere made themselves masters of the ground on which they stood (May–August, 1918). This meant that they practically controlled the Trans-Siberian Railway, and politically the Trans-Siberian Railway was Siberia. England, after a futile negotiation with the Bolshevist government for joint action against Germany, seized Murmansk and Archangel and set up a Socialist Revolutionary government. This *coup de main* was too late to help a rising of Russian officers organized from Moscow at Yaroslavl (July 6–21).

The Czechs also entered Ekaterinburg a week too late to save the Imperial family from assassination. It had been sent for its safety by Kerensky to Tobolsk in Siberia and had been brought back to the Urals by the Bolshevist government, which also sent to this neighbourhood from Petrograd and Moscow the Grand Duke Michael, the Grand Duchess Elizabeth, and several other Grand Dukes. Nicholas and his family, who had suffered their change of fortunes with remarkable patience, were butchered in a cellar at Ekaterinburg on July 16, and the next day a number of other Romanovs were thrown down a mine at Alapayevsk.

Admiral Kolchak, who had offered his sword to the Allies, was utilized by them to form an Eastern Front in Siberia. In September 1918 a Directory, chosen from various parties, was established at Ufa, to coordinate the struggle against the Bolsheviks. From the start it was powerless; some of its members never appeared there; Chernov, the leader of the S.R.'s, had nothing in common with the military chiefs. The Directory was violently displaced in favour of a dictatorship of Kolchak (November 18), who was later recognized as supreme ruler by the various other centres of resistance and was assisted by military and civil missions of the Allies. The Czechs had brought to Siberia the gold reserve of Russia, which they had captured at Kazan. Kolchak in the early months of 1919 took Perm and advanced nearly to the Volga; in the north he was not far from Kotlas, where he could have effected a junction with the British at Archangel. When Kornilov was killed in action and Alexeyev died, the resistance in South Russia was headed by Denikin.

All these efforts came to nothing; and the reasons were everywhere the same. The counterattacks from every side served to prolong that reign of force which made possible such a sharp centralization, such an absolute dictatorship, as that of the Bolsheviks. In their apartness and their isolation from the rest of the world, opposition stimulated them and kept them united. It set the maximum of value on the distinctive qualities of their leader, a stern theory and relentless will. Lenin had the devotion of his small band of followers. The conditions of a besieged city and the frequent nearness of ruin kept initiative at high pitch. Trotsky, who showed marked courage and leadership in the suppression of the rising at Yaroslavl, where for a time it was touch and go, now as War Commissary set about a thorough organization of the Red Army. Officers became proscript unless they registered in the service of the Soviet government; the shortage of food in the towns enabled the government to make subsistence depend on service; categories were established, by which the advantage in the distribution went first to manual workers, and next to brain-workers in the service of the government; little was left for the rest. Endless ingenuity, enterprise, and money were expended on an immense system of propaganda which almost superseded and absorbed the ordinary work of education. This propaganda did more than anything else to break up the forces of resistance in Russia, and produced for a time unexpectedly successful results even among the populations of the Allied countries which supported them.

Above all, ruthless terrorism was applied wherever the Bolshevist arm reached. Large numbers of officers had been killed from the very outset of the Bolshevist movement; and when Uritsky, the director of the Bolshevist police, was assassinated and a Socialist Revolutionary, Dora Kaplan, lodged a bullet in Lenin himself (August 30, 1918), whole massacres were immediately conducted in the prisons. Thus the ordinary system of justice with trained judges and a regular procedure was superseded by a code in which the first of crimes was opposition in deed, word, or thought to Communism or to the Communist rulers. The peasantry at first kept up a series of local risings, which were with difficulty crushed by the most ruthless measures. Their conspirative experience in the past enabled the Bolsheviks by a system of universal espionage, especially in the factories and in the army, to anticipate any movement against them. Free use was also made of a system of hostages. As such perished two of Russia's finest generals, Ruzsky and Radko Dmitriev.

All this, however, if taken alone, would in no way account for the Bolshevist success. The peasants themselves at last possessed the whole of the land and were deeply suspicious of any risk of its restoration to its former owners. In the general breakdown of all the past—the futility of the last Tsar, the corruption of the church government under Rasputin—Lenin appeared to the young generation like Moses descending from the mountain with the tablets of the new law, in whose defence no effort seemed too great and no exploit impossible. One of the outstanding features of the Revolution, now and later, was the release of energy in the vast masses of the population. As in the French Revolution, new forces emerged from the lower ranks of the army, and everywhere there was a premium on a bold and fearless initiative. The operations did not have the numbers and consistency of regular warfare. The man of brains or courage seized his chances. The Red Army produced its own new values in the strategic instinct of Frunze, the cavalry leadership of Budenny, and the resource and courage of Chapayev.

On the opposing side there was everywhere weakness and confusion. It was while the civil war was developing that the Germans made their last great onslaught on Amiens and, coming to the end of their reserves, were driven back and compelled to ask for an armistice on any terms (November 11, 1918). The inevitable reaction from the horrors of the war began at once in those countries which had already triumphed, and this, together with the able Bolshevist propaganda, knocked the bottom out of the Allied interest in Russian affairs. The German projects for the economic domination of Russia, which had been made so plain in the Treaty of Brest-Litovsk, became for the present inexecutable and could therefore be disregarded. Semenov, Kolchak, Miller (in Archangel), Denikin, Yudenich, and Wrangel were in turn dropped by the Allies. Ground for this was found in the futility of which the Allies saw so much in the anti-Bolshevist efforts. Kolchak and Denikin were disinterested patriots, but in each anti-Bolshevist force there were reactionary officers who had learned nothing and of whom some committed atrocities quite comparable to those of their enemies, while in the rear there were governments consisting of ineffective politicians, of the most varied opinions, possessed of no real authority. In the troops, except those composed of ex-officers, there was an absence of any binding morale; they were easily traversed by the Bolshevist propaganda. The bankruptcy of Allied interest and the bankruptcy of Russian morale constantly interacted on each other and helped to turn every temporary reverse into a permanent one. In Russia as a whole, nerves were gone to pieces, and public interest was worn out; the comparatively small opposing forces, fighting, so to speak, in a political wilderness, advanced in turn through the void by operations in which decisive actions were replaced by wide outflanking manœuvres. The crisis came in May and June 1919, when a close and apparently satisfactory examination of Kolchak's intentions by the Allied governments was not followed by his definite recognition; at the first reverse, with the dissensions of his generals complicated by political differences, he was driven back in increasing disorder first to the Urals and then to Irkutsk, where he was disgracefully surrendered to his enemies and met his death with great gallantry (February 7, 1920). His rout robbed of all reason the presence of the British at Archangel, which was evacuated on February 21.

Denikin had meanwhile advanced from South Russia nearly as far as Tambov; the tide turned with the defence of Tsaritsyn, in which prominent parts were played by Stalin and Voroshilov. In October 1919 Yudenich, starting from a neighbouring base in Estonia, actually fought his way almost into the suburbs of Petrograd, but he was driven out and defeated through a vigorous concentration of troops, due to the energy of Trotsky. Wrangel, probably the most capable of all the anti-Bolshevist leaders, taking over the remainder of Denikin's forces, continued to defend Crimea and at one time was able to advance again northward;

but ultimately a daring Bolshevik force crossed the Straits of Perekop on the ice, and he was compelled to withdraw his army from Russian territory (November 15, 1920).

There remained the question of Russia's relations with the small States on her western border, several of which were new and had been formed at her expense. The peace had more than realized the aspirations of many of these small peoples. Finland, in a war against her own and Russian Bolsheviks, had fought herself into independence from Russia under General Mannerheim in 1918. In consequence of the triumph of the Entente Powers, Livonia (resuming its original name of Latvia) and Estonia had for the first time gained their independence, which was still precarious, as they blocked Russia's outlet to the Baltic achieved by Peter the Great after centuries of efforts. Neither of these new little States, left high and dry by the almost simultaneous collapse of Russia and Germany, was capable of defending itself whenever these two Great Powers revived, and they could look for protection only to distant England and France. Lithuania, which had even fewer of the elements of security, was made independent by the Treaty of Versailles, but, containing a large Polish community in and around Vilna, it was invaded by a Polish partisan leader, Zeligowski (October 1920), and a large part of its territory, including Vilna, was eventually absorbed by Poland.

The Poles, possessing no geographical frontier and hardly an ethnographical one, were trying to secure as much as they could of Lithuania, White Russia, and Ukraine. These ambitions were materially furthered by France, who, with old traditions of friendship for Poland, wished to create in her a strong bulwark against Bolshevism, separating Russia from Germany. England and America on the other hand strongly discountenanced the Polish advance into Russian territory, as certain to produce trouble in the future. England, on September 20, 1920, suggested as a basis of armistice the so-called Curzon Line, which roughly represented the demarcation between the two nationalities, but neither side accepted it. The security of a restored Poland must depend normally on her having a friend either in Russia or in Germany. At this time she could have neither. Militant international Bolshevism urgently required contact with the new revolutionary Germany, and this could be won only over the body of Poland. The Poles had advanced to Kiev, but had to retreat in haste before the impetuous squadrons of the Bolshevist cavalry leader Budenny. The Red Army advanced in turn, and even reached the gates of Warsaw; but Pilsudski, assisted by General Weygand, dispatched from Paris, turned the tide, and the Poles went for-

FRONTIER CHANGES IN EASTERN EUROPE
AFTER WORLD WAR I

ward again, the Red Army breaking up before them. Again Lenin cut
his losses by the Treaty of Riga (March 18, 1921). About ten million
Ukrainians and White Russians passed under Polish rule; White Russia
was almost exactly bisected, and an artificial corridor was set up to
separate Russia from Lithuania. Such were the consequences of placing
world revolution before the interests of Russia.

By 1921, military operations were over, and the Communist government had practically established its authority over what remained of
Russia. But with the pressure withdrawn, the failure of the anti-Bolshevist forces and of their allies was followed by a failure of Communism,
which, as a principle of government, had for the present to be abandoned, at least in large part, by the Communists themselves.

Lenin had accurately gauged his moment for the seizure of power.
His eyes were on the outside world, and it was to it that he looked for
success. He had long realized that the Russian peasants, so far from
being material for Communism, were by all their instincts *petits
bourgeois*. They were to be under the leadership of the factory workers,
and in the national Soviet elections the peasant's vote counted for only
one fifth of the workman's. Russia was seized in order to create a general
headquarters for a Communist revolution in industrial countries. With
this object, though Lenin spoke vaguely of a future in which the State
would itself wither away, the centralized government, taken over from
the war period, was deepened and strengthened. But a centrifugal reaction, after the tight pressure of war collectivism, was in process in other
countries. In England and the new Czechoslovakia, the two healthiest
States in Europe, the success of Bolshevist propaganda reached its culmination in the middle of 1920 and then rapidly declined, ending, for
the time at least, in evident and admitted failure. France and America
also held firm against it; and in Italy, Spain, and Poland came reaction
and Fascism. After the crisis of the Polish War, the new Germany also
seemed immune, though Communist hopes were again to rise with the
occupation of the Ruhr in 1923.

Meanwhile Russia was ruined. The ruin had begun in the Great
War, and more particularly under the Empress and Stürmer. It grew in
dimensions under the almost nominal rule of the Provisional Government. The wild initial experiments of the Bolsheviks were fast completing it. Fantastic inflation and hopeless deficits marked the abandonment of all conventional principles of exchange. Industry was more
than five sixths gone, which in an industrial country would have meant
the final ruin of the whole project. Transport had worn out most of its

existing reserves and, in the failure of repair and production, except for
military purposes it had broken down almost completely. Private trade
had been suppressed at the outset, but in default of any adequate substitute it continued illegally through the most curious channels. Not only
the threat of world revolution, the Civil War, and the foreign intervention, but the initial confiscation of all private property even of foreigners
and the repudiation of government debts, were entirely prohibitive of
all foreign trade. The fact that lay at the bottom of all other facts was
that during the Civil War productive work had almost stopped, and
that the country was living on its reserves from a preceding period.

The peasants, often with great brutality, had themselves made a
wholesale clearance of the country gentry; many of these were "smoked
out" and no trace of their former estates was left; at last all the land
was in peasant hands. The government had had to concede in practice
that the land belonged to the village communities, because at that time
it would have been impossible to impose by force any other settlement.
But the State, if it could not own the land, could still make claim to its
produce; a certain proportion of foodstuffs was assigned as the wages
of the peasant, and the rest, instead of being sent to market, was to be
surrendered to the State without payment. The answer of the peasants
—which, though quite unorganized, was practically identical all over the
country—was very simple, and its effects were decisive. For the most
part they ceased to produce any more than they consumed. This meant
famine for the towns, whose population fell with the most alarming
rapidity. That of the abandoned capital, Petrograd, went down to one
third. Town markets became so empty that even dogs and pigeons
stopped coming to them, and town-dwellers made long railway journeys
to find peasants who could give them food in return for boots, clothes,
or other articles. As all such trade was illegal, the traveller was liable
to see his hard-won supply taken from him before he could get back
home.

The Communist government had attempted, through Committees of
Poverty in the villages, to base its power on the most impoverished.
Another part of its policy was to take back estates from the peasants
and establish large state farms. Here again it met with failure. These
farms were often managed by Communists quite ignorant of farming.
They found themselves in an ocean of hostile peasantry, and ultimately
the experiment was, for the time, more or less abandoned. Peasant risings had throughout been an incessant commentary on Communist
rule; yet it was increasingly necessary to send punitive expeditions to

seize grain for the towns; and when these expeditions seized the stores which the peasant required for himself, including even the seed corn, famine was the inevitable result. When it came, it was on a staggering scale. The breakdown of transport and a great drought added to its virulence. First in the grain-growing provinces on the Volga and later in Ukraine and Crimea, whole masses of the population broke loose from their moorings in their hunt for food, and cases of cannibalism were reported. A terrible epidemic of malaria added to the devastation. The ARA (American Relief Administration, led by Herbert Hoover) did especially able work among the starving.

Already in the early months of 1921, fully appreciating the critical character of his situation, Lenin, who alone in the Party had authority equal to such a strain, carried through the so-called New Economic Policy (NEP), or economic retreat, which attempted to retain Communism as the principle of government while shelving it as far as was necessary in practice (March 15, 1921). He retained, it is true, three "dominating heights": the monopoly of political power, of the press, and of foreign trade. State trusts had already replaced the mass management of factories. The peasants, after paying a heavy tax in kind, were now allowed to sell their remaining products. Factories were handed over to trusts or even to individuals; private trade was licensed, but under conditions which did not guarantee its stability. The vast officialdom created at the outset by the Bolsheviks was reduced by the abolition of numbers of superfluous posts. The government turned eagerly to the capitalist world (which it did not cease to threaten) for the resources required to maintain its own control in Russia. The New Economic Policy was Lenin's last achievement. He had a stroke in the spring of 1922 and retired. A partial recovery in October was followed by a relapse and ultimately by his death on January 21, 1924. The old capital was renamed Leningrad in his honour, and, by a strange inversion, his tomb, which was built into the wall of the Kremlin, became the official shrine of a new religion. The general direction was taken over by a triumvirate consisting of Stalin, Kamenev, and Zinoviev.

The period opened by the New Economic Policy of 1921 was one of contradictions, of concessions and mental reservations, and of mingled threats to the Old World, appeals for its money, and compromises with it. The shock of the retreat from principle was a terrible one for the young people who had fought through all hazards to victory in the Civil War; several of them, when they knew that the peasant market was again open and the trains running for money, even committed suicide.

Equally equivocal was the position of capitalists and of governments who, attracted by the undoubtedly enormous potentialities of Russian resources, sought to utilize this more favourable mood. By a commercial treaty with England (March 1921), trade missions were exchanged; the lead of England was followed in 1922 by Germany and Norway, and in 1924 by most other European countries. In that year the Soviet government was recognized by England, Italy, and France. Every attempt was made to play off one capitalist country against another. Hostile propaganda was continued, mobilized at various times in different directions but especially emphatic in Afghanistan and India. Russia sent an imposing deputation to a European conference at Genoa (1922), with a request for credits from foreign governments, while the question of the payment of debts and the return of confiscated foreign property was complicated by the most extreme counter-claims. The Soviet spokesman, Rakovsky, told his suspicious audience that in Russia they would now find Communists but not Communism. This was quite correct, and it remained so: the only period of Soviet history that bears that name—"the period of War Communism"—was that which ended in 1921; but the change brought little confidence abroad. More importance was attached to the growing friendship between Russia and Germany, signalized by the Treaty of Rapallo, concluded at the same time. This was a perfectly reasonable development of policy. Both countries, for different reasons, were in disgrace with the rest of Europe and were therefore sure to draw together. But the closest foreign observers of Russia began to see the spectre of an alliance for a war of revenge.

The New Economic Policy soon began to produce a new bourgeoisie, the so-called "Nepmen," not unlike the business adventurers who appeared in the France of 1795 under the Directory. This development, and indeed the whole policy of compromise, caused great alarm to the sincerest Communists, who made a vigorous stand in the spring of 1923 and prevailed in the Party Congress in April. Rigorous purges were several times carried out in the Party; dissensions began to arise among the political leaders, some of whom saw that, with a reversion toward capitalism, the Terror and the Bolshevist Revolution itself had lost their justification. Thus the more extreme wing again prevailed, though on condition of not disturbing the foreign trade relations. Sometimes the Nepmen were swept up with their profits.

In the realm of ideas, however, the extremists were left free, and they still had control of the machinery of repression. While abridging the practice of Communism, they hoped to educate a new generation in its principles, and with this object the universities were filled with their nominees, and numbers of the more independent professors were expelled from the country, especially in the autumn of 1922. The humanities, as tending to independent thought, had been almost crushed by the government; a premium had been put on technical studies, such as medicine and engineering, and here trained men were an absolute necessity to fill the sadly depleted services of the State. The extermination of the Great War and the Civil War had borne especially hard on the educated classes. The Russian officer had led his men into action; the bulk of the educated had been with the Whites; but these losses were now to be read in terms of teachers and technicians. Contradictions followed the rulers into the new policy. Professions of Communism could not be a substitute for a university entrance examination; and the new students, if they spent their time on propaganda, did not complete their studies. Nor were the improvised *rabfaks* or university classes for workmen an adequate substitute. The secondary schools were disorganized and demoralized by changing experiments; but a new type of primary school, introduced everywhere, gave interesting results in places where there were found funds and teachers to keep it in existence.

Even more dangerous than the universities to the hope of creating a new Communist generation was the national Orthodox Church. Readers will remember the dislike of Peter the Great for a rival authority and his abolition of the Patriarchate, his lay commissioner for the Church, and the long reign of Pobedonostsev over religion in Russia from 1881 to 1905. In that year the Church had made a gallant bid for freedom; it called for a church council and the restoration of the Patriarchate. What followed was the domination of the vile Rasputin, who ruled the Church in the years immediately preceding the Revolution. Both the war and the Revolution of March 1917 had produced a quickening of the religious sense and also promoted a tendency towards independent inquiry. Under the Provisional Government a Church Congress was called and the Patriarchate was restored, signifying before all things the independence of the Church from the State. The free legislation of this short period was marked not only by complete tolerance but by a striking sympathy with religion in general. As has been truly said, the fall of the Tsar marked the final end of the Byzantine period of history in its last stronghold, Russia. Now it was not only possible but imperative to organize the Church on the basis of broad cooperation with the laity, and this hope stimulated and inspired many ardent churchmen. The new Patriarch, Tikhon, was chosen in Moscow at the very moment when the

Bolsheviks were capturing the Kremlin, and his first appearance in his new office was among the combatants in an effort to save lives (November 1917).

The attitude of the Communists was entirely different. Their views, as defined by Marx and Lenin, took no account of the historical origins of Christianity, and they regarded not only this but all other religions as a mystification offered to the poor by their rulers in order to keep them in submission and subjection. The Patriarch declared that the Church had no concern with political parties and accepted any government "that came from God," but he excommunicated the Soviet government on the ground of its professed atheism. After the Civil War there followed a lull in the persecution, and the Commissary for Education, Lunacharsky, even engaged in public debates with the eccentric Bishop Antonin. Now, however, the extremists launched a new crusade. A decree of June 13, 1921, had forbidden the teaching of religion to any person under eighteen, except at home. Mocking anti-religious processions of the Communist League of Youth were organized in Moscow, at Christmas 1922. A trial of Catholic clergy was staged for the Western Easter week of 1923, and the public mind was prepared for the trial of the Patriarch in the week that followed, that of the Russian Easter. He had been compelled to suspend his functions, and on the initiative of Bishop Antonin and others of less repute a number of new church groups were formed under the protection of the atheistic government.

In each of the two trials the accused were charged with refusal or unwillingness to surrender church vessels as a contribution to famine relief (though other property of the churches had been willingly offered for this purpose); but they were also called upon to give an undertaking to obey the decree, already mentioned, restricting the teaching of religion. The Catholic priests were indeed tried, and firmly refused to give this pledge; they were sent to prison; Archbishop Cieplak and Monsignor Budkiewicz were condemned to death, and the latter was executed (March 1923). But a general outcry in Europe and America, together with alarm for the trade agreement with England, so impressed the Communist leaders that the trial of the Patriarch was postponed. He was deposed by a packed Congress of Clergy in May 1923, but was later liberated on signing a retractation of hostility to the government; after which, the rival groups such as the Living Church, which never had any vitality, were more or less dropped by the Communists. The persecution, which was directed against all forms of religion—Orthodox, Catholic, Protestant, Jewish, and Moslem—was continued in less conspicuous forms, such as exclusion of Christian children from schools, and exile of the more devoted of the bishops and clergy to the far north or Siberia. The Patriarch died, worn out, on April 7, 1925, and his funeral was an immense demonstration of affection which lasted nearly the whole day. Any regular election of a successor was impossible; but deputies continued to be appointed and were imprisoned, one after another, by the government. Under this stress, religion easily lost its more formal adherents; but the nucleus of believers was strengthened in its faith; and in the enforced absence of the bishops, its organization came to rest on the devotion and activity of the parishioners.

Another striking failure was to be seen in the matter of child welfare, which from the first had been one of the sincerest objects of the Party. Persistent attempts to break up the family, in the case of the peasants, met with material complications. With its continual shortage in finance, the government was unable to make any adequate provision for the children whom the Revolution and Civil War had separated from their homes or who had been "given to Lenin," and Lunacharsky had to announce that there were hundreds of thousands of these waifs. They were entirely demoralized and inoculated with all sorts ot disease; they huddled together in groups at night, migrated according to the season, and beset foot-travellers, robbing and killing.

On the other hand it was in primary instruction that the Soviet government achieved one of its most signal successes. At the Revolution, the figures for illiteracy were in European Russia roughly 75 per cent and in Siberia 85 per cent; in Russian central Asia literacy had practically to start from scratch. As soon as the country could revert to the tasks of peace, this problem was attacked with great vigour. The Soviets had two advantages from the start. The Russian mind, especially the clever child-mind, longed for knowledge. The old Zemstva or county councils had, in their small way, done all they could to satisfy this thirst. Now children themselves played a large part in the success. They cut out the letters of the alphabet, hunted down their ignorant elders, and insisted on teaching them. In the factories there was little use for workmen who could not read their instructions; their names were written up on a board to shame the malingerers into learning. Ultimately—in a surprisingly short time for such an achievement—in the European provinces it was rare to find an illiterate younger than fifty-five. In Asia—and this was even more striking—the proportion of literates rose before the Second World War to 72 per cent. By no means did the battle stop short at literacy; it became the foundation for a thorough and all-round educational system.

Under the NEP the country recovered with surprising rapidity. Shops and cafés had reappeared in the towns as if by magic at the beginning of 1922, and the peasants, especially the more thrifty of them, now the masters of their increased holdings, prospered more and more. Many new schools were opened. The budget was successfully balanced at the beginning of 1925. But the lines of this evolution had little or nothing in common with the principles of the government, or indeed with those of any political party. They represented rather an effort to return to the normal economics which had marked the period of increasing prosperity before the war. Lenin, as he himself avowed, had been defeated only by the silent opposition of the peasants. Giving up all attempt at open conflict, they defended themselves by a dogged if passive opposition which nullified the action of the government. They were now allowed to lease land for twelve years, to hire labour, and to sell their products on the market, in lieu of surrendering them to the State, for which was substituted a heavy but definite tax in grain. They held up this tax, of which the arrears were forty per cent in 1925, and successfully claimed a reduction of it. They met the heavy prices asked for the scanty supply of manufactured goods by a kind of buyers' strike which induced Lenin's successors to put peasant needs in the forefront of their policy. They wrecked by their mistrust a scheme devised to meet those needs by foreign credits derived from the profits of a large export of grain; they would not supply the grain, and the credits could not materialize. Most ironical of all, they abolished widely, under a Communist government, the communal land tenure which had lasted through centuries of Tsardom, and replaced the obsolete strip system with allotments which were to all intents and purposes personal and heritable property. In 1923 the government itself felt impelled to issue a land law largely based on individual farming; and in 1925 the peasantry was able to give expression to a program including an open market, no special taxes on thrift, equalization of the peasant's vote with the town worker's, restoration of the ballot, and abolition of the practice of sending down from the Communist Party the names of candidates to be elected. The industrial workers had also developed a greater independence of attitude, which showed itself in strikes, especially at the outset of 1925. In 1926 wages were twice what they had been before the war, but perhaps with no more buying value. Though rural industries were now prospering, there was a healthy backward movement to the towns.

A typical saying of the period was that "the corpse had proved stronger than the surgeon."

Perhaps an even greater change was to be seen in the outlook of the new intelligentsia. Theories and visions were now at a discount and were replaced by steady, practical work. In the inevitable dominance of economic needs, experts received more and more favour and attention, and some of them even believed they were gradually getting the working of the state machinery more and more into their own hands. Seeing no alternative government, evading all open opposition to the authorities, the population desired above all things to be left to itself to manage its own local affairs, a task for which the bitter school of material necessity had trained more pupils than had ever existed before.

The formula which had held so far through the story of Communist rule in Russia was an alternation of tugs to the left and drifts to the right. The Communists were idealists, and in their effort to equalize the general well-being they were intent to eliminate the demand for industrial profit and, by an unhistorical inference, to eradicate the idea of religion. But they were also realists who took careful account of what might be achieved at a given time. Still, it was not possible that the sincerest of them could be satisfied with the great drift of the NEP. The peasants, who were being rapidly differentiated in prosperity, were becoming the masters of the situation, and were in a position to dominate the town population by holding up supplies. The successes of individual agriculture were much more evident than those of semi-socialized industry, and it was clear that the two were incompatible if a real victory were to be won for Communism. Dissensions, long concealed, began to appear in the Party. There was a rank-and-file movement for democracy within its framework, which had already been once suppressed and was not allowed to become very articulate.

Meanwhile, what was the progress of the long-awaited world revolution abroad? It had degenerated into a game of hide-and-seek, disingenuous on all sides. Contact with foreign trade was sought as indispensable to Russia; but the trading agencies, in spite of precise engagements, were utilized for propaganda. Unable to realize their principles in Russia, the Communists clung to the hope that they might triumph in one or more of those industrial countries for which Marx had designed them. In answer to protests, the Soviet government disclaimed responsibility for the acts of the Comintern or Third International, founded in 1919 for the purpose of world revolution; but both organizations were alike instruments of the Communist Party which, whatever its interpretation of Communism, was the real ruler of Russia.

In 1923 there were rumours in Germany of an approaching Communist seizure of power, but they came to nothing; and the further political development of Germany was the story of the anti-Communist crusade of Adolf Hitler. In England, where lay the acid test of Communist success, the Labour government in February 1924 had recognized that of the Soviets; but it was driven from power at the end of the year, largely by the sudden publication during a general election of a letter attributed to the head of the Comintern, Zinoviev. The letter contained internal signs of forgery; its contents more or less corresponded to Zinoviev's known program. In September 1925, the head of the Russian trade unions, Tomsky, as guest of the British trade unions at their congress at Scarborough, secured their adherence to a prescription of policy such as that which had brought the Communists into power in Russia. This led, in May 1926, to a General Strike in England, which in Moscow was expected to bring about a transference of power to the British trade unions. But the latter, with their honest record of past organization and accomplishment, were themselves much too conservative to proceed to an open conflict, and the result was a complete fiasco. The news of this failure was described by Radek in Moscow as equivalent to a bomb-shell. The British reply was a sharp note from Austen Chamberlain on propaganda (February 24, 1927); and a futile search for incriminating propaganda at the Soviet Trade Delegation in London, Arcos, was followed on May 17 by a complete breach of relations. This lasted till October 1930, when the Labour Party returned to power. Rakovsky, the Soviet Ambassador in Paris, was forced to withdraw, for alleged propaganda in the French army. In 1927 propaganda was principally concentrated on China where, rather in the form of culture, it seemed at first to attain spectacular successes, but here too, after Chiang Kai-shek broke with the Communists, the result was another failure. Thenceforward, Communist propaganda had no further major success abroad. Not a single country outside Russia was won over to Communism. It is to be noted that not even any of the little States on the Russian borders, all of which were instinctively nationalist, was successfully overrun by this propaganda.

Since Lenin's death, as will be remembered, Russia had been governed by a triumvirate consisting of Stalin, Kamenev, and Zinoviev, to the exclusion of Trotsky. Among these the man who had far the strongest hold on the ruling party was its General Secretary, Stalin. This was one of the many conspirative names of Joseph Djugashvili, the son of a Georgian cobbler. He broke the bounds of a training college for the lower clergy, and was deeply impressed by the writings of Lenin. Unlike the early Bolshevik leaders, of whom he was not considered one, he did not live abroad; in fact, but for a few short trips for conferences, he never left his own country. There he was Lenin's principal executive for the collection of funds for the Party. He had remarkable executive ability and conspicuous daring, and carried out sensational seizures of government money. He was jailed five times, and was constantly escaping. Like his fellows, he was trained in a school of conspiracy, from which atmosphere it is difficult to escape; but his was the roughest school of all, with the most immediate sense of danger. He seems to have been little interested in the hair-splitting theoretical debates of his emigrant colleagues, and his pragmatic mind developed a mastery of tactical and later of political manœuvre. At the time of the Revolution he was still in Siberia. He was at first regarded in the Party merely as a man who carried out the instructions of Lenin. During the long boycott of Russia by Europe, there was gradually growing up a tendency to irritation against those who had not shared the struggle at home and, when it was over, returned to rule the country.

Stalin's first post in the Soviet government was that of Commissary for the one hundred and eighty-odd minor nationalities of Russia of which his native Georgia, with a population of some three million, was one. None of these had obtained any kind of political recognition under the Tsars, yet they amounted to nearly half the population of the State. In 1922 he was entrusted with the all-important post of Secretary of the Party, and till the eve of the Second World War his work was only indirectly concerned with the official government. Its every act was submitted in advance to the Politburo or inner ring in the Communist Party, consisting then of seven persons, of whom practically all except Stalin were returned emigrants.

The first result of his elevation was seen in 1923 in a revised structure of the State, of which he was the author. Russia now took a new title: "The Union of Soviet Socialist Republics" (USSR). In this new structure racial discrimination, so marked a feature in the Tsars' regime and later so vital a factor in that of Hitler in Germany, was entirely eliminated. Any man or woman in the country was as good as another. The State was divided up solely by nationalities, provision being made even for the smallest, and in each unit the language of teaching was that of the racial group. It was the more backward nationalities of the Union that gained most from the change, to which some owed even their first alphabets. New republics were set up for Turcomans, Uzbeks, Kirghiz, and, later, the Tadjiks on the Chinese frontier; and each of the many tiny racial units of the Caucasus received some measure of autonomy. Among the more backward peoples, the primary work of the new federal government was largely cultural; and with the exception of religion, which was repressed everywhere, each was encouraged to develop its national traditions, of which Georgia at least had a historic store. On the other hand the grip of the ruling party was everywhere, and each group was taught to build up its own Communist Party, entirely under the control of Moscow. The centre also exercised complete control over the economic resources of the whole State, and, as time went on, the new regime certainly justified itself by the far-reaching benefits which it conferred. The new structure was equally in line with purely Communist policy, for it provided also an international system of Soviet Republics which any other country could enter at will.

Stalin's position as General Secretary was greatly changed first by the growing illness and then, in 1924, by the death of Lenin, the unquestioned head of the Party, who could not be replaced. Lenin, in his anxiety as to the future, had left an estimate both of Stalin and of Trotsky. Stalin, he thought, was much too rough and "uncomradely" (he would not have used so mild a word later) and had better be replaced as Secretary. Trotsky he regarded as a weathercock on whose changing opinions reliance could not be placed. Trotsky, as the more recent recruit to the party but its next most prominent member, seems to have regarded Stalin as merely a henchman, and spent his acid wit on him. The two men had quarrelled violently during the Civil War: Trotsky was for using the Tsar's former generals under close control, Stalin for trusting to men of their own. It was to Stalin that members had to go for inquiries as to Party tactics, it was he who held the records and had much the best chance of influencing appointments, which, with acute tact and patience, he later learned to shuffle at will. We can imagine him thinking what use he could make of this position; he had from the first the clearest sense of what really constituted power. The contrast between the methods of the two men, in the light of details from inside the Politburo and other sources, is most interesting. Trotsky might even sometimes address this small group of close colleagues as if it were a public meeting. Stalin let him go ahead with his fireworks and make his mistakes and his enemies; he would hold his own hand, listen to everyone else, watch faces, and then suggest the conclusion which seemed most likely to carry the rest. Thus his would be the Party line.

There are some early indications that Stalin had not much faith in the effectiveness of outside propaganda for world revolution. Trotsky has ascribed to Stalin's indifference the failure to utilize the three opportunities already mentioned—in Germany, England, and China. Stalin changed his ground, as he was to do several times, as occasion demanded: indeed, he later laid it down that Marxism, if it is a live doctrine, must necessarily adapt itself to its environment, and even that Marx obviously could not have foreseen what the world would be like one hundred years after his time. Trotsky was all for industrialization and for close contact with the working world outside. Stalin, with the support of the "Rights" of the Party, was at first for taking full account of the peasantry. But as the issues clear, the contrast of views becomes plain. Trotsky still preaches "permanent revolution" and maintains that without a world victory Communism cannot hold out in Russia. Stalin opposes to this a purely national program: "Socialism [he does not say Communism] in one country"—that is, in Russia. Later he consistently adds: "We are quite ready for working relations with any foreign government, even capitalist, that is friendly to the Soviet Union." This principle was later to serve as the foundation of alliance in the Second World War.

The Party was none too numerous, and it was a long time before it let the outside public get any clear view of its dissensions. In 1924 Trotsky revealed them in his *Lessons of October*. At the thirteenth Party Congress, Kamenev spoke with alarm of the growth of private trade: while Rykov, Lenin's successor as Soviet Premier, was horrified by the idea of ending the compromise of the NEP. The orthodox revolutionary view prevailed at the Fifth Congress of the Comintern in July. In April 1925, Trotsky was dismissed from the War Commissariat, where he had many military friends, and was sent on "sick leave"; on his return he was transferred to a much less influential department, that of National Economy. In December, Kamenev and Zinoviev attacked Stalin at the Party Congress and were beaten by nearly ten to one. Zinoviev was dethroned from his dictatorship in Leningrad. At meetings early in 1926 Stalin again had the support of the Rights, and the opposition was significantly described as "a gang of European adventurers." After the failure of the General Strike in England, Zinoviev lost the headship of the Comintern. Trotsky attacked the government in public speeches and was ordered to keep silence. Kamenev and Zinoviev made insincere recantations, but Trotsky stuck to his guns. In July 1927, he again denounced Stalin to the Party Central Committee and was expelled from it; but he turned to conspirative organization, of which he was a past master. He even tried to disturb the celebration of the tenth anniversary of the Communist Revolution. He was turned out of the Party and was exiled to Alma Ata in Asia. Here he still kept up his connections, and the Opposition even appealed to the organ of German Communism, *Die Fahne des Kommunismus*. In the end, still protesting, he was pushed over the western frontier in 1929. It cannot be reasonably doubted that he left a strong underground organization behind him, and he continued to fight back with vigour from his various foreign refuges till he was murdered in Mexico. Stalin had throughout the backing of the Party and of the young, and he had won outright. After his triumph he did not allow the Comintern, to which Trotsky had appealed against him, to meet again for six years, and when at last it reappeared, it was as an agent abroad not of world revolution, but of Soviet national policy.

But Stalin quickly made it clear that this was no victory of the Rights, no mere surrender to facts. "Socialism in one country" implied the socialization of agriculture. If in an agricultural country, he said, only industry was socialized, then Socialism had failed in Russia. It was in this program that he found his answer to the growing independence and authority of the leaders of the peasantry. In this he was confirming the view of Trotsky. It was the same when he preached an intensification of the development of socialized industry. The distinction between them, as Trotsky well recognized, was that Russia now came first and world revolution was in effect shelved. Henceforth, Communism was an ideal, a dream of the future, even in Russia.

Stalin's program was not likely to satisfy his recent allies of the Right, and they reacted strongly under the leadership of Rykov, the Soviet Premier; Bukharin, author of the *ABC of Communism*; and Tomsky, head of the trade unions. Early in 1929 Bukharin and Tomsky called on Stalin to resign. In November, Stalin turned Bukharin out of the Politburo and the next summer drove Rykov out of the premiership, replacing him with his trusted follower, V. Molotov. In all this he was supported by the Party and also by the Komsomol, or Communist League of Youth, of whom practically all had never been outside Russia. The same came to be true of the Politburo, which ultimately did not include a single former emigrant. Stalin was now supreme and issued his trumpet call for a Soviet industrialization which had two objects: to raise the level of living for the whole country, and to make it defensible against any invader. The benefits to accrue would go not to individuals but to the community as a whole. This appeal restored the unity and enthusiasm both of the Party and of the Komsomol.

CHAPTER XXVI

Stalin's Russia

[*1928–41*]

From this time onwards, the story of Russian policies was that of the mind and purposes of Stalin. Politically, as was to be proved in the event, it was a mind of the first quality, but far more akin to that of the Russian peasant than to that of the intellectual. Stalin was capable of long and lucid expositions of policies, and not only of policies but even of doctrine, but his was essentially the business mind, with a shrewd and eminently practical common sense which, with experience, mounted more and more to high statesmanship. His intentions were to be ascertained much better from what he did than from what he said. As compared with other dictators, he was much the closest to the ground. He listened to the country just as he had earlier listened to his more prominent colleagues around the table of the Politburo. It must in no way be assumed that he was untrue to the teaching of his master, but Lenin himself had clearly recognized that Socialism must move forward by stages, and that each stage was in itself a serious study.

Lenin's creation, the Communist Party, was the one real force in the country and only through it could power be achieved and maintained. The first three years of the Soviet regime had belonged to its left arm, the Comintern—that is, to the returned internationalist emigrants. That was the one period of Communist rule. After 1921, Russia was ruled by Communists but not necessarily on the principles of Communism. The one principle which was firmly established was the national ownership of the means of production. The initial complete sacrifice of Russia to world revolution, for instance in the Treaty of Brest-Litovsk, had taken its revenge. The new direction was back to nationalism.

How did Stalin handle this situation? Not by pulling down the flag, though the watchwords were frequently changed. Whatever the character of the Party, he had to make of it the instrument which he wanted.

As his post was that of its Secretary, he was under a continuous cross fire from those who associated the Party name with its original revolutionary purpose, and from those who regarded him as untrue to that purpose. One of his greatest embarrassments lay in the Communist parties abroad and in their so-called "fellow travellers" among foreign intellectuals. To them the arm of his power did not reach, and not Trotsky himself need have less authority. Those of them who remained loyal to Stalin were often completely baffled by what he did; those who opposed him wished him out of the way, for the resumption of world revolution. And sometimes he used an old name for a new idea. "The United Front" was originally one of a workers' class war in all countries; it came later to mean an alliance against the enemies of Russia. The old methods were used with new purposes. After six years of discipline, in 1935 the Comintern was allowed to emerge again as a kind of "Fifth Column" against Russia's actual or potential enemies; and this form of interference aroused as much resentment abroad as the earlier had.

Stalin's first task was to prove the falsity of Trotsky's argument that a Socialist Russia could not live in the world without the success of world revolution. There was every encouragement to the attempt, and it would, if successful, greatly increase the Russian's initiative and his pride in his country. Russia still had about one sixth of the land surface of the world, so that the recent sacrifice of territory might be disregarded. She was immensely rich in resources, more than rich enough to make her economically self-sufficient. So far these vast potentialities had been generally left unworked. There had only been two periods when anything like energetic attention had been given to production. The first was that of Stalin's natural model, Peter the Great, and of his predecessor, Ordyn-Nashchokin, Minister of Peter's father Alexis, who in many directions showed the way to Peter. The other period immediately preceded the First World War and was the natural outcome of the liberation of labour by the emancipation of the peasants in 1861; and but for the War and the Revolution, it would of itself have gone on to greater strength. Here the successive leaders were three enlightened administrators at the Tsar's Ministry of Finance: Vyshnegradsky, Witte, and Kokovtsev—above all, Witte.

Lenin, who gave constant thought to production, had created the first elements of state planning. These were now developed into an enormous organization with thousands of trained scientists, called the *Gosplan* (the State Plan). It covered every side of the national life, not only industry and agriculture but public health and education; in Soviet

Russia, from the first, all medical attendance was free of charge. As this huge organization got into working order, it functioned on a kind of shuttle system. The scientists planned and sent their directions down through the various organs of government to the individual factories. These were keenly discussed in full and regular meetings of the workers, who had every opportunity of suggesting alterations, not in the task but in the methods of its execution. The suggestions passed up to the top and came down again with corrections.

But the principal need had to be supplied from outside. Russia had very, very little heavy plant of her own. This had reduced her to what Lenin described as a "colonial" dependence on industrial countries, and had made her incapable of manufacturing her own munitions in the last War. This was the first thing required, whether to raise the level of living or to make the country defensible; and Stalin had his eye firmly fixed on both these objects. The Soviet government had been born in conditions of war and civil war; and the foreign intervention of 1919–20, long after its futility had been exposed, left a conviction that the attempt would be repeated, which the Soviet propaganda did its best to reinforce. A world coalition of the capitalist world against a Socialist Russia was no longer in the realm of probability, but the danger was now taking a narrower though more concrete form. Hitler was already actively at work preaching the resurrection of Germany, and his program was already before the public in his book *Mein Kampf*. Here was what he had written about Russia: "When we talk of more ground and room in Europe [that is, for German settlement], we can in the first place think only of Russia and the border States depending on her [that is, the territory lost to Russia in the Great War]. . . . The gigantic empire in the East is ripe for collapse, and the end of the Jewish domination in Russia will be the end of the Russian State itself." [1] (The "Jewish domination," by the way, had ended decisively with the triumph of Stalin.) If we look at Russia's task in the light of this threat, we shall see the magnitude of Stalin's undertaking. In a broken country, still only emerging from revolution, he set himself the apparently impossible goal of bringing up the war output of Russian industry to the level of the German.

If the German threat to Russia's front door was still in the clouds, the threat to her back door took shape much earlier. Even in 1917 a German pamphlet, with a program later followed closely by Hitler, marked out for a war of revenge a future alliance between Germany and

[1] *Mein Kampf*, II, 742–3.

Japan. During the intervention, Japan did little more than disturb the harmony of the Allies. She had her chance during the breakdown of Russia, but she did not take it. Annoyed though she was at the discrimination against her naval armaments at the Washington Conference of 1922, she ultimately came out of Siberia like the rest: the Japanese are ill suited to that climate. But in 1927, in connection with the last serious success of Communist propaganda, then centred on China, there was a wave which spread to Japan itself and called down the sternest reprisals from the government: in that year the Japanese Premier, Tanaka, presented to the Mikado a systematic program of aggression and conquest which, under the ever increasing dominance of the military forces, became the textbook of Japanese policy. It aimed at the conquest of China, Burma, and India but it began with the threat of "again crossing swords with the Russians in Manchuria."

In September 1931, Japan actually seized Manchuria and converted it into a puppet State under her protection. Russia was not yet strong enough to react to this. For a nominal price, which for a long time was not paid, she surrendered the Chinese Eastern Railway, the fruit of her own enterprise and credit, which gave her direct communication with Vladivostok. Japan even called also for the demilitarization of the Russian frontier, now pushed back far northward along the Amur, and there followed a number of border conflicts which were neither peace nor open war. Russia on her side took Outer Mongolia under her protection, and established her practical control over the province of Sinkiang (Chinese Turkestan).

Meanwhile the first industrial Five Year Plan, starting almost from scratch and aiming before all things at speed and quantity, was pounding along through its enormous initial difficulties. The foreign capitalist was indispensable, as the heavy plant had to be obtained from abroad, but he was attracted by the possibilities of this practical program. The foreign technician was equally indispensable at the outset, and he too was attracted by the scope for his enterprise. Confiscation had long since been abandoned as senseless, but its evil memory still remained and loans could be obtained only at limited credit and on hard terms. To buy the heavy plant at all, Russia had to export raw materials, including foodstuffs, greatly needed at home. The rapid recovery of the country under the NEP was again cut short, and famine again claimed millions of victims. Belts had to be tightened all round until the expected consumers' goods should actually materialize. Haste precluded solid construction; there were many mistakes in the Plan, which allowed for no margins, for Russia was learning by trial and error to become industrial. The machinery often fell into incompetent hands, and there were many serious accidents. The feverish haste allowed for no delays: works were constructed before quarters for the workmen, who repeatedly left their jobs in search of better accommodation. At one time, forty per cent of what was produced was reckoned as "scrap." Nothing was to be accomplished save under the most ruthless compulsion, but this did not shake Stalin's purpose.

Both Lenin and Stalin had set for Russia the remote goal of getting level in production with America, and this was a stimulating challenge to a socialist community in a hostile capitalist environment. The Russian workman was notoriously lazy: it took three Russians to do the job of one American. In this tremendous drive for production, in which Stalin anticipated and exceeded all that was later to be done by any country that valued its independence, he was attempting his greatest task: he was remoulding the character of the whole people and creating a new Russia—not of world dreamers, but of technicians, administrators, and men of business; and this has proved to be the most marked distinction between the old Russia and the new.

There were inevitably defaulters of all sorts. The Plan itself often demanded sheer impossibilities. Not only malingering but even interference with the hated new machinery might be the unwilling worker's reaction. But beyond that, it is clear that there was often a political purpose. Until the consumers' goods should arrive, there was always the chance of upsetting the ruthless dictator, abandoning the Plan, and perhaps returning to the old internationalist policy. In any case there were innumerable victims, for no lapse was pardoned and the Plan was not to be proved wrong. John D. Littlepage, a higher American technical expert in the Soviet service, laid the blame for certain grave accidents with serious loss of life not on negligence but on the deliberate removal of some essential piece of machinery. There followed a whole series of trials of "wreckers" of a demonstrative kind in which great masses of innocents were swept into the police net. It was the police custom to interrogate prisoners without remission for endless hours day and night until they would admit that the blame was theirs. In the case of the British firm Metro-Vickers this led to a temporary breach of relations with England.

The whole ordeal passed in an atmosphere of war; and the most devoted and trustworthy of the government's forces was the so-called Komsomol, or League of Communist Youth, the reserve of the Communist Party. This had grown out of the Civil War, which was its first great school. It had shown an alarming degeneration under the more comfortable NEP, during which it seemed to be becoming merely a new privileged class; but it was repeatedly "purged" by wholesale exclusions. These young people, like their leader, were familiar with no other country than their own, and their enthusiasm had been entirely recaptured by his appeal to make the great potential resources of Russia available to the community as a whole. These were the optimists, confident in their success, prepared for any sacrifice in the great enterprise. When the Plan was "breached" on any industrial "Front," they were thrown in masses into it, ignorant, but very quick to learn; and the initial Five Year Plan, which went through with such violence, was the second great school that produced the braced and hardened new generation of Russians. Any young boy or girl would want to be admitted to the Komsomol and could arrive at this through the junior party organizations of Young Octobrists and Pioneers. They were proud of their restrictions, their discipline, their hazards, and the unprecedented scope for their daring and energy.

Enormous new works and great new towns sprang up almost like mushrooms. Such were the Harkov tractor works, the Moscow lorry factory (1931), the Moscow rubber and ball-bearing factory, the Dnieper Dam, the Stalingrad tractor works, the Nizhny motor works, the furnaces of Magnitogorsk (in the Urals) and of Kuznetsk (in Turkestan) linked by the new Turk-Sib railway, and the Solikamsk fertilizer works in the Urals (1932).

With full foresight, the new works were for the most part set up far out of reach of an invader's attack. This was the first real attention given to the hitherto uncharted potentialities of Siberia. In 1917 a serious study of these resources had appeared in Germany under the title *The March Eastward, or Russian Asia as the Goal of German Military and Economic Policy*; and Hitler, for whom Siberia was the ideal new "German living-room," certainly had its great spaces in view. But it was the Russians, supposed to be incapable of industrial initiative, who moved before him and began its complete transformation. With the help of research, ice-breakers, and aviation, the Arctic Ocean from the North Cape to the Bering Strait could ultimately be kept open for two months of the year. Vegetables and fruit were grown inside the Arctic Circle, and new and unsuspected mineral wealth of all sorts was discovered in that neglected region.

The First Five Year Plan, completed before its time limit, did not reach all the extravagant goals which it had set itself, but its results were more than astonishing. It was announced that the next Five Year Plan would be concentrated on quality. In 1933 the canal linking the White Sea with the Baltic was after twenty months completed by convict labour. Over ninety new towns owed their origin to the first Five Year Plan, some of them in areas which till then had remained practically unutilized, such as the Kuznetsk district in the neighbourhood of Tashkend. The industry of the Urals, the earliest in Russia, was amplified fivefold. The industrial output increased yearly, by twenty per cent in 1929, thirty-eight per cent in 1930, and by similar large figures later. More attention could now be given to accessory considerations such as the living conditions of the workers and the provision for experts; but the compelling hand exercised its control throughout.

But Stalin, simultaneously with this enormous task of haste and compulsion, attacked another far more difficult, and it was precisely the wholeness of his effort that drew all these young people after him. This task was one before which even Lenin himself had called a halt. It was entirely logical to declare that a socialized industry with an individualist agriculture spelt the failure of Socialism in Russia; but here Stalin was fighting not sloth but the most rugged instincts of the peasantry as a whole, and they were still the bulk of the population. It was this, too, that brought an inevitable break with the Rights, the allies of his recent victory over Trotsky and the Lefts. The peasants under their natural leaders, the more prosperous, had shown plainly what they wanted, and every little peasant wished he could be one of the prosperous. Lenin had arbitrarily divided them into the poor, the middle, and the *kulaks*—a term used before the Revolution for the hard-fisted and the usurers; but even the *kulak* was far below the level of an American or British farmer. The word *kulak* now came to be applied to anyone who had his own machinery and hired labour, as had been allowed during the retreat of the NEP. It was these more prosperous peasants who had supplied the surplus of grain for export which had brought within possibility the purchase of the heavy plant. Stalin's arithmetic was to make good the loss to be caused by their elimination through a vast scheme for the mechanization of agriculture, in which there was the widest possible field for improvement. This was a second revolution, much more vital than the first.

In the spring of 1928 the Central Committee had decided to carry through its system of collective farming. The first step was to crush individual farmers with ever increasing taxation; the right to rent land was withdrawn; they were expelled from the *mir* or village assembly, and later the *mir* itself was abolished. Already, a number of government agents established in the villages as "country correspondents" had been assassinated; and now the peasant reply took open form in frequent murders, arson, and even small battles, which the government met with wholesale shooting and execution (forty a day in February 1930). Those who in sheer despair tried to escape across the frontier were treated in the same way.

At the close of 1929 the government announced a new "socialist offensive on all fronts" with "ruthless war" and a "ruthless class policy," and formed shock brigades of town workers. By a decree of February, 1930, about a million of the more prosperous peasants, with their families, were to be eliminated as farmers, and all their possessions confiscated. The innumerable tragedies of this immense process can be seen in the life in the faithful pages of Maurice Hindus.[1] By now all the towns were rationed for bread, and these regulations were extended to one new article of food after another. By March 1, 1930, the government forces of OGPU, town brigades, and Komsomol had succeeded in driving fifty-five per cent of the peasantry into the new farms; but these, as farms, existed for the most part on paper and, without a far greater measure of organization, could not supply the country with food. With ruin threatening the crop, Stalin called off his men in an article entitled "Dizziness from Success," and thereupon many of the new artificial farms collapsed. But the task was then resumed with greater preparation and more method. It was made almost impossible for the individual peasant to work with profit on the old lines; on the other hand, every favour was shown to the collective farms, and the looser forms of association were emphasized. The poorest of the peasants stood to gain by the experiment, for they corporately inherited the property of their thriftier neighbours; but even so, there was a wholesale slaughter of livestock, as the peasant proposed to enter the new farm with empty hands. Masses of peasantry, as in the great famine of 1922–3, broke loose from their moorings in a vague search for better conditions elsewhere, and it was with difficulty that the government maintained its hold over the country. The confiscated property for a time made possible a large export of grain; but the tables were soon turned, and in 1932 famine conditions reappeared on a large scale and grain had to be imported.

The new farms were now being built up more slowly. The government, while aiming at a State-owned agriculture, admitted, for the time

[1] Maurice Hindus: *Red Bread*.

being, three types: the state farm, the collective farm, and the artel, of which the last two approached rather more nearly the model of Western cooperative agriculture and allowed of varying degrees of personal property. By October 1, 1930, 25 per cent of agricultural Russia had been collectivized on a more permanent basis; by March 10, 1931, 37 per cent; by November 30, 1931, 60 per cent, and 60 to 90 per cent in the more fertile districts. Livestock and farming implements were now less rare. Pressure was now forbidden; for it was considered enough, as it well might be, for the peasant to be "faced with the choice." Premiums were introduced, with a very minute system of piece-work, to which the peasant himself objected, as taking no account of the number of mouths which he had to feed. Large numbers of workers were drafted from the farms to meet the very pressing needs of construction in industry.

But peasant ingenuity reappeared in the organization of the farms themselves: even religious communities had been found to be utilizing the new type. Inside the farms, the government was faced with a recurrence of the opposition which it had been fighting outside them, and ultimately felt it necessary to declare "war to a finish" against it (April 29, 1933). Many local managers were mainly influenced by their environment, and therefore had to be kept under close inspection and frequently replaced. The farm workers were now organized in brigades, with definite tasks assigned to each; and the retention of grain was met by a decree which punished with death the so-called "grain thieves," who made attempts on what was now declared to be "socialized property" (March 2, 1932). Special "brigades" for guarding the crops were used in 1933. Ultimately, special sections of political police were set up on the larger centres of farming.

The wholesale expulsions of peasants brought a new type of labour to the concentration camps of the north and east, very different from the suspected "counter-revolutionaries" of the educated class; and these camps were now put upon a business footing. With impounded peasants and impounded technical labour, they could now undersell the foreign timber market, causing grave loss to Scandinavia and Canada.

The government at times relaxed its pressure, but the main purpose remained unchanged. Repression culminated in 1932–3 when workers in factories were by decree expelled for one day's unexplained absence, with loss of food and quarters (November 10, 1932). The cooperative stores were closed, and the food was transferred for distribution to the factories themselves (December 4, 1932). A new system of internal passports was introduced—a revival of a creation of Peter the Great, which had been one of the most odious features of the old serfdom—and tens of thousands of persons were expelled from the larger cities without any apparent provision for their future (December 27, 1932). It was in this period that the political sections were established, first on the machine and tractor stations (January 13, 1933), which were now the centre of the new agriculture, and soon afterwards on the railways (July 11, 1933).

There was a third important aspect of the new offensive: a renewal of the attack on religion, which was regarded as the principal obstacle to the training of a new generation in the ideals of Socialism. Religion, though its organization and training had suffered grievously, had triumphantly survived the first intense persecution, and spiritually it had come out so much stronger that in 1928 the Commissary of Education, Lunacharsky, had himself admitted the futility of attack on it. As the persecution was now directed against all forms of religion and indeed of idealist thought, it was noted with alarm that traces of revival had appeared in all of them. The Baptists, at first excepted and even favoured, were now a special cause of apprehension. Something like a common religious front had appeared, which, in the common danger, minimized differences of belief and confession. Some new Orthodox churches had been built by workmen themselves, to replace those that had been closed. A Union of the Godless, which had been founded in April 1925, at first languished in comparison with the activity of the believers.

In the spring of 1929 drastic steps were taken. The Constitution was altered to exclude the freedom of religious propaganda (May 1929). A new and comprehensive law forbade any kind of religious activity except worship (April 6). The Commissariat of Education replaced the policy of non-religious teaching in schools by orders for definitely anti-religious instruction. Anti-religious museums were set up, and all the forces of broadcast, cinema, and stage were enlisted in this cause. The leader of this campaign, Yaroslavsky, a friend of Stalin's youth, reorganized the Union of the Godless on a much broader scale. While instructing his followers to avoid irritating the population, he directed all the energy of the attack on the ministers of all religions as such. Their lot was made intolerable: they were without the right to rations or housing, and the most active of them disappeared in great numbers into the concentration camps. First a five-day week was introduced (September 24, 1929), with holidays by shifts; and when this irritated the workers, it was replaced by a six-day week, of which one day was for rest.

Thus, by eliminating Sunday, attendance at worship was made much more difficult and dangerous. Far more churches were closed, and the process of collectivization was employed to convert churches to other uses. This last was probably much the most serious and most practical blow aimed against religion. Yet Yaroslavsky himself in his instructions to his followers in 1937 admitted that more than half the population was still religious.

Learning also, logically, had to suffer during the new offensive. It was now an offence in a teacher not to introduce Communism into his teaching. The Academy of Sciences, the highest learned institution in the country, with a splendid tradition of two hundred years, was made a special object of attack and was ultimately remodelled on Communist lines. Many of the finest scholars in Russia—some of whom, like the historians Platonov, Lyubavsky, and Tarlé, were men with European reputations—were imprisoned or exiled. The list of those who perished by shooting or in prison or exile was a long necrology of Russian scholarship. Purges were more frequent than ever in the Party itself.

By 1932 Stalin felt strong enough on his new basis to summon the Trade Union Congress after an interval of three years. The amount to be expended on social insurance had been doubled. The contribution of the collective farms to the State was reduced, and an open market allowed on the new footing (May 6). The meat due was halved (May 10), and free sale allowed (May 20), but middlemen were not tolerated. In 1933 the pay of engineers was greatly raised. The output of coal, which had given so much trouble earlier, had risen by thirty-three per cent.

Stalin was barely in time, with his first and roughest period of planning. By January 1933, Adolf Hitler was master of Germany. The threat contained in *Mein Kampf* became direct, and in all of Hitler's suggestions for world peace there was a systematic evasion of any guarantee on the side of Russia; it was England and Italy that he sought as his allies. The threat of Communism to the world—a threat that Stalin himself had emasculated in Russia itself—was taken as a smokescreen to cover sheer territorial conquest. There were explicit reports of military conferences between Germany and Japan. This, of itself, cut short the period of Russo-German collaboration initiated in 1922 by the Treaty of Rapallo and removed the prospect of a Russo-German alliance for a war of revenge.

In harmony with previous German and Austrian designs, German aggression was expected to be directed toward Ukraine. In 1918 the Central Powers, for the time triumphant, had at Brest-Litovsk temporarily forced Ukrainian separation on Russia in the guise of separate peace treaties with Ukraine and with Russia. Now Poland, restored to the map of Europe with a large slice of White Russian and Ukrainian territory, lay between Germany and Russia. Poland was geographically compelled to secure herself by agreements of some kind with both; and the German-Polish agreement of January 28, 1934, which was almost the last act of the Polish dictator, Marshal Pilsudski, was in Moscow suspected of implying cooperation in a joint aggression in Ukraine.

Stalin from the first kept the closest eye on this growing danger. There was by now no doubt that the Soviet government, absorbed in its reconstruction of the whole life of Russia and so dependent on foreign help, was sincerely desirous of maintaining world peace. But Stalin had found himself practically at war with the peasants—the main body of the population and the main source of his army; at one time their contribution to it had been reduced to thirteen per cent. History might ask, what was the wisdom of waging war on his own people between two major foreign wars. It was war that had overthrown Tsardom; in a new war the first-class citizens, the Communist Party, would have to lead, and this élite numbered only two millions in a population of about 160,-000,000. Would the peasants defend their country? Would they defend Stalin as their ruler? Hitler reckoned otherwise. It became imperative to Stalin to have them with him; and, for this, he had to give substantial satisfaction to their primary instincts. His action was in some ways reminiscent of the NEP; but there was this big difference: that in this case it was the government itself that took the lead in a return to greater freedom.

Significantly, this new direction began, in December 1933, with exemptions to the peasants on the Far East frontier. Among the sharpest acts of the period of repression had been the socialization of cattle (March 27, 1932). Now peasants were allowed to possess as many as three cows and an unlimited number of sheep, pigs, and poultry. The houses and the kitchen gardens were now, as under the Tsars, recognized as their property; in addition, they received small allotments for personal work and profit. They might not use hired labour, but their own earnings were guaranteed by the State as personal property and could be invested in interest-bearing bonds. As for centuries under the Tsars, ploughing, sowing, and reaping were done in common, though now infinitely better organized; but by now the peasants' share in the profit was reckoned by the most rigorous book-keeping according to the amount of work which they had put into it. Agricultural cooperation had always been the habitual practice of the Russian peasants. What they were concerned about was that the initiative should be left as far as possible to themselves. It was only the looser forms of cooperation that had been really found effective, and the standard articles of association of artels (February 13, 1935) now gave a larger share of the management to the members.

With the workers in industry, too, Stalin was passing from compulsion to encouragement. Piece-work was the basis of payment throughout the country. A Donets miner, Stakhanov, by rationalizing his task and organizing a system of cooperation, had greatly exceeded his assignment. His superiors saw a danger in this, but Stalin set him up as a model for general imitation, and "Stakhanovites" (or record-breakers) were honoured by having their names displayed on factory boards. The substantial reward was a progressive over-pay, reckoned on the excess above the assignment; soon some workers were earning more than their foremen. This helped the government to raise the standards of the tasks assigned. The custom of cooperative competition in output between rival factories was also further developed.

Another substantial change was that the family, which had somehow lived through these hard times, was fully restored to honour. Along with the strictest legislation against juvenile hooliganism went the restoration of full authority to parents and teachers; parents were called to help in school discipline; the pupils were put into uniform; the memory of the times when schoolchildren could even dismiss their teachers passed into oblivion. Delays were introduced into divorce procedure, and it was ultimately subjected to a progressive tax. Abortion, once so common, was now made a penal offence save in exceptional circumstances.

These were big things. With them went a substantial reversion to the past in the system of education. The theoretical bias of the preceding period was denounced by Stalin himself, and a decree of April 24, 1934, was directed against the "overburdening of schoolchildren and Pioneers with civic and political training." By a series of decrees which followed was re-established the old system of the teaching of history and geography, with its emphasis on facts, events, and personalities—in a word, on the concrete.

With the family, the past of Russia was also brought back to honour. At the outset an attempt had even been made to reckon Russian chronology from the Revolution of November 1917. The one outstanding Communist historian, Michael Pokrovsky, friend of Lenin, in his loyalty to "economic determinism," had even tried to eliminate the influence on Russia of the tremendous personality of Peter the Great. Now, Peter was extolled in first-class films, and with him all who had by their military exploits brought honour to Russia: St. Alexander Nevsky, who in the thirteenth century defeated the Order of Teutonic Knights; the Grand Duke Dmitry of the Don, who in 1380 won the first great victory over the Tartars; and Suvorov of the eighteenth century, the greatest of Russian generals. These pictures were presented with remarkable historical fidelity and with an honesty that took full account of the religious consciousness of the times. In the Red Army the old ranks of officers, with the exception of generals, were brought back. The military oath, which had engaged soldiers to the service of the international workers of the world was replaced by one which called for "the defence of the Soviet Motherland" (formerly an opprobrious term) and obedience to the military chiefs. These changes did not all come at once, but they represented a settled tendency in all succeeding legislation.

By 1934 there had been a very notable advance of heavy industry, with a greater output at a lesser cost. New great works were opened at Kramatorsk. Original defects in the Plan had been corrected, and the new constructions were based on calculations which took account of climatic conditions, and even created large new tracts of water. A new barrack town was established in the Far East. By 1933 the new agriculture had concentrated all output primarily on the towns. But more thorough methods of collection were established; and in 1935, in spite of a drought in South Russia, it appeared that the new system might even hope to defy the vagaries of the crops. In January 1935, the rationing of grain, which had lasted for five years, was abolished, and its price fixed at a mean between that of the former rations and that of the illegal free market; this practice was later extended to meat and other foodstuffs. The new farms got a better price for their grain. The budget now assigned a larger proportion to consumers' goods than to production, and light industry was also favoured. The effect came to be seen in a wide distribution, at least in Moscow, of the products of the new heavy plant, particularly of means of transport. The Metro underground railway, a work of great magnificence, was opened on May 15, 1935.

In 1935 Stalin, who had always to remember that his post was that of Secretary to the Communist Party, could again venture to allow the Comintern to meet; though, in accordance with the whole direction of his policy from the international to the national, it now reappeared in a new and chastened form, as an organ not of world revolution but of national defence. He had declared for "working relations with any foreign government, even capitalist, which was friendly to the Soviet Union." The Comintern was now therefore an agency for influencing the foreign policies of friendly nations and for disturbing those of actual or prospective enemies. The change was not likely to be readily noticed outside Russia, least of all perhaps by foreign Communist parties themselves; and in any case the intrusion of Russian influence in other countries under directions from Moscow continued to be sharply resented.

The great domestic success of 1935 enabled Stalin at the outset of 1936 to proclaim something like a general holiday. He spoke to his people by means of red posters carrying short, incisive phrases in large white letters; and Moscow was told: "Now, comrades, life is better, life is brighter." There was a mood of almost surprised satisfaction in the celebration of the New Year in January 1936. It was clear, at least in Moscow, that the Plan had taken effect. Now that the heavy plant was there, consumers' goods were being poured out at a great rate; the government stores showed an abundance of the more necessary and useful goods; motor traffic filled the streets. At the New Year a further attempt was made to stabilize the foreign exchange by fixing an arbitrary mean between the fantastically high legal rate and the fantastically low free market, which was clearly another step in the right direction. While we cannot accept the ignorant and insipid adulation of everything that was Soviet which so many travellers brought back from escorted tours, there was by now no question that the generation formed in the rough, through the ruthless years, had now something to be proud of. While such lines as the persecution of religion, always alien to the Russian character, had lost all interest (according to the testimony of the President of the Godless himself), the initial root principle of Communism, national ownership of the more substantial means of production, had taken a firm hold on the imagination as the most fundamental recognition of the oneness of the whole community. The care of Mother Russia for all whose support must depend on others had by now passed into full effect. The best medical attendance was free to all, even visitors; the number of doctors had been multiplied many times, and medical science, with the constant support of the State, had made enormous strides. Education was now compulsory and free of any charge; it had been completely modernized and was now centred around biology, always the favourite subject of Russian children. A complete system of insurance covered accidents, old age, and vocational disabilities. Unemploy-

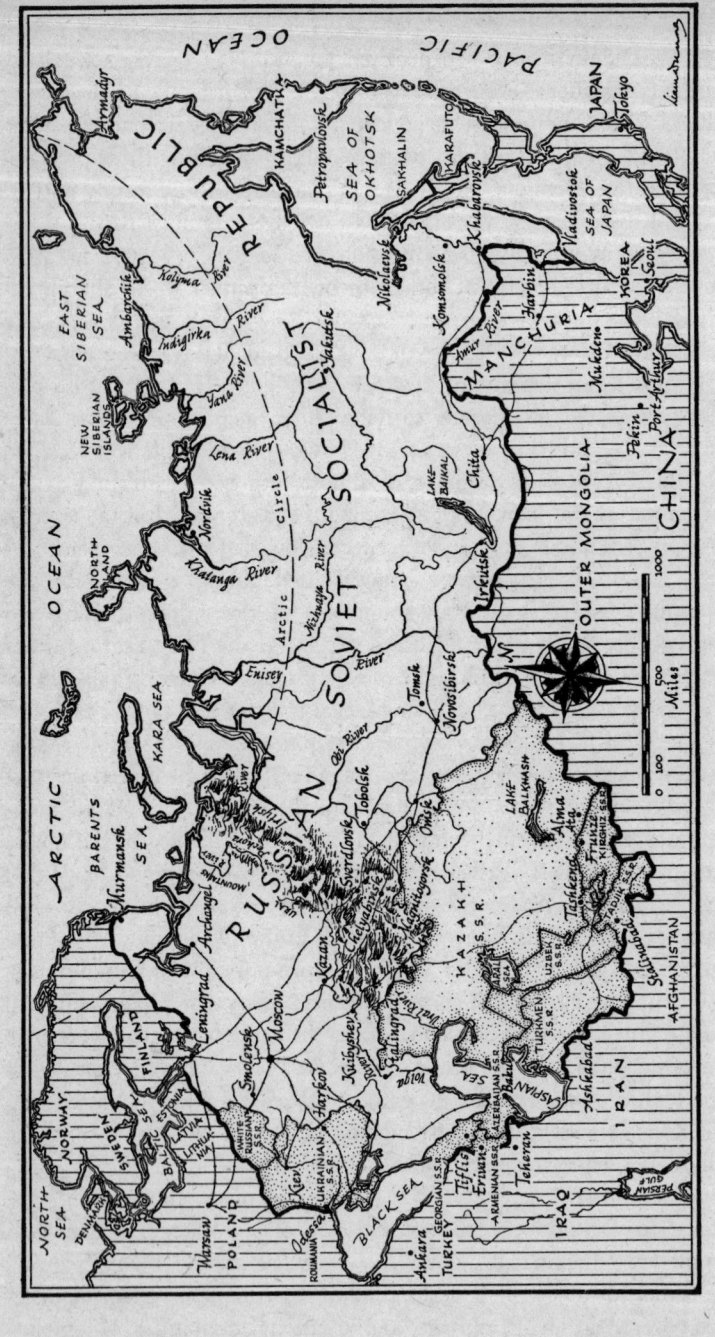

SOVIET UNION IN 1936

ment had been abolished by the Five Year Plans, with their enforcement of compulsory labour for those capable of it. The individual no longer felt a dependence on the chances of the future: and this very practical application of equality in a country so long accustomed to the caprices of absolute rule seemed an effective compensation for the loss of the right to criticize the government. Criticism of the way in which the intentions of the State were carried out was more systematically encouraged in Russia than elsewhere. Above all, Russia was now a country of the young; in fact, the average age of the population was near thirty; and the care of the young, in all its forms, always congenial to the Russian instinct, was that feature of the life of the country which was the principal charm for all who visited it.

The All-Union Congress of Soviets was called again after an interval of four years, and some of the restrictions of the franchise were abolished. The Congress met on January 28 and discussed the dangers which threatened from Germany and Japan. On February 6, Premier Molotov announced the drafting of a new Constitution with universal, equal, direct, and secret suffrage and the restoration of the ballot. This was in fact the famous "four-tailed formula" which had practically swept the country in the liberal period before the war. The peasant's vote, which had so far had one fifth of the value of the town worker's, was now to be equalized with it.

The draft of the proposed new Constitution, principally the work of Stalin himself, was on May 15, 1936, brought before the Central Executive Committee, which approved it and referred it for amendment or ratification to an All-Union Congress to be held before the end of the year. It was published in the official press on June 12, and proved to be the culminating point in the growing movement of conciliation already described.

It admitted of three kinds of property. The major means of production belonged to the State, the minor were the property of corporations, such as collective farms, together with assured tenure of their land; but the earnings of individuals and other limited rights of family property were guaranteed to them. As before, no place was left for the middleman. The old formula, as long since revised in practice, now read: From each according to his ability, to each according to his work.

The new Constitution was a very important further step on the lines of Stalin's earlier elimination of all racial inequality and presented in greater detail his distinction between the rights of the central government and those of autonomous republics. A Supreme Council was instituted, consisting of two Chambers equal in authority, of which one represented the whole State, and the other represented the various nationalities of the Soviet Union. The first is elected on the principles of universal, direct, equal, and secret suffrage from equal constituencies of the whole population; the second, in the same way by the national assemblies of the federal republics respectively. In case of disagreement between the Chambers, a joint commission is appointed. When no agreement is obtained, the Chambers are dissolved, and new elections conducted within two months; provision is made for a referendum where required. Normally, the Supreme Council sits for four years, in two sessions a year. In time of vacation its authority is exercised by a presidium elected by itself.

All appointments are made by the Supreme Council, including those of the People's Commissaries or Ministers. Deputies cannot be prosecuted without the agreement of the Council; they have the right to present interpellations to the government, which must be answered within three days. The Union as a whole reserves to itself the province of heavy industry; but the federal republics, which also have their own representative assemblies, have some latitude to deal with finance, police, and justice. They are to draft their own constitutions, which must, however, conform in general to that of the Union as a whole.

All judges are appointed for five years by the Supreme Council, except those of the People's Courts, who are elected. The judges are declared to be "independent, and subject only to the law," and the law officers are authorized to enforce their decisions, with authority in this respect over administrative officials.

Every citizen has the right to work, to holiday with pay, to social services such as free medical help, and to free education. In striking identity with the demands made by the Liberal movement of 1905 are laid down the principles of freedom of conscience, speech, press, meetings, and association. The place reserved to the Communist Party is that of an association, which acts as a leading nucleus or vanguard in all departments of public endeavour.

Arrests are to be made only on the authority of the law courts, and the text even declares the inviolability of dwelling and correspondence. The socialized property of the State remains inviolable, and "defence of the Fatherland" is a sacred duty of all.

All citizens over eighteen, male or female, have the vote, or can be elected, "independently of race, creed, education, place of dwelling, social origin, property status, or past activity." Candidates are put forward by any association, such as the Communist Party, trade unions, cooperatives, youth organizations, or cultural societies. Deputies are responsible to their constituents and can be recalled. Changes in the constitution require a majority of two thirds in both Chambers.

All this, on paper, was unexceptionable and represented an acceptance of the principles of Western democracy. But before the first election a supplementary article was introduced: that in each constituency there would only be one candidate, and the elections were carried out on this basis. Unqualifying apologists of the Soviets, when they did not shut their eyes to this article, were flabbergasted, and the sceptical were more sceptical than ever. It is not known whether Stalin from the start had this limitation in mind, but in any case the course of events can be interpreted by the darkening shadows of coming war. Stalin was still dealing with bitter enemies both at home and abroad.

There is a partial explanation in the way in which this single candidate was chosen: not behind the scenes, but through prolonged discussion in the press of the claims of the persons suggested. In each case, the discussion turned on his or her record of public service, though political activity was not stressed. Many indications tend to show that Stalin, who was already in other ways carrying through a wholesale transformation of the ruling party, was looking everywhere for key men and women, active and successful in public work. He issued a call for "nonparty Bolsheviks"—and "Bolsheviks" now meant those who put devotion and ability into executing the government's purpose. The slogan that his posters displayed at the election ran: "The union of Party and non-Party." Following out his definition of national policy as "Socialism in one country," he was everywhere broadening his hold on all national activities, by a process that might be described as turning the Party into the nation, and the nation into the Party. The best comparison will be with the vigorous football coach who seeks out talent in the lower games. The Supreme Council thus elected, though certainly more like the voice of the nation, had yet to show itself to be a deliberative assembly, affecting the course of policy.

For obvious reasons Stalin was now sincerely seeking a "United Front" against Hitler and Japan, and for this purpose he naturally turned to the democracies, who were threatened by exactly the same enemies. The dates are in themselves significant: 1933 marked the end of the first Five Year Plan by which, among other things, Stalin aimed at making his country defensible; but it was also the year in which Hitler became master of Germany. On November 16, 1933, through

Litvinov he renewed relations with the United States. On September 15, 1934, he brought Russia into the League of Nations. In 1932 he had concluded a Pact of nonaggression with France, which was converted into an alliance on May 2, 1935, and supplemented by an alliance between Russia and Czechoslovakia. Yet his post was still that of General Secretary of the Communist Party, and he could not expect anyone outside to understand what he was doing with the Party. Still largely unapproachable by foreign diplomats, he could not complain if other countries, and especially their Labour parties, recalled that Russia had earlier sought a quite different "United Front"—a Front of the world's workers against capitalism; the more so as the Comintern remained (it is true, with a different purpose), and the method of Communist infiltrations into national organizations abroad still continued. Both his own aloofness—quite intelligible in his strange position—and the traditional secretiveness of Russian diplomacy did much to hinder his success.

The Japanese invasion of Manchuria in 1931, which robbed Russia of her direct connection with Vladivostok, was condemned by the League of Nations, and Japan simply left the League. In April 1935—when Hitler was threatening the independence of Austria—England, France, and Italy held a conference for joint opposition at Stresa; but Russia, though already in the League, was not invited to join or cooperate. This suggested a distinction between two Europes, West and East, and Litvinov at Geneva was constantly insisting on the indivisibility of peace and the establishment for eastern Europe of some equivalent for the Locarno Agreement of 1925. When Mussolini invaded Ethiopia, Litvinov also called persistently, though in vain, for the sternest application of "sanctions" against Italy. It was Laval who was most responsible for this inaction, and the Franco-Soviet alliance was never followed up by any military consultations. Litvinov again strongly criticized the weakness of the League when Hitler, without opposition, remilitarized the Rhineland in March 1936.

A severer threat to Russian collaboration with the democracies was presented by Franco's rebellion in Spain in the summer of 1936, and the ensuing two and a half years of civil war there. Although the legal Spanish parliament, which fought back vigorously, had a few Communist members, these were greatly outnumbered by the champions of local autonomy; but, owing to the nature of the struggle and the compactness of their doctrine and organization, they became more and more prominent in the picture. German and Italian support of Franco was at first countered with energy by Russia. But Spain was not under Russian control; moreover, beneath the main struggle there was proceeding a subterranean continuation of the duel between Stalin and Trotsky—and Trotsky might claim to be the truer representative of doctrinaire Communism. To the interests of world revolution, Stalin preferred the support of England and France in his coming struggle with Hitler and Japan; and it is this preference that explains the patience with which Russia continued its membership of the futile Non-Intervention Committee in London, whose policy of appeasement left the way open for armed intervention by Germany and Italy in Spain, and thereby for the victory of Franco.

Meanwhile, Russian home policy had taken a sharp turn backwards which was negative to the realization of democracy and highly prejudicial to foreign collaboration. It could hardly have been without influence in the radical alteration of the new Constitution, as first announced. On December 1, 1934, just as Stalin's great industrial push was beginning to bear fruit, his right-hand man and favourite lieutenant, Kirov, whom he had sent to Leningrad to replace the dethroned dictator Zinoviev, was assassinated. On this Stalin went savage. Over one hundred survivors of the old regime, who could not have been responsible, were shot elsewhere. The assassin, Nikolayev, was a Communist whose wife had been Kirov's secretary, and the blame was later fixed on Zinoviev and Kamenev who, unlike Trotsky, had crawled back into the Party by repeated recantations and worked against Stalin from within. This was the first time that two of the original Bolshevist leaders were sent to prison. Sharp regulations as to trials were issued, reminiscent of the old field courts-martial of Stolypin.

There followed a feverish search for evidence of complicity with the absent Trotsky. There was a series of great political trials and executions, to which was given a resounding publicity, with verbatim reports of the proceedings. In the first, in August 1936, Kamenev and Zinoviev were retried with fourteen others and executed as having aimed at the assassination of Stalin and some of his colleagues. It has to be remembered that these men, like Stalin himself, had grown up in conspiracy in which political assassination was not excluded. Zinoviev, in particular, had terrorized Leningrad, as its dictator, with innumerable executions. In January, 1937, among seventeen accused were ex-leaders as distinguished as Pyatakov, Radek, and Sokolnikov. All of these were charged with having received and tried to carry out instructions of Trotsky for wrecking the work of construction. That he should have sent such instructions and known how to send them was not necessarily inconsistent with his past conspirative activity or with his present attitude. In March 1938, among twenty-one accused were Bukharin and Rykov of the Rights (Tomsky had committed suicide), accused of plotting with the Lefts for the overthrow of Stalin. That Bukharin, with the help of Sokolnikov, had sought the collaboration of Kamenev appears to be established apart from this trial.

Nearly all admitted having conspired against the life of Stalin and others, and on this point it is not necessary to doubt them. The bulky verbatim report was received abroad with sharp criticism. Hardly any outside evidence was adduced in these trials and no documents were submitted, but some of the statements—particularly the so-called "last words" of Bukharin, who was executed, and of Radek, who was not— carried conviction to others. Bukharin admitted in full the conspiracy against Stalin, but indignantly repudiated any suggestions of contact with foreign agents. Radek, who spoke with consummate lucidity, gave what is probably a true picture. When arrested he was about to consult his colleagues as to whether Trotsky, still in Mexico, should not be told that now that the consumers' goods had arrived, a plot against Stalin's life had lost its point. The most doubtful part of the evidence related to complicity with German and Japanese agents; some of this was refuted as clearly untrue. It was only later, when so much more was known of Hitler's methods of penetration in other countries, that some took this charge more seriously.

In June 1937, seven of the most distinguished generals in Russia, including Marshal Tukhachevsky, were condemned for treason and shot. This was a court-martial, and no full report was published. During the Rapallo period, when community in the boycott of Europe had thrown Russia and Germany together, it was natural for the two General Staffs to confer on the possibilities of future joint action. There was common ground of policy between the two staffs, for among the military an alliance had been favoured on both sides. But after Hitler came into power, with his program of conquest of Russia, further contact became absurd and was prohibited. There is good reason to think that the conversations continued, and that each Staff had its own views about its own ruler. It is by no means unlikely that there was a plot; the additional details supplied for public consumption may be disregarded, but the result was received in Germany with something like dismay. General Blomberg passed out of office there at the same time.

These trials were only a part of a vast purge, including the Party and the army, of all suspected of sympathy either with Trotsky or with Germany. It extended to the autonomous republics, many of whose highest officials disappeared at this time. The plea that Stalin acted first to disrupt a potential Fifth Column, especially in view of the contrast between the subsequent Russian resistance and the impotence of other countries, is by no means unwarranted. The one thing which comes out quite clearly is that the victims in the Party were precisely the champions of world revolution. The purge completed the Party's thorough transformation; it was now simply the party of Stalin, and only a minority could date their membership from its earlier days. Mr. Chamberlin, the principal critic of these purges, concurs in this when he writes: "It would be no exaggeration to say that the casualties read like a Communist *Who's Who* of the Twenties." [1] It was these who were the real enemies of Stalin inside Russia.

Outside, war was well on the way. On November 25, 1936, an Anti-Communist Pact was concluded between Germany and Japan, later joined by Italy. As all these three States had effectively suppressed Communism within their own borders, it was evident that Russia was the target.

On July 7, 1937, in full accordance with the Tanaka program, a manufactured "incident" outside Pekin provided the jumping-off point for a Japanese conquest of China. In 1912, Kaiser Wilhelm II, on a visit to Nicholas II, had warned the Russian Foreign Minister that, if Russia did not take a hand in the organization of China, Japan would do so and that the Russians would lose their hold on the Pacific. At one time it had looked very much as if this might happen; but Stalin's Russia was already very different from that of Lenin.

On March 10, 1938, Hitler made his first actual aggression by the forcible seizure of Austria. The Soviet government had been little interested in the dictatorship of Dollfuss since he had fired on the workmen of Vienna. But Hitler's act resulted in an almost complete German encirclement of Russia's ally Czechoslovakia. The Czechs, who were extremely well organized and equipped, were determined to defend themselves, however hopeless the task, and felt sure that sooner or later their friends would come to their help. But France, which was definitely committed, was not ready, and England, which had not definitely committed itself, was still less ready. It was France which, with the acquiescence and support of England, had built up a ring of small States on the circumference of Germany, and these had every right to look to the two

[1] W. H. Chamberlin: *The Russian Enigma*, p. 208.

Powers for help; but the British and French Premiers set themselves to stave off war at any cost—which meant at the cost of Czechoslovakia. Neville Chamberlain made three hectic visits by air to Hitler for this purpose. He did not visit Prague, and the Czechs were not invited to the decisive conversations at Munich. Neither was Russia, although a member of the League: was it to be assumed that she had ceased to be one of the Great Powers? On September 23 Litvinov at Geneva repeated the Russian pledge to the Czechs; and even after the disastrous decision Russia, though released from her treaty obligations by the French default, still offered her support. The Czechs were left helpless, with their strong mountain defence taken from them. Their ruin was completed on March 14, 1938, by Hitler's sudden forcible seizure of Prague itself, carried through with the most sinister details of deceit and brutality. Nothing was done to redeem the Anglo-French pledge to the remainder of Czechoslovakia.

The British Premier, indeed, now at long last realized the true nature of the man in whose word he had trusted, but of this fact Stalin needed more convincing proof. Not without reason, he discriminated between the ruling classes and public opinion in England; but he was prepared to wait for a change of policy before locking his own doors and seeing to his own defences. Meanwhile Hitler went forward. By fostering a movement for independence, he was able to lay hands on Slovakia. This meant the outflanking of Poland, evidently marked as his next victim. In Carpathian Russia, which is Ukrainian, he even set up a little show window for the "liberation" of Ukraine. He also moved against the new independent State of Lithuania from which, by ultimatum alone, he extracted the cession of Memel. Poland was already half conquered.

France was long since allied with Poland and on March 31, 1939, England gave her a unilateral pledge of help, guaranteeing her independence. On April 13 she added similar guarantees to Greece and Roumania. Clearly, the Western Powers could do nothing at all against Germany in eastern Europe without the cooperation of Russia. British Labour became insistent, and Churchill pointed vigorously to the need of an understanding. Russia was approached, and as France was already allied with her, England took the leading part in the negotiations. On April 17, Russia offered a triple alliance against aggression, with a joint guarantee of the Baltic States, Poland, and Roumania; the little Baltic States, on which Hitler was already encroaching, were the obvious German land route to Leningrad. To this proposal, which was repeated, no direct answer was given. From May to August, long and unsatisfactory parleyings dragged on in Moscow. On the British side the task was left to a subordinate official of the Foreign Office. There were no general conferences of all concerned. The Russians concluded that England and France were interested only in the defence of Poland and the small States—or, as they put it later, in Russia's willingness to "pull the chestnuts out of the fire" for them. The Poles imposed limitations on Russian help, which the British passed on to the Russians: for instance, they were not to be allowed to enter Poland. The Russians proposed a military conference to speed things up; but this was putting the cart before the horse, and it was carried out in a very halfhearted way. The question of the Baltic States also hung up any decision; for they refused to accept a joint occupying force of the prospective allies: Russia, Britain, and France. Polish objections had only with difficulty been overcome, when Molotov broke off the discussions by announcing that Ribbentrop, who had for some time been in touch with him, was arriving next day to conclude a nonaggression pact between Russia and Germany, by which on August 22 Russia contracted herself out of the coming war. By relieving Germany of all anxiety as to a second main front, this pact made the war inevitable, and on September 1 the Germans invaded Poland.

Throughout, the Russo-German Pact was never an alliance, either political or military. Both sides were playing an elaborate game of poker, as was quite clear to those aware of the issues at stake between them. It has been well called "the pact which was also a duel." Hitler had difficulty in explaining to his people his elaborate demonstrations of friendship with the "Bolsheviks"; and Molotov had to devise an equally artificial explanation to the effect that the word "aggression" had changed its meaning when England and France refused to accept the almost immediate defeat of Poland. Russia spent only words on pleasing the Germans. The Soviet press emphasized the landmarks of the British intervention only twenty years before, as they came up, without reference to the almost simultaneous German intervention in Finland and elsewhere; but there was a unanimous omission of the name of its chief leader, Churchill, who might be useful later on. Stalin's gains from the Pact were substantial. He was well aware that the German attack on Russia was only deferred. Military production was feverishly speeded up and Russia was converted into a wholesale "defence in depth"; every new German military device, as practised in France, was carefully studied and the right antidote sought in realistic practice.

By September 17 the Polish army and government were in rapid retreat from Warsaw. The chief issue left was the fate of those White

Russian and Ukrainian populations which Pilsudski had conquered in the period of Russian exhaustion in 1921. It was self-evident that Hitler must conquer these too, unless he was anticipated. The Red Army marched in. Polish soldiers and landlords fled, and the large Polish estates were divided up among the White Russian and Ukrainian poor. Soviet institutions were introduced, including the extensive social services, but for the present excluding collective farming. The German and the Russian armies were racing towards each other, to see which could cover most ground, and a clash seemed near. A line of military demarcation was set up running through Warsaw, which was the most direct challenge to the British pledge to Poland; but the Russians retired to a limit approximate to the Curzon line, suggested by England in 1920, though they still included within it some three or four million Poles.

Stalin was taking advantage of Hitler's preoccupation in the West to regain, under the cover of neutrality, what he could of the strategic positions of Russia in 1914. The side which next claimed his attention was the Baltic. By the last World War, Russia had lost the principal conquest of Peter the Great and the approaches which guarded his new capital. The little States set up at that time could not defend themselves against either Russia or Germany, and the war had converted them into a *glacis*, still neutral, between the two great armies. Stalin began by demanding of them the naval bases which Russia had possessed in 1914. Resistance was impossible, and he secured them by a series of separate ultimata (September 29–October 10). In each case he gave the most explicit pledge against interference in their internal affairs. But by June 15, 1940, he had annexed and Sovietized all of them. The most extraordinary part of this story is that Hitler himself removed the German population of these States, to plant them in the old Polish Corridor near Danzig.

This accounted for the left side of Peter's sea road to Europe. On the right side lay Finland, which was a very different affair; and here Stalin made his worst miscalculation. Finland, though never wholly independent till 1918, had always shown herself capable of standing up for her own liberties and enjoyed well-deserved sympathies in America and in England. At this time her rulers represented those "White" Finns who with substantial German aid had triumphed over the "Red" Finns in their civil war of 1918. Russia asked first for the old naval bases which she had held before 1914, offering in return an extension of the Finnish frontier in Karelia. But the Finns felt they could not place their defences in Russian hands, and the negotiations lagged. Stalin scraped a

quarrel and invaded (November 30, 1939). Counting on the support of
the Red Finns he sent in one of them, Otto Kuusinen, who had taken
refuge in Russia after the Finnish Civil War, and declared him to be the
ruler of Finland. He even made a treaty with Kuusinen, by which in return for the naval bases he granted the extension of territory which he
had earlier suggested to the legal Finnish government. In an appeal for
a Finnish rising it was not expedient to overemphasize the military character of the invasion. But the Finns, to their credit, remained united.
They put up the sturdiest resistance, and the invasion was halted. Germany did nothing to help them. In December Russia was voted out of
the League of Nations as an aggressor. At one moment it looked as if
England would send a force to help the Finns, and Russia might have
found herself on the German side in the western war. The operations
were now entrusted to Timoshenko; and, once these were serious, the
Finns stood no chance. They were attacked by day and night until their
reserves were exhausted. But Stalin cut his losses; Kuusinen was dropped,
and the legal Finnish government was again recognized. The frontier
was put back somewhat further from Leningrad, and also on the north
on the side of Russian Karelia (March 12, 1940).

The Russian outlook was radically altered by Hitler's spectacular
successes in the spring and early summer in Denmark, Norway, Holland,
Belgium, and France. After the fall of France, with England defending
her own beaches, Russia, originally Hitler's first target, now came next
on the list and the continual pinpricks of the period of the Pact could
be avenged. The totalitarian Soviet press, through which Stalin talked
to his people, now discouraged the conclusion that England's fall was
inevitable. British war news came first, and the Battle of Britain and
defence of London received full recognition. The world was now back
in the times of Napoleon. When England held firm, Hitler, like Napoleon, turned eastward. At each step the rift in the Pact widened and
the Russian reaction to his advance became more articulate. The old interest in the "younger brothers," the lesser Slavonic nations, once discouraged in the Soviet press as a bourgeois anachronism, resumed its
force, and Hitler's New Order for Europe was more clearly challenged.

Hitler was seriously embarrassed by the ill-advised attack of his ally
Mussolini on Greece, and by the Italian reverses which followed. To
come to his aid, he had quickly to find a road to Greece, and this set
him to work on Hungary and Roumania. Hungary, as a loser at Versailles, was not a difficult obstacle. In Roumania, Stalin anticipated him
by demanding and getting back by ultimatum alone Bessarabia, lost to

Russia in the First World War, as well as Ukrainian parts of Bukovina, never yet under Russian rule (June 27, 1940). Hitler now adjudicated between the impossibly complicated claims of Roumania and Hungary. He transferred Transylvania from Roumania to Hungary, which gave him a favourable approach towards Russia (August 30). Roumania threw herself on the mercy of Hitler, and by February 1941, German guns were set up on the coast of the Black Sea. Russia made an official remonstrance to Hungary.

Next on Hitler's road came Bulgaria and Yugoslavia, both of which were strongly pro-Russian. He cajoled and threatened their rulers, and by March 1, 1941, Bulgaria joined his so-called "New Order." Russia sent her sharp disapproval on March 3. The Yugoslavs on the other hand overthrew their regent, Prince Paul, and rose to resist the German demands. They showed their hopes clearly enough by carrying British and Soviet flags side by side through the streets of Belgrade. Russia responded with a pact of friendship which was too late to be of service, and not only the Yugoslavs but the Greeks, in spite of the help of British troops, were overwhelmed.

Turkey was now threatened by Germany, and received a reassurance of friendship from Russia (March 24). In her rear, British authority in Irak was shaken by a revolt led by a German protégé, Rashid Ali; but England managed to re-establish her control. Everywhere the interests of England and Russia were becoming more closely identified, since Hitler was now master of almost all the rest of Europe.

Danger had also threatened from Japan. In July 1938, incessant frontier clashes led to hard and prolonged fighting on the Chang-Kuping hills near Lake Hasan. In the end the Russians won decisively. No real settlement followed, and Russia steadily continued her support of the independence of China, supplying her with arms from the new Asiatic base in Kuznetsk. In July 1940, a single National Party was set up in Japan, and on September 28 the Anti-Communist Pact of Germany, Japan, and Italy was converted into a Tripartite Alliance, which was to establish the "New Order" throughout the world. Russia repeated her intention to support China, but she had no wish to see herself attacked on two fronts, and the major danger was in the West. The Japanese Minister, Matsuoka, came to reconnoitre in Europe and attended a ceremony of the New Order in Vienna. On his way back through Moscow, he signed with Russia a pact of reinsurance (April 13, 1941) which promised to preclude a Japanese attack.

Could Russia, like Roumania and other smaller fry, be cajoled into joining the New Order too? If so, her independence would be finished, and the German program of 1917—a German-Japanese alliance, with Russia as a junior partner—would have come into being. An extensive economic treaty, which had accompanied the Russo-German Pact of 1939, had not resulted in satisfying either party. The Soviet regime would not survive if the Germans could come freely into Russia to work and transport their own supply of oil. In November 1940, Molotov went by invitation to Berlin; but the only result of the visit was the patching up of the economic treaty with new promises on January 10, 1941.

On May 6 a significant pointer was offered. Stalin for the first time assumed the Premiership of the Soviet government. So far he had stayed outside it. This was a further sign of the shifting of the whole centre of gravity to the nation, another step toward the "Union of Party and non-Party," on what might be the eve of a great national ordeal.

In the early morning of June 22, 1941, Hitler cut the Gordian knot and repeated the cardinal mistake of Napoleon and Wilhelm II by invading Russia. On the same evening Churchill, in the British Parliament, made England the ally of Russia.

What followed was the full manifestation of Stalin's new Russia, and the explanation of everything he had done.

CHAPTER XXVII

The Second Fatherland War

[*1941–5*]

THIS brings us to events of the utmost portent to the whole world. The first major factor for the future was Russia's resistance to the invader, anticipated only by those who without prejudice had closely followed her past and understood her present.

There are certain constant elements in the history of Russian military defence. Russia is always far stronger in defence than in attack, for defence is always the affair of the whole people. With no protective sea frontier or formidable geographical boundaries, Russia has always had to retire before a sudden aggression. Normally it takes fifteen days for her real strength to gather on her western border. But as soon as the enemy passes the frontier, it is not only the regular Russian army, but the whole people and even the country itself that rise to resist him. This involves vast and uncalculating sacrifices, especially at the outset; and Stalin at once (July 3) ordered a strategy of "scorched earth," by which nothing of value should be left to the invader. The unstinting thoroughness with which this was carried out was the first great surprise to Hitler and to everyone else.

On the other hand, Russia's vast distances are in themselves a great defence. The object of any invader must be to bring the Russian army to a real decision—to encircle it and destroy it. So long as the army is in being and is supplied, Russia is not beaten. It is this that inspired the tactics of Peter the Great against Charles XII and of Kutuzov against Napoleon. But every advance is contested, and in this "back fighting," especially at night, the Russian is a past master. Even the army of 1915, threadbare of all supplies except the bayonet, was never encircled.

This, for the enemy, results in a constant wastage of effective strength. Here the country is almost more important than the army. Napoleon lost more in this way than in any other. Russia, especially in the north and centre, has a greater proportion of marsh than any other country in Europe; in the treeless south, rain churns up the rich black soil into a sea of mud, peculiarly obstructive to mechanized transport; even in the initial stages of the new campaign the early autumn rains brought pitiful complaints from the broadcaster accompanying the German forces. Instead of the metalled roads and built-up areas of France, the invader was surrounded, in the north and centre, by vast and mysterious tracts of no-man's land—forest or marsh or both together—where only the patient Russian peasant could feel at home or find a way. This gave abundant cover for guerrilla warfare all along the German lines of communication, with easy contact, often by parachute, with the Russian rear. Russian agriculture, almost throughout Russian history, had been collective; and now, replacing the antique village communes, which were so effective against Napoleon in day or night warfare at any point on his road, there were the new collective farms, far better organized and led, and with a far closer interest in the soil that they were defending. In the First World War peasant hoarding of food was one of the primary causes of the collapse of the Imperial machine. In the Second it was the Soviet collectivization of agriculture that maintained the regular distribution of food to both army and people.

From the first was vindicated the wisdom of Stalin's long-considered policy of military defence against a long-anticipated invasion. By his pact of nonaggression with Germany in 1939,[1] "the pact which was also a duel," [2] he had put off the evil day for a year and a half. He had himself recovered that *glacis* of independent territory—a large part of what Russia had lost in the preceding war—that lay between the two great States, and of which Hitler had been thinking in *Mein Kampf* when he spoke of his designs on "Russia and the border states formerly dependent on her." [3] He had been able to watch the novelties of German warfare in France, tank formations, dive-bombers, and so on, to study in the most assiduous practice methods of opposing them, and to turn Russia into an almost wholesale "defence in depth." The Russian plan was to cut off the advancing tanks from their supporting infantry, a task requiring signal individual courage that had not so far been seriously attempted. If one goes further back, he had eliminated in advance the nucleus of that "Fifth Column" on which Hitler, largely encouraged by Russian emigrant advisers, still placed such reliance, and the sincerity of the Russian resistance showed that this hope was illusory.

[1] Treaty of Berlin.
[2] Walter Duranty in *The Kremlin and the People*.
[3] *Mein Kampf*, Vol. II, pp. 742–3.

All the same, through those vast spaces the tremendous German machine pounded its way, taking masses of prisoners, but always at a cost that gravely upset the timetable Hitler had announced. The newly acquired *glacis* was quickly overrun, for its defences were recent and incomplete, but it served a purpose in giving time to recover from the first effects of the shock. The passages of the Pruth and Dniester were contested with special vigour, for the country that lay behind them was comparatively open and easy. Kiev in the First World War was not a fortress, but it was now the first town in Europe to hold the dreaded Panzers at bay (August 7 to September 20).[1] It held out long after it had been outflanked; it had to be carried against desperate street-fighting, leaving the ruins of this ancient and lovely city to the conquerors. Every kind of booby-trap was left to the incoming Germans. Odessa, though close to the frontier, held out even longer with the help of the Red fleet (August 14 to October 16), and long after its occupation Russian suicide squads in underground refuges continued to blow up German troops on the top of them. On August 24 the retreating Russians themselves blew up the Dnieper Dam, perhaps the most outstanding achievement of Soviet industry. The defence of Sevastopol was even more memorable than that of the Crimean War; soldiers would buckle grenades to them and throw themselves under the German tanks; the civil population, men, women, and children, took the fullest share in the fighting (November 1, 1941 to July 1, 1942). Russian military production had been furiously speeded up in the years preceding the invasion, and measures of which this people would earlier have been thought incapable were largely successful in removing whole factories with their staffs to places far in the rear. Leningrad lay perilously close to the frontier. The neighbouring Finns joined in the German assault on it; but that great hive of war industry held out and continued to function, though almost ringed round by the enemy, fighting off the beleaguerers in incessant and prolonged counterattacks.

Hitler had challenged comparison with Napoleon, invading one day earlier in the year, and his main interest was concentrated on the road to Moscow; for it was there that a real decision might be reached. Thither, beside the new metalled track, still runs the old road of Catherine the Great—the "big 'un," as the peasants still call it—with its double line of silver birch, enveloped by forests of birch, pine, and fir. Russia is full of strong local traditions, and at each natural barrier on this road the fighting flared up stronger. The invader was held up for

---

[1] The dates given in each case include the period of encirclement.

days on the Berezina, which winds in silver streams among a half-mile stretch of peat bog (July 1). Smolensk, with its old walls of Boris Godunov—"the precious necklace of Russia," as he called them—had kept Napoleon at bay till it was all on fire, and it did the same with Hitler (July 17 to August 11). Here in Great Russia, where peasant patriotism is at its strongest, the advance slowed down until it was brought to a standstill at two historic spots, Mozhaisk and Malo-Yaroslavets. Mozhaisk is almost identical with Napoleon's battlefield of Borodino, and at Malo-Yaroslavets in 1904 I found a tablet commemorating his other great check after he left Moscow. It reads: "End of offensive, beginning of rout and ruin of enemy." These two small towns eventually also stopped Hitler and remained the buttresses of the Russian line (October 19 to January 19).

This turn of the tide came in the early days of December. The Germans had captured the ancient city of Novgorod in the Valday hill district (August 26) and had cut the road from Leningrad to Moscow, occupying Kalinin (Tver) street by street (October 23), and pushing forward a great pincer for the envelopment of Moscow as far east as Dmitrov. They also threatened the capital from the south with another great pincer which penetrated past Kaluga as far as Orel. It looked as if Russia was being cut up into pieces, which were to be encircled in turn. On November 23 the enemy reached Rostov, which was occupied only after the fiercest street-fighting; but Timoshenko, with a brilliant flank movement, drove them out in something very like rout and followed them up in swift pursuit. It was at this point (December 6) that on the order of Stalin, as Commander-in-Chief, Russia, with fresh reserves, launched a great counterattack in the whole Moscow area, winning back one point after another by desperate fighting, often bypassing the "hedgehog" strong points that the Germans had set up, but gradually pressing their whole line westwards.

Hitler would have liked to call a halt on his Russian front, but this the Russians did not allow. They continued the most vigorous counter-attacks throughout the winter, making appreciable gains at different points of the line and leaving none of it in peace. Zhukov, in turn, threatened Vyazma with two formidable converging pincers. Timoshenko reconquered a large part of the Donets coal and iron region, where sixteen mines were even set working again.

Hitler had failed to supply his troops with the necessary winter clothing, and this winter was peculiarly severe. Russian energy did not relax, and for the first time the Germans had most to suffer; sometimes whole numbers of men were found frozen stiff at their posts. The long, hard winter culminated in a peculiarly bitter March, when Berlin admitted (March 23) that the invaders were faced with their hardest trials. A promised German spring offensive was anticipated and rendered impossible; Russian initiative was eating up reserves destined for later German attacks, and Hitler had to scour conquered Europe for new unwilling cannon-fodder.

Throughout the winter the guerrilla bands, in which Russian women played a great and fearless part, engaged in enterprises of amazing audacity, cutting off German supplies, destroying isolated detachments, wrecking tanks or aerodromes, and making the German soldier's life a burden to him day and night. Again clear evidence of this occasionally came through in the plaintive accounts of the German field broadcaster to the only less harassed population at home. In May, Berlin announced that, despite the many punitive expeditions, these guerrilla bands kept springing up everywhere again like mushrooms.

In England, it was now evident to all that success both in the war and in the achievement of a lasting peace settlement depended on keeping this new-found friend. The initial lead had come from the British Prime Minister. Now he and President Roosevelt, meeting in the Atlantic on August 14, 1941, issued a joint declaration, the Atlantic Charter, which Russia accepted (September 4); indeed, some of these were principles in which she was herself specially interested. At the same time came the offer to Stalin of a joint Russo-British-American conference in Moscow for the pooling of military supply and its distribution according to the most pressing needs of the Allies as a whole. This generous offer was cordially welcomed; and the practical realism with which this business was carried through probably did more than anything else could have done to create an atmosphere of reciprocal confidence. From that time onward a great stream of British and American supplies flowed into Russia past bitter and ever increasing Axis opposition, with silent but immense sacrifices of the naval forces involved. Later the Russian Foreign Minister, Molotov, himself came to London, and his visit led to the conclusion of a treaty of twenty years between Britain and Russia, for the joint achievement both of victory and of a permanent peace settlement. This was announced on June 12, 1942.

It was just at the time when Stalin was turning the tide in Russia that the scope of the war became world-wide. The United States of America has normally been in friendly relations with Russia. Under the old regime there was one great disturbing factor: Russia's treatment of her minor nationalities, which were strongly represented in America, and especially of her Jewish population, kept under by almost impossibly oppressive legislation. The hideous pogroms or armed attacks on Jews were definitely stirred up by the Imperial Department of Police. Nowhere has the new regime been more happy than in its complete solution of this question of nationalities. All of them are now, both in principle and in practice, equal in rights and responsibilities, and this solution was peculiarly the work of Stalin himself, at first as Commissary for the Minor Nationalities, and later as the drafter of the new federal constitution of the Union of Soviet Socialist Republics (1936).

America took relatively little part in the intervention of 1918–21. She barely associated herself with the settlement of Versailles, which Russia has never recognized. She was foremost in the work of relief in the great famines that followed in Russia. She has played a far larger part in Stalin's industrialization than any other country. Definitely, Russia took her as her model in this whole work of construction and owes to her the most substantial of all foreign contributions, both in machinery and technicians. The sudden rise of English to the first place among foreign languages in the Russian school system is, in the main, a recognition of the importance of industrial collaboration with America. According to Litvinov, it was an American Ambassador, Joseph E. Davies, who has published the most important contribution in English to a sane understanding of present-day Russia.

With the withdrawal of the Russian menace in the Far East and the consistent support which the Soviets gave to China, American and Russian interests in the Pacific became for the time almost identical, and both powers alike stood for peace. To both the threat of danger came from Japan. Japanese policy had led naturally to alliance with Nazi Germany. Japan was evidently not the leading power in this alliance, and she hesitated for a long time to cast the die, but this she did when it was perhaps least expected, with the usual Axis preface of negotiation and deception, by a sudden attack on the American naval base at Pearl Harbor (Sunday, December 7, 1941). War between Britain and Japan followed automatically, for Britain's interests in the Pacific were generally the same as America's. On December 11 Hitler announced the full solidarity of Germany and Italy with Japan; that is, Germany and Italy were now at war with America. Russia still had a nonaggression treaty with Japan, and it could not be expected that she should challenge an extra conflict when her military resources in the Far East were so important for the reinforcement of the defence of her capital. Two events in

Russia followed naturally enough in this period of friendship: the dissolution of the Comintern on May 22, 1943 and the restoration of the Patriarchate on September 4, 1943. The Russian Church had convincingly shown both its vitality and its patriotism.

In May and June 1942, after a tremendous and far-probing effort of German organization, Hitler was at last able to resume the offensive in colossal force, with thousands of tanks and dive-bombers in a double drive for the Lower Volga and the Caucasus. After Sevastopol had at last been taken, house by house (July 1, 1942), it was possible to cross the narrow outlet of the Sea of Azov and push on even into the foothills of the Caucasus. By the fall of Novorossiisk the Russian fleet was deprived of almost its last refuge in the Black Sea. On the road to Baku the Russians were compelled to destroy and abandon the valuable oil wells of Maikop, and Grozny was seriously threatened. At one moment it seemed to be touch and go whether the invader did not secure the master key of the passage through the Caucasus range.

Close northward, Rostov was again outflanked and taken, the Don crossed at the point where it comes nearest to the Volga, and by sheer weight of metal and of numbers, through country that offered few possibilities for defence, the invaders forced their way to the outskirts of Stalingrad. There was no Stalingrad in the First World War: this new and immense industrial city, like the Dnieper Dam, was purely an achievement of Soviet industry. Here the Russians of today were fighting for what was very specially their own. If ever in history some vital event was required to fix a new place-name decisively on the map, it was to be found in the weeks and months that followed. The Germans had reached the Volga—in fact, at tremendous sacrifices, they actually held short stretches of its western shore—but this great eastern city remained unconquered. By the nature of things, the German tanks could never have free play in the rubble created by the German artillery, and the dive-bombers were largely hampered by the presence of the attacking battalions, thrown separately or in whole divisions into this death-pit. Always at their best in conditions that call for individual initiative, courage, and resource, the Russians held on to every shelter in their battered factories and cellars.

It was now that General Zhukov and his Chief of Staff, Vasilevsky, planned a war of manœuvre which in the end sealed the fate of the besieging Sixth and Fourth (tank) German Armies. In mid-November 1942 the British victory of El Alamein in North Africa and the pursuit of the beaten Germans stopped the flow of reinforcements to the German armies in front of Stalingrad. The Russians were enabled by the greatly superior reserves of their manpower to bring into action fresh troops, finely trained, which could change the balance and draw a line behind the besieging armies of von Paulus in a combined "pincer" action from both north and south.

By November 15 Rokossovsky, supported by Vatutin, was moving, chiefly at night, from the north across the great bend of the Don towards Kalach, which is due west of Stalingrad. Towards this point of junction Yeremenko also moved from the south of the city; he broke the enemy line on November 20 and almost closed the gap. On December 10 a German relief force under Mannstein came up from the southwest, but it was successfully held by Yeremenko, and the Russians now launched a new great thrust from the north directed against the relieving force. The gap behind Stalingrad was finally closed, and Mannstein was sturdily driven back. Further Russian successes opened the way to the west; and in the south Mannstein was pinned down to a narrow front running east to west along the Black Sea, with only a precarious connection with the German forces still remaining in the Caucasus. On January 8 an ultimatum was sent to von Paulus; it was rejected, and on February 2, 1943, after further attacks grinding down their strength, came the final surrender of the pitiful remains of the great besieging armies along with twenty-four generals.

In the Caucasus the Germans were already retreating; the region of the oil fields was abandoned at the end of January, and they were hard pressed to hold Rostov. To the north the Russians cleared Voronezh of the enemy and were pressing on victoriously westward to attack the line of the Donets, with its great industrial resources. General Golikov on the road to Kursk was taking hosts of prisoners. At every turn the great gaps in the German manpower were becoming more evident. Kursk fell on February 7 and Belgorod on February 9. The Donets coal and iron region was recovered and the Germans were pushed back towards the Dnieper. Even Harkov, industrial centre of Ukraine, fell on February 14. On the same day Rostov, now far to the east, was finally recovered.

To the south of these new Russian gains Mannstein was organizing a fine defence along his far-extended eastward line: the Dnieper was his one road of escape. At last, strongly reinforced, he was able to threaten the flank of the Russians advancing westward through their newly regained territory to the north of him. The speedy successes of the Russians had dispersed their troops, and they were held up by heavy thaws, which made coordination very difficult. Mannstein was thus enabled to make considerable gains, and on March 15 he even recaptured Harkov. Meanwhile, on their northern front the Germans had been compelled to shorten their line. Around Leningrad the besieged Russians opened up a corridor ten to twenty miles wide, which greatly eased their communications and supply. The strong German "hedgehog" at Rzhev was at last captured on March 3, and directly afterwards the strongpoint of Vyazma, from which the Germans had so long threatened Moscow. No recourse was left to them but a rapid retreat to Smolensk.

Floods and marshes caused a long lull at this point. The Germans had by now lost something like half of their original striking force and three quarters of the satellite forces with which they had in 1942 tried to replace the heavy losses of their own regular army. What remained of that army was of noticeably poorer quality. The Russian losses must by now have been some five million men from their army alone, without counting a far greater number of sacrifices both of partisan forces and of the civil population of the vast occupied territory; but with their advantage in manpower, their replacements were far more efficient and better trained than the enemy's; in fact, the general quality was improved.

By now the Germans could do no more than try to forestall the next Russian attack, which, they knew, would come from the watershed district of Kursk. This they attempted on July 5 with half a million men, as compared with the million of the Stalingrad offensive of 1942 or the two million of their original advance in 1941. At a tremendous cost they gained some initial success; but after ten days of furious fighting the Russians were able to counterattack westward toward the enemy strongpoint of Orel. On the 22nd, after further desperate fighting, imposed by Hitler's refusal to face events and retreat in time, the Germans began to withdraw from in front of Kursk. This was their only offensive of 1943. Orel, earlier a cornerstone of the German advance on Moscow in 1941, fell to the Russians. Harkov was recovered on August 23, and the road lay open for an advance to the famous Pinsk Marshes, which have figured so prominently in every western invasion of Russia, and also to the Dnieper. The German forces were all the more restricted, especially in the air, by the Allied successes in North Africa and Sicily and their new threat to the French coast and to the Balkans, but far the greater part of the German strength was still on the Russian front. There they still had strongpoints at the extremities of their long winding southern line in Bryansk and Taganrog, but they could hardly hope for a strong offensive by Mannstein from this side.

It was with a great sweep and splendour that the Russian mass now rolled forward. They began their next move with Tolbukhin's capture of Taganrog at the far eastern end of Mannstein's line on August 30; but their main drive was on the Dnieper. Rokossovsky, suddenly plunging southwestward, thrust in the direction of Kiev. To either side of him seven great Russian army groups were on the move. The Germans had no choice but to retreat on the Dnieper with heavy delaying actions. Day by day the Russians swept up more successes: on one single day, twelve hundred towns and villages were liberated. Five army commanders joined in this southern advance: Rokossovsky, Vatutin, Konev, Malinovsky, and Tolbukhin. Poltava, scene of Peter the Great's historic victory over Charles XII of Sweden, fell on September 22. To the north, the formidable German hedgehog of Bryansk was abandoned on the 20th. On the 25th, Sokolovsky entered the key fortress of Smolensk. The Russians were advancing all along the line. On the 24th Rokossovsky's men had reached the Dnieper and sighted the belfries of Kiev, and Vatutin also reached the great river lower down at Cherkasy, with Konev at Kremenchug (September 28) and Malinovsky at Dnepropetrovsk. All eastern Ukraine except the very south was now liberated. Fine summer weather still prevailed, and no respite was given.

Mannstein's tenuous southern line to the Sea of Azov had been heavily entrenched. At its western end it joined the Dnieper at Zaporozhe near the formidable Dnieper rapids. Behind this cover the Germans were hurrying back to the river, pressed hard by Tolbukhin. Mannstein, one of their best generals, might still try to counterattack the long exposed flank of the Russian advance. Above the rapids, along the high cliffs of the western bank, the German defence was largely entrusted to mobile troops. North of Kiev, where the river is narrower and more exposed, Rokossovsky reached the bank before a bridgehead could be established on it and also occupied an island in midstream. Here the east bank had forest cover, and here Rokossovsky, assisted by excellent repair work on the available railways and by a good supply of motor vehicles, attacked on October 5 and made a surprise crossing in boats and rafts collected under cover on the east bank. More crossings followed south of Kiev. Zaporozhe, the all-important bridgehead, was captured on October 14. On the 17th, Konev, who had already crossed the river, advanced from near Kremenchug westward towards the great iron centre of Krivoy Rog. Malinovsky, with another surprise crossing, captured Dnepropetrovsk. This brought the far-eastern wing of Mannstein hastening back to the river, thus isolating the weak German forces still left in

Crimea. Vatutin, with another unexpected advance, enveloped and entered Kiev on November 6 and hastened on westward, but he was himself to die of his wounds in Kiev.

The fall of the Dnieper barrier transferred the next main Russian attack to the marshy district northwards, where the frost had already made advance possible. A Russian thrust here would of itself cut the connections between the Germans to the north and to the south. The whole Russian line was now on the move. First Rokossovsky, who was nearest to Kiev, enveloped and took the hornets' nest of Gomel. North of him Popov, with mobile columns followed by infantry, was penetrating the frozen marsh of White Russia and quickly approaching the old frontier of 1939.

The last German hold on the Dnieper was soon broken by the capture of Kremenchug (December 6), the Kherson bridgehead (December 20), and Kreshchatik (February 5, 1944). Important gains followed: Nikopol with its manganese (February 8) and Krivoy Rog with its iron ore (February 22). On February 14 ten German divisions were encircled and eliminated at Korsun. The lot of the Germans still at Sevastopol was by now hopeless. The Russian fleet was again complete master of the Black Sea, and the German attempt to escape resulted in a terrible massacre. The Russian mass streamed on to the Dniester and entered Bessarabia on March 19. On the 24th the frontier of Bukovina was reached; on the 26th, that of Roumania; and on the 30th Chernovets was captured. On January 3 the First Ukrainian Army reached the Polish border of 1939, and on the 12th it captured Sarny, nearly forty miles beyond. On January 15 the Russians began to break out of besieged Leningrad. On the 20th they cut off the German corridor to the Gulf of Finland, thus isolating the Finns from German help. On the 27th Leningrad celebrated the end of two and a half years of siege. To the south the last German hold on the railway to Moscow was broken, and on February 2 the Russians entered Estonia.

This was really the end of the Fatherland War, as such; but there was to follow such a manifestation of Russian military power beyond the frontiers as had never before been witnessed in Europe. The Germans were in effect already crushed. They held on much too long on the southern coast of the Baltic in order to keep Finland in the war as long as possible. The powerful northern Russian armies of Govorov and Bagramyan systematically carved up the coast territory still in enemy hands, and an enormous pocket of German troops was isolated in a corner of Latvia. Next westward came that hornets' nest of European history, home of the old Teutonic Order, East Prussia, with its great fortress of Königsberg. The Russians were evidently out for more than a merely military settlement. The province was traversed by the tank columns of a gifted young Jewish general, Chernyakhovsky, who died of wounds at his task, and the great Junker fortress was completely pounded to ruins. While the war still lasted and the going was good, the Russians, as will be seen, were digging the grave of their immemorial enemies, the feudal lords of Prussia, Poland, and Hungary.

Next to the south lay the complex and multi-national realm of the proud Polish landlords. The conquests of Pilsudski, made at the time of Russia's greatest weakness, were for a second time eliminated, and the Russian population of Poland were again liberated from their Polish masters. It was a different story with the Polish capital, Warsaw. Here politics came in; and the central armies of the great Russian mass, those of Rokossovsky, Zhukov, and Konev, were at least partially halted. The fugitive Polish government of 1939, mainly rooted in the landed classes, had taken refuge first in Roumania, next in France and, after the collapse of 1940, in England. While Stalin and Hitler were racing through Poland under the Russo-German Pact, there were voices in England calling for a breach with Russia. With the Anglo-Russian Alliance of 1941 the position of the Poles in England became peculiarly difficult. Churchill's government did what it could to reconcile Russian and Polish interests, and until the Polish Premier, General Sikorski, perished in a plane disaster near Gibraltar (July 27, 1943) there seemed hopes of success. These hopes rose again during the premiership in London of the peasant leader Mikolajczyk; but the terms which he obtained in Moscow in August 1944 were rejected by his more reactionary colleagues in London. And he resigned his office. In Russia there was a Polish "National Committee of Liberation" under the wing of the Kremlin, and this group moved with the Russian troops into Poland and took the title of "The Polish Provisional Government of National Unity," centred at Lublin. The underground forces of the London faction were dominated by General Sosnowski, a bitter enemy of Russia. There is evidence that he ordered his forces to oppose the incoming Russians as they had opposed the conquering Germans—a policy that was hopeless unless England and America were ever to be persuaded to fight both. It was more than manifest that the liberation of Poland from the Germans could only come from the Red Army.

There followed a period that still requires to be elucidated. General Bor (Komorowski), head of the Polish underground forces in Warsaw,

seems to have received orders to rise and drive the Germans out before
the Russians came in. The Poles made a very fine attempt in the terribly battered city. The Russians stopped in front of it and waited till the
rising was crushed (August 1–October 2, 1944). They even refused their
landing-space to planes that came from the west to bring arms and provisions to the insurgents in the city, thus compelling these airmen to
make a journey doubled in distance and in danger. It is true, of course,
that the Russian way of taking a stronghold was not to batter their heads
against it but to bypass and isolate it by going round it. Nothing could
be more formidable than the eastern front of Warsaw, enthroned on
high cliffs with the broad Vistula in front of it; in 1831 Paskevich had
been compelled to cross the river and outflank it, but now the Russians
stayed where they were. After the rising had been crushed, they ultimately took the city; but even now they did not hurry forward on the
flat and easy road towards Berlin.

Again it would seem that behind the operations there was a broad
and definite policy of more than military purpose, which could hardly
have been other than the concept of Stalin and Molotov. Konev, it is
true, still following the plain, was advancing to fight his way solidly
through the industrial district of Silesia, partly Polish but also one of
the greatest centres of the German military industry. But to the south of
him Petrov was set the formidable task of following the mountain line
that had formerly separated Germany from the Austro-Hungarian
monarchy—in other words, the mountain spine of Czechoslovakia. To
the south of him Malinovsky fought straight over the eastern Carpathians into the bottleneck of Hungary. It must have been the Russian purpose to settle once for all with those time-honoured enemies of Russia,
the feudal landlords of Hungary, by conquering their country, establishing a government of friendly pattern, and distributing their great estates,
as it now proved easy to do both in Poland and in East Prussia. Anyhow
Malinovsky fought through against bitter resistance into the very heart
of Budapest and left it a heap of ruins (February 13, 1945).

To the south of Malinovsky the remaining great army of Tolbukhin
evidently also followed a definite purpose. This was to fight its way past
Bulgaria, which was never hostile to Russia except for its German
dynasty, to the friendly country of Yugoslavia, always devoted to Russia and now awaiting relief from the tremendous underground struggle
that it had throughout waged with such gallantry against the occupying
Germans. Tolbukhin, following the Danube, was in the end able to join
hands with the Yugoslav leader Tito, which meant in the long run that

Russian influence now extended to the Adriatic. It followed of itself that this junction also liberated Greece on the south, from which the occupying forces escaped as best they might. From Hungary Malinovsky and Tolbukhin pushed on to the conquest of Vienna (April 13, 1945).

All this cleared the ground for the grand finale at Berlin. Something like three million Russians now stood in front of the German capital on easy military ground, lined up without a break and leaving no weak spot to inspire a counterattack. Let us imagine what this presupposes. The advance from Stalingrad to Berlin had proceeded almost uninterruptedly except for weather hindrances and inevitable re-formations; and behind that advancing line every railway had to be changed back from the German gauge to the Russian, factories repaired and again set in action, and almost a miracle of supply carried out, to follow without delay the stupendous offensive. To the south everything was already secure. To the north Rokossovsky had carried the Russian triumph to Stettin, at the mouth of the Oder, thus making the Russians militarily the masters of the settlement of Poland's new western frontier.

And now the end of all things, Berlin. The great mass closed in on the doomed enemy capital. The British and the Americans, triumphant onward from D-day, closed in on the other side. Berlin did not prove a Stalingrad, and Adolf Hitler was driven to take his life in the cellar of his own chancellery before his victorious enemies stormed in above him. By May 1945 came the final unconditional surrender of the Nazi realm to the conquering Allies. Was there ever a cleaner finish?

Epilogue

On the Russian Attitude to the United Nations Organization

THIS book, first published in 1926, has already been four times brought up to date. The various chapters in Russian history mark themselves out very clearly. In this revision a new chapter, "The Second Fatherland War," has been completed. But I also have to make a beginning of a much more difficult chapter on the peacemaking. This new chapter will be long, and I can only at present touch the fringe of it. It would be profitless to dwell on the wearisome and inconclusive meetings and conferences. The only guidance one can offer is by trying to get behind the slow progress of events, to give some idea of what is blocking the way. The full details of the peace treaties will be given when the time has come to replace this epilogue by a new chapter.

It is far harder to make peace than to make war. War is the simplest and most primitive of human activities, and the highest qualities of devotion to one's community come out spontaneously. The more dangerous the enemy, the greater is the compulsion to a collective loyalty. And how often do the combatants realize what they are going to lose in loyalty with the removal of the one bond that holds them together? But peacemaking and peace-keeping demand a thousand special requisites that are neither simple nor common—in the first place a full understanding of the claims of one's allies and a forbearance towards their ideas.

This was of course foreseen; and in the days of the greatest danger the Allies tried to make such provision as they could for the future. England and Russia made a treaty, announced on June 12, 1942, by which they agreed to hold together for twenty years. The war tasks, of themselves, imposed the necessity of frequent conferences—of the Foreign Ministers of the "Big Three" (Russia, England, and the United States) at Moscow on November 1, 1943, and of the Heads of State themselves at Teheran on December 1, 1943 and at Yalta on February 3, 1945. The last named was the last activity of that supreme world statesman President Franklin Roosevelt, who died on April 12, 1945. A standing committee of all three Powers was set up in London. What could be settled in advance at the time of common unity of purpose was, however vaguely, foreseen. The Big Three promised cooperation in peacetime.

But thinkers all over the world called for something more. After the first overthrow of Napoleon in 1814 his principal enemy, Alexander I of Russia, found to his dismay that at the peace congress of Vienna Talleyrand, the brilliant representative of conquered France, had split up the conquerors and had carried off a treaty of offensive and defensive alliance of France with England and Austria, directed against Russia and Prussia, an experience that in changed conditions could happen again. After Waterloo he rose from his bed one night, in deep distress, to draft a sacred engagement between sovereigns called the Holy Alliance. After the First World War the same passionate world urge to peace produced the League of Nations. The wish is father to the thought—the burning wish that a world of savagery shall be transformed straight off into a world of angels.

No signatures on a piece of paper can of themselves give a permanent guarantee of peace. Bismarck, who certainly had experience enough in treaty-making, writes: [1] "International policy is a fluid element which under certain conditions will solidify, but on a change of atmosphere reverts to its original diffuse condition. The clause *rebus sic stantibus* (things standing as they were) is tacitly understood in all treaties that involve performance. The Triple Alliance [his own treaty] is a strategic position, which, *in the face of the perils that were imminent at the time when it was completed,*[2] was politic, and, under the prevailing conditions, feasible. It has from time to time been prolonged, and may be yet further prolonged; but eternal duration is assured to no treaty between Great Powers, and it would be unwise to regard it as affording a permanently stable guarantee against all the possible contingencies which in the future may modify *the political, material, and moral conditions under which it was brought into being* . . . it does not dispense us from the attitude of *toujours en vedette.*" The reason, as he gives it, is that the world is not static and cannot be stopped from moving on; and the record of treaty after treaty confirms him to the full.

[1] *Reflections and Reminiscences*, Vol. II, p. 280 (English edition of Smith & Elder).
[2] My italics.

The improvisation of "the United Nations," which came into being at San Francisco on June 26, 1945, as the answer to the world urge for peace, suffered from the first from the contrast between principle and practice. The thinkers sought for a world of equality, which in practice does not exist. Ethiopia and England, Holland and Russia, Roumania and the United States, alike count for one vote each, which is simply ridiculous. Who will suggest that one Roumanian is as important a pillar of world peace as ten Americans? But this fantastic arithmetic, of course, could be no more than window-dressing. In reality, each of the greater Powers had its train of followers, whether they were to be called good neighbors or satellites. England, in all, had a train of six, including India, to which she was soon to offer independence. The United States, thanks to the Monroe Doctrine and the Good Neighbor Policy, could ordinarily muster more than twenty. Russia, after an unwilling admission of Ukraine and White Russia (and when was White Russia ever independent?), still has no full recognition of nearly two hundred millions of population, which are in themselves a kind of League of Nations. With all this, everyone knew that there could be no peace, least of all for the smaller states, without agreement between the Big Three; each of these therefore was armed with a veto, which could bring all debates to a standstill. Even China, which is more of a commitment than a power, has the same privilege.

This was all that was left of the idealizing of "democracy" and the magnifying of the "small Powers," and more was not to be obtained, without the rupture of the whole organization. Certainly UN is a great step forward in providing a forum of debate, some kind of articulation of a "world opinion," and even the Russians would not wish to be left out of it; but as a promise of a world state, it means nothing at all until the big Powers are ready to accept the new arithmetic as a substitute for their own sovereignty, which not one of them can be expected to do.[1] That is the whole point of the veto, which is in practice the most substantive part of the entire organization. And the Russians are well aware that, even with the reservation of real authority to the Security Council, on which they have insisted, they are at best likely to be outvoted there every time, say by seven to four. That is why they remain with one leg in and one leg out, and fight every detail till the moment might come that they would prefer to leave altogether. The mere fact that they are still half in is some kind of evidence that they wish to be in if they can

[1] Apparently, not even South Africa.

FRONTIER CHANGES IN EASTERN EUROPE, 1939–47

get what they think essential inside, and therefore of a relative success of UN.

For myself, I can see no wisdom in winding up a great coalition by breaking up the world of authority into as many small units as possible or by a series of clamorous meetings ("quack, quack, quack, quack, quack")[1] to find out what holes you can all pick in each other. For that to be anything else but disastrous, it would be necessary, first of all, to shut off some of the noise (quack, quack) and then for there to be an understanding by each and all of us of everyone else's affairs, which at present simply does not exist and will take a very long time to acquire. There is still wisdom in the famous judgment of Solomon who ingeniously suggested a different arithmetic; or, to take a more recent illustration, an Englishman must still have a poignant memory of the time when he was left alone to face the common enemy with such remnants of resources as pacifism and idealism had left to him.

This, in the rough, is the framework within which the Russians have had to act, and I must say that here, at least, I have much general sympathy with them. Here were the main points that Molotov had to drive home to a hopelessly uninformed world; they will be self-evident to anyone who studies the record of fact contained in this book:

That there was a Russia before 1914, whether we knew it or not, built up by centuries of effort;

that Russia had no hand in the settlement of Versailles, which marked the most humiliating defeat and the greatest loss of territory in her history;

that this is not to be the first war in history after which a return is automatically made to the entirely bankrupt settlement of the war before;

that this time Russia is a major winner: that she does not, for instance, acquiesce in an eternal deprival of the principal lifework of Peter the Great in opening her sea road to Europe, which she lost at a moment of chaos in 1918;

that so far most of the sharp debates in the UN concern some territory or some title that Russia had before the last war and now insists on recovering;

that as one of the major winners, she has just the same right to preach her ideas as we have to preach ours, though we have an equal right to say that we disagree with them.

[1] Quotation from Mr. W. S. Jordan, delegate from New Zealand to the Peace Conference in Paris.

The methods chosen by Molotov to teach these simple lessons, so obvious to anyone who knew anything about Russia before 1914, naturally seemed irritating, and the Russians will have reason to regret later that they paid far too little attention to the loss of good will which these tactics have cost them. Nevertheless, they have met with considerable success. Molotov, it will be remembered, replaced the Russian advocate of cooperation with the Western democracies, Litvinov, in the spring of 1939, when England quite failed to realize the implications of a frank alliance with Russia against Hitler and expected to limit Russian cooperation to military aid to Poland. Molotov was appointed to talk "plain Russian" to us. I picture him now as having in his portfolio a number of "poker points," designed to correct Western misapprehensions. We talk of free elections in Bulgaria, a country liberated by Russia from Turkey at a time of intolerable oppression in 1878, a country that settles her political questions in other ways, where, to quote a Balkan diplomat, "the minority does not accept the verdict"; and Molotov suggests that Russia is interested in Argentina and in democracy as practised in South Carolina or, he might say, Mississippi or Georgia. We go back to the old traditional English policy of keeping Russia from the Straits, by which England insists on placing an international watch on Russia's main outlet to the sea, and Molotov suggests that Russia might be interested in participating in an international control of the Panama Canal.

Unfortunately, nearly all the sharpest debates in the UN are challenges to a Russian recovery of what she had before 1914 or to questions that are to be solved on her doorstep. And what a ground to choose for the next quarrel—just where it is least possible to challenge her with success! As has been pointed out in the last chapter, Russia went out of her way to settle such questions in her own favour while war conditions still prevailed and the going was good; and "possession," we are told, is "nine points of the law."

It is quite clear that Russia is succeeding in the tasks she has set herself and is replacing our own earlier idea of a *cordon sanitaire* with a ring of "friendly" neighbours on her western frontier. It is also clear that she has met the claim to set up "one world," an Anglo-Saxon one, backed by the flimsy franchise of the United Nations, by direct attack on the revived English policy of keeping Russia from the sea. This was the policy of England from 1801 to 1907, interrupted only by the alliance of 1812. Even Lord Salisbury, one of the chief authors of the blocking policy of the Treaty of Berlin in 1878, lived to declare that

England, in supporting Turkey, had "backed the wrong horse";[1] and later, both the Conservatives and the Liberals supporting him, Sir Edward Grey reversed this policy by the Convention of 1907 on Persia (Iran), which left the northern zone of influence to Russia. This led up to the British alliance with Russia in the First World War. And in December 1916 both England and France publicly agreed that the Tsar should acquire Constantinople.[2] Two world wars in which both England and America were allied with Russia brought home to us the difficulties of carrying help to her which our own blocking policy had set up. But what we were willing to grant to the tottering Tsar we would not allow to the Bolsheviks; for them we had the *cordon sanitaire*, or policy of blocking off Russia from Europe, which lasted till a new war forced on us a new alliance.

Now less than ever can England keep Russia from the sea. In Iran her summons to stop is an empty pistol, even if the United States were ready to save for Britain her old colonial system, which she has no right to expect. To have continued on the lines of Sir Edward Grey might have saved all this trouble. It is on the seas themselves, and not on the approaches to them, that Britain may still count on holding her own. For it will take much more than the emergence of Russia at a given point to make her a great naval power.

And now we are already faced by the greatest danger of all in the unfinished peace work for a settlement of Germany; and the protagonists of the "peacemaking," Molotov, Byrnes, and Bevin, have all plainly shown that they have recognized this.

When I started serious work in Russia in 1904, my apprehension was that, if Germany and Russia were united in a world war against England, they would be invincible. I found that a large number of the key posts of mastery there were held by Germans—whether at court, in the administration, in trade and industry, or even with the stewards of absentee landlords on country estates—and that they fully shared the unpopularity of the government. It followed that the masters of the moment in Russia were mortally anxious not to offend Imperial Germany and feared before all things anything that would bring the Russians themselves into the management of their own affairs. This meant that any

[1] See above, pp. 394–9.
[2] England ratified her agreement on March 27, 1915. The agreement of England and France was announced in the Duma on December 2, 1916, by the Russian Premier, A. F. Trepov. The Russian government at this last date was practically under the control of the Empress and Rasputin. See S. Sazonov: *Fateful Years*, p. 245; Bernard Pares: *Fall of the Russian Monarchy*, pp. 215 and 396. In this book, p. 485.

movement in the direction of reform was inevitably accompanied by one of friendship for Britain, France, and America, if only as an alternative to a German monopoly of their country. This was an arithmetic that has never failed me in all my work in Russia. From the danger I have indicated, of a united Germany and Russia, we were only delivered by Germany herself, when she was so foolish as to exchange a successful penetration for sheer domination, by invading in 1914 and again in 1941. But we have no right to count on the same mistakes, should the old motto of "Germany and Russia," at one time popular in the higher command of both countries, be exchanged for a new motto of "Russia and Germany"; and we have already reached the moment when Germany, with her population of sixty-six millions, including so many efficient potential agents of policy and commerce, is coming back right into the middle of the picture, with the split that is developing so fast between her recent conquerors.

It appears that the only solution to be found is in a direction very different from that so far followed by the United Nations. The United Nations in the long run, and with patience all round, can be very useful in reducing the margins of disagreement. There is no doubt that it gained greatly in prestige with the mutual exchange of Christmas presents at the close of 1946. But instead of two divergent ideologies seeking each to win a purely formal "majority" for its own conception of "one world," safety is often only to be maintained by agreement, where necessary, to disagree, which is surely the test of any ordinary friendship.

The real gap between the two camps is one of knowledge. England, after many long tussles with Russia, has far less excuse for the lack of it. An America in isolation had no urge to study Russia, and it is intelligible that she should start her study from the moment when she first fixed her eyes on the subject, which probably dates from 1914. While America took no action of her own, her criticisms, well or ill founded, were not necessarily taken as serious politics. The amazing achievements of American landings, first in North Africa and then in Normandy, have radically changed all that; and now the poverty of knowledge is in pathetic contrast with the might that waits on it for its direction. Irresponsible criticism is generally self-confident; but no one cares to be told: "I am holier than thou," especially by anyone who doesn't know his facts. The Russians, on their side, are themselves responsible for the unintelligent secrecy with which they cover all their moves. Till they find the sense to open their doors to foreign inquiry, they cannot expect to be understood. Many are the journalistic reputations that have been ruined by the senseless prohibitions of the Soviet censorship, which is like a sore that poisons Russia's foreign relations at the source. And even more important is the senseless exclusion of foreign students. It is a terrible sign of weakness. Triumph for the Soviet conception of the world is not to be won by a policy of closed doors. On the other side, the newspaper chains in the Western democracies, which can control what news and views they will pass on to the public, are thus enabled to live on sensations instead of facts, and malignity to everything Russian becomes a profitable profession. Thus on both sides is precluded the one remedy: namely, constant and objective study.

And a little knowledge will tell us that in the actual course of life, as contrasted with word-slinging, things are not necessarily at all as bad as they are painted. It will tell us that the original fantastic experiments of the militant Communism of 1917 were abandoned in 1921, for the simple reason that they did not work and led of themselves to a colossal and devastating famine; that the authors of those wild experiments have all been eliminated by the present holder of power in Russia; that he publicly countered Trotsky's program of "permanent revolution" with one of common-sense construction at home and, to use his own words, of "working relations with any foreign government, even capitalist, which is friendly to the Soviet Union"; that he definitely preferred to a foreign policy of revolution the association of the Western democracies against Hitler (especially during the Spanish Civil War) and that it was more our fault than his if they did not accept his proffered hand up to 1939 (when Litvinov was replaced by Molotov); that the present product of his rule is not a generation of world revolutionists but a new race of technicians, each with a vigour of purpose that was new to Russia in her work of home construction; that with this program he not only outmanned but, with plentiful Allied aid, even outequipped Hitler's Germany and carried his country to such a complete triumph as Russia had never known before; and, lastly, that anyone who has live contact with Russia today will not find anyone there, official or unofficial, who will maintain that Russia, herself, has actually achieved that system of Communism which she is so freely credited abroad with seeking to impose on the rest of the world.

If we go back to the facts, there is much to comfort us. The main fact in the world is the crying demand for world peace, and nowhere more than in Russia. The main opportunity now is in cooperative reconstruction of a broken world. It is always emphasized in Stalin's pronouncements, but this part of them is sometimes minimized or distorted in the foreign press as not sensational and therefore not "news." For the newspaper, "Peace" can be a headline, but only once, and soon to be forgotten again. Stalin's record in history, however, will tell us that, like Peter the Great, he brought to life for the benefit of his whole community the enormous neglected resources of his own country; and that is a task which for its success must depend before all things on world peace and world cooperation. Russia is waiting ardently for this, and Stalin is not one who has failed to read the needs and hopes of his own people.

For us, the high road to peace with Russia is equally simple; it is study. World opinion, to have its effect on Russia, as on others, must be frank, but it cannot afford to be ignorant. Cannot we pay to that immense and to us unknown country the very small compliment of crediting her with a separate and independent life of her own, with a course of development which she alone can determine for herself? That is the real subject for our study, and it is a task that we have hardly begun.

And knowledge alone is not enough without understanding, which is much more hardly won. To no country does this apply more than to Russia. Some things are so very hard to guess; and others, which often do not express themselves at all, are so abundantly clear. One can always see at once whether anyone talking of Russia has really lived there; it is a kind of freemasonry, entirely independent both of class and of views. It is that real knowledge which we have got to win. At present we are far away from anything of the kind.

This gap has to be filled, or it will cost us dear.

On the recent policy of stopping the expansion of Communism by financial bolstering of Greece and Turkey, the view of this observer, which can only be an individual opinion, will be anticipated from this Epilogue, which was written before its announcement. I have always been directly opposed to World Revolution in any form. I cannot see how opinions can be halted at a frontier. By bolstering weak States we take over the responsibility for all their weakness; this responsibility cannot be limited, and I think this step can only lead to the opposite result to that intended. For Russia, this would only mean a return to the *cordon sanitaire*, which is a direct geographical challenge. I do not think my country had a right to impose a deadline on aiding Greece. If England had to give up that century-old policy in a great hurry, it seems a pity that the United States should now be called upon to shoulder it in a hurry, without a full realization that it is really a geographical far more than an ideological challenge. I do not think the transfer could have been put over without an altogether fantastic exaggeration of the present danger to American democracy, which has been puffed up to monstrous proportions in the press: I cannot think so poorly of American democracy. One thing seems to me quite clear: that there is no surer road back to World Revolution than a third world war between America and Russia, a war in which all the geographical advantage is with Russia.

*Appendixes, Bibliography,
and Index*

FAMILY OF VLADIMIR MONOMAKH

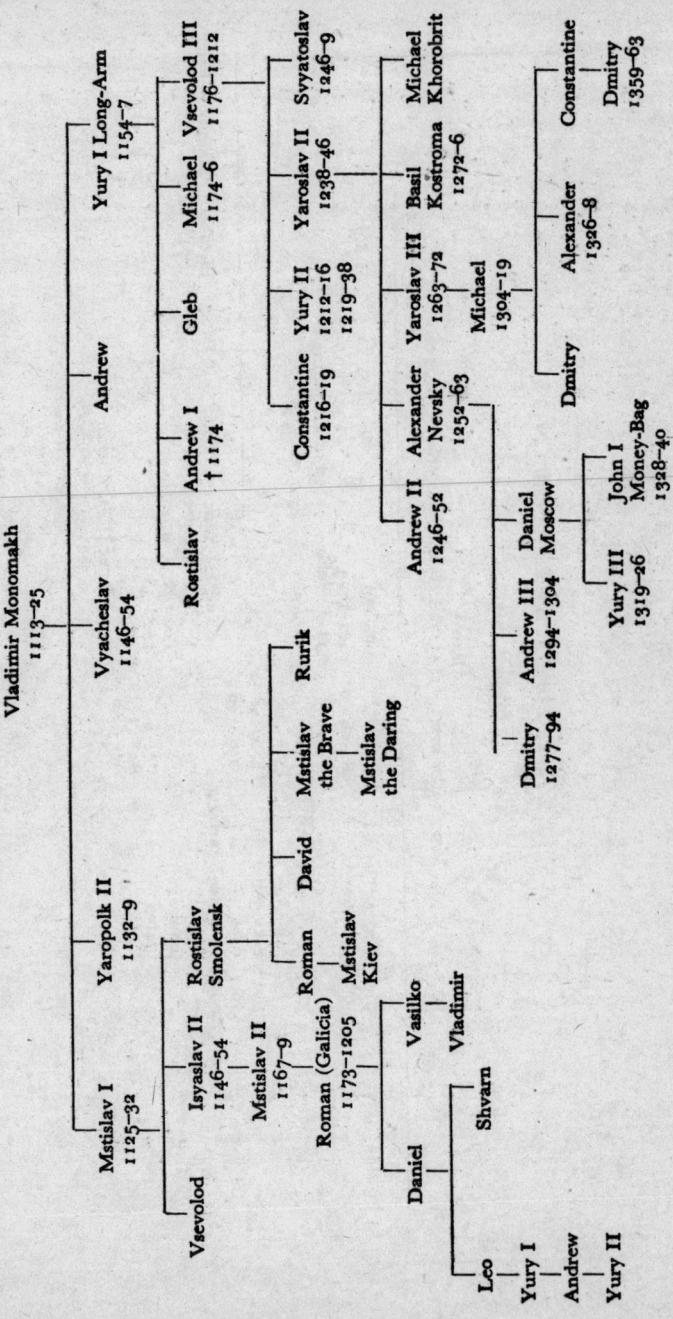

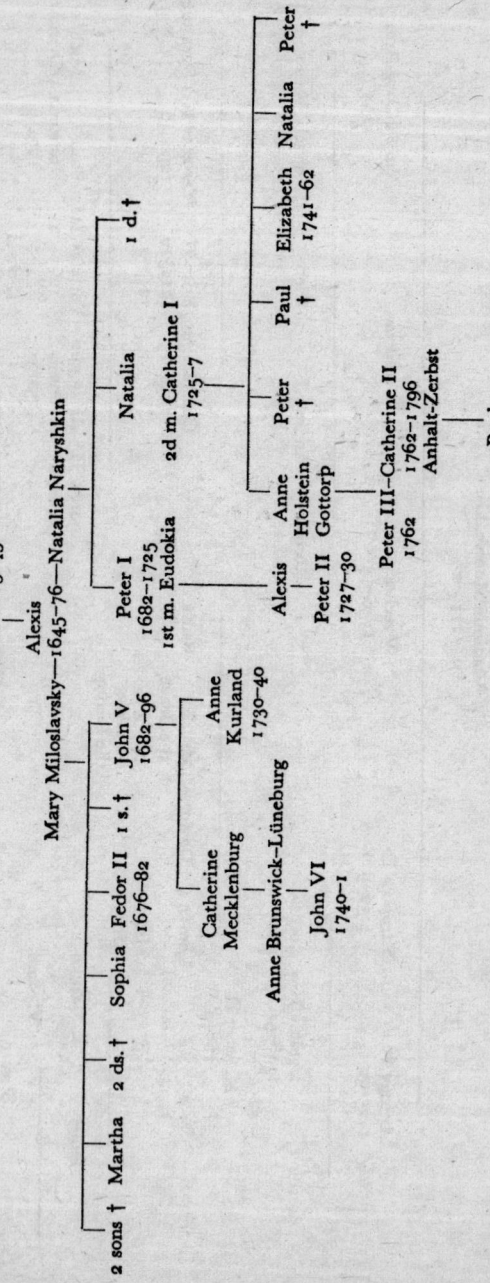

FAMILY OF MICHAEL ROMANOV

FAMILY OF PAUL

PAUL—Princess Würtemberg
Mary Fedorovna

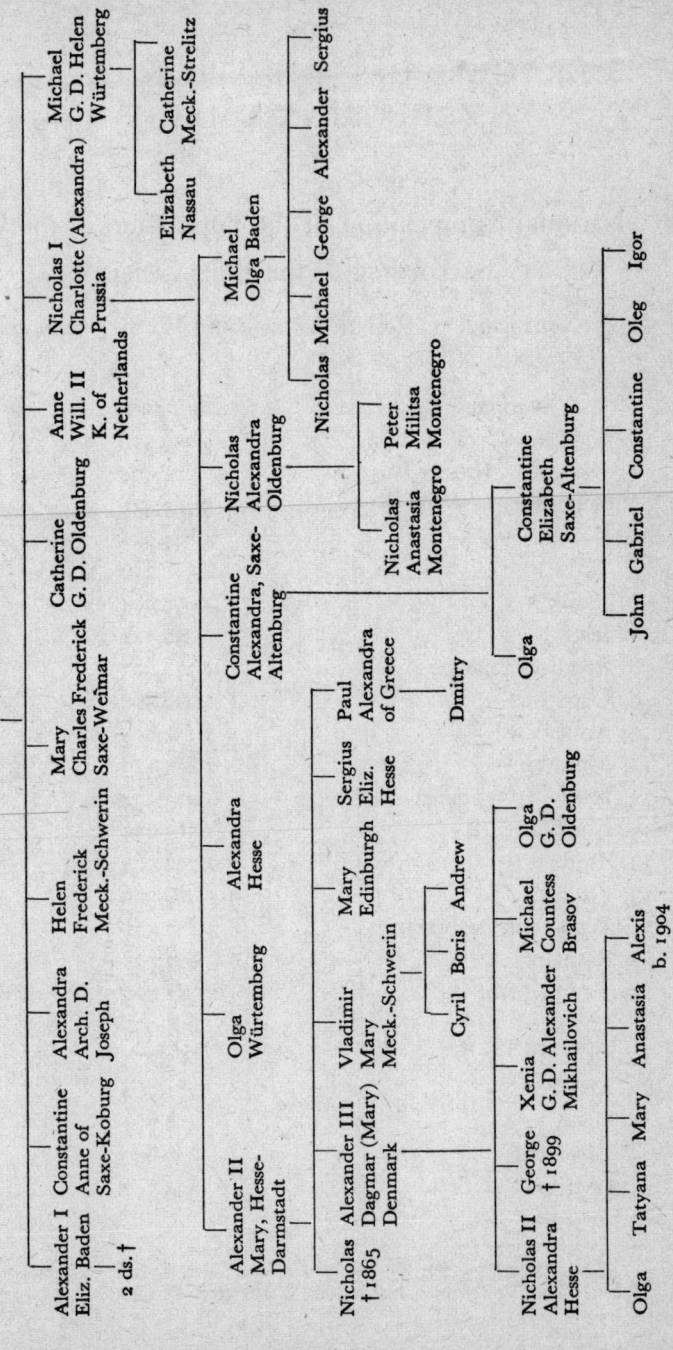

RACIAL DISTRIBUTION OF THE RUSSIAN EMPIRE

National Composition of the Population of the USSR according to the 1939 Census[1]

(Not including Western Ukraine and Western Belorussia)

Nationalities	Number	Percentage of Total
1. Russians (Great Russians)	99,019,929	58.41
2. Ukrainians (Lesser Russians)	28,070,404	16.56
3. Belorussians (White Russians)	5,267,431	3.11
4. Uzbeks	4,844,021	2.86
5. Tartars	4,300,336	2.54
6. Kazakhs	3,098,764	1.83
7. Jews	3,020,141	1.78
8. Azerbaidjanians	2,274,805	1.34
9. Georgians	2,248,566	1.33
10. Armenians	2,151,884	1.27
11. Mordvians	1,451,429	0.86
12. Nemtsy (Germans)	1,423,534	0.84
13. Chuvash	1,367,930	0.81
14. Tajiks	1,228,964	0.72
15. Kirghiz	884,306	0.52
16. Peoples of Daghestan	857,371	0.50
17. Bashkir	842,925	0.50
18. Turkmenians	811,769	0.48
19. Poles *	626,905	0.37
20. Udmurts	605,673	0.36
21. Mariitsy	481,262	0.28
22. Komy	408,724	0.24
23. Chechentsy	407,690	0.24
24. Osetians	354,547	0.21

* At large.

---

[1] From Aleš Hrdlička: *The Peoples of the Soviet Union*, by permission of the publisher, The Smithsonian Institution, Washington, D. C.

Racial Distribution

Nationalities	Number	Percentage of Total
25. Greeks	285,896	0.17
26. Moldavians	260,023	0.15
27. Karelians	252,559	0.15
28. Karakalpaks	185,775	0.11
29. Koreans	180,412	0.11
30. Kabardinians	164,016	0.10
31. Finns *	143,074	0.08
32. Estonians *	142,465	0.08
33. Kalmyks	134,327	0.08
34. Latvians and Latgols *	126,900	0.07
35. Bolgars	113,479	0.07
36. Ingush	92,074	0.05
37. Adygeitsy	87,973	0.05
38. Karachayevtsy	75,737	0.04
39. Abkhasians	58,969	0.03
40. Khakasy	52,062	0.03
41. Oirots	47,717	0.03
42. Kurds	45,866	0.03
43. Balkartsy	42,665	0.03
44. Iranians	39,037	0.02
45. Lithuanians *	32,342	0.02
46. Chinese	29,620	0.02
47. Czechs and Slovaks	26,919	0.02
48. Arabs	21,793	0.01
49. Assyrians	20,207	0.01
50. Native Siberians and other small groups	807,279	0.48
Total	169,519,127	100.00

* At large.

Bibliography

NOTE ON

SOME OF THE PRINCIPAL MATERIALS

THE fountainhead of this study is to be found in the old Russian Chronicles. They were kept year by year, at first in the Pechersky Monastery of Kiev (Monastery of the Caves), from near the end of the eleventh century. Later every individual district possessed its own chronicle. The earliest materials were used to make a compilation, probably the work of the monk Sylvester about 1110. It is generally agreed by those acquainted with them that no other country of their time possesses a more vivid and faithful record of its public life. The compilers, who were monks, regarded the task as a work of conscience; and their object was to let the events teach their own lesson in the eternal struggle between good and evil. The Chronicles have left the strongest impress on all succeeding Russian historians. They continue in one form or another as far down as the sixteenth, seventeenth, and even the eighteenth century. The two manuscripts which are most complete and authoritative are those known as the *Lavrentyevskaya* and *Ipatyevskaya Letopisi*.

The foundations of Russian history were laid in modern times by Professor Sergius Solovyev, Professor in the University of Moscow. Though other important attempts had been made before him to collect and coordinate historical materials (notably by Tatishchev in the eighteenth century), Professor Solovyev must be regarded as the first real historian of Russia. In a life work lasting for over twenty years, he issued in all twenty-nine successive volumes ending in 1773, on the eve of the rebellion of Pugachev. His *History of Russia* is based throughout on a laborious study of the first materials which he was the first to bring into order; where possible the originals, such as letters or acts, are given in full; the book is written in a lucid and attractive style which forms an excellent vehicle.

Solovyev's successor in his Chair at Moscow was his pupil Vasily Klyuchevsky, the greatest of Russian historians. Designed at first for the priesthood, he began his historical studies about the time of the Emancipation of the Serfs and concentrated at the start on the records of the *Boyarskaya Duma* (Council of Boyars) that is, on the first elements of Russian constitutional history. His *Course of Russian History* was circulated in students' manuscripts up to the Liberation Movement of 1904–5; one could see in the successive volumes, as they came out, the effects of the comparative but increasing relaxation of the censor's control; Klyuchevsky was almost the only man of learning consulted by the Emperor when he was fixing the regulations which were to govern the Russian Duma; in the best sense he was Conservative and he was strongly patriotic; yet freedom of speech was during the publication of his work only in course of acquisition. The fourth volume, starting with the accession of Peter the Great, was accessible outside Russia only in 1910, and the fifth, dating from the accession of Catherine and giving only a sketch of Russian history from her death to the present time, was published in Russia under the Soviet government, which has nationalized the history of Klyuchevsky as a possession of the people as a whole. Klyuchevsky assumes in his readers such a knowledge of detail as would be expected of a student who has passed through a Russian secondary school. The work is in the nature of a historical essay; and from the materials made accessible by Solovyev the erudition and the genius of Klyuchevsky have created a picture of the story of Russia convincing and consistent enough to stand the test of the tremendous cataclysm which followed his death. He is lordly in his disregard of all that does not serve his purpose. Of the Tartar conquest, despite its tremendous consequences, he does little more than make mention. To foreign policy he sometimes seems almost indifferent. He sets himself to tell the economic story of the Russian people.

The authorities so far mentioned are those without which no history of Russia could be attempted, but they carry the student little further than halfway through the scope of this book. Among the major authorities for the modern period, Platonov's study of the Time and Troubles (*Ocherki po istorii smuty v Moskovskom Gosudarstve*) has received an additional value from the analogy of that time with our own days. Brückner's History of Catherine the Great is particularly valuable for the use to which it puts her correspondence in the study of her diplomacy. The industrious and talkative Schilder in three large works on the reigns of Paul, Alexander I, and Nicholas I has collected testimony from every side on the puzzling personalities of the two first-named of these emperors. Dr. Theodor Schiemann has written in German a masterly and scholarly account of the reign of Nicholas I. Kornilov's *Course on the History of the 19th Century*, which has been translated into English, has but little perspective and has serious gaps, especially for instance in foreign policy; but it is useful for the study of the Emancipation of the Peasants and of economical developments.

Of studies relating to special aspects of Russian history, some of the most valuable are the following: Engelmann in his History of Serfdom, published both in German (*Leibeigenschaft in Russland*) and in Russian (*Istoria Krepostnago Prava*) has made an excellent and very handy compilation of the chief laws relating to the peasants, besides giving an informing sketch of their economic conditions. One of the most scholarly of Russian historical studies is the *History of Russian Factories* by Tugan-Baranovsky. Ivanov-Razumnik's *History of Russian Social Thought*, in spite of a terribly pedantic phraseology, seems to me to have charted in the main truly an extraordinarily difficult field of study.

Among Russian school textbooks, besides the abridgements of Solovyev and Klyuchevsky, of which the first is a miracle of packing, should be specially mentioned that of Platonov; that of Elpatyevsky is also useful; an excellent schoolbook of early Russian history was published in 1918 by Matthew Lyubavsky, formerly Rector of Moscow University; at each contentious question he stops to summarize the views of the rival schools. The same writer has rendered a great service to Russian leaders by his objective and lucid sketch of the history of the Western Slavs published in the same year.

Rambaud's *Histoire de la Russie*, though in its condensation and rapidity of judgment it partakes of the character of a textbook, is also much more than that; it is so good that it was translated, with the expurgations imposed by the Tsarist censorship, and used in Russian schools. It is of immense service to foreign readers; however, it hardly ever gets away from the point of view of a brilliant and admirably informed foreigner. The original work retains its value only up to the death of Alexander II; a continuation by Professor Haumant brings it down to 1917.

Two books, accessible to readers of English, will be found to be of great use. In his *Slavic Europe; a Bibliography*, Professor Robert J. Kerner has made a very valuable survey of materials dealing with Russian history in other languages than Russian. Professor Leo Wiener's *Anthology of Russian Literature* includes a very well chosen selection of extracts, unfortunately very short, from those writers who have most importance for the study of Russian history.

In his own studies the present writer has chiefly concentrated on the contemporary period, making much use of country travel, for instance in the study of local self-government, communal land-tenure, the land settlement of Stolypin, and the campaign of 1812. He has also had the advantage of frequent consultation with very many of the principal actors in this period, of which he has witnessed many of the chief events.

BERNARD PARES

NOTE ON
THE ENLARGED BIBLIOGRAPHY

THIS bibliography was prepared by Eleanor Buist, Research Assistant in Russian Studies, Columbia University. It is an expanded and reorganized version of the bibliography prepared by Sir Bernard Pares for previous editions of this book.

* indicates a title that appeared in the 1947 edition of the bibliography.

[ ] indicates either annotations made by the author in earlier editions, or remarks by the present compiler added for clarity.

The bibliography is organized under the following general heads:

In the section on history by period, documents in translation together with accounts by participants and observers appear first under each subhead, followed by historical studies and interpretations.

In the section on history by subject, books relating to the period prior to 1917 appear first, followed by those concerning the Soviet period.

I. GENERAL BIBLIOGRAPHY AND HISTORIOGRAPHY

GAPANOVITCH, J. J. *Historiographie russe hors de la Russie*. Paris: Payot, 1946.

GRIERSON, P. *Books on Soviet Russia 1917–1942; a Bibliography and a Guide to Reading*. London: Methuen, 1943.

KERNER, R. J. *Northeastern Asia; a Selected Bibliography . . . of the Relations of China, Russia, and Japan . . . in Oriental and European Languages*. 2 vols. Berkeley: University of California Press, 1939.

*KERNER, R. J. *Slavic Europe; a Selected Bibliography in the Western European Languages*. . . . Cambridge: Harvard University Press, 1918.

KOVALEVSKY, P. E. *Manuel d'histoire russe; étude critique des sources et exposé historique d'après les recherches les plus récentes*. Paris: Payot, 1948.

MAZOUR, A. G. *An Outline of Modern Russian Historiography*. Berkeley: University of California Press, 1939.

MORLEY, C. *Guide to Research in Russian History*. Syracuse: Syracuse University Press, 1951.

New York Public Library, Slavonic Division. *A Bibliography of Slavonic Bibliography in English*. New York: New York Public Library, 1947. (Reprinted from the Bulletin of the New York Public Library, April 1947.)

STRAKHOVSKY, L., ed. *A Handbook of Slavic Studies*. Cambridge: Harvard University Press, 1949.

U. S. Dept. of State, Division of Library and References Services. *Soviet Bibliography*. Washington, D. C., 1950–

U. S. Library of Congress, Division of Bibliography. *Soviet Russia; a Selected List of Recent References*. Washington, D. C., 1943.

◇◇◇◇◇◇◇◇◇◇◇◇

II. GEOGRAPHY AND ETHNOGRAPHY

BALZAK, S. S., V. F. VASYUTIN, and YA. G. FEIGIN, eds. *Economic Geography of the USSR*. New York: Macmillan, 1949. (Russian Translation Project Series of the American Council of Learned Societies.)

BERG, L. S. *Natural Regions of the USSR*. New York: Macmillan, 1950. (Russian Translation Project Series of the American Council of Learned Societies.)

CAMENA D'ALMEIDA, P. *Russie*. Paris: Colin, 1932. (*Géographie universelle*, ed. P. VIDAL DE LA BLACHE and L. GALLOIS, Vol. V.)

CRESSEY, G. B. *The Basis of Soviet Strength*. New York: McGraw-Hill, 1945.

GOODALL, G., ed. *Soviet Russia in Maps; Its Origins and Development*. Chicago: Denoyer-Geppert, 1942. [Includes historical maps of Russia.]

JOCHELSON, V. I. *Peoples of Asiatic Russia*. New York: American Museum of Natural History, 1928.

*LEROY-BEAULIEU, A. *The Empire of the Tsars and the Russians*. 3 vols. New York: Putnam, 1902–3. [Part I: The Country and Its Inhabitants.]

SHABAD, T. *Geography of the USSR; a Regional Survey*. New York: Columbia University Press, 1951.

◇◇◇◇◇◇◇◇◇◇◇◇

III. ANTHOLOGIES

COURNOS, J., ed. *A Treasury of Russian Life and Humor*. New York: Coward-McCann, 1943.

FEDOTOV, G. P. *A Treasury of Russian Spirituality*. New York: Sheed and Ward, 1948.

GUERNEY, B. G., ed. *A Treasury of Russian Literature*. New York: Vanguard, 1943.

WALSH, W. B. *Readings in Russian History*. Enl. ed. Syracuse: Syracuse University Press, 1950.

*WIENER, L. *Anthology of Russian Literature*. 2 vols. New York: Putnam, 1902–03.

YARMOLINSKY, A. T., ed. *A Treasury of Russian Verse*. New York: Macmillan, 1949.

❖❖❖❖❖❖❖❖❖❖❖

IV. GENERAL HISTORY

GITERMANN, V. *Geschichte Russlands.* 3 vols. Zürich: Gutenberg, 1944–9.

HARCAVE, S. *Russia, a History.* Philadelphia: Lippincott, 1952.

*KLYUCHEVSKY, V. O. *A History of Russia.* 5 vols. New York: Dutton, 1911–31. [English translation is abridged and inadequate. See Note on Materials. There are several Russian editions, among them: V. O. KLIUCHEVSKII. *Kurs russkoi istorii.* 5 vols. Ann Arbor: Edwards, 1948. (Russian Reprint Project Series of the American Council of Learned Societies.)]

KUCHARZEWSKI, J. *The Origins of Modern Russia.* New York: Polish Institute of Arts and Sciences in America, 1948. [An abridged translation of a seven-volume work.]

*LEROY-BEAULIEU, A. *L'Empire des tsars et les russes.* 3 vols. Paris: 1881–9; English translation New York: Putnam, 1902–3. [A scholarly and exhaustive work. English translation to be used with caution.]

MAZOUR, A. *Russia Past and Present.* New York: Van Nostrand, 1951.

MILIUKOV, P., C. SEIGNOBOS, and L. EISENMANN. *Histoire de Russie.* 3 vols. Paris: Leroux, 1932–3.

MIRSKY, D. S. *Russia, A Social History.* London: Cresset, 1931.

PASCAL, P. *Histoire de la Russie des origines à 1917.* Paris: Presses univer sitaires, 1946.

PLATONOV, S. F. *History of Russia.* New York: Macmillan, 1929.

POKROVSKY, M. N. *History of Russia from the Earliest Times to the Rise of Commercial Capitalism.* New York: International Publishers, 1931.

*RAMBAUD, A. *Histoire de la Russie, revue et complétée jusqu'en 1917 par E. Haumant.* Paris: Hachette, 1918. [See Note on Materials.]

STÄHLIN, K. *Geschichte Russlands von den Anfängen bis zur Gegenwart.* 5 vols. Stuttgart: Deutsche Verlagsanstalt, 1923–9.

SUMNER, B. H. *A Short History of Russia.* Rev. ed. New York: Harcourt Brace, 1949.

VERNADSKY, G. *History of Russia.* 3rd rev. ed. New Haven: Yale University Press, 1951.

V. BY PERIOD

Beginnings (to 1533)

CROSS, S. H., ed. *The Russian Primary Chronicle.* Cambridge: Harvard University Press, 1930.

JAKOBSON, R., and others. *La Geste du Prince Igor, épopée russe du douzième siècle.* (*Annuaire de l'Institut de Philologie et d'Histoire Orientales et Slaves,* Université de Bruxelles, VIII, 1945–7.) New York: distr. by Columbia University Press, 1948. [Includes English translation.]

*MICHELL, R., and N. FORBES. *The Chronicle of Novgorod, 1016–1471.* (Vol. 25, Camden 3rd Series) London: Royal Historical Society, 1914. [Excellently translated and edited. See Note on Materials.]

VERNADSKY, G., tr. *Medieval Russian Laws.* New York: Columbia Univercity Press, 1947.

. . .

CHADWICK, N. K. *The Beginnings of Russian History: an Enquiry into Sources.* Cambridge: Cambridge University Press, 1946.

ECK, A. *Le Moyen âge russe.* Paris: Maison du livre étranger, 1933.

FEDOTOV, G. P. *The Russian Religious Mind: Kievan Christianity.* Cambridge: Harvard University Press, 1946.

GREKOV, B. D. *The Culture of Kiev Rus.* Moscow: 1947.

*HOWORTH, H. H. *History of the Mongols from the Ninth to the Nineteenth Century.* 5 vols. London: Longmans, Green, 1876–1927.

KERNER, R. J. *The Urge to the Sea; the Course of Russian History. The Role of Rivers, Portages, Ostrogs, Monasteries, and Furs.* Berkeley: University of California Press, 1942.

*NIEDERLE, L. *Manuel de l'antiquité slave.* 2 vols. Paris: Champion, 1923–6. [The classical work on the subject.]

PRAWDIN, M. *The Mongol Empire; Its Rise and Legacy.* New York: Macmillan, 1940.

VASILIEV, A. A. *The Russian Attack on Constantinople in 860.* Cambridge, Mass.: Medieval Academy of America, 1946.

VERNADSKY, G. *Ancient Russia.* New Haven: Yale University Press, 1944.

VERNADSKY, G. *Kievan Russia.* New Haven: Yale University Press, 1946.

1533–1682

BADDELEY, J. F. *Russia, Mongolia, China.* . . . 2 vols. London: Macmillan, 1919. [1600–76.]

EPSTEIN, F., ed. *Heinrich von Staden, Aufzeichnungen über den Moskauer Staat.* . . . Hamburg: Friederichsen, de Gruyter, 1930.

*FLETCHER, G., and J. HORSEY. *Russia at the Close of the Sixteenth Century.* London: Hakluyt Society, 1856. [Like Herberstein, Fletcher is accounted a first source by Russian historians.]

*HAKLUYT, R. *The Principal Navigations, Voyages, Traffiques and Discoveries of the English Nation.* 10 vols. New York: Dutton, 1927–8. [Selected parts of Vols. 2 and 3.]

HARRISON, J., and H. MIRRLEES, tr. *The Life of the Archpriest Avvakum, by Himself.* London: Woolf, 1924.

*HERBERSTEIN, S. VON. *Notes upon Russia.* 2 vols. London: Hakluyt Society, 1851–2. [One of the earliest foreign observers; is accounted an authority by Russian historians.]

*JENKINSON, A., and others. *Early Voyages and Travels to Russia and Persia.* 2 vols. London: Hakluyt Society, 1886.

*OLEARIUS, A. *Adam Olearii ausführliche Beschreibung der Kundbaren Reyss nach Muscow und Persien . . . in den Jahren 1633–1639.* New Ger. ed. Berlin: 1927.

STÄHLIN, K., ed. *Der Briefwechsel Iwans des Schrecklichen mit dem Fürsten Kurbskij, 1564–1579.* Leipzig: Schraepler, 1921.

.   .   .

BAIN, R. N. *The First Romanovs, 1613–1725.* New York: Dutton, 1905.

FLEISCHHACKER, H. *Russland zwischen zwei Dynastien, 1598–1613.* Vienna: Rohrer, 1933.

GRAHAM, S. *Boris Godunof.* London: Senn, 1933.

NOWAK, F. *Medieval Slavdom and the Rise of Russia.* New York: Holt, 1930.

PASCAL, P. *Avvakum et les débuts du Raskol; la crise religieuse au xvii* siècle en Russie.* Paris: Centre d'études russes "istina," 1938.

PLATONOV, S. F. *La Russie moscovite.* Paris: Boccard, 1932.

VERNADSKY, G. *Bogdan, Hetman of Ukraine.* New Haven: Yale University Press, 1941.

VIPPER, R. *Ivan the Terrible.* 3rd ed. Moscow: 1947.

WALISZEWSKI, K. *Ivan the Terrible.* Philadelphia: Lippincott, 1904.

1682–1796

*CATHERINE II, EMPRESS. *Memoirs.* New York: Knopf, 1927.

*GORDON, P. *Tagebuch während seiner Kriegsdienste unter den Schweden und Polen 1655–1661, und seines Aufenthaltes in Russland, 1661–1699.* 3 vols. Moscow: 1849–52.

PETER I, THE GREAT. *Beytraege zur Geschichte Peters des Grossen. Tagebuch Peters des Grossen.* 3 vols. Riga: Hartnoch, 1774–84.

PUTNAM, P., ed. *Seven Britons in Imperial Russia, 1698–1812.* Princeton: Princeton University Press, 1952.

RADISHCHEV, A. N. *Reise von Petersburg nach Moskau* (1790). Leipzig: Schraepler, 1922.

REDDAWAY, W. F., ed. *Documents of Catherine the Great; the Correspondence with Voltaire and the Instruction of 1767.* Cambridge: Cambridge University Press, 1931.

*SHCHERBATOV, M. M., ed. *Journal de Pierre le Grand depuis l'année 1698 jusqu'à la conclusion de la paix de Neustadt.* Berlin: 1773.

*SEGUR, COUNT L. DE. *Memoires, souvenirs et anecdotes.* 2 vols. Paris: 1879. [Ambassador of France in the reign of Catherine.]

BAIN, R. N. *The Daughter of Peter the Great; a History of Russian Diplomacy and of the Russian Court under the Empress Elizabeth Petrovna, 1741–1762.* Westminster: Constable, 1899.

BAIN, R. N. *The Pupils of Peter the Great; a History of the Russian Court and Empire from 1697 to 1740.* Westminster: 1897.

*BRÜCKNER, A. *Iwan Possoschkow; Ideen und Zustände in Russland zur Zeit Peters des Grossen.* Leipzig: Duncker, 1878. [Pososhkov was a peasant trader who supported the reforms of Peter the Great and gave expression to the wishes of the working classes.]

*BRÜCKNER, A. *Katharina die Zweite.* Berlin: Grote, 1883. [See Note on Materials.]

*HOETSCH, O. "Catherine II." *Cambridge Modern History*, VI, xix. New York: Macmillan, 1925.

MENSHUTKIN, B. N. *Russia's Lomonosov: Chemist, Courtier, Physicist, Poet.* Princeton: Princeton University Press, 1952. (Russian Translation Project Series of the American Council of Learned Societies.)

O'BRIEN, C. B. *Russia under Two Tsars, 1682–1689; the Regency of Sophia Alekseevna.* Berkeley and Los Angeles: University of California Press, 1952.

*SCHUYLER, E. *Peter the Great, Emperor of Russia; a Study of Historical Biography.* 2 vols. New York: Scribner's, 1884.

SOLOVEYTCHIK, G. *Potemkin: Soldier, Statesman, Lover and Consort of Catherine of Russia.* New York: Norton, 1947.

SUMNER, B. H. *Peter the Great and the Emergence of Russia.* New York: Macmillan, 1951.

*WALISZEWSKI, K. *The Romance of an Empress: Catherine II of Russia.* New York: Appleton, 1929.

*WALISZEWSKI, K. *Peter the Great.* New York: Appleton, 1897.

1796–1881

CAULAINCOURT, A. A. L. *Memoirs of General Caulaincourt, Duke of Vicenza.* 2 vols. London: Cassell, 1935–8.

CUSTINE, A. L. L. *Journey for our Time; the Journals of the Marquis de Custine.* New York: Pellegrini and Cudahy, 1951.

CZARTORYSKI, A. J. *Memoirs of Prince Adam Czartoryski and his Correspondence with Alexander I.* 2nd ed. 2 vols. London: Remington, 1888.

HERZEN, A. *My Past and Thoughts; the Memoirs of Alexander Herzen.*
6 vols. New York: Knopf, 1924–8.

*KROPOTKIN, P. A. *Memoirs of a Revolutionist.* Boston and New York:
Houghton Mifflin, 1930. [A scholar and revolutionary; deals with the
period of Alexander II.]

*MAISTRE, J. *Correspondance diplomatique, 1811–1817.* 2 vols. Paris: Levy,
1860. [An acute analyst of the Russian mentality from the reactionary
and religious point of view.]

MAISTRE, J. *Les soirées de Saint-Pétersbourg.* Paris: Garnier, 1929.

*SÉGUR, P. P. *La campagne de Russie; mémoires du Général de Ségur (aide
de camp de Napoleon) de l'Académie française.* Paris: Nelson, 1910.
[A brilliant psychological account; the author was with Napoleon
throughout.]

TOLSTOY, L. *War and Peace.* New York: Simon and Schuster, 1942.

*TURGENEV, N. I. *La Russie et les Russes.* 3 vols. Brussels: Meline, Cans,
1847. [One of the best of the Decembrists and historian of the movement.]

.   .   .

GRUNWALD, C. DE. *La vie de Nicolas I*". Paris: Calmann-Lévy, 1946.

*HAXTHAUSEN-ABBENBURG, A. *The Russian Empire; Its People, Institutions
and Resources.* 2 vols. London: 1856.

KARPOVICH, M. *Imperial Russia, 1801–1917.* New York: Holt, 1932.

*KORNILOV, A. *Modern Russian History, from the Age of Catherine the
Great to the End of the Nineteenth Century.* New York: Knopf, 1943.

*LEROY-BEAULIEU, A. *Un homme d'état russe (Nicolas Milutine) d'après
sa correspondance inédite; étude sur la Russie et la Pologne pendant le
règne d'Alexandre II (1855–1872).* Paris: Hachette, 1884. [A personal
account of the notable participant in the Emancipation.]

MAZOUR, A. G. *The First Russian Revolution, 1825; the Decembrist Movement, Its Origins, Development and Significance.* Berkeley: University of
California Press, 1937.

NECHKINA, M. V., ed. *Russia in the Nineteenth Century.* Ann Arbor:
Edwards, 1952. (Russian Translation Project Series of the American
Council of Learned Societies.)

*NIKOLAI MIKHAILOVICH, GRAND DUKE. *L'Empereur Alexandre I*"; essai
d'étude historique.* 2 vols. St. Petersburg: 1912.

*SCHIEMANN, T. *Geschichte Russlands unter Kaiser Nikolaus I.* 4 vols.
Berlin: Reimer, 1904–19. [See Note on Materials.]

*SCHILDER, N. K. *Histoire anecdotique de Paul I*". Paris: 1899. [A summary
of the exhaustive personal record of the life of Alexander I, mentioned
in Note on Materials.]

TARLE, E. V. *Napoleon's Invasion of Russia, 1812.* New York: Oxford
University Press, 1942.

VERNADSKY, G. *La Charte constitutionnelle de l'empire Russe de l'an 1820.*
Paris: Libraire du Recueil Sirey, 1933.

1881–1914

GURKO, V. I. *Features and Figures of the Past; Government and Opinion in the Reign of Nicholas II.* Stanford: Stanford University Press, 1939.

IZVOLSKII, A. P. *Recollections of a Foreign Minister.* Garden City: Doubleday, Page, 1921.

KOKOVTSOV, V. N. *Out of My Past; the Memoirs of Count Kokovtsov, Russian Minister of Finance, 1904–1914, Chairman of the Council of Ministers, 1911–1914.* Stanford: Stanford University Press, 1935.

*MELNIK, J., ed. *Russen über Russland; ein Sammelwerk.* Frankfurt a. M.: 1906. [A series of sketches, by experts, of the defects of the autocratic régime.]

MOSOLOV, A. A. *At the Court of the Last Tsar; Being the Memoirs of A. A. Mossolov, Head of the Court Chancellery, 1900–1916.* London: Methuen, 1935.

PALÉOLOGUE, M. *An Ambassador's Memoirs.* 3 vols. London: 1924–5.

*POBÉDONOSTSEV, K. P. *Reflections of a Russian Statesman.* London: Richards, 1898. [The maker of the official creed of reactionary Nihilism under Alexander III and Nicholas II; a very good translation.]

POBEDONOSTSEV, K. P. *L'Autocratie russe; mémoires, politiques, correspondance officielle et documents inédits relatifs à l'histoire du règne de l'empereur Alexandre III de Russie* (1881–1894). Paris: Payot, 1927.

ROSEN, BARON R. *Forty Years of Diplomacy.* 2 vols. London: Allen and Unwin, 1922.

SAVINKOV, B. V. *Memoirs of a Terrorist.* New York: Boni, 1931.

SAZONOV, S. D. *Fateful Years, 1909–1916. Reminiscences.* London: Cape, 1928.

*WITTE, S. IU. (VITTE). *The Memoirs of Count Witte.* Garden City: Doubleday, Page, 1921.

. . .

BADAEV, A. E. *The Bolsheviks in the Tsarist Duma.* New York: International Publishers, 1932.

*BARING, M. *A Year in Russia.* London: Methuen, 1907. [The most objective and informing picture of the important year 1905–6.]

*HOETSCH, O. *Russland; eine Einführung auf Grund seiner Geschichte von japanischen bis zum Weltkrieg.* Berlin: Reimer, 1917. [A work of German historical scholarship.]

LEVIN, A. *The Second Duma; a Study of the Social-Democratic Party and the Russian Constitutional Experiment.* New Haven: Yale University Press, 1940.

*MILYUKOV, P. N. *Russia and Its Crisis.* Chicago: University of Chicago Press, 1905. [A plea for liberal principles of government.]

*MAURICE, F. B. "The Russo-Japanese War." *Cambridge Modern History,* XII, xix. New York: Macmillan, 1920. [A very good short account.]

*MAYNARD, J. *Russia in Flux.* New York: Macmillan, 1948.

OWEN, L. A. *The Russian Peasant Movement, 1906–1917.* London: King, 1937.

*PARES, B. "Reaction and Revolution in Russia." "The Reform Movement in Russia." *Cambridge Modern History,* XII, xii, xiii. New York: Macmillan, 1920. [A record of Russian history from 1861 to 1909.]

ROBINSON, G. T. *Rural Russia under the Old Regime; a History of the Landlord-Peasant World and a Prologue to the Peasant Revolution of 1917.* New York: Macmillan, 1949.

SETON-WATSON, H. *The Decline of Imperial Russia, 1855–1914.* New York: Praeger, 1952.

*WALLACE, D. M. *Russia.* Rev. ed. London: Cassell, 1912. [The greatest of foreign observers; admirable scope and judgment.]

*WILLIAMS, H. W. *Russia of the Russians.* New York: Scribner, 1914. [An admirable and scholarly guide to contemporary Russian culture.]

WOLFE, B. D. *Three Who Made a Revolution; a Biographical History.* New York: Dial, 1948. [Lenin, Trotsky, Stalin.]

World War I

BUCHANAN, G. *My Mission to Russia and Other Diplomatic Memoirs.* 2 vols. London: Cassell, 1923.

La Chute du régime tsariste; interrogatoires des ministres, conseillers, généraux, hauts fonctionnaires de la cour impériale russe par la Commission extraordinaire du gouvernement provisoire de 1917. Paris: 1927.

FRANCIS, D. *Russia from the American Embassy, April 1916–November 1918.* New York: Scribners, 1921.

GANKIN, O. H., and H. H. FISHER. *The Bolsheviks and the World War; the Origin of the Third International.* Stanford: Stanford University Press, 1940.

GOLDER, F. A. *Documents of Russian History, 1914–1917.* New York: Century, 1927.

Letters of the Tsar to the Tsaritsa, 1914–1917. New York: Dodd, Mead, 1929.

Letters of the Tsaritsa to the Tsar, 1914–1916. London: Duckworth, 1923.

*PALÉOLOGUE, M. *La Russie des tsars pendant la grande guerre.* 3 vols. Paris: Plon-Nourrit, 1921–2. [A brilliant diary of Russian history in the Great War, by the French Ambassador in Petrograd.]

RODZIANKO, M. V. *The Reign of Rasputin: an Empire's Collapse; Memoirs.* London: Philpot, 1927.

·   ·   ·

ANTSIFEROV, A. N., and A. D. BILIMOVICH. *Russian Agriculture during the War.* New Haven: Yale University Press, 1930.

ASTROV, N. I., and P. P. GRONSKY. *The War and the Russian Government.* New Haven: Yale University Press, 1929.

CHURCHILL, W. S. *The Unknown War; the Eastern Front.* New York: Scribner's, 1931.

DANILOW, Y. *La Russie dans la guerre mondiale, 1914–1917.* Paris: Payot, 1927.

FAINSOD, M. *International Socialism and the World War.* Cambridge: Harvard University Press, 1935.

FLORINSKY, M. T. *The End of the Russian Empire.* New Haven: Yale University Press, 1931.

GOLOVINE, N. N. *The Russian Army in the World War.* New Haven: Yale University Press, 1931.

KOHN, S., and A. MEYENDORFF. *The Cost of the War to Russia.* New Haven: Yale University Press, 1932.

NOLDE, B. E. *Russia in the Economic War.* New Haven: Yale University Press, 1928.

PARES, B. *The Fall of the Russian Monarchy; a Study of the Evidence.* New York: Knopf, 1939.

POLNER, T. I. *Russian Local Government during the War and the Union of Zemstvos.* New Haven: Yale University Press, 1930.

STRUVE, P. B., and others. *Food Supply in Russia during the World War.* New Haven: Yale University Press, 1930.

WHEELER-BENNETT, J. W. *The Forgotten Peace: Brest-Litovsk, March, 1918.* New York: Morrow, 1939.

ZAGORSKY, S. O. *State Control of Industry in Russia during the War.* New Haven: Yale University Press, 1928.

Revolution, Civil War, and Intervention (1917–23)

BUNYAN, J., and H. H. FISHER. *The Bolshevik Revolution, 1917–1918; Documents and Materials.* Stanford: Stanford University Press, 1934.

BUNYAN, J. *Intervention, Civil War and Communism in Russia; April–December 1918; Documents and Materials.* Baltimore: Johns Hopkins Press, 1936.

CHERNOV, V. M. *The Great Russian Revolution.* New Haven: Yale University Press, 1936.

DENIKIN, A. I. *The Russian Turmoil; Memoirs, Military, Social and Political.* London: Hutchinson, 1922.

HARD, W. *Raymond Robins' Own Story.* New York: Harper, 1920.

KERENSKY, A. F. *The Catastrophe: Kerensky's Own Story of the Russian Revolution.* New York: Appleton, 1927.

LENIN, V. I. *Collected Works.* Vol. XX, Parts 1 and 2. "The Revolution of 1917 (March–July)." New York: 1929. Vol. XXI, Parts 1 and 2. "Toward the Seizure of Power (July–October 1917)." New York: 1933.

LOCKHART, R. H. B. *British Agent.* New York: Putnam, 1933.

REED, J. *Ten Days That Shook the World.* New York: Modern Library, 1935.

STALIN, J. *The October Revolution: a Collection of Articles and Speeches.* New York: International Publishers, 1934.

TROTSKY, L. *The History of the Russian Revolution.* 3 vols. New York: Simon and Schuster: 1932.

U. S. Dept. of State. *Papers Relating to the Foreign Relations of the United States. 1918. Russia.* 3 vols. Washington: U. S. Government Printing Office, 1931–2.

U. S. Dept. of State. *Papers Relating to the Foreign Relations of the United States. 1919. Russia.* Washington: U. S. Government Printing Office, 1937.

VARNECK, E., and H. H. FISHER. *The Testimony of Kolchak and Other Siberian Materials.* Stanford: Stanford University Press, 1935.

WRANGEL, P. N. *Memoirs of General Wrangel, the Last Commander-in-Chief of the Russian National Army.* New York: Duffield, 1930.

        .   .   .

CARR, E. H. *The Bolshevik Revolution, 1917–1923.* 2 vols. New York: Macmillan, 1951–2.

*CHAMBERLIN, W. H. *The Russian Revolution, 1917–1921.* 2 vols. New York; Macmillan, 1947. [The result of an arduous study in Russia.]

FISHER, H. H. *The Famine in Soviet Russia, 1919–1923; the Operations of the American Relief Administration.* New York: Macmillan, 1927.

GORKY, M., and others, eds. *History of the Civil War in the USSR.* London: Lawrence and Wishart, 1937–47. [Vol. 1: 1914–October, 1917; Vol. II: October–November 1917.]

GRAVES, W. S. *America's Siberian Adventure, 1918–1920.* New York: P. Smith, 1941.

KAZEMZADEH, F. *The Struggle for Transcaucasia, 1917–1921.* New York: Philosophical Library, 1951.

RADKEY, O. H. *The Election to the Russian Constituent Assembly of 1917.* Cambridge: Harvard University Press, 1950.

RESHETAR, J. S. *The Ukrainian Revolution, 1917–20; a Study in Nationalism.* Princeton: Princeton University Press, 1952.

STEWART, G. *The White Armies of Russia; a Chronicle of Counter-Revolution and Allied Intervention.* New York: Macmillan, 1933.

STRAKHOVSKY, L. I. *The Origins of American Intervention in North Russia.* Princeton: Princeton University Press, 1937.

STRAKHOVSKY, L. I. *Intervention at Archangel.* Princeton: Princeton University Press, 1944.

1923–39

Communist Party of the Soviet Union, Central Committee. *History of the Communist Party of the Soviet Union (Bolsheviks).* Short Course. New York: International Publishers, 1939.

Communist Party of the Soviet Union, Eighteenth Congress. *Land of Socialism Today and Tomorrow. Reports and Speeches at the Eighteenth Congress of the CPSU(b), March 10–21, 1939.* Moscow: Foreign Languages Publishing House, 1939.

MEISEL, J. H., and E. S. KOZERA, eds. *Materials for the Study of the Soviet System.* 2nd rev. ed. Ann Arbor: Wahr, 1953.

STALIN, J. V. *Leninism; Selected Writings.* New York: International Publishers, 1942.

VYSHINSKY, A. Y. *The Law of the Soviet State.* New York: Macmillan, 1948. (Russian Translation Project Series of the American Council of Learned Societies.)

* * *

*CHAMBERLIN, W. H. *Russia's Iron Age.* Boston: Little, Brown, 1934. [The period of the First Five Year Plan.]

*DAVIES, J. E. *Mission to Moscow, by Joseph E. Davies, U. S. Ambassador to the Soviet Union from 1936 to 1938.* Garden City: Garden City Publishing Co., 1943.

FISCHER, L. *Men and Politics, an Autobiography.* New York: Duell, Sloan and Pearce, 1941.

*HINDUS, M. *Red Bread.* New York: Cape and Smith, 1931. [A brilliant and poignant picture of the peasant under collectivization.]

LIBERMAN, S. *Building Lenin's Russia.* Chicago: University of Chicago Press, 1945.

*LITTLEPAGE, J. D., and D. BESS. *In Search of Soviet Gold.* New York: Harcourt Brace, 1938. [On industrial planning and on "wrecking."]

LYONS, E. *Assignment in Utopia.* New York: Harcourt Brace, 1937.

*SCOTT, J. *Behind the Urals; an American Worker in Russia's City of Steel.* Boston: Houghton Mifflin, 1942. [Life and work at Magnitogorsk.]

TROTSKY, L. *My Life.* New York: Scribner's, 1930.

*TROTSKY, L. *The Revolution Betrayed.* Garden City: Doubleday Doran, 1937.

* * *

*ANDERSON, P. B. *People, Church and State in Modern Russia.* New York: Macmillan, 1944. [A special study, similar in value to Maynard's work.]

BASILY, N. DE. *Russia under Soviet Rule; Twenty Years of Bolshevik Experiment.* London: Allen and Unwin, 1938.

BERGSON, A. *Soviet National Income and Product in 1937.* New York: Columbia University Press, 1953.

DEUTSCHER, I. *Stalin; a Political Biography.* London: Oxford University Press, 1949.

FLORINSKY, M. T. *Toward an Understanding of the USSR; a Study in Government, Politics and Economic Planning.* Rev. ed. New York: Macmillan, 1951.

FREUND, H. A. *Russia from A to Z; Revolution, State and Party, Foreign Relations, Economic System, Social Principles and General Knowledge.* London: Angus and Robertson, 1945.

*KARLGREN, A. *Bolshevist Russia.* London: Allen and Unwin, 1927. [The pest picture in English of the peasantry, 1921–7.]

*MAYNARD, J. *Russia in Flux.* New York: Macmillan, 1948. [See Preface, p. xx.]

MOORE, B., JR. *Soviet Politics, the Dilemma of Power*. Cambridge, Harvard University Press, 1950.

PARES, B. *Russia*. New York: New American Library, 1949.

SCHUMAN, F. L. *Soviet Politics at Home and Abroad*. New York: Knopf, 1946.

*SOUVARINE, B. *Stalin; a Critical Survey of Bolshevism*. New York: Alliance, 1939.

TIMASHEFF, N. *The Great Retreat; the Growth and Decline of Communism in Russia*. New York: Dutton, 1946.

WHITE, D. F. *The Growth of the Red Army*. Princeton: Princeton University Press, 1944.

World War II

CHURCHILL, W. S. *The Second World War*. 3 vols. Boston: Houghton, Mifflin, 1948–50.

DEANE, J. R. *The Strange Alliance*. New York: Viking, 1947.

STALIN, J. *The Great Patriotic War of the Soviet Union*. New York: International Publishers, 1945.

STETTINIUS, E. R. *Lend-Lease, Weapon for Victory*. New York: Macmillan, 1944.

STETTINIUS, E. R. *Roosevelt and the Russians; the Yalta Conference*. Garden City: Doubleday, 1949.

WERTH, A. *The Year of Stalingrad; an Historical Record and a Study of Russian Mentality, Methods and Policies*. London: Hamilton, 1946.

.   .   .

FISCHER, G. *Soviet Opposition to Stalin*. Cambridge: Harvard University Press, 1952.

GUILLAUME, A. *La guerre germano-soviétique, 1941–1945*. Paris: Payot, 1949.

LA FARGE, H., ed. *Lost Treasures of Europe*. New York: Pantheon, 1946. [See Nos. 60–83.]

SHERWOOD, R. E. *Roosevelt and Hopkins*. New York: Harper, 1948.

WERNER, M. (A. SCHIFFRIN). *The Great Offensive; the Strategy of Coalition Warfare*. New York: Viking, 1942.

1945–

BARGHOORN, F. L. *The Soviet Image of the United States*. New York: Harcourt Brace, 1950.

GRULIOW, L., ed. *Current Soviet Policies; a Documentary Record of the 19th Party Congress and the Reorganization after Stalin's Death*. New York: Praeger, 1953.

ROUNDS, F. *Window on Red Square*. New York: Houghton Mifflin, 1953.

SMITH, W. B. *My Three Years in Moscow*. Philadelphia: Lippincott, 1950.

STALIN, J. *Economic Problems of Socialism in the USSR.* New York: International Publishers, 1952; and Special Supplement to *Current Digest of the Soviet Press,* October 18, 1952.

STEVENS, E. *This is Russia, Uncensored.* New York: Didier, 1950.

.   .   .

BERGSON, A., ed. *Soviet Economic Growth: Conditions and Perspectives.* Evanston, Row, Peterson, 1953.

BERMAN, H. *The Russians in Focus.* Boston: Little, Brown, 1953.

CRANKSHAW, E. *Cracks in the Kremlin Wall.* New York: Viking, 1951.

GURIAN, W., ed. *The Soviet Union: Background, Ideology, Reality.* Notre Dame: University of Notre Dame Press, 1951.

MOORE, B., JR. *Soviet Politics; the Dilemma of Power.* Cambridge: Harvard University Press, 1950.

MOSELY, P. E., ed. The Soviet Union since World War II. *The Annals of the American Academy of Political and Social Science,* vol. 263, May 1949.

SCHLESINGER, R. *The Spirit of Postwar Russia: Soviet Ideology.* London: Dennis Dobson, 1947.

SCHWARTZ, H. *Russia's Postwar Economy.* Syracuse: Syracuse University Press, 1947.

STEINBERG, H., ed. V*erdict of Three Decades.* New York: Duell, Sloan and Pearce, 1950.

◇◇◇◇◇◇◇◇◇◇◇◇

VI. BY SUBJECT

Economy

*KOVALEVSKY, V. I., ed. *La Russie à la fin du 19ᵉ siècle.* Paris: Dupont, 1900.

KRYPTON, C. *The Northern Sea Route: Its Place in Russian Economic History before 1917.* New York: Research Program on the USSR, 1953.

LYASHCHENKO, P. I. *History of the National Economy of Russia to the 1917 Revolution.* New York: Macmillan, 1949. (Russian Translation Project Series of the American Council of Learned Societies.)

*MAVOR, J. *An Economic History of Russia.* 2d ed. rev. and enl. 2 vols. New York: Dutton, 1925. [A thorough work which makes good use of Klyuchevsky and other materials.]

MILLER, M. S. *The Economic Development of Russia, 1905–1914; with Special Reference to Trade, Industry and Finance.* London: King, 1926.

ROBINSON, G. T. *Rural Russia under the Old Regime; a History of the Landlord-Peasant World and a Prologue to the Peasant Revolution of 1917.* New York: Macmillan, 1949.

*TUGAN-BARANOWSKY, M. I. *Geschichte der russischen Fabrik*. Berlin: Felber, 1900. [See Note on Materials.]

TURIN, S. P. *From Peter the Great to Lenin: the History of the Russian Labour Movement with Special Reference to Trade Unionism*. London: King, 1935.

WITTSCHEWSKY, V. *Russlands Handels- Zoll- und Industriepolitik von Peter dem Grossen bis auf die Gegenwart*. Berlin: Mittler, 1905.

• • •

BAYKOV, A. *The Development of the Soviet Economic System*. New York: Macmillan, 1946.

BERGSON, A., ed. *Soviet Economic Growth: Conditions and Perspectives*. Evanston: Row, Peterson, 1953.

BERGSON, A. *Soviet National Income and Product in 1937*. New York: Columbia University Press, 1953.

BIENSTOCK, G., S. SCHWARZ, and A. YUGOW. *Management in Russian Industry and Agriculture*. New York: Oxford University Press, 1944.

CARR, E. H. *The Bolshevik Revolution, 1917–23*. Vol. II: "The Economic Order." New York: Macmillan, 1952.

DEUTSCHER, I. *Soviet Trade Unions; Their Place in Soviet Labor Policy*. New York: Royal Institute of International Affairs, 1950.

DOBB, M. *Soviet Economic Development since 1917*. New York: International Publishers, 1948.

JASNY, N. *The Socialized Agriculture of the USSR; Plans and Performance*. Stanford: Stanford University Press, 1949.

JASNY, N. *The Soviet Economy during the Plan Era*. Stanford: Stanford University Press, 1951.

LORIMER, F. *Population of the Soviet Union: History and Prospects*. Geneva: League of Nations, 1946.

SCHWARTZ, H. *Russia's Soviet Economy*. New York: Prentice Hall, 1950.

SCHWARZ, S. M. *Labor in the Soviet Union*. New York: Praeger, 1951.

SHIMKIN, D. B. *Minerals, a Key to Soviet Power*. Cambridge, Harvard University Press, 1952.

TIMOSHENKO, V. P. *Agricultural Russia and the Wheat Problem*. Stanford: Food Research Institute, 1932.

VOLIN, L. *A Survey of Soviet Russian Agriculture*. Washington: U. S. Government Printing Office, 1951.

VUCINICH, A. S. *Soviet Economic Institutions: the Social Structure of Production Units*. Stanford: Stanford University Press, 1952.

Political and Social Institutions

CHASLES, P. *Le Parlement russe; son organisation, ses rapports avec l'empereur*. Paris: Rousseau, 1910.

ELNETT, E. *Historic Origin and Social Development of Family Life in Russia*. New York: Columbia University Press, 1926.

GRIBOWSKI, V. M. *Das Staatsrecht des Russischen Reiches.* Tübingen: Mohr, 1912.

HANS, N. A. *History of Russian Educational Policy* (1701–1917). London: King, 1931.

JOHNSON, WM. H. E. *Russia's Educational Heritage: Teacher Education in the Russian Empire, 1600–1917.* Pittsburgh: Carnegie Press, 1950.

KAIDANOVA-BERRY, O. *Public Education in Russia since 1850.* Ann Arbor: Edwards, 1952. (Russian Translation Project Series of the American Council of Learned Societies.)

KENNAN, G. *Siberia and the Exile System.* 2 vols. New York: Century, 1891.

*KORKUNOV, N. M. *General Theory of Law.* 2nd ed. New York: Macmillan, 1922.

*KOVALEVSKY, M. M. *Russian Political Institutions; the Growth and Development of these Institutions from the Beginnings of Russian History to the Present Time.* Chicago: University of Chicago Press, 1902.

LEARY, D. B. *Education and Autocracy in Russia from the Origins to the Bolsheviks.* Buffalo: University of Buffalo, 1919.

VASSILYEV, A. T. *The Ochrana: the Russian Secret Police, by A. T. Vassilyev, the Last Chief of Police under the Tsar.* Philadelphia: Lippincott, 1930.

*VINOGRADOFF, P. *Outlines of Historic Jurisprudence.* 2 vols. New York: Oxford University Press, 1920–2.

*VINOGRADOFF, P. *Self-government in Russia.* London: Constable, 1915.

· · ·

BABB, H., and J. N. HAZARD, eds. *Soviet Legal Philosophy.* Cambridge: Harvard University Press, 1951.

BALDWIN, R. N. *Liberty under the Soviets.* New York: Vanguard, 1928.

BATSELL, W. R. *Soviet Rule in Russia.* New York: Macmillan, 1929.

BAUER, R. A. *The New Man in Soviet Psychology.* Cambridge: Harvard University Press, 1952.

BECK, F., and W. GODIN. *Russian Purge and the Extraction of Confession.* New York: Viking, 1951.

BERMAN, H. J. *Justice in Russia.* Cambridge: Harvard University Press, 1950.

GORER, F., and J. RICKMAN. *The People of Great Russia; a Psychological Study.* New York: Chanticleer, 1950.

GSOVSKI, V. *Soviet Civil Law.* 2 vols. Ann Arbor: University of Michigan Law School, 1948–9.

*HARPER, S. N. *Civic Training in Russia.* Chicago: University of Chicago Press, 1929. [By the foremost American authority on his contemporary Russia.]

HARPER, S. N., and R. THOMPSON. *The Government of the Soviet Union.* 2nd ed. New York: Van Nostrand, 1949.

HAZARD, J. N., and M. L. WEISBURG. "Cases and Readings in Soviet Law."

New York: Parker School of Foreign and Comparative Law, Columbia University, 1950. [Mimeographed.]

INKELES, A. *Public Opinion in Soviet Russia; a Study in Mass Persuasion.* Cambridge: Harvard University Press, 1950.

KONSTANTINOVSKY, B. A. *Soviet Law in Action; the Recollected Cases of a Soviet Lawyer.* Cambridge: Harvard University Press, 1953.

MEAD, M. *Soviet Attitudes toward Authority; an Interdisciplinary Approach to Problems of Soviet Character.* New York: McGraw-Hill, 1951.

MEISEL, J. H., and E. S. KOZERA, eds. *Materials for the Study of the Soviet System.* 2nd enl. ed., including the Nineteenth Party Congress. Ann Arbor: Wahr, 1953.

RUNES, D. D. *The Soviet Impact on Society.* New York: Philosophical Library, 1953.

SCHLESINGER, R., ed. *Changing Attitudes in Soviet Russia; Documents and Readings.* Vol. I: "The Family in the USSR." London: Routledge and Kegan Paul, 1949.

SCHLESINGER, R. *Soviet Legal Theory, Its Social Background and Development.* 2nd ed. London: Routledge and Paul, 1951.

SHORE, M. J. *Soviet Education, Its Psychology and Philosophy.* New York: Philosophical Library, 1947.

Soviet Science: a Symposium . . . 1951. Washington: American Association for the Advancement of Science, 1952.

TOWSTER, J. *Political Power in the USSR, 1917–1947; the Theory and Structure of Government in the Soviet State.* New York: Oxford University Press, 1948.

VYSHINSKY, A. Y. *The Law of the Soviet State.* New York: Macmillan, 1948. (Russian Translation Project Series of the American Council of Learned Societies.)

ZINOVIEV, M. A. *Soviet Methods of Teaching History.* Ann Arbor: Edwards, 1952. (Russian Translation Project Series of the American Council of Learned Societies.)

Literature, Language, Music, and Art

ABRAHAM, G. *On Russian Music. Critical and Historical Studies.* New York: Scribner, 1939.

BUNT, C. E. *A History of Russian Art.* London and New York: Studio, 1946.

DE BRAY, R. G. A. *Guide to the Slavonic Languages.* London: Dent, 1951.

ENTWISTLE, W. J., and W. A. MORISON. *Russian and the Slavonic Languages.* London: Faber and Faber, 1949.

GUDZY, N. K. *History of Early Russian Literature.* New York: Macmillan, 1949. (Russian Translation Project Series of the American Council of Learned Societies.)

HAUMANT, E. *La Culture française en Russie, 1700–1900.* 2nd rev. ed. Paris: Hachette, 1913.

HOLME, C. *Peasant Art in Russia.* London: "The Studio," 1912.

JAKOBSON, R., and E. J. SIMMONS, eds. *Russian Epic Studies.* Philadelphia: American Folklore Society, 1949.

KONDAKOV, N. P. *The Russian Icon.* Oxford: Clarendon, 1927.

*MILIUKOV, P. N. *Outlines of Russian Culture.* 3 vols. Philadelphia: University of Pennsylvania Press, 1948. [Vol. II: "Literature." Vol. III: "Architecture, Painting and Music."]

MIRSKY, D. S. *A History of Russian Literature; Comprising a History of Russian Literature and Contemporary Russian Literature.* Ed. and Abr. New York: Knopf, 1949.

MONTAGU-NATHAN, M. *A History of Russian Music; Being an Account of the Rise and Progress of the Russian School of Composers, with a Survey of Their Lives and a Description of Their Works.* 2nd ed. rev. London: Reeves, 1918.

RALSTON, W. R. S. *The Songs of the Russian People as Illustrative of Slavonic Mythology and Russian Social Life.* London: Ellis, 1872.

RÉAU, L. *L'Art russe.* Paris: Larousse, 1945.

RICE, T. R. *Russian Art.* London: Penguin, 1949.

RUBISSOW, H. *The Art of Russia.* New York: Philosophical Library, 1946. [Painting.]

SIMMONS, E. J. *English Literature and Culture in Russia, 1553–1840.* Cambridge: Harvard University Press, 1935.

SLONIM, M. *The Epic of Russian Literature: from Its Origins through Tolstoy.* New York: Oxford University Press, 1950.

SOKOLOV, Y. M. *Russian Folklore.* New York: Macmillan, 1950. (Russian Translation Project Series of the American Council of Learned Societies.)

VARNEKE, B. V. *History of the Russian Theater, Seventeenth through Nineteenth Century.* New York: Macmillan, 1951. (Russian Translation Project Series of the American Council of Learned Societies.)

·   ·   ·

BORLAND, H. *Soviet Literary Theory and Practice during the First Five Year Plan, 1928–1932.* New York: King's Crown Press, 1950.

Current Digest of the Soviet Press, eds. *The Soviet Linguistic Controversy.* New York: King's Crown Press, 1951.

LONDON, K. *The Seven Soviet Arts.* New Haven: Yale University Press, 1937.

MACLEOD, J. *The New Soviet Theater.* London: Allen and Unwin, 1943.

MATTHEWS, W. K. *Languages of the USSR.* Cambridge: The University Press, 1951.

REAVEY, G. *Soviet Literature Today.* New Haven: Yale University Press, 1947.

SIMMONS, E. J., ed. *Through the Glass of Soviet Literature; Views of Russian Society.* New York: Columbia University Press, 1953.

STRUVE, G. *Soviet Russian Literature, 1917–50.* Norman, Okla.: University of Oklahoma Press, 1951.

VOYCE, A. *Russian Architecture: Trends in Nationalism and Modernism.* New York: Philosophical Library, 1948.
WERTH, A. *Musical Uproar in Moscow.* London: Turnstile, 1949.

Religion

CONYBEARE, F. C. *Russian Dissenters.* Cambridge: Harvard University Press, 1921.
CURTISS, J. S. *Church and State in Russia . . . 1900–1917.* New York: Columbia University Press, 1940.
FEDOTOV, G. P. *The Russian Religious Mind.* Cambridge: Harvard University Press, 1946–   . [Vol. I: Kievan Christianity.]
FRERE, W. H. *Some Links in the Chain of Russian Church History.* London: Faith Press, 1918.
LATIMER, R. S. *Under Three Tsars: Liberty of Conscience in Russia, 1856–1909.* New York: Revell, 1909.
MEDLIN, W. K. *Moscow and East Rome: a Political Study of Relations of Church and State in Muscovite Russia.* Geneva: Librairie E. Droz, 1952.
MILIUKOV, P. N. *Outlines of Russian Culture.* 3 vols. Philadelphia: University of Pennsylvania Press, 1942. [Vol. I: Religion and the Church.]
PALMER, WM. *Notes of a Visit to the Russian Church in the Years 1840–1841.* London: Kegan Paul, 1882.
SCHULTZE, B. *Russische Denker: ihre Stellung zu Christus, Kirche, und Papstum.* Vienna: Herder, 1950.
*SOLOVYEV, V. *Russia and the Universal Church.* London: Bles, 1948.

·   ·   ·

*ANDERSON, P. B. *People, Church and State in Modern Russia.* New York: Macmillan, 1944.
CASEY, R. P. *Religion in Russia.* New York: Harper, 1946.
CURTISS, J. S. *The Russian Church and the Soviet State.* Boston: Little, Brown, 1953.
LIEB, F. *La Russie évolue, le peuple russe entre le communisme et le christianisme.* Neuchâtel: Delachaux & Niestlé, 1946.
SPINKA, M. *Christianity Confronts Communism.* New York: Harper, 1936.
TIMASHEFF, N. S. *Religion in Soviet Russia, 1917–1942.* New York: Sheed and Ward, 1942.

Philosophy and Ideology

BERDYAEV, N. *The Origin of Russian Communism.* 2nd ed. London: Bles, 1948.
BERDYAEV, N. *The Russian Idea.* New York: Macmillan, 1948.
BRESHKO-BRESHKOVSKAIA, E. *Hidden Springs of the Russian Revolution: Personal Memoirs.* Stanford: Stanford University Press, 1931.
CARR, E. H. *Michael Bakunin.* London: Macmillan, 1937.

HARE, R. *Pioneers of Russian Social Thought: Studies of Non-Marxian Formation in Nineteenth Century Russia and of Its Partial Revival in the Soviet Union.* New York: Oxford, 1951.

HECHT, D. *Russian Radicals Look to America, 1825–1894.* Cambridge: Harvard University Press, 1947.

KOYRÉ, A. *Études sur l'histoire de la pensée philosophique en Russie.* Paris: Vrin, 1951.

LOSSKY, N. O. *History of Russian Philosophy.* New York: International Universities Press, 1951.

*MASARYK, T. C. *The Spirit of Russia; Studies in History, Literature and Philosophy.* New York: Macmillan, 1919.

*MILIUKOV, P. N. *Le Mouvement intellectuel russe.* Paris: Bossard, 1918.

QUÉNET, C. *Tchaadaev et "Les Lettres philosophiques"; contribution du mouvement des idées en Russie.* Paris: Champion, 1931.

RIASANOVSKY, N. V. *Russia and the West in the Teachings of the Slavophiles; A Study of Romantic Ideology.* Cambridge: Harvard University Press, 1952.

TOMPKINS, S. R. *The Russian Mind from Peter the Great through the Enlightenment.* Norman, Okla.: University of Oklahoma Press, 1953.

WEIDLÉ, W. *La Russie absente et présente.* Paris: Galliamard, 1949.

WILSON, E. *To the Finland Station.* New York: Harcourt Brace, 1940.

ZENKOVSKII, V. V. *Russian Thinkers and Europe.* Ann Arbor: Edwards, 1953. (Russian Translation Project Series of the American Council of Learned Societies.)

ZENKOVSKY, V. V. *History of Russian Philosophy.* New York: Columbia University Press, 1953.

.   .   .

BAUER, R. A. *The New Man in Soviet Psychology.* Cambridge: Harvard University Press, 1952.

COUNTS, G. S., and N. LODGE. *The Country of the Blind; the Soviet System of Mind Control.* Boston: Houghton Mifflin, 1949.

GRAY, A. *The Socialist Tradition, Moses to Lenin.* New York: Longmans, Green, 1947.

GURIAN, W. *Bolshevism; an Introduction to Soviet Communism.* Notre Dame: University of Notre Dame Press, 1952.

HUNT, R. N. C. *The Theory and Practice of Communism.* New York: Macmillan, 1951.

KELSEN, H. *The Political Theory of Bolshevism.* Berkeley: University of California Press, 1949.

LA PIRA, G., and others. *The Philosophy of Communism.* New York: Fordham University Press, 1952.

LASSWELL, H. D., N. LEITES, and others. *Language of Politics; Studies in Quantitative Semantics.* New York: Stewart, 1949.

LEITES, N. *The Operational Code of the Politburo.* New York: McGraw-Hill, 1951.

MOORE, B., JR. *Soviet Politics; the Dilemma of Power.* Cambridge: Harvard University Press, 1950.

PHILIPOV, A. *Logic and Dialectic in the Soviet Union.* New York: Research Program on the U.S.S.R., 1952.

ROSENBERG, A. *A History of Bolshevism from Marx to the First Five Years' Plan.* London: Oxford, 1934.

RUSSELL, B. *The Practice and Theory of Bolshevism.* 2nd ed. London: Allen and Unwin, 1949.

SOMERVILLE, J. *Soviet Philosophy; a Study of Theory and Practice.* New York: Philosophical Library, 1946.

WETTER, G. *Der dialektische Materialismus, seine Geschichte und sein System in der Sowjetunion.* Wien: Herder, 1952.

Expansion and Foreign Relations

ANDREYEV, I. A., ed. *Russian Discoveries in the Pacific Ocean and North America in the Eighteenth and Nineteenth Centuries.* Ann Arbor: Edwards, 1952. (Russian Translation Project Series of the American Council of Learned Societies.)

*BADDELEY, J. F. *Russia, Mongolia and China; Being Some Record of the Relations between them from the Beginning of the Seventeenth Century to 1676. . . .* 2 vols. London: Macmillan, 1919.

BADDELEY, J. F. *The Russian Conquest of the Caucasus.* New York: Longmans, 1908.

*BAIN, R. N. *Slavonic Europe; a Political History of Poland and Russia from 1447 to 1796.* Cambridge: Cambridge University Press, 1908.

BARTOLD, V. V. *La découverte de l'Asie; histoire de l'orientalisme en Europe et en Russie.* Paris: Payot, 1947.

DALLIN, D. J. *The Rise of Russia in Asia.* New Haven: Yale University Press, 1949.

DEBENHAM, F., ed. *The Voyage of Capt. Bellingshausen to the Antarctic Seas: 1819–1821.* London: Hakluyt Society, 1946.

*EVERSLEY, G. J. *Partitions of Poland.* London: Unwin, 1915. [1763–96.]

FISCHEL, A. *Der Panslawismus bis zum Weltkrieg.* Stuttgart: Cotta, 1919.

*GOLDER, F. A. *Russian Expansion on the Pacific, 1641–1850.* Cleveland: Clark, 1914. [An important contribution towards filling a very large gap.]

HABBERTON, W. *Anglo-Russian Relations concerning Afghanistan, 1837–1907.* Urbana: University of Illinois Press, 1937.

HOWARD, H. N. *The Partition of Turkey; a Diplomatic History, 1913–1923.* Norman: University of Oklahoma Press, 1931.

KOHN, HANS. *Panslavism, Its History and Ideology.* Notre Dame: University of Notre Dame Press, 1953.

KONOVALOV, S., ed. *Russo-Polish Relations; an Historical Survey.* Princeton: Princeton University Press, 1945.

KRAUSSE, A. S. *Russia in Asia . . . 1558–1899.* New York: Holt, 1899.

LANGER, W. L. *The Diplomacy of Imperialism, 1890–1902.* New York: Knopf, 1951.

LANGER, W. L. *European Alliances and Alignments, 1871–90.* 2nd ed. New York: Knopf, 1950.

LANTZEFF, G. V. *Siberia in the Seventeenth Century; a Study of the Colonial Administration.* Berkeley: University of California Press, 1943.

LATTIMORE, O. *Inner Asian Frontiers of China.* 2nd ed. New York: American Geographical Society, 1951.

LOBANOV-ROSTOVSKY, A. *Russia and Asia.* Rev. ed. Ann Arbor: Wahr, 1951.

*LORD, R. H. *Second Partition of Poland; A Study in Diplomatic History.* Cambridge: Harvard University Press, 1915.

LUBIMENKO, I. *Les relations commerciales et politiques de l'Angleterre avec la Russie avant Pierre le Grand.* Paris: Champion, 1933.

MARTENS, F. F., ed. *Recueil des traités et conventions . . . conclus par la Russie avec les puissances étrangères.* 15 vols. St. Petersburg: 1874–1909.

MASTERSON, J. R., and H. BROWER. *Bering's Successors, 1745–1780: Contributions of Peter Simon Pallas to the History of Russian Exploration toward Alaska.* Seattle: University of Washington Press, 1948.

MITCHELL, M. *The Maritime History of Russia, 848–1948.* London: Sidgwick and Jackson, 1949.

MOSELY, P. E. *Russian Diplomacy and the Opening of the Eastern Question in 1838 and 1839.* Cambridge: Harvard University Press, 1934.

OKUN, S. B. *The Russian-American Company.* Cambridge: Harvard University Press, 1951. (Russian Translation Project Series of the American Council of Learned Societies.)

PAVLOVSKY, M. N. *Chinese-Russian Relations.* New York: Philosophical Library, 1949.

PORTAL, R. *L'Oural au xviii° siècle; étude d'histoire économique et sociale.* Paris: Institut d'études slaves, 1950.

POTEMKIN, V. P., ed. *Histoire de la diplomatie.* 3 vols. Paris: Librairie de Médicis, 1946–7. [Vol. I: To 1871. Vol. II: 1872–1919. Vol. III: 1919–1939.]

PURYEAR, V. *England, Russia and the Straits, 1844–1856.* Berkeley: University of California Press, 1931.

ROMANOV, B. A. *Russia in Manchuria* (1892–1906). Ann Arbor: Edwards, 1952. (Russian Translation Project Series of the American Council of Learned Societies.)

SCHELTING, A. *Russland und Europa im russischen Geschichtsdenken.* Bern: A. Francke, 1948.

SHOTWELL, J. T., and F. DEÁK. *Turkey at the Straits; a Short History.* New York: Macmillan, 1940.

*SKRINE, F. H. B. *Expansion of Russia, 1815–1900.* 3rd ed. Cambridge: The University Press, 1915.

*SKRINE, F. H. B., and E. D. ROSS. *The Heart of Asia: a History of Russian Turkestan and the Central Asian Khanates from the Earliest Times.* London: Methuen, 1899.

SUMNER, B. H. *Peter the Great and the Emergence of Russia.* New York: Macmillan, 1951.

SUMNER, B. H. *Russia and the Balkans, 1870–1880.* Oxford: Clarendon, 1937.

TARLE, E. V. *Napoleon's Invasion of Russia, 1812.* New York: Oxford University Press, 1942.

TEMPERLEY, H. W. V. *The Crimea.* London: Longmans, Green, 1936.

THOMAS, B. P. *Russo-American Relations, 1815–67.* Baltimore: Johns Hopkins Press, 1930.

VERNADSKY, G. *Political and Diplomatic History of Russia.* Boston: Little, Brown, 1936.

ZABRISKIE, E. H. *American-Russian Rivalry in the Far East, 1895–1914.* Philadelphia: University of Pennsylvania Press, 1946.

.   .   .

ARMSTRONG, H. F. *Tito and Goliath.* New York: Macmillan, 1951.

BAILEY, T. A. *America Faces Russia; Russian-American Relations from Early Times to Our Day.* Ithaca: Cornell University Press, 1950.

BARGHOORN, F. C. *The Soviet Image of the United States.* New York: Harcourt Brace, 1950.

BELOFF, M. *The Foreign Policy of Soviet Russia.* 2 vols. New York: Oxford University Press, 1947–9. [Vol. I: 1929–36. Vol. II: 1936–41.]

BISHOP, D. G. *Soviet Foreign Relations; Documents and Readings.* Syracuse: Syracuse University Press, 1952.

CARR, E. H. *The Soviet Impact on the Western World.* New York: Macmillan, 1947.

DALLIN, D. *Soviet Russia and the Far East.* New Haven: Yale University Press, 1948.

*DALLIN, D. *Soviet Russia's Foreign Policy, 1939–42.* New Haven: Yale University Press, 1942.

DEDIJER, V. *Tito.* New York: Simon and Schuster, 1952.

DEGRAS, J. *Calendar of Soviet Documents on Foreign Policy, 1917–1941.* New York: Royal Institute of International Affairs, 1948.

DEGRAS, J., ed. *Soviet Documents on Foreign Policy.* New York: Oxford University Press, 1951–   . [Vol. I: 1917–24. Vol. II: 1924–32.]

DENNETT, R., and J. E. JOHNSON, eds. *Negotiating with the Russians.* Boston: World Peace Foundation, 1951.

FISCHER, L. *The Soviets in World Affairs, 1917–1929.* 2nd ed. 2 vols. Princeton: Princeton University Press, 1951.

KENNAN, G. F. *American Diplomacy, 1900–1950.* Chicago: University of Chicago Press, 1951.

LASERSON, M. M., ed. *The Development of Soviet Foreign Policy in Europe, 1917–1942; a Selection of Documents.* New York: Carnegie Endowment for International Peace, 1943. (*International Conciliation,* January 1943, No. 386.)

LENCZOWSKI, G. *Russia and the West in Iran, 1918–1948; a Study in Big-Power Rivalry.* Ithaca: Cornell University Press, 1947.

LENIN, V. I., J. STALIN, V. MOLOTOV, and others. *The Soviet Union and the Cause of Peace.* New York: International Publishers, 1936.

LIPPMANN, W. *The Cold War; a Study in U. S. Foreign Policy.* New York: Harper, 1947.

LITVINOV, M. *Against Aggression: Speeches . . . together with Texts of Treaties and of the Covenant of the League of Nations.* New York: International Publishers, 1939.

MILIUKOV, P. N. *La Politique extérieure des Soviets.* 2nd ed. Paris: Librairie génerale de droit et de jurisprudence, 1936.

MOORE, H. L. *Soviet Far Eastern Policy, 1931–1945.* Princeton: Princeton University Press, 1945.

SCHUMAN, F. L. *Soviet Politics at Home and Abroad.* New York: Knopf, 1946.

SETON-WATSON, H. *The East European Revolution.* 2nd ed. London: Methuen, 1952.

SHAPIRO, L., ed. *Soviet Treaty Series.* Washington: Georgetown University Press, 1950– . [Vol. I: 1917–1928.]

SHOTWELL, J. T., and M. M. LASERSON. *Poland and Russia, 1919–1945.* New York: King's Crown Press, 1945.

SONTAG, R. J., and J. S. BEDDIE, eds. *Nazi-Soviet Relations, 1939–1941; Documents from the Archives of the German Foreign Office.* Washington: U. S. Department of State, 1948.

The Soviet-Yugoslav Dispute; Text of the Published Correspondence. New York: Royal Institute of International Affairs, 1948.

TARACOUZIO, A. T. *War and Peace in Soviet Diplomacy.* New York: Macmillan, 1940.

U. S. Department of State. *Foreign Relations of the United States: The Soviet Union, 1933–1939.* Washington: U. S. Government Printing Office, 1952.

WHEELER-BENNETT, J. W. *Munich: Prologue to Tragedy.* New York: Duell, Sloan and Pearce, 1948.

WU, AITCHEN K. *China and the Soviet Union; a Study of Sino-Soviet Relations.* New York: J. Day, 1950.

Neighboring Peoples and National Minorities

ALLEN, W. E. D. *The Ukraine.* Cambridge: The University Press, 1940.

ALLEN, W. E. D. *A History of the Georgian People from the Beginning down to the Russian Conquest in the Nineteenth Century.* London: Paul, 1932.

BARTOLD, V. V. *Turkestan down to the Mongol Invasion.* 2nd ed. London: Luzac, 1928.

BILMANIS, A. *A History of Latvia.* Princeton: Princeton University Press, 1951.

DYBOSKI, R. *Poland in World Civilization.* New York: Barrett, 1950.

*DYBOSKI, R. *Outlines of Polish History.* 2nd ed. London: Allen & Unwin, 1941. [Able and clear.]

DUBNOW, S. M. *History of the Jews in Russia and Poland.* 2 vols. Philadelphia: Jewish Publication Society of America, 1916–20.

GREENBERG, L. *The Jews in Russia; the Struggle for Emancipation.* 2 vols. New Haven: Yale University Press, 1944–51.

HALECKI, O. *Borderlands of Western Civilization; a History of East Central Europe.* New York: Ronald, 1952.

*HRUSHEVSKY, M. *History of the Ukraine.* New Haven: Yale University Press, 1941. [The most prominent Ukrainian historian.]

KIRIMAL, E. *Der nationale Kampf der Krimtürken mit besonderer Berücksichtigung der Jahre 1917–1918.* Emsdetten: Lechte, 1952.

KOHN, HANS. *Nationalism in the Soviet Union.* London: Routledge, 1933.

KOLARZ, W. *Russia and Her Colonies.* New York: Praeger, 1952.

KULISCHER, E. M. *Europe on the Move: War and Population Changes, 1917–1947.* New York: Columbia University Press, 1948.

REDDAWAY, W. F., and others, eds. *Cambridge History of Poland.* Cambridge: The University Press, 1941–50. [Vol. I: "From the Origins to Sobieski (1696)"; Vol. II: "From Augustus II to Pilsudski (1697–1935)."]

SCHWARZ, S. M. *The Jews in the Soviet Union.* Syracuse: Syracuse University Press, 1951.

STALIN, J. *Marxism and the National Question; Selected Writings and Speeches.* New York: International Publishers, 1942.

YARMOLINSKY, A. *The Jews and other National Minorities in the Soviet Union.* New York: Vanguard, 1928.

World Communism

BORKENAU, F. *Der europäische Kommunismus; seine Geschichte von 1917 bis zum Gegenwart.* Munich: Lehnen, 1952.

BORKENAU, F. *World Communism; a History of the Communist International.* New York: Norton, 1939.

BRANDT, C., B. SCHWARTZ, and J. K. FAIRBANK. *Documentary History of Chinese Communism.* Cambridge: Harvard University Press, 1952.

CROSSMAN, R. H. S., ed. *The God that Failed.* New York: Harper, 1950.

EINAUDI, M. *Communism in Western Europe.* Ithaca: Cornell University Press, 1951.

CHAMBERLIN, W. H., ed. *Blueprint for World Conquest, as Outlined by the Communist International.* Washington: Human Events, 1946.

CIANFARRA, C. M. *The Vatican and the Kremlin.* New York: Dutton, 1950.

FISCHER, R. *Stalin and German Communism; a Study in the Origins of the State Party.* Cambridge: Harvard University Press, 1940.

FISHER, M. J., ed. *Communist Doctrine and the Free World; the Ideology of Communism according to Marx, Engels, Lenin and Stalin.* Syracuse: Syracuse University Press, 1952.

JAMES, C. L. R. *World Revolution 1917–1936; the Rise and Fall of the Communist International.* London: Secker and Warburg, 1937.

KOESTLER, A. *The Yogi and the Commissar.* New York: Macmillan, 1945.

LEITES, N. *The Operational Code of the Politburo.* New York: McGraw-Hill, 1951.

MONNEROT, J. *Sociology and Psychology of Communism*. Boston: Beacon, 1953.

RECORD, W. *The Negro and the Communist Party*. Chapel Hill: University of Norfh Carolina Press, 1951.

ROSSI, A. *A Communist Party in Action; an Account of the Organization and Operations in France*. New Haven: Yale University Press, 1949.

SALVADORI, M. *The Rise of Modern Communism*. New York: Holt, 1952.

SELZNICK, P. *The Organizational Weapon: a Study in Bolshevik Strategy and Tactics*. New York: McGraw-Hill, 1952. (RAND Series.)

STALIN, J. *The Economic Problems of Socialism*. New York: International Publishers, 1952; also published as Special Supplement to *Current Digest of the Soviet Press*, October 18, 1952.

SWEARINGEN, R., and P. LANGER. *Red Flag in Japan; International Communism in Action, 1919–1951*. Cambridge: Harvard University Press, 1952.

U. S. Eightieth Congress, Second Session. *The Strategy and Tactics of World Communism*. House Document 619. 1948.

INDEX

*Russian names are accentuated when necessary to assist
in their pronunciation*

Abbas the Great, Shah of Persia, 133

Abdul Hamid, Sultan of Turkey, 397

Aberdeen, Lord, 351

Abyssinia, 435, 540

Academy of Sciences, 230; communized, 531

Adáshev, Minister of John IV, 107, 108, 111, 112–13

Adrianople, Treaty of, in 1828, 335–6

Aehrenthal, Baron, 470

Afghanistan, Anglo-Russian conflict in, 435

Agricultural Committees of Witte, 424

Agricultural Society of Poland, 374

Agriculture: development of, 44; transferred to north, 49; frontier agriculture, 122; *pomestya*, 123; military conditions of tenure, 123; depletion of centre, 127; condition of, after the Troubles, 156–60; on verge of famine, 159; effects of poll tax, 220; embarrassments of, 242–3; difficulties after Emancipation, 386–7; import of agricultural implements favoured, 415; impoverishment of centre, 423; Bolsheviks urge seizure of land, 492; agrarian revolution of 1917, 496–7; individual land tenure, 513; collectivized, 526 ff.; *see also* Peasants

Ahmed, Tartar Khan, 94

Aix-la-Chapelle, Congress of, 325, 328

Aksákov, Constantine, writer, 346

Aksákov, Ivan, Slavophil publicist, 346, 350, 375, 378, 379, 399, 407

Aládin, Labour leader, 455, 459

Aland, isle of, 206–7, 305, 358

Alans, 10, 11

Alexander, Prince of Lithuania, then King of Poland, 98, 104

Alexander, Prince of Tver, 79–80

Alexander of Battenburg, Prince of Bulgaria, 402; deals with Russian intrigues, 432; unites Eastern Rumelia,

Alexander of Battenburg (*continued*)
432; defeats Serbs, 432; kidnapped, 432; abdication, 432

Alexander Nevsky: defeats Jarl Birger, 57; defeats German Knights, 57; Grand Prince, 57; mediations with Khan, 58; death, 58; honoured by Soviets, 534

Alexander I, Emperor: educated by Laharpe, 263–4; and question of succession, 286; and murder of Paul, 297; character of, an enigma, 297–8; two alien worlds, an actor, 298; Liberal views, 298; peace with England, 298; joint mediation with Napoleon in Germany, 298; his friends: the Private Committee, 299; reforms and schools, 299–301; breaks with Napoleon, 301; in Third Coalition, 301; at Austerlitz, 301–3; helps Prussia, 303; makes friends with Napoleon at Tilsit, 304; and Speransky, 306; breach with Napoleon, 308–10; his resolution, 311; with the army, 312; in Moscow, 312; in St. Petersburg, his firmness, 315; passes into Europe, 318; soul of coalition, 319–20; enters Paris, 320; his predominant role there, 320; his magnanimity, 320; insists on a French Constitution, 320; generosity to Poles, 320–1; becomes dictatorial, 321; and Metternich, 321; obtains large part of Poland, 322; Quadruple Alliance against revolution, 322; his Holy Alliance, 322–3; grants a Polish Constitution, 323; emancipation, but not yet for Russia, 323; military colonies, 324–5; reaction in education, 325; Liberal speech at Polish Diet, 325; inconsistencies, 328; follows Metternich at Troppau, 328; disavows Ypsilanti, 329; at Polish Diet, 330; at Taganrog, his death, 330–1

i

A NOTE ON THE TYPE

This book was set on the Linotype in ELECTRA, *designed by W. A. Dwiggins. The Electra face is a simple and reddable type suitable for printing books by present-day processes. It is not based on any historical model, and hence does not echo any particular time or fashion. It is without eccentricities to catch the eye and interfere with reading—in general, its aim is to perform the function of a good book printing-type: to be read, and not seen.*

VINTAGE HISTORY—WORLD

V-286   **ARIES, PHILIPPE** / Centuries of Childhood
V-563   **BEER, SAMUEL H.** / British Politics in the Collectivist Age
V-620   **BILLINGTON, JAMES H.** / Icon and Axe: An Interpretive History of Russian Culture
V-44   **BRINTON, CRANE** / The Anatomy of Revolution
V-391   **CARR, E. H.** / What Is History?
V-628   **CARTEY, WILFRED AND MARTIN KILSON (eds.)** / Africa Reader: Colonial Africa, Vol. 1
V-629   **CARTEY, WILFRED AND MARTIN KILSON (eds.)** / Africa Reader: Independent Africa, Vol. 1
V-522   **CHINWEIZU** / The West and the Rest of Us: White Predators, Black Slavers and the African Elite
V-888   **CLARK, JOHN HENRIK (ed.)** / Marcus Garvey and the Vision of Africa
V-507   **CLIVE, JOHN** / Macauley
V-261   **COHEN, STEPHEN F.** / Bukharin and the Bolshevik Revolution: A Political Biography
V-843   **DAUBIER, JEAN** / A History of the Chinese Cultural Revolution
V-227   **DE BEAUVOIR, SIMONE** / The Second Sex
V-726   **DEBRAY, REGIS AND SALVADOR ALLENDE** / The Chilean Revolution
V-746   **DEUTSCHER, ISAAC** / The Prophet Armed
V-748   **DEUTSCHER, ISAAC** / The Prophet Outcast
V-617   **DEVLIN, BERNADETTE** / The Price of My Soul
V-471   **DUVEAU, GEORGES** / 1848: The Making of A Revolution
V-702   **EMBREE, AINSLIE (ed.)** / The Hindu Tradition
V-2023   **FEST, JOACHIM C.** / Hitler
V-225   **FISCHER, LOUIS** / The Essential Gandhi
V-927   **FITZGERALD, FRANCES** / Fire in the Lake: The Vietnamese & The Americans in Vietnam
V-914   **FOUCAULT, MICHEL** / Madness & Civilization: A History of Insanity in the Age of Reason
V-935   **FOUCAULT, MICHEL** / The Order of Things: An Archaeology of the Human Sciences
V-97   **FOUCAULT, MICHEL** / The Birth of the Clinic: An Archaeology of Medical Perception
V-152   **GRAHAM, LOREN R.** / Science & Philosophy in the Soviet Union
V-529   **HALLIDAY, FRED** / Arabia Without Sultans
V-114   **HAUSER, ARNOLD** / The Social History of Art (four volumes—through 117)
V-979   **HERZEN, ALEXANDER** / My Past and Thoughts (Abridged by Dwight Macdonald)
V-465   **HINTON, WILLIAM** / Fanshen
V-328   **HINTON, WILLIAM** / Iron Oxen
V-2005   **HOARE, QUINTIN (ed.) AND KARL MARX** / Early Writings
V-878   **HOLBORN, HAJO (ed.)** / Republic to Reich: The Making of the Nazi Revolution
V-201   **HUGHES, H. STUART** / Consciousness and Society
V-514   **HUNTINGTON, SAMUEL P.** / The Soldier and the State
V-790   **KAPLAN, CAROL AND LAWRENCE** / Revolutions: A Comparative Study
V-708   **KESSLE, GUN AND JAN MYRDAL** / China: The Revolution Continued
V-628   **KILSON, MARTIN AND WILFRED CARTEY (eds.)** / Africa Reader: Colonial Africa, Vol. I
V-629   **KILSON, MARTIN AND WILFRED CARTEY (eds.)** / Africa Reader: Independent Africa, Vol. II
V-728   **KLYUCHEVSKY, V.** / Peter the Great
V-246   **KNOWLES, DAVID** / Evolution of Medieval Thought
V-939   **LEFEBVRE, GEORGES AND JOAN WHITE (trans.)** / The Great Fear of 1789: Rural Panic in Revolutionary France
V-533   **LOCKWOOD, LEE** / Castro's Cuba, Cuba's Fidel
V-787   **MALDONADO-DENIS, MANUEL** / Puerto Rico: A Socio-Historic Interpretation

V-380	**JOYCE, JAMES** / Ulysses
V-991	**KAFKA, FRANZ** / The Castle
V-484	**KAFKA, FRANZ** / The Trial
V-841	**KANG-HU, KIANG AND WITTER BYNNER** / The Jade Mountain: A Chinese Anthology
V-508	**KOCH, KENNETH** / The Art of Love
V-915	**KOCH, KENNETH** / A Change of Hearts
V-467	**KOCH, KENNETH** / The Red Robbins
V-82	**KOCH, KENNETH** / Wishes, Lies and Dreams
V-134	**LAGERKVIST, PAR** / Barabbas
V-240	**LAGERKVIST, PAR** / The Sibyl
V-776	**LAING, R. D.** / Knots
V-23	**LAWRENCE, D. H.** / The Plumed Serpent
V-71	**LAWRENCE, D. H.** / St. Mawr & The Man Who Died
V-329	**LINDBERGH, ANNE MORROW** / Gift from the Sea
V-822	**LINDBERGH, ANNE MORROW** / The Unicorn and Other Poems
V-479	**MALRAUX, ANDRE** / Man's Fate
V-180	**MANN, THOMAS** / Buddenbrooks
V-3	**MANN, THOMAS** / Death in Venice and Seven Other Stories
V-297	**MANN, THOMAS** / Doctor Faustus
V-497	**MANN, THOMAS** / The Magic Mountain
V-86	**MANN, THOMAS** / The Transposed Heads
V-36	**MANSFIELD, KATHERINE** / Stories
V-137	**MAUGHAM, W. SOMERSET** / Of Human Bondage
V-720	**MIRSKY, D. S.** / A History of Russian Literature: From Its Beginnings to 1900
V-883	**MISHIMA, YUKIO** / Five Modern Nō Plays
V-151	**MOFFAT, MARY JANE AND CHARLOTTE PAINTER** / Revelations: Diaries of Women
V-851	**MORGAN, ROBIN** / Monster
V-926	**MUSTARD, HELEN (trans.)** / Heinrich Heine: Selected Works
V-925	**NGUYEN, DU** / The Tale of Kieu
V-125	**OATES, WHITNEY J. AND EUGENE O'NEILL, Jr. (eds.)** / Seven Famous Greek Plays
V-973	**O'HARA, FRANK** / Selected Poems of Frank O'Hara
V-855	**O'NEILL, EUGENE** / Anna Christie, The Emperor Jones, The Hairy Ape
V-18	**O'NEILL, EUGENE** / The Iceman Cometh
V-236	**O'NEILL, EUGENE** / A Moon For the Misbegotten
V-856	**O'NEILL, EUGENE** / Seven Plays of the Sea
V-276	**O'NEILL, EUGENE** / Six Short Plays
V-165	**O'NEILL, EUGENE** / Three Plays: Desire Under the Elms, Strange Interlude, Mourning Becomes Electra
V-125	**O'NEILL, EUGENE, JR. AND WHITNEY J. OATES (eds.)** / Seven Famous Greek Plays
V-151	**PAINTER, CHARLOTTE AND MARY JANE MOFFAT** / Revelations: Diaries of Women
V-907	**PERELMAN, S. J.** / Crazy Like a Fox
V-466	**PLATH, SYLVIA** / The Colossus and Other Poems
V-232	**PRITCHETT, V. S.** / Midnight Oil
V-598	**PROUST, MARCEL** / The Captive
V-597	**PROUST, MARCEL** / Cities of the Plain
V-596	**PROUST, MARCEL** / The Guermantes Way
V-600	**PROUST, MARCEL** / The Past Recaptured
V-594	**PROUST, MARCEL** / Swann's Way
V-599	**PROUST, MARCEL** / The Sweet Cheat Gone
V-595	**PROUST, MARCEL** / Within A Budding Grove
V-714	**PUSHKIN, ALEXANDER** / The Captain's Daughter and Other Stories
V-976	**QUASHA, GEORGE AND JEROME ROTHENBERG (eds.)** / America a Prophecy: A New Reading of American Poetry from Pre-Columbian Times to the Present

VINTAGE HISTORY—AMERICAN

VINTAGE BELLES—LETTRES